Technologies Shaping Instruction and Distance Education:
New Studies and Utilizations

Mahbubur Rahman Syed
Minnesota State University Mankato, USA

Information Science
REFERENCE
INFORMATION SCIENCE REFERENCE
Hershey · New York

Director of Editorial Content: Kristin Klinger
Senior Managing Editor: Jamie Snavely
Assistant Managing Editor: Michael Brehm
Publishing Assistant: Sean Woznicki
Typesetter: Michael Brehm, Carole Coulson
Cover Design: Lisa Tosheff
Printed at: Yurchak Printing Inc.

Published in the United States of America by
Information Science Reference (an imprint of IGI Global)
701 E. Chocolate Avenue
Hershey PA 17033
Tel: 717-533-8845
Fax: 717-533-8661
E-mail: cust@igi-global.com
Web site: http://www.igi-global.com/reference

Library of Congress Cataloging-in-Publication Data

Technologies shaping instruction and distance education : new studies and utilizations / Mahbubur Rahman Syed, editor.
p. cm.
Includes bibliographical references and index.
Summary: "This book covers the use of technology and the development of tools to support content exchange, delivery, collaboration and pedagogy used in distance education delivery"--Provided by publisher.
ISBN 978-1-60566-934-2 (hardcover) -- ISBN 978-1-60566-935-9 (ebook) 1. Distance education--Computer-assisted instruction. 2. Education--Effect of technological innovations on. 3. Educational technology. I. Syed, Mahbubur Rahman, 1952-
LC5803.C65T43 2010
371.35'8--dc22

2009043357

British Cataloguing in Publication Data
A Cataloguing in Publication record for this book is available from the British Library.

Editorial Advisory Board

Table of Contents

Detailed Table of Contents

The authors of this chapter propose a novel data distribution framework for developing a large Web-based course forum system. In the distributed architectural design, each forum server is fully equipped with the ability to support some course forums independently. The forum servers collaborating with each other constitute the whole forum system. Therefore, the workload of the course forums can be shared by a group of the servers. With the secure group communication protocol and fault tolerance design, the new distribution framework provides a robust and scalable distributed architecture for the large course forum system. The forum servers can be settled in anywhere as long as a broadband network connection to Internet is provided. The experimental performance testing results show that the large forum system is a high performance distributed system with very low communication overhead cost. In addition, all course forums are classified by their teaching content relevance. Relevant course forums can be arranged on the same forum server together. Hence this distribution framework also provides a knowledge-based taxonomic storage solution to build a large digital course teaching material library.

In recent years, with the rapid development of communication and network technologies, distance learning has been popularized and it became one of the most well-known teaching methods, due to its practicability. Over the Internet, learners are free to access new knowledge without restrictions on time or location. However, current distance learning systems still present restrictions, such as support to interconnection of learning systems available in scalable, open, dynamic, and heterogeneous environments. This chapter introduces a distance learning platform based on grid technology to support learning in distributed environments, where open source and freely available learning systems can share and exchange their learning and training contents. The authors have envisioned such distance learning platform in heterogeneous environment using grid technology. A prototype is designed and implemented, to demonstrate its effectiveness and friendly interaction between learner and learner resources used.

A traditional distance learning system requires supervisors or teachers always available on online to facilitate and monitor a learner's progress by answering questions and guiding users. This chapter presents an English chat room system in which students discuss course contents and ask questions to and receive from teachers and other students. The mechanism contains an agent that detects syntax errors in sentences written by the online the user and also checks the semantics of a sentence. The agent can thus offer recommendations to the user and, then, analyze the data of the learner corpus. When users query the system, this system will attempt to find the answers from the knowledge ontology that is stored in the records of previous user comments. With the availability of automatic supervisors, messages can be monitored and syntax or semantic mistakes can be corrected to resolve learner-related problems.

Cooperative learning has been proven to be helpful in enhancing the learning performance of students. The goal of a cooperative learning group is to maximize all members' learning, which is accomplished via promoting each other's success, through assisting, sharing, mentoring, explaining, and encouragement. To achieve the goal of cooperative learning, it is very important to organize well-structured cooperative learning groups, in which all group members have the ability to help each other during the learning process. In this chapter, a concept-based approach is proposed to organize cooperative learning groups, such that, for a given course each concept is precisely understood by at least one of the students in each group. An experiment on a computer science course has been conducted in order to evaluate the efficacy of this new approach. From the experimental results, the authors conclude that the novel approach is helpful in enhancing student learning efficacy.

Collaborative e-learning delivers many enhancements to e-learning technology; it enables students to collaborate with each other and improves their learning efficiency. Semantic blog combines semantic Web and blog technology that users can import, export, view, navigate, and query the blog. The authors of this chapter developed a semantic course blog for collaborative e-learning. Using this semantic course blog, instructors can import the lecture course. Students can team up for projects, ask questions, mutually discuss problems, take the comments, support answers, and query the blog information. This semantic course blog provided a platform for collaborative e-learning framework. This chapter described some collaborative e-learning and semantic blog technology, and then introduced functions, implementation and how collaborative e-learning appears in semantic course blog.

Natural computing is a terminology used to describe computational algorithms developed by taking inspiration from information processing mechanisms in nature, methods to synthesize natural phenomena in computers, and novel computational approaches based on natural materials. The virtual laboratory on natural computing (LVCoN) is a Web environment to support the teaching and learning of natural computing, and whose goal is to provide didactic contents about the main themes in natural computing, in addition to interactive simulations, videos, exercises, links for related sites, forum, and other materials. This chapter describes an experiment with LVCoN during a School of Computing in Brazil. The results are presented in four parts: Self-Evaluation, Evaluation of LVCoN, Evaluation of the Simulations (Applets), and Interviews. The results allowed the authors to positively evaluate the structure and contents of LVCoN, in the sense that most students were satisfied with the environment. Besides, most students liked the experience of working with a virtual laboratory, and considered a hybrid teaching approach; that is, one mixing lectures with virtual learning, very appropriate and productive.

This work describes a Java-based virtual laboratory accessible via the Internet by means of a Web browser. This remote laboratory enables the students to build both direct and alternating current circuits. The program includes a graphical user interface which resembles the connection board, and also the electrical components and tools that are used in a real laboratory to build electrical circuits. Emphasis has been placed on designing access patterns to the virtual tools as if they were real ones. The virtual laboratory developed in this study allows the lecturer to adapt the behaviour and the principal layout of the different practical sessions during a course. This flexibility enables the tool to guide the student during each practical lesson, thus enhancing self-motivation. This study is an application of new technologies for active learning methodologies, in order to increase both the self-learning and comprehension of the students. This virtual laboratory is currently accessible at the following URL: http://personales.upv.es/jogomez/labvir/ (in Spanish).

This chapter proposes a knowledge representation model which judiciously serves the remediation process to students' errors during learning activities via a virtual laboratory. The chapter also presents a domain knowledge generator authoring tool which attempts to offer a user-friendly environment that allows modelling graphically any subject-matter domain knowledge according to the proposed knowledge representation and remediation approach. The model is inspired by artificial intelligence research on the computational representation of the knowledge and by cognitive psychology theories that provide a fine description of the human memory subsystems and offer a refined modelling of the human learning processes. Experimental results, obtained thanks to practical tests, show that the knowledge representation and remediation model facilitates the planning of a tailored sequence of feedbacks that considerably help the learner.

A multipoint, multimedia conferencing system called FocusShare is described. It uses IPv6/IPv4 multicasting for real-time collaboration, enabling video, audio, and group-awareness and attention-sharing information to be shared. Multiple telepointers provide group-awareness information and make it easy to share attention and intention. In addition to pointing with the telepointers, users can add graphical annotations to video streams and share them with one another. The system also supports attention-sharing using video processing techniques.

model. After the pose recovery, a similarity measurement function is proposed to locate the neighborhood for the given image in the 3D face database. The scope of neighborhood can be determined adaptively using the authors' cross-validation algorithm. Furthermore, the individual 3D shape is synthesized by neighborhood interpolation. Texture mapping is achieved based on feature points. The experimental results show that the authors' algorithm can robustly produce 3D facial models from images captured in various scenarios to enhance the lifelikeness in distant learning.

The computer software education in vocational schools in Taiwan can hardly be deemed as effective. To increase students' learning motivation and develop practical skills, innovative learning designs such as problem-based learning (PBL) and self-regulated learning (SRL) are on trial in this specific context. The authors conducted a series of quasi-experiments to examine effects of these designs mediated by a web-based learning environment. Two classes of 106 freshmen in a semester course at Institute of Technology in Taiwan were chosen for this empirical study. Results reveal that effects of web-enabled PBL, web-enabled SRL, and their combinations, on students' skills of application software have significant differences. The implications of this study are also discussed.

This chapter is aimed at giving an introduction to computer game-based learning. Besides discussing computer games' intrinsic educational traits favouring constructivist learning from different perspectives, the authors also review a number of instances of two recent foci in the game-based learning domain. The first one is education in games that involves the adoption of existing recreational games in the commercial market for educational use. The second is games in education that entails designing and developing educational games articulated with different constructivist learning paradigms or pedagogical approaches.

The authors of this chapter designed and implemented new functions such as: a new ranking function, automatic interface change function, vibration function, room light control function and sound emission function in order to improve the performance of their Web-based e-learning system. By using these new functions, the proposed e-learning system can increase learner's efficiency by stimulating learner's motivation. The experimental results showed that the implemented system has better performance than previous systems.

A personalized e-learning framework based on a user-interactive question-answering (QA) system is proposed, in which a user-modeling approach is used to capture personal information of students and a personalized answer extraction algorithm is proposed for personalized automatic answering. In this approach, a topic ontology (or concept hierarchy) of course content defined by an instructor is used for the system to generate the corresponding structure of boards for holding relevant questions. Students can interactively post questions, and also browse, select, and answer others' questions in their interested boards. A knowledge base is accumulated using historical question/answer (Q/A) pairs for knowledge reuse. The students' log data are used to build an association space to compute the interest and authority of the students for each board and each topic. The personal information of students can help instructors design suitable teaching materials to enhance instruction efficiency, be used to implement the personalized automatic answering and distribute unsolved questions to relevant students to enhance the learning efficiency. The experiment results show the efficacy of this user-modeling approach.

Distance learning in advanced military education can assist officers around the world to become more skilled and qualified for future challenges. Through well-chosen technology, the efficiency of distance-learning can be improved significantly. This chapter presents the architecture of Advanced Military Education – Distance Learning (AME-DL) prototype for advanced military distance-learning, it combines advanced e-learning tool, simulation technology, and Web technology to provide a set of military learning and training subjects that can be accessed easily anywhere, anytime through a Web browser. The major goal of AME-DL is to provide a common standard framework for military training program, and the major contribution for such a prototype is to reduce training cost while providing high quality learning experience.

Chapter 18
Virtual On-Line Classroom for Mobile E-Learning over Next Generation Learning Environment .. 268
Tin-Yu Wu, Tamkang University, Taipei, Taiwan, ROC

This chapter develops an environment for mobile e-Learning with interactive courses, virtual online labs, interactive online test, lab-exercise training platform and the identification of learning information by next generation tag on the 4th generation mobile communication system. The term that the Next Generation Learning Environment (NeGL) promotes is "knowledge economy". At present, inter-networking has become one of the most popular technologies in Mobile e-Learning for the Next Generation Networks (NGN) environment. This system uses various computer embedded devices to ubiquitously access multimedia information like smart phones and PDAs; and the most important feature is its greater available bandwidth. The future learning mode will include an immediate, virtual, interactive classroom with personal identification that enables learners to learn and interact. (Wu et al. 2008)

Chapter 19
A Methodology for Developing Learning Objects for Web Course Delivery 280
Karen Stauffer, Athabasca University, Canada
Fuhua Lin, Athabasca University, Canada
Marguerite Koole, Athabasca University, Canada

This chapter presents a methodology for developing learning objects for web-based courses using the IMS Learning Design (IMS LD) specification. The authors first investigated the IMS LD specification, determining how to use it with online courses and the student delivery model, and then applied this to a Unit of Learning (UOL) for online computer science courses. The authors developed an editor and runtime environment to apply the IMS LD to a UOL. The authors then explored the prospect for advancement of the basic IMS LD UOL. Finally, the chapter discusses how to construct ontology-based software agents to use with the learning objects created with the IMS LD Units of Learning.

Chapter 20
A Chinese Interactive Feedback System for a Virtual Campus 290
Jui-Fa Chen, Tamkang University, Taiwan
Wei-Chuan Lin, Tak Ming College, Taiwan
Chih-Yu Jian, Tamkang University, Taiwan
Ching-Chung Hung, Tamkang University, Taiwan

Considering the popularity of the Internet, an automatic interactive feedback system for Elearning websites is becoming increasingly desirable. However, computers still have problems understanding natural languages, especially the Chinese language, firstly because the Chinese language has no space to segment lexical entries (its segmentation method is more difficult than that of English) and secondly because of the lack of a complete grammar in the Chinese language, making parsing more difficult and complicated. Building an automated Chinese feedback system for special application domains could solve these problems. This chapter proposes an interactive feedback mechanism in a virtual campus that can parse, understand and respond to Chinese sentences. This mechanism utilizes a specific lexical database according to the particular application. In this way, a virtual campus website can implement a special application domain that chooses the proper response in a user friendly, accurate and timely manner.

Preface

The impact of technology on distance education is revolutionary. Distance education delivery started with exchange of printed material using postal mail with negligible or no interactions. The explosive growth of technology and the support for Internet based interactive communication has opened new avenues for the participants of distance education to collaborate, exchange messages, content, etc. This is an introductory chapter that discusses how technology has shaped and continues to shape instruction and distance education. It also introduces chapters included in this book, which covers the use of technology and the development of tools to support content exchange, delivery, collaboration and pedagogy used in distance education delivery.

INTRODUCTION

There is remarkable growth in the development, delivery and quality of distance education. In depth study would reveal that this growth phenomenon occurred in parallel to and may be credited to the innovation and development of the Internet, network transmission, computer processing technology, streaming video technology, and data and information storage capacity. Distance education has been evolving since the mid 19th century with a vision to spread education to those who could not have access to the traditional education systems because they were separated from educational institutions in distance (space), and in affordability of time. The advancement of the Internet and other related technologies have significantly changed the distance education system as a whole. It has changed the mode of teacher-student communication, student-student communication and reshaped teaching and leaning environments and coverage of distance education offerings. However, the objectives of distance education have remained the same.

This chapter includes reviews of important literature related to distance education since the beginning of distance education systems. This will help us to become familiarized with the evolution of the distance education, its concepts and implementations, and lead us to i) investigate the factors that are contributing to general shifting to online education, ii) identify issues, effectiveness and reasons for a rise in the number of institutions providing distance education, iii) find the cause of the increase in the number of people enrolling in distance education.

This chapter is organized in seven sections. Section two discusses the evolution of distance education and its development through the three generation of distance education. Section three explains the role of technology that contributed to rapid development of distance education delivery followed by its comparison with face to face education in section four and issues yet to be solved. Section five discusses the reasons for the increasing trend in student numbers shifting to distance education. Section six introduces the chapters included in this book. Conclusions and summaries are included in section seven.

EVOLUTIONS OF DISTANCE EDUCATION & TECHNOLOGY

In a report for the National Center for Education Statistics (NCES), Zandberg and Lewis (2008) defined distance education as a formal education process "where the teachers and students are in different locations and courses are delivered via audio, video (live or prerecorded), or Internet or other computer technologies."

Sloan Consortium, which conducts research on contemporary distance learning, defines distance education as "an online course as one with at least 80% of the course delivered online without face-to-face meetings." (Dykman, C. A., et. al., 2008)

These definitions of distance education focus mainly on the current Internet based online method of distance education and overlook historic methods of distance education.

The following paragraphs provide a brief discussion of the history of distance education and then continue to introduce the evolution of technology that contributed to widening the prospect of distance education over the years and dramatically changed the way teachers and students involved in distance education delivery can interact.

First Generation Distance Education

A literature review reveals that Sir Isaac Pitman of England first started a correspondence course in 1837 using postal mail, transported by railway, to send the printed instructional materials to those who were interested in learning the new form of short hand—the "Pitman Shorthand" (also known as "stenographic code"). In the United States, the first distance education delivery started in 1852 when the Phonographic Institute of Cincinnati (OH) initiated a correspondence course on Pitman Stenography. The participants received a certificate on shorthand after successful completion of the course. In 1892, the Queen of England awarded Pitman the highest honor, known as the Knight title, for developing shorthand code and spreading knowledge to the people who had the desire to learn it and delivered at a cost of mailing fee. (Matthews, 1999)

Following the correspondence model, Anna Eliot Ticknor in 1873 founded the Society to Encourage Studies at Home to educate women who had to stay home to take care of their children and did not get opportunities to attend conventional educational institutions. The printed course materials sent to members through the mail were the only method of communication for teaching and learning at that time.

In 1878, John H. Vincent created the Chautauqua Literary Scientific Circle (CLSC) to provide vocational and safety training courses to improve the knowledge/skills of the adults in their respective carriers. William Rainey Harper, the first president of the University of Chicago, first initiated college level distance education in 1892 in the US. The University of Wisconsin followed a similar model and started offering distance education in 1892 using postal mailing systems (Emmerson, 2004). Several other universities started offering correspondence education using postal mail to send materials to the students, which further opened university level educational opportunities to a wider group of students. One major problem with the postal mail was slow communication between teachers and learners which affected student. Postal services, printing technology and railways transportation played a significant role in the expansion of correspondence education during the first generation of distance education between the middle of the 19th century to the beginning of the 20th century.

Second Generation Distance Education: Evolution of Technology

Radio Broadcasting: Radio broadcasting technology was first introduced in 1921 to deliver educational programs for distance students and eventually became a popular and a cheaper method of communication. Teachers offered courses and discussed topics on the radio (asynchronous mode of communication) and simultaneously sent course materials and test materials by postal systems. The combination of these two methods helped students better learn the topics. Since radio was relatively cheaper and more available to remote areas it helped to expand the coverage of distance education. Many developing countries started to introduce distance education using this technology.

Television Broadcasting: The University of Iowa first used television broadcasting in 1934. Use of satellite television communications started in1960 and the Instructional Television Fixed Service (ITFS) was introduced in 1963 to provide low-cost licensing systems for educational institutions to offer distance education (Casey, D. M. 2008). Educational institutions started offering satellite television programs to facilitate distance learning, which was considered a cost effective method of offering distance education. Businesses also found satellite technology very cost effective for training their employees and improving their professional skills. At this time radio, television and satellite communication systems were the available and popular method of communication. These also included some form of postal communication until the latter part of the 20th century. This development of distance education, guided mainly by technology, is considered the second generation of distance education.

Third Generation Distance Education: Influence of the Internet

The Internet: Using the Internet for distance education was still not a consideration when the Advanced Research Projects Agency (APRA), through its ARPANET project, built the foundation of the Internet in 1969 with the development of the first 50 Kbps circuit network that linked four universities: University of California at Los Angeles, SRI (in Stanford), University of California at Santa Barbara, and University of Utah. The development of applications on the Internet was accelerated after Tim Berners-Lee at the European Laboratory for Particle Physics (CERN) introduced Hyper Text Markup Language (HTML) technology for internal management and linking of files over the Internet. With the use of this technology, a commercial version of the first Web browser Mosaic, known as Netscape, became available in 1993. Further developments of different browsers including Internet Explorer facilitated the transfer of text, graphics, sound and video over the Internet. HTML remains the standard tool to link, transfer and view the files on the Internet. Universities and businesses got connected to the Internet. It grew at a tremendous rate as the cost of computers became more affordable, and individuals and homes started getting connected to the internet.

Significant changes have occurred in the 21st century due to new innovations and availability of more advanced technologies such as the Internet, the World Wide Web, email, high speed telecommunication network systems, management software, computer networks, and teleconferencing. These new and more affordable technologies, providing interactive learning opportunities with the potential of breaking the barrier of distance, are considered the third generation of distance education.

Internet media along with other supporting technologies helped to provide more flexible education at a lower cost and with more improved accessibility and ability to expand around the globe.

ROLE OF TECHNOLOGY

A study of historical development reveals that technology is one of the most important contributors to the dramatic transformation in the evolution of distance learning from inception to its current role in the 21st century. Technology has even changed the concept of distance education, enabling learners to access a variety of resources at anytime from anywhere around the globe. It has broken the geographical and socioeconomic barriers. It has made time affordable and resources which were available only to on-campus students until recently available to distance students. The concept of and approach to education systems is experiencing rapid changes with the introduction of computer assisted instructions, video courses, videoconferencing, Web-based instructions, and online delivery and learning with the help of course management software. Now, thousands of educational institutions are offering online courses using high speed Internet connections, World Wide Web and several types of course management software such as WebCT, Blackboard, Angela, Desire to Learn (D2L), etc. This has created educational opportunities to busy working people and non-traditional students. They have now the option to choose universities and courses located far from their residence or workplace without the feeling of being significantly disadvantaged compared to the on-campus students.

The advancements of technology and new software have facilitated a radical change in the method of delivery of education, instructional design and pedagogy. The use of email, chat rooms, and discussion boards has changed the approach to distance education (Beldarraian, 2006). The first generation of Web technologies helped the innovation of the new paradigm of teacher-student communication. It was further developed for student-student communication, enabling students to get support from each other and complete group tasks through email, chat rooms, and discussion boards (Godwin-Jones, 2003). Student-student communication was not possible in the first two generations of distance education.

The second generation of Web tools that includes Weblogs, wikis, podcasts or vlogs for video materials and audio blogs for audio materials is contributing to the creation of engaging learning environments. Blogs, Wiki, and Podcasts are the tools that the educators are embracing to improve collaborative learning. Ulises Mejias is a type of software that teachers can use to manage blogs posted by the students. Several institutions and teachers are embracing these technologies to promote collaboration and interactivity in distance education. Columbia University's teachers college in the US uses software where students post their blogs and their learning progress for the course is recorded (Mejias, 2006). Educators in the Auburn University School of Architecture and Bowdain College in the US, and Deakin University in Australia also use Wikis to promote collaborative learning, complete group projects and facilitate teamwork that needs collaborative work among the students similar to a classroom environment and can be managed by the teachers or the students. Podcasting using RSS technology can deliver audio or video created by the teachers or students, which helps in exchanging course materials and also keeps participants up to date and allows them to feel connected.

DISTANCE EDUCATION AND FACE TO FACE MODE OF EDUCATION

The performance of students and the effectiveness of distance learning versus traditional teaching methods has been a subject of debate and discussion, and a matter of research for long time. In spite of the fact that communication technologies and new applications have revolutionized the delivery of distance education to anyone at anytime and anywhere in the world at a cheaper cost, the quality of the distance education incorporating proper and genuine evaluation is still debated.

Student Performances

Bartini (2008) conducted an empirical study delivered to a 200 level psychology course to compare student performance in a traditional face-to-face course and a Web-based online course. One instructor offered the course using the same content, same quizzes, and same exams for the traditional face-to-face classroom and the online class using course management software. Exams were given on the same day to the students studying in both modes of delivery. The mean score on exams taken by distance education students was 80.68%, and the mean score obtained by the face-to-face students was 72.67%. This indicates that the distance education students performed better compared to the traditional face-to-face students. The probable cause of success of the distance education students may be attributed to the fact that online students received prompt feedback that helped them to understand difficult topics and perform better on the exams. The study report stated that there is a correlation between the proportions of online quizzes completed with the unit exam scores. However, no correlation was found between completion of in-class assignments and exam scores in either section. The research analysis concludes that students may benefit by taking the quiz and getting feedback rather than participating in an in-class activity. Online students had expressed favorable views of online quizzes. Nothing has been mentioned about the type of questions included in the quizzes and exams, or repetition of questions in quizzes to exams, or about the reasons for lower performance of the face-to-face students on the exams (Oskar and Lames, 2008).

Quality of Distance Education

A widespread concern among educators and employers is about the quality of distance education, as they believe that academic misconduct is increasing (Hard, Conway, and Moran 2006). Several studies have been conducted about student perceptions of cheating in online courses, and some reported that chances of cheating in online courses are higher, because there is no screening process that can check student identification (Kennedy, Nowak, and Raghuraman, 2000). It is impossible to know who has enrolled in the course, who is submitting and/or working on the assignments or posting discussions and who is taking the exams, especially when exams are taken in unproctored environments.

A large number of researchers have been working on the issue of quality of distance education and cheating in online classes. A study conducted by Oskar and James (2008) carried out an empirical study to find out the extent of cheating and the effectiveness of online instruction and face-to-face instruction in a "Principles of Economics" course. The authors collected data from two courses, which were identical in every respect, offered during summer 2004 and 2005. The only difference was that the final exam in the summer 2004 course was not proctored, and the final exam in the summer 2005 course was proctored. Student characteristics were considered independent variables and R-squares statistics were compared for each exam. The assumptions include that if there was no cheating took place, then same scores will be attained for all exams and, conversely, if cheating occurred in the exams that were unproctored then the scores will be different. The comparison of the R-squared statistics revealed that the variation in test scores in the unproctored format compared to the proctored environment indicate an incidence of academic dishonesty in online courses when compared to face-to-face courses. The results suggest that online exams administered in a proctored environment might equalize the incidence of academic dishonesty between online courses and face-to-face courses. The authors included findings from several other studies to evaluate the cheating and how to improve the online courses. There are several interesting studies on the testing process for distance education. Studies carried out by Edling (2000), Rovai (2001), and Deal (2002) suggested that campus proctored tests and open book testing with time constraints can improve the quality of tests and the evaluation process of distance education.

Acceptability of Distance Education

Internet technology that is not limited to any boundaries and multimedia technology based on high performance microprocessors are now widely used in distance education. Educational institutions, academicians and learners around the globe are gaining interest in distance education due to the application of these advanced technologies. The popularity of online courses has been increasing, which is demonstrated by the tremendous increase in the number of institutions offering online courses. Even prestigious universities such as Harvard, Stanford, Oxford, the University of Texas and many other universities around the globe have been offering degrees partially or entirely through online coursework. Participation in large numbers and by well known universities is contributing to the wider acceptance of distance education degrees.

SHIFT TO DISTANCE EDUCATION

The US National Center for Education Statistics (NCES), the primary entity of the federal government that publishes reports on education in the United States and other nations, reported that during 2006-07 the total enrollment for distance education courses was about 12.2 million (USDoE, 2008). According to this report, out of a total 4200 institutions, about 61% of the institutions offer online courses. About 35% offer hybrid courses (which is a combination of online and face to face courses) and 26% offer other types of college level credit granting education. These institutions include both two-year and four-year, and public and private institutions. In a report for the NCES, Zandberg and Lewis (2008) stated that during 2004-05 about 37% of school districts had offered courses on distance education, which was 9% higher than the previous year, and that the Internet was the primary mode of communication.

In an article for the Sloan Consortium, which is an online education forum that conducts research and publishes reports about contemporary online educational practices, C.A. Dykman et al (2008) stated that "the number of students in the United States taking at least one online course per year is increasing at a rate exceeding 20% in recent years, reaching more than 3.2 million in Fall of 2005."

The reason for the shift toward online education is a research question. This is a complex issue that involves the rise in demand for flexible schedules, questions of educational access, paradigms for teaching and learning, competition and globalization among universities, the development of new and better online technologies, and the financial pressures facing higher education. A huge transition is underway (Dykman and Davis, 2008).

Financial Constraints and Technology Advances

Traditionally, higher education has been self-regulating and relatively independent of centralized governmental authority and control (Berdahl and McConnell, 1999; King, 2007). In the United States, for example, state governments have provided most of the funding for state universities, and the federal government has provided substantial research funding based upon various research grant programs to both public and private universities (Dill, 2001; Spellings, 2006). These sources of funding are tax-based and have been weakening in recent years under political pressures. Universities have been forced to look elsewhere for significant funding. Similar situations have been developing in Europe and other parts of the world (Weiler, 2000).

Higher education is expensive and government support in real terms has been on the decline (Cantor and Courant, 2003; Hemsley-Brown and Goonawardana, 2007; Longanecker, 2006). As budgets get tighter, there is a new focus on financial accountability (Broadbent, 2007). In many cases, student tuition and fees have risen at an alarming rate, as well (Jacobs, 2005). Faced with the choice of further tuition and fee increases or expanding markets, many administrators turn entrepreneurial and see online education as a possible salvation. Distance education, now equipped with advancing technology and the level of acceptance, is considered a mostly untapped route to important new markets (Mok, 2005).

Leveraging Existing Technological Resources

Computer and network architectures (especially in universities) are already established and being maintained with mostly state-of-the-art equipment. Virtually everyone in every university is already highly computer literate and connected to the Internet. Adding distance learning over the Internet for a typical university will require relatively little incremental cost, especially compared to the resulting potential for market expansion. It is essentially a case of leveraging and better utilizing an already large investment in existing resources. This is a totally new strategic development that has never been possible on such a scale before. Universities can potentially increase student enrollment without significantly expanding campus facilities for classroom space, dormitories, etc. But it is not as straightforward as it sounds. One major issue is the faculty development for distance education. Teaching online is very different from conventional teaching and is not easy. Planning online coursework is much more demanding and student-teacher relationships are much more complex. Once mistakes are made, it is difficult to recover fully in an online environment. And once a professor, a department, or a student body has soured on Internet-based online education, it may take a long time to get any of them to reconsider pursuing it again.

TOPICS COVERED IN THIS BOOK

More details of recent developments in some specific areas are covered in different chapters of this book. The major topic areas include:

- Web Based distributed course forums and content sharing
- Cooperative learning
- A virtual laboratory on natural computing: A learning experiment
- Multimedia tools and conferencing systems
- Facial animation in distance education
- Pedagogy and technology in distance education
- Mobile e-learning

The following paragraphs provide a brief introduction to each of the areas included in different chapters of this book.

Web Based Distributed Course Forums and Content Sharing

The development of the Internet has extended to the distance learners of today an opportunity that was never even a dream to the learners in the earlier generations of distance education. One very important aspect is to interact with other fellow learners and with the instructors whether in asynchronous or synchronous mode. Web-based education application systems have affected the traditional teaching-learning concepts, models and methods for both distance education and face-to-face mode. By breaking the barrier of time zones and geographic locations, these systems provide synchronous or asynchronous interactive learning environments for the teachers and students as well as among the students themselves.

In this book, the chapter by Hung Chim and Xiaotie Deng proposes a novel data distribution framework for developing a large Web-based course forum system. The proposer's university has 3,983 different kinds of courses covering over 150 different academic programs. The major objective of this work is to build a high performance distributed Web based BBS forum system with very low communication overhead cost and also with the least hardware cost as possible. In the distributed architectural design, each forum server is fully equipped with the ability to support some course forums independently. The forum servers collaborating with each other constitute the whole forum system. All course forums are classified by their teaching content relevance. Relevant course forums are arranged on the same forum server together. The distribution framework also provides a knowledge-based taxonomic storage solution to build a large digital course teaching material library.

Over the Internet, learners are free to access new knowledge without restrictions of time or location. But there are still restrictions considering support in interconnection of learning systems available in scalable, open, dynamic, and heterogeneous environments. The chapter by Kuan-Ching Li et al introduces a distance learning platform based on grid technology to support learning in distributed environments, where open source and freely available learning systems can share and exchange their learning and training contents. A prototype is designed and implemented.

The chapter by Ying-Hong Wang and Chih-Hao Lin presents an English chat room system in which students discuss course contents and ask questions to and receive feedback from teachers and other students. The developed system checks the semantics of a sentence and contains an agent that detects syntax errors in sentences. It can also offer recommendations to the user. The system attempts to find the answers to a user query from the knowledge ontology that is stored in the records of previous user comments. It is aimed to automatically perform the tasks like in a traditional distance learning system where supervisors or teachers are available online to facilitate and monitor a learner's progress by answering questions and guiding the users. An automatic supervisor can help monitor messages, check syntax or semantic mistakes and attempt to correct and to resolve learner-related problems.

Cooperative E-Learning

Technology developments have extended the opportunity for distance learners to be involved in cooperative learning. Cooperative learning requires creation of an environment where a group of heterogeneous students may support their own learning as well as that of others in the same group. In this instructional paradigm, the students recognize that all group members share a common fate, but also retain individual accountability by having assignments of vital, distinct yet overlapping tasks. Research has shown that cooperative learning techniques have the potential to promote student learning and enhance learning performance of students through improved information acquisition and retention, increased self efficacy, higher motivation and development of higher-level thinking skills. It also helps to improve interpersonal and communication skills, social skills and self-confidence, which were not available in the traditional first or second generation distance education delivery. In this book, the chapter by Pei-Jin Tsai et al discusses a concept-based approach and proposes a computer-assisted approach to organizing cooperative learning groups based on complementary concepts to maximize students' learning performance. In this approach, in a given course, each concept is precisely understood by at least one of the students in each group. To evaluate the performance of the proposed approach, an experiment has been conducted on a computer course entitled, "Management Information System." The experimental results conclude that this approach is helpful in enhancing student learning efficacy.

The chapter by Lai-Chen Lu and Ching-Long Yeh discusses some collaborative e-learning and semantic blog technology, and then introduces functions, implementation and how collaborative e-learning appears in semantic course blog. Using a developed semantic course blog, instructors can import the course lectures. Students can team up for projects, ask questions, mutually discuss problems, take the comments, support answers, and query the blog information. Semantic blog combines semantic Web and blog technology that the users can import, export, view, navigate, and query the blog. It provides a platform for collaborative e-learning framework.

Virtual Laboratories: Learning Experiments

In most current Web-based applications virtual labs are designed to provide students some practice in theory, allow them to complete pre-experiments and review contents of experiments. The emergence of high speed Internet has opened the possibility for the development of powerful Web based multimedia applications and integration of virtual reality into these applications. These applications have raised the expectations of implementing more effective virtual laboratories to provide students access via the Internet to experiments in various fields including science and engineering laboratories, which are regarded to be challenging to complete over the Internet. The Carnegie Mellon Virtual Lab and the University of Virginia's Virtual Lab represent innovations in the educational use of information technology.

In this book, the chapter by *Leandro Nunes de Castro* et al discusses a virtual laboratory on natural computing (LVCoN) to support the teaching and learning of natural computing whose goal is to provide didactic contents about the main themes in natural computing in addition to interactive simulations, videos, exercises, links for related sites, forums, and other materials. Natural computing is a terminology used to describe computational algorithms developed by taking inspiration from information processing mechanisms in nature, methods to synthesize natural phenomena in computers, and novel computational approaches based on natural materials. This chapter describes an experiment with LVCoN in a school of computing in Brazil. Most students liked the experience of working with a virtual laboratory, and considered a hybrid teaching approach (i.e. one mixing lectures with virtual learning) very appropriate and productive.

The chapter by *J.A. Gómez Tejedor et al* in this book describes a Java-based virtual laboratory. This remote laboratory enables students to build both direct and alternating current circuits. A graphical user interface resembles the connection board, and also the electrical components and tools that are used in a real laboratory to build electrical circuits. The design of access patterns to the virtual tools is attempted to replicate real touch and allow the lecturer to adapt to the behavior and the principal layout of the different practical sessions during a course.

Learning by means of virtual laboratories tools would be more effective if they were specifically tailored to each student's needs. The virtual teaching process would be well adapted if an artificial tutor could identify the correct acquired knowledge, recognize the erroneous learner's knowledge and suggest a suitable sequence of pedagogical activities to improve the performance of the student. The chapter by Mehdi Najjar proposes a knowledge representation model which judiciously serves the remediation process to students' errors during e-learning activities. The model is inspired by recent research on computational representation of knowledge and by cognitive psychology theories that offer a refined modeling of the human learning processes. Experimental results, obtained via practical tests, show that the knowledge representation and remediation approach facilitates the planning of tailored sequences of feedback that considerably help the learner.

Multimedia Tools and Conferencing Systems

Multimedia systems have opened a wide range of applications by combining a variety of information sources, such as voice, graphics, animation, images, audio, and full-motion video. The integration of high speed network and multimedia helped to develop important tools used in distance education. In this book, the chapter by Noritaka Osawa and Kikuo Asai describes a multipoint, multimedia conferencing system called FocusShare that uses IPv6/IPv4 multicasting for real-time collaboration, enabling video, audio, and group awareness information to be shared. Multiple telepointers provide group awareness information and make it easy to share attention and intention. In addition to pointing with the telepointers, users can add graphical annotations to video streams and share them with one another. The system also supports attention sharing using video processing techniques. Users evaluated FocusShare more positively than conventional video conferencing.

The chapter by S- A. Selouani et al presents systems that use speech technology to emulate the one-on-one interaction a student can get from a virtual instructor. A Web-based learning tool, the Learn IN Context (LINC+) system, designed and used in a real mixed-mode learning context for a computer (C++ language) programming course taught at the Université de Moncton (Canada) is described in this chapter. It integrates an Internet Voice Searching and Navigating (IVSN) system that helps learners search and navigate both the Web and their desktop environment through voice commands and dictation.

The chapter by Sami Habib and Maytham Safar presents an Internet tool called WEBCAP that can schedule the retrieval of multimedia Web documents in time while considering the workloads on the WWW resources by applying capacity planning techniques. The results shown demonstrate the effectiveness of WEBCAP in scheduling the refreshing of multimedia Web documents.

Facial Animation in Distance Education

Several researchers consider emotion deficiency as an issue in distance education systems. Facial emotion recognition and speech emotion recognition technologies are countermeasures proposed in Web based education systems. Online interaction with 3D facial animation is an alternative way. The chapter by Yushun Wang and Yueting Zhuang presents a novel 3D facial modeling solution that facilitates quasi-facial communication for online learning. The experimental results show that the proposed algorithm can robustly produce 3D facial models from images captured in various scenarios to enhance the lifelikeness in distant learning.

Pedagogy and Application of Technology in Distance Education

Successful education delivery requires an understanding of how technology relates to pedagogy and content. Technology, pedagogy and content can not be seen in isolation. (Mishra & Koehler, 2006; Koehler & Mishra, 2008).

The chapter by Pei-Di Shen et al discusses use of innovative learning designs such as problem-based learning (PBL) and self-regulated learning (SRL) to increase students' learning motivation and develop practical skills. A series of quasi-experiments were conducted in two classes of 106 freshmen in a semester course at the Institute of Technology in Taiwan to examine effects of these designs mediated by a Web-based learning environment. The results of the experiment revealed that effects of Web-enabled PBL, Web-enabled SRL, and their combinations on students' skills of application software have significant differences.

Computer games technology can be used to make learning more interesting. Attempts are being made to employ games for constructivist learning and teaching. The chapter by Morris S. Y. Jong et al in this book introduces game-based learning and its intrinsic educational traits from motivational, cognitive and socio-cultural perspectives. It also reviews two recent foci of game-based learning : i) "education in games" which is an approach for adopting existing commercial games for educational use and ii) "games in education" in which the games are designed specifically with underlying pedagogy for some curricula.

The chapter by Keita Matsuo et al discusses design and implementation of new functions such as interface changing function, new ranking function and learner's learning situation checking function to improve the system performance of a previously implemented e-learning system that was able to increase the learning efficiency by stimulating learners' motivation.

The chapter by Dawei Hu et al proposes a personalized e-learning framework based on a user-interactive question-answering (QA) system, in which a user-modeling approach is used to capture personal information of students and a personalized answer extraction algorithm is used for personalized automatic answering. The experimental results show the efficacy of the proposed user-modeling approach.

The chapter by Huan-Chao Keh et al presents an application of distance education in advanced military education with well-chosen technology to assist officers around the world in becoming more skilled and qualified for future challenges. The chapter presents a prototype of the architecture of 'Advanced Military Education – Distance Learning' (AME-DL). It combines advanced e-learning tools, simulation technology, and Web technology to provide a common standard framework for a military training program and a set of military learning and training subjects that can be accessed easily from anywhere, at anytime through a Web browser. It is aimed at reducing training costs while providing a high quality learning experience.

Mobile E-Learning

A relatively development is mobile technology. This technology has the potential to make real use of the fundamental terminology in distance education "education anytime and anywhere." Learners may be at work, in a meeting, on the road on a bus or a train, shopping at a store, or eating, etc. However, with flexibility comes more issues: a small screen with limitations for reading a large amount of content, viewing graphics, or seeing moving graphics in a distracted environment where mobile devices are mostly used. Accordingly, much research and review is needed for technology, content and pedagogy in mobile environment.

In this book, the chapter by Tin-Yu Wu develops an environment for mobile e-learning that includes an interactive course, virtual online labs, an interactive online test, and lab-exercise training platform on the fourth generation mobile communication system. This system uses a variety of computer embedded devices to ubiquitously access multimedia information, such as smart phones and PDAs.

Inter-networking has become one of the most popular technologies in mobile e-learning for the next generation communication environment. The learning mode in the future will be an international, immediate, virtual, and interactive classroom that enables learners to learn and interact.

Other Web-Based Tools for Distance Education

Research is being done to define learning objects, their standards, and building tools for developing Web-based courses. Research in this area also includes the use of agents and ontologies with learning objects employing their intelligent search and selection capabilities.

The chapter by Karen Stauffer et al presents a methodology for developing Extensible Markup Language (XML) based learning objects for courses using the IMS LD specification and to design a runtime environment for these learning objects. The chapter first investigates the IMS LD specification, determining how to use it with online courses and the student delivery model, and then applies this to a Unit of Learning (UOL) for online computer science courses. This chapter also looks at how the specification used for the learning objects can be extended by using intelligent agents and more advanced levels of the IMS LD.

The chapter by Jui-Fa Chen et al proposes an interactive feedback mechanism in a virtual campus that can parse, understand and respond to Chinese sentences. This mechanism utilizes a specific lexical database according to the particular application. The aim of this work is to develop an automatic interactive feedback system for e-learning Websites.

SUMMARY AND CONCLUSION

In this chapter, we have observed that technology has significantly contributed to shaping instruction and the future. In discussing how technology is shaping instruction and distance education, we looked back to the past history of distance education in America and other countries around the world. The major highlights include:

- how technology has helped to change the communication media and contributed to growth of distance education;
- development of course management technology that created virtual distance education systems which extended educational opportunities to all who desire education and who cannot afford to attend institutions due to socio-economic reasons, time constraints or geographical separation.

Over the last few decades, the innovation of new technology and revolutionary changes in communication systems has played a convincing role in changing peoples' attitudes towards distance education. This has contributed to changes in educational policy, increased support by academics and acceptance of degrees by institutions around the globe. Over the past decade, we have seen a significant growth in numbers of institutions offering distance education and also an increase in the number of students of all ages and races seeking a degree.

The development of new technology and changing dynamics of delivery options, interaction and collaboration using asynchronous or synchronous mode of communications created a new dimension to distance learning of the 21st century.

It is expected that more sophisticated communication and teaching tools that would help to further improve the quality of distance education will be available in the future. The growth of technology, its availability, and its affordability will contribute to overcoming the limitations of quality of test and evaluation process of student's knowledge. It appears that educational institutions will need to adopt one or more iterations of distance education to maintain and fulfill the expectations and requirements of current and future students.

Mahbubur R Syed
Department of Information Systems and Technology
Minnesota State University Mankato, USA

REFERENCES

Ashby, M (2002, September 26). *Growth in Distance Education Programs and Implications for Federal Education Policy* (Testimony before the committee on Health, Education, Labor and Pension, U.S senate).

Bartini, M. (March 2008). An Empirical Comparison of Traditional and Web-enhanced Classrooms. Journal of Instructional Psychology, *35*(1), 3-11.

Beldarrain, Y. (2006). Distance education Trends: Integrating new technologies to foster student interaction and collaboration. *Distance Education, 27*(2), 139-153.

Casey, D. M. (2008). The Historical Development of Distance Education through Technology. *TechTrends, 52*(2), 45-51.

Dykman, C.A., & Davis, C.K. (2008). Part One - The Shift Toward Online Education. *Journal of Information Systems Education, 19*(1), 11-16.

Charlesworth, P., Charlesworth, D. D., & Vlcia, C. (2006). Students' perspectives of the influence of Web-enhanced coursework on incidences of cheating. *Journal of Chemical Education, 83*(9), 1368-75.

Deal, W. F., III. (2002). Distance learning: Teaching technology online. *Technology Teacher, 61* (8), 21-27.

Edling, R. J. (2000). Information technology in the classroom: Experiences and recommendations. *Campus-Wide Information Systems, 17*(1), 10-15.

Emmerson, A.M. (2004). *A history of the changes in Practices of Distance education – The United States from 1852-2003*. PhD thesis submitted at Dowling College, Oakdale, New York. (UMI Number: 3157941).

Godwin-Jones, R. (May, 2003). Emerging technologies, blogs, and wikis: Environment for online collaboration. *Language Learning & Technology.* 7, 12-16. Retrieved October 15, 2005 from http://LLt.msu.edu/vol17/num2/pdf/emerging.pdf

Harmon, O. R., & Lambrinos J. (2008). Are Online Exams an Invitation to Cheat? *The Journal of Economic Education*, 39(2), 116-25. Retrieved May 10, 2009 from http://www.heldref.org/ (retrieved May10, 2009).

Hard, S. F., J. M. Conway, and A. C. Moran. (2006). Faculty and college student beliefs about the frequency of student academic misconduct. *Journal of Higher Education*, *77* (6), 1058-80.

Kennedy, K., Nowak, S., Raghuraman, R., Thomas, J. & Davis, S. F. (2000). Academic dishonesty and distance learning: Student and faculty views. *College Student Journal*, *34*(2), 309-14.

Koehler, M. J., & Mishra, P. (2008). Introducing Technological Pedagogical Knowledge. In AACTE (Eds.), *The Handbook of Technological Pedagogical Content Knowledge for Educators*. Routledge/ Taylor & Francis Group for the American Association of Colleges of Teacher Education.

Mejias, U. (2006). *Social software affordance, course blog*. Columbia University. Retrieved from http://ssa05/blogpost.com

Mishra, P., & Koehler, M. J. (2006). Technological Pedagogical Content Knowledge: A new framework for teacher knowledge. *Teachers College Record, 108*(6), 1017-1054.

Potashnik, M., & Capper, J. (n.d.). *Distance Education: Growth and Diversity*. Retrieved April 28, 2009 from http://www.worldbank.org/fandd/english/0398/articles/0110398.htm (Adapted from J.S. Daniel, 1996, Mega Universities and Knowledge Media: Technology Strategies for Higher Education; London: Kogan Page).

Rovai, A. P. (2001). Online and traditional assessments: What is the difference? *Internet and Higher Education*, *3*(3), 141-51.

USDoE (U.S. Department of Education, National Center for Education Statistics). (2008). *Distance Education at Degree-Granting Postsecondary Institutions: 2006-07*. Retrieved from http://nces.ed.gov/pubsearch/pubsinfo.asp?pubid=2009044

Zandberg, I., & Lewis, L. (2008). *TBDE - Technology-Based Distance Education Courses for Public Elementary and Secondary School Students: 2002-03 and 2004-05*. National Center for Education Statistics, Institute of Education Sciences, U.S. Department of Education. Washington, DC. Retrieved April 28, 2009 from http://nces.ed.gov/pubsearch/pubsinfo.asp?pubid=2008008

Chapter 1
A Semantics-Based Information Distribution Framework for Large Web-Based Course Forum System

Hung Chim
City University of Hong Kong, Hong Kong

Xiaotie Deng
City University of Hong Kong, Hong Kong

ABSTRACT

We propose a novel data distribution framework for developing a large Web-based course forum system. In the distributed architectural design, each forum server is fully equipped with the ability to support some course forums independently. The forum servers collaborating with each other constitute the whole forum system. Therefore, the workload of the course forums can be shared by a group of the servers. With the secure group communication protocol and fault tolerance design, the new distribution framework provides a robust and scalable distributed architecture for the large course forum system. The forum servers can be settled in anywhere as long as a broadband network connection to Internet is provided. Our experimental performance testing results show that the large forum system is a high performance distributed system with very low communication overhead cost. In addition, all course forums are classified by their teaching content relevance. Relevant course forums can be arranged on the same forum server together. Hence our distribution framework also provides a knowledge-based taxonomic storage solution to build a large digital course teaching material library.

INTRODUCTION

Rapid advance of Web technology has changed not only the initially proposed role of the Web as the medium of information communication but also human life in various ways. Web learning has become one of the hot research topics in recent years. Many Web-based education application systems have been introduced and affected the traditional teaching-learning concepts, models and methods. Without the limitations of time zones and geographic locations, these systems provide synchronous or asynchronous interactive learning environment for the teachers and students as well as among the students themselves. We started working on online Web-based Bulletin Board System (BBS) forums in 2003, and have developed a Web-based BBS forum system named Teaching Assistant System (TAS) (Hung Chim, 2004; Hung Chim, 2005). Currently, we are planning to extend the BBS forum system to a large course forum system with the capacity to support the tutorial of all teaching courses in our university. Having reviewed our original TAS system design, we devise an innovative information distribution framework to build a large Web-based course forum system as presented in this article.

Nowadays, almost all Web-based BBS forum systems use quite similar conventional client-server database design shown in Figure 1(a). This kind of design produces a tight system architecture. The biggest benefit from this architecture is the lower maintenance cost. However, this tight architecture apparently has its limitation as all forum servers must be allocated in a protected local network. Consequently, the performance of a forum will be unavoidably affected by the other forums that are sharing the same hardware or network bandwidth.

Our approach provides a solution to overcome the limitation and build up a high-performance, large-course forum system which can work over the Internet. The large forum system consists of several forum servers with the same system architecture. Each forum server (also called a *node*) is a fully equipped Web-based forum system (similar to Figure 1 (a)) which works independently to support the forums on it. Additionally, a new module called Node Communication Module is developed to provide the communications for data exchange and synchronization among the *nodes*. Therefore, all *nodes* collaborating with each other construct a large forum system to hold up all course discussion forums. Certainly, a particular *node* has to be assigned as a coordinator (called *main node*) to manage the collaborative communication among the *nodes*.

We believe that fault tolerance capability is a crucial issue for the distributed forum system. As a mature system design technique which we are using in the Forum Processing Module development, the conventional client-server database design is widely used in Web service applications. Thus we assume that each *node* in our forum system has sufficient stability in handling all local forum operations and works against the security attacks. On the other hand, nobody can guarantee that the network between two *nodes* will never be broken or jammed if and when the two *nodes* are located in two different cities. How to guarantee that each *node* can provide adequate forum services even if it temporarily loses network connections to other *nodes* is the major concern in our approach. We solve the problem with two methods. First, we apply a partial data replication in the database model design, the essential data for maintaining the local forum services are replicated in each *node*. Second, secure group communication protocols are developed to keep the consistency of the replicated data on all *nodes*. Therefore, our approach provides a robust and high scalable distribution framework to meet the demand and nature characteristic of Web distance education.

Communication is a key issue in distributed system, since efficiency can only be achieved when the communication overhead is small. Based on the results of investigating the ordinary operations of registered users and corresponding forum programs, we develop a hierarchical tree structure to define the relationships of forum data, so that we can apply a horizontal fragmentation schema on the distributed database (Rothnie, 1980) to partition the forum data by the forum identifier. The database fragmentation schema is transparent to almost all forum operations and the corresponding programs. Therefore, almost all data submitted to a forum can be saved into the *node* which supports the forum locally. The necessary data accessed by most ordinary forum operations are also limited in the local database. Only a few essential data must be replicated over the *nodes* to maintain the running up of entire forum system.

Besides considering the above technical design issues, we also considered the behavior and interests of forum members as an important issue of affecting the communication overhead in the distributed forum system. Let us imagine an ordinary scenario: a member is currently interested in the topics of two discussion forums located in two different *nodes*. He may frequently shift himself between the two forums and *nodes*. As such, these actions of the forum members inevitably increase the cost for the replicated user data update and synchronization. In fact, the majority of the communication overhead costs in the distributed forum system are involved in the replicated user data update and synchronization. Moreover, we consider the forum system as a big digital library to store all course teaching material. We introduce a semantics-based clustering algorithm to classify the relevant courses into the same group according to their semantic similarities. Then we can allocate the relevant course forums to the same node according to the clustering results. The initial semantic similarities of the courses are computed from the course introduction pages. The relevance of the information content (posts) in the forum also will be taken into account of the semantic similarities in our future work. We believe that this allocation strategy is helpful in reducing the communication overhead costs for the replicated user data update and synchronization. The statistical data we collected from real online forum communities also proves that most forum users have strong preferences in choosing their favorite topics and joining the forum discussions. Further, this strategy also speeds up the information assessment and distillation, and reduces the complexity of the work for topic-oriented summary in constructing the knowledge digital library. Because we have already provided a knowledge-based taxonomy storage framework to settle the information and knowledge before the contributors (teachers and students) submitting them.

RELATED WORK

Bulletin Board System (BBS) first appeared in the middle of 70s and was essentially "a personal computer, not necessarily an expensive one, running inexpensive BBS software, plugged into an ordinary telephone line via a small electronic device called modem" (Howard, 1993). With advent of the Internet, the World Wide Web brought more new multimedia technologies to the BBSs. Millions of BBSs sprang up across the world. BBS online community also became an interesting research topic to attract many researchers. Data Grid (Wolfgang, 2000; Stockinger, 2001) presented a distributed database management system for the mass-replicated data accessing in the large scientific computing community. We met the same problems in handling data replication and synchronization over a WAN or Internet, however the replicated data in our work were formalized relation tuples stored in a RDBMS. We preferred to use a distributed database model to represent the architecture of our distributed forum system than a middleware infrastructure, although we used a similar system design idea in the similar working environment. There is some relevant research work exploring the important role of BBS forum systems in their e-learning approaches (Zhang, 2004; Wang, 2004). Like that in our previous work, they used a BBS forum system as an interactive platform in their e-learning approaches and never concerned the performance problem in the forum system. During the forum system development, we studied the codes of two Web-based BBS forum systems (XMB and Discuz! Board). We also have observed that some world class IT companies such as Yahoo! and Google are launching their large online BBS forums this year. However, up to now we have not found any research paper or technical report proposing a similar system design to our approach.

Conventional database replication protocols are well known and their correctness has been studied in much detail. Eager replication protocols use update everywhere (e.g., *read-one/write-all-available*) and quorums to minimize overhead cost (Bernstein, 1987). They are mainly designed for fault tolerance. These protocols coordinate each operation individually, use distributed locking and two-phase commit. As a result, when the number of nodes increases, transaction response times, conflict probability and deadlock rates grow significantly (Gray, 1996). In practice, most commercial database systems prefer to use lazy approaches (updates are only propagated after the transaction commits) to achieve better performance with a tradeoff on fault tolerance and replica correctness. Several improvement protocols have been proposed in recent years. Esther Pacitti (2000) proposed an approach to combine the total order concept with a lazy replication protocol. Yair (2002) implemented replication at the middleware layer using a *black-box* approach that has been tested in a LAN and in a WAN. Almost all these work are based on an important assumption: there exist some stable network trunks among the servers. Contrarily our work tries to solve a quite tough and different problem: how to handle the temporary network breakdown and partition is the major concern in our information distribution framework and replication protocols design.

SEMANTICS-BASED INFORMATION DISTRIBUTION FRAMEWORK

Background and Motivation

Our original TAS forum system uses a conventional client-server database design as shown in Figure 1(a). In the client-server architecture, the Web server acts as a pre-processor to process the data carried by the HTTP requests, and the database server handles all data storing and accessing. Figure 1(b) illustrates a popular cluster system design. It uses a workload balancer to dispatch the HTTP requests into two Web servers; each Web server cooperates with its database respectively. The data consistency is kept by the database cluster technique. Thus the workload is shared by two similar forum systems. This design provides a robust and scalable capacity to the Web-based forum system. The particular cluster technique is also helpful in enhancing the reliability of the entire forum system. However both system architectures have a limitation: all servers have to be located in a high speed internal network because of the heavy data communication among the servers.

The major objective of our work is to build a high performance distributed Web-based BBS forum system with the least hardware cost as possible. We find that the above system design solutions are not suitable for building our large course forum system. Firstly, there are 3,983 different kind of courses in our university, covering over 150 different academic programs. To fulfill the demand of supporting these courses, at least two expensive high grade servers are needed if we use the conventional client-server system design. Secondly, when we consider that some course forum sites will be located in the community college outside the main campus, the cluster system architecture also presents its server settling limitation even if it can provide a cheaper solution with Linux cluster techniques.

Figure 1. System architecture of a Web-based BBS forum system

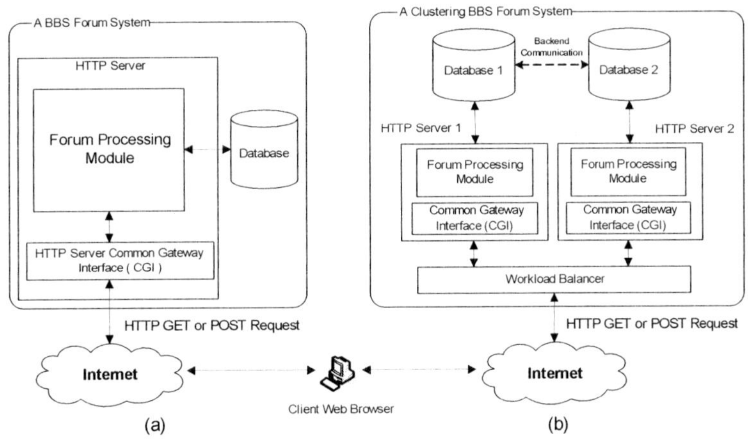

The distributed forum system consists of several server nodes in our approach. We are planning to choose several low grade servers as the *nodes*. Because the hardware budget of the whole system costs is around 25%-30% for purchasing one enterprise grade server, but the computing power we can obtain at least doubles such a server, both the CPU power and disk storage capacity. Additionally, using multiple servers also makes it feasible to settle the forum servers in different places over a WAN. Settling the servers as near to the users as possible is considered as a helpful strategy to reduce the total communication costs via localizing the network traffic between the servers and the clients within a sub-network.

Horizontal Fragmentation Schema for Database Distribution

The original TAS system was developed with PHP, Apache Web server and MySQL database server on the Linux system platform. At the beginning of designing the new distribution framework, we reviewed the codes, database structure of the TAS system and investigated the ordinary operations of forum users in participating in the forum discussion. Our investigation yields two results:

1. The course forum system uses a catalog tree to compose and arrange all dynamic content Web pages. The index page of the forum site is the root of the tree, it lists all uniform resource locators (URL) links of the courses; the forum index page of each course becomes a child of the root, it lists the URL links for the forums of a course; then each topic index page is a child of the corresponding forum index page, it lists URL links of the topic threads in the forum; finally all topic thread pages are the leaves of the tree: they list the content of the posts by the topics. The catalog tree is transparent to the forum users since the URL links are hidden in the Web pages. To visit a discussion forum, all the user has to do is click the corresponding URL link. Even an experienced user might not perceive that the URL link has led him to another forum site if the two forum sites use the same user interface. This hidden URL link technique makes using multiple servers to construct a large forum system possible and user friendly.
2. Despite the forum management operations (these operations seldom occur), the ordinary operations of a user in TAS forum system can be concluded as browsing courses index, checking topics list in a forum, read-

Figure 2. The database tables and forum programs are involved in the ordinary forum operations

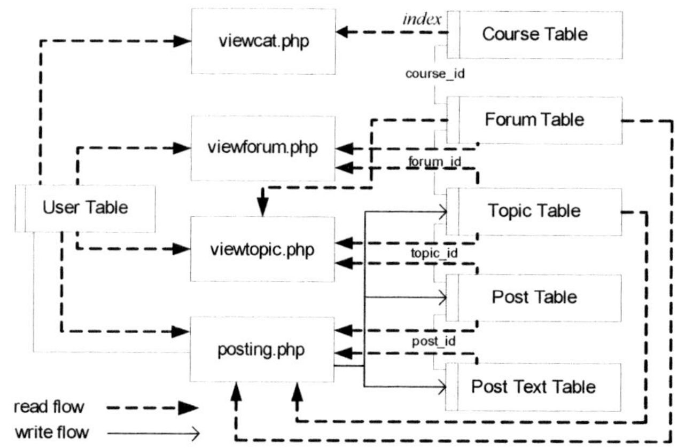

ing posts of a topic thread, and writing a post to disseminate information. Inside the corresponding forum programs, the tables accessed by the programs also follow the order of the catalog tree from the root to the leaves, except *USER* table containing the data of registered users.

Based on the above investigation, we use a horizontal fragmentation schema (Rothnie, 1980) (Ceri, 1985) to partition the relevant database tables by forum identifier. Hence each *node* of the distributed forum system only needs to maintain the part of database data with respect to the course forums supported by itself. As illustrated in Figure 2, the tuples of five tables must be partitioned in our fragmentation schema. If there are *n nodes* and a total of *m* forums in the distributed forum system, then we can partition *COURSE* and *FORUM* table into *n* subsets by the *node identifiers* (*node_id*: N_1, N_2, ..., N_n), the *TOPIC*, *POST* and *POST_TEXT* tables into *m* subsets by the forum identifiers (*forum_id*: 1, 2, 3, ..., *m*). Thus we get the final fragmentation schema as illustrated in Figure 3, where a new table named *NODE* containing the data of all *nodes* is added in order to completely reconstruct the global relations in the fragmentation schema. All tuples of *NODE* and *COURSE* tables need to be replicated around the *nodes*. In practice, we choose to partition the tuples of these tables by *node_id*. However we can move a forum and its data from one *node* to another without damaging the data integrity, since the minimum fragments of the horizontal

Figure 3. The fragmentation tree of global relation of COURSE, FORUM and TOPIC (the sub-trees of POST, POST_TEXT are same to TOPIC)

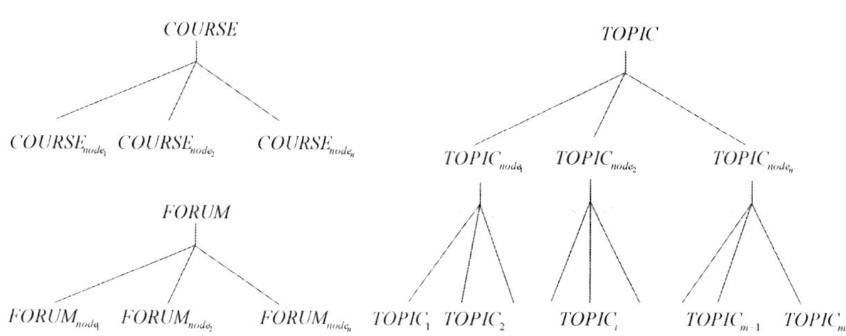

Figure 4. Session ID propagation protocol

node N_i

```
BEGIN: A client submits $username, $password
  T1: SELECT ALL FROM USER
          WHERE username = $username;
  IF T1: PASSWORD = ms5($password), THEN
      $session_id = new md5(IP);

          T2: UPDATE USER SET session_id=$session_id
                  WERE username=$username;
  ELSE $session_id = ANONYMOUS ;
  Deliver $session_id to the client;
END
BEGIN: receives $session_id from node N_j;
  T4: SELECT ALL FROM USER
          WHERE session_id = $session_id;

  Deliver T4 to node N_j;
END
```

node N_j

```
BEGIN: A client submits $session_id
  T3: SELECT ALL FROM USER
          WHERE session_id = $session_id;
  IF T3 = NIL AND $session_id<>ANONYMOUS, TEHN
      Deliver $session_id to node N_i;

  Waiting until receive T4 from node N_i;
  IF T4 <> NIL, THEN
      T5: UPDATE USER SET T4
              WERE session_id=T4:session_id;
  ELSE $session_id = ANONYMOUS ;
  Deliver $session_id to the client;
END
```

fragmentation schema are generated by *forum_id*. Thus we can adjust the workload of the *nodes* by moving the forums around the *nodes* on the fly.

User Data Partial Cache Mechanism for System Fault Tolerance

The user authentication for a Web service is quite different from other network services, since HTTP protocol is a stateless application protocol. Almost all Web servers cannot track a user's progress over the HTML pages. Most of Web-based BBS forum systems reply on a HTTP session technique to solve the user authentication problem. The forum system generates a unique session identifier (ID) for a user while he logs in. The session ID is returned and kept in the user's Web browser locally, thereafter the Web browser combines the session ID in every HTTP request sent to the forum, then the forum system can validate the user's HTTP requests by the session ID. Consequently *USER* table becomes the busiest table in the forum database; that is why we have to replicate the data of this table over all *nodes*. On the other hand, there are few users who visit every forum of the forum system, and few or no users would like to submit their posts in every forum. For example, a student of the Department of Computer Science might never visit the course forums of the Physics Department. Thus a partial tuples replication for *USER* table may be reasonable to reduce the communication costs for the user data update and synchronization in whole forum system. This partial tuples replication is called a *user data partial cache mechanism* in our work. This cache mechanism is implemented as follows: The *main node* maintains a full copy of *USER* table, and other *nodes* keep an empty *USER* table at the initial stage. When a course forum moderator (course lecturer or tutor) uploads a student list, the corresponding *node* sends a *pull* request to the *main node* to fetch the corresponding user tuples of these students, and keeps them in *USER* table locally. For other registered users, the *node* will send a *pull* request to the *main node* to fetch the record at his first login on the *node*. The user data partial cache mechanism allows all *nodes* to obtain a capability to tolerate the temporary network breakdown or traffic jam. Each *node* can keep on providing normal forum service to the members whose records have been cached locally when it loses the network connection to the *main node*.

Figure 5. Node communication module's architecture and group communication model

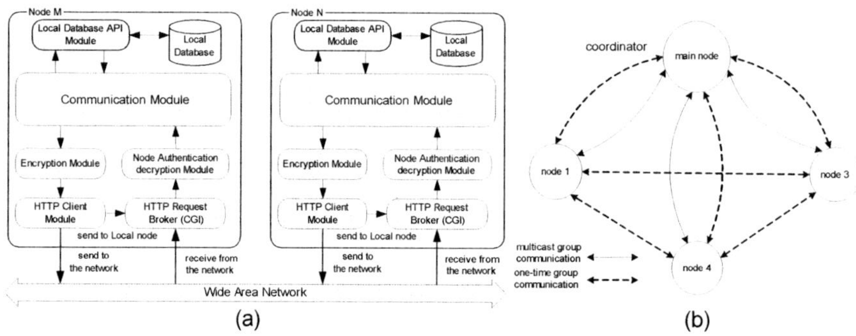

Replication Protocol for Forum Management Data Update

In general, data replication is a key component to spread the workload across several servers, mask failures of individual servers and increase the processing capacity of the whole database system. We studied the data replication problem with a group communication model as shown in Figure 5(b), which is derived from the entire forum system architecture. All group communications are classified into two types: multicast communications and one-time communications. The multicast communications are mainly involved in the global forum management operations and global user data synchronization. The one-time communications are mainly involved in the individual user authentication and data update.

We define a global forum management operation as the administrative operations for adjusting the forum configuration parameters that affect the entire forum system, such as inserting a new server *node*, or adding a new course. They are only manipulated by the system administrators (not forum moderators) and not common in ordinary forum management. We implement a simple lazy replication protocol to keep the consistency of the replicas in global forum management operations: all these operations are limited on the *main node* only, where the primary copies are updated locally. Then the updated primary copies will be propagated to other *nodes* by multicast messages. Since there is only one primary copy among all replicas, all multicast messages for replicas propagation are also coordinated by the *main node*. Each multicast message is labeled a sequence number and sent to each *node* at a serialization order (Birman, 1991). Thus the data consistency can be guaranteed.

Replication Protocol for User Data Update and Synchronization

We classify the fields in replicated *USER* table into two kinds of replicas according to their purpose in the distributed forum system. The first replica contains the fields for user authentication, for example, *user_id, username, password and session_id*. They are considered as the essential data for the *nodes* to maintain the normal forum service even if the network around the *nodes* is breakdown or partitioned. The second replica contains the fields to store historical records of the forum members. The forum system keeps the records of a member, such as his total number of posts (*posts*), experience value (*exp*) and credit value (*credit*). The current values of these fields are also online listed in some forum pages. Here we use $AUTH_{N_i}$ to denote the fields in first replica in *node* N_i, $STATE_{N_i}$ to denote the fields in the second replica.

$AUTH$ = *USER(user_id, username, password, session_id)*

STATE = USER(user_id, posts, exp, credit)

The updating urgencies for the two kinds of replicas are studied in the replication protocol design. It is impractical to keep a strict consistency for the replicas in the large forum system due to the communication overhead that is unable to be expected as pointed out in Gray (1996). We have to keep a balance between the data consistency and efficiency in the replicas control. Clearly, the data consistency depends on the frequency of updates and the amount of data items covered by an update. The replicas of *AUTH* are considered as the essential data for fault tolerance of the nodes, they might require an immediate update when one of the replicas is changed. On the other hand, *STATE* is not a kind of essential data. The replica of *STATE* on each node is accessed and updated by the local forum operations independently. None of them can be considered as the primary copy. Thus the replicas of *STATE* require a global data synchronization to collect the updates of each replica and calculate their latest sum as the primary copy; after that the primary copy will be propagated to all nodes. Such a requirement leaves us large room for choosing the data update frequency in consideration of the system efficiency in the replication protocols design.

Replication Protocol for User Authentication (AUTH)

As described in the previous sections, a *node* in the distributed forum system can identify a registered user by either his username-password or a session ID. The username-password authentication often occurs at the time when a user logs into the forum system. The session ID authentications happen in all forum operations of the user in the current session after his login. The session ID propagation between two *nodes* is implemented by a one-time group communication with *pull* methodology as illustrated in Figure 4.

The password replication handles the field *password* update for an individual user when he has changed his password. We also implement the replication protocol with *pull* methodology as that in session ID propagation. We make all URLs for changing password point to the user profile page on the *main node*, then all users have to go to the site of the *main node* to change their password. Only the *main node* maintains a primary copy of the replicas. When the user logs into a *node* which keeps an incorrect replica, the *node* will forward the user request to the *main node* after it fails in the local password verification. If the *main node* verifies the password successfully, the *main node* returns the *node* a positive acknowledgement message with a new primary copy of the user. Otherwise a negative acknowledgement message with the primary copy is returned.

Thus the corresponding user record on the *node* is updated along with the password or session ID delivery. When the user goes to another *node*, his current user record is also forwarded to the *node*. In such scenes the intermediate *node* works as a router to forward a network packet to its destination. In other words, some temporary network partitions will be covered in our distribution framework.

Replication Protocol for Statistic User Data (STATE)

The replication protocols for *STATE* deal with a more complicated situation, since we cannot find a primary copy among the replicas. A user may visit any *node's* site at any time. Consequently, the replica of *STATE* on the *node* might be updated independently. In fact, the replica control for *STATE* is to implement a global user data synchronization to calculate the aggregated sums for the fields in *STATE* replicas on all *nodes*. The global user data synchronization must execute periodically to keep an online update for the replicas (e.g., *1 hour* in our approach).

To implement the replica control of *STATE*, we add a new table named *STUSER* to store the sums of the fields in *STATE* for each forum member. The *main node* maintains the primary copy. Any update on the primary copy will be propagated to all other *nodes*. Then the global user data synchronization can be considered as a transaction to complete the replicas update for *STATE* and *STUSER*.

A global user data synchronization transaction includes several multicast messages. To tolerate the temporary network interruption or partition, we use group communication primitive to provide total order semantics for the multicast message deliveries in the transaction. Additionally, since the transaction is concurrently executed along with other local forum operations and data replications, we introduce a snapshot isolation (SI) solution to avoid these read/write conflicts entirely in the transaction (Kemme, 2000). In the SI solution, all replicas of *STATE* as well as the transaction must be labeled by a timestamp of BOT (beginning of the transaction). The timestamp of the *main node* is used as a sequence number to label each transaction and its multicast messages.

The replication protocol for the global data synchronization executes its transaction in four phases. We implement the group communication layer with HTTP application protocol, each message delivery procedure also includes two phases: a *node* sends its data by a HTTP request (*send phase*), the opposing *node* responses a XML document containing its data as the acknowledgement (*ack phase*).

- **Prepare phase:** The *main node* sends a *prepare* multicast message to all *nodes* (including itself). On *node* N_i, a snapshot of *STATE* is created as *TS*: $STATE_{N_i}$ by a *SQL* query to the local database after receiving the *prepare* message (we assume that there are a total of *n nodes*).

SELECT *user_id*, *posts*, *exp*, *credit* FROM *USER* WHERE *posts* >0 *OR exp* >0 *OR credit* >0 INTO *TS*: $STATE_{N_i}$;

Then *TS*: $STATE_{N_i}$ is returned to the *main node* as the acknowledgement of the *prepare* message. The *main node* goes to next *phase* only if the number of acknowledgements that it receives is larger than $n - 2$. Otherwise the *main node* will cancel the transaction and start it again after a defined timeout (e.g., 10 minutes).

- **Local update phase:** The *main node* labels the failure *node* if there exists one. Then it computes the sum of each field in all *TS*: $STATE_{N_i}$ and saves all sums into *TS*: *STUSER*.
- **Replication phase:** The *main node* sends a *replica* multicast message containing *TS*: *STUSER* to all active *nodes*. Each *node* must return *commit ready* message as a positive acknowledgement after receiving *TS*: *STUSER* completely. If there is a message reporting failure, the message will be sent again until the delivery succeeds. If the *replica* message cannot be delivered to all active *nodes* within a defined timeout, the transaction will be cancelled too.
- **Commit phase:** After acknowledging that all active *nodes* have received a copy of *TS*: *STUSER*, the *main node* sends a *commit* multicast message to all active *nodes* (the message will be sent again if a message delivery fails). Each *node* begins to execute its *local commit phase* when it receives the message. The *local commit phase* on a *node* N_i covers updating local *STATE* with *TS*: $STATE_{N_i}$ and updating its local *STUSER* with *TS*: *STUSER*.

UPDATE *USER* SET *posts=posts-TS:posts*, *exp=exp - TS:exp*, *credit=credit - TS:credit*, *ts = TS* WHERE *user_id=TS:user_id*;

DELETE FROM *STUSER*;
INSERT INTO *STUSER* (*user_id, posts, exp, credit, ts*)
SELECT ALL FROM *TS:STUSER*;

Since that the global user data synchronization is only executed by the *main node* with a long interval time (e.g., 1 hour), the total order of multicast messages is certainly guaranteed. However, the long interval time for the global user data synchronization presents a tradeoff of a large data update latency. In particular, the global user data synchronization might be cancelled due to a serious network interruption or partition. As the complement for reducing the user data update latency, we also implemented an individual user data replication protocol.

Actually, the session ID propagation also plays a similar role of the individual user data replication protocol by transferring a full copy of a user tuple from one *node* to another. We use the same idea for the session ID propagation to implement the individual user data replication protocol.

At first, we add a new table named *USERSTATE* consisting of fields: *user_id, posts, exp, credit, ts, node_id* into the database on each *node, ts* is the timestamp of the latest update for the tuple. The table enables each *node* N_i to keep a set of replicas $STATE_{N_j}$ of other *nodes* ($j=1,2,...,n$ and $j \neq i$),

$$USERSTATE_{N_i} = TS_1{:}\,STATE_{N_1} \text{ UN } TS_2{:}\,STATE_{N_2} \ldots \text{ UN } TS_n{:}\,STATE_{N_n}$$

$TS_j{:}\,STATE_{N_j}$ is the latest replica obtained from a remote *node* N_j at time TS_j. Certainly *node* N_i also has a local replica $STATE_{N_i}$. Then the *node* N_i can compute the sums of all fields in *STATE* for user *m* by the following formula.

$$STATE_m = SUM(USERSTATE_{N_{j,m}}) + STATE_{N_{i,m}} + TS_i{:}\,STUSER_{N_{i,m}}$$
$$(j=1, 2, \ldots, n \text{ and } j \neq i)$$

Assuming that there are two *nodes* N_i and N_j have cached the session ID of a user *m* locally, the session ID propagation for user *m* will not occur again between the two *nodes* in the current session. We use TS_1 to denote the timestamp of latest session ID propagation or individual user data replication, *RST* denote the interval data refresh time for the individual user data replication. The individual user data replication will be executed when the user *m* moves from *node* N_i to *node* N_j.

In the node N_j
BEGIN
TS= current time;
IF $TS - TS_1 \geq RST$, THEN
  send *update* message containing *user_id* = *m* to *node* N_i;
  waiting for the response message with TS_2: $STUSER_{N_{i,m}}$, TS_i: $STUSER_{N_{i,m}}$ and $USERSTATE_{N_i}$
IF $TS_2 > TS_1$, THEN
  update TS_1: $STUSER_{N_{i,m}}$ with TS_2: $STUSER_{N_{i,m}}$;
IF $TS_i > TS_j$, THEN
  update TS_j: $STUSER_{N_{j,m}}$ with TS_i: $STUSER_{N_{i,m}}$;
FOR each TS_{id}: $STUSER_{id,m}$ in $USERSTATE_{N_{i,m}}$ ($id \neq i, j$)
  update $USERSTATE_{N_{j,m}}$ with TS_{id}: $STUSER_{id,m}$ IF $TS_{id} > TS_j$;
END

In the node N_i
INPUT: *user_id* = *m*
BEGIN
  get TS_2: $STUSER_{N_{i,m}}$ for user *m* with a current timestamp TS_2 = current tim;
  get TS_i: $STUSER_{N_{i,m}}$ for user *m* with its original time stamp TS_i;
  get $USERSTATE_{N_{i,m}}$;
  send TS_2: $STUSER_{N_{i,m}}$, TS_i: $STUSER_{N_{i,m}}$ and $USERSTATE_{N_{i,m}}$ to *node* N_j;
END

SEMANTICS-BASED COURSES CLUSTERING

Since the minimum fragment in the database fragment schema is partitioning the forum data by *forum_id*, we can apply different strategies to allocate the forums around the server *nodes* to cope with different practical situations and optimization targets, for example, balancing the workload, or localizing the network traffic between the servers and the clients. The semantics-based course clustering algorithm is one of the solutions for optimizing the whole performance of the distributed forum system by assigning relevant courses into the same *node*.

In our university, each teaching course has provided a course introduction page. These introduction pages provide a lot of useful information to the students, including course code, title, teaching pattern, credit unit and so on. To compute the semantic similarities of the courses, we parse the layout of the course introduction pages and extract the semantic features as: title (*T*, consists of the departmental code and name), aims & objectives (*O*), keyword syllabus (*S*), pre-requisites (*RC*), pre-cursors (*PC*) and equivalent courses (*EC*).

Since the semantic features *T*, *O* and *S* are plain text, we compute the similarity of each pair of semantic features with the following formula based on vector space model (VSM) (Salton, 1968; 1971):

$$sim(\vec{d}_i, \vec{d}_j) = \frac{\vec{d}_i \times \vec{d}_j}{|\vec{d}_i| \bullet |\vec{d}_j|}$$

Then we can compute the overall similarity of three pairs of features by the following formula.

$$sim(C_i, C_j) = a*sim(T_i, T_j) + b*sim(O_i, O_j) + c*sim(S_i, S_j)$$

where a, b, c are the coefficient weights to satisfy $a+b+c=1$, they are currently set to 0.2, 0.3, and 0.5 respectively in our final clustering algorithm. Combining with all other semantic features, we get the final pairwise distance of two courses C_i and C_j as seen in Box 1, where α, β, ν are the coefficient weights to satisfy $\alpha + \beta + \nu = 1$ too. $sim(RC_i, RC_j)$, $sim(PC_i, PC_j)$, and $sim(EC_i, EC_j)$ will be 1 while the corresponding course exists, otherwise be 0.

Finally, all these pairwise distances constitute a distance matrix for hierarchical clustering (Jain, 1988). The results derived from the clustering algorithm are used to allocate the courses, so that the relevant course knowledge and information content can be settled on the same *node*.

IMPLEMENTATION ISSUES

The distributed Web-based course forum system is developed based on the original TAS System. The major improvement of the new system is that we designed and implemented a node communication module for each *node* to establish a group communication layer for data exchange and update in the distributed forum system. All

Box 1.

$$dist(C_i, C_j) = \begin{cases} \dfrac{1}{\alpha * sim(C_i, C_j) + \beta * sim(RC_i, RC_j) + \nu * sim(PC_i, PC_j)} & if\ sim(EC_i, EC_j) = 0 \\ 0 & if\ sim(EC_i, EC_j) = 1 \end{cases}$$

replication protocols discussed in this article are working on the group communication layer. Thus the efficiency of node communication module has an immediate impact on the performance of a *node* and further the overall performance of the distributed forum system.

Node Communication Module Architecture

Figure 5(a) presents the architecture of the node communication module and demonstrates how it works in transferring data between two *nodes*. Instead of using conventional Socket programming or client-server RPC technique, we choose an application layer protocol - HTTP protocol to implement our data transport protocol at the group communication layer. The basic component in the node communication module is a HTTP Web client. The Web client encapsulates transmitted data into a HTTP request and sends it to the Web server of another *node*, and receives the response data. The Web client masks temporary network connection interruption by re-sending the same HTTP request for several times until the Web client gets a right response or after a defined timeout. The node communication module works as a *black-box* to other forum programs. When a forum program submits sent data to the module, the module encapsulates data into a XML document firstly, then encrypts the XML document with the *node's* session key and sends it. If the node communication module cannot receive a response after a timeout, it returns a failure notification to the forum program. Otherwise the module decrypts the received XML document and parses the data. Finally, the data is returned to the forum program.

Secure the Group Communication Data

Some replicated data are involved in personal information of forum members, such as password, gender, e-mail box and so on. To protect these private user data and improve the security of the whole forum system, we introduce a RSA+3DES encryption solution to secure the transmitted data among the nodes (Mcrypt, 2006). 3DES (TripleDES) symmetrical encryption schema is used to protect the transmitted data. All XML documents must be encrypted with the *node's* session key before delivery, and decrypted by the session key in the receiver. The receiver (*node*) identifies the sender (*node*) by the IP address then retrieves its session key on the local *NODE* table.

Figure 6. The statistical analysis results for two online Web-based forum communities

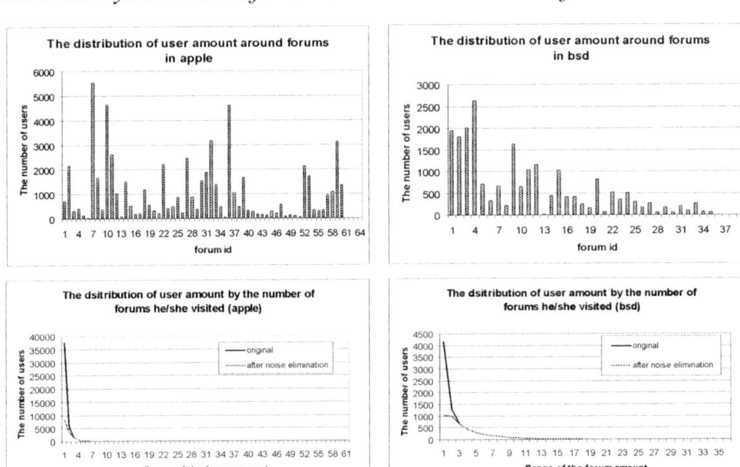

Each *node* keeps a replica of the session keys. Each session key is only valid in a prescribed period (e.g., 2 days). The *main node* periodically generates a set of new session keys for each *node*. The set of session keys is propagated to all *nodes* with a two-phase commit protocol to guarantee that each active *node* has received the new session key set before using them. RSA private-public key encryption schema is used to secure the transmission of the session key set. Thus we not only implement a secure data transport protocol for the group communication but also provide a solution for the *node* authentication in the distributed forum system.

To reduce the cost for data encryption, decryption and delivery, we apply a lossless ZLIB compression algorithm in compressing the XML documents before the encryption. Our experimental data shows that the compression algorithm can achieve 2:1-8:1 compression ratio in compressing different transmitted XML documents. It is also suggested to enable the ZLIB (or GZIP) compression feature of Web servers for improving the network transmission efficiency in HTTP 1.1 protocol specification and other technical reports for tuning Web servers.

EXPERIMENTAL RESULTS

Statistic Data for Forum Members' Behavior Analysis

To investigate human behavior in online forum communities, we need a large amount of real forum data from some large online forums. We chose two online forum sites for our study. One is Apple Discussions Community (discussions.apple.com), a commercial technical support forum site for the products of Apple Company (called *apple* in this article). Another site (called *bsd*) is a nonprofit forum community for freeBSD (www.freebsdforums.org). We wrote a Web crawler to get the posts in 61 topic forums in *apple*, and all posts in *bsd*. There are a total of 189,926 posts in *apple* submitted by 46,590 different registered users, and a total of 159,419 posts cover 36 different topic forums in *bsd* submitted by 7,783 different registered users.

The statistic results from above data, as shown in Figure 6, provide an evidence to support the partial user data cache mechanism design in our approach. The distribution of user amount also explores that some topic forums attract more forum members to join the discussions as well as some topic forums draw less attention in a forum community. The two figures below illustrate the distribution for the total number of distinct users by counting the amount of forums that they have participated in (have submitted at least one post in each forum). Only 115 users have submitted posts in more than 10 different topic forums in *apple* site. In *bsd* site, the amount of users who have submitted posts in more than 10 topic forums is 380. They are two small numbers as compared with the total number of users in two forum communities.

Single Node Throughput Benchmark

We choose CentOS Linux 4.2 as the platform to set up the experimental forum system for performance testing. The experimental forum system consists of 10 server nodes connected with a 100M Fast Ethernet Switch. Two DELL PE-2850 servers (Dual Xeon 3.8GHz Processors with 4 GB RAM and two 73GB SCSI disks with Raid 1 configuration) work as the *main node* and the *backup node*. Eight Pentium D 3.0GHz PC with 1 GB RAM and 80 GB disk work as the *nodes*.

Before the performance testing, we set up ten course links in the forum system. Each course has four discussion forums. Then each node serves one course and its four forums independently. There are a total of 40,000 members and 40,000 posts on each *node*. In particular, we have developed a multithread HTTP Web client program which can simulate all ordinary forum operations of a Web browser manipulated by a forum member.

In the single node throughput benchmark test, we chose DELL PE-2850 (main node) for the single node throughput benchmark testing. We used the Web client program to send the same forum operations concurrently. The response time of a forum operation was counted from sending a HTTP request to receiving a response page completely. We increased the number of concurrent forum operations until the Web client program received a failure notification page, which declared the overload of the server. In each response time data collection, the Web client program keeps sending the same forum operation requests for 2 hours. The average response times of the seven most common forum operations are finally listed in Table 1 (∞ in column "op-2" denotes the overload of a server node).

The benchmark results declare that a single node can handle at least 2,500 local forum operations within 1 minute except local user login operation. The maximum response time of each forum operation is no more than 20 seconds (A local user login operation is a more complicated and contains two forum operations, receiving a redirect URL and following it to get an index page).

Figure 7 presents the performance benchmark results of two remote login operations with comparison of single *node's* local login operation. The benchmark is used to test the efficiency of two replication protocols for user authentication data. This benchmark test is conducted with the *main node* and the *backup node*. Before starting the test, the *backup node* keeps an empty *USER* table. Consequently, the *node* has to execute a full user data replication or a session ID propagation to get a user's tuple from the *main node*. The result shows the cooperation of two *nodes* can increase the maximum throughput of the same login operation on one *node* and achieve a response time in much shorter than that of a single *node*.

Table 1. Single node throughput benchmark Testing (seven kinds of local forum operations, op-1:viewing the index page; op-2: local login; op-3: viewing the forum list page of a course; op-4: Viewing a topic list page of a forum; op-5: Reading a topic thread; op-6: Posting a topic; op-7: Posting a reply)

Number of clients	op-1	op-2	op-3	op-4	op-5	op-6	op-7
10	0.0730	1.1422	0.0680	0.0861	0.0889	0.2221	0.2188
25	0.0775	1.4264	0.0691	0.0853	0.0895	0.2122	0.2514
50	0.0725	1.7865	0.0706	0.0870	0.0927	0.2010	0.2618
100	0.0781	6.1850	0.0737	0.0915	0.1027	0.5119	0.52303
150	0.0768	14.574	0.0838	0.1038	0.1167	0.5992	0.5502
175	0.0782	23.353	0.0934	0.1196	0.1444	0.6359	0.5630
200	0.0732	28.445	0.1455	0.1205	0.1763	0.6739	0.6773
250	0.0965	34.216	0.2015	0.1650	0.2583	0.8713	0.9067
300	0.0887	∞	0.1643	0.1920	0.5128	1.1491	1.1710
500	0.1518	∞	0.2211	0.1981	0.6200	1.1752	1.1848
1000	0.4080	∞	0.6473	0.4982	1.0307	2.4737	3.3140
1500	1.868	∞	0.8556	1.6841	2.7461	5.1547	7.1719
2000	4.9368	∞	2.2570	4.3436	5.5202	5.2453	8.2244
2500	9.7270	∞	4.6747	7.7021	8.4198	19.121	19.289

Figure 7. User authentication operations benchmark for testing the performance of the session ID propagation and the password replication protocols

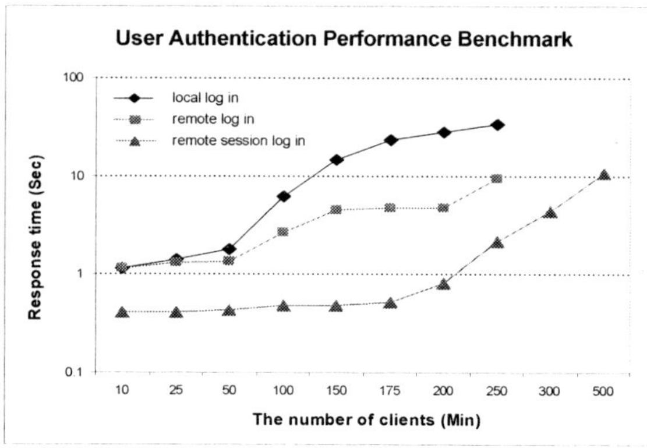

Communication Overhead Cost Evaluation

We take all communication network traffic among the *nodes* into account of the communication overhead cost. The communication overhead cost can be concluded in two kinds of overhead costs: computing cost and networking cost.

We assume that there are n active *nodes* in our distributed forum system. The interval time for the global user data synchronization is T_{sync}, the interval data refresh time for the individual user data replication protocol is T_r. There are M active forum members who are online among the sites of the *nodes*, $m(m < M)$ forum members who have done at least once posting or voting during a time slot T. Then there are a total of T/T_{sync} global user data synchronization occurred within T.

Each global user data synchronization manipulates a replica of *STUSER* for m users and n snapshots of the replica *STATE* for m users. If we assume the data size for transferring the *STATE* of one forum member to be L_{STATE}, the data size for transferring the *STUSER* for one user to be L_{STUSER}. The networking overhead cost in T can be computed as follows:

$$COST_{sync} = (n-1)\cdot m\cdot (L_{state} + L_{stuser}) / T_{sync}$$

The maximum communication overhead cost in the session ID propagation and individual user data replication is only occurred in an extreme situation: The M active online forum members are doing nothing except walking around the sites of n nodes frequently after logging into the forum. In fact, all actions of these M members are in two forum operations only: getting the index page of a node and randomly choosing a course link (a node) to get the forum list page. We suppose that each member has visited all nodes at least once after T_r. It needs $n-1$ session ID propagations to transfer the current session ID of a member over all nodes. Thereafter the individual user data replication protocol will be used for refreshing the user data. The user data replication for each member is occurred at least once within $2T_r$, since all these members continue to move around all nodes along the time of T. Therefore, there are a total of $M \cdot (n-1)$ session ID propagation and $M \cdot (n-1) \cdot T / T_r$ individual user data replication during the time slot T. If we assume the transmission data size in a session is ID propagation L_s, the transmission data size for individual user data replication is L_s, then we can calculate the maximum networking overhead cost with the following formula.

$$COST_{refresh} = M \cdot (n-1) \cdot (L_s + T \cdot L_s / T_r)$$

We simulated the extreme case in our experimental forum system: 400 registered users are doing nothing except moving around the 10 *nodes* frequently. Figure 8 illustrates the results for four different interval data refresh times.

In the corresponding forum programs, there are eight different SQL queries in generating an index page, and eight queries in generating a forum list page too. A session ID propagation contains a total of five SQL queries on two *nodes*, and an individual user data replication contains six SQL queries as well. To simplify the computing overhead cost calculation, we assume each SQL

Figure 8. The maximum communication overhead cost evaluation test

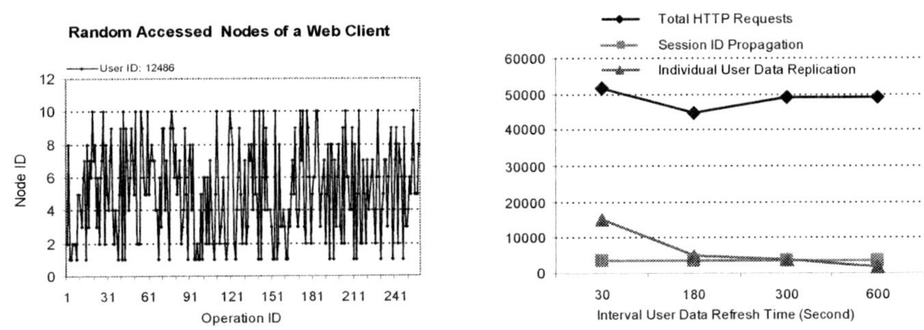

query has the same computing cost regardless of the computing cost for pre-processing data. When we count the transmission data size with both the HTTP request and its HTTP response in each operation, the total data for a session ID propagation is about 4.5 KBytes. The total data in an individual user data replication is about 1.2 KBytes. The average data size is about 100 KBytes for getting an index page, and 95 KBytes for getting a forum list page. Then the computing overhead cost and networking overhead cost in the simulation result can be computed and presented in Table 2. The simulation result demonstrates that the distributed forum system is highly efficient with low computing overhead cost and trivial networking overhead cost in the extreme situation, if we choose a reasonable data refresh time.

Table 3 presents a result for verifying the precisions of the semantics-based course clustering algorithm. It lists two clusters with respect

Table 2. The maximum communication overhead cost

Data refresh time (sec)	Total requests	Session ID propagation	Individual user data replication	Computing overhead ratio	Networking overhead ratio
30	51661	3600	15103	29.18%	1.084%
180	44719	3600	5162	15.55%	0.651%
300	49169	3600	3906	11.06%	0.525%
600	49051	3600	1805	7.627%	0.441%

Table 3. A result for the semantics-based course clustering algorithm

Cluster ID	Course Code	Course Title
cluster 183	CS 5286 CS 4395	Algorithms & Techniques for Web Searching Web Publishing
cluster 240	CS 3102 CS 3103 CS 3161 CS 4183 CS 3151 CS 3171 CS 3185 CS 5102 CS 5101	Operating Systems Operating Systems Operating System Principles Advanced Operating Systems Computer Systems System Software Computer Architecture Operating Systems Computer Organisation and Architecture

Figure 9. The courses aggregation in the semantics-based clustering algorithm

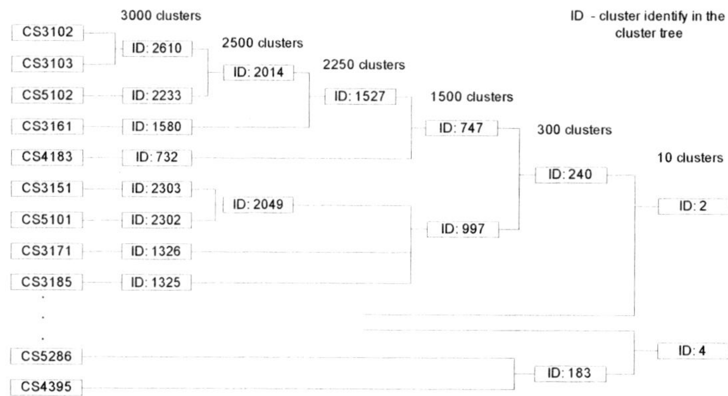

to course CS5286 and course CS3102 when all courses are clustered into 300 clusters. There are a total of 3,983 course documents in the data set. Readers who are interested in the result can check it at the university site. Figure 9 demonstrates how the corresponding courses aggregate into the same cluster in the clustering algorithm. Because the course data corpus is collected from real online Web pages, we will not expect there to exist a benchmark standard to verify exact precision and recall for the semantics-based clustering algorithm.

CONCLUSION

A Web-based course forum system not only provides a dynamic interactive learning environment for teachers and students to allow off-class discussion beyond the limited classroom teaching but also conducts a knowledge collaboration to build a big digital teaching material library.

We summarize our work in four points. First, by analyzing the member's behavior in a forum community, we investigate the possibility of designing and implementing a distributed forum system. Second, we present a taxonomy storage framework to partition the forum database. The partition is based on the knowledge and information relevance of the courses' content. Third, a partial data cache mechanism is implemented based on the analysis results of the behavior of forum members. The data cache mechanism makes the forum system a robust and high-scalable-distributed forum system with fault tolerance to the failure of network and computer hardware. Fourth, we implement an innovative secure group communication approach for the forum data exchange on the Internet. In fact, the distribution framework in this article is not only suitable for implementing our distributed course forum system but also a promising business solution for a large commercial forum application product.

ACKNOWLEDGMENT

The research work described in this article is partially supported by a City University TDF grant [Project No. 6980080] and a SRG grant of City University of Hong Kong [Project No. 7001975].

REFERENCES

Amir, Y. (2002). From total order to database replication. *Proceedings of the 22nd international conference on distributed computing systems (ICDCS'02)* (p. 494).

Bernstein, P., & Hadzilacos, V. (1987). *Concurrency control and recovery in database systems.* Reading, MA: Addison-Wesley.

Birman, K., & Schiper, A. (1991). Lightweight causal and atomic group multicast. *ACM Transactions of Computer Systems, 9*(2), 272-314.

Ceri, S. (1985). *Distributed databases principles & systems.* McGraw-Hill.

Gray, J., & Helland, P. (1996). The dangers of replication and a solution. *Proceedings of the 1996 ACM SIGMOD international conference on management of data.*

Howard, R. (1993). *The virtual community: Homesteading on electronic frontier.* USA: Harper Perennial Paperback.

Hung Chim, L. (2004). The design and implementation of a Web-based teaching assistant system. *International Journal of Information Technology & Decision Making, 3*(4), 663-672.

Hung Chim, X., & Jie Liu, B (2005). A group decision approach for information assessment. *Proceeding of EUROIMSA* (p. 7-13). Switzerland: IASTED.

Jain, A. (1988). *Algorithms for clustering data.* Englewood Cliffs, NJ: Prentice Hall.

Kemme, B. (2000). A new approach to developing and implementing eager database replication protocols. *ACM Transactions on Database Systems, 25*(3), 333-378.

Mcrypt, L. (2006). *A crypotography library as the replacement for the old UNIX crypt under the GPL.* http://sourceforge.net/projects/mcrypt.

Pacitti, E. (2000). Update propagation strategies to improve freshness in lazy master replicated databases. *VLDB Journal: Very Large Data Bases, 8*(3), 305-318.

Rothnie, B. (1980). Introduction to a system for distributed databases (SDD-1). *ACM Transactions on Database Systems, 5*(1), 1-17.

Salton, G. (1968). Computer evaluation of indexing and text processing. *Journal of the ACM, 15*(1), 8-36.

Salton, G. (1971). *The smart retrieval system.* Englewood Cliffs, NJ: Prentice Hall Inc.

Stockinger, H. (2001). Distributed database management systems and the data grid. *18th IEEE Symposium on Mass Storage Systems and 9th NASA Goddard Conference on Mass Storage Systems and Technologies.*

Wang, Y., & Li, X. (2004). Web-based adaptive collaborative learning environment designing. *Proceedings of ICWL 2004.* Beijing, China.

Wolfgang, H., & Javier, J. (2000). Data management in international data grid project. *1st IEEE, ACM International Workshop on Grid Computing.*

Xinyu Zhang, D., & Luo, N. (2004). Web-based collaborative learning focused on the study of interaction and human communication. *Proceedings of ICWL 2004.* Beijing, China.

This work was previously published in International Journal of Distance Education Technologies, Vol. 6, Issue 1, edited by S. Chang; T. Shih, pp. 10-31, copyright 2008 by IGI Publishing (an imprint of IGI Global).

Chapter 2
Toward Development of Distance Learning Environment in the Grid

Kuan-Ching Li
Providence University, Taiwan

Yin-Te Tsai
Providence University, Taiwan

Chuan-Ko Tsai
Providence University, Taiwan

ABSTRACT

In recent years, with the rapid development of communication and network technologies, distance learning has been popularized and it became one of the most well-known teaching methods, due to its practicability. Over the Internet, learners are free to access new knowledge without restrictions on time or location. However, current distance learning systems still present restrictions, such as support to interconnection of learning systems available in scalable, open, dynamic, and heterogeneous environments. In this chapter, we introduce a distance learning platform based on grid technology to support learning in distributed environments, where open source and freely available learning systems can share and exchange their learning and training contents. We have envisioned such distance learning platform in heterogeneous environment using grid technology. A prototype is designed and implemented, to demonstrate its effectiveness and friendly interaction between learner and learner resources used.

INTRODUCTION

In recent years, with the rapid development in communication and network technologies, e-learning has been popularized and become one of the most popular teaching methods in educational community. Along with the gradual improvements found in network bandwidth and quality, real-time transmission of high-quality video and audio has become possible and true reality. Because of these major transitions, conventional methods of school education have also followed this trend.

Distance learning utilizes electronic devices to assist the education or training process, taking advantage of the internet or any other communication channel to connect other devices, to deliver information and knowledge. According to Capuano, Gaeta, Laria, Orciuoli, and Ritrovato, (2003), this model of learning has many advantages with respect to traditional models:

- A better interaction between the learners and the learning resources they use, that is, the learning is not passive,
- Learning can happen anytime and anywhere, that is, there are not boundaries tied to time and place,
- Tutors, or learners themselves, are able to monitor the progress and to customize the learning experience basing on learner skills and preferences.

Unfortunately, there are drawbacks related to current learning solutions. First, they are mainly focused on the content delivery. Second, current learning platforms only support a specific learning-domain and are not able to support learning in different domains (Capuano, et al. 2003; Gaeta, Ritrovato, & Salerno, 2003). Third, many e-learning platforms and systems have been developed and commercialized, though, with limitations in scalability, availability, and distribution of computing power as well as storage capabilities (IMS Global Learning Consortium, 2002).

Grid computing has emerged as an important new field, distinguished from conventional distributed computing by focusing on large-scale resource sharing. Grid technology addresses issues related to access provisioning coordinated resource sharing and problem solving in dynamic, multi-institutional virtual organizations (Foster, Kesselman, & Tuecke, 2001).

In distance learning researches, it is a crucial problem the support of existing learning systems in scalable, open, dynamic, and heterogeneous environments. The scenario is a large scale and interconnected computing environment of learning management systems, learning content management systems and virtual classroom systems of different organizations.

Linking the drawbacks presented in learning systems with the advantages grid technology offers, we present in this chapter the design and implementation of a collaborative distance learning architecture based on grid technology in heterogeneous environment. With the combination of grid technology with distance learning, it is possible to build up an effective and ubiquitous learning system with impressive potential, to share learning resources in heterogeneous and geographically distributed environments. Learners can take course of their choice from a distributed virtual content repository and have it delivered to them anytime and any place of their choice in a personalized fashion with support available as and when they need it.

The remainder of this chapter is organized as follows: In the Background section, we introduce generic learning management systems, brief concepts of grid computing and web services. In the next section, it is discussed the proposed architecture for distance learning in the Grid, while following that, the design and implementation of the prototype. Finally, conclusions and future works are presented.

BACKGROUND

E-Learning Systems

General distance learning systems have four components: People, Authoring System, Run-Time System, and Learning Management System (LMS), as shown in Figure 1. People in these systems are the learners and authors, while others may include trainers and administrators. Authors (which may be teachers or instructional designers) create content, which is stored under the control of a LMS, and typically in a database. Existing content can be updated, and it can also be exchanged with other systems (Capuano, et al., 2003; Gaeta, et al., 2002; Pankratius & Vossen, 2003).

A LMS is managed under the control of an administrator, and it interacts, with a run-time environment which is addressed by learners, who in turn may be coached by a trainer. These components of a learning system can be logically and physically distributed. In order to make such a distribution feasible, standards such as IMS and SCORM have been proposed, to ensure plug-and-play compatibility (Wesner & Wulf, 2003; Advanced Distributed Learning, 2006).

A learning platform requires an LMS, to store and manage the teaching content. It is a collection of learning tools available through a shared administrative interface. A learning management can be thought as the platform in which online courses or components of courses are assembled and used from. Hall (2006) defines a LMS as, "software that automates the administration of training events. All Learning Management Systems (LMSs) manage the log-in of registered users, manage course catalogs, record data from learners, and provide reports to management".

Grid Computing

The grid computing paradigm essentially aggregates the view on existing hardware and software resources. The term Grid is chosen as an analogy to a power Grid that provides consistent, pervasive, dependable, transparent access to electricity irrespective of its source (Adelsberger, Collis, & Powlowski, 2002; Berman, Fox, & Hey, 2003). The concept of Grid computing focuses on resource sharing, which is not primarily file exchange, but rather direct access to computers, software, data, and other resources, as is required by a range of collaborative problem-solving and resource-

Figure 1. Generic view of learning systems

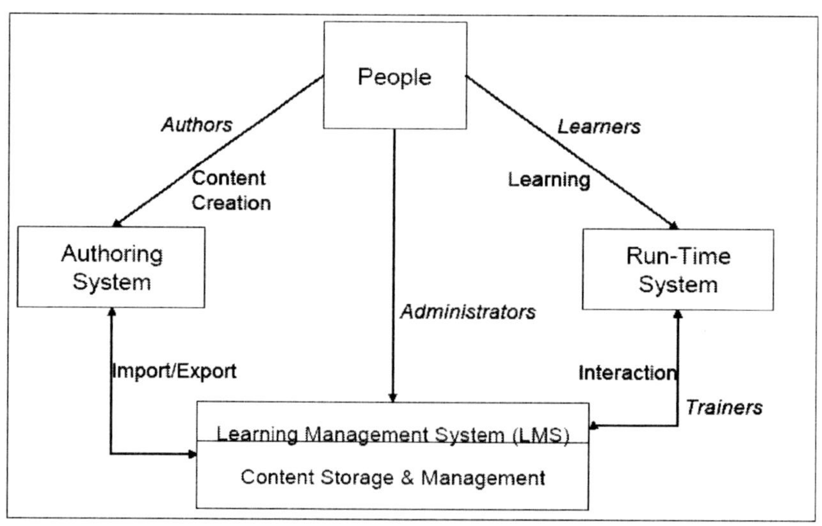

Figure 2. The grid architecture

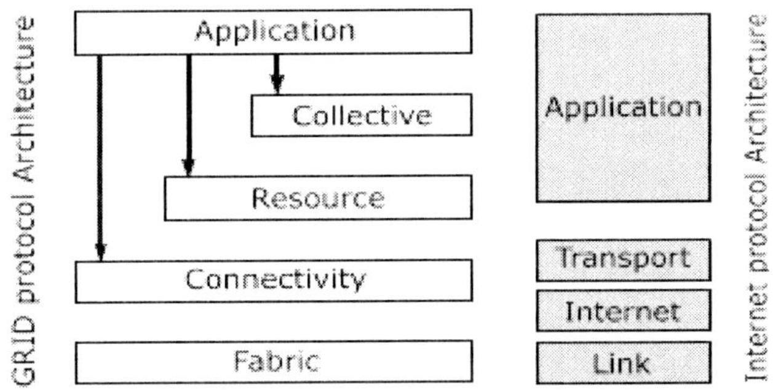

brokering strategies emerging in industry, science and engineering.

This description of Grid architecture identifies requirements for general classes of component. The result is an extensible, open architectural structure within which can be placed solutions to key user requirements. The architecture is organized into component layers, as shown below. Components within each layer share common characteristics, but can build on capabilities and behaviors provided by any lower layer (Foster & Kesselman, 2004; Li, Wang, Chen, Liu, Chang, Hsu, et al. 2005). The architectural description is high level and places few constraints on design and implementation. The layered Grid architecture and its relationship to the Internet protocol architecture are shown in Figure 2.

The Grid Fabric layer contains the resources that are to be shared. This could include computational power, data storage, sensors, and so on. This sharing is controlled by Grid protocols but the resource could include local networks. In this case, the local protocols take over at this point. The Grid system is just concerned with access above this point.

The Connectivity layer contains the communication and authentication protocols required for Grid-specific network transactions. Communication protocols enable the exchange of data between different Fabric layer resources. Authentication protocols build on communication services to provide secure mechanisms for verifying the identity of users and resources.

The Resource layer uses the communication and security protocols of the Connectivity layer to control the secure negotiation, initiation, monitoring, control, accounting, and payment of sharing operations on individual resources. Resource layer protocols call Fabric layer functions to access and control local resources. Resource layer protocols are concerned entirely with individual resources.

While the Resource layer is focused on interactions with a single resource, the Collective layer contains protocols and services that are global in nature and capture interactions across collections of resources. Collective components are designed that they implement a wide variety of sharing behaviors without placing new requirements on the fabric resources being shared such as: a directory service may allow users to query for resources by name or by attributes such as type, availability, or load.

The final layer in the Grid architecture comprises the user applications. Applications are constructed in terms of, and by calling upon, services defined at each layer in the Grid structure. At each layer, well-defined protocols provide access to some useful service: resource management, data access, resource discovery, and so forth. At each layer, protocols and services are used to perform desired actions.

Web Services

Web services define a technique for describing software components to be accessed via Internet,

Figure 3. Web services architecture

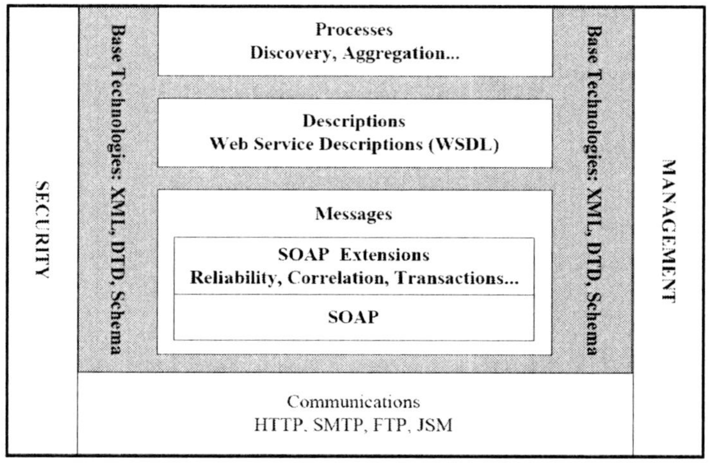

a communication media between different platforms. Web services standard is defined within the W3C, that has the support of large number of industries, and the components interact between in the service processes that are based on XML, SOAP, WSDL and UDDI (The Globus Alliance, 2006). The architecture of Web services standard is depicted in Figure 3.

Web services are described by XML that covers all the details that is necessary to interact among services, including message formats, transport protocols and location. Simple object access protocol (SOAP) provides a means of messaging between a service provider and a service requestor. It is independent of underlying the transport protocol. SOAP can carry on HTTP, FTP and SMTP. WSDL is an XML-based language to describe a Web service how to access them, to provide a formal framework to describe services in terms of protocols servers, ports and operations that can be invoked, the specification that provides a SOAP binding which is the most natural technology to be used for implements a web services. Universal description, discovery and integration (UDDI) provides the registry and search mechanism for Web services. Concisely, WSDL describes the format SOAP messages, and UDDI serves as a discovery service for the WSDL descriptions.

The Grid emphasizes the usage of Web services, and it does not use SOAP for all communications. If needed, alternate transport can be utilized, for example, to achieve higher performance or to be able to collide with a specialized network protocols.

One critical point is on how to combine the different heterogeneous resources in Grid. XML-based metadata is a popular problem solving, so it has been widely used. The XML document can not only help manage facilities, but also interchange between different databases. The interface based on Web services can integrate not only the web resources easily, but also make the occurrence much faster to duplicate. The process of duplication becomes much easier, since it is based on the open structure of web service.

PROPOSED ARCHITECTURE FOR DISTANCE LEARNING SYSTEM OVER GRID

The architecture contains five layers from bottom to up, as shown in Figure 4. The infrastructure layer, at the lowest layer, supports basic networking environment, including computing devices, networking and networking protocols, and so on.

Figure 4. An e-learning grid architecture

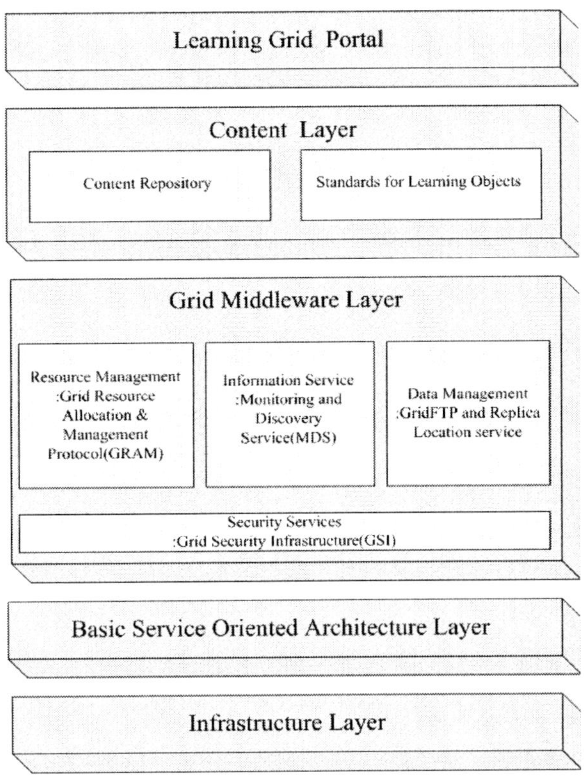

Secondly, the basic service oriented architecture for implementing the basic web services related protocols such as XML, UDDI/SOAP/WSDL, and so on. This layer provides the elementary connectivity, interoperation, reliability and flexibility for the layers on top of it. As next layer, the grid middleware layer is the core of the architecture where the basic grid problems such as distribution, dynamic, open and cross-organization are resolved. The content layer is on top of grid middleware layer to store all of learning contents in our platform. At last, the learning grid portal supports single user sign on the system. In next subsections, brief introduction of these layers will be discussed.

Grid Middleware Layer

This layer is a crucial layer to build a grid environment and should be on existing OGSA compliant middleware such as Globus Toolkit 4 (GT4). The Globus project provides open source software toolkit that can be used to build computational grids and grid-based applications (The Globus Alliance, 2006). It allows sharing of computing power, databases, and other resources securely across corporate, institutional and geographic boundaries, without sacrificing local autonomy. It implements services for resource management, information services and data management in the Grid. The main functions of them are: it enables single sign-on, authorization and security mechanism based on the grid security infrastructure (GSI).

Resource Management

Grid resource management involves the coordination of a number of components, including resource registries, staging of executable files, discovery, monitoring, allocation, and data access. The Globus toolkit includes a set of components to help users have a standard set of interfaces for the coordination of the above activities. Grid resource allocation and management (GRAM) is used for allocation of computational resources and for monitoring and control of computation on those resources. GRAM provides a set of standard interfaces and components to collectively manage a job task, and to provide resource information including job status and resource configuration.

Information Services

Information services have to fulfill the following requirements: a basis for configuration and adaptation in heterogeneous environments; uniform and flexible access to static and dynamic information; scalable and efficient access to data; access to multiple information sources; and decentralized maintenance capabilities. The monitoring and discovery service (MDS) provides a uniform framework for discovering and accessing configuration and status information such as compute server configuration, network status, and the capabilities and policies of services.

Data Management

The data management services provide standard means for helping to manage the Grid computing environment. GridFTP is a standard extension to the normal file transfer protocol (FTP) that works with the Grid Computing data requirements. This is a high-performance, secure, reliable, data transfer protocol that is optimized for high bandwidth across wide area networks. This is a standard that provides GSI security, parallel transfer capabilities, and channel reusability.

Replica management service in grid middleware layer provides guarantee for better quality of resource sharing, which implements functions of transparent data transfer/copy, transparent copy selection in grid. The replica location service (RLS) maintains and provides access to mapping information from logical names regarding data items to target names. These target names may represent physical locations of data items, or an entry in the RLS may map to another level of logical naming for the data item. The RLS is intended to be one of a set of services for providing data replication management in grids.

Content Repository Layer

This layer is on top of grid middleware layer to store all of contents in our platform. An e-learning system needs a learning management system (LMS) to store and manage its teaching content. However, every LMS platform runs its own learning materials, which cannot be exchanged with those of other LMSs. To deal with this problem, the U.S. government launched the Advanced Distributed Learning Initiative (ADL) The Globus Alliance (2006) is unifying e-learning specifications emerging from the international standards organizations into a single specification referred to as the sharable content object reference model (SCORM). SCORM aims to establish a mechanism for repeated use and sharing of courseware as a way to reduce the time and cost of developing courseware and to make courseware reusable and acceptable to different LMSs.

The SCORM standard is divided into 2 parts: the content aggregation model (CAM) and runtime environment (RTE). CAM-produced courseware is based on the principles of reusability, interoperability, and shareability, and it includes three major modules: content model, metadata, and content packaging. Courseware elements are defined as content objects in the content model and must be properly arranged to make a reusable course, also known as an sharable content object (SCO). SCO elements, such as html files, graphic files, and multimedia files, are known as *assets*. Metadata files describe courseware information using XML. The description of courseware and elements made by metadata enables further management of course resources. Content packaging uses the Manifest XML files, denominated as imsmanifest.xml, to arrange and package SCOs in a course framework.

Some LMSs will be used as learning grid nodes when implementing a complete learning grid platform in which each node is provided with an interface for linkage between the Grid interface and the LMS.

Although an SCO meets the SCORM standards and can be run in every LMS, it may still be inconvenient for sharing among multiple LMSs because of the lack of a fast, safe, and secure mechanism. Each SCO Repository in the LMS is linked through Globus Middleware, and each and every LMS node can share SCOs with other LMSs. Based on Grid Middleware Globus which is in the middle of the communication between nodes is conducted via the Learning Grid Portal, which is the interface between grid nodes.

Learning Grid Portal

Learning grid portal is the unified entry for all grid platform users. Users from different organizations who login can could share learning resources without knowing actually where the information comes from.

THE DISTANCE LEARNING SYSTEM OVER GRID

Execution Flow

In this section, we describe the main execution flow of a learner when utilizing the proposed learning platform, also briefly shown in Figure 5.

1. A learner enters the grid portal, the grid portals have a user database which store user information and access rights. When a user wants to enter the grid environment, the system will checks the user's login name and password against the values stored in the database;
2. If the login was successful, the system will show a list of all resources currently available in the grid and the status and type of all resources in the grid. It then requests from each computer (if each computer has it own LMS) some status information (e.g., unused storage space, how many learning content);
3. Furthermore, a broker is assigned which can handle requests to distribute computation or data across other computers in the grid;
4. For the distribution of data it uses the GridFTP to access the other computer's resource;
5. For the resource have a high speed access performance, Replica Location Service supports multiple locations for the same file throughout the grid.

Prototyping

In our learning grid platform, Globus Toolkit version 4.0 was installed on each site. Three different versions of open source learning management systems have been installed in these sites in our grid platform: ILIAS is installed in site A, Dokeos in site B, while Claroline in site C. The Grid Portal has been developed using GridSphere in OGCE Release 2 (Gridsphere, 2006).

ILIAS (ILIAS Open Source E-Learning System, 2006) is a powerful web-based learning management system that allows users to create, edit and publish learning and teaching material

Figure 5. Execution flow of a learner utilizing distance learning platform

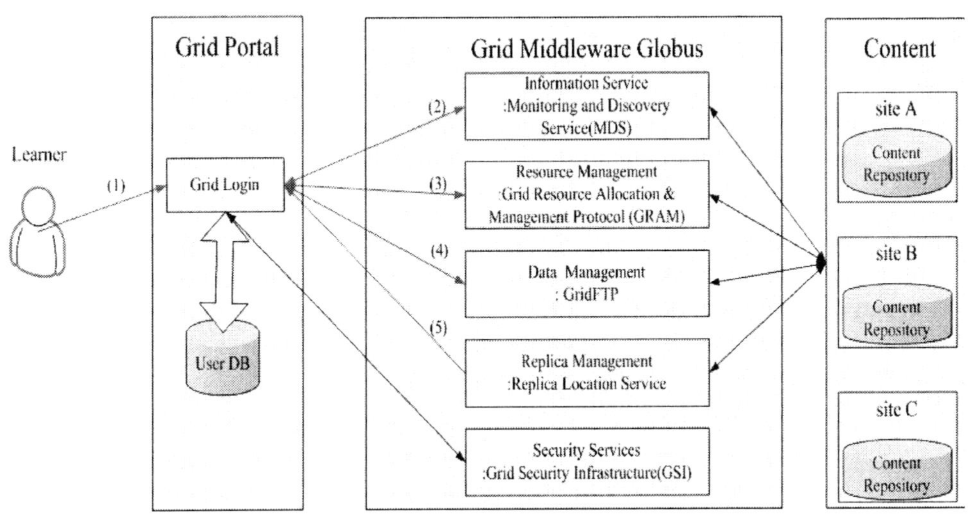

in an integrated system with their normal web browsers. Tools for cooperative working and communication are included as well. ILIAS is available as open source software under the GNU general public license (GPL). Universities, educational institutions, private and public companies, and every interested person may use the system free of charge and contribute to its further development. ILIAS is the first free software LMS that has reached SCORM 1.2 Conformance Level LMS-RTE3 and therefore guarantees platform independent re-use of contents. Due to a modular and object oriented software architecture; ILIAS allows easy customization of the platform for specific purposes.

Claroline (2006) is a free application based on PHP/MySQL allowing teachers or education organizations to create and administrate courses through the web. Developed from teachers to teachers, Claroline is built over sound pedagogical principles allowing a large variety of pedagogical setup including widening of traditional classroom and online collaborative learning.

Dokeos (Dokeos Open Source E-Learning System, 2006) is an Open Source e-learning and course management Web application translated in 34 languages and helping more than 1,000 organizations worldwide to manage learning and collaboration activities.

The NSF Middleware Initiative's (NMI's) OGCE portal provides access to Grid technologies through sharable and reusable components (NMI OGCE Open Grid Computing Environment, 2006), whereas the GridSphere portal framework provides an open-source portlet based Web portal. With the GridPortlets Web application (Gridsphere, 2006; NMI OGCE Open Grid Computing Environment, 2006), users upload their Grid credentials and utilize them to gain access to a variety of Grid services.

We have placed different topics of multimedia educational contents in each site's repository. In site A, we have placed parallel programming topic coursewares, while in site B, contents related to bioinformatics, and site C for bioinformatics related contents, as depicted in Figure 7.

Figure 6. Distance learning system over grid prototype architecture

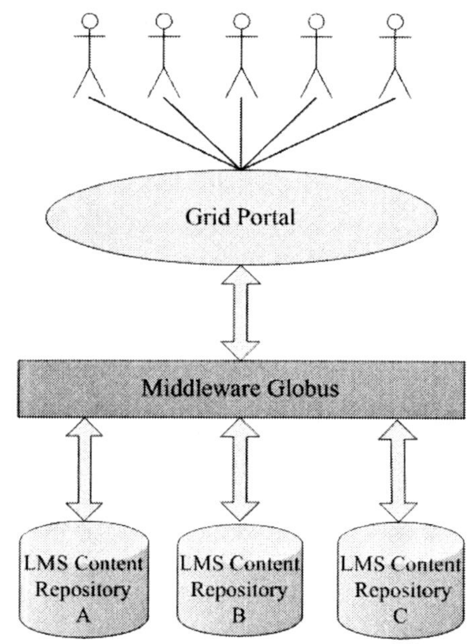

CONCLUSION AND FUTURE WORK

In this research, we have designed and implemented a Grid portal interconnecting a number of well known and open source distance learning systems, and taking advantages of grid technology. In a grid environment, learner can learn in scalable, open, dynamic, and heterogeneous environments. At present, most e-learning environment architectures use single computers or servers as their structural foundations. The distance learning architecture introduced and presented in this chapter is innovative and effective, since it can solve scalability issues of currently available learning systems, improving the collaboration and cooperation where technology Grid provides. We expect that the implementation of Grid Portal, as also the integration of learning systems utilizing Grid technology, may enable people to process

Figure 7. Implementation of distance learning system over grid, running real applications

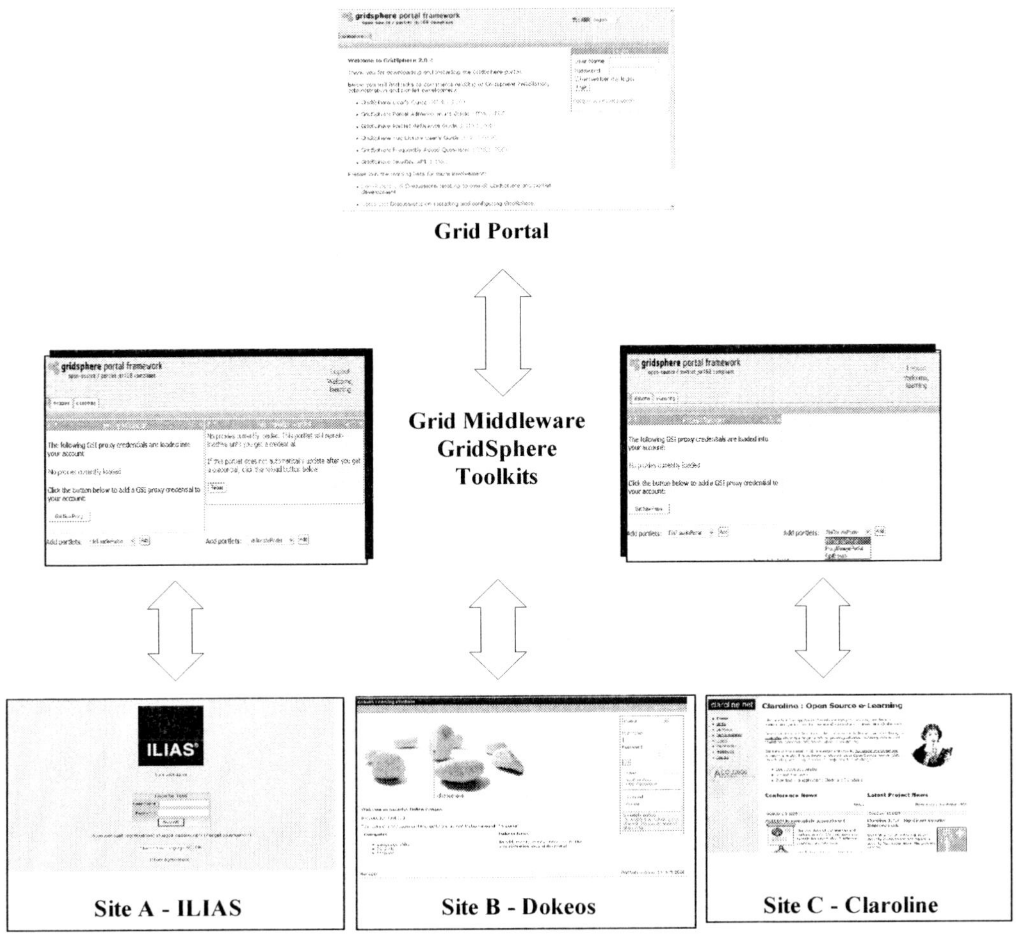

interactions and opinion exchanges through video and audio simultaneously, in situations such as training, teaching, conferences and seminars.

As of present stage of investigation, we have successfully built the learning system over Grid inside our campus. We will include other different topics of contents inside our repository, as also include other open source distance learning systems.

As future work, some challenges where we will go through our investigations can be listed as development of adaptive middleware, large scale data management, fault tolerance, high availability, homogeneous access to heterogeneous information, tools, among several others.

In near future, our plan is to promote the use of this technology among groups or universities that maintain collaborative research projects or other purposes, such as Association of Christian Universities, *sister* universities, among innumerous others definitions of groups that exists. In addition, we have already started to collaborate with distance learning developing groups and investigate the viability of improving overall learning transmission quality, with the utilization of high speed and fiber networking technologies, the development of adequate and productive authoring tools, as also the use of wireless devices for the learning purpose.

ACKNOWLEDGMENT

This article is based upon work supported in part by National Science Council (NSC), Taiwan, under grants NSC95-2221-E-126-006-MY3, NSC96-2221-E-126-004-MY3, NSC96-2745-E-126-005-URD and NSC96-2218-E-007-007. Any opinions, findings, and conclusions or recommendations expressed in this material are those of the authors and do not necessarily reflect the views of the NSC.

REFERENCES

Adelsberger, H. H., Collis, B., & Pawlowski, J. M. (Eds.) (2002). *Handbook on information technologies for education and training.* Berlin: Springer-Verlag.

Advanced Distributed Learning (2006). Retrieved from http://www.adlnet.org/

Berman, F., Fox, G., & Hey, T. (Eds.) (2003). *Grid computing: Making the global infrastructure a reality.* New York: John Wiley and Sons, Inc.

Capuano, N., Gaeta, A., Laria, G., Orciuoli, F., & Ritrovato, P. (2003). How to use GRID technology for building the next generation learning environments. In *Proceedings of the 2nd International LeGE-WG Workshop: A Fundamental Challenge for Europe*, France.

Claroline.net – Open Source E-Learning System (2006). Retrieved from http://www.claroline.net/

Dokeos Open Source E-Learning System (2006). Retrieved from http://www.dokeos.com/

Foster, I., Kesselman, C., & Tuecke, S. (2001). The Anatomy of the grid enabling scalable virtual organizations, *International J. Supercomputer Applications, 15*(3).

Foster, I., & Kesselman, C. (2004). *The grid: Blueprint for a new computing infrastructure*, Amsterdam: Elsevier.

Gaeta, M., Ritrovato, P., & Salerno, S. (2002). Implementing new advanced learning scenarios through GRID technologies, In *Proceedings of the 1st International LeGE-WG Workshop: Educational Models for GRID Based Services*, Switzerland.

The Globus Alliance (2006). Retrieved from http://www.globus.org

Gridsphere (2006). Retrieved from http://www.gridsphere.org/

Hall, B. (2006). New Technology Definitions. *Brandon Hall Research.* Retrieved from http://www.brandonhall.com/public/glossary/index.htm

ILIAS Open Source E-Learning System (2006). Retrieved from http://www.ilias.de/ios/index-e.html

IMS Global Learning Consortium, Inc. (2002). Draft Standard for Learning Object Metadata, *IEEE Publication P1484.12.1/D6.4.*

Li, K. C., Wang, H. H., Chen, C. N., Liu, C. C., Chang, C. F., and Hsu, C. W., et al. (2005). *Design issues of a novel toolkit for parallel application performance monitoring and analysis in cluster and grid environments.* Paper presented at I-SPAN 2005, The 8th IEEE International Symposium on Parallel Architectures, Algorithms, and Networks, U.S.

NMI OGCE Open Grid Computing Environment (2006). Retrieved from http://www.ogce.org/index.php

Pankratius, V. & Vossen, G. (2003). Towards e-learning grids: Using grid computing in electronic learning. In *Proceeding of IEEE Workshop on Knowledge Grid and Grid Intelligence,* Canada.

Web Services Architecture (2004 February 11). *W3C Working Group Note*, Retrieved from http://www.w3.org/TR/we-arch/

Wesner, S., & Wulf, K. (2003). How GRID could improve e-learning in the environmental science domain. In *Proceedings of the 2nd International LeGE-WG Workshop: A Fundamental Challenge for Europe*, France.

This work was previously published in International Journal of Distance Education Technologies, Vol. 6, Issue 3, edited by Q. Jin, pp. 45-57, copyright 2008 by IGI Publishing (an imprint of IGI Global).

Chapter 3
Applying Semantic Agents to Message Communication in E-Learning Environment

Ying-Hong Wang
Tamkang University, Taiwan

Chih-Hao Lin
Asia University, Taiwan

ABSTRACT

A traditional distance learning system requires supervisors or teachers always available on online to facilitate and monitor a learner's progress by answering questions and guiding users. We presents an English chat room system in which students discuss course contents and ask questions to and receive from teachers and other students. The mechanism contains an agent that detects syntax errors in sentences written by the online the user and also checks the semantics of a sentence. The agent can thus offer recommendations to the user and, then, analyze the data of the learner corpus. When users query the system, this system will attempt to find the answers from the knowledge ontology that is stored in the records of previous user comments. With the availability of automatic supervisors, messages can be monitored and syntax or semantic mistakes can be corrected to resolve learner-related problems.

INTRODUCTION

Distance Learning has become a hot topic in the disciplines of computer science and education in the recent years (Tsang, Hung, Ng, 1999). Furthermore, online learning technologies operating through the Web interface have been developed during the past decade. Because of its ability to incorporate multimedia, the World Wide Web has become an ideal platform for distance learning (Adhvaryu, & Balbin, 1998). Through the Internet, distance learning allows students to enroll in courses and acquire new knowledge. It is a good solution for anyone who does not have enough time to attend traditional classes. Therefore, distance learning now plays a very important role in education (Harris, Cordero, & Hsieh, 1996; Willis, n.d.; Goldberg, 1996; Goldberg & Salari, 1997; Goldberg, Salari, & Swoboda, 1996).

The advantage of the Internet is information sharing. Many applications on the Internet support information interchange, including Telnet, FTP, e-mail, BBS, and chat-rooms. Each participant can communicate with other participants through text-, voice-, and even video-based messages.

However, it is difficult for instructors trace the activities and behaviors of learners in distance learning environments. For example, instructors may need answers to the following questions:

- Do the learners understand the teaching context?
- Are learners talking about the issues indicated by the instructor?
- Do the learners really understand the issues being studied in the course?

Therefore, it is quite useful if there are some automatic supervising mechanisms. These mechanisms can monitor discussions and detect mistakes in grammar. This helps students obtain educational training without the need to go to a classroom. Thus, people can teach or learn anywhere any time.

However, there are many problems with distance learning systems. For example, instructors cannot control learners' activities, instructors cannot stay online forever—the Instructor-off problem—and instructors cannot track of frequent answers and questions (FAQs); thus, learners cannot learn from previous learners and other learners.

To solve the problems mentioned above, this study built up an ontology-based Semantic Agent system that provides supervision and learning-assistance for textual chat rooms. This system was built based on Agent, Link grammar, XML, a learner corpus, and other supporting functions to solve the Instructor-off problems. The system provides a Learning_Angel agent and a Semantic agent. Also, the QA sub-system can collect/analyze frequent mistakes and problems. The Learning_Angel agent is designed to provide monitoring and syntax checking functions online. While discussing in the class, if learners fall behind the topic of discussing courses, Semantic agent can make some comments and/or suggestions. The statistical analyzer then records, classifies, and analyzes the learners' discussion. Furthermore, this discussion can be used to generate QA pairs and update the learner corpus. By means of these resources, instructors can revise or enhance their teaching materials. Learners can also learn from the experience of the previous learners and other learners.

This article is organized as follows: we first describe related works and introduce link grammar and ontologies. The next section presents the architecture of proposed system. The chief processes in the proposed system and evaluations of several related systems then are given. The last part of this article gives conclusions and discusses future researches.

THEORETICAL BACKGROUND

Link Grammar

Link grammar is an English grammar parser system that was proposed by researchers at the School of Computer Science of Carnegie Mellon University (CMU). Link grammar is a scheme for describing natural language (Sleator & Temperley, 1991). Link grammar defines a set of ***words***, which are the terminals of grammar, and each has some ***linking requirements***. The linking requirements of each word are gathered in a ***dictionary***. Figure 1 illustrates the linking requirements defined in a simple dictionary for the following words: *a/the, cat/mouse, John, ran, and chased.*

Each intricately shaped labeled box is defined as a ***connector***. A pair of compatible connectors will join, given that they correspond to the same type. For each black dot, only one connector can be selected. Figure 2 shows that the linking requirements are satisfied in the sentence, *"The cat chased a mouse."*

The linkage can be perceived as a graph, and the words can be treated as vertices, which are connected by labeled arcs. Thus, the graph is connected and planar. The labeled arcs that connect the words to other words on either their left or right sides are ***links.*** A set of links that proves that a sequence of words is in the language of a link grammar is called a ***linkage.*** Thus, Figure 3 shows a simplified form of the diagram, indicating that *the cat chased a mouse* is part of this language.

Table 1 presents an abridged dictionary, which encodes the linking requirements of the above example.

The linking requirement for each word is expressed as a formula that includes the operators *"&"* and *"or," parentheses,* and *connector names.* The "+" or "–" suffix after a connector indicates the direction in which the matching connector must be laid. Thus, the farther to the left a connector is in an expression, the nearer the word to which it connects must be.

A sequence of words is a *sentence* form a language defined by the grammar. If links can be established among the words so as to satisfy the formula of each word, then they must satisfy the following ***meta-rules:***

1. **Planarity:** The links do not cross when draw above the words.
2. **Connectivity:** The links suffice to connect all the words of the sequence together.
3. **Ordering:** When the connectors of a formula are traversed from left to right, the words to which they connect proceed from near to far. To understand this, consider a word, and consider two links connecting that word to the word on its left. Compared with the other word, the link connecting the closest word (the shorter link) must satisfy a connector that appears to the left (in the formula) of that connector in the other word. Similarly, a link to the right must satisfy a connector to the left (in the formula) of a longer link to the right.

Figure 1. Words and connectors in a dictionary

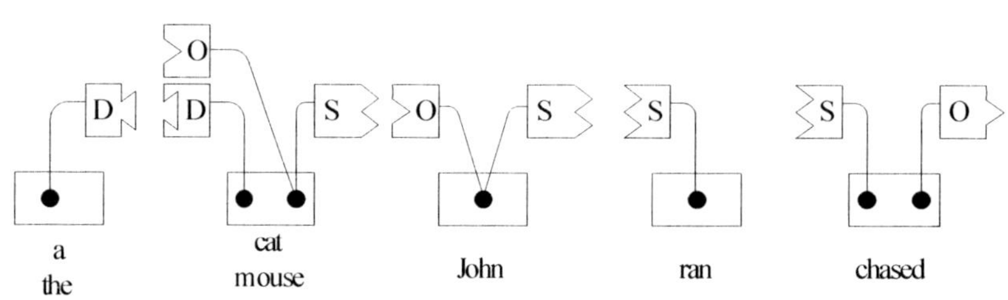

Figure 2. All linking requirements are satisfied

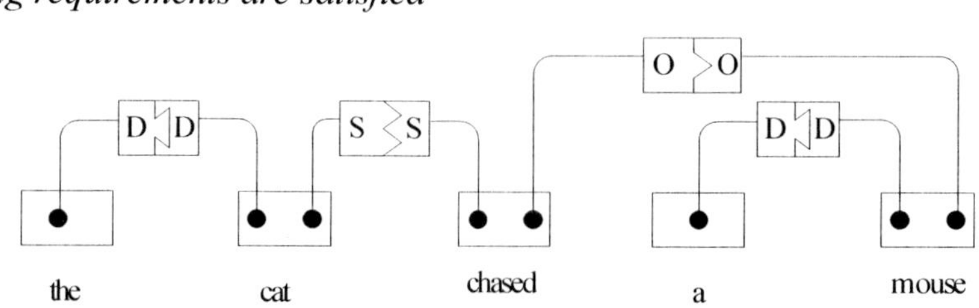

Figure 3. A simplified form of Figure 2

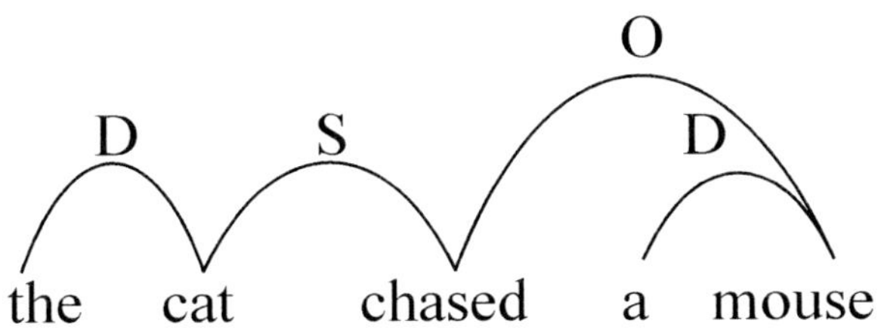

4. **Exclusion:** No two links may connect the same pair of words.

Using a formula to specify a link grammar dictionary is convenient for creating natural language grammars. However, it is cumbersome for mathematical analysis of link grammars and for describing algorithms for parsing link grammars. Therefore, an alternate method of expressing link grammar is known as ***disjunctive form***, in which each word has an associated set of disjuncts. In disjunctive form, each word of the grammar has a set of disjuncts associated with it. Each disjunct corresponds to one particular way of satisfying the requirements of a word. A disjunct consists of two ordered lists of connector names: the ***left list*** and ***right list***. The left list contains connectors that connect to the left of the current word, and the right list contains connectors that connect to the right of the current word. A disjunct is denoted as

$$((L_1, L_2, \ldots, L_m)(R_n, R_{n-1}, \ldots, R_1)),$$

where $L_1, L_2, \ldots, L_m$ and $R_n, R_{n-1}, \ldots, R_1$ are the connectors that must connect to the left and right, respectively.

Thus, it is easy to see how to translate a link grammar in disjunctive form to one in standard form. Translating a link grammar from disjunctive to standard form can be accomplished as follows:

$$(L_1 \& L_2 \& \ldots \& L_m \& R_1 \& R_2 \& \ldots \& R_n).$$

Table 1. The words and linking requirements in a dictionary

words	formula
a / the	D+
cat / mouse	D- & (O- or S+)
John	O- or S+
ran	S-
chased	S- & O+

By enumerating all the ways in which the formula cab be satisfied, we can translate a formula into a set of disjuncts. For example, the formula

(A- or ( )) & D- & (B+ or ( )) & (O- or S+)

corresponds to the following eight disjuncts, which may be used in some linkages:

((A,D) (S,B))
((A,D,O) (B))
((A,D) (S))
((A,D,O) ( ))
((D) (S,B))
((D,O) (B))
((D) (S))
((D,O) ( )).

To streamline the difficult process of writing the dictionary, we incorporate several other features into the **Dictionary Language**. It is useful to consider connector-matching rules that are more powerful than those which simply require that the strings of the connectors be identical. The most general matching rule is simply a table—part of the link grammar—that specifies all the pairs of connectors that match. The resulting link grammar is still context-free. In the dictionary, a matching rule is used that is slightly more sophisticated than simple string matching. This rule is described below.

A connector name begins with one or more upper case letters, followed by a sequence of lower case letters or *s. Each lower case letter (or *) is a ***subscript***. To determine if two connectors match, we delete the trailing + or - and append an infinite sequence of *s to both connectors. The connectors match if and only if these two strings match under the proviso that * matches a lower case letter (or *).

For example, S matches both Sp and Ss, but Sp does not match Ss. The formula "((A- & B+) or ( ))" is satisfied either by using both A+ and B-, or by using neither of them. Conceptually, then, the expression "(A+ & B-)" is optional. Since this situation occurs frequently, we denote it with curly braces, as follows: {A+ & B-}.

It is useful to give certain connectors to be ability connect to one or more links. This makes it easy, for example, to allow any number of adjectives to attach to a noun. We denote this by putting a "@" before the connector name, and we call the result a ***multi-connector***. A dictionary consists of a sequence of ***entries***, each of which is a list of words separated by spaces, followed by a colon, followed by the formula defining the words, followed by a semicolon.

If a word (such as **move** or **can**) has more than one distinct meaning, then it is useful to be able to give it two definitions. This is accomplished by defining several versions of the word with differing suffixes. The suffix always begins with a "." followed by one or more characters. We use the convention that ".v" indicates a verb and ".n" indicates a noun (among others). When the user types the word "move," the program uses an expression that is equivalent to that obtained by oring the expressions for the two versions of the word. When it prints out the linkage, it uses whichever version is appropriate for that particular linkage. As of this writing, there is no macro facility in the dictionary language. There is reason to believe that using macros would significantly reduce the size of the dictionary while making it easier to understand.

Ontology

Ontologies are important in various fields, such as knowledge engineering, natural language processing, intelligent information integration, and knowledge management. An ontology provides a shared, common representation of a domain that can be communicated between heterogeneous and widespread application systems. Ontologies have been developed in AI to facilitate knowledge sharing and reuse. An ontology provides an explicit conceptualization that describes the semantics of data. (Ide, 2003; Ide, Reppen, & Suderman, 2002).

Current computer systems are changing from single isolated devices to entry points into a worldwide network of information exchange. Therefore, support for data exchange, information, and knowledge is becoming a key issue in communication technology. It can facilitate communication between people and application systems. The provision of shared, common domain structures is becoming essential for describing the structure and semantics of information exchange. Now, Internet technology and the World Wide Web comprise the main technology infrastructure for online information exchange. It is not surprising to see that a number of initiatives are providing notations for data structures and semantics. These include:

- the resource description framework (RDF);
- the Extendible Markup Language (XML);
- XML schemes providing standards for describing the structure and semantics of data;
- the transformation language of XSL (XSL-T); and
- various querying languages for XML (XQL, XML-QL).

With the large number of online documents, several document management systems have entered the market. However, these systems have several weaknesses, which are explained below:

- Searching information: Existing keyword-based search schemes retrieve irrelevant information about the use of certain word in a different context, or they may miss information when different words about the desired content are used.
- Extracting information: Human browsing and reading is currently required to extract relevant information from information sources, as automatic agents lack the common sense knowledge required to extract such information from textual representations and fail to integrate information spread over different sources.
- Maintaining weakly structured text resources is difficult and time-consuming when the amount of resources becomes hug. Keeping these resources consistent, correct, and up-to-date requires a mechanized representation of semantics and constraints that help to detect anomalies.
- Automatic document generation takes advantage of the usefulness of adaptive Web sites, which enable dynamic reconfiguration according to user profiles or other relevant aspects. The generation of semi-structured information presentations from semi-structured data requires a machine-accessible representation in semantic information sources.

In the near future, semantic annotations will make structural and semantic definitions of documents possible, thus opening up new possibilities:

- intelligent search instead of keyword matching;
- query answering instead of information retrieval;
- document exchange between departments via XSL translations; and
- definitions of views on documents.

Depending on their level of generality, different types of ontologies may be identified and play different roles. The following are some ontology types:

- Domain ontologies: these capture knowledge that is valid for a particular type of domain.
- Metadata ontologies: these, such as Dublin Core (Weibel, Gridby, & Miler, 1995), provide a vocabulary for describing the content of on-line information sources.
- Generic or common sense ontologies: these aim to capture general knowledge about the world.
- Representational ontologies: these do not commit themselves to any particular domain.

Ontological engineering is concerned with the principled design, modification, application, and evaluation of ontologies. Ontologies can be adopted in situations where the capability for representing semantics is important to overcome XML's disadvantages in terms of maturity.

One well-known ontology language—the OWL Web Ontology Language (McGuinness & Harmelen, 2004)—is designed to process information instead of just presenting information to humans. OWL facilitates greater machine interpretability of Web content by providing additional vocabulary along with formal semantics.

OWL has three increasingly-expressive sublanguages: OWL Lite, OWL DL, and OWL Full. OWL is used when the information is contained in documents and needs to be processed by applications. It also opposes situations in which the content only needs to be presented to humans. OWL can be used to explicitly represent the meanings of terms in vocabularies and the relationships between those terms. This representation of terms and their interrelationships is called an ontology. OWL has more facilities for expressing meaning and semantics than XML, RDF, and RDF-S do; thus, OWL goes beyond these languages in its ability to represent machine interpretable content on the Web. OWL is a revision of the DAML+OIL Web ontology language and incorporates lessons learned from the design and application of DAML+OIL.

SYSTEM ARCHITECTURE

This section introduces the proposed Chat Room System, which is shown in Figure 4. The left part of the figure shows the components of the Augmentative Chat Room, the flow of Chat Room supervisors, and the Ontology Definition process. This system has two kinds of online supervisors: (1) Learning_Angel Agent and (2) Semantic Agent. The right part of the figure shows the database, which includes the Distance Learner Ontology, Learner Corpus Database, and User Profile Database. The Question and Answer System analyzes the Corpus and user profile to collect questions that are frequently asked by learners. Finally, the data is sent to the FAQ system, which generates new OA-pairs.

The following sections describe the chief components of the proposed system.

Domain Specific Sentences

Before introducing each chief sub-system of the proposed chat room, we first will explain why this reason is restricted the research to specified domain. Domain specific sentences refer to those

Figure 4. The system architecture and operation flow

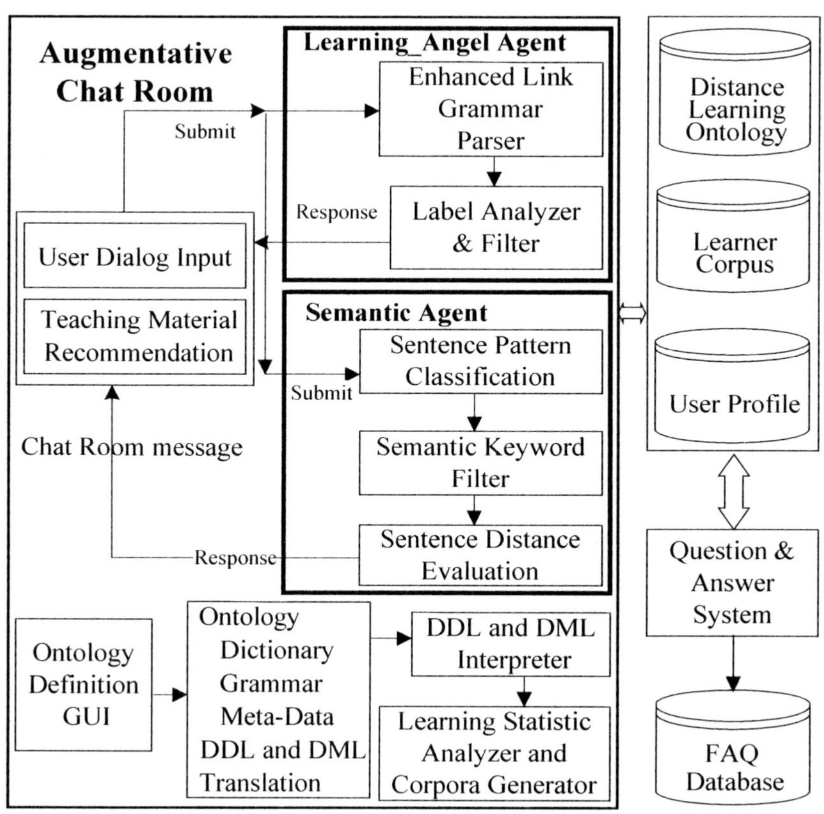

sentences that frequently appear in certain application domain texts but rarely in others. The following are some characteristics domain specific sentences (Li, Zhang, & Yu, 2001):

1. the vocabulary set is limited;
2. word usage is based on patterns;
3. semantic ambiguities are rare; and
4. term and jargon appear frequently in the domain.

It is fairly hard to apply semantic-level analysis to common language conversation. Take the following two sentences as examples. The syntax of the two sentences "The car is drinking water" and "The data is pushed in this heap" is correct. But the meaning of these sentences is incorrect. In the real world, a car cannot drink water. In a data structure course, a heap cannot be pushed. In fairy tales, cars perhaps can drink water or maybe even cola. Therefore, in different situation, the meaning of such a sentence might be different. For this reason, the domain must be restricted. Thus, the proposed system deals with only the "Data Structure" domain. The same scheme can be extended to other domains.

For the above reasons, the class topic and user messages are all restricted in a domain. Thus, the terms in the data structure are limited and can be pre-defined in the system ontology to support the functions of syntax and semantic analysis.

Furthermore, the system manager can load pre-defined terms about the Data Structure through the Ontology Definition GUI during system initialization. This Ontology Definition GUI interface is designed to provide the ability to generate another scaffolding teaching material. The ontology built for this system includes the Dictionary, Grammar, and Meta-Data. This process of ontology creation is designed to transform the pre-defined ontology into DDL and DML form. Finally, the DDL and DML Interpreter can interpret the ontology and then send the data to the Corpora Generator, which records the data to the Distance Learning Ontology and Learner Corpus databases.

Learning_Angel Agent

The Learning_Angel Agent is designed to be a supervisor. It can constantly detect syntax errors online as online users submit messages to the system. It can then correct the learners' errors.

The Learning_Angel Agent workflow is shown in Figure 5. Strictly speaking, when learners in the Augmentative Chat Room submit sentences to the Learning_Angel Agent, it will forward them to the Link Grammar Parser. Then, the Link Grammar Parser will query the ontology to get the tags for the input sentences (Wible, Kuo, Chien, & Taso, 2001). Meanwhile, the Link Grammar Parser will send the tags and sentences to the Label Analyzer & Filter, which can find out if there are any incorrect linkages. In addition, if the input messages have grammar errors, the Label Analyzer & Filter can detect them, search for suitable sentences from the Learner Corpus, and convey them to the online learners. In addition, the Label Analyzer & Filter analyzes the links of input words' sequences sent by the Link Grammar Parser to check whether the links between words satisfy the meta-rules in terms of planarity, connectivity, ordering, and exclusion. If the input words' sequences have received particular tags from the Learning_Angel Agent, the Label Analyzer & Filter will record them in the Learning Corpus and efficiently send the correct information to the online learners.

Semantic Agent

This section describes the Semantic Agent. The Semantic Agent is also designed to be an online supervisor. It can check the semantics of each sentence. In the distance-learning environment, learners sometimes may fall behind the in courses discussions. They may not understand the course topic clearly and, thus, may make some semantic

Figure 5. Workflow of the Learning_Angel agent

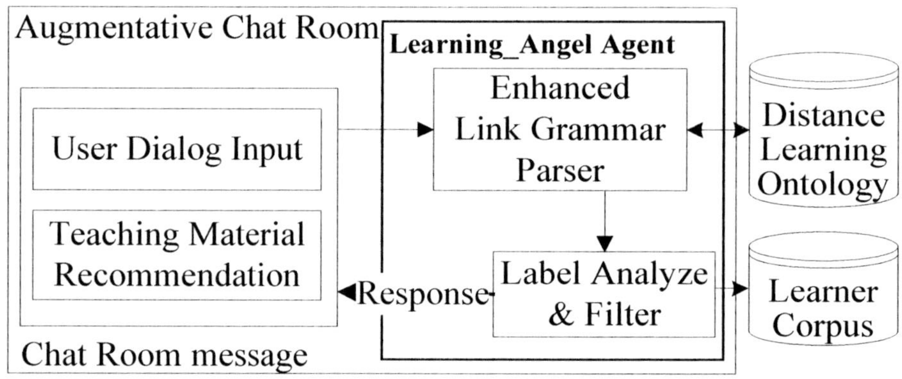

level mistakes. For example, learners may submit sentences that do not make sense of the course topic. The Semantic Agent can analyze the data in the Learner Corpus and make some comments or give suggestions to the users.

Two proposed methodologies for constructing the Semantic Agent are proposed in this article. One is the Semantic Link Grammar, which is based on Link Grammar, and the other is the Semantic Relation of Knowledge Ontology, which is based on ontology technology. The Semantic Link Grammar can use the algorithm from the Link Grammar to parse sentences. However, it is quite difficult to modify the dictionary, which consists of correct semantic meanings. It will take a lot of money and time for linguistic classification and the performance is not very good.

In this article, we will employ the second method: the **Semantic Relation of Knowledge Ontology**. This method can be used to evaluate the distance between specified keywords. The Semantic Agent subsystem shown in Figure 6 contains three processes.

1. Sentence Pattern Classification

Firstly, the sentence pattern classification process classifies input sentence patterns. Currently, this process can only identify Simple and Negative Sentence Patterns. Other types of sentence patterns are ignored. After classification is completed, each sentence will be tagged with its sentence pattern information and passed to the Semantic Keyword Filter to be processed.

Figure 6. Workflow of the Semantic Agent

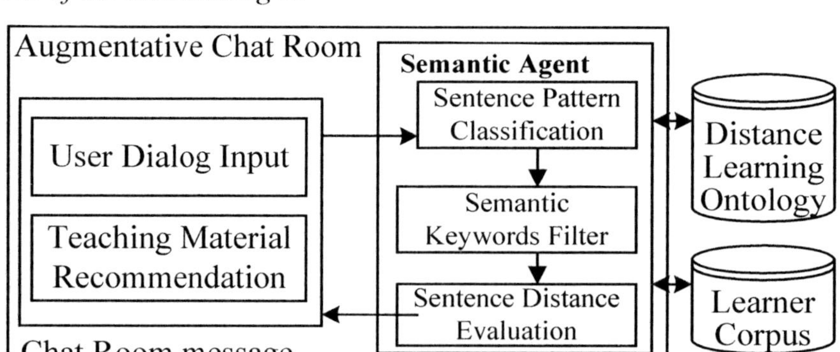

2. Semantic Keywords Filter

According to the sentence pattern information, the Semantic Keyword Filter will extract the sentence's keywords and query the ontology (in this article, the Data Structure Ontology) to get the keywords' IDs.

3. Sentence Distance Evaluation

We have designed a tree structure that can be used to encode the Data Structure Ontology shown in Figure 7. Each node (i.e., keyword) in the ontology has its unique ID number. The Sentence Distance Evaluation component uses the ID information to calculate the distance between two keywords.

For example, consider: **The tree doesn't have pop method.** After the sentence is processed by the Semantic Keyword Filter, the keywords will be "tree" and "pop." Table 2 shows some of the predefined IDs and keywords in the ontology. Here, we know that the ID number of the keyword "tree" is 4 and that of "pop" is 33.

And the following Figure 8 shows the tree-view of the above keyword ontology structure shown in Table 2. In the Schema of the Data Structure Course, the depth value of the ID indicates the keyword's distance from the root node. For example, the depth value between "Stack" the "Course" is 2 and that of "pop" and "Course" is 3. Thus, we transfer the depth value calculation to string comparison with the keywords' ID values. We examine the ID string from left to right. The left-most digit represents the top category in the domain of the Data Structure. The following digit represents the subcategory related to its parent and so on. According to the design of the ontology structure, the problem of evaluating the distance between two nodes can be simplified as the string comparison problem. If the left most digits of two keywords' IDs are not equal, then we conclude that the two keywords are absolutely unrelated.

As Figure 8 shows, the ID of the keyword "tree" is 4 and that "pop" is 33. We discover that the left-most digits of the two keywords' IDs are not the same. So "tree" and "pop" in the example sentence is not related. This information is then combined with the pattern classification obtained from Sentence Pattern Classification component. Since the result for this example sentence is negative, the semantic checker will conclude that the semantics of this sentence are still correct.

In our discussion of Sentence Pattern Classification, we will focus on the semantic checking of a simple sentence pattern and a negative sentence pattern. Based on the analysis performed by the Link Grammar, Tables 3 and 4 show the sentence

Figure 7. Schema of the data structure course

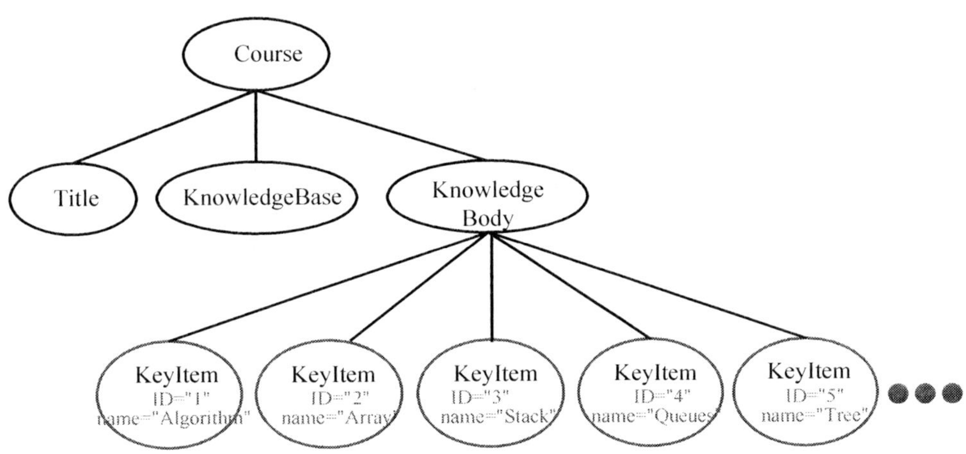

Table 2. The ID of keywords in the knowledge ontology

Keywords	Stack	Tree	pop	Push
ID	3	4	33	34

pattern classifications of simple sentence pattern and negative sentence pattern. Based on these two tables, the keywords can be extracted from learners' sentences.

Other examples of such sentences are as follows:

- I push the data into a tree.

This is a simple sentence pattern. In this simple sentence pattern, we find the ID of the keyword "push" is 32 and that of "tree" is 4. This means that these two words are not in the same branch. Thus, we know that they are not mutually related, so there is a semantic mistake with this sentence:

- The tree doesn't have pop method.

This is a negative sentence, even though the IDs of "tree" and "pop" are not in the same branch. Thus, the semantics meaning of this sentence is still correct.

However, in the Sentence Pattern Classification process, if learners submit the following W/H sentence pattern or yes/no sentence pattern sentences, it will be hard to determine the relationships between the subjects and objects in the sentence patterns:

- How can I push data in to Stack?
- Is Tree has a method pop?
- What method can be used in link-list?

In this section, we have ignored this kind of question pattern checking. But in the following section, we will use the Question and Answer System to answer learners' questions based on the learning ontology and learning corpus.

Question and Answer System

In chat room systems, learners can ask questions of each other or direct questions to the system. In this system, the domain knowledge that is in the Distance Learning Ontology and Learning Corpus can provide answers for users. When

Figure 8. Knowledge ontology representation of the Data Structure (taking "tree" and "push" as examples)

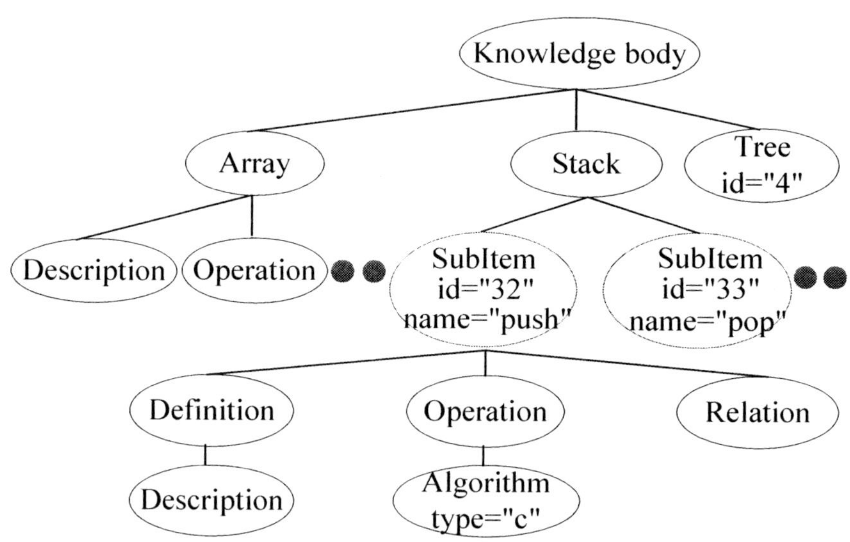

Table 3. Simple sentence pattern and link grammar tags

		Active voice	Passive voice
Simple pattern	present past future	Ss or Sp Ss or Sp Ss or Sp + I	Ss or Sp + Pv Ss or Sp + Pv Ss or Sp + Ix + Pv
Continuous pattern	present past future	Ss or Sp + PP Ss or Sp + PP Ss + If + PP	Ss or Sp + ppf + Pv Ss or Sp + ppf + Pv Ss or Sp + If + ppf + Pv
Proceed pattern	present past future	Ss or Sp + Pg Ss or Sp + Pg Ss or Sp + Ix + Pg	Ss or Sp + Pg + Pv Ss or Sp + Pg + Pv none
Perfective continuous pattern	present past	Ss or Sp + ppf + Pg Ss or Sp + ppf + Pg	
Comments: Ss and Sp: connects subject nouns to finite verbs. I: connects infinitive verb forms to certain words, such as modal verbs and "to." PP: connects forms of "have" with past participles. PV: connects forms of the verb "be" with past participles. Pg: connects forms of the verb "be" with present participles. ppf: connects forms of the verb "be" with the past participle "been."			

Table 4. Negate sentence pattern

		Original+not	"Not" condensation
Simple pattern	present past future	Ss or Sp + N Ss or Sp + N Ss or Sp + N + I	Ss or Sp + I*d Ss or Sp + I*d Ss or Sp + I
Continuous pattern	present past future	Ss or Sp + N + PP Ss or Sp + N + PP Ss or Sp + N + If + PP	Ss or Sp + PP Ss or Sp + PP Ss or Sp + If + PP
Proceed pattern	present past future	Ss or Sp + N + Pg Ss or Sp + N + Pg Ss or Sp + N + Ix + Pg	Ss or Sp + Pg Ss or Sp + Pg Ss or Sp + Ix + Pg
Perfective continuous pattern	present past	Ss or Sp + N + ppf + Pg Ss or Sp + N + ppg +Pg	Ss or Sp + ppf + Pg Ss or Sp + ppf + Pg
Comments: There must be a label "N" in the negative sentence pattern. N: connects the word "not" to preceding auxiliaries.			

users query the system, the system will attempt to find answers from the Knowledge Ontology or Learner Corpus. Also, if a sufficient number of QA pairs have been accumulated, the FAQ can act as a powerful learning tool for learners. Based on these corpora, instructors can revise or enhance their teaching materials. Learners can also learn from the experience of previous learners and other learners.

As discussed in a previous section, we used the knowledge ontology based approach, the **Semantic Relation of Knowledge Ontology**, to construct the Semantic Agent. This methodology can detect sentence patterns and find the positions

Figure 9. Workflow of questions and answers system

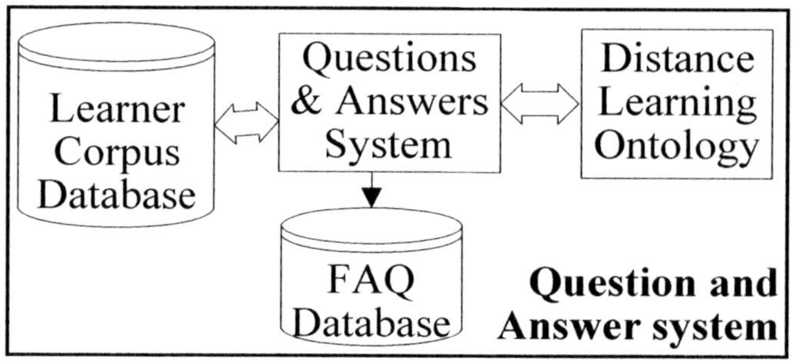

of the keywords in the Knowledge Ontology. This is a new way to design a Question and Answer system (QA system). The workflow of the QA system is shown in Figure 9.

When the QA system receives a question pattern sentence, it can find the IDs of keywords in the Data Structure Ontology and find their related information (for example, "description" and "algorithm") and then try to answer the learner's question.

The question sentence analysis process is illustrated in Tables 5 and 6.

Some examples of such sentences are as follows:

- What is Stack?
- Which data structure has the method push?
- Does stack have pop method?

According to the Yes/No question sentence pattern and WH question sentence pattern, when the QA system receives the question "***What is Stack***" from a learner, the sentence will first be recognized as a type of question sentence pattern. Then, the QA system will extract the keyword "stack" to find its ID in the Knowledge Ontology. With its ID and the question sentence pattern type "***What is,***" The system will understand the semantic meaning of this question is to ask the definition of stack. Then, it will try to find the definition or description of "stack" for the user. Then, the system will collect this question and answer into the FAQ database. Some examples of Knowledge Ontology are as follows:

\- <KeyItem id="**3**" name="**stack**">
\- <Definition>
<Description>**A stack is a Last In, First Out(LIFO) data structure in which all insertions and deletions are restricted to one end. There are three basic stack operations: push, pop, and stack top.**</Description>
<Symbol name="**top**">**A stack is a linear list in which all additions and deletions are restricted to one end, which is called the top.**</Symbol>
<Symbol name="**overflow**">**There is one potential problem with the push operation: We must resure that there is room for the new item. If there is not enough room, then the stack is in an overflow state.**</Symbol>
<Symbol name="**underflow**">**When the last item in the stack is deleted, the stack must be set to its empty state. If pop is called when the stack is empty, then it is in an underflow state.**</Symbol>
</Definition>

There are some question templates for the question and answer system:

- What is
- The relations of
- Is ... has ...
- Which ... has

Table 5. Yes/No question sentence

		Yes/No question sentence
Simple pattern	present past future	Qd + SIs + I*d Qd + SIs + I*d Qd + SIs + I
Continuous pattern	present past future	Qd + SIs + PP Qd + SIs + PP Qd + SIs + If + PP
Proceed pattern	present past future	Qd + SIs + Pg Qd + SIs + Pg Qd + SIs + Ix + Pg
Perfective continuous pattern	present past	Qd + SIs + ppf + Pg Qd + SIs + ppf + Pg
Comments: A Yes/no question sentence pattern must be labeled as "Qd".		

Table 6. WH question sentence

		What	Where and how
Simple pattern	present past future	Wq + Sid + I*d + Bsw Wq + Sid + I*d + Bsw Wq + SIs + I + Bsw	Wq + Q + SIs + I*d Wq + Q + SIs + I*d Wq + Q + SIs + I*d
Continuous pattern	present past future	Wq + SIs + I + Bsw Wq + SIs + I + Bsw	Wq + Q + SIs + PP Wq + Q + SIs + PP
Proceed pattern	present past future	Wq + SIs + Pg + Bsw Wq + SIs + Pg + Bsw	Wq + Q + SIs + PP Wq + Q + SIs + PP
Perfective continuous pattern	present past	None	none
Comments: A WH question sentence, such as where/when/why questions, must be labeled as "Wq." Sid: connects subject nouns to finite verbs in cases of subject-verb inversion Bsw: connects auxiliary verb will have/has/had to past participle.			

Moreover, the FAQ database can also use the data mining technology to accumulate question and answer pairs received from learners while learners are engaged in discussions using this proposed system. If a sufficient number of QA pairs have been accumulated, the FAQ system will obtain the statistics of questions and answers and then get the most frequently Question and Answer pairs. The system can also show these QA pairs to learners. This can be a powerful learning assistant for online learners.

EVALUATION

Several related systems are surveyed in the following:

- IwiLL(Wible, Kuo, Chien, & Taso, 2001), which is a Web-based language-learning platform, consists of several tightly interwoven components. This is a learner corpus for students in Taiwan. Students can write article on the Web and then send then to teachers. The teachers also can check the homework online. Teachers cannot only check for spelling errors and grammar mistakes but also semantic problems. IwiLL also provides some multimedia data to help students learn English. And it can store articles written by students in the learner corpus. However, it is not an automatic system. Teachers need to go online frequently.
- The American National Corpus (Ide, 2003; Ide, et al.. 2002; American National Corpus, n.d.; British National Corpus, n.d.) includes, ideally, a balanced representation of texts and transcriptions of spoken data. Samples of other major languages of North America, especially Spanish and French Canadian, should also comprise a portion of the corpus and, ideally, be aligned with parallel translations in English. ANC comprises approximately 100 million words that include additional texts in a wide range of styles from various domains. It is designed to be a word corpus.
- The British National Corpus, which is a 100-million-word collection of samples of written and spoken language from a wide range of sources, is designed to represent a wide cross-section of current British English, both spoken and written. BNC is an online service that is different from ANC. It is also designed to be a word corpus only.
- CRITIQUE is a system provided by Yael Ravin (1988). The methodology employed in this system is grammar error detection. The system analyzes the grammar and style weaknesses, as the terms "error" and "weakness" suggest. CRITIQUE can detect five categories of grammar errors and eight categories of style weaknesses. This system uses rule-based methodology. But it is only an application; users cannot use this system on the Web. The system can record information from users, but its functions are not upgradeable.
- The Microsoft Office Word grammar checker is a well-known system. When one uses the Word system, there is a "paper clip" agent or something else to provides help. If one makes a spelling or grammar mistake, the agent will show the error and can correct the mistake. The system uses several dictionaries like ActiveGrammarDictionary, ActiveHyphenationDictionary, ActiveSpellingDictionary, and ActiveThesaurusDictionary to return corresponding Dictionary objects. The system also uses the statistical methodology to detect and correct errors (Microsoft MSDN). But this system cannot collect user information when people use the system. It will also be difficult to upgrade its capability unless upgrade the Word system to next version.

The Table 7 shows the functionalities comparisons between our system and other systems.

IwiLL is also a learning system, whose goal and functionality are very similar to those of our proposed system. We first compare the IwiLL system with ours based on the functions listed in the table. Next, we compare the capability of our corpus with that of ANC and BNC. Lastly, we compare the about the grammar checking capabilities of our system with those of CRITIQUE and the MS Grammar checker. If there is no value in the comparison grid, then means that this function in here can't be compared between our system and the corresponding system.

Table 7. Evaluation of our system and other systems

Comparison	**Learning Assistance**		**Corpus Capability**		**Grammar**	
System	**Semantic Chat Room**	**IwiLL**	**ANC**	**BNC**	**CRITIQUE**	**MS Grammar checker**
Corpus	Lerner Corpus	Lerner Corpus	Standard Corpus	Standard Corpus		
Words Capability	Words are updatable	Words are updatable	1,00 Millions Words	1,00 Millions Words		
Grammar check	Automatic	Manual			Automatic	Automatic
Number Disagreement	Y	⊙			Y	Y
Wrong Pronoun	Y	⊙			Y	Y
Wrong Verb Form	Y	⊙			Y	Y
Wrong Article	Y	⊙			N	Y
Punctuation	Y	⊙			Y	Y
Web Application	Y	Y	N	Y		
Support Multimedia	Y	Y				
Semantic Analysis	Y	N				
FAQ collection	Automatic	N				
Online teachers supervising	Not always	Always				

⊙ *Manually checked by teacher*

CONCLUSION

In our proposed system, learners can send messages to each other in an English environment. They can discuss courses with each other and ask teachers questions. We have designed the Learning_Angel Agent and Semantic Agent to be online supervisors. These two agents automatically can help learners to practice English conversation and engage in discussions. The Learning_Angel Agent automatically can detect syntax errors. Then, the Semantic Agent can check the semantics of sentences in dialogues if learners fall behind in discussing courses. Thus, online teachers and tutors do not always have to wait for students to submit questions. In other words, this system can solve the Instructor-off problems.

The Link Grammar, a word-based parsing mechanism, is designed to be an accurate grammar checker. However, it fails to focus on fault tolerance. Different from the Link Grammar, our system is particularly useful for non-native English speakers. In addition it can parse sentences, make comments, and suggest corrections to users.

The original Link Grammar does not have these functions, and it appears that the idea proposed herein can be applied in other domain specific applications.

With the system constantly serviced online, it is important for philologists to analyze sentences accumulated from students' dialogues. Then, the system can easily point out common or special mistakes. Subsequently, online teachers can refine their learning materials.

In conclusion, this system provides a better and more interactive environment for teachers and students. Words are the basic communication units in natural language texts and speech-processing activities. When teaching English, teachers always want to know the types of mistakes that their students make. The proposed system also can be extended to encompass more scalable domain. The concepts presented herein can aid in the development of other similar applications. In the future, we will focus on finding better approaches to semantic analysis by evaluating the accuracy of the proposed Semantic Agent and trying to make our system adaptable with famous distance-learning standards.

REFERENCES

Adhvaryu, S., & Balbin, I. (1998). How useful is multimedia on the WWW for enhancing teaching and learning? *Proceedings of International Conference on Multimedia Computing and Systems (ICMCS'98)*, Austin, TX, June 28-July 31.

American National Corpus. (n.d.). http://american-nationalcorpus.org/

British National Corpus (n.d.). http://www.nat-corp.ox.ac.uk/

Goldberg, M. W. (1996). Student participation and progress tracking for Web-based courses using WebCT. *Proceedings of the Second International N.A. Web conference*, Fredericton, NB, Canada, October 5-8.

Goldberg, M. W., & Salari, S. (1997). An update on WebCT (World-Wide-Web Course Tools) – A tool for the creation of sophisticated Web-Based learning environments. *Proceedings of NAU-Web'97 – Current Practices in Web-Based Course Development*, Flagstaff, AZ, June 12-15.

Goldberg, M. W., Salari, S., & Swoboda, P. (1996). *World Wide Web course tool: An environment for building WWW-based courses.* Computer Networks and ISDN Systems.

Harris, D., Cordero, C., & Hsieh, J. (1996). High-speed network for delivery of education-on-demand. *Proceeding of Multimedia Computing and Networking Conference (MCN'96)*, San Jose, CA, January 29-31.

Ide, N. (2003). The American National Corpus: Everything you always wanted to know...and weren't afraid to ask. Invited keynote, Corpus Linguistics 2003, Lancaster, UK.

Ide, N., Reppen, R., & Suderman, K. The American National Corpus: More than Web can provide proceedings of the third Language Resources and Evaluation Conference (LREC). Las Palmas, Canary Islands, Spain, 839-844.

Labrou, Y. & Finin, T. (1999). Yahoo! as an ontology—Using Yahoo! categories to describe documents. *Proceedings of the 8th International Conference on Information and Knowledge Management*, Kansas City, MO, November, 180-187.

Li, J., Zhang, L., & Yu, Y. (2001). Learning to generate semantic annotation for domain specific sentences. *In the Workshop on Knowledge Markup and Semantic Annotation at the 1st International Conference on Knowledge Capture (K-CAP 2001)*, October, Victoria, B.C., Canada.

McGuinness, D.L. & Harmelen, F.V. (2004). OWL Web ontology language overview. W3C Recommendation, February 10.

Microsoft MSDN online Library. http://msdn.microsoft.com/vstudio/

Ravin, Y. (1988). Grammar errors and style weaknesses in a text-critiquing system. *IEEE Transactions on Professional Communication, 31*(3), 1988, 108-115.

Sleator, D. K. & Temperley, D. (1991). Parsing English with a link grammar. October, CMU-CS-91-196.

Tsang, H.W., Hung, L.M., & Ng, S.C. (1999). A multimedia distance learning system on the Internet. *Proceedings of IEEE International Conference on Systems, Man, and Cybernetics (SMC), 2*, 243-246.

Wang,Y.H., Wang, W.N., & Lin, C.H. An intelligent semantic agent for e-learning message communication. *Journal of Information Science and Engineering, 21*(5), 1031-1051.

Wang, Y.H. & Lin, C.H. (2004). A multimedia database supports English distance learning. *An International Journal Information Sciences, 158*, 189-208.

Wang,Y.H., Lin, C.H., & Wang, W.N. (2007). Semantic enhanced QA system architecture use link grammar parser for e-learning environment. *Proceeding of Conference Taiwan E-Learning Forum (TWELF) 2007*, May, 18-19.

Weibel, S., Gridby, J., & Miler, E. (1995). *OCLC/NCSA metadata workshop report,* Dublin, EUA. Retrieved from http://www.oclc.org:5046/oclc/research/conferences/metadata/dublin_core_report.html

Weible, D., Kuo, C.-H., Chien, F.-Y., & Taso, N.L. (2001). Automating repeated exposure to target vocabulary for second language learners, Advanced Learning Technologies. *Proceedings,of the IEEE International Conference on,* August 6-8, 127-128.

Willis, B. (n.d.). Distance education at a glance. Engineering Outreach at the University of Idaho, http://www.uidaho.edu/evo/distglan.html

This work was previously published in International Journal of Distance Education Technologies, Vol. 6, Issue 5, edited by S. Chang; T. Shih, pp. 14-33, copyright 2008 by IGI Publishing (an imprint of IGI Global).

Chapter 4
A Computer-Assisted Approach to Conducting Cooperative Learning Process

Pei-Jin Tsai
National Chiao Tung University, Taiwan

Gwo-Jen Hwang
National University of Tainan, Taiwan

Judy C.R. Tseng
Chung-Hua University in Hsinchu, Taiwan

Gwo-Haur Hwang
Ling Tung University, Taiwan

ABSTRACT

Cooperative learning has been proven to be helpful in enhancing the learning performance of students. The goal of a cooperative learning group is to maximize all members' learning, which is accomplished via promoting each other's success, through assisting, sharing, mentoring, explaining, and encouragement. To achieve the goal of cooperative learning, it is very important to organize well-structured cooperative learning groups, in which all group members have the ability to help each other during the learning process. In this article, a concept-based approach is proposed to organize cooperative learning groups, such that, for a given course each concept is precisely understood by at least one of the students in each group. An experiment on a computer science course has been conducted in order to evaluate the efficacy of this new approach. From the experimental results, we conclude that the novel approach is helpful in enhancing student learning efficacy.

INTRODUCTION

In past decades, cooperative learning researchers have shown that positive peer relationships are an essential element of success during the learning process, and isolation and alienation will possibly lead to failure (Tinto, 1993). Hundreds of relevant studies have been conducted to compare the effectiveness of cooperative, competitive, and individualistic efforts by a wide variety of researchers in different decades using many different methods (Smith, 1995; Keyser, 2000; Ramsay et al., 2000; Rachel & Irit, 2002; Veenman et al., 2002). Results have shown cooperation among students typically results in higher achievement and greater productivity, more caring, supportive, and committed relationships, and greater psychological health, social competence, and self-esteem (Johnson et al., 1991; Veenman et al., 2002).

Even though many researchers have proposed a variety of cooperation learning methods, and have defined various constraints on achieving the expected results, there are however, many complex human factors that cannot be fully controlled during the cooperative learning process, including the construction of cooperative learning groups and the designed activities for the promoting of constructive cooperation, which all are known to be difficult without proper aid.

In this article, we shall propose a computer-assisted approach to organizing cooperative learning groups based on complementary concepts to maximize students' learning performance. In the approach, for a given course, each concept is well learned and completely understood by at least one of the students in each group. That is, in each cooperative learning group, the students will have an enhanced capability of learning all of the concepts, if they know how to learn from each other, via proper designed learning activities.

To evaluate the performance of the proposed approach, an experiment has been conducted on a computer course entitled, "Management Information System". One hundred and four students were separated into a control group and an experimental group. In the control group, the cooperative learning groups were organized by averaging the pre-test scores of each group; in the experimental group, the concept-based grouping method was applied; dividing the students into cooperative learning groups based on their well-learned and poorly-learned concepts. From the experimental results, it can be seen that the cooperative learning groups constructed by the concept-based grouping method are able to achieve significantly better performance, and hence, we conclude that the new approach is helpful in enhancing student learning efficacy.

RELEVANT RESEARCH

In human societies, it can be seen that the more one learns from other people's experiences, the higher the possibility of success. People often take advice, interact, consult with each other and observe others to learn from their activities and experiences; that is, people cooperate to learn (Ahmadabadi & Asadpour, 1980). "Cooperation" in this context means working together to accomplish common goals. Within the realm of cooperative activities, individuals seek outcomes that are beneficial to all members of the group. Cooperative learning is the instructional use of small groups so that students work together in order to maximize the learning efficacy of all group members (Johnson et al., 1991; Johnson & Johnson, 1999; Huber, 2003). Well-organized cooperative learning involves people working in teams to accomplish a common goal, under conditions in which all members must cooperate in the completion of a task, whereupon each individual and member is accountable for the absolute outcome (Smith, 1995).

In a cooperative learning group, students are assigned to work together with the awareness that success fundamentally depends upon the efforts of all group members. The group goal of maximizing all members' learning abilities provides a compelling common purpose, one that motivates members to accomplish achievements beyond their individual expectations. Students promote each other's success through helping, sharing, assisting, explaining, and encouraging. They provide both academic and personal support based on a commitment to and caring about each other. All of the group members are taught teamwork skills and are expected to use them to coordinate their efforts and achieve their goals (Smith, 1996).

Various studies have documented the effectiveness of cooperative learning in the classroom (e.g., Mevarech, 1993; Ghaith & Yaghi, 1998; Klingner & Vaughn, 2000; Porto, 2001; Swain, 2001; Ghaith, 2002) and its problems such as the 'free-rider effects,' (e.g., Johnson & Johnson; 1990; Hooper, 1992). Some of the results from these studies and design strategies derived from empirical data may serve as a basis for constructing an interactive cooperative/collaborative learning system. For example, Adams and Hamm (1990) suggested a group size of three or four is appropriate for solving mathematical problems cooperatively; Slavin (1989) and Sun and Chou (1996) stated that clear group goals and conscious self-accountability among students are the necessary factors for the success of cooperative learning; Hooper (2003) compared the effects of grouping students with different levels of persistence on their ability to learn in cooperative learning groups while working at the computer.

So far, cooperative learning has been applied to the learning design of various courses. For example, an application was presented by Dibiasio and Groccia (1995) on a sophomore level chemical engineering course that was redesigned to emphasize active and cooperative learning. The structure used in the course was a peer-assisted cooperative learning model, and was compared to a control course taught by the passive lecture method. The control and test courses were compared using student performance, attitudes, an evaluation of the course and instructor, and faculty time. The experimental results showed that the student learning performance can be improved via conducting cooperative learning; moreover, faculty time was reduced by 24% using the peer-assisted cooperative learning model. In the meanwhile, another example was reported by McDonald (1995), who demonstrated the use of cooperative learning in a junior-level analog electronics course by arranging the students to work in assigned groups on complex homework problems and laboratory projects. Dietrich and Urban (1998) also reported the use of cooperative learning concepts in support of an introductory database management course. The database practice is realized through the use of cooperative group projects.

Researchers have presented several ways for implementing cooperative learning in classrooms, including informal cooperative learning groups, formal cooperative learning groups, and cooperative-based groups (Smith, 1996; Klein & Schnackenberg, 2000). Formal cooperative learning can be used in content-intensive classes, where the implementation of conceptual or procedural material is essential. Base groups are long-term, heterogeneous cooperative learning groups with stable membership whose primary responsibility is to provide students with the support, encouragement, and assistance they need to make academic progress. Base groups personalize the work required and the course learning experiences. These base groups remain unchanged during the entire course and longer if possible. When students have success, insights, questions or concerns they wish to discuss; they can contact other members of their base group.

In recent years, some cooperative learning activities have been performed on Web-based learning environments, so that the students in different locations can cooperate to learn (Kirschner, 2000; Johnson et al., 2002; Sheremetov & Arenas, 2002; Macdonald, 2003). CORAL is a well-known system that promotes cooperative and collaborative learning by providing windows that convey both verbal messages, such as voice, and nonverbal messages (e.g., facial expressions) to increase the social presence of the system (Sun & Chou, 1996). That is, the degree to which the system permits users to interact with others, as if they are face to face (Fulk et al., 1987). Moreover, CORAL also provides private a bookmark function and a shared discussion function. Students were asked to form teams of two or three to work on group projects, such as programming tasks. Since the CORAL system keeps track of each student's progress, via recording the number of nodes visited, the number of projects done, and examination scores, it retrospectively assigns advanced students to help slower students. Students who help others will get extra credits.

It can be seen that network-based learning not only preserves the advantage of providing individualized learning but also supports competitive and cooperative learning. Moreover, from a variety of practical applications, it has been noted that well-structured cooperative learning groups are differentiated from poorly structured ones (Sun & Chou, 1996). Therefore, it is an important issue to know how to organize cooperative learning groups in a way that can benefit all of the students in the class. To cope with this problem, a teacher not only needs to promote the advantages of cooperative learning to the students, but also requires knowledge of the learning status of each student. Without proper aid, it is difficult for the teacher to organize effective cooperative learning groups. In this article, a concept-based grouping approach is proposed, which is capable of effectively determining well-structured cooperative learning groups in a class.

COOPERATIVE LEARNING BASED ON CONCEPT RELATIONSHIP MODEL

A course can be regarded as a collection of concepts to be learned and understood. In Hwang (2003), a concept-based model was proposed to detect the poorly-learned and well-learned concepts for individual students. It is obvious that a student is capable of helping other group members if he or she has learned some concepts

Table 1. Illustrative example of an original ASST

			Test item Q_k									
			Q_1	Q_2	Q_3	Q_4	Q_5	Q_6	Q_7	Q_8	Q_9	Q_{10}
Student S_i	S_3	Mary	1	1	1	1	1	1	1	0	1	1
	S_7	David	1	1	0	1	1	1	1	1	1	1
	S_2	Tom	1	1	1	1	1	0	1	0	1	1
	S_6	Paul	1	1	1	0	1	1	0	1	1	1
	S_5	Susan	1	0	1	1	0	1	1	0	1	1
	S_8	Olivia	1	1	1	1	0	1	0	1	1	0
	S_9	Carol	0	1	1	0	1	0	0	1	1	1
	S_{10}	Jade	0	1	0	0	1	0	0	1	1	1
	S_1	John	0	1	0	0	1	0	0	1	1	1
	S_4	Peter	0	1	0	0	1	0	0	1	1	1
Fail-to-Answer[Q_k]			4	1	4	4	2	5	6	3	0	1
P_k			0.6	0.9	0.6	0.6	0.8	0.5	0.4	0.7	1	0.8
D_k			0.3	0	0.2	0.2	0	0.2	0.3	-0.2	0	0

well. Therefore, it may be a good idea to arrange a student who has well learned a certain concept in the group with those who have poorly-learned the same concept. In this section, we implement the idea by proposing a new approach to organize cooperative learning groups based on the analysis results of the well-learned and poorly-learned concepts for each student.

Generate the Answer Sheet Statistic Table

An answer sheet statistic table (ASST) is an (N+3)×M table which records the answers of the test given by the students, where M is the number of test items and N is the number of students. If a student correctly answers a test item, the corresponding entry value in ASST is marked "1", otherwise, the entry value is marked "0". An illustrative example of ASST is given in Table 1, where S_i and Q_k represent student and test item, respectively, and Fail-to-Answer[Q_k] represents the number of students who did not answer correctly Q_k. For example, four students failed to correctly answer Q_1, that is, "John", "Peter", "Carol" and "Jade", and hence, Fail-to-Answer[Q_k] = 4.

$$P_k = \sum_{i=1}^{N} \left(ASST\left[S_i, Q_k\right] \right) / \mathrm{N},$$

represents the difficulty degree of test item Q_k. D_k represents the discrimination degree of test item Q_k, and is computed by taking the difference of the "correct answer" rate for the students who achieved the top-27% score and the "incorrect answer" rate for the students who rated the lowest-27% score, divided by the number of students. Consider test item Q_1 given in Table 1, the top-27% score students are "Mary", "David" and "Tom", and the lowest-27% score students are "Jade", "John" and "Peter"; therefore, $D_1 = (3 - 0) / 10 = 0.3$ and $D_2 = (3 - 3) / 10 = 0$.

After constructing the initial ASST, the test items that are not influential in determining student learning status must be removed. This can be done by observing the Fail-to-Answer[Q_k], difficulty degree and discrimination degree of each test item. For example, researchers indicated that the ideal values of P_k and D_k are $0.4 < P_k < 0.8$ and $D_k \geq 0.19$, respectively (Chase, 1978; Ebel & Frisbie, 1991). While P_k and D_k focus on describing the ability of the test item for discriminating high achievement students from the low achievement students. If Fail-to-Answer[Q_k], the number of students who failed to correctly answer Q_k, is smaller than a threshold, Q_k may not be influential in the determining of learning status for overall students. In this article, if two of Fail-to-Answer[Q_k], P_k and D_k values cannot satisfy the corresponding ideal values, Q_k will be removed from ASST. For example, assume that the threshold for Fail-to-Answer[Q_k] is 3, as Fail-to-Answer[Q_2]=1<3, P_2=0.9 > 0.8 and D_2=0< 0.19, Q_2 is removed from ASST, so do Q_5, Q_9 and Q_{10}. After removing those test items, a reduced ASST can be obtained, as shown in Table 2.

Generation of the Test Item-Concept Statistic Table

A test item-concept statistic table (TCST) records the relationship between each test item and each concept. The value of TCST [Q_k, C_j] ranges from 0 to 1, indicating the degree of relevance for the test item to each concept. Table 3 shows an illustrative example of a TCST originating from Table 2, consisting of six test items and six concepts.

In the sequel, the concepts with small total weight will be removed from TCST, since effective use of the calculation concerning determining student learning status is limited. For example, assume that the threshold for removing concepts is 0.5; TCST is reduced as shown in Table 4.

Identifying Student Learning Status

A student-concept relationship table (SCRT) is used to record the well-learned and poorly-learned

Table 2. Illustrative example of a reduced ASST

			Test item Q_k					
			Q_1	Q_3	Q_4	Q_6	Q_7	Q_8
Student S_i	S_3	Mary	1	1	1	1	1	0
	S_7	David	1	0	1	1	1	1
	S_2	Tom	1	1	1	0	1	0
	S_6	Paul	1	1	0	1	0	1
	S_5	Susan	1	1	1	1	1	0
	S_8	Olivia	1	1	1	1	0	1
	S_9	Carol	0	1	0	0	0	1
	S_{10}	Jade	0	0	0	0	0	1
	S_1	John	0	0	0	0	0	1
	S_4	Peter	0	0	0	0	0	1
Fail-to-Answer[Q_k]			4	4	4	5	6	3
P_k			0.6	0.6	0.6	0.5	0.4	0.7
D_k			0.3	0.2	0.2	0.2	0.3	-0.2

Table 3. Illustrative example of a TCST

		Concept C_j					
		C_1	C_2	C_3	C_4	C_5	C_6
		Data vs. Information	Computer Equipment	Re-engineering	Productivity	Accounting	Groupware
Test Item Q_k	Q_1	1	-	-	-	-	-
	Q_3	-	-	-	-	-	1
	Q_4	-	-	0.7	0.3	-	-
	Q_6	-	0.8	-	0.2	-	-
	Q_7	-	-	-	-	-	1
	Q_8	-	-	1	-	-	-
Total weight		1	0.8	1.7	0.5	0	2

concepts for each student. If S_i correctly answered most of the test items relevant to C_j, SCRT[S_i, C_j]=1, which implies that S_i has well learned C_j; otherwise SCRT[S_i, C_j]=0.

SCRT is derived by composing the contents of ASST and TCST. Figure 1 shows the graphical representation of ASST, and each connection line represents an "incorrectly-answer" relationship. For example, it can be read from Figure 1 that four students, for example, "John", "Peter", "Carol" and "Jade", have incorrectly answered Q_l. Figure 2 is the graphical representation of TCST, and each connection line represents the "implication" relationship between each test item and each concept, which is marked as $\{Q_k\} \rightarrow C_j$ and is interpreted as, "if one failed to correctly answer Q_k, then he/she did not learn concept C_j satisfactorily." For example, $\{Q_l\} \rightarrow$ "Data vs. Information", $\{Q_6\} \rightarrow$ "Computer Equipment", and $\{Q_4, Q_8\} \rightarrow$ "Re-engineering".

Table 4. Illustrated example of a reduced TCST - by removing the concepts with total weight being lower than 0.5

		Concept C_j				
		C_1	C_2	C_3	C_4	C_6
		Data vs. Information	Computer Equipment	Re-engineering	Productivity	Groupware
Test Item Q_k	Q_1	1	-	-	-	-
	Q_3	-	-	-	-	1
	Q_4	-	-	0.7	0.3	-
	Q_6	-	0.8	-	0.2	-
	Q_7	-	-	-	-	1
	Q_8	-	-	1	-	-
Total weight		1	0.8	1.7	0.5	2

Figure 1. Graphical representation of the reduced ASST

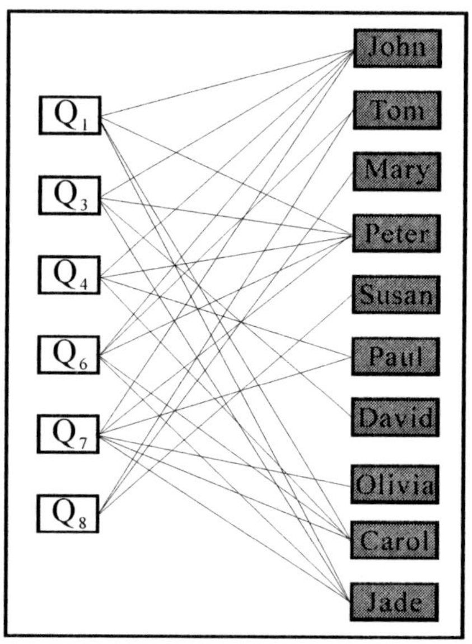

By composing Figure 1 and Figure 2, Figure 3 can be derived. For example, {John, Peter, Carol, Jade}→ Q_1 and {Q_1}→ "Data vs. Information", and hence, {John, Peter, Carol, Jade}→ "Data vs. Information" in Figure 3; therefore, the final SCRT can be derived as shown in Table 5, where SCRT [S_i, C_j]=0 represents student S_i who has poorly-learned concept C_j. For example, in Table 5, it can be observed that Tom failed to learn the concepts "Computer Equipment", "Re-engineering" and "Productivity".

Constructing the Concept-Based Cooperative Learning Groups

Based on the information given in SCRT, a concept-based method is proposed to organize the cooperative learning groups. To count the common concepts that the students failed to learn, an inverse SCRT is defined as, SCRT'[S_i, C_j]=(1 - SCRT[S_i, C_j]), in which SCRT' [S_i, C_j]=1 implies that student S_i has poorly learned concept C_j. The basic idea of the approach is to place a student who has well learned a concept in the

Figure 2. Graphical representation of the reduced TCST

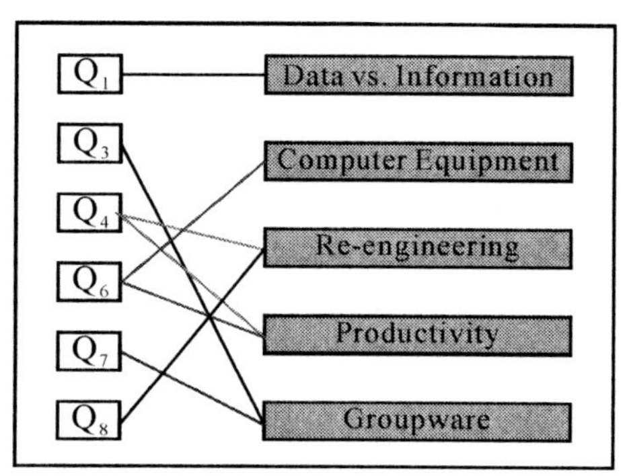

Figure 3. Graphical representation from Figure 1 and Figure 2

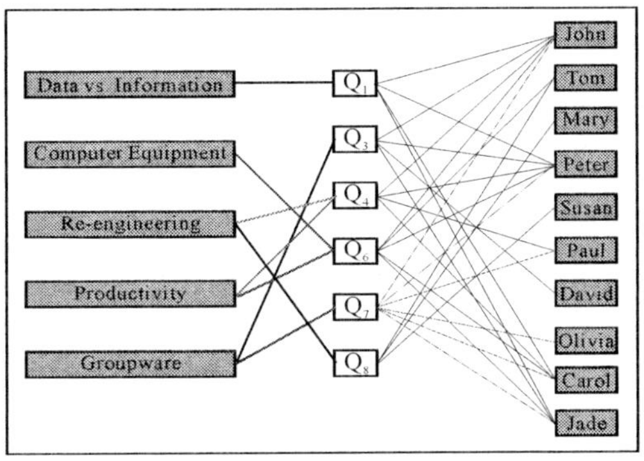

same group with those who have poorly learned the concept. Moreover, for each concept, at least one of the students in each group has well learned that concept, so the students in the same group will have the ability to assist each other in learning all of the concepts well.

An N×N matrix CCRM (Common Concept Relation Matrix) is used to record the group assignment relationships among the students. Figure 4 is an illustrative example of a CCRM matrix. The value of CCRM [S_i, S_j] represents the number of common concepts that both students S_i and S_j failed to correctly answer. For example, CCRM [John, Tom] = 3 means that both students "John" and "Tom" failed to correctly answer three concepts, that is, "Computer Equipment", "Re-engineering", and "Productivity" as shown in Table 5.

To organize cooperative learning groups for students such that the group members have the ability to help each other to learn all of the concepts, it is straightforward to allocate the pair of students with minimum value in CCRM, which implies they have the complementary ability to help each other. Therefore, the proposed algorithm finds S_i and S_j with minimum CCRM value by searching CCRM row by row from top to bottom. Once S_i and S_j are allocated to a cooperative learning group, say G_r, the corresponding information are removed from CCRM. The operation is repeated until all of the students have been assigned to the specified learning groups. Assuming the students in Figure 4 are to be divided into three groups, say G_0, G_1 and G_2. Since CCRM [*Tom, David*] = 0 is the minimum value in CCRM, and hence "Tom" and "David" are selected into G_0 and the corresponding rows and columns in CCRM are eliminated. In the second iteration, "Mary" and "Olivia" are selected into G_1 and the corresponding rows and columns in CCRM are eliminated since CCRM [Mary, Olivia]=0. After several iterations, three cooperative learning groups, that is, G_0= {Tom, David, John, Paul}, G_1 = {Mary, Olivia, Peter, Carol} and G_2= {Susan, Jade}, are constructed.

If the cooperative learning groups were constructed by considering the average scores of the students, the students will be divided into three different groups, say {John, David, Paul}, {Peter, Mary, Olivia, Jade} and {Carol, Tom, Susan}, which reveals several problems:

- In {John, David, Paul}, none of the students learned concept "Groupware" well, and hence it is difficult for them to learn "Groupware" during the cooperative learning process.

Figure 4. Illustrative example of a CCRM

	John	Tom	Mary	Peter	Susan	Paul	David	Olivia	Carol	Jade
John		3	1	4	1	3	1	1	4	3
Tom			1	3	1	2	0	0	3	2
Mary				1	1	1	0	0	1	0
Peter					1	3	1	1	5	4
Susan						1	0	0	1	0
Paul							1	1	3	2
David								1	1	1
Olivia									1	1
Carol										4
Jade										

- {Carol, Tom, Susan} have the same problem that none of the students learned concept "Re-engineering" well, and hence it is difficult for them to learn "Re-engineering" during the cooperative learning process.

Those problems can be solved by applying the concept-based approach; that is, by dividing the students into {Tom, David, John, Paul}, {Mary, Olivia, Peter, Carol} and {Susan, Jade}, such that in each group, each concept is well learned by at least one of the group members.

DEVELOPMENT OF A COMPUTER-ASSISTED TOOL

It can be seen that for a teacher to decide if a student has well learned a concept or poorly learned a concept could be very complicated and not feasible. To cope with this problem, a Web-based tool has been implemented to assist those teachers who want to construct concept-based cooperative learning groups.

Figure 5 shows the user interface for assisting the teachers in identifying the relationships between subject concepts and test items. Once the students have submitted their answers, the computer-assisted tool collects the answers, processes the inference flow, and then determines the well-learned concepts and poorly-learned concepts for each student.

Based on the learning status of the students to each concept, the system is able to construct cooperative learning groups based on the teacher's request (as shown in Figure 6).

EXPERIMENTS AND EVALUATION

To evaluate the efficacy of our novel approach, an experiment was conducted from September 2002 to January 2003 on a computer science course, namely "Management Information System". One hundred and four sophomore students participated in the experiment, and were separated into two groups, each of which contained fifty-two students. Both the control group and experimental group were divided into ten cooperative learning groups, each of which contained four to six students taught by the same teacher.

The goal of Management Information Systems is to provide a real-world understanding of information systems (ISs) for business and computer

Table 5. Illustrative example of SCRT

		C_1	C_2	C_3	C_4	C_6	Number of poorly-learned concepts
		Data vs. Information	Computer Equipment	Re-engineering	Productivity	Groupware	
S_1	John	1	0	0	0	0	4
S_2	Tom	1	0	0	0	1	3
S_3	Mary	1	1	0	1	1	1
S_4	Peter	0	0	0	0	0	5
S_5	Susan	1	1	0	1	1	1
S_6	Paul	1	1	0	0	0	3
S_7	David	1	1	1	1	0	1
S_8	Olivia	1	1	1	1	0	1
S_9	Carol	0	0	0	0	0	5
S_{10}	Jade	0	0	1	0	0	4

Figure 5. User interface of the computer-assisted tool

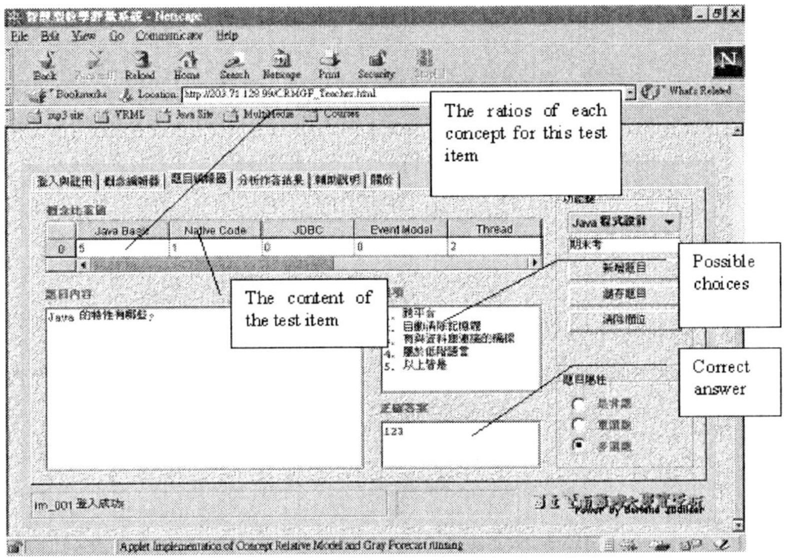

Figure 6. Cooperative learning groups constructed by the system

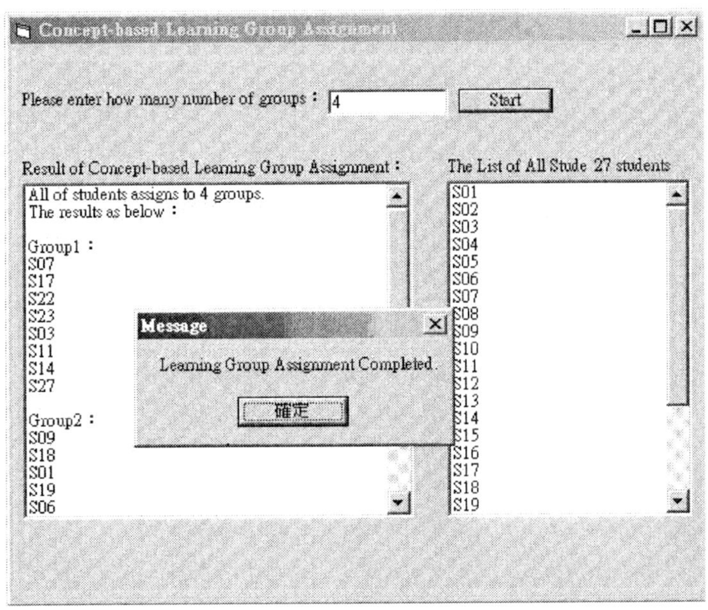

science students. In this course, students learn how to formulate strategic plans in executive suites, optimizing operations in businesses or on factory floors, fine-tuning plans for their own entrepreneurial ventures, designing information systems to optimize their organization's operations, working as consultants, augmenting business activities on the Web, or creating valuable new information products in any number of industries (Oz, 2002).

In Group A (the control group), ten cooperative learning groups were constructed by averaging the pre-test scores among the learning groups; while in Group B, the concept-based approach was applied to organize other ten cooperative learning groups based on the pre-test.

Table 6. TCST of the MIS course pre-test

	Test item Q_k																				Total Weight
	Q_1	Q_2	Q_3	Q_4	Q_5	Q_6	Q_7	Q_8	Q_9	Q_{10}	Q_{11}	Q_{12}	Q_{13}	Q_{14}	Q_{15}	Q_{16}	Q_{17}	Q_{18}	Q_{19}	Q_{20}	
Data vs. Information	1	0.8	-	-	-	-	-	-	-	-	-	-	-	-	-	-	-	-	-	-	1.9
Computer Equipment for Information Systems	-	-	1	0.5	0.2	-	-	0.1	-	-	-	-	-	-	-	-	-	-	-	-	1.8
Closed system	-	-	-	-	0.8	-	-	-	-	-	-	-	-	-	-	-	-	-	-	-	0.8
Computer components	-	-	-	-	-	0.5	0.5	-	-	-	-	-	-	-	-	-	-	-	-	-	1
Human-Computer Synergy	-	-	-	-	-	0.5	0.5	-	-	-	-	-	-	-	-	-	-	-	-	-	1
Information system	-	0.2	-	-	-	-	-	0.9	-	-	0.2	-	-	-	-	-	0.2	-	-	-	1.5
Personal computers	-	-	-	0.5	-	-	-	-	0.4	-	-	-	-	-	-	-	-	-	-	-	0.9
Strategic advantage	-	-	-	-	-	-	-	-	0.6	-	-	-	0.3	1	-	-	-	-	-	-	1.9
Strategic alliance	-	-	-	-	-	-	-	-	-	1	-	-	-	-	-	-	-	-	-	-	1
Strategic information system (SIS)	-	-	-	-	-	-	-	-	-	-	0.8	-	0.7	-	-	-	-	-	-	-	1.5
Re-engineering	-	-	-	-	-	-	-	-	-	-	-	1	-	-	-	-	-	-	-	-	1
Productivity	-	-	-	-	-	-	-	-	-	-	-	-	-	-	1	-	-	-	-	-	1
Accounting	-	-	-	-	-	-	-	-	-	-	-	-	-	-	-	1	-	-	-	-	1
EDP (Electronic Data Processing)	-	-	-	-	-	-	-	-	-	-	-	-	-	-	-	-	0.8	-	-	-	0.8
CNC (Computerized Numeric Control)	-	-	-	-	-	-	-	-	-	-	-	-	-	-	-	-	-	1	-	-	1
MPS (Master Production Scheduling)	-	-	-	-	-	-	-	-	-	-	-	-	-	-	-	-	-	-	1	-	1
Groupware	-	-	-	-	-	-	-	-	-	-	-	-	-	-	-	-	-	-	-	1	1

Pre-Test

The pre-test aims to ensure that the students in Groups A and B have the equivalent basis for learning the course, including the concepts "Data vs. Information", "Human-Computer Synergy", "Closed system", "Computer Equipment for Information Systems", "Information system",

Table 7. Relationships between cooperative learning groups and concepts

Concepts \ Cooperative learning groups	A_1	A_2	A_3	A_4	A_5	A_6	A_7	A_8	A_9	A_{10}	B_1	B_2	B_3	B_4	B_5	B_6	B_7	B_8	B_9	B_{10}
Data vs. Information	•	√	•	√	√	√	•	•	√	√	√	√	√	√	√	√	√	√	√	√
Computer Equipment for Information Systems	√	√	√	√	√	√	√	√	√	√	√	√	√	√	√	√	√	√	√	√
Closed system	•	•	√	√	√	√	√	√	•	√	√	√	√	√	√	√	√	√	√	√
Computer components	√	√	√	√	√	√	√	√	√	√	√	√	√	√	√	√	√	√	√	√
Human-Computer Synergy	√	√	√	√	√	√	√	√	√	√	√	√	√	√	√	√	√	√	√	√
Information system	√	√	√	√	√	√	√	√	√	√	√	√	√	√	√	√	√	√	√	√
Personal computers	√	√	√	√	√	√	√	√	√	√	√	√	√	√	√	√	√	√	√	√
Strategic advantage	√	√	√	•	√	•	√	√	√	√	√	√	√	√	√	√	√	√	√	√
Strategic alliance	√	√	√	√	•	√	√	√	√	•	√	√	√	√	√	√	√	√	√	√
Strategic information system (SIS)	√	√	√	√	•	√	√	√	√	•	√	√	√	√	√	√	√	√	√	√
Re-engineering	√	√	•	√	√	√	√	•	•	√	√	√	√	√	√	√	√	√	√	√
Productivity	√	•	√	√	•	√	√	√	√	√	√	√	√	√	√	√	√	√	√	√
Accounting	√	√	√	•	√	√	√	√	√	√	√	√	√	√	√	√	√	√	√	√
EDP (Electronic Data Processing)	√	√	√	√	√	√	√	√	√	√	√	√	√	√	√	√	√	√	√	√
CNC (Computerized Numeric Control)	√	√	√	√	√	√	√	√	•	√	√	√	√	√	√	√	√	√	√	√
MPS (Master Production Scheduling)	√	√	√	√	•	√	•	√	√	√	√	√	√	√	√	√	√	√	√	√
Groupware	√	√	•	√	√	•	√	√	√	•	√	√	√	√	√	√	√	√	√	√

"Personal computers", "Strategic alliance", "Strategic information system", "Re-engineering", "Productivity", "Accounting", "Groupware", "EDP (Electronic Data Processing)", "CNC (Computerized Numeric Control)", and "MPS (Master Production Scheduling)". The test sheet of the pre-test contained twenty multiple-choice questions. Table 6 depicts the TCST of the MIS course pre-test, in which the total weight of each concept ranged from 0.8 to 1.9. If the students correctly answered test items related to a concept with total weight ≥ 0.6 (the threshold defined by the teacher), they were said to have well learned that concept (Hwang 2003). For example, if a student correctly answered Q_4, Q_5 and Q_8, the total weight for concept "Computer Equipment

Table 8. Statistic results of pre-test

	Group A	Group B
N	52	52
Mean	49.81	54.42
Std. Dev.	13.93	13.45
t=1.718 sig.=0.089		

for Information Systems" is $0.5 + 0.2 + 0.1 = 0.8 \geq 0.6$, and hence the student was said to have well learned the concept.

Table 7 shows the relationship between each cooperative learning group and each concept. The symbol "√" implies that at least one of the members in the cooperative learning group has well learned the concept, and "•" indicates that none of the members in the cooperative learning group has well learned the concept. For example, at least one of the members in the cooperative learning group A_2 has well learned concept "Data vs. Information", while none of the members in A_2 has well learned concept "Closed system".

The t-test for the pre-test results of Groups A and B is shown in Table 7. The t-value is 1.718 and p-value is 0.089. Consequently, the pre-test results of Groups A and B are not significant at a confidence interval of 95%. That is, the students in Groups A and B have the equivalent ability when learning the course.

Post-Test

The students in both of the control group and the experimental group have received the same course content with a series of relevant projects. After six weeks, a post-test was performed to compare the learning performance of the students in both groups. In the post-test, the same concepts of the MIS course were tested. In this test, the students received thirty true/false questions, thirty multiple-choice questions and seven short-answer questions.

Table 9 shows the improvement ratios of the students whose learning status changed from "poorly-learned" to "well-learned" in each cooperative learning group. The ratio was derived by computing the number of students whose learning status changed from "poorly-learned" to "well-learned" divided by the number of students who initially poorly learned the concept in each cooperative learning group. For example, in cooperative learning group A_3, there were six students who failed in learning the concept "Data vs. Information" well in the pre-test, and three of them changed the learning status for "Data vs. Information" from "poorly-learned" to "well-learned" after receiving the post-test; therefore, the improvement ratio was 0.5. Note that a "-" in the table indicates that no student has poorly learned the concept.

From Table 9, it can be seen that, for a given concept, the improvement ratios for the cooperative learning groups without any student who well learned the concept in the beginning derived lower improvement ratios than those groups with at least one student who well learned the concept. Moreover, the improvement ratios were much lower for the more advanced concepts, such as "Re-engineering" and "MPS (Master Production Scheduling)".

The t-test for the post-test results of Groups A and B is shown in Table 10. The t-value is 6.115 and p-value is 0.000. Consequently, the post-test results of Groups A and B are significant at a confidence interval of 95%. From the experimental results, it can be seen that the students in Group B (the experimental group) have achieved significantly improved performance than that of Group A (the control group) in learning the advanced concepts of the MIS course, and hence we conclude the new approach is helpful in enhancing student learning efficacy.

Table 9. Ratio of students whose learning status changed from 'poorly-learned' to 'well-learned' in each cooperative learning group

Cooperative learning groups	A_1	A_2	A_3	A_4	A_5	A_6	A_7	A_8	A_9	A_{10}	B_1	B_2	B_3	B_4	B_5	B_6	B_7	B_8	B_9	B_{10}
Number of students / Concepts	6	6	6	5	5	5	5	5	5	4	6	6	5	4	4	6	6	6	5	4
Data vs. Information	**0.3**	1	**0.5**	1	0.75	1	**0**	**0.2**	1	0.67	1	1	0.75	1	1	0.67	1	1	0.75	1
Computer Equipment for IS	-	-	-	-	-	-	-	-	-	-	-	-	-	-	-	-	-	-	-	-
Closed system	**0**	**0.3**	1	1	1	1	0.67	1	**0.2**	0.8	1	1	0.67	1	1	1	0.76	1	1	0.5
Computer components	-	-	-	-	-	-	-	-	-	-	-	-	-	-	-	-	-	-	-	-
Human-Computer Synergy	1	1	0.67	1	1	1	0.75	1	1	0.75	1	1	1	0.5	1	1	0.75	0.67	1	1
Information system	-	-	-	-	-	-	-	-	-	-	-	-	-	-	-	-	-	-	-	-
Personal computers	-	-	-	-	-	-	-	-	-	-	-	-	-	-	-	-	-	-	-	-
Strategic advantage	1	1	0.75	**0.2**	0.76	**0**	1	1	1	1	1	1	0.75	0.67	1	1	1	1	1	1
Strategic alliance	0.75	1	1	0.67	**0.2**	1	1	1	1	**0.25**	1	1	1	1	1	0.75	1	0.75	1	0.5
Strategic information system (SIS)	1	1	1	1	**0.2**	0.75	1	1	1	**0**	0.75	1	0.67	1	1	1	1	0.67	0.67	1
Re-engineering	0.75	0.67	**0**	0.67	0.67	0.5	0.67	**0**	**0.2**	1	1	1	0.75	0.67	1	0.3	0.67	0.67	0.75	0.5
Productivity	1	**0.**	0.5	0.67	**0.2**	0.75	1	0.75	1	0.67	0.75	1	1	0.67	0.75	1	1	1	1	1
Accounting	1	1	1	**0.4**	1	1	1	1	1	0.75	1	1	1	0.67	1	0.67	1	0.75	1	1
EDP (Electronic Data Processing)	-	-	-	-	-	-	-	-	-	-	-	-	-	-	-	-	-	-	-	-
CNC (Computerized Numeric Control)	0.67	0.75	0.75	1	0.75	1	0.75	0.75	**0**	0.67	1	1	1	0.67	0.75	1	1	1	0.67	0.67
MPS (Master Production Scheduling)	1	1	0.5	0.75	**0**	2	**0**	0.5	0.5	1	0.75	1	0.5	0.75	0.67	0.67	0.75	1	0.67	0.67
Groupware	1	1	**0.3**	1	0.75	**0.2**	0.5	1	1	**0.5**	1	1	1	1	0.5	1	0.67	1	1	1

Table 10. Statistic results of post-test

	Group A	Group B
N	52	52
Mean	81.33	86.54
Std. Dev.	5.69	2.33
t=6.115 sig.=0.000		

CONCLUSION

To achieve the goal of cooperative learning, it is very important to organize well-structured cooperative learning groups, in which all group members have the ability to help each other during the learning process. In this article, a concept-based approach is proposed to organize cooperative learning groups such that for a given course, each concept is well learned by at least one of the students in each group. An experiment has been conducted on a computer science course to evaluate the efficacy of the novel approach. From the experimental results, we found that the improvement ratios for the cooperative learning groups constructed by applying our approach were higher than those constructed by conventional approach; moreover, the t-test results of the pre-test and the post-test have shown that the cooperative learning groups in the experimental group have achieved significantly better improvement than those in the control group. Therefore, we conclude that the concept-based approach is helpful in enhancing students' learning performance.

In an ideal scenario, each concept should be well learned by at least one of the students in each cooperative group, such that the students will be capable of learning the entire concepts well, via accurately designed learning activities. However, sometimes there might be some concepts that only a few students have learned well. For example, as there are only three students who have learned some of the concepts well, it is impossible to assign a student who has well learned that concept to each of the ten learning groups. Therefore, in the future, it may be plausible to allow some students to be assigned to more than one cooperative learning group, since they are the ones who have well learned some of the most important concepts.

ACKNOWLEDGMENT

This study is supported in part by the National Science Council of the Republic of China under contract numbers NSC 95-2524-S-024 -002 and NSC 95-2520-S-024 -003.

REFERENCES

Adams, D., & Hamm, M. (1990). *Cooperative learning: Critical thinking and collaboration across the curriculum.* Springfield, IL: Charles C. Thomas.

Ahmadabadi, M., & Asadpour, M. (2002). Expertness-based cooperative Q-learning. *IEEE Transactions on Systems, Man, and Cybernetics-Part B: Cybernetics, 32*(1), 66-76.

Aronson, E. (1978). *The jigsaw classroom.* Beverly Hills, CA: Sage Publication.

Chase, C. (1978). *Measurement for educational evaluation.* Reading MA: Addison-Wesley.

Dibiasio, D., & Groccia, J. (1995). Active and cooperative learning in an introductory chemical engineering course. *IEEE Conference on Frontiers in Education,* 3c2.19-3c2.22.

Dietrich, S., & Urban, S. (1998). A cooperative learning approach to database group projects: Integrating theory and practice. *IEEE Transactions on Education, 41*(4), 346.

Ebel, R., & Frisbie, D. (1991). *Essentials of educational measurement.* Englewood Cliffs, NJ: Prentice-Hall.

Fulk, J., Steinfield, C., Schmitz, J., & Power, J. (1987). A social information processing model of media use in organizations. *Journal of the Communication Research, 14*(5), 529-552.

Ghaith, G., & Yaghi, H. (1998). Effect of cooperative learning on the acquisition of second language rules and mechanics. *System, 26*(2), 223-234.

Ghaith, G. (2002). The relationship between cooperative learning, perception of social support, and academic achievement. *System, 30*(3), 263-273.

Hiltz, S. (1994). *The virtual classroom: Learning without limits via computer networks.* Norwood, NJ: Ablex.

Hooper, S. (1992). Cooperative learning and computer-based instruction. *Journal of the Educational Technology Research & Development, 40*(3), 21-38.

Hooper, S. (2003). The effects of persistence and small group interaction during computer-based instruction. *Computers in Human Behavior, 19*(2), 211-220.

Huber, G. (2003). Processes of decision making in small learning groups. *Learning and Instruction, 13*(3), 255-269.

Hwang, G. (2003). A concept map model for developing intelligent tutoring systems. *Computers & Education, 40*(3), 217-235.

Johnson, D., & Johnson, R. (1987). *Learning together and alone: Cooperative, competitive, and individualistic learning.* Englewood Cliffs, NJ: Prentice-Hall.

Johnson, D., & Johnson, R. (1990). *Cooperative learning and achievement, cooperative learning: Theory and research.* New York, NY: Praeger.

Johnson, D., Roger, T., & Smith, K. (1991). *Active learning: Cooperation in the college classroom.* Edina, MN: Interaction Book Company.

Johnson, D., & Johnson, R. (1999). Making cooperative learning work. *Theory into Practice, 38*(2), 67-73.

Johnson, S., Suriya, C., Yoon, S., Berrett, J., & Fleur, J. (2002). Team development and group processes of virtual learning teams. *Computers & Education, 39*(4), 379-393.

Kelley, T. (1939). The selection of upper and lower groups for the validation of test item. *Journal of the Educational Psychology, 30*(1), 17-24.

Keyser, M. (2000). Active learning and cooperative learning: Understanding the difference and using both styles effectively. *Research Strategies, 17*(1), 35-44.

Klein, J., & Schnackenberg, H. (2000). Effects of informal cooperative learning and the affiliation motive on achievement, attitude, and student interactions. *Contemporary Educational Psychology, 25*(3), 332-341.

Klingner, J., & Vaughn, S. (2000). The helping behaviors of fifth graders while using collaborative strategic reading during ESL content classes. *TESOL Quarterly, 34*(1), 69-98.

Kirschner, P. (2000). Using integrated electronic environments for collaborative teaching/learning. *Research Dialogue in Learning and Instruction, 2*(1), 1-10.

Macdonald, J. (2003). Assessing online collaborative learning: process and product. *Computers & Education, 40*(4), 377-391.

McDonald, D. (1995). Improving student learning with group assignments. *IEEE Conference on Frontiers in Education,* 2b5.9-2b5.12.

Mevarech, Z. (1993). Who benefits from cooperative computer-assisted instruction?. *Journal of the Educational Computing Research, 9*(4), 451-464.

Oz, E. (2002). *Management information systems,* 3rd ed. Boston, MA: Course Technology.

Porto, M. (2001). Cooperative writing response groups and self-evaluation. *ELT Journal, 55*(1), 38-46.

Rachel, H., & Irit, B. (2002). Writing development of Arab and Jewish students using cooperative learning (CL) and computer-mediated communication (CMC). *Computers & Education, 39*(1), 19-36.

Ramsay, A., Hanlon, D., & Smith, D. (2000). The association between cognitive style and accounting students' preference for cooperative learning: An empirical investigation. *Journal of Accounting Education, 18*(3), 215-228.

Sheremetov, L., & Arenas, A. (2002). EVA: An interactive Web-based collaborative learning environment. *Computers & Education, 39*(2), 161-182.

Slavin, R. (1989). Research on cooperative learning: Consensus and controversy. *Journal of the Educational Leadership, 47*(4), 52-54.

Smith, K. (1996). Cooperative learning: Making groupwork work. *New Directions for Teaching and Learning, 67,* 71-82.

Sun, C., & Chou, C. (1996). Experiencing CORAL: Design and implementation of distant cooperative learning. *IEEE Transactions on Education, 39*(3), 357-366.

Swain, M. (2001). Integrating language and content teaching through collaborative tasks. *The Canadian Modern Language Review, 58*(1), 44-63.

Tinto, V. (1993). *Leaving college: Rethinking the causes and cures of student attrition,* 2nd ed. Chicago, IL: University of Chicago Press.

Veenman, S., Benthum, N., Bootsma, D., Dieren, J., & Kemp, N. (2002). Cooperative learning and teacher education. *Teaching and Teacher Education, 18*(1), 87-103.

This work was previously published in International Journal of Distance Education Technologies, Vol. 6, Issue 1, edited by S. Chang; T. Shih, pp. 49-66, copyright 2008 by IGI Publishing (an imprint of IGI Global).

Chapter 5
Collaborative E-Learning Using Semantic Course Blog

Lai-Chen Lu
Tatung University, Taiwan

Ching-Long Yeh
Tatung University, Taiwan

ABSTRACT

Collaborative e-learning delivers many enhancements to e-learning technology; it enables students to collaborate with each other and improves their learning efficiency. Semantic blog combines semantic Web and blog technology that users can import, export, view, navigate, and query the blog. We developed a semantic course blog for collaborative e-learning. Using our semantic course blog, instructors can import the lecture course. Students can team up for projects, ask questions, mutually discuss problems, take the comments, support answers, and query the blog information. This semantic course blog provided a platform for collaborative e-learning framework. In this chapter, we described some collaborative e-learning and semantic blog technology, and then we introduced functions, implementation and how collaborative e-learning appears in semantic course blog.

INTRODUCTION

The World Wide Web demonstrates a new era for e-learning; it can disseminate knowledge around the world in near-real time. E-learning provides learning resources in electronic media and makes them available anywhere, and anytime. In the last few years, the Web has been increasingly used to not only share existing knowledge, but to create opportunities for knowledge-generation through collaboration. Collaborative learning's biggest impact occurs when the technology enables an individual person, students, or parties to build their understanding collaboratively on the Web. Many students find that their learning is most effective when they actively construct knowledge during group social interaction and collaboration. In this article, we demonstrated the collaborative e-learning using semantic course blog. Through the semantic course blog, instructors can import the lecture course; students can team up for project, ask the questions, mutually discuss the problems, take the comments, support the answers, and query the blog information. Students and instructors can use semantic course blog as a collaborative e-learning platform. In this article, first we describe some collaborative e-learning concepts. Then we introduce the relevant technology. Third, we show our semantic course blog architecture. After that we present our implement method and some collaborative e-learning usage in semantic course blog. Finally, we present our conclusions and propose future work.

COLLABORATIVE E-LEARNING

E-learning delivers many enhancements to the teaching and learning experience. Collaborative learning change the learning technology; it enables individual person, students or parties to build their understanding collaboratively on the Web. E-learning provides learning resources in electronic media and makes them available anywhere, anytime. Many students find that their learning is most effective when they actively construct knowledge during group social interaction and collaboration. These approaches have various calls like social constructivism, social learning, and collaborative learning, or aggregated learning. The theories of social constructivist epistemology and Vygotsky's *zone of proximal development* provide a rigorous study of pedagogies. Garrison's study (1993) was implemented, a theoretical framework for collaborative learning in an online environment, and the research study provided results that supported and extended a theoretical framework from the perspective of social constructivism. Harasim and her colleagues, Hiltz, Teles, and Turoff (1995) repeated and supported conferencing as an ideal environment for collaborative interaction. They stated:

"These shared spaces can become the locus of rich and satisfying experiences in collaborative learning, an interactive group knowledge building process in which learners actively construct knowledge by formulating ideas into words that are shared with and built on through the reactions and responses of others".

Henri and Rigault (1996) described this medium as a framework for true collaborative group work in distance education. Ragoonaden and Bordeleau (2000) found that some students resented having to communicate with others whose work habits were different from theirs. Collaborative e-learning provides more intense communication than face-to-face groups. If the students have the social pressure and the greater freedom to express their views and ideals in Internet, they can have better performance in learning. In collaborative e-learning, instructor can easily view input from students, make assessments online and, in most cases, full of audits of the learning cycle for later analysis. These ways of learning activities are also extremely effective for instructor to use them for collaboration at college or other learning areas.

Collaborative e-learning (Lindsay, 2007) contains following items:

- Collaboration occurs in a group of geographically different students and/or learners (and possibly diverse) who have a mutual goal.
- Collaboration occurs when collaborators actively interact, discuss, synthesize and then construct new knowledge (in the form of original work).
- Collaboration occurs as students and teachers share the decision making process.
- Collaboration occurs as meaningful friendships are made that become relevant in the context of learning.

Figure 1. RDF graph

RELEVANT BACKGROUND AND TECHNOLOGY

In this section, we first describe the Resource Description Framework (RDF) metadata technology. Then we describe the concept of semantic blog..

RDF

RDF is a W3C standard for data interchange in World Wide Web (Beckett, 2004). RDF is an XML-type data to provide a mechanism for describing data and resource on the Web. RDF provides a model that we can describe Web information in a standard and machine-readable format. It represents Web resource in a set of RDF statements (triples). The RDF triples consist of three parts: a subject, a predicate, and an object. A set of such triples is called an RDF graph. This can be illustrated by a node and directed-arc like Figure 1.

To imagine trying to state that someone named Laichen Lu created a particular Web page, a straightforward way to state this in a natural language, such as English, would be in the form of a simple statement such as: *http://www.cse.ttu.edu.tw/laichenlu* has an Author whose value is Laichen Lu.

The RDF terms for the various parts of the statement are

- the *subject* is the URL: http://www.cse.ttu.edu.tw/laichenlu
- the *predicate* is the word "Author"
- the *object* is the phrase "Laichen Lu"

Representing in XML becomes as follows:

```
<rdf:RDF
xmlns:rdf='http://www.w3.org/1999/02/22-rdf-syntax-
    ns#'
xmlns:t='http://www.cse.ttu.edu.tw/sw'>
<rdf:Description about='http://www.cse.ttu.edu.tw/
    laichenlu'>
  <t:author>Laichen Lu</t:author>
</rdf:Description>
</rdf:RDF>
```

The information layer represented by using RDF is a generic relational data model, describing the relationship between resources or between resource and atomic values. The meaning of the resources can then be found in the domain knowledge base, that is, ontology. The representation of ontology in the Semantic Web is an extension of RDF, OWL (Bechhofer, S., van Harmelen, F., Hendler, J., Horrocks, I., McGuinness, D. L., Patel-Schneider, P., et al., 2004). The RDF enables Web information to be expressed in a formal way that computer software can read, process, and store. The Web can be annotated to a RDF metadata then we can use the knowledge base technology to manipulate it.

Semantic Blog

The term *blog* is a portmanteau of the words Web and log (Web log). Blogs are user-oriented, providing personal spaces for users on the web. Users can publish and share their news, stories, good food, and so on, in the Web. Blogs enable users to publish information in small, discrete notes, in contrast to large, carefully-organized Web sites. Blog entries are primarily kept together based on common authorship, not common subject. In other words, the content author is the one who controls publication and *bloggers* write on a variety of topics and categorize their content as they choose. There are not systematic rules and relations between blogs, but billions of blog information in the Internet. If you want to find some relative news or publications in the blogs, you just can use keyword search and you cannot exactly find the information you need.

Semantic blog takes the advantage of RDF extensibility by adding additional semantic structures to Really Simple Syndication (RSS) (in RDF) (Winer, 2003). The richer semantic structures have two effects. First, they enable richer, new subscription, discovery, and navigation behaviors. Second, by accessing vocabularies in ontologies, they provide richer annotations sharing of higher level structures and encouraging peer commentary and recommendation activity.

Semantic blogging (Cayzer, 2004) is a technology that builds upon blogging and adds semantic structure to the blog items. Blog items can add some metadata then we can process it by machine. Semantic blogging can provide a way to write blog entries as annotations or comments to other blog entries or publications. The design of a Semantic blog emphasizes three key features. First is viewing the blog content schematically, including Record Card view, Table view and Normal view.

Figure 2. Functional view of Semantic blog

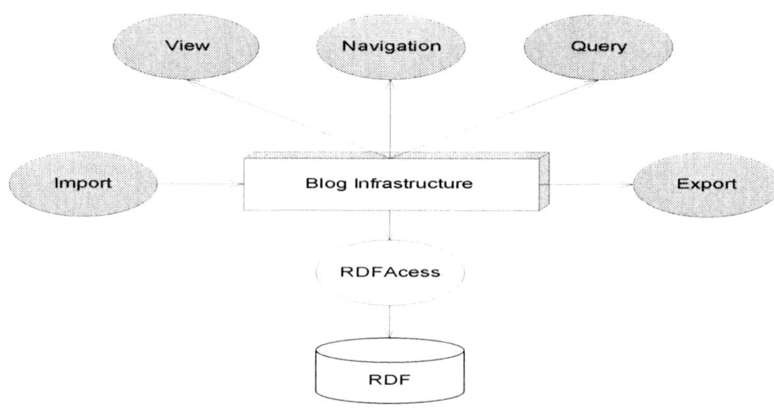

Figure 3. Architectural view of Semantic blog system

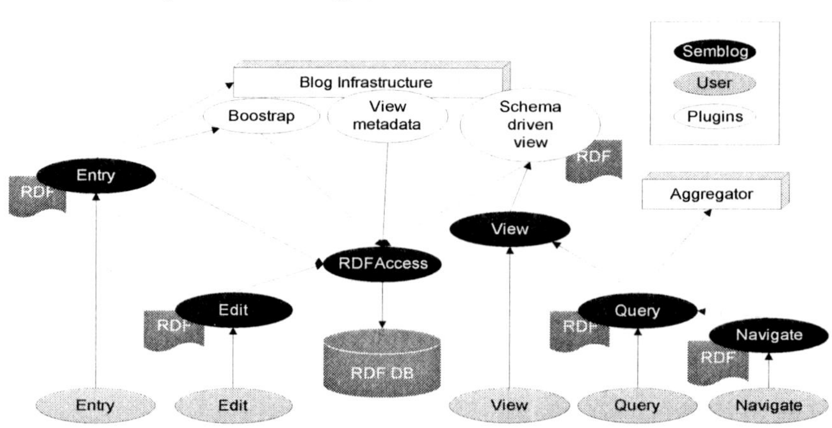

Second is navigating the blog content according to the semantic schema. Third is schema-driven query, allowing queries over user-selectable metadata. The functional view of Semantic blog is summarized as shown in Figure 2. It is built upon existing blogging platform and its semantic processing capabilities are made by accessing the RDF backend. The management functions, including importing, exporting, viewing, navigating and querying are implemented upon the blog infrastructure. The detailed architectural view is shown in Figure 3.

SYSTEM ARCHITECTURE

In Tatung University, we develop a Semantic course blog for students and teachers to use in the campus information system. Through the Semantic course blog students and instructors can import the lecture course, navigate the course, ask questions, take comments, support answers, and query the blog information. Our Semantic blog in Figure 4 contains the following items: the Homepage, Instructor, Announcement, Outline, Schedule, Grade Book, Discussion, and Query functions. Figure 5 is the semantic course blog of Tatung University.

Homepage: This function shows the course homepage, instructor can put the course home page into this course homepage function. The contents of homepage will be stored in homepage RDF file. Instructor only has to change the contents of RDF file then he or she can change the homepage presentation. The students also can add bookmarks in this course homepage. Other students can read the bookmark about this course.

Instructor: represents the instructor who creates this course. Students also can add bookmark for the instructor.

Announcement: is the announcement about this course, something like the homework, date of test, course changing announcement, and so on, Instructor can put the course announcements into this page and students can read the announcement and add comments and questions about the announcement.

Outline: displays related important items of this course. Students also can add their comments for these outlines.

Schedule: shows the course schedule about this course. All schedule data is a RDF data file, so the instructor just has to change the schedule RDF file then it will change the schedule of the course. Students can read the course schedule and they are allowed to add the bookmark about the schedule.

Grade Book: represents the student score of this course. Instructor can make the score for students about this course. He also can query the student activities in this Semantic course blog and score students' contributions in this course.

Figure 4. System architecture of Semantic course blog

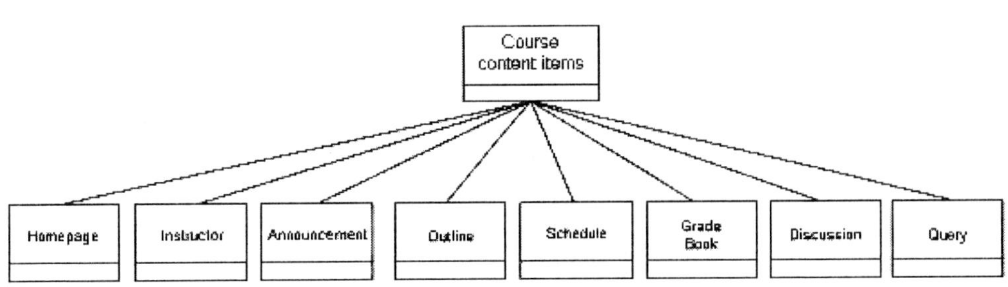

Figure 5. The Semantic course blog of Tatung University

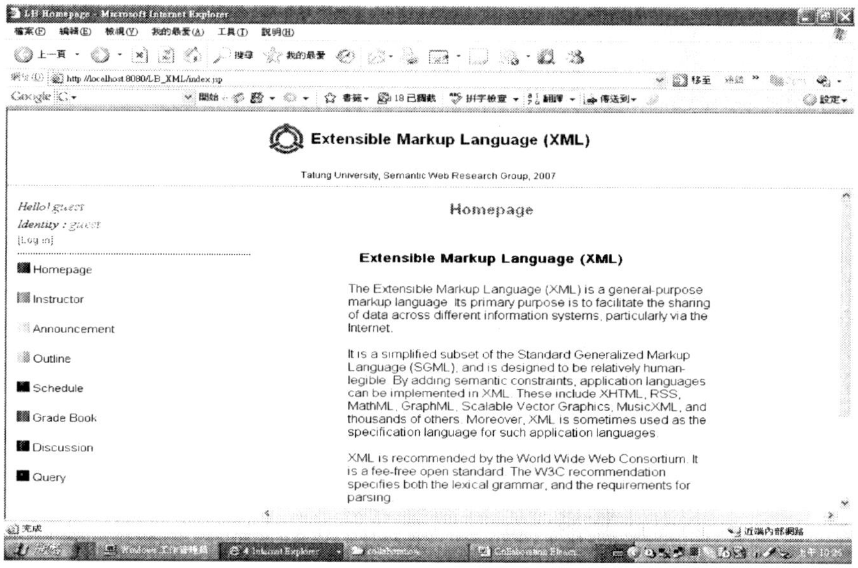

Students also can make their opinions about their scores. Instructor will read their opinions and give them answers.

Discussion: The Instructor and students can ask the questions about this course. Every one can give answers or comments to the question. Figure 6 is the discussion homepage of Semantic course blog. In the project collaboration, all students can present their contributions in this page and make solutions for the project. Of course, all students can give their opinions and comments to their classmates.

Query: As you see in Figure 7, the query page of Semantic course blog, instructor and students can use the function to query the course contents, the creator, outlines, schedule, and discussions. Because all the information is stored by RDF format and we make the metadata ontology about this Semantic course blog, users can query the information by different conditions. This is the main benefit of the Semantic blog. We make some annotation for blog homepages and they will appear meaningfully.

SYSTEM IMPLEMENTATION

Semantic course blog is built over the Java-based blog platform and uses Jena for its capabilities (Jena, n.d.). First, we use the CommonKADS Methodology to define our knowledge model (Schreiber, et al., 2002). CommonKADS is a complete methodological framework for the development of a knowledge-based system (KBS). It supports knowledge management, knowledge analysis, knowledge acquisition, and modeling. Second, we use the Protégé 3.2.1 for ontology definition (Protégé, 2008). Protégé is a free, open-source ontology editor and knowledge-base framework. The Protégé platform supports two main ways of modeling ontologies via the Protégé-Frames and Protégé-OWL editors. Protégé ontology can be exported into a variety of formats, including RDF(S), OWL, and XML Schema. Third we use the Apache Tomcat as our web server platform (Apache Tomcat, 2007). Apache Tomcat is a web application server developed at the Apache Software Foundation (ASF). Apache Tomcat provides an environment for Java code to run in cooperation with a web server. Then we use JSP called Jena API as our rule-based

Figure 6. The discussion page of Semantic course blog

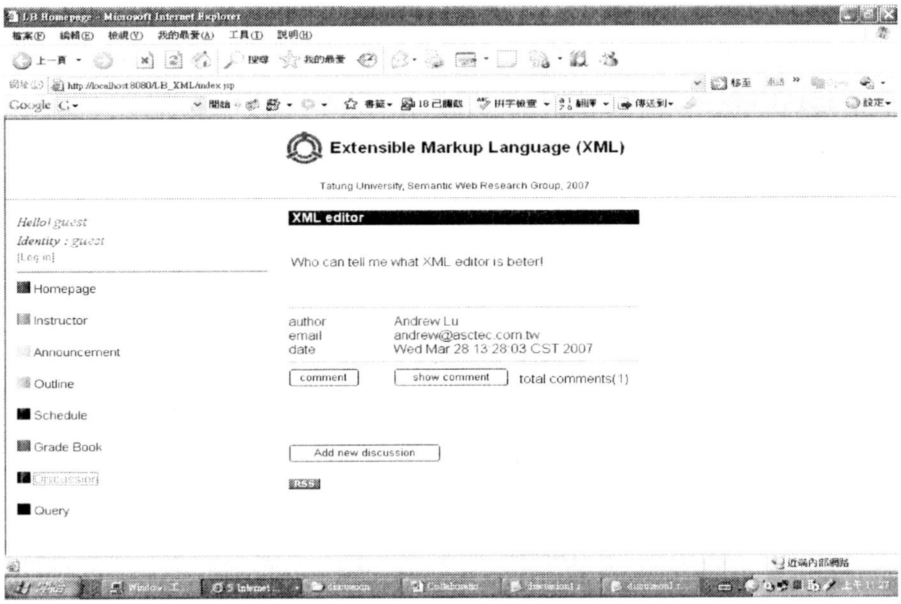

Figure 7. The query page of Semantic course blog

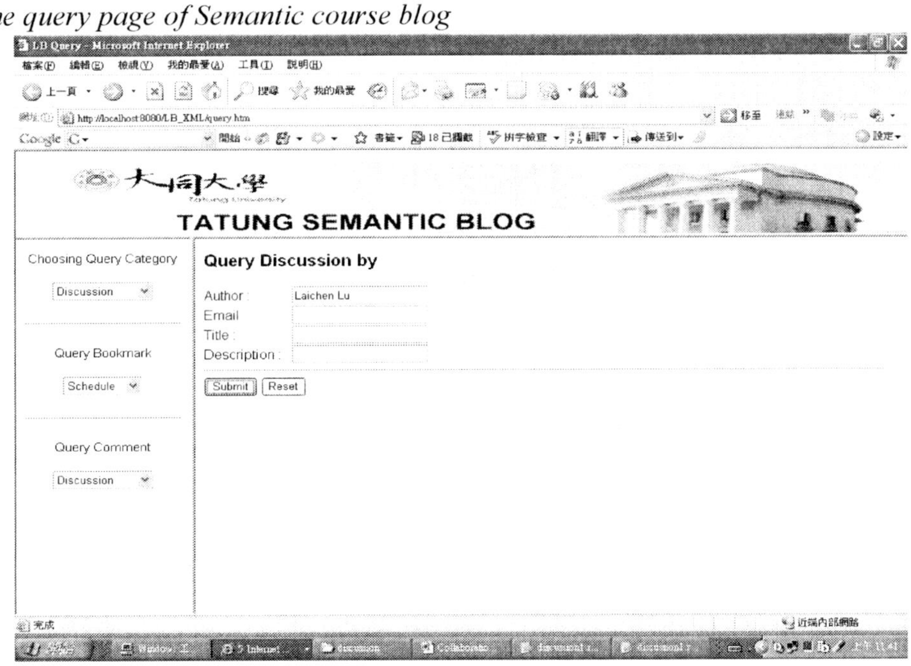

inference engine. Jena is a Java framework for building Semantic Web applications. It provides a programmatic environment for RDF, RDFS and OWL, SPARQL and includes a rule-based inference engine. Figure 8 is our Jena ontology internal structure. Our Semantic course blog also provide RSS feeds which are understood by RSS readers. The metadata in Semantic blog can be embedded in the RSS feeds and users can use their RSS readers to get the update information from our Semantic course blog.

Figure 8. Jena ontology internal structure including imports

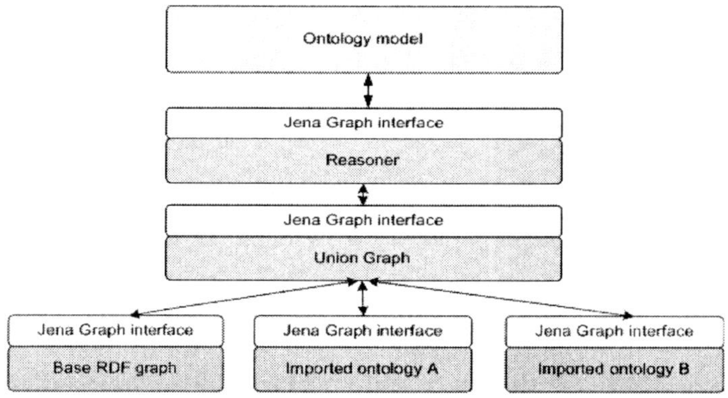

COLLABORATION SCENARIO

Through the Semantic course blog, instructors can import the lecture course; students can team up for project, ask questions, mutually discuss problems, take comments, support answers, and query the blog information. Here, we present some collaboration scenarios for instructors and students using our Semantic course blog.

1. When students ask questions in a discussion page at the end of some learning course section, their classmates in distance can team up and give them answers and suggestions. They can discuss collaboratively and make solutions for the problems on this Semantic course blog.
2. If instructors want to get opinions from students when making decisions, then they can display the message in announcement page and the students can use the comment function to deliver their opinions.
3. If instructors create some team projects for students, then they can create some discussion topic in discussion page. All the team members of the project can give their contribution to the project and make some comments for that discussion topic. Students can learn the mutual collaboration on their project and learn how to team up for the project.
4. Instructors can use the query page to monitor the students' activities and collaboration representations in the course and give students the scores of the course.
5. Professional or social interaction can encourage and persuade people to share information and know-how which in turn, can lead to ad-hoc collaboration. Using our Semantic course blog, students and instructors can invite some professional experts to participate the course and give students some motivation.
6. If instructors want to investigate the opinion of the students, they can have a vote on our Semantic course blog. Through the query function of the blog, instructors can collect the results of the vote and get the opinions from the students.

DISCUSSION AND FUTURE WORK

In this article, we design a Semantic course blog and present some collaborative e-learning usage in our Semantic course blog. For the Web 2.0 trend, the collaborative e-learning is very important; some call it collaboration 2.0. Our Semantic course blog adds semantic structure to the blog items and the blog items can add some metadata, that we can process it by machine. Using the advantages of Semantic blog, we can combine it with the collaborative e-learning. Here, we presented some collaboration activities in a semantic course blog. The semantic blog takes the advantage of RDF extensibility by adding additional semantic structures to RSS (in RDF). Students can use their RSS readers to get the update information from our semantic course blog. Now the mobile e-learning is another important topic in e-learning area. Using the mobile RSS readers, users can read the update course information in their mobile devices. In the future we hope we can combine the collaborative e-learning, semantic course blogs, and mobile technology to the collaborative mobile e-learning.

Finally in the semantic web service and e-learning research, trust and security control is an important topic in the future (Kagal et al., 2004). We have to support the information privacy for the students and instructors, such as the research results, private discussions, student score, or students' private information. There is so much confidential information and must supporting privacy. In the e-learning system we have to guarantee that who can access private information and under what conditions. In the future we will improve our semantic course blog with the trust and security control.

CONCLUSION

In this article we developed a semantic course blog using the CommonKADS knowledge engineering and RDF semantic blog technology. We used the JSP, Protégé ontology and Jena rule-based inference engine to implement our semantic course blog. Collaborative e-learning is the biggest impact occurs when the technology enables students to collaborate with each other and improves their learning efficiency. We designed a semantic course blog to realize the concepts of collaborative e-learning. Through the semantic course blog, students and instructors can import the lecture course, navigate the course, ask questions, take comments, support answers, and query blog information. We demonstrated some collaborative e-learning examples by using our semantic course blog. Combining the semantic blog technology and e-learning will improve some technology usages in e-learning researches. We hope our studies can make some contributions for future collaborative e-learning researches.

REFERENCES

Apache Tomcat (2007). *The Apache Software Foundation*. Retrieved from http://tomcat.apache.org/

Bechhofer, S., van Harmelen, F., Hendler, J., Horrocks, I., McGuinness, D. L., Patel-Schneider, P., et al. (2004 February 10). W3C OWL Web Ontology Language Reference, *W3C Recommendation*.. Retrieved from http://www.w3.org/TR/owl-ref/

Beckett, D. (Ed.) (2004, February 10). RDF W3C, *W3C Recommended*.. Retrieved from http://www.w3.org/TR/2004/REC-rdf-syntax-grammar-20040210/

Cayzer, S. (2004). Semantic blogging and decentralized knowledge management. Communications of the ACM, 47(12).

Garrison, D. R. (1993). A cognitive constructivist view of distance education: An analysis of teaching-learning assumptions. *Distance Education, 14*(2), 199-211.

Harasim, L. M., Hiltz, S. R., Teles, L., & Turoff, M. (1995). *Learning networks: A field guide to teaching and learning online*. Cambridge, MA: MIT Press.

Henri, F., & Rigault, C. (1996). Collaborative distance education and computer conferencing. In T. Liao (Ed.), *Advanced educational technology: Research issues and future potential* (pp. 45-76). Berlin: Springer-Verlag.

Jena – A Semantic Web framework for Java (n.d.). Retrieved from http://jena.sourceforge.net/index.html

Kagal, L., Paoucci, M., Srinivasan, N., Denker, G., Finin, T., and Sycara, K. (2004, July). Authorization and privacy for semantic Web services. *IEEE Intelligent Systems* (Special Issue on Semantic Web Services).

Lindsay, J. (2007, April 2). Shall we call it Collaboration 2.0? *E-Learning Journeys.* Retrieved from http://123elearning.blogspot.com/2007/04/shall-we-call-it-collaboration-20.html

Protégé (2008). Retrieved from http://protege.stanford.edu/

Ragoonaden, K., & Bordeleau, P. (2000). Collaborative learning via the Internet. *Educational Technology and Society, 3*(3), 1-16.

Schreiber, A., et al. (2002). Knowledge engineering and management: The CommonKADS methodology. Cambridge, MA: MIT Press.

Winer, D. (2003, July 15). RSS 2.0 Specification. *RSS 2.0 at Harvard Law.* Retrieved from http://blogs.law.harvard.edu/tech/rss

This work was previously published in International Journal of Distance Education Technologies, Vol. 6, Issue 3, edited by Q. Jin, pp. 85-95, copyright 2008 by IGI Publishing (an imprint of IGI Global).

Chapter 6
A Virtual Laboratory on Natural Computing: A Learning Experiment

Leandro Nunes de Castro
Catholic University of Santos, Brazil

Yupanqui Julho Muñoz
Catholic University of Santos, Brazil

Leandro Rubim de Freitas
Catholic University of Santos, Brazil

Charbel Niño El-Hani
Federal University of Bahia, Brazil

ABSTRACT

Natural computing is a terminology used to describe computational algorithms developed by taking inspiration from information processing mechanisms in nature, methods to synthesize natural phenomena in computers, and novel computational approaches based on natural materials. The virtual laboratory on natural computing (LVCoN) is a Web environment to support the teaching and learning of natural computing, and whose goal is to provide didactic contents about the main themes in natural computing, in addition to interactive simulations, videos, exercises, links for related sites, forum, and other materials. This article describes an experiment with LVCoN during a School of Computing in Brazil. The results are presented in four parts: Self-Evaluation, Evaluation of LVCoN, Evaluation of the Simulations (Applets), and Interviews. The results allowed us to positively evaluate the structure and contents of LVCoN, in the sense that most students were satisfied with the environment. Besides, most students liked the experience of working with a virtual laboratory, and considered a hybrid teaching approach; that is, one mixing lectures with virtual learning, very appropriate and productive.

INTRODUCTION

Natural computing (de Castro, 2007) is a terminology that has been used to describe three main areas of research: (1) methods that take inspiration from nature to develop problem-solving algorithms; (2) computational approaches to synthesize natural phenomena; and (3) the use of natural materials (e.g., molecules) to compute.

The Virtual Laboratory on Natural Computing (LVCoN) presents many important features of virtual laboratories for supporting teaching and learning activities, such as the use of high-quality didactic contents associated with the many subjects of natural computing, interactive algorithms implemented in applets, availability of links to related works and subjects, and a Learning Matrix so that students and instructors can develop their own study agendas.

This article presents the results of a learning action with the Portuguese version of LVCoN conducted during a School of Computing held in Brazil in April, 2007. This action was performed in limited time, for although the learning matrix of LVCoN suggests 100 hours to complete the course, only 10 hours were available for the action during School of Computing. Therefore, some specific topics had to be selected for the experiments, and the time and shape of each activity had to be substantially reduced or altered. In such a scenario, it is possible to investigate the impact of a work under pressure in the group of students, to assess the degree of satisfaction of the students with the environment, to evaluate the potential of LVCoN as a self-learning and self-evaluation tool, and to evaluate the usefulness of LVCoN as a tool for supporting the teaching and learning of natural computing.

This article is organized as follows. Section 2 makes a brief introduction to natural computing, and Section 3 describes LVCoN. Section 4 describes the experimental protocol used, and the results are presented in Section 5. The article is concluded in Section 6. Appendices 1 to 6 present the learning matrices, the self-evaluation form, the form to assess LVCoN, and the interviews protocol.

NATURAL COMPUTING

Natural computing is the computational version of the process of extracting ideas from nature to develop computational systems, or using natural materials (e.g., molecules) to perform computation. It can be divided into three main branches (de Castro, 2006, 2007; de Castro & Von Zuben, 2004):

1. *Computing inspired by nature*: It makes use of nature as inspiration for the development of problem solving techniques. The main idea of this branch is to develop computational tools (algorithms) by taking inspiration from nature for the solution of complex problems.
2. *The simulation and emulation of nature by means of computing*: It is basically a synthetic process aimed at creating patterns, forms, behaviors, and organisms that (do not necessarily) resemble "life-as-we-know-it." Its products can be used to mimic various natural phenomena, thus increasing our understanding of nature and insights about computer models.
3. *Computing with natural materials*: It corresponds to the use of novel natural materials to perform computation, thus constituting a true novel computing paradigm that comes to substitute or supplement the current silicon-based computers.

Therefore, natural computing can be defined as the field of research that, based on or inspired by nature, allows the development of new computational tools (in software, hardware, or "wetware") for problem solving, leads to the synthesis of natural patterns, behaviors, and organisms, and may result in the design of novel computing systems that use natural media to compute (de Castro, 2006).

Natural computing is thus a field of research that testifies against the specialization of disciplines in science. It shows, with its three main areas of investigation, that knowledge from various fields of research are necessary for a better understanding of life, for the study and simulation of natural systems and processes, and for the proposal of novel computing paradigms. Physicists, chemists, engineers, biologists, and computer scientists, among others, all have to act together or at least share ideas and knowledge in order to make natural computing feasible.

Most of the computational approaches natural computing deals with are based on highly simplified versions of the mechanisms and processes present in the corresponding natural phenomena. The reasons for such simplifications and abstractions are manifold. First of all, most simplifications are necessary to make the computation with a large number of entities tractable. Also, it can be advantageous to highlight the minimal features necessary to enable some particular aspects of a system to be reproduced and to observe some emergent properties. Which level is most appropriate for the investigation and abstraction depends on the scientific question asked, what type of problem one wants to solve, or the life phenomenon to be synthesized.

Natural computing usually integrates experimental and theoretical biology, physics, and chemistry, empirical observations from nature and several other sciences, facts and processes from different levels of investigation into nature so as to achieve its goals, as summarized in Figure 1.

LVCON: THE VIRTUAL LABORATORY ON NATURAL COMPUTING

In order to maximize the learning experience within LVCoN, a specific program for the teaching and learning of natural computing using the virtual laboratory is provided. An average of 100 hours of study is suggested. In spite of suggesting a sequential and ordered study, the program is flexible, so that either the student or the instructor decides the order in which to study. This is because there is no strict order to be followed while using LVCoN; each module may be studied independently. Overall, there are seven main

Figure 1. Many approaches are used to develop natural computing and its main branches

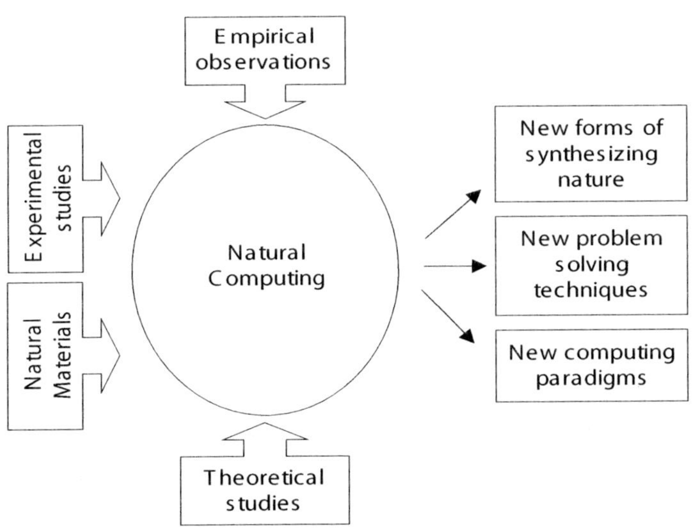

themes within LVCoN: Evolutionary Computing, Artificial Neural Networks, Swarm Intelligence, Artificial Immune Systems, Fractal Geometry, Artificial Life, DNA Computing, and Quantum Computing. Each theme has:

- *Didactic contents*: In most themes, a biological motivation is provided, allowing the student to understand the biological inspiration for the design of a given algorithm. Besides, pictures, references, and pseudocodes complement the themes.
- *Simulations*: With the exception of DNA and Quantum computing, all other themes have one or more applets simulators available. These applets are interactive, allowing a better comprehension of the theory and the algorithms presented. A brief tutorial describing the inputs, outputs, and expected results of the simulations is also available.
- *Exercises with responses*: With the exception of DNA and Quantum computing, all other themes have a set of exercises with their respective answers that allow the students to self-evaluate. In some cases, exercises for further research are presented, and references to useful works are provided.

Figure 2. Main page of LVCoN (English version)

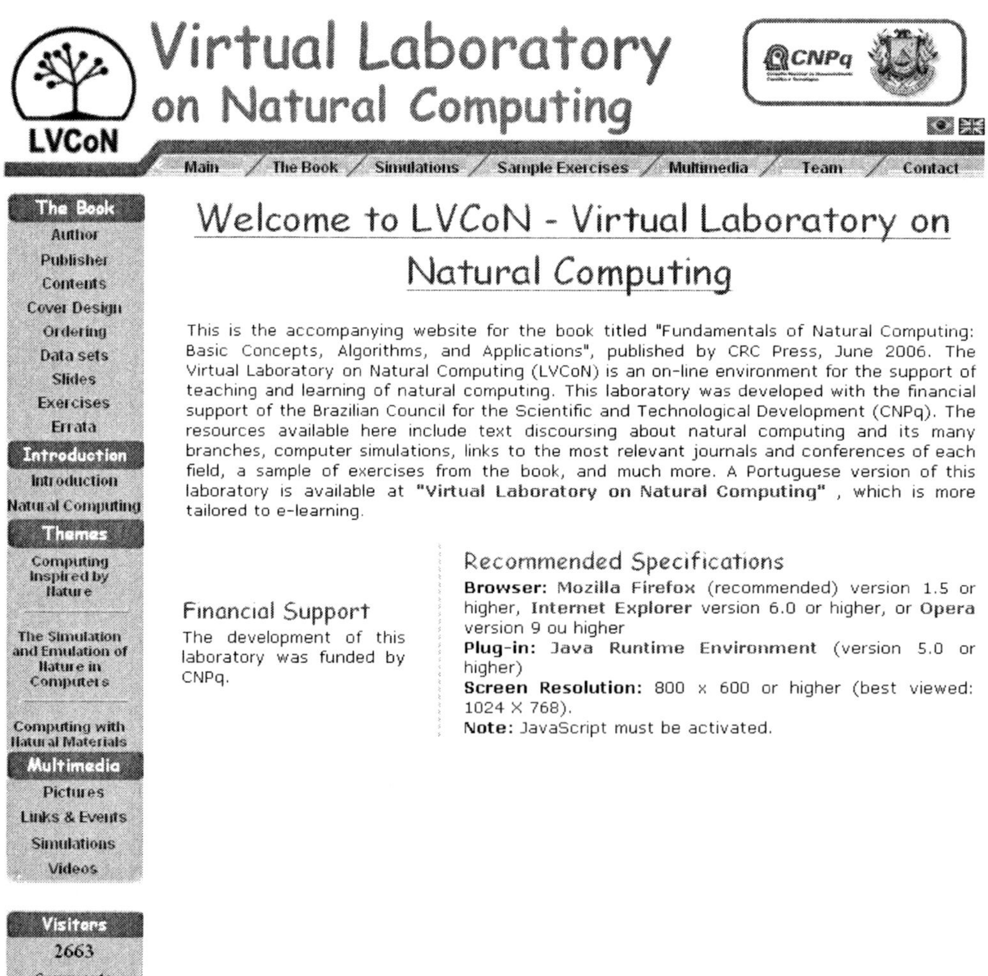

LVCoN also has a forum that allows students and instructors to exchange ideas, references, and results remotely. There are also lists with the most important conferences and periodicals of each area; videos and images concerning the main themes are provided in the multimedia link. Figure 2 illustrates the main page of LVCoN in English (LVCoN, 2007).

Related Works

Although there is a large variety of virtual laboratories, very few were found dealing with the main themes discussed in LVCoN. Furthermore, none of them is designed as a tool to support the teaching and learning of a subject—they are basically a virtual environment with which to do some experiments or find a specific content. Under this perspective, LVCoN is a pioneer virtual laboratory. Below is a brief description of three virtual laboratories that have a theme slightly related with LVCoN's main themes.

VLAB is a Web-based resource for the research and education about complex systems, developed by the Monash University in Australia (Vlab, 2007). It provides numerous simulations, in most cases Java applets, together with related tutorials, exercises, references, and Web links. The themes available include cellular automata, swarm intelligence, evolution, networks, and nonlinear dynamic systems.

The accompanying Web site for the book titled "The Computational Beauty of Nature: Computer Explorations of Fractals, Chaos, Complex Systems, and Adaptation" (CBofN, 2007) can also be viewed as a type of virtual laboratory. Although the contents of the themes are not available in the site, it includes source code for simulations involving fractals, chaos, complex systems, and adaptation. Furthermore, it presents hints for educators, glossary, and references, amongst other extra book contents.

The Virtual Laboratory of Artificial Intelligence (VLAI, 2007) is a Website developed by the AGH University of Science and Technology in Poland, whose aim is to present the fundamentals and some specific applications of artificial intelligence. The materials available emphasize neural networks, include simulations and conceptual descriptions, and can be used as teaching aids to artificial neural networks.

A LEARNING EXPERIMENT AT A SCHOOL OF COMPUTING

LVCoN is structured for 100 hours of study, as can be seen at the learning matrix in Appendix 1. This matrix illustrates the main features of LVCoN, such as the availability of research questions, theoretical questions, and computational exercises for the nature-inspired computing, and the synthesis of natural phenomena areas. DNA and Quantum computing only have didactic contents associated.

To assess the usefulness of LVCoN as a tool to support the teaching and learning of natural computing, a case study was performed in which a summarized learning action was elaborated and applied to a group of students at the Regional School of Computing in Bahia-Alagoas-Sergipe, named ERBASE, was held in Vitória da Conquista, Bahia, Brazil, from the 16th to the 20th of April, 2007. Appendix 2 presents the summarized learning matrix implemented during ERBASE 2007. Due to time constraints, only five themes out of eight (neural networks, immune systems, swarm intelligence, fractal geometry, and artificial life) were selected for the experiment at ERBASE 2007. The time available for the course was 10 hours, divided in five classes of two hours each, being two on the 16th of April, and three on the 17th of April, 2007.

As can be observed from Appendix 2, the pedagogical model adopted was a hybrid between distance learning and traditional classroom learning. The instructor was responsible for briefly introducing the theory about each theme, and then the students had to perform three different activities: (1) to answer the *research questions*, whose answers are not available at LVCoN; (2) to answer the theoretical questions, whose correct answers are available and are also subsided by the explanations (contents) available at LVCoN; and (3) to practice the interpretation of the contents by *experimenting with the applets* available. It must be noted that this format of laboratory is inherently incomplete, for the students did not have sufficient time to study the theory available. However, this type of experiment allows us to assess the usefulness of LVCoN to support the teaching and learning of natural computing.

The experiment performed aims at evaluating four main aspects of LVCoN: (1) its usefulness as a self-learning and self-evaluation tool; (2) the quality of LVCoN in relation to its structure, content, and the usefulness of its forum, and so on; (3) the quality of the simulations implemented as applets; and (4) the usefulness of LVCoN as a tool for supporting the distance learning of natural computing.

For the first three aspects above, a specific questionnaire was prepared and should be filled by the students either during or after the learning action. For the first aspect, a *Self-Evaluation Questionnaire* was prepared, and the students had to mark each of the questions answered (see Appendix 3) right after studying a certain theme. For aspects 2 and 3, the students filled in some forms indicating their degree of satisfaction with LVCoN and the applets available, as shown in Appendices 4 and 5, respectively. To evaluate the usefulness of virtual laboratories like LVCoN as tools to support teaching and learning, some interviews were made and recorded with the students at ERBASE 2007, following the protocol presented in Appendix 6. All students agreed to have their interviews recorded.

The experiment performed during ERBASE 2007 had 33 students registered, 27 participants, and 25 filling in the forms and being interviewed. All participants were undergraduate students in Brazil from the courses Computer Engineering (CE), Computer Science (CS), Information Systems (IS) and System Analysis (SA) of five different universities. Table 1 presents the profile of the students that participated in the experiment, including the semester they are taking the course and the course name.

Table 1. List of students participating at the LVCoN experiment during ERBASE 2007

Student	Semester	Course
1.	6°	CS
2.	4°	IS
3.	8°	CE
4.	7°	CS
5.	8°	CE
6.	4°	IS
7.	4°	CE
8.	8°	IS
9.	2°	CE
10.	6°	IS
11.	8°	CE
12.	2°	CE
13.	7°	CS
14.	4°	CE
15.	4°	CE
16.	2°	CE
17.	3°	CS
18.	8°	CE
19.	7°	CS
20.	6°	SA
21.	2°	CE
22.	10°	CS
23.	4°	CE
24.	2°	CE
25.	2°	CS
26.	8°	CE
27.	2°	CE

CS: computer science
IS: information systems
CE: computer engineering
SA: system analysis

EXPERIMENTAL RESULTS

The results will be presented in four distinct parts: (1) Self-assessment; (2) LVCoN evaluation; (3) Simulations' evaluation; and (4) Interviews. The experimental settings are as follows:

- A single instructor conducted the whole experiment without the aid of any assistant, and remained within the lab during all the experiments. The instructor answered the students' questions.
- The laboratory contained 20 AMD Celeron PCs with 624MB of RAM running either Windows XP or Linux. The browsers used were Internet Explorer and Mozilla Firefox, and the Internet connection was high-speed (over 1Mbps).
- Due to the limited number of PCs in the lab, some students performed the experiments individually, while others did it in couples.
- The self-assessment questions were marked right after answering, and the simulations' evaluations were performed after playing with an applet. The interviews and LVCoN evaluation were made at the end of all activities. More details are provided in each separate session below.

Self-Assessment

All questions available at LVCoN have their respective answers and marks available. Therefore, it is possible for each student to evaluate him/herself. A Self-Assessment Form was thus created for the ERBASE learning experiment, as presented in Appendix 3. The students themselves were responsible for marking their exercises anonymously, but identifying their year and course. Self-assessment is an interesting exercise for the students, because it transfers the responsibility of evaluating learning to the students themselves, forcing them to create their own marking standards. However, this makes it difficult to standardize the results, for each student defines his/her own standards.

From among the 25 students that answered the questions, only 19 identified their year and course in the form. A summary of the marks obtained are shown in Table 2. The value for each question was the same as the ones available in LVCoN, resulting in a maximum of 27.5 points. It can be observed, from Table 2, that the students marked, on average, 18.74 points, corresponding to 68.15% of the total, a value that can be considered good for the constrained learning time. The computer engineering students performed worse than the computer science and information systems students, which may be explained by the

Table 2. Average performance for each course based on the self-assessment form. The maximal mark possible is 27.5 points; σ: standard deviation

Course	Number of answers	Average mark ± σ
Computer Science	05	19,24 ± 3,30
Information Systems	03	20,12 ± 1,85
Computer Engineering	10	17,06 ± 2,61
System Analysis	01	18,95 ± 0,00
Unidentified	06	17,64 ± 3,24
Total	25	18,74

fact that most of them are in the early stages of their undergraduate course.

LVCoN Evaluation

To evaluate LVCoN, a questionnaire about LVCoN was prepared, as shown in Appendix 4. This questionnaire has four objective questions concerning the students' satisfaction (Questions 1 to 4), one technical and functional question (Question 5), two questions that allow comments (Questions 6 and 7), and an objective question aimed at comparing the traditional teaching method with the ones using virtual laboratories (Question 8).

Table 3 summarizes the students' answers for this questionnaire. The answers to Questions 1, 3, and 4 allowed us to conclude that most students, around 90% of them, were satisfied with the experiment, the contents, and the structure of LVCoN. Concerning the forum available (Question 2), only 21 students answered the question, and 43% of them were not satisfied with it. It is important to remark, though, that a forum is an asynchronous communication tool, which makes it difficult to be used in an experiment such as the one performed at ERBASE 2007. A synchronous communication tool, such as a *chat,* would be more appropriate in this case.

According to the answers to Question 5, 40% of the students found technical or functional problems in LVCoN—the main aspects being applets malfunctioning—insufficient explanations, and grammar errors in the text. All students that answered Question 6 considered that the instructor encouraged them to make a good use of the resources available at LVCoN. The answers to Question 7 showed that 28% of the students found the exercises did not help to evaluate the contents studied, mainly due to the lack of time to go through the contents. Finally, comparing to a standard lecturing course, 32% of the students preferred LVCoN, 48% considered them equivalent, 16% found it a little worse, and 4% found the use of LVCoN worse than a traditional lecture.

Table 3. LVCoN evaluation. Percentage relative to the number of answers.

Question	Number of answers	Evaluation Number of votes (percentage)				
		VS	S	LS	U	VU
1	25	04 (16%)	18 (72%)	02 (8%)	---	01 (4%)
2	21	01 (5%)	11 (52%)	09 (43%)	---	---
3	25	14 (56%)	10 (40%)	01 (4%)	---	---
4	25	12 (48%)	11 (44%)	02 (8%)	---	---
		Yes			No	
5	25	10 (40%)			15 (60%)	
6	25	25 (100%)			---	
7	25	18 (72%)			07 (28%)	
		B	E	LW	W	Un
8	25	08 (32%)	12 (48%)	04 (16%)	01 (4%)	---

VS: very satisfied
S: satisfied
LS: little satisfied
U: unsatisfied
VU: very unsatisfied

B: better
E: equal to
LW: little worse
W: worse
Un: unsatisfactory

Simulations' Evaluation

The simulations available at LVCoN, and the respective marks to be attributed by the students, are presented in Appendix 5. Table 4 summarizes the students' evaluations. It is interesting to observe that most students did not evaluate the simulations; in some cases, only nine students out of 25 marked the simulations. Overall, most students positively evaluated the simulations, exceptions being ap-

Table 4. Results from the simulations' evaluations at ERBASE 2007

Simulation	Number of answers	Concept Number of votes (percentage)			
		Very Good	Good	Medium	Poor
[A.4-01] Compet	16	---	09 (56%)	05 (31%)	02 (13%)
[A.4-03] Perceptron for character recognition	17	06 (35,3%)	05 (29,4%)	06 (35,3%)	---
[A.5-02] ACA-Ant Clustering Algorithm	13	03 (23%)	09 (69%)	01 (8%)	---
[A.5-03] PSO-Particle Swarm Optimization	09	02 (22,2%)	05 (55,6%)	02 (22,2%)	---
[A.6-01] NSA-Negative Selection Algorithm	13	01 (7,7%)	08 (61,5%)	03 (23,1%)	01 (7,7%)
[A.6-02] CLONALG-Clonal selection algorithm	13	05 (38,5%)	05 (38,5%)	03 (23%)	---
[A.7-01] Cellular automata	14	05 (35,7%)	05 (35,7%)	04 (28,6%)	---
[A.7-02] Lindermayer Systems	18	15 (83,3%)	02 (11,1%)	01 (5,6%)	---
[A.7-03] Particle Systems	14	07 (50%)	05 (35,7%)	02 (14,3%)	---
[A.8-01] Boids	10	---	04 (40%)	06 (60%)	---
[A.8-02] Traffic Jam	16	01 (6,2%)	11 (68,8%)	02 (12,5%)	02 (12,5%)
[A.8-03] Game of Life	15	04 (26,7%)	09 (60%)	02 (13,3%)	---

plets A.4-01, A.6-01, and A.8-01, corresponding to the Competitive Network, the Negative Selection Algorithm, and the Boids, respectively. In the case of the positive evaluation of applet A.7-02 (Lindermeyer System), it must be stressed that the students had a little more time to play with this simulation, which may have favoured a deeper understanding and better exploration of the tool, thus resulting in better assessments.

Interviews

One last assessment of LVCoN was based on an interview with the students. The interviews were performed either individually or in groups, depending on the time constraints. The individual and group interviews were distributed as follows: five individual interviews, two interviews in groups of three students, two interviews in groups of four students, and one interview with a group of five students, leading to a total of 24 students interviewed. In the group interviews, each student initially presented himself for the records, and every student replied to the questions after saying their names. The *Interview Protocol* is presented in Appendix 6.

For Question 1, a single student said LVCoN did not motivate him to study natural computing. In Question 2, the preferred themes were: fractal geometry (16.7%), swarm intelligence (12.5%), and neural networks (8.3%). The preferred simulations were A.7-04—Particle Systems (16.7%), A.7-02—Lindermeyer Systems (12.5%), A.8-03—The Game of Life (8.3%), A.8-02—Traffic Jam (4.2%), and A.8-01—Boids (4.2%). All students interviewed found the LVCoN interface easy to use and/or intuitive, but several suggestions were made, such as improving the text layout to enhance readability and attractiveness, to use more icons, and to maintain a single menu. Concerning the experience of working with a virtual laboratory (Question 4), it was considered good by everybody, and the main benefits stressed were the availability of good-quality and didactic content, and the interactivity of the environment. Besides, 20.8% of the students stressed the need and importance of tutors during the learning action. The main difficulties (Question 5) raised by the students were insufficient time (45.8%), difficulties with math (29.2%), and applets with problems or little intuitiveness (12.5%). In Question 6, the students were unanimous about the usefulness of LVCoN as a tool to support the teaching and learning of natural computing. The main suggestions made to improve LVCoN (Question 7) were related to the interface (25%), the need to add more simulations (8.3%), the need to add more content (4.2%), the addition of a chat tool (4.2%), and the need to add links to related high-quality sites (4.2%). The students were also unanimous in relation to their preference for a hybrid course involving traditional lectures and e-learning activities.

DISCUSSION AND PERSPECTIVES

The experiment described in this article had several goals:

- To evaluate the usefulness of LVCoN as a self-learning and self-evaluation tool;
- To evaluate the usefulness of LVCoN as a tool to support the teaching and learning of natural computing;
- To evaluate the quality of the structure and contents of LVCoN; and
- To evaluate the functioning and simulations available at LVCoN.

The results obtained allowed us to positively evaluate the structure and contents of LVCoN, mainly because most students were satisfied with these aspects. Among the themes studied during ERBASE 2007, the students preferred fractals, swarm intelligence, and neural networks. Its interface was considered simple and intuitive, though suggestions for improvements have been made, particularly in relation to readability and the use of icons. The students also indicated the need to extend the explanations of some topics, and detected applets with malfunctioning. Considering the positive evaluation of the Lindermayer Systems applet, which had a longer time for experimentation, we may infer that having more time to play with the applets could have resulted in more positive evaluations to other, not so well evaluated, applets. From among the many improvements to be made at LVCoN, the following will be of particular attention to us: readability, correction of specific applets, and the inclusion of new simulations and links. Also, a chat will be included in order to allow for instant communication among students, and between them and the tutor.

LVCoN users are responsible for their own assessment, and this was investigated during the experiment at ERBASE 2007. Self-assessment experiments make it difficult to maintain the marking standards, and deeply rely on the students' responsibility and subjectivity of evaluating themselves. By contrast, they have a series of positive aspects that depend on the motivation and engagement of the students. Self-assessment makes the students take the responsibility to themselves in relation to how to evaluate their degree of success in a given activity, thus making them responsible for their own learning. It may favour the motivation and engagement of students, due to the higher control they have of the learning process (Pintrich, Marx, & Boyle, 1993), and also stimulates the students to get involved in the metacognitive processes in which they analyse their own cognitive processes, improving their critical and reflexive capabilities (White & Gunstone, 1989).

The students' performance in the experiment described here can be considered good, once they marked 68% of the total, even in a limited time experiment as the one described here. Undoubtedly, the lack of time was a constraining factor for the students' performance, and this was even noted by the students themselves. The self-assessment experiment performed showed that the computer science and information systems students performed better than the computer engineering students. Table 1 shows, however, that most computer engineering students were either at the first or the second year, different from the other courses that were at a more advanced level in their degrees. This may justify the poorer performance of the computer engineering students.

Finally, the results concerning the comparison between lecture-based courses and the learning experience with LVCoN are very relevant. Most students considered both methods equivalent in terms of learning experience, though some students preferred the use of LVCoN, while only 20% found it worse than a traditional lecture-based course. It must be acknowledged, however, that all students liked working with a virtual laboratory, detaching many benefits related to the availability of high-quality content available on the Web, and the interactivity of the environment. When taken altogether, these results suggest that the limited time to the learning actions may be an intervenient factor in the evaluation, though we should never forget the potential differences in the learning styles and preferences of students. This indicates the importance of investigating the results of using LVCoN with its full learning matrix, involving 100 hours of activities. Concerning Question 1, a single student said LVCoN did not take his/her interest in natural computing. Concerning the nature of the learning action, most students stressed the need and importance of tutors to follow the virtual laboratory use, and everybody showed a preference for a hybrid learning combining lectures and virtual learning, which has important implications for the pedagogical use of LVCoN in the future.

ACKNOWLEDGMENT

The authors thank CNPq, Fapesp, and Fapesb for the financial support.

REFERENCES

CBofN. (2007). *The computational beauty of nature.* Retrieved January 20, 2008, from http://mitpress.mit.edu/books/FLAOH/cbnhtml/

Dalgarno, B., Bishop, A. G., & Bedgood, D. R. (2003). The potential of virtual laboratories for distance education science teaching: Reflections from the development and evaluation of a virtual chemistry laboratory. In I. Johnston (Ed.), *Improving Learning Outcomes Through Flexible Science Teaching.* Uniserve Science Conference, Sydney, Australia.

Dasgupta, D., & Michalewicz, Z. (1997), *Evolutionary algorithms in engineering applications.* Springer-Verlag.

de Castro, L. N. (2006). *Fundamentals of natural computing: Basic concepts, algorithms, and applications.* Chapman & Hall/CRC.

de Castro, L. N. (2007). Fundamentals of natural computing: An overview. *Physics of Life Reviews, 4*(1), 1–36.

de Castro, L. N., & Von Zuben, F. J. (2004). *Recent developments in biologically inspired computing.* Hershey, PA: Idea Group.

Ertugrul, N. (2000). Towards virtual laboratories: A survey of LabVIEW-based teaching/learning tools and future trends. The Special Issue on Applications of LabVIEW in Engineering Education, *International Journal of Engineering Education, 16*(3), 171–179.

Federl, P., & Prusinkiewicz, P. (1999). Virtual laboratory: An interactive software environment for computer graphics. In *Proceedings of Computer Graphics International* (pp. 93–100).

Gomez, F. J., Cervera, M., & Martinez, J. (2000). A world wide Web based architecture for the implementation of a virtual laboratory. In *Proceedings of The 26th EUROMICRO Conference (EUROMICRO'00)* (Volume 2, pp. 2056).

Kouzes, R. T. J. D., Myers, J. D., & Wulf, W. A. (1996). Collaboratories: Doing science on the Internet. *IEEE Computer, 29*(8), 40–46.

LVCoN. (2007). *Virtual laboratory on natural computing.* Catholic University of Santos (UniSantos). Retrieved January 20, 2008, from http://lsin.unisantos.br/lvcon (Portuguese version), http://lsin.unisantos.br/lvcon_en (English version)

Lawson, E. A., & Stackpole, W. (2006, October 19–21). Does a virtual networking laboratory result in similar student achievement and satisfaction? In *Proceedings of the 7th conference on Information technology education (SIGITE'06).* Minneapolis, MN.

Leitner, L. J., & Cane, J. W. (2005, October 20–22). A virtual laboratory environment for online IT education. In *Proceedings of the 6th conference on Information technology education (SIGITE'05)* (pp. 283–289). Newark, NJ.

Paton, R. (1994). *Computing with biological metaphors.* Chapman & Hall.

Paton, R., Bolouri, H., & Holcombe, M. (2003). *Computing in cells and tissues: Perspectives and tools of thought.* Springer-Verlag.

Pintrich, P. R., Marx, R. W., & Boyle, R. A. (1993). Beyond cold conceptual change: The role of motivational beliefs and classroom contextual factors in the process of conceptual change. *Review of Educational Research, 63*(2), 167–199.

VLAB. (2007). *Monash University's complexity virtual lab.* Retrieved January 20, 2008, from http://vlab.infotech.monash.edu.au/

VLAI. (2007). *Virtual laboratory of artificial intelligence.* Retrieved January 20, 2008, from http://galaxy.agh.edu.pl/~vlsi/AI/

Way, T. P. (2006, March). A virtual laboratory model for encouraging undergraduate research. In *SIGCSE Technical Symposium (SIGCSE 2006).*

White, T. R., & Gunstone, R. F. (1989). Metalearning and conceptual change. *International Journal of Science Education, 11*, 577–586.

Yokomori, T. (2002). Natural computation – new computing paradigm learned from life phenomena. *IPSJ Magazine*, *41*, 08–11.

Zimmermann, H.-J. (1999). *Practical applications of fuzzy technologies*. Kluwer Academic Publishers.

APPENDIX 1: LEARNING ACTION MATRIX FOR LVCON

THEME	ACTIVITY	GOAL	GRADE	TIME
Introduction	Didactic content	Introduce natural computing and its main branches	----	1 hour
Basic concepts	Didactic content	Study the main concepts of natural computing	----	3 hours
	Research questions	Search related subjects	10 points	2 hours
Evolutionary computing	Didactic content	Study the theoretical content available	----	6 hours
	Research questions	Search related subjects	3 points	4 hours
	Theoretical questions	Evaluate the contents studied	7 points	2 hours
	Computational exercises	Evaluate the behavior of the simulations	----	2 hours
Neural networks	Didactic content	Study the theoretical content available	----	6 hours
	Research questions	Search related subjects	1 point	2 hours
	Theoretical questions	Evaluate the contents studied	9 points	2 hours
	Computational exercises	Evaluate the behavior of the simulations	----	2 hours
Swarm intelligence	Didactic content	Study the theoretical content available	----	6 hours
	Research questions	Search related subjects	4 points	4 hours
	Theoretical questions	Evaluate the contents studied	6 points	2 hours
	Computational exercises	Evaluate the behavior of the simulations	----	2 hours
Artificial immune systems	Didactic content	Study the theoretical content available	----	6 hours
	Research questions	Search related subjects	3 points	4 hours
	Theoretical questions	Evaluate the contents studied	7 points	2 hours
	Computational exercises	Evaluate the behavior of the simulations	----	2 hours
Fractal geometry	Didactic content	Study the theoretical content available	----	6 hours
	Research questions	Search related subjects	2 points	4 hours
	Theoretical questions	Evaluate the contents studied	8 points	2 hours
	Computational exercises	Evaluate the behavior of the simulations	----	2 hours
Artificial life	Didactic content	Study the theoretical content available	----	6 hours
	Research questions	Search related subjects	3 points	4 hours
	Theoretical questions	Evaluate the contents studied	7 points	2 hours
	Computational exercises	Evaluate the behavior of the simulations	----	2 hours
DNA computing	Didactic content	Study the theoretical content available	----	6 hours
Quantum computing	Didactic content	Study the theoretical content available	----	6 hours
			TOTAL	100 hours

APPENDIX 2: LEARNING ACTION MATRIX FOR LVCON AT ERBASE 2007

THEME	ACTIVITY	GOAL	GRADE	TIME (MIN)
Presentation	Introduce LVCoN	Introduce LVCoN	----	30
Introduction	Didactic content	Introduce natural computing and its main branches	----	15

Basic concepts	Didactic content	Lecture	----	25
	Research questions	Questions 1 e 4	5 points	20
Neural networks	Didactic content	Lecture	----	30
	Research questions	Question 1	1 point	10
	Theoretical questions	Questions 4 e 5	3,5 points	30
	Computational exercises	A.4-01, A.4-03	----	20
Swarm intelligence	Didactic content	Lecture	----	30
	Research questions	Question 1	1 point	10
	Theoretical questions	Questions 2 e 3	6 points	30
	Computational exercises	A.5-02, A.5-03	----	20
Artificial immune systems	Didactic content	Lecture	----	30
	Research questions	Question 1	0,5 point	10
	Theoretical questions	Questions 1, 2 e 3	3,5 points	30
	Computational exercises	A.6-01, A.6-02	----	20
Fractal geometry	Didactic content	Lecture	----	30
	Research questions	Question 2	1 point	10
	Theoretical questions	Questions 4, 5 e 6	2 points	30
	Computational exercises	A.7-01, A.7-02, A.7-04	----	30
Artificial life	Didactic content	Lecture	----	30
	Research questions	Question 3	1 point	10
	Theoretical questions	Questions 1 e 4	3 points	30
	Computational exercises	A.8-01, A.8-02, A.8-03	----	20
LVCoN	Evaluate LVCoN	Evaluate LVCoN	----	50
			TOTAL	600 minutes

APPENDIX 3: SELF-ASSESSMENT FORM

THEME	ACTIVITY	GOAL	GRADE (POINTS)	MARK
Basic concepts	Research questions	Questions 1 e 4	5	
Neural networks	Research questions	Question 1	1	
	Theoretical questions	Questions 4 e 5	3,5	
Swarm intelligence	Research questions	Question 1	1	
	Theoretical questions	Questions 2 e 3	6	
Artificial immune systems	Research questions	Question 1	0,5	
	Theoretical questions	Questions 1, 2 e 3	3,5	
Fractal geometry	Research questions	Question 2	1	
	Theoretical questions	Questions 4, 5 e 6	2	
Artificial life	Research questions	Question 3	1	
	Theoretical questions	Questions 1 e 4	3	
		TOTAL	27,5	

APPENDIX 4: QUESTIONNAIRE ABOUT LVCON

1. What is your satisfaction degree with the experience of using LVCoN?

( ) Very Satisfied ( ) Satisfied ( ) Little Satisfied
( ) Unsatisfied ( ) Very Unsatisfied

2. What is your satisfaction degree with LVCoN's Forum as a tool for exchanging ideas and discussing results?

( ) Very Satisfied ( ) Satisfied ( ) Little Satisfied
( ) Unsatisfied ( ) Very Unsatisfied

3. What is your satisfaction degree with the didactic content available at LVCoN?

( ) Very Satisfied ( ) Satisfied ( ) Little Satisfied
( ) Unsatisfied ( ) Very Unsatisfied

4. What is your satisfaction degree with LVCoN's structure (organization, information available, etc.)?

( ) Very Satisfied ( ) Satisfied ( ) Little Satisfied
( ) Unsatisfied ( ) Very Unsatisfied

5. Did you find any technical or functional problem in LVCoN? If yes, which one(s)?

( ) No ( ) Yes: ____
____
____

6. The instructor encouraged you to use well LVCoN's resources?

( ) No ( ) Yes

7. Did the exercises help you to evaluate the contents studied? If not, why?

( ) Yes ( ) No: ____
____
____

8. Compared with a traditional course, how would you evaluate LVCoN?

( ) Better ( ) Equivalent ( ) A Little Worse
( ) Worse ( ) Unsatisfactory

APPENDIX 5: SIMULATIONS EVALUATIONS

Simulations	Usefulness
[A.4 - 01] Compet	[ ] Great [ ] Good [ ] Reasonable [ ] Poor
[A.4 - 03] Perceptron for pattern recognition	[ ] Great [ ] Good [ ] Reasonable [ ] Poor
[A.5 - 02] ACA - Ant Clustering Algorithm	[ ] Great [ ] Good [ ] Reasonable [ ] Poor
[A.5 - 03] PSO - Particle Swarm Optimization	[ ] Great [ ] Good [ ] Reasonable [ ] Poor
[A.6 - 01] NSA - Negative Selection Algorithm	[ ] Great [ ] Good [ ] Reasonable [ ] Poor
[A.6 - 02] CLONALG - Clonal Selection Algorithm	[ ] Great [ ] Good [ ] Reasonable [ ] Poor
[A.7 - 01] Cellular Automata	[ ] Great [ ] Good [ ] Reasonable [ ] Poor
[A.7 - 02] Lindermayer System	[ ] Great [ ] Good [ ] Reasonable [ ] Poor
[A.7 - 03] Particle Systems	[ ] Great [ ] Good [ ] Reasonable [ ] Poor
[A.8 - 01] Boids	[ ] Great [ ] Good [ ] Reasonable [ ] Poor
[A.8 - 02] Traffic Jam	[ ] Great [ ] Good [ ] Reasonable [ ] Poor
[A.8 - 03] Game of Life	[ ] Great [ ] Good [ ] Reasonable [ ] Poor

APPENDIX 6: INTERVIEW PROTOCOL

Has LVCoN made you feel more interested about natural computing?
Which theme or simulation was most interesting to you? Why?
Did you find the interface intuitive? Which improvement would you suggest?
How did you like working with a virtual environment? Did you notice any benefit?
Did you have any specific difficulty? If yes, has it affected your learning?
Would you use LVCoN as a tool to support the learning of natural computing?
Would you add anything to LVCoN?
Would you like to have the whole course by distance, or a hybrid between lectures and e-learning?

This work was previously published in International Journal of Distance Education Technologies, Vol. 6, Issue 2, edited by Q. Jin, pp. 55-73, copyright 2008 by IGI Publishing (an imprint of IGI Global).

Chapter 7
Online Learning of Electrical Circuits Through a Virtual Laboratory

J.A. Gómez-Tejedor
Polytechnic University of Valencia, Spain

G. Moltó
Polytechnic University of Valencia, Spain.

ABSTRACT

This work describes a Java-based virtual laboratory accessible via the Internet by means of a Web browser. This remote laboratory enables the students to build both direct and alternating current circuits. The program includes a graphical user interface which resembles the connection board, and also the electrical components and tools that are used in a real laboratory to build electrical circuits. Emphasis has been placed on designing access patterns to the virtual tools as if they were real ones. The virtual laboratory developed in this study allows the lecturer to adapt the behaviour and the principal layout of the different practical sessions during a course. This flexibility enables the tool to guide the student during each practical lesson, thus enhancing self-motivation. This study is an application of new technologies for active learning methodologies, in order to increase both the self-learning and comprehension of the students. This virtual laboratory is currently accessible at the following URL: http://personales.upv.es/jogomez/labvir/ (in Spanish).

INTRODUCTION

The idea of web-based virtual laboratories is not new (Hoffman, 1994; Potter, 1996; Preis 1997). However, this topic has received much attention over the last few years due to the implementation of new teaching technologies in the classroom, and the widespread adoption of the Internet. Currently, a large number of virtual laboratories can be found online. These virtual laboratories cover different fields of study: measurement of hardness in metals (Hashemi, 2006), microbiology (Sancho, 2006), earthquake engineering (Gao, 2005), environmental applications (Ascione, 2006), manufacturing engineering education (Jou, 2006), photonics (Chang, 2005), robot control (Sartorius, 2006) and electronic circuit simulation (Butz, 2006; Moure, 2004; Yang, 2005), to name but a few.

DOI: 10.4018/978-1-60566-934-2.ch007

All of these virtual laboratories are based on computer simulations, and have been developed with different programming languages such as Java (Gao, 2005), Matlab (Sartorius, 2006) or Macromedia Flash (Hashemi, 2006). This paper describes a virtual laboratory for electric circuit simulation developed in Java and deployed as an applet which can be accessed through a web browser.

One of the main topics of the Fundamentals of Physics for Computer Science subject at the Faculty of Computer Science (Faculty of Computer Science, 2007) and HTS of Applied Computer Science (HTS of Applied Computer Science, 2007) at the Polytechnic University of Valencia (Polytechnic University of Valencia, 2007) is the study of elementary electrical circuits, with both direct and alternating currents. The electrical circuit is also an important topic in other engineering studies at many universities. These studies are performed both from a theoretical point of view and a more practical one through applied lessons in a laboratory.

In these lessons, the students become familiarized with a series of devices, tools and techniques, and they learn to analyse data, thus achieving skills and expertise. However, the students also face a lack of tools for their individual work, since they are unable to perform electrical experiments outside the laboratory. In addition, some students cannot attend the laboratory during their allocated time slot. Furthermore, the financial costs related to maintaining and updating the laboratory with modern equipment is also a major handicap.

With the simulation software described in this paper (Gómez Tejedor, 2002; Gómez Tejedor, 2005), the students are supplied with a useful and versatile tool for performing some of the practical lessons online (Gómez Tejedor, 2007). One important question related to virtual laboratories is "Can the fundamental objectives of the instructional laboratories be met via software and computers?" (Hashemi, 2006). In order to overcome this problem, we propose that virtual lessons should be complemented with real ones. On the one hand, the students can train themselves in the virtual environment before working in the laboratory and even improve their skills before examination. On the other hand, different practical lessons can be available online which, due to timetabling problems, cannot be performed in the real laboratory.

The main novelty of this work is that the students can make electrical circuits in a similar way as they do at a real laboratory. Only the virtual laboratories of (Butz, 2006) and (Moure, 2004) have this built-in feature. In addition, another original point of our virtual laboratory is the possibility of configuring the program by the teacher by only editing a file, where the main options of the program are defined. This easy approach to configure the virtual laboratory makes it ideal to perform different practical lessons, where the environment is customised. Besides, our virtual laboratory is friendly accessible through the web by only means of a web browser.

This paper is related to teaching the Fundamentals of Physics for Computer Science through the Internet (Mas, 2002), which, since 2000/2001, has been part of the curriculum at the Faculty of Computer Science and HTS of Applied Computer Science at the Polytechnic University of Valencia. This approach is linked to the current trend of developing applications for active learning methodologies, to leverage self-learning and comprehension skills for the students. In this field, this work can be considered to be a pioneering one.

METHODOLOGY INNOVATIONS

This study introduces an important innovation in the teaching methodology used within the laboratory, since it enables the students to train their skills using any computer connected to the Internet. The virtual laboratory allows students to learn how to operate the different devices found in a laboratory by means of a comprehensive user manual. Subsequently, they practice with virtual devices which resemble real ones. Practice is conducted either individually or in small groups, and without a schedule. This enables students to self-regulate their learning procedure, investing as much time as required.

It could be argued that using a virtual environment does not fully help the students to interact with real devices. However, our proposal combines both virtual and real lessons so that students can gradually become used to the actual technology employed in university laboratories.

Moreover, the virtual laboratory facilitates the design of more challenging practical lessons. Hence, the students can practise in the virtual laboratory before working in the real laboratory. Therefore, they can achieve a greater number of objectives given the expertise gained using the software tools.

Finally, as previously mentioned, the students can use the virtual laboratory as a useful tool to prepare for the laboratory exam. Also, its ubiquitous access is of great benefit to those students that cannot attend the practical lessons in the laboratory.

THE VIRTUAL LABORATORY OF ELECTRICITY

The virtual laboratory has been entirely developed in Java (Newman, 1996). The usage of Java represents a two-fold strategy. On the one hand, its portability enables the application to be executed on virtually any platform for which a Java Virtual Machine exists (Sun Microsystems, 2007). On the other hand, a Java application can be deployed as an applet in order to access its functionality via a Java-enabled web browser. This involves only minimal requirements from the students, who are only required to install the Java Virtual Machine on their PCs.

On the other hand, the use of the object-oriented skills of Java has enabled the simplification of application extensibility by using a modularized approach for separating the different functionalities of the application.

Implemented Functionality

Nowadays, the virtual laboratory allows for the creation of direct and alternating current circuits on the connection board using cables, resistances, capacitors and inductors. It is important to point out that, with this software, the student must completely set-up the circuit, by linking all the elements and devices on the connection board, as if these were actually in a real laboratory. This is a major advantage compared with other virtual laboratories found on the Internet, where the circuit is almost completely implemented and the student can only change some parameters and different configurations. As far as the authors are aware, only the virtual laboratories of (Butz, 2006) and (Moure, 2004) have this built-in feature.

The virtual laboratory permits voltages to be measured in direct currents by means of the analogical voltmeter. The digital multimeter allows both voltage and intensity to be measured in direct and alternating currents, and frequencies in alternating currents and resistances.

The established virtual laboratory includes a circuit resolution kernel that computes all the voltages and intensities in the circuit by using the matrix method for knot tensions, both in the direct current and in the alternating sinusoidal current (Llinares, 1987).

In this method, given an electrical circuit with $n+1$ electric knots, the circuit is solved by the following method:

1. All potential generators are transformed to intensity generators. For this purpose, we take into account that the short-circuit intensity of the intensity generator is given by the following expression:

$$I_0 = \frac{\varepsilon}{r_\varepsilon} \qquad (1)$$

where ε is the generator electromotive force and r_ε corresponds to its internal resistance. The internal resistance of the intensity generator is the same as the voltage generator one.

2. The voltage of one knot is taken arbitrary to 0 volts. In our case, this is the knot number n+1.
3. Then, a system of linear equations, with dimension $n\times n$, is assembled:

$$\begin{pmatrix} I_1 \\ I_2 \\ \vdots \\ I_n \end{pmatrix} = \begin{pmatrix} Y_{11} & Y_{12} & \cdots & Y_{1n} \\ Y_{21} & Y_{22} & \cdots & Y_{2n} \\ \vdots & \vdots & \ddots & \vdots \\ Y_{n1} & Y_{n2} & \cdots & Y_{nn} \end{pmatrix} \begin{pmatrix} V_1 \\ V_2 \\ \vdots \\ V_n \end{pmatrix} \qquad (2)$$

where I_i stands for the short-circuit intensity of intensity generators connected to knot i, Y_{ii} are the admittances connected to knot i, Y_{ij} with $i\neq j$ are the admittances simultaneously connected to knots i and j. V_i corresponds to the voltage at knot i. The admittance is defined as the inverse of the impedance. The calculations are performed with complex numbers for alternating current, whereas real numbers are employed for direct current circuits.

4. Then, the matrix equation is solved in order to obtain V_i. This way, the potential difference between any pair of knots can be calculated. The intensities measured by the multimeter are calculated as the potential difference between the knots where the multimeter is connected divided by the resistance of the multimeter in ammeter function.

The resolution of circuits, when the generator supplies a square wave, requires special resolution techniques. In this case, the program performs a Fourier's development of the square wave given by the following expression (Zwillinger, 2003):

$$u(t) = \frac{4U_m}{\grave{A}} \sum_{n=0}^{\infty} \frac{\cos\left[(2n+1)\acute{E}_0\, t - 90^0\right]}{2n+1} \qquad (3)$$

U_m stands for the amplitude and ω_0 is the signal pulsation. For example, by taking the first 100 terms of the Fourier series, we obtain the results shown in Figure 1.

With this input voltage, the program solves the circuit for each one of the harmonics of the Fourier series as described before, and finally gathers the obtained results to determine the

Figure 1. Square wave computed with the first 100 terms of the Fourier series

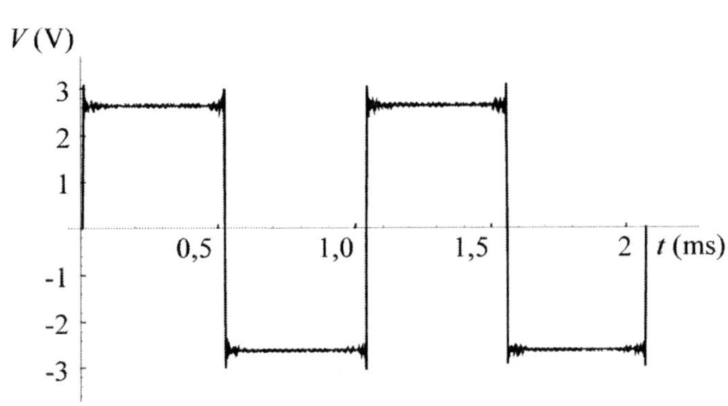

voltage in each of the circuit knots. Experimental observations have revealed that using the first 50 terms of the Fourier series provides an appropriate representation of the potential difference. Using only 10 terms of the series reveals that a satisfactory reproduction of the potential difference in the terminals of the capacitor in a resistance-capacitor circuit is provided. However, with these terms, the potential difference in the generator terminals is not satisfactorily represented when compared to real measurements in the laboratory. Therefore, the final decision regarding the number of terms of the Fourier's development to be employed should depend on the performance capabilities of the client computer. Finally, using 50 terms is an appropriate value for most cases, since it combines a moderate execution time with a satisfactory voltage performance in the electrical circuit.

The elements and devices that have been currently implemented in the virtual laboratory are summarised in the following paragraphs:

Connection board: This has six electric knots, each one of them with three or four pins, allowing the set-up of a great variety of circuits. Two different models of connection boards, as illustrated in Figure 2 and 3, have been implemented. On the left hand side of the figures, a picture of a real connection board is given. On the right hand side, the graphical aspect of a simulated one is shown.

Resistances, capacitors and inductors: These have a known nominal value, and an unknown real value: The program assigns a random value to each impedance close to its nominal value, between the element tolerance margins. The real values are ignored by the user, who is only aware of the nominal value. In addition, "unknown resistances" can also be used, the nominal value of which is ignored by the user, in order to produce a practical session for determining the value of resistances.

Cables: Employed to link devices and elements to create electrical circuits. They are shown, together with resistances, in Figure 4.

Figure 2. First connection board

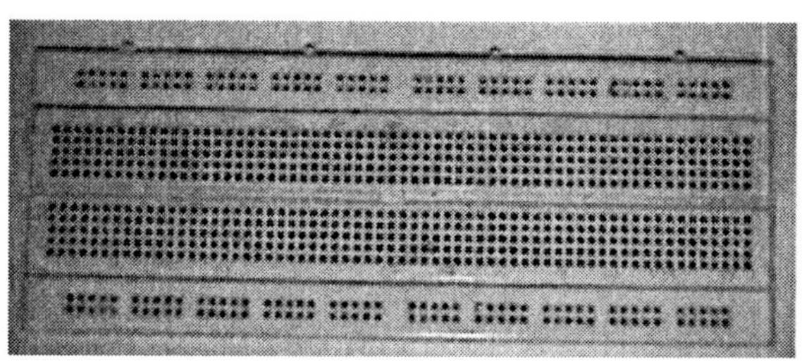
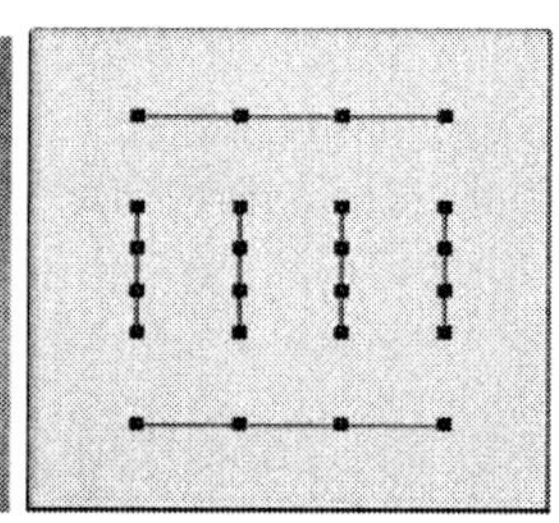

Figure 3. Second connection board

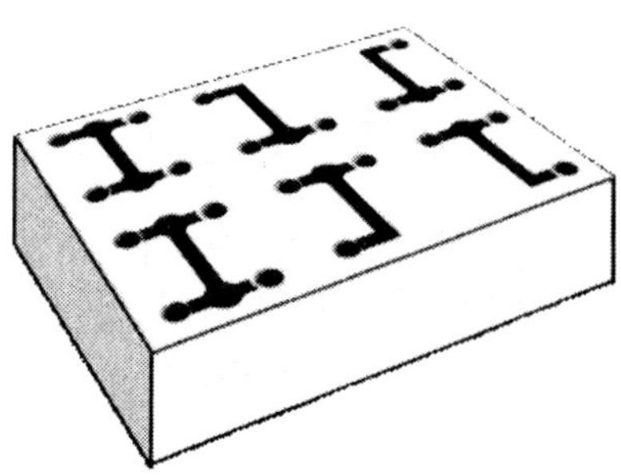
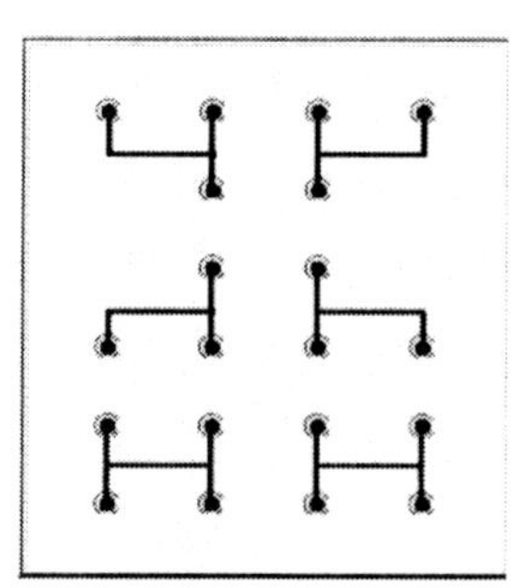

Figure 4. Elements used in the program: two cables, two resistances of 22 Ω and 47 Ω, a capacitor of 4.4 μF and an inductor of 9.0 mH

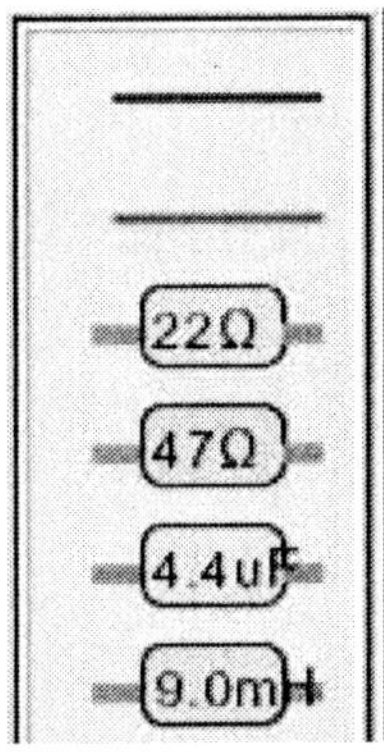

Power supply source in direct current: Composed of three independent power supply sources. Two of these supply a variable potential difference between 0 and 30 V, and the third one supplies a constant voltage of approximately 5 V. In the program, the 5 V power supply, shown in Figure 5, is modelled in a similar manner to an intensity generator, with intensity in the short circuit of 0.4618 A, and internal resistance of 10.9 Ω.

Function generator: Employed to create circuits in alternating current. It allows the generation of a sinusoidal signal or a square wave of a

Figure 5. Power supply source in direct current

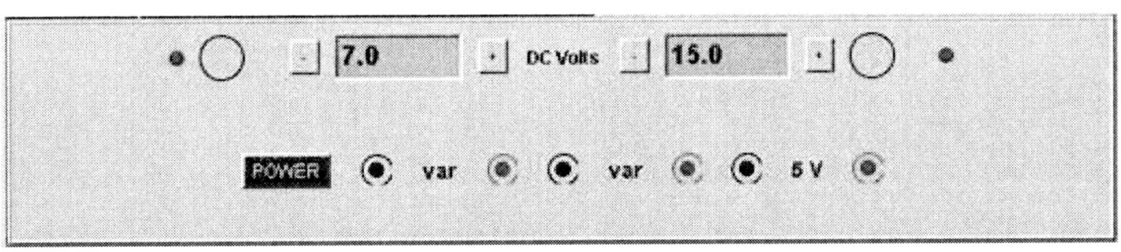

Figure 6. Function generator

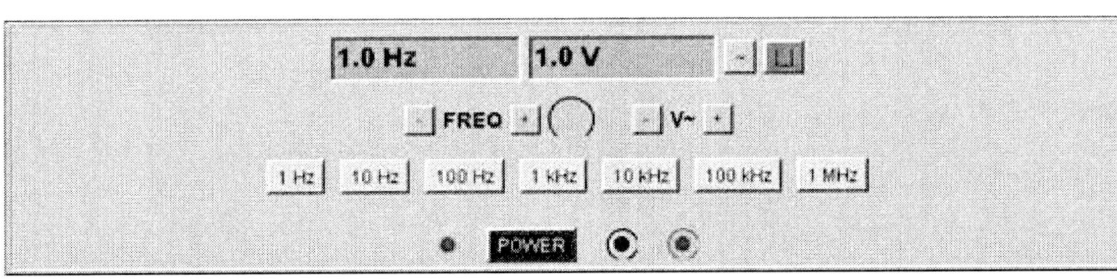

Figure 7. Digital multimeter

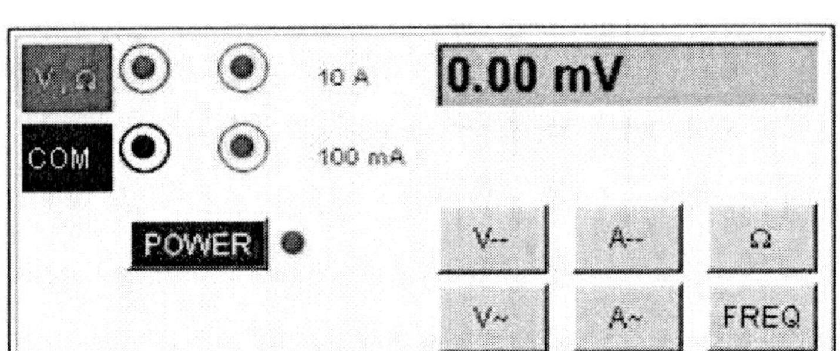

Figure 8. Analogical voltmeter

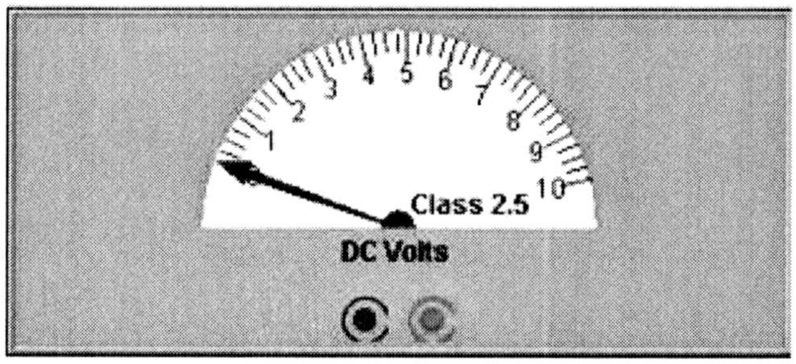

given amplitude and frequency. Its visual aspect is shown in Figure 6.

Digital multimeter: It is shown in Figure 7, and it measures potential differences and intensities in both direct and alternating current. It also measures resistances and frequencies. The internal resistance of the device has been considered in the circuit resolution kernel (10 MΩ in voltmeter mode, and 0.003 Ω in ammeter mode).

Analogical voltmeter: This is a very useful device for observing systematic errors, as shown in Figure 8. It has a small internal resistance (15 kΩ).

Scope: The program uses the virtual scope developed by (Benlloch, 2002) to measure time-dependent potential differences.

Given all the implemented functionality, the virtual laboratory can currently simulate most of the practical laboratory sessions of the Physics for Computer Science module at the University Polytechnic of Valencia, (Gómez Tejedor, 2006):

- **Practical session 1: Equipment and measure devices**. Circuit set-ups in direct current. Measurement of the potential difference, intensity and resistances at different circuit points.
- **Practical session 2: Accidental and systematic errors.** Evaluation of different techniques to measure resistances by means of Ohm's law in two different circuit set-ups. In the first set-up (Figure 9) the emphasis is placed on accidental errors in the measurements introduced by the devices. In the second set-up (Figure 10) an important systematic error appears due to the internal voltmeter resistance of 15 kΩ.
- **Practical session 3: Scope**. Measurement of amplitude, period and difference of phase in a resistance-capacitor circuit (*RC* circuit) with a sinusoidal alternating current.
- **Practical session 4: Transitory phenomena. Capacitor charge and discharge**. Time constant measurement in the *RC* circuit. A square wave is supplied in the *RC* circuit. Subsequently, the virtual scope shows how the capacitor is charged and then discharged. The time constant of the charge and discharge processes can be measured from the curves obtained.
- **Practical session 5: Resonance and filters in the alternating current**. Measurement of the impedance in a series inductor-capacitor-resistance circuit (series *LCR* circuit) as a frequency function, and calculation of the resonance frequency. Filter use: low-pass, high-pass and band-pass filters by means of an *LCR* circuit. Measurement of the ratio between the output and input potential difference as a frequency function, and the determination of the quality factor.

Nowadays, the user manual of the virtual laboratory is very detailed, guiding the student

Figure 9. Virtual laboratory: First set-up for resistance measurement

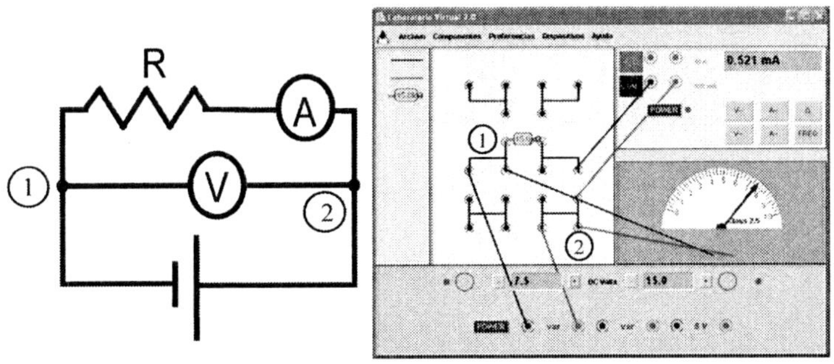

during the practical session, in addition to the teacher's manual which explains how to configure the program for the implementation of new practical sessions in the laboratory. It is possible to access the program and the documentation at the following web page (in Spanish): http://personales.upv.es/jogomez/labvir/.

Usage Examples of the Virtual Laboratory

The following section describes some examples which show the functionality of the virtual laboratory. The first example illustrates how to determine the value of a resistance by measuring the potential difference and the intensity in the electrical circuit. There are two different configurations for this circuit. The first layout sets the ammeter in serial with the resistance. The voltmeter is in parallel to both elements (see Figure 9).

In this case we have selected 7.5 V in the generator. A measure of 7.5 V in the analogical voltmeter and 0.521 mA in the digital ammeter is obtained. Subsequently, *R,* the resistance is given by:

$$R = \frac{V}{I} = 14.40\ \text{k©} \qquad (4)$$

In addition, we should take into account that the nominal resistance value is 15 kΩ, with 5% tolerance, and that the program selects a random resistance around the nominal value and between the tolerance limits. Subsequently, the measured resistance of 14.40 kΩ, falls within the expected 15.00 ± 0.75 kΩ interval.

In this case it is important to point out that the intensity through the resistance has been measured. However, the potential difference measurement corresponds to the resistance + ammeter set. In this case, the measure is very precise due to the fact that the internal resistance of the ammeter (3 mΩ) is negligible when compared to the circuit resistance of 15 kΩ.

In the second layout, the voltmeter has been linked in parallel to the resistance, and the ammeter in serial with both elements (see Figure 10).

Once again, a value of 7.5 V was selected on the generator, and measurements of 7.5 V on the analogical voltmeter and 1.021 mA on the digital ammeter were obtained. This configuration produces an important systematic error because the measured resistance is 15 kΩ. This is of the same order of magnitude as the internal voltmeter resistance, which is considered in the calculations, obtaining a measured resistance of:

$$R_{measured} = \frac{V}{I} = 7.32\ \text{k©} \qquad (5)$$

corresponding to the parallel association of both resistances:

Figure 10. Virtual laboratory; Second set-up for resistance measurement

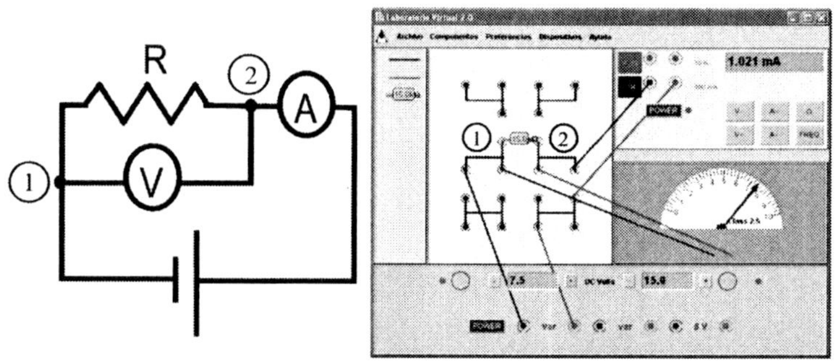

Figure 11. Left: Set-up for tension-intensity characteristic curve measurement for power supply source in direct current. Right: Results obtained for tension-intensity, and linear fit to data

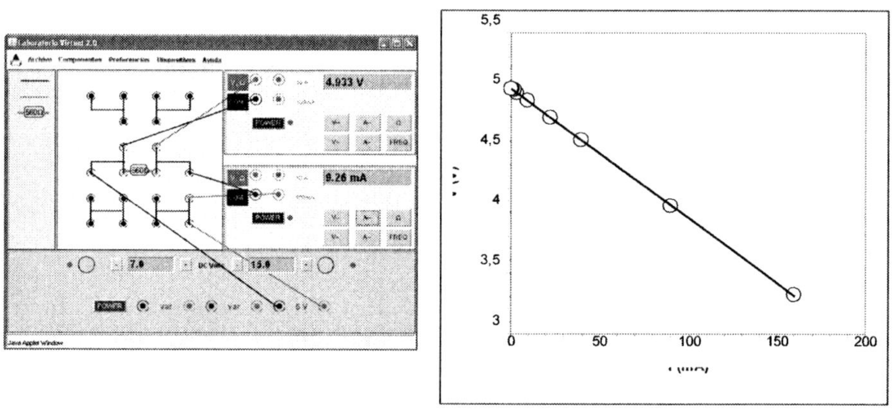

$$R_{measured} = \left(1 / R + 1 / R_V\right)^{-1} = 7.5 \text{ k©} \qquad (6)$$

The difference between both results can be explained by the fact that the real value of the circuit resistance is randomly taken around the nominal value of 15 kΩ, as previously mentioned.

In Figure 11 another example of the program in the direct current is given. In this case, the relation between the tension and intensity in the DC generator is obtained (the so called "characteristic curve").

The electric potential difference in a DC generator is given by the expression:

$$V_A - V_B = \varepsilon - rI \,,$$

Where ε is the electromotive force and r the internal resistance of DC power supply source.

For this purpose, the DC generator is connected to a resistance, and the electric potential difference in DC generator and the intensity in the circuit is measure. Changing the resistance value, we obtained different pair values of tension-intensity for the generator. From the experimental data obtained from the virtual laboratory, that are shown in Figure 11, making a linear data fit, we have obtained the parameters of the characteristic curve:

$$\varepsilon = 5{,}032\ V \qquad r = 10{,}7\ \Omega$$

In this way, the intensity of the equivalent intensity generator is given by:

$$I_0 = \frac{\varepsilon}{r} = \frac{5,032\ V}{10,7\ \Omega} = 0,470\ A$$

Note that the values obtained through the virtual laboratory for the intensity and the internal resistance differ slightly from those discussed above, due to experimental errors committed in the measurement. These errors are also taken into account in the simulation, and is a very important part of the program.These are the same errors that the students face in a real electricity laboratory.

In Figure 12 an example of the program working with alternating current is given. The figure on the right shows the *LCR* series circuit in alternating current. The figure on the left shows the measured intensity as a function of frequency, where the resonance frequency can be clearly observed at around 800 Hz. R =120 Ω, C =4.4 μF and L = 9 mH.

In Figure 13 another example of the program for alternating current is shown. The *RLC* series circuit acting as a high-pass filter. In this case, the electric potential difference at the entrance *Vi* (in the generator), and the output (at terminals of the inductor) as a function of frequency are measured. The figure represents the results of the ratio *Vo/Vi* obtained through the virtual laboratory, depending on the frequency. In the figure, it is clear that the voltage on the output is much

Figure 12. Circuit LCR series in the alternating current configured in the virtual laboratory. Intensity evaluated in the circuit as a function of frequency. R =120 Ω, C =4.4 μF and L = 9 mH

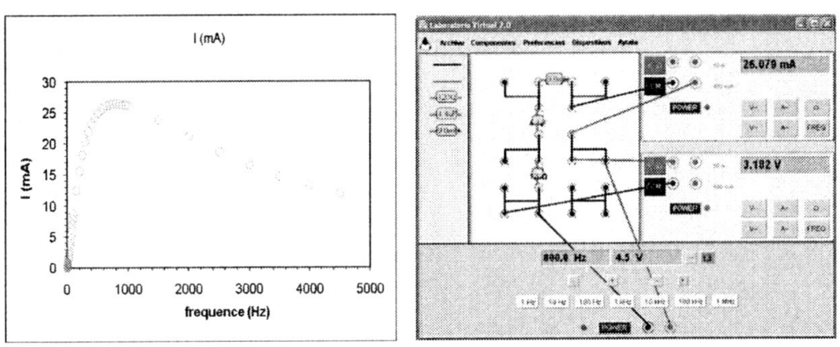

Figure 13. Circuit LCR series in the alternating current configured in the virtual laboratory as a high-pass filter. The graph represents the ratio Vo/Vi as a function on the frequency. That is, the relationship between the voltage at the output Vo (at the inductor terminals) and the entrance Vi (at the terminals of the generator), as a function of frequency. R =47 Ω, C =4.4 μF and L = 9 mH.

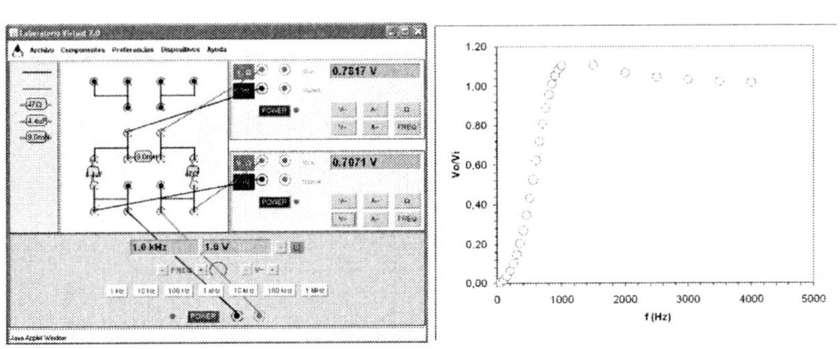

smaller than at the entrance for low frequencies (below 800 Hz). Above that frequency the output voltage is approximately equal to the entrance voltage. In this way, the student can learn the role of the high-pass filter performed by the circuit. In a similar way, the student can make setups of low-pass filter and band-pass filter through the virtual laboratory.

Web Integration

Not only can the virtual laboratory seamlessly run as a stand-alone application, but it can also be deployed as an applet accessible via the Internet. Figure 14 shows the interaction diagram between the student and the virtual laboratory. The students only require a web browser with Java Virtual Machine support to access the application, which is deployed onto a web server. This also simplifies the work of the tutors, who have total control of the application. Whenever an updated version of the application is available, the students can automatically use it, without having to reinstall the application. In addition, online access enables to gather statistics regarding application usage.

The usage of the virtual laboratory enables the student to follow a two-fold learning strategy (online and presential). Both approaches should have appropriate feedback as the online training is expected to be reinforced by presential lessons in the laboratory. This combination stands out as an ideal platform to increase the students' skills. Notice that the virtual laboratory should also be coherent with the real laboratory so that the students do not face a steep learning curve when using new devices and components.

The application has been designed to be easily configurable without requiring a source code modification. This allows the basic behaviour and layout of the application to be adapted to various practical lessons. This is a very useful asset for laboratory training, as each practical lesson requires a different set of devices and elements. This configuration is currently supplied

Figure 14. Overview of the Virtual Laboratory and interaction diagram with the student

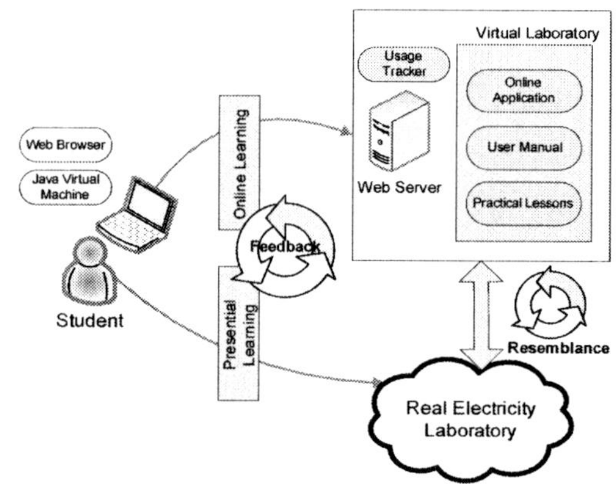

via arguments to the applet, specified in the web page which launches the applet.

The program currently allows for the modification of the following parameters:

- **Resistances, capacitors and inductors:** A list of these elements, indicating the nominal value and the tolerance can be specified. If the tolerance is not specified, then a value of 5% is assumed. The program assigns a random value between the margins of tolerance to these components. In the case of resistances, if the tolerance is greater than 19%, then the program considers this to be an unknown resistance, whose nominal value is not known by the student.
- **Connection board:** Two different types of connection board are available. Furthermore, the electric connections between the different connection points can be shown or hidden.
- **Voltage source:** A direct current generator and a function generator are available. The latter has three independent exits. The short circuit intensity and the internal resistance of the 5 V generator can be defined. The number of terms used in the Fourier's

development for the square wave in the function generator can also be selected.

- **Analogical voltmeter:** The maximum potential difference value, the class error, the divisions of the scale and their internal resistance can be specified. The class error of the voltmeter is visible to the student in order to acquire the error estimate, but does not influence the calculations.
- **Devices:** It allows the devices that will be available when the application starts, to be specified. Either two digital multimeters, a digital multimeter with the analogical voltmeter or one with the virtual scope can be selected
- **Digital multimeter:** The resistance values in the voltmeter and ammeter modes of the digital multimeter can be established.

CONCLUSION AND AREAS FOR FUTURE STUDIES

During the 2005-2006 course, the program was introduced as a pilot study with a group of approximately 250 students from the Polytechnic University of Valencia. Nowadays, the virtual laboratory is freely accessible through the web to the general public. Therefore, students from other universities can also use this tool to train their skills in electrical circuits.

In order to analyse the impact on student achievement, as well as student satisfaction, we made a questionnaire to a group of 40 students and also gathered user experiences. According to the results, we can conclude that the students are satisfied with the laboratory skills gained using the virtual laboratory. The virtual laboratory interface was easy to use although it could be improved by using real images of the devices. It is also worth to point out that there was a strong disagreement between students comparing this on-line learning with a conventional presential laboratory: some students prefer the on-line learning; most of them think that they are equivalent and few of them consider worse the on-line learning.

On the other hand, it is important to mention that students think that minor technical problems have interfered with the learning of the content covered. At this moment, we are enhancing the user interface as well as the robustness of the application.

The results reveal that students who used the virtual laboratory significantly improved their knowledge level of the objectives of the Physics for Computer Science subject. Using a self-training approach in the virtual laboratory, through different practical lessons, enables the students to repeat the same actions they do in the real laboratory. It has been observed that learning by means of the virtual laboratory has assisted students when carrying out laboratory work involving real devices. Therefore, we can conclude that the virtual laboratory has helped the students to learn in a more effective way.

This environment provides the student with the opportunity to learn through free exploration, although a specific performance criteria guides the learning process. In virtual laboratories, the student has the freedom to explore different parameters, observing their effects inside the virtual laboratory. Our results show that Web-based experiments that are designed to be interactive and allow the user to be involved in the learning process are effective for distance education. The help students learn about the procedure and analysis of data. In conditions where physical laboratory facilities are not available, virtual modules are a suitable replacement.

It is also important to point out that since the website has been online (established more than 3 years ago) it has received more than 9,100 visits. These include students from our university and also from other universities, since the virtual laboratory is available for the general public.

Areas for future development include increasing the simulator functionality by incorporating new components and devices in order to increase the number of practical sessions that can be accomplished with the program. For example:

- Diodes and a transistor to obtain its characteristic curves
- A Chronometer to perform capacitor charge and discharge with a large time constant, by measuring the potential difference with a multimeter as a function of time
- The inclusion of a variable resistance in order to perform a practical session of Wheatstone's bridge, where an unknown electrical resistance is measured by balancing two legs of a bridge circuit

In addition, we are planning to migrate the virtual laboratory to a client-service architecture in order to create a remote laboratory. The idea is to prepare a connection board with real components and devices, thereby producing desirable connections through the use of commutators. Subsequently, the student would be able to set-up the circuit via the web interface of the virtual laboratory. Hence, instead of simulating the circuit, this could be carried out on the connection board with the help of commutators. Therefore, the devices would perform real measurements which would be accessible to students through a web interface.

ACKNOWLEDGMENT

The support of the Institute of Education Sciences of the Polytechnic University of Valencia through project numbers PID 10.041, PID 13.085 and PAEEES 04-030 is gratefully acknowledged. We would also like to acknowledge the valuable discussions with Professor Lenin Lemus Zúñiga of the Department of Systems Data Processing and Computers at the Polytechnic University of Valencia, and the authors of Virtual Scope (J.V. Benlloch Dualde et al.,) for allowing us to integrate the Virtual Scope into the Virtual Laboratory. We would like to thank the R&D+i Linguistic Assistance Office at the Universidad Politécnica de Valencia for their help in revising and correcting this paper.

REFERENCES

Ascione, I. (2006). A Grid computing based virtual laboratory for environmental simulations. *Euro-Par 2006 Parallel Processing* (. *LNCS, 4128*, 1085–1094.

Benlloch Dualde, J. V., et al. (2002). *Osciloscopio Virtual*. Retrieved from http://www.eui.upv.es/ineit mucon/Applets/Scope Osciloscopio.html

Butz, B. P., Duarte, M., & Miller, S. M. (2006). An intelligent tutoring system for circuit analysis. *IEEE Transactions on Education, 49*(2), 216–223. doi:10.1109/TE.2006.872407

Chang, G. W. (2005). Teaching photonics laboratory using remote-control web technologies. *IEEE Transactions on Education, 48*(4), 642–651. doi:10.1109/TE.2005.850716

Faculty of Computer Science. (2007). Retrieved from http://www.fiv.upv.es/default_i.htm

Gao, Y. (2005). Java-Powered Virtual Laboratories for Earthquake Engineering Education. *Computer Applications in Engineering Education, 13*(3), 200–212. doi:10.1002/cae.20050

Gómez Tejedor, J. A., et al. (2002). Laboratorio virtual. In *Proceedings of I Jornadas de Innovación Educativa. Metodologías activas y educación* (pp. 559-564). Institute of Education Sciences and the Vice-rectorate for Academic Organisation and Teaching Staff of the Polytechnic University of Valencia.

Gómez Tejedor, J. A., et al. (2003). *Prácticas de Fundamentos Físicos de la Informática: Facultad de Informática*. Polytechnic University of Valencia.

Gómez Tejedor, J. A., Barros Vidaurre, C., & Moltó Martínez, G. (2005). Laboratorio virtual. In *Proceedings of the "IV Jornadas de Didáctica de la física, III Encuentros de Investigación"* (pp. 197-202). Polytechnic University of Valencia.

Gómez Tejedor, J. A., Barros Vidaurre, C., & Moltó Martínez, G. (2007). Laboratorio virtual. Retrieved from http://personales.upv.es/jogomez/labvir

Hashemi, J., Chandrashekar, N., & Anderson, E. E. (2006). Design and development of an interactive Web-based environment for measurement of hardness in metals: A distance learning tool. *International Journal of Engineering Education, 22*(5), 993–1002.

Hoffman, C. M. (1994). Soft lab - a virtual laboratory for computational science. *Mathematics and Computers in Simulation, 36*(4-6), 479–491. doi:10.1016/0378-4754(94)90080-9

HTS of Applied Computer Science. (2007). Retrieved from http://www.ei.upv.es/webei/english/in_english/in_english.php

Jou, M., & Zhang, H. W. (2006). Interactive web-based learning system for manufacturing technology education. *Progress on Advanced Manufacture for Micro/Nano Technology 2005, Parts 1 and 2, Materials Science Forum* (pp. 505-507; 1111-1116).

Lawson, E. A., & Stackpole, W. (2006). Does a virtual networking laboratory result in similar student achievement and satisfaction? *Conference On Information Technology Education* (pp. 105-114).

Llinares, J., & Page, A. (1987). *Curso de Física Aplicada. Electromagnetismo y semiconductores.* Polytechnic University of Valencia.

Mas, J., et al. (2002). Una experiencia sobre enseñanza distancia de asignaturas básicas de primer curso. In *Proceedings of the I Jornadas de Innovación Educativa en la UPV* (pp. 705-711).

Moure, M. J. (2004). Virtual Laboratory as a Tool to Improve the Effectiveness of Actual Laboratories. *International Journal of Engineering Education, 20*(2), 188–192.

Newman, A. (1996). *Special edition using Java.* Que Cooperation, Indianapolis, IN.

Polytechnic University of Valencia. (2007). Retrieved from http://www.upv.es

Potter, C. (1996). EVAC: A virtual environment for control of remote imaging instrumentation. *IEEE Computer Graphics and Applications, 16*(4), 62–66. doi:10.1109/38.511856

Preis K. (1997) et al. A virtual electromagnetic laboratory for the classroom and the www. *IEEE Transactions on Magnetics, 33*(2), 1990-1993, Part 2.

Sancho, P. (2006). A blended learning experience for teaching microbiology. *American Journal of Pharmaceutical Education, 70*(5), 120.

Sartorius, A. R. S. (2006). Virtual and remote laboratory for robot manipulator control study. *International Journal of Engineering Education, 22*(4), 702–710.

Sun Microsystems. (2007). *Java Plugin.* Retrieved from http://java.sun.com/products/plugin/

Yang, O. Y. (2005). ECVlab: A web-based virtual laboratory system for electronic circuit simulation. *Computational Science - ICCS 2005, pt 1 LNCS, 3514*, 1027–1034.

Zwillinger, D. (2003). Standard CRC Mathematical Tables and Formulae (31st ed.). Chapman & Hall/CRC Press LLC.

Chapter 8
A Case Study on Scaffolding Adaptive Feedback within Virtual Learning Environments

Mehdi Najjar
Interdisciplinary Research Center on Emerging Technologies, University of Montreal, Canada

ABSTRACT

Despite a growing development of virtual laboratories which use the advantages of multimedia and the Internet for distance education, learning by means of such tutorial tools would be more effective if they were specifically tailored to each student needs. The virtual teaching process would be well adapted if an artificial tutor (integrated into the lab) could identify the correct acquired knowledge. The training approach could be more personalised if the tutor is also able to recognise the erroneous learner's knowledge and to suggest a suitable sequence of pedagogical activities to improve significantly the level of the student. This chapter proposes a knowledge representation model which judiciously serves the remediation process to students' errors during learning activities via a virtual laboratory. The chapter also presents a domain knowledge generator authoring tool which attempts to offer a user-friendly environment that allows modelling graphically any subject-matter domain knowledge according to the proposed knowledge representation and remediation approach. The model is inspired by artificial intelligence research on the computational representation of the knowledge and by cognitive psychology theories that provide a fine description of the human memory subsystems and offer a refined modelling of the human learning processes. Experimental results, obtained thanks to practical tests, show that the knowledge representation and remediation model facilitates the planning of a tailored sequence of feedbacks that considerably help the learner.

DOI: 10.4018/978-1-60566-934-2.ch008

INTRODUCTION

Virtual laboratory-based learning is likely to have a profound impact on the whole area of education by affecting the way we learn, what we know and where we acquire knowledge. In the educational community a large amount of enthusiasm has been engendered for highly interactive virtual laboratories, exploiting the multimedia features and the web advantages for a remote teaching purpose and which behave according to laws and constraints of subject-matter domains, permitting the student to experience the nature of those domains through free/guided exploration or scaffolding adaptive learning.

The original notion of scaffolding assumed that a more knowledgeable tutor helps an individual learner, providing him/her with exactly the help s/he needs to move forward. A key element of scaffolding is that the tutor provides appropriate support based on an ongoing diagnosis of the learner's current level of understanding. This requires that the tutor should not only have a thorough knowledge of the task and its components, the subgoals that need to be accomplished, but should also have knowledge of the student's capabilities that change as the instruction progresses.

Considerable success has been achieved in the development of software scaffolding that has been employed within interactive learning environments and virtual labs to offer a means of enabling learners to achieve success beyond their own independent ability (Hammerton & Luckin, 2001). Jackson et al. (1996) showed that an approach which attempts to design adaptable learning environments which offer learners guidance and tools to make decisions for themselves also should address the importance of maintaining the fine balance between system guidance and learner control. However, evidence from other researches into learners' use of scaffolding assistance has indicated that less able and knowledgeable learners are ineffective at selecting appropriately challenging tasks and seeking appropriate quantities of support and guidance (Luckin & du Boulay, 1999; Wood, 1999). This led, among others, to explore the way that Vygotsky's Zone of Proximal Development (Vygotsky, 1986) can be use in the design of learner models.

To provide appropriately challenging activities and the right quantity and quality of assistance, du Boulay, Luckin & del Soldato (1999) have presented a categorisation which suggest three principled methodologies for developing teaching expertise in artificial tutoring. First is the Socratic tutoring that provides a number of detailed teaching tactics for eliciting from and then confronting a learner with her/his misconceptions in some domain. The second methodology is the contingent teaching which aims to maintain a learner's agency in a learning interaction by providing only sufficient assistance at any point to enable her/him to make progress on the task. The third methodology is an amalgam of the above two. This builds a computational model of the learner and derives a teaching strategy by observing the learner's response to deferent teaching prompts selected with regards to the model. Scaffolding in the form of prompts to help students reflect and articulate has been developed under different types, either by varying the activities according to their difficulty or content of the task (Bell & Davis, 1996; Jackson et al., 1998; Puntambekar & Kolodner, 2005; Luckin & Hammerton, 2002).

Furthermore, it is a generally held position that the process of learning will improve when learners are given virtual tutoring that allow for interactive access tuned to the specific needs of each individual learner. If we aim to develop virtual laboratories in complex domains which are equipped with tutorial strategies able to interact with learners having various levels of intelligence and different abilities of knowledge acquisition, then understanding the human learning mechanism and the manner of structuring and handling knowledge in the course of this process is a fundamental task.

Recent multidisciplinary researches (Wang, 2003; Wang et al., 2003; Wang & Wang, 2006; Wang & Kinsner, 2006) – that study processes of the brain and that investigate how human beings acquire, interpret and express knowledge by using the memory and the mind – lead to seriously consider the idea to adopt a memory-based approach which perceives the memory as the foundation for any kind of intelligence. Incontestably, representing the acquired/handled knowledge of students during learning constitutes a real challenge. One solution to the outcome issues expressed above could be offered thanks to the adoption of a cognitive, computational and human memory-based knowledge representation approach that (1) formalise the structuring of the domain knowledge which is handled and/or acquired by students during learning activities via virtual labs and (2) represent accurately the cognitive activity (in term of knowledge processes) of each learner.

This chapter describes a computational model of knowledge representation which judiciously serves the remediation process to students' errors during learning activities via a virtual laboratory (VL). The approach is based on a learner model-based tutoring methodology with the aim of scaffolding feedbacks according to a student model and of providing adapted teaching prompts to help the learner. This approach of knowledge representation and reasoning is inspired by artificial intelligence researches on the computational modelling of the knowledge and by cognitive theories which offer a fine modelling of the human learning processes. The reminder of the chapter is organised as follows. First, the computational model of knowledge representation, theoretically based on the human memory (HM) subsystems and on theirs processes, is expounded. Second, the principle of errors' personalised remediation is described and its experimental validation is presented. The fourth section presents a domain knowledge generator authoring tool which attempts to offer a user-friendly environment that allows modelling graphically any subject-matter domain knowledge according to the proposed knowledge representation and remediation approach. The fifth section discusses some originalities of the approach. Finally, by way of conclusion, the current work is briefly mentioned.

THE HUMAN MEMORY-BASED COMPUTATIONAL MODEL

If we are interested in education and teaching, and have the ambition to endow an artificial system with competence in those fields, it is not possible to be unaware of all that concerns training, cognition and memory. The latter is one of the most enthralling properties of the human brain. If it is quite true that it governs the essence of our daily activities, it also builds the identity, the knowledge, the intelligence and the affectivity of human being (Baddeley, 1990). Rather than being a simple hardware device of data storage (as in the computer's case), the principal characteristic of this memory is carrying out categorisation, generalisation and abstraction processes (Gagné et al., 1992). However, if the human memory has its extraordinary faculties of conservation, it sometimes happens to us to forget. This phenomenon occurs when information did not undergo suitable treatment. Indeed, the organisation process is essential in the success of the mechanism of recall. In other words, chances to find a recollection (a fact in the memory) depend on the specificity of elements with which it has been linked. Those facts can be acquired explicitly (for example, we can acquire them by speech). They correspond to an explicit memory called declarative memory (whose contents in knowledge are declarative, according to the AI paradigm). Moreover, our practice and *savoir-faire* are largely implicit. They are acquired by repetitive exercises rather than consciously. They correspond to an implicit memory called procedural memory. Whereas the latter is mainly made up of procedures acquired by practice, declarative memory can be subdivided in several types such as, semantic memory and episodic memory.

Different approaches in cognitive psychology propose various sets of knowledge representation structures. Nevertheless, these sets are not necessary compatible. Depending on authors, the semantic memory is sometimes called "declarative memory" and it may contain an episodic memory (Anderson & Ross, 1980). The episodic/semantic distinction debate was open during many decades. Sophisticated experiments (Herrmann & Harwood, 1980; Tulving, 1983) tried to show that the two memory subsystems are functionally separate. Other surveys were against the distinction between them (Anderson & Ross, 1980). Recent neurological research (Shastri, 2002) proved that the episodic memory is distinct, by its neuronal characteristics, from the semantic memory. However, it seems that at least there is significant overlap between the two memories, even if they are functionally different (Neely, 1989).

Basically, it has been argued that knowledge is encoded in various memory subsystems not according to their contents but according to the way in which these contents are handled and used, making the memory a large set of complex processes and modules in continual interactions (Baddeley, 1990). These subsystems are mainly divided in three main sections presenting – each one – a particular type of knowledge: (1) semantic knowledge (Neely 1989), (2) procedural knowledge (Anderson, 1993) and (3) episodic knowledge (Tulving, 1983). Although there is neither consensus on the number of the subsystems nor on their organisation, the majority of the authors in psychology mentions – in some form or in another – these three types of knowledge.

The Semantic Knowledge Representation

The knowledge representation approach regards semantic knowledge as concepts taken in a broad sense. Thus, they can be any category of objects. Moreover, concepts are subdivided in two categories: primitive concepts and described concepts. The first is defined as a syntactically non-split representation; i.e., primitive concept representation can not be divided into parts. For example, in propositional calculus, symbols "a" and "b" of the expression "(a & b)" are non-split representations of the corresponding proposals. On the other hand, described concept is defined as a syntactically decomposable representation. For example, the expression "(a & F)" is a decomposable representation that represents a conjunction between proposal "a" and the truth constant "False" (two primitive concepts). Symbol "&" represents the conjunction logic operator (AND) and is a primitive concept. In this way, the semantic of a described concept is given by the semantics of its components and their relations (which take those components as arguments to create the described concept). Thus, it would be possible to combine primitive or described concepts to represent any other described concept.

The Procedural Knowledge Representation

The procedural memory subsystem serves to automate problem solving processes by decreasing the quantity of handled information and the time of resolutions (Sweller, 1988). In opposition to semantic knowledge, which can be expressed explicitly, procedural knowledge becomes apparent by a succession of actions achieved automatically – following internal and/or external stimuli perception – to reach desirable states. A procedure is a mean of satisfying needs without using the attention resources. For example, procedural knowledge enables us to recognise words in a text, to write by means of the keyboard, to drive a car or to add mechanically "42 + 11" without being obliged to recall the algorithm explicitly, i.e., making mentally the sum of the units, the one of the tens and twinning the two preceding sums. Performing automatically the addition of "42" and "11" can be seen as procedural knowledge which was acquired by the repetitive doing. This automation – via the use of procedures – reduces the cognitive complexity of problems solving. In its absence, the entire set of semantic knowledge must be interpreted in order to extract relevant knowledge, able to specify real or cognitive actions that are necessary to achieve the task. In that case, the semantic knowledge interpretation often lies beyond of the numerical capacities. This surpassing is one of the most frequent causes of student's errors during the resolution of problems (Sweller, 1988). However, a procedure can be transformed into semantic knowledge by means of reification. For example, a teacher who explains the sequence of actions to solve a problem reifies the corresponding procedure. Nevertheless, these two types of knowledge (semantics and procedural) can coexist, since automation is not made instantaneously. It is done rather in the course of time and with the frequency of use (Anderson, 1993). In the proposed approach, procedures are subdivided in two main categories: primitive procedures and complex procedures. Executions of the first are seen as atomic actions. Those of the last can be done by sequences of actions, which satisfy scripts of goals. Each one of those actions results from a primitive or complex procedure execution; and each one of those goals is perceived as an intention of the student cognitive system.

The Episodic Knowledge Representation

The episodic memory retains details about our experiences and preserves temporal relations allowing reconstruction of previously experienced events as well as the time and context in which they took place (Tulving, 1983). Note that the episode, seen as a specific form of knowledge, has been extensively used in various approaches in a wide variety of research domains, such as modelling cognitive mechanisms of analogy-making (Kokinov & Petrov, 2000), artificial intelligence planning (Garagnani et al. 2002), student modelling within ITS (Weber & Brusilovsky, 2001) and neuro-computing (Shastri, 2002). In the proposed approach, the episode representation is based on instantiation of goals. These are seen as generic statements retrieved from semantic memory. Whereas the latter contains information about classes of instances (concepts), the episodic memory contains statements about instances of concepts (cognitions). As the episodic knowledge is organised according to goals, each episode specifies a goal that translates an intention and gives a sense to the underlying events and actions. If the goal realisation requires the execution of a complex procedure, formed by a set of "n" actions, then the goal will be composed of "n" subgoals whose realisation will be stored in "n" sub-episodes. Thus, executions of procedures are encoded in episodic memory and each goal realisation is explicitly encoded in an episode. In this way, the episodic memory of a student model can store all facts during a learning activity.

The Explicit Representation of Goals

In theory, a goal can be described using a relation as follows: (R X, A1, A2, .. An). This relation (R) allows to specify goal "X" according to primitive or described concepts "A1, A2, .. An" which characterise the initial state. Nevertheless, in practice, the stress is often laid on methods to achieve the goal rather than the goal itself; since these methods are, in general, the object of practising. Consequently, the term "goal" is used to refer to an intention to achieve the goal rather than meaning the goal itself. Thus, procedures become methods carrying out this intention, which is noted "R (A1 A2.. An)"; and a goal can be seen as a generic function where the procedures play the role of methods. To underline the intention idea, the expression representing "R" is an action verb. For example, the goal "reduce (F & T)" means the intention to simplify the conjunction of the truth constant "False" with the truth constant "True".

THE ERRORS REMEDIATION PRINCIPLE

When interacting with a VL during the problem solving activities, and when a learner makes an error, satisfying the goal that s/he wished to accomplish was realised by means of an erroneous procedure. This error results from bad interpretation of the situation, causing a choice of procedure which (i) can be correct but whose application cannot be done in the current context or (ii) is invented and completely false. The procedure is regarded as erroneous if the final result obtained by the learner is different from that of the tutor. In this case, the procedure will be labelled (within an episode in which the erroneous result is stored) as a "procedure-error" which has a unique identifier and which will lead to formulate a set of valid procedures that the learner should have used to achieve the goal. At this stage, learning and mastering these correct procedures will be one of the immediate objectives of the tutorial strategy. More precisely, as the episode containing the "procedure-error" comprises an instance of the goal, a set of valid procedures which satisfy it will be deduced starting from the goal prototype. The valid procedures contain the didactic resources necessary to teach their usage. In the case that those procedures are complex, each procedure specifies a set of subgoals whose each one contains its own set of valid procedures. In this recursive way, the tutor easily conceives an ordered sequence of valid procedures allowing the correct accomplishment of any goal. Particularly, those for which the learner has failed.

EXPERIMENTAL VALIDATION

"Red-Bool" is a virtual laboratory (VL) which presents a problem solving milieu related to the simplification of Boolean expressions by using algebraic reduction rules. These are generally taught to undergraduate students. The goal of the VL is to help students to learn Boolean reduction techniques. Preliminary notions, definitions and explanations (in the "Theory" section) constitute a necessary knowledge background to approach the Boolean reduction problem. This knowledge is organised into sub-sections and is available through exploration via clicking buttons. In the examples section, examples are given. Those are generated randomly with variable degree of difficulty chosen by the learner. Students can also enter, by means of a visual keyboard, any Boolean expression they want and ask the system to solve it. The problem solving steps and the applied rules are shown on a blackboard. Examples show optimal solutions to simplify expressions and are provided to guide learner during the problem solving, which begins by clicking on the exercise button, allowing to access to the corresponding section. In this latter – and via the visual keyboard – students reduce a randomly generated or a specifically shaped (by the tutor) Boolean expression by choosing suitable simplification rules to apply in the order they want. Figure 1 shows the resolution steps made by a student (Marie) to reduce an expression. Although various tutorial strategies are to be considered, the choice fell on the "Cognitive Tutor" strategy (Anderson et al., 1995), implemented within several intelligent tutoring systems and which its effectiveness has been largely proven (Aleven & Koedinger, 2002; Corbett et al., 2000). Consequently, in the case of erroneous rule choice (or application) on any of the sub-expressions forming the initial given expression, the system notifies the learner and shows her/him – in the "advices" window – (i) the selected sub-expression, (ii) the applied rule to reduce it, (iii) the resulted simplified sub-expression and (iv) the current state of the global expression. If there were mistakes, then at the end of each exercise, the tutor proposes to the student a related example or suggests to her/him to solve another exercise. In this last case, the Boolean expression suggested to reduce is considered as a personalised feedback with regards to the made errors.

Figure 1. The problem solving steps made by Marie to simplify the given expression

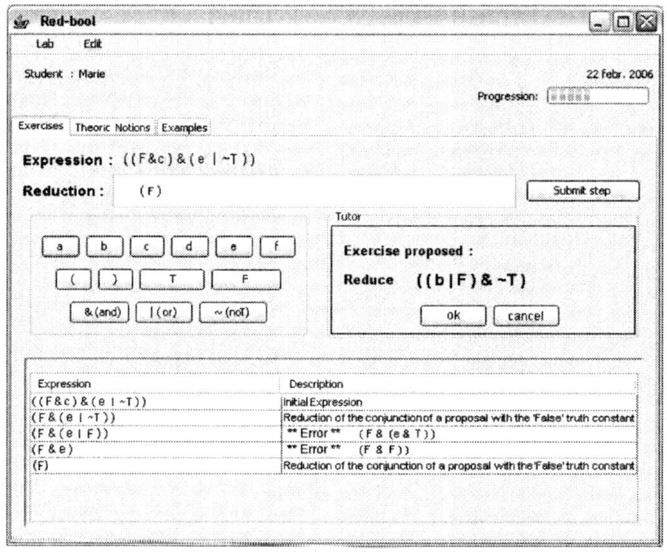

Students in mathematics who attend the courses "MAT-113" or "MAT-114" dedicated to logic calculus and discrete math were asked to practice the reduction of Boolean expressions using "Red-Bool". By this experiment, the interest was to record the resolution's traces of each learner during problems solving tasks (in the "exercises" section) in order to evaluate the aptitude of the feedbacks' model to enlighten the tutor when making tutorial decisions. Data and parameters of this experiment are reported in Table 1.

Figure 2 illustrates the exponential evolution of the errors made by students with regard to the complexity of the exercises offered by the tutor. The probability of having distinct errors' types is highly conceivable as the complexity raises.

According to the proposed theoretical approach described above, each step in a learner's resolution process (during a solving task) corresponds to a transition realisable by means of primitive or complex procedure which was applied to satisfy a goal or a subgoal. This procedure handles primitive and/or described concepts such as rules, proposals, logical operators and truth constants. For each student and each exercise made, the system deduces (starting from the low-level observations sent by the graphical interface of the VL) the procedures used as well as the instances of knowledge created and handled. Since a procedure is generally called to achieve a goal, the collected data allows deduction of goals (and their subgoals) formulated during the Boolean reduction process. At the end of the exercise, the system saves the trace of the resolution in an "episodic" XML file which serves for the errors' analysis. For example, let's consider the case of John who tried to reduce the expression "(a & ~T)" by (1) applying the simplification rule of the "True" truth constant negation which substitutes "(~T)" by "(F)" transforming "(a & ~T)" into "(a & F)" and (2) changing the resulted expression into "(a)". Here, John makes a mistake. Theoretically, the reduction of "(a & F)" is correctly made by applying the conjunction

Table 1. Main parameters of the experiment

Complexity	1	2	3	4	5
Number of exercises	4	4	5	6	6
Number of stuents	10	10	10	10	10

Figure 2. The Complexity vs. Errors diagrams

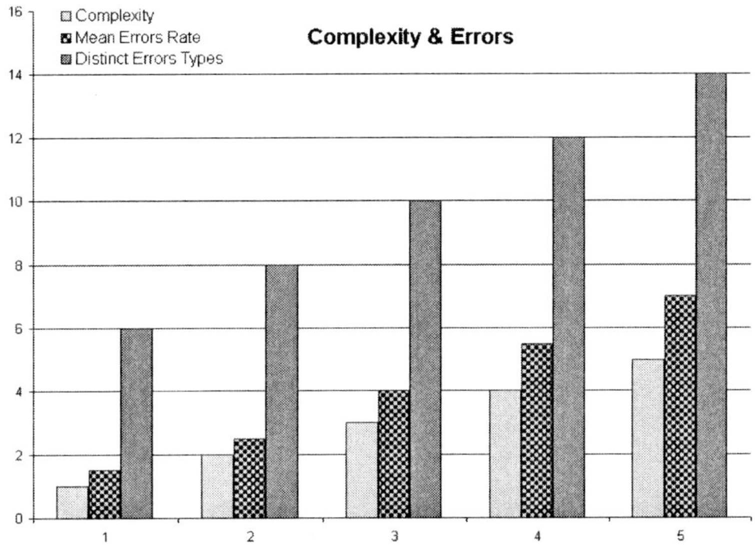

rule of a proposal with the "False" truth constant (p & F → F, where p is a proposal) which results in transforming "(a & F)" into "(F)". In this case, the main goal "reduce (a & ~T)" was achieved by a complex procedure giving rise to two subgoals: (1) "substitute (~T ; F)", which was achieved by the primitive procedure "P_SubNegTrue" calling the substitution rule of the "True" truth constant negation; and (2) "reduce (a & F)" which was achieved by a procedure calling an unknown erroneous rule (noted in figure 3 and figure 4 by Dx#4) unseated of the primitive procedure "P_ReduceConjunctionFalse" which call the conjunction rule of a proposal with the "F" truth constant. Figure 3 illustrates the episodic history related to this exercise. "Episode1" reflects the main goal realisation which was split into two sub-events: "Episode2" and "Episode3". The

Figure 3. A part of the John's episodic history related to the reduction of the expression "(a & ~T)"

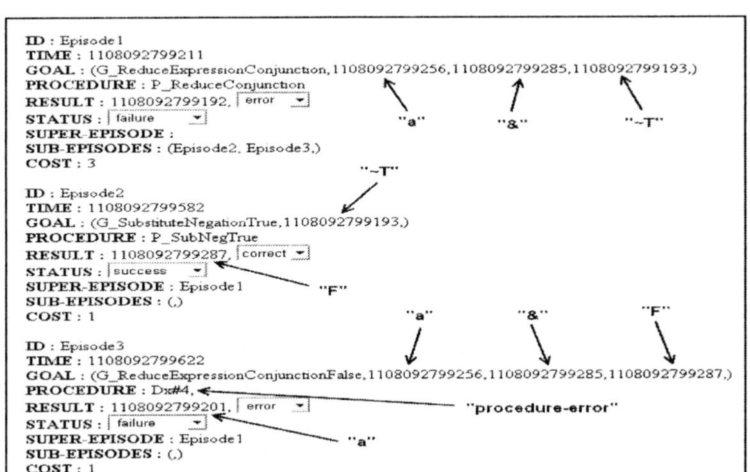

Figure 4. Some slots of the goal "G_ReduceExpressionCunjonctionFalse"

ID : RedBoolLab.xmltools.content.B_125487996
NAME : G_ReduceExpressionConjunctionFalse
DESCRIPTION :
The goal to reduce the conjunction of an expression with the truth constant "False".
AUTHOR : Mehdi Najjar
TYPE : concept décrit
GOALS : add prototype_but
SUPER-CONCEPTS : ca.usherbrooke.astus.knowledgebase.standardknowledge.Goal,
SUB-CONCEPTS : add idconcept
CONSTRUCTOR : CGoal_ReduceExpressionConjunction_False,
COMPONENTS : add comp
TEACHING :
add facettes_fct GOAL SLOTS :
SKILL : The capability to reduce correclty the conjunction of an expression with the truth constant "False".
PARAMETERS : ca.usherbrooke.astus.knowledgebase.standardknowledge.Expression_Abstract,
ca.usherbrooke.astus.knowledgebase.standardknowledge.Operator_Logic,
ca.usherbrooke.astus.knowledgebase.standardknowledge.Constant_False,
PROCEDURES : (P_ReduceConjunctionFalse, Dx#4),
DIDACTIC STRATEGY : (RedBoolLab.Goals.Strategies.STR#1, RedBoolLab.Goals.Strategies.STR#2),

former represents the substitution of the "True" truth constant negation and the latter corresponds to the "(a & F)" erroneous simplification. Figure 4 shows the slots' content of the goal "G_Reduce-ExpressionConjunctionFalse" that John attempts erroneously to achieve.

The analysis of errors consists in (1) scanning the content of the XML file to research the errors occurred during the reduction of the expression and, for each detected error, (2) identifying a valid procedure ("P_valid") allowing to achieve the student goal and which could have been used instead of the erroneous procedure ("P_error"). The identification of a correct procedure – which makes use of Boolean reduction rules – is made thanks to a second XML file that contains the domain knowledge. In that case, the tutor proposes to the learner a new Boolean expression ("Expr_FBack") that the simplification will (in theory) make use of "P_valid". In this sense, "Expr_FBack" can be seen as a personalised remediation following the occurrence of "P_error".

The Individualised Feedback Generation Process

The slot "exercises" defined in the structure of the valid procedure includes a script containing dynamic (not predefined) didactic resources. i.e., a generic model of exercises. In order to propose an exercise to resolve, the generic model specifies a sequence of goals which are of the type "G_build". The type "G_build" enables to create (1) a primitive object (concept) starting from its class or (2) a complex object starting from the classes of its components. Arguments of each goal of the type "G_build" are formulated starting from clues discovered in the episodic XML file. In other words, the structure of the episodic memory permits to the tutor to find, thanks to the erroneous procedures, the episodes in which errors have occurred. These episodes contain indices which are taken as parameters by the goal of the type "G_build"; and thus, which are useful to scaffold an exercise with regards to the generic model. For example, and as shown in Figure 1 which illustrates the steps made by Marie to reduce the expression "((F & c) & (e | ~T)), the student deals firstly with the sub-expression "(F & c)" and applies the conjunction rule of a proposal with the "False" truth constant to obtain "(F)". At step 2, she simplifies the sub-expression "(~T)" to "(T)". Here, Marie makes a mistake. Theoretically, the reduction of "(~T)" is correctly made by applying the negation rule of the "True" truth constant. At step 3, another error was made when Marie simplifies the sub-expression "(e | F)" to "(F)". The reduction of "(e | F)" is correctly made by applying the disjunction rule of a proposal with the "F" truth constant (p | F → p, where p is a proposal), which results in transforming the sub-expression into "(e)", not into "(F)". At the last step, Marie applies the conjunction rule of a proposal with the "False" truth constant to reduce "(F & e)" into "(F)".

At the end of the exercise, and in consequence with the two made errors, the objective of the tutorial strategy is to teach Marie (1) the use of the simplification rules of the negation of a truth constant and (2) the application of the reduction rule of the disjunction of a proposal with the "False" truth constant. To this end, the generic model of the didactic resources of each valid procedure which allows achieving a failed goal (i.e., the intention to simplify the negation of the "True" truth constant or that to reduce the disjunction of a proposal with the "False" truth constant) is requested to scaffold an exercise that will be proposed – to the learner – as a tailored feedback. To remedy her two gaps, the tutor proposes to Marie to practice the simplification of the expression "((b | F) & ~T)". This one is formulated starting from the scripts of the slots "exercises" of the procedures "P_Apply_ReductionNegation_True" and "P_ReduceExpressionDisjonction". Figure 5 shows some slots of the latter which simplifies the disjunction of a proposal with the "False" truth constant. For example, Table 2 comprises feedbacks generated following the resolution of the expression "(((F | c) & (E & ~V)) & (~a | ~F))" which was given as exercise to all students. Because of the difference of the made errors, feedbacks (provided in terms of suggested exercises) are dissimilar.

Figure 6 shows diagrams illustrating dissimilar feedbacks (mean of generated feedbacks following the resolution of a same expression by all students) in relation to the complexity of exercises. Figure 7 shows the students improvement brought about the proposed feedbacks.

Figure 5. Some slots of the procedure "P_ReduceExpressionDisjonction"

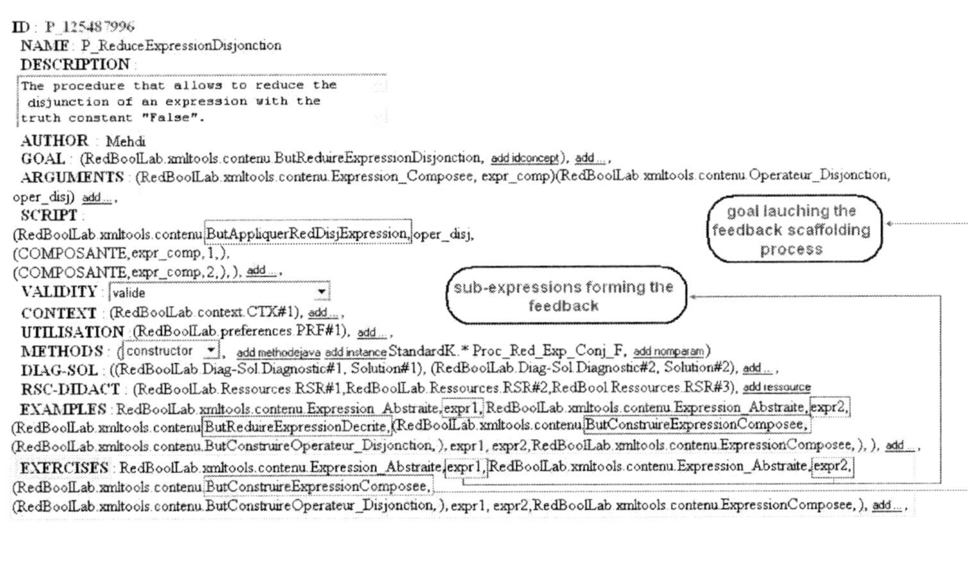

Table 2. Generated feedbacks following the resolution of a same expression

Expression:	(((F|c)&(e&~T))&(~a|~F))
Feedback:	Proposed Exercise
1	((T&d)&(~T&(T|a)))
2	(~F & (c & F))
3	(~F & ((T | e) | (F & F)))
4	((c | T)&~T)
5	((~F)&(~T))
6	((F & ~a) & (T & (b|F)))

THE AUTHORING TOOL

A domain knowledge generator authoring tool has been designed. It attempts to offer a user-friendly environment that allows to model graphically any subject-matter domain knowledge (according to the proposed knowledge representation approach) and to transpose it automatically into related XML files. Those are generated to serve as a knowledge support for a tutor reasoning purpose. The authoring tool eases representing and modeling the knowledge by experts without the obligation of high capabilities in computer science at their disposal (for example, the mastery of specification (e.g., UML) and/or programming languages). This section uses the description of the authoring tool environment (1) to point out (to the reader) in minute detail the various knowledge representation structures proposed by the theory and (2) to highlight the ergonomic aspect of the assisted modelling.

The Graphical Part

The left-hand side of the environment consists of a drawing pane where the various types of knowledge can be represented. Concepts and cognitions are represented by triangles. As mentioned, cognitions are concrete instances of concepts and are taken as parameters by goals which pass them to procedures (that achieve goals). Procedures are represented by circles and goals by squares. Abstract concepts and abstract goals are delimited by dashed contours. These abstract objects stand for categories of similar knowledge entities. Thus, they don't have any concrete instances. Complex procedures and described concepts are delimited by bold contours.

Figure 6. Dissimilar feedbacks of a same expression

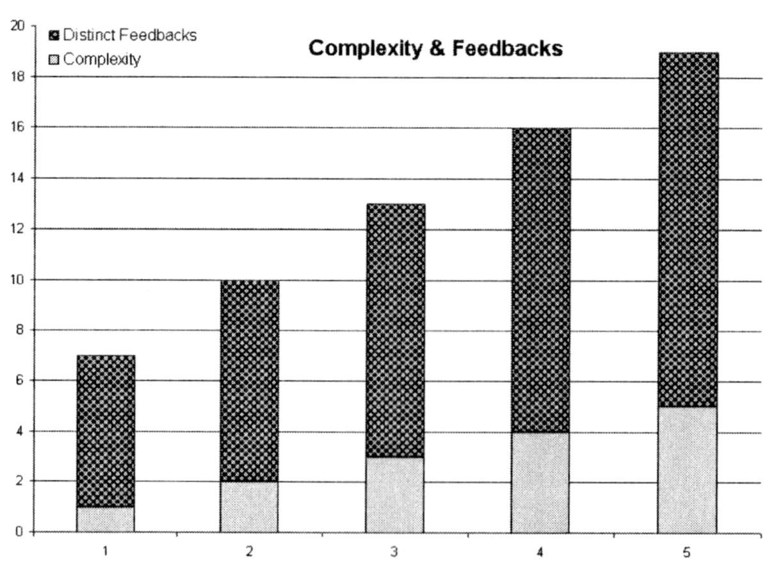

Figure 7. Improvement brought about the tutor intervention

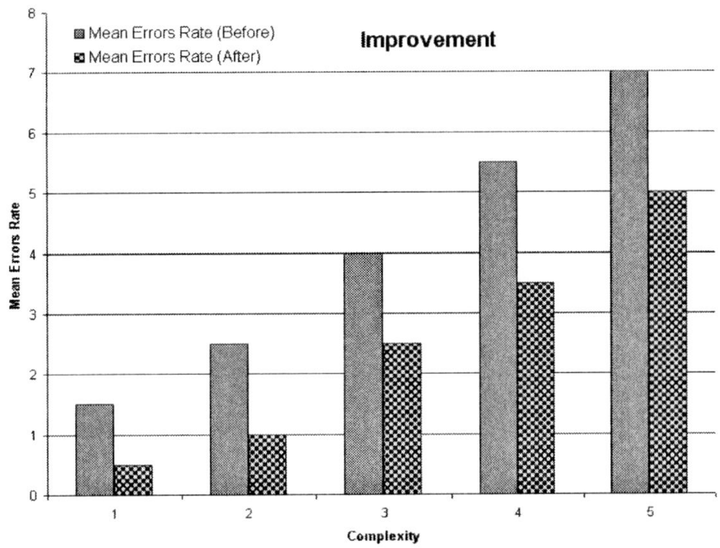

The structural model offers two types of diagrams: procedural diagrams and conceptual diagrams. The former contain (1) specification links connecting a complex procedure to all subgoals that it specifies, (2) satisfaction links associating a goal with all the procedures which attempt to achieve it, and – optionally – (3) handling links involving a goal and its handled cognitions. Figure 8 shows a general view of the authoring tool environment in which a procedural diagram defines that the goal "reduce (F & T)" (a specification of the abstract goal "reduce_Expression-Conjunction") can be achieved by means of two procedures: "AppRedConjTrue" and "AppRedConjFalse". The former is the procedure that applies the reduction rule of a conjunction with the "True" truth constant. The latter reduces conjunctions of expressions with the "False" truth constant. The diagram also defines that the goal "reduce (F & T)" handles three cognitions: "cst_t", "cst_f" and "oper_and". The first is a concrete instance of the concept "Constant_True", the second is of the concept type "Constant_False" and the third is an instance of the concept "Operator_Conjunction".

Conceptual diagrams specify hierarchical links ("is-a") and aggregation links ("part-of") between primitive and/or described concepts of the domain knowledge. Figure 6 illustrates that concepts "Constant_False" and "Constant_True" are specifications of the primitive concept "Truth_ Constant" which inherits from the abstract concept "Object" and the latter is a specification of the primitive concept "Logical_ Operator", also a sub-concept of "Object".

The Data Specification Part

The right-hand side of the environment permits to author(s) to specify detailed information about the knowledge entities. This information is organised in slots (see figure 8 and figure 9). The first four slots of a concept are metadata that provide general information about the concept. The "Identifier" slot is a character string used as a unique reference to the concept, "Name" contains the concept name (as it is presented to the learner), "Description" specifies its textual description and "Author" refers to its creator. The remaining slots are specific concept data. "Type" indicates the concept type

Figure 8. A general view of the authoring tool environment

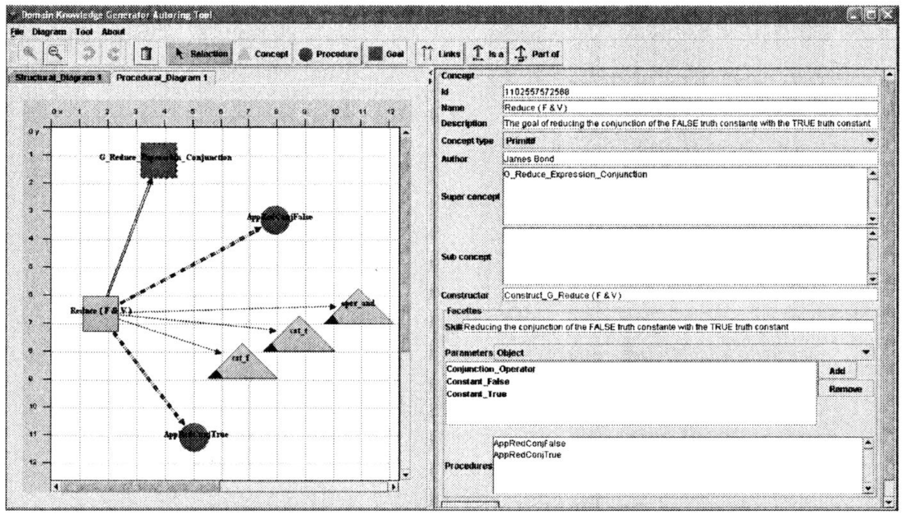

which can be either primitive or described. The "Goals" slot contains a goals prototypes list. The latter provides information about goals that students could have and which use the concept. While "Super-concepts" contains the list of concepts from which the concept inherits, "Sub-concepts" contains the list of concepts which inherit from that concept. This notion of inheritance between concepts can be seen as a shortcut available to authors to simplify modelling, but should not be regarded as a way to model the organisation of concepts in the semantic memory. The organisation of the latter that is currently accepted by the majority of psychologists is the Collins and Loftus model of spreading activation (Collins & Loftus, 1975) which states that inheritance links are a particular form of semantic knowledge that can be acquired and encoded as concepts.

Figure 9. An example of a conceptual diagram

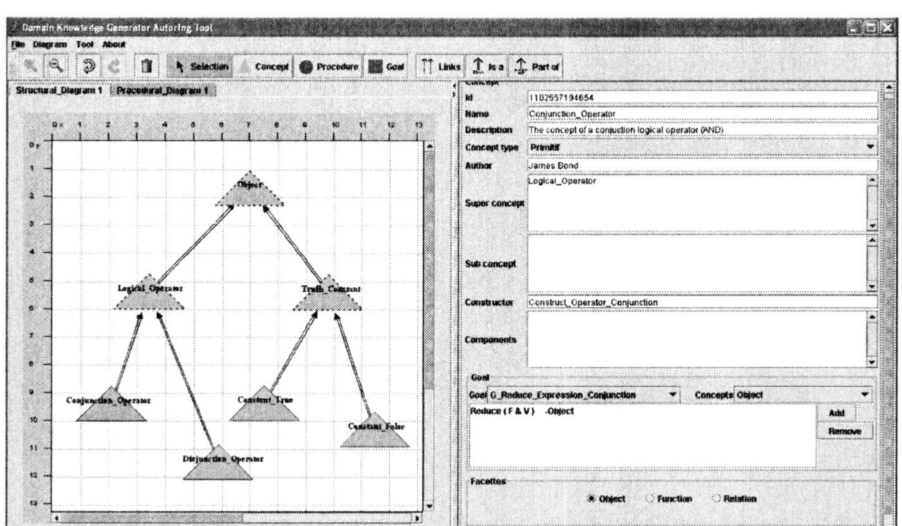

The "Components" slot is only significant for described concepts. It indicates, for each concept component, its concept type. Finally, "Teaching" points to some didactic resources which can be used to teach the concept.

Goals have four specific slots (in addition to all the concept's slots). "Skill" describes the necessary skill to accomplish the goal, "Parameters" indicates the types of its parameters, "Procedures" contains a set of procedures which can be used to attain it and "Didactic-Strategies" suggests strategies to teach how to realise that goal. Other than the metadata slots where "Description", "Author" and "Name" are slots identical to those of concepts and goals, each procedure is characterised by its specific data. The "Goal" slot indicates the goal for which the procedure was defined. "Parameters" specifies the concepts type of the arguments. For complex procedures, "Script" indicates a sequence of goals to achieve. For primitive procedures, "Method" points to a Java method that executes an atomic action. "Validity" is a pair of Boolean values. Whereas the first indicates if the procedure is valid and so it always gives the expected result, the second indicates if it always terminate. "Context" fixes constraints on the use of the procedure. "Diagnosis-Solution" contains a list of pairs [diagnosis, strategy] indicating for each diagnosis, the suitable teaching strategy to be adopted. Finally, "Didactic-Resources" points to additional resources (examples, tests, etc.) to teach the procedure.

DISCUSSION

Promising Interdisciplinary researches have proved that it is very beneficial to integrate into the new generation of software the encouraging knowledge that studies of internal information processing mechanisms and processes of the brain have accumulated (Shao & Wang 2003; Wang, 2005). In this sense, it would be advantageous and practical to be inspired by a psychological cognitive approach, which offers a fine modelling of the human process of the knowledge handling, for representing both the learner and the domain knowledge within virtual laboratories. The hypothesis is that the proposed knowledge structures because they are quite similar to those used by human beings, offer a more effective knowledge representation (for example, for a tutoring purpose). In addition, we chose a parsimonious use of cognitive structures suggested by psychology has been chosen to encode knowledge. Indeed, these structures have been divided into two categories: on one hand, semantic and procedural knowledge which is common, potentially accessible and can be shared – with various mastery degrees – by all learners; and, on the other hand, episodic knowledge which is specific for each learner and whose contents depend on the way with which the common knowledge (semantic and procedural) is perceived and handled. More precisely, primitive units of semantic and procedural knowledge – chosen with a small level of granularity – are used to build complex knowledge entities which are dynamically combined in order to represent the learner knowledge. The dynamic aspect is seen in the non-predefined combinations between occurrences of concepts and the applied procedures handling them translating the learner goals. Generally, the complex procedure "P" selected to achieve a given goal "G" determines number and order of subgoals of "G" (whose each one can be achieved, in turn, by a procedure called, in this case, a sub-procedure of "P"). The choice of "P" depends of the learner practices and preferences when s/he achieves the task. This means that goal realisation can be made in various ways, by various scenarios of procedures execution sequences. Therefore, number and chronological order of subgoals of "G" are not predefined. Thus, the learner cognitive activity is not determined systematically, in a static way, starting from her/his main goal. Traces of this cognitive activity during problems solving are stored as specific episodic knowledge. This allows a tutor to scan the episodic knowledge model that the system formulates in its representation of the learner to determine – via reasoning strategies – the degree of mastery of procedural knowledge and/or the acquisition level of semantic knowledge.

Another original aspect of the proposed approach is the explicit introduction of goals into the knowledge representation. Although they are treated by means of procedures, goals are considered as a special case of knowledge that represents intentions behind the actions of the cognitive system. i.e., a goal is seen as a semantic knowledge which describes a state to be reached. The fact that there exists a particular form of energy employed to acquire goals distinguishes them from any standard form of knowledge. This distinction involves a different treatment for goals in the human cognitive architecture (Altman & Trafton, 2002). The proposed approach offers to treat goals explicitly to reify them as particular semantic knowledge which is totally distinct from those which represent objects.

Finally, note that a practical study (Najjar & Mayers, 2007; Najjar et al., 2006) has validate – in the scope of the expressivity and efficiency contexts – a model based on the HM-based computational knowledge representation theory. Here, the interest was on modelling interrupted activities and the interruptions' consequence on the task achievement and the focus was on the cognitive aspects of the designed model in comparison with ACT-R (Anderson, 1993), a famous and widely acknowledged cognitive architecture. The model of interrupted activities has been conceived using the authoring tool.

CONCLUSION

This chapter described an HM-based knowledge representation approach which is inspired by the artificial intelligence research on the computational modelling of the knowledge and by cognitive theories that offers a fine modelling of the human learning processes. The chapter introduced an original principle of personalised remediation to students' errors when interacting with a virtual laboratory which presents a problem solving milieu related to the simplification of Boolean expressions by using algebraic reduction rules. By means of experimental results obtained thanks to practical tests, it was shown that the knowledge representation model facilitates the planning of a tailored sequence of feedbacks that significantly help the learner. Our research group is actually refining the knowledge representation structures – by taking into account pedagogical and didactic knowledge – and setting about new experiments with others teaching domains; such as, teaching heuristic techniques in operational research and teaching the resolution by refutation in the predicate calculus.

ACKNOWLEDGMENT

The author thanks André Mayers for his instructive comments, Philippe Fournier-Viger for his help on the realisation of the "Red-Bool" graphical interface and Jean Hallé for his collaboration on the design of the authoring tool.

REFERENCES

Aleven, V., & Koedinger, K. (2002). An Effective Metacognitive Strategy: Learning by doing and explaining with computer-based Cognitive Tutors. *Cognitive Science*, *26*(2), 147–179.

Altmann, E., & Trafton, J. (2002). Memory for goals: An Activation-Based Model. *Cognitive Science*, *26*, 39–83.

Anderson, J. R. (1993). *Rules of the mind.* Lawrence Erlbaum.

Anderson, J. R., Bothell, D., Byrne, M. D., Douglass, S., Lebiere, C., & Qin, Y. (2004). An integrated theory of the mind. *Psychological Review, 111*(4), 1036–1060. doi:10.1037/0033-295X.111.4.1036

Anderson, J. R., Corbett, A. T., Koedinger, K. R., & Pelletier, R. (1995). Cognitive Tutors: Lessons learned. *Journal of the Learning Sciences, 4*(2), 167–207. doi:10.1207/s15327809jls0402_2

Anderson, J. R., & Ross, B. H. (1980). Evidence against a semantic-episodic distinction. *Journal of Experimental Psychology. Human Learning and Memory, 6*, 441–466. doi:10.1037/0278-7393.6.5.441

Baddeley, A. (1990). *Human Memory: theory and practice*. Hove, UK: Lawrence Erlbaum.

Bell, P., & Davis, E. A. (1996). Designing an Activity in the Knowledge Integration Environment. In *Proceedings of the Annual Meeting of the American Educational Research Association, New York, NY, USA*.

Brusilovsky, P., & Peylo, C. (2003). Adaptive and intelligent Web-based educational systems. *International Journal of AI in Education, 13*(2), 159–172.

Collins, M., & Loftus, F. (1975). A spreading activation theory of semantic processing. *Psychological Review, 82*, 407–428. doi:10.1037/0033-295X.82.6.407

Corbett, A., Mclaughlin, M., & Scarpinatto, K. C. (2000). Modeling Student Knowledge: Cognitive Tutors in High School and College. *Journal of User Modeling and User-Adapted Interaction, 10*, 81–108. doi:10.1023/A:1026505626690

de Rosis, F. (2001). Towards adaptation of interaction to affective factors. *Journal of User Modeling and User-Adapted Interaction, 11*(4), 176–199.

du Boulay, B., Luckin, R., & del Soldato, T. (1999). Human teaching tactics in the hands of a machine. In *Proceedings of the international conference on artificial intelligence in education. Le Mans, France* (pp. 225-232).

Gagné, R., Briggs, L., & Wager, W. (1992). *Principles of Instructional Design*. (4th ed.). New York: Holt, Rinehart & Winston.

Garagnani, M., Shastri, L., & Wendelken, C. (2002). A connectionist model of planning as back-chaining search. *The 24th Conference of the Cognitive Science Society. Fairfax, Virginia, USA* (pp 345-350).

Halford, G. S. (1993). *Children's understanding: The development of mental models*. Hillsdale, NJ: Lawrence Erlbaum Associates.

Hammerton, L. S., & Luckin, R. (2001). You be the computer and I'll be the learner: Using the 'Wizard of Oz' technique to involve children in the software design process. In *Artificial Intelligence in Education*. San Antonio, TX, USA.

Heermann, D., & Fuhrmann, T. (2000). Teaching physics in the virtual university: The Mechanics toolkit. *Computer Physics Communications, 12*, 11–15. doi:10.1016/S0010-4655(00)00033-3

Hermann, D., & Harwood, J. (1980). More evidence for the existence of separate semantic and episodic stores in long-term memory. *Journal of Experimental Psychology, 6*(5), 467–478.

Humphreys, M. S., Bain, J. D., & Pike, R. (1989). Different ways to cue a coherent memory system: A theory for episodic, semantic and procedural tasks. *Psychological Review, 96*, 208–233. doi:10.1037/0033-295X.96.2.208

Jackson, S. L., Krajcik, J., & Soloway, E. (1996). A learner-centred tool for students building models. *Communications of the ACM, 39*(4), 48–50. doi:10.1145/227210.227224

Jackson, S. L., Krajcik, J., & Soloway, E. (1998). The Design of Guided Learner-Adaptable Scaffolding in Interactive Learning Environments. *CHI 98 Human Factors in Computing Systems* (pp. 187-194).

Kokinov, B., & Petrov, A. (2000). Dynamic extension of episode representation in analogy-making in AMBR. *The 22nd Conference of the Cognitive Science Society*, NJ. (pp. 274-279).

Lintermann, B., & Deussen, O. (1999). Interactive Structural and Geometrical Modeling of Plants. *IEEE Computer Graphics and Applications*, *19*(1), 48–59. doi:10.1109/38.736469

Luckin, R., & du Boulay, B. (1999). Ecolab: the Development and Evaluation of a Vygotskian Design Framework. *International Journal of Artificial Intelligence in Education*, *10*(2), 198–220.

Luckin, R., & Hammerton, L. (2002). Getting to know me: helping learners understand their own learning needs through metacognitive scaffolding. In S. A. Cerri & G. Gouarderes & F. Paranguaca (Eds.), *Intelligent Tutoring Systems* (pp. 759-771). Berlin: Springer-Verlag.

Najjar, M., Fournier-Viger, P., Lebeau, J. F., & Mayers, A. (2006). Recalling Recollections According to Temporal Contexts – Applying of a Novel Cognitive Knowledge Representation Approach. *The 5th International Conference on Cognitive Informatics*. July 17-19, Beijing, China.

Najjar, M., & Mayers, A. (2007). AURELLIO – A Cognitive Computational Knowledge Representation Theory. *International Journal of Cognitive Informatics and Natural Intelligence*, *1*(3), 17–34.

Najjar, M., Mayers, A., Vong, K., & Turcotte, S. (2007). Tailored Solutions to Problems Resolution – An Experimental Validation of a Cognitive Computational Knowledge Representation Model. [iJET]. *The International Journal on Emerging Technologies in Learning*, *2*(1), 28–32.

Neely, J. H. (1989). Experimental dissociations and the episodic/semantic memory distinction. *Experimental Psychology: Human Learning and Memory*, *6*, 441–466.

Puntambekar, S., & Kolodner, J. L. (2005). Toward implementing distributed scaffolding: Helping students learn science by design. *The International Journal of Research in Science Teaching*, *42*(2), 185–217. doi:10.1002/tea.20048

Richards, D. D., & Goldfarb, J. (1986). The episodic memory model of conceptual development: an integrative viewpoint. *Cognitive Development*, *1*, 183–219. doi:10.1016/S0885-2014(86)80001-6

Rzepa, H., & Tonge, A. (1998). VChemlab: A virtual chemistry laboratory. *Journal of Chemical Information and Computer Sciences*, *38*(6), 1048–1053. doi:10.1021/ci9803280

Shao, J., & Wang, Y. (2003). A New Measure of Software Complexity based on Cognitive Weights. *IEEE Canadian Journal of Electrical and Computer Engineering*, *28*(2), 69–74. doi:10.1109/CJECE.2003.1532511

Shastri, L. (2002). Episodic memory and cortico-hippocampal interactions. *Trends in Cognitive Sciences*, *6*, 162–168. doi:10.1016/S1364-6613(02)01868-5

Sweller, J. (1988). Cognitive load during problem solving. *Cognitive Science*, *12*, 257–285.

Tulving, E. (1983). *Elements of Episodic Memory*. Oxford University Press, New York.

Vygotsky, L. S. (1986). *Thought and Language*. Cambridge, MA: MIT Press.

Wang, Y. (2003). Cognitive Informatics: A New Transdisciplinary Research Field. *Transdisciplinary Journal of Neuroscience and Neurophilosophy*, *4*(2), 115–127.

Wang, Y. (2005). The Development of the IEEE/ACM Software Engineering Curricula. *IEEE Canadian Review*, *51*(2), 16–20.

Wang, Y., & Kinsner, W. (2006). Recent Advances in Cognitive Informatics. *IEEE Transactions on Systems, Man, and Cybernetics*, *36*(2), 121–123. doi:10.1109/TSMCC.2006.871120

Wang, Y., Liu, D., & Wang, Y. (2003). Discovering the Capacity of Human Memory. *Transdisciplinary Journal of Neuroscience and Neurophilosophy*, *4*(2), 189–198.

Wang, Y., & Wang, L. (2006). Cognitive Informatics Models of the Brain. *IEEE Transactions on Systems, Man, and Cybernetics*, *36*(2), 203–207. doi:10.1109/TSMCC.2006.871151

Weber, G., & Brusilovsky, P. (2001). ELM-ART: An adaptive versatile system for Web-based instruction. *International Journal of AI in Education*, *12*(4), 351–384.

Wells, L. K., & Travis, J. (1996). *LabVIEW for Everyone: Graphical Programming Made Even Easier*. NJ: Prentice Hall.

Wood, H. A., & Wood, D. (1999). Help seeking, learning and contingent tutoring. *Computers and Education.*

Chapter 9
Multipoint Multimedia Conferencing System for Efficient and Effective Remote Collaboration

Noritaka Osawa
Chiba University, Japan

Kikuo Asai
The Open University of Japan, Japan

ABSTRACT

A multipoint, multimedia conferencing system called FocusShare is described. It uses IPv6/IPv4 multicasting for real-time collaboration, enabling video, audio, and group-awareness and attention-sharing information to be shared. Multiple telepointers provide group-awareness information and make it easy to share attention and intention. In addition to pointing with the telepointers, users can add graphical annotations to video streams and share them with one another. The system also supports attention-sharing using video processing techniques. FocusShare is a modularly designed suite consisting of several simple tools, along with tools for remotely controlling them. The modular design and flexible management functions enable the system to be easily adapted to various situations entailing different numbers of displays with different resolutions at multiple sites. The remote control tools enable the chairperson or conference organizer to simultaneously change the settings for a set of tools distributed at multiple sites. Evaluation showed that the implemented attention-sharing techniques are useful: FocusShare was more positively evaluated than conventional video conferencing systems.

INTRODUCTION

Conventional videoconferencing standards using Internet protocols (IPs), such as H.323 (ITU-T, 2007), are widely used and commercial videoconferencing products based on H.323 are widely available. Microsoft NetMeeting (Summers, 1998), Ekiga (Sandras 2001), and other videoconferencing software systems based on H.323 can be used on personal computers (PCs). Video chat systems, such as Yahoo! Messenger and Windows Messenger,

DOI: 10.4018/978-1-60566-934-2.ch009

and Skype video can also be used on PCs. While these systems can be used in distance education, they are inadequate and inefficient for large-scale distance education, as explained below.

Conventional videoconferencing systems based on H.323 do not adequately provide group-awareness and attention-sharing information to participants. Such information would enable participants to better understand the situations and intentions of others. We think that this basic information is important in distance education and remote collaboration. There are various methods for providing group-awareness and attention-sharing information. For example, group-awareness can be provided by pointing using telepointers and attention-sharing by using either telepointers or video processing techniques like zooming. Telepointers play an important role in interactive distance education (Adams et al., 2005).

Conventional videoconferencing systems only support one telepointer or none at all. While some systems allow it to be shared among users, it is usually controlled by one user at a time. Before someone else can use it, the current user must relinquish control. This control transfer is time-consuming and slows down communications. Multiple telepointers would eliminate this problem, so multiple telepointers should be supported.

Conventional H.323-compliant systems are designed for point-to-point connections. Since these systems cannot use the multicast capability of IPv6/IPv4 (Internet protocol version 6/version 4) networks, they are not efficient for large-scale distance education on multicast-capable networks. Multicast support is an important requirement for large-scale distance education.

Moreover, as large numbers of people can attend lectures in distance education, differences in system settings for the different locations can be a problem. Instructing participants individually about settings via video and/or audio is tedious and time-consuming. Remote adjustment would facilitate the preparation and management of remote lectures. Although general-purpose remote control software tools are available, they generally cannot handle multiple sites simultaneously. Tools that can handle multiple sites are thus needed.

Conventional videoconferencing systems restrict display and window configurations and are not easily adapted to differences in environments. They usually support only one type of display. Some conventional systems are based on H.239 (ITU-T, 2003), which defines dual video stream functions, such as People+Context, and data collaboration. They support one main display and another display, but the use of dual video stream functions requires two displays at every site. Any site with only one display cannot participate in a conference that uses dual video stream functions. Moreover, any site with more than two displays cannot fully utilize the available displays even when multiple sites send and receive videos simultaneously. To process multiple video streams, a conventional videoconferencing system usually uses a multipoint control unit (MCU), which composes one video stream from multiple video streams and sends it to the receivers. The resolution of the composed video stream is inferior to a total resolution of the original streams. It would obviously be better if all displays could be effectively used when multiple displays are available and multiple video streams are received even if the display resolutions differ between sites.

Conventional videoconferencing systems usually display a video as a full screen or in a window. They do not allow the users to view multiple videos in multiple windows on a display. In other words, they lack flexibility in their display configuration.

To overcome the above inadequacies and inefficiencies for large-scale distance education, we developed a multipoint multimedia conferencing system called FocusShare that supports group-awareness using multiple telepointers and other attention-sharing techniques using video processing like partial zooming and nonlinear zooming. FocusShare enables video, audio, and telepointers to be shared using IPv4/IPv6 multicasting.

The various combinations of tools and functions provided by the system efficiently support flexible configurations. Moreover, the remote control functions enable the chairperson or conference organizer to simultaneously change the settings of a set of tools distributed at multiple sites.

We conducted experiments designed to evaluate the attention-sharing techniques supported in FocusShare. The results show that they are useful and that users prefer FocusShare to conventional conferencing systems.

This paper describes all the main features of FocusShare and presents evaluation results. It also complements previous work (Osawa, 2004) that mainly described the multicasting capability and flexibility of FocusShare.

The rest of the paper is organized as follows. The next two sections describe related work and the flexibility, scalability and adaptability of FocusShare. Then, three sections describe its major functions: group-awareness support using telepointers, attention-sharing display techniques using video processing, and remote management and flexible configuration support. Then, the minor, but still important, functions are described. After that, experiences using FocusShare are described and evaluation results are presented. The final section concludes with a brief summary.

RELATED WORK

The Alkit Confero multimedia collaboration software tool (Alkit Communications, n.d.; Johanson, 2001) supports synchronous audio, video, and text communication. It also supports both point-to-point and multipoint communication. Multipoint communication uses either IP multicasting or a real-time transport protocol reflector and mixer. Although Confero has many functions, it does not support multiple shared telepointers, pointer labels, attention-sharing views using video processing, simultaneous display of multipoint videos, or remote control functions, which are all supported by our system.

Access Grid (Childers et al., 2000) is an ensemble of resources for multimedia interactive communications. It can be used for group-to-group interactions such as large-scale distributed meetings and collaborative work. It has group communications functions similar to those supported in FocusShare but does not have similar attention-sharing functions.

The ConferenceXP platform (Beavers, J. et al., 2004) provides software modules for developing collaborative tools and applications as well as client and server tools that enable users to interact and collaborate in a virtual space. It has various functions like Alkit Confero and Access Grid but lacks functions supporting advanced attention-sharing in live videos and remote management of groups, which are implemented in FocusShare.

Other conventional systems generally do not support advanced attention-sharing—they support only simple communication functions and simple conference management functions. While such basic functions are important in conference systems, they are not sufficient to effectively enhance remote group collaboration.

FOCUSSHARE

FocusShare provides users with real-time collaboration-support functions that support multimedia conferencing. It lets them simultaneously exchange multiple video streams, audio streams, and group-awareness information. For example, multi-angle video streams can be transmitted, and one PC can simultaneously receive all of them. It is also possible for different PCs to receive different video streams captured from different angles. Conventional videoconferencing software systems based on H.323 such as Ekiga cannot receive multi-angle video streams simultaneously on a PC without the help of video mixing at the MCU because the H.323 protocol uses fixed IP ports, so only one instance of the software can be executed on a PC.

Flexibility

To enhance the flexibility of our system, we developed it using a modular design. It is not a monolithic tool but a suite of several small tools. It is composed of (1) a sender, (2) a receiver with pointer sharing, which will be referred to simply as the '*receiver*' although it also sends pointing and annotating information, (3) a multipoint viewer, (4) a recording/replaying/relaying tool, (5) a vote-counting tool, (6) a remote control tool for the sender, (7) a remote control tool for the receiver, and (8) a remote control tool for the multipoint viewer. By using different combinations of the tools, users can prepare various configurations for remote conferences and collaboration.

In FocusShare, a sender and a receiver are separated on the basis of the modular design. In this design, receivers need to share group-awareness information by means of telepointers. It is inefficient for a sender to collect all information from all receivers and then send back the collected information to all receivers. Therefore, each receiver needs to send its own pointing and annotating information as well as receive others' pointing and annotating information through multicasting. This is different from conventional conferencing systems.

FocusShare uses DirectShow technologies (Microsoft, n.d.), so it can use existing DirectShow-based video/audio codecs that use state-of-the-art technologies. Moreover, we developed and used several basic DirectShow filters (i.e., software modules) that are powerful components for effective distance education.

FocusShare simplifies multipoint remote sharing of video, audio, and focus information by using IPv6/IPv4 multicasting. It also improves the transmission efficiency of multipoint conferences. The FocusShare system thus provides a simple and efficient means of sharing such information among multiple remote sites.

Figure 1. Multicasting a remote lecture

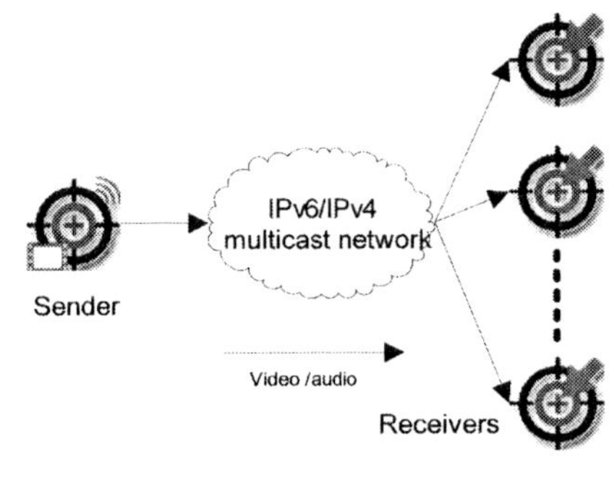

Figure 2. Point-to-point conferencing with attention-sharing and group-awareness information (transmission of self-image videos is monitored using a receiver tool at the local site)

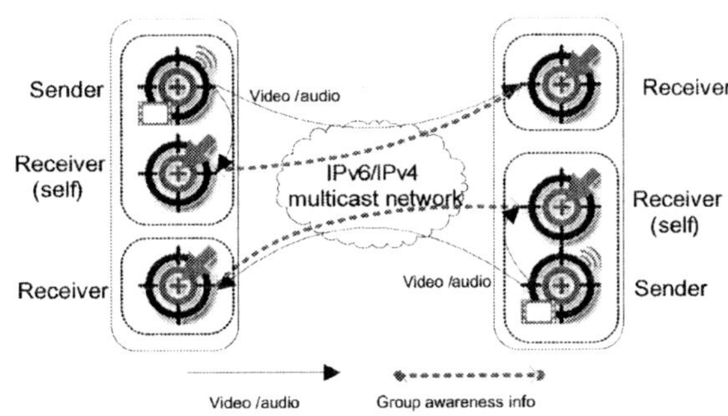

For example, FocusShare can be used to broadcast remote lectures. A lecturer sends video and audio information, which the participants receive simultaneously. The configuration for a multicast remote lecture is shown in Figure 1. Any number of receivers can be added.

When FocusShare is used for a point-to-point conference, a sender/receiver pair can be set up at each site for both sending a self-image video stream and monitoring the sender's self-image video (Figure 2). The two sites share two pointers, with each receiver sending its pointer information to the other.

Scalability

FocusShare achieves scalability by using multicasting. It uses UDP (user datagram protocol) packets to send video/audio information as well as group-awareness, attention-sharing, and control information, which are also multicast. The use of multicasting minimizes the bandwidth required for a multipoint videoconference. FocusShare supports both IPv6 and IPv4.

A group can use FocusShare to discuss a topic. An example of a small group videoconference without monitoring of the self-image video transmission is shown in Figure 3. Each site has one sender and multiple receivers. In this configuration, each member can see all the other members. If this were implemented with a conventional videoconferencing system using point-to-point communication and an MCU without video composition, or a simple reflector, the required bandwidth at the MCU could be extremely large. Let N be the number of members in the group and B be the required bandwidth per sender. FocusShare requires a total bandwidth of only NB, whereas a conventional system requires $N(N-1)B$ at the reflector because each member must send his or her own video data to all the other members. Thus, in a conventional system, the MCU performance and the bandwidth of the network connected to the MCU become the limiting factors for scalability. As a result, conventional systems do not support this configuration well. They usually support only one set of video data, which may be a selected video feed or a video stream composed of the members' video streams combined at the MCU.

FocusShare can allocate a multicast IP address randomly for a session, and it arbitrates if the allocated address conflicts with that of another session although the possibility of conflicts is low in IPv6. This mechanism exploits the huge address space of IPv6, a key feature of that protocol.

Figure 3. Example of group videoconference

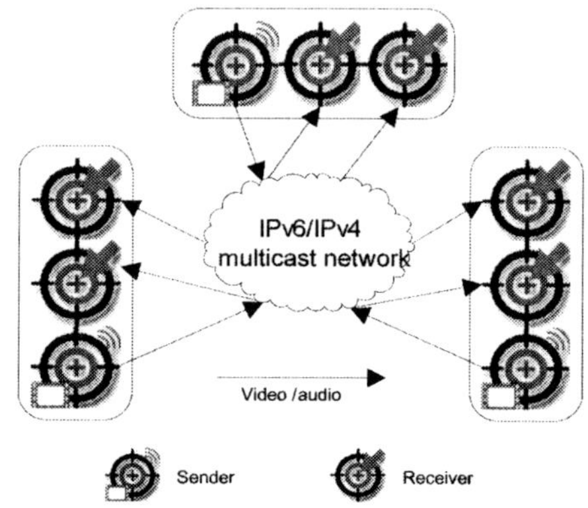

Adaptability

The compression method, resolution, transmission rate, and input device can be flexibly selected in FocusShare. For example, high-definition video and high-fidelity audio can be transmitted. Compression methods are implemented in codecs, and several video codecs can be used with FocusShare:

- HDV (1920×1080 pixels for HD)
- DV (720×480 pixels for NTSC)
- H.264
- MPEG-4
- Motion JPEG
- MPEG-2
- MPEG-1.

The DV- and HDV-based codecs are mainly used for high-resolution, high-frame-rate video transmission, while the MPEG-4-based codecs are mainly used for low-bit-rate video transmission. The supported audio formats include PCM, MP3, CCITT μ-Law, and G.723.1.

Most other DirectShow-compatible codecs, including a user's own codec if it is compatible, can be used with FocusShare. A FocusShare sender transmits the encoding information to the receivers by multicasting, and the receiver tool automatically chooses an appropriate decoder.

The current version of FocusShare supports various video formats: SQCIF (128×96 pixels), QCIF (176×144), CIF (352×288), QQVGA (160×120), QVGA (320×240), VGA (640×480), Quarter SDTV (360×240), SDTV (720×480), HDTV (1920×1080), XGA (1024×768), SXGA (1280×1024), and UXGA (1600×1200).

The maximum transmission rates for video streams and attention-sharing information can be specified, and the frame rates of video streams or the data updating rates of attention-sharing information can be adjusted. Although it is possible to specify a maximum transmission rate for audio, the output of an audio encoder should be sent without delay and omissions because long delays or omissions cause bad sound quality, so they are not acceptable in audio transmission.

FocusShare also supports various input devices, including NTSC video capture devices, DV/HDV camcorders, USB (Web) cameras, and screen capture devices.

GROUP-AWARENESS SUPPORT

Our system supports various functions that provide group-awareness information using telepointers. These functions can also be used for attention-sharing.

Telepointers

A telepointer is a cursor, usually shaped as an arrow, used to indicate where on a display a participant is pointing. It is useful for explicitly and clearly indicating interesting points or areas. The telepointer is usually controlled by a mouse. Telepointer movements can be used as gestures to communicate with other participants. In other words, telepointers are important for sharing information through embodiment, gestures, and coordination in collaborative environments (Gutwin & Penner, 2002). People involved in synchronous distance education and collaborative work can use telepointers to promote group-awareness and attention-sharing (Adams et al., 2005).

Our system enables each participant to have his/her own telepointer. A participant can share multiple telepointers with other users in the same session. The receiver tool can transmit local mouse information as telepointer information in the same session. The telepointers appear in the video windows on the receivers while transmission is in progress.

Most conventional videoconferencing systems do not enable users to manipulate a telepointer on a live video stream although some enable them to use a telepointer for data-sharing applications such as a shared whiteboard based on T.120 (ITU-T, 1996). Moreover, most conventional systems do not enable users to manipulate their telepointers simultaneously. Whereas only one or no telepointer can be used at a time in conventional videoconferencing systems, our system enables the use of multiple shared telepointers on a video stream, enabling users to show explicit points. For example, they can discuss a scene using telepointers on a live video stream from a microscope being captured in a biology lecture. Such a lecture and discussion are impossible with a conventional system.

Telepointers with Different Appearances and Labels

The telepointers can take different shapes and colors. They can be statically or dynamically shaped to enable them to be easily distinguished and to attract the attention of participants. A dynamically shaped pointer is visually similar to the moving spot of a laser pointer. Furthermore, brief labels can be specified for telepointers. A label can be entered by typing it directly into a text field of a setting panel or by selecting it from a history list of items that have been entered. As will be described, different shapes, colors, and labels can be assigned to each mouse button state. These differences make it easy to distinguish the pointers. A screenshot of five differently specified telepointers is shown in Figure 4.

Hand-Raising Action

Our system provides a function that simulates the action of raising a hand. Pressing one of the mouse buttons causes a shape representing a hand to appear in the video windows on the receivers. This is implemented by assigning a different mouse button state to a pointer with a different shape, color, and label. A screenshot containing various hand-raising actions is shown in Figure 5.

This capability is simple yet effective for attracting attention. Conventional systems do not have this capability. Moreover, appropriate labels assigned to buttons can clearly indicate the user's intention.

Telepointer Traces

Trace images of pointers can also be used to improve the understanding of pointing gestures (Gutwin & Penner, 2002). When this setting is turned on, trace images of the telepointer appear in the video window on the receivers, as can be seen in Figure 6. The transparency of the telepointer traces increases as time passes.

Graphical Annotation

Our receiver tool also enables lines to be drawn on videos. The lines are shared with all receivers. This function can be used for simple graphical annotation, as illustrated in Figure 7. Multiple users can draw on video displays simultaneously.

When the left mouse button is clicked and dragged while this setting is turned on, telepointer trails appear in the video window on the receivers. Clicking the right mouse button erases the trails. Users can erase only their own drawings or trails.

ATTENTION-SHARING DISPLAY USING VIDEO PROCESSING TECHNIQUES

In addition to telepointers, FocusShare supports various attention-sharing display actions using

Figure 4. Differently specified telepointers

Figure 5. Various hand-raising actions with labels

Figure 6. Telepointer traces

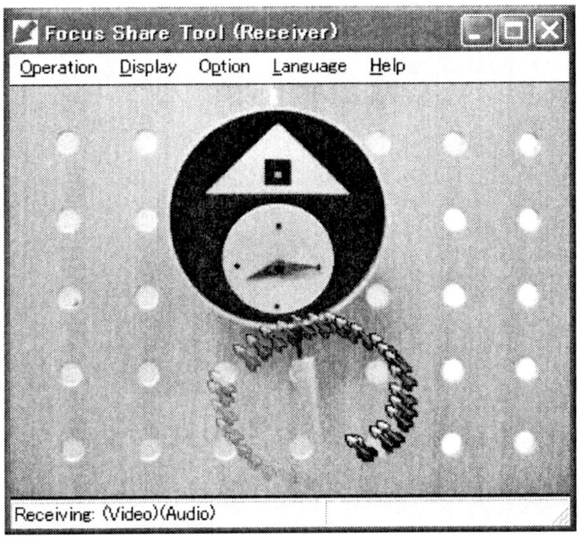

Figure 7. Graphical annotation

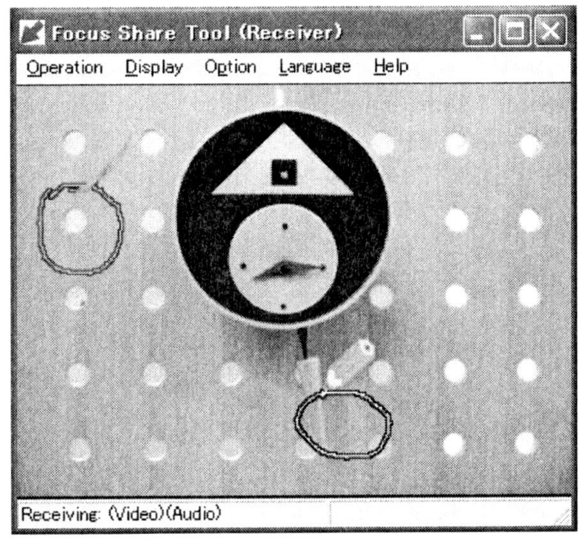

video processing techniques: (1) partial zooming, (2) linear zooming, (3) nonlinear zooming, (4) video composing with different qualities, and (5) video mosaicing. These techniques are not implemented in other videoconferencing systems—they are unique to FocusShare.

Partial Zooming

A region of interest (ROI) in a video is extracted on the basis of the location of the mouse pointer of the sender and displayed on the receivers, as illustrated in Figure 8. The region enclosed by the red rectangle on the sender's screen (Figure 8(a)) is shown on the receivers' screens (Figure 8(b)).

Figure 8. Partial zooming

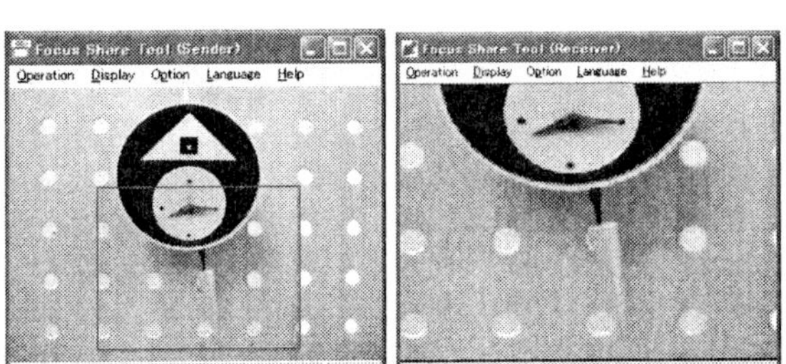

(a) Sender (b) Receiver

Linear Zooming

Linear zooming is a kind of Focus+Context visualization technique (Card, Mackinlay & Shneiderman, 1999). An ROI extracted from a video is controlled using the mouse pointer and overlaid on the video, as illustrated in Figure 9. The ROI is enlarged, but the whole image can also be seen, except for the portion hidden by the ROI. A rectangular ROI, as in Figure 9, or an oval ROI can be specified in the following techniques as well as in linear zooming.

Nonlinear Zooming

Nonlinear zooming is also a kind of Focus+Context visualization technique. As shown in Figure 10, the extracted part of the video is displayed at the original resolution, while the area surrounding the extracted video is nonlinearly reduced and displayed. This type of zooming displays not only the zoomed region but also its surroundings. While this display technique does not hide anything, there is some distortion. The non-distorted ROI of the video moves depending on the location of the mouse pointer of the sender.

Figure 9. Linear zooming

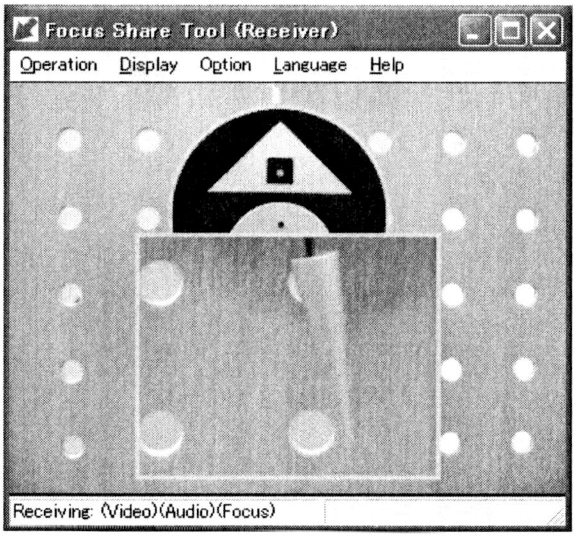

Figure 10. Nonlinear zooming

Video Composition with Different Qualities

An ROI can be shown with high quality while the area surrounding it is shown with low quality. In this context, quality includes frame rate as well as resolution. In this technique, the frame rate of the ROI is set higher than that of the surrounding area. Such videos cannot be created at the sender unless a codec that can encode a video containing areas with different frame rates is available there. Since such codecs are not readily available, we have developed a simple and effective mechanism to compose a video containing areas of different quality. The sender transmits an overview low-resolution video at a low frame rate and transmits a high-resolution ROI of the video at a higher frame rate along with information specifying the pointer location. The ROI is extracted on the basis of the pointer's location. Each receiver creates a composite view from these two video streams using the pointer location information.

This mechanism allows an ROI to be shown in detail while reducing the bandwidth needed to send the video. The resolution and other parameters are controlled on the basis of the ROI in question while using existing codecs. This technique enables Focus+Context display through cooperation between the sending and receiving sides. An example of a video composed of areas with different qualities is shown in Figure 11.

Video Mosaicing

Part of a video can be concealed by mosaicing, as shown in Figure 12. The sender specifies the area to be mosaiced by moving the mouse pointer.

This function can be used, for example, to hide answers on quizzes. While conventional systems enable a window to be hidden, they do not support partial hiding at positions controlled by mouse movement.

REMOTE MANAGEMENT AND FLEXIBLE CONFIGURATION SUPPORT

Remote Window Control

As explained in the introduction, many general-purpose remote-control software tools are avail-

Figure 11. Video with areas of different qualities

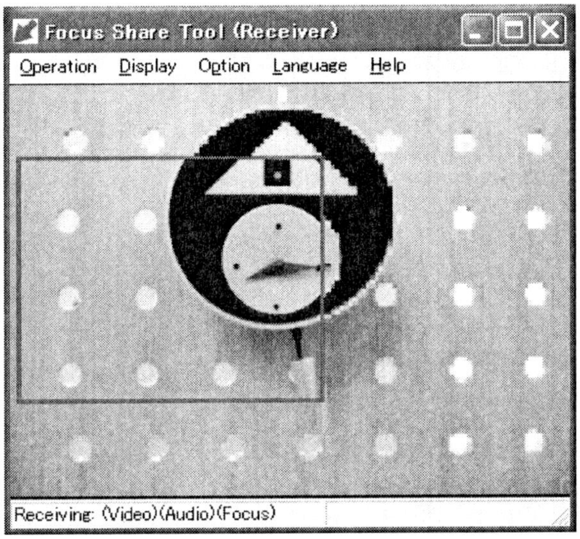

Figure 12. Video with mosaiced area

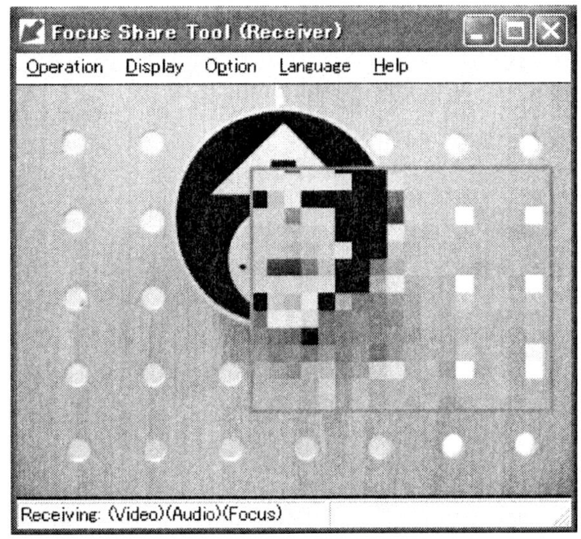

able, but they cannot simultaneously control a large numbers of clients. The remote control tool in FocusShare lets a lecturer or chairperson remotely control each type of tool at all locations at the same time. This makes managing numerous software clients easier. For example, a chairperson can remotely allocate unique shapes and colors to telepointers at multiple sites. Moreover, a lecturer can control the receiving windows at multiple sites: maximizing or minimizing them, moving them to the front or back, or creating other window arrangements, as shown in Figure 13. This function enables the use of various display configurations even if the displays at different sites vary in size. The regions in each display can thus be fully utilized. Consider the situation where a display at one site has a different size or resolution from that of a display at another site and that two receiver windows are shown on each display. When one receiver window is moved to the front, the other window may be hidden by the front window; however, by arranging the windows appropriately, the lecturer can ensure that a large part or possibly all of the rear window can be seen if the display is large. Our system thus makes it possible to utilize the display regions more fully.

Voice-Activated Window Control

The layering of the receiver windows can be changed on the basis of the sound levels. If the voice-activated window control is turned on, a receiver window is moved to the front when its sound level exceeds a specified limit for a specified duration. This function automatically positions the window of the person currently speaking at the front. In conventional videoconferencing systems, an MCU is needed for this function to be implemented.

Volume Indicator

Sound levels during multipoint conferences are often problematic. Inappropriate sound levels can often cause howling and other similar problems. Sound problems are generally more difficult to solve than visual problems. This is because sound cannot be seen, which makes tracking down sound problems a time-consuming process. Visualization of the sounds would facilitate the diagnosis of sound problems. We thus included a sound visualization function, a volume indicator, in our tools.

Figure 13. Window control menu in remote control tool

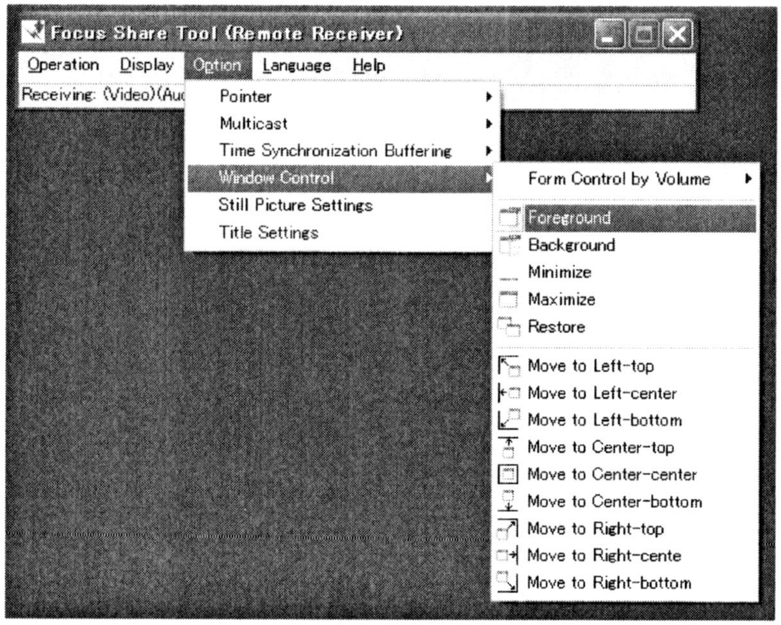

The volume indicator provides a graphical representation of the audio data transmitted or received during a session. In remote conferences, it is important to adjust the sound volume at every site appropriately. This tool can be used to adjust the volumes before the lecture or conference. Moreover, lecturers and speakers can confirm their vocal volume level during the lecture or conference. A screenshot of the volume indicator is shown in Figure 14. The horizontal axis denotes time, while the vertical axis denotes volume. The time scale can be changed.

The remote control tools can be used to show the volume indicators at the remote sites. This lets users check whether the input and output sound levels at both senders and receivers are appropriate. This reduces the time needed to confirm sound settings at remote sites and to solve sound problems.

Figure 14. Volume indicator

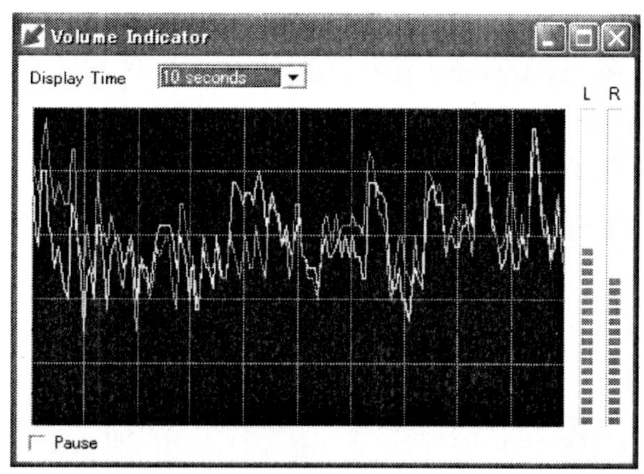

ADDITIONAL FUNCTIONS AND TOOLS

FocusShare has additional tools and functions that are useful for large-scale conferences.

Recording/Replaying/Relaying Tool

The multicasting scheme enables the monitoring of all the data sent. The recording/replaying/relaying tool can capture multiple videos, audios, and group-awareness and attention-sharing information multicast from senders and receivers and store them as a file on a PC. It can replay the recorded data and transmit it synchronously. It can also select types of data for replay. The tool can relay the received data to a different multicast group; i.e., it can work as a reflector. Moreover, it can transcode received data and transmit it by multicasting in real time. This promotes the distribution of functions over the network and enables flexible system configuration.

A screenshot of this tool is shown in Figure 15. Lecturers can use this tool to help save their lectures, including pointer movements and line drawings, and reuse them. Furthermore, the relay function enables the multicast data to be used in different network environments.

Multipoint Viewer

The multipoint viewer can receive videos from multiple sites and show them in one application window. It enables users to see multipoint videos in one window.

A screenshot of the multipoint viewer is shown in Figure 16. In the figure, all the video images are displayed at the same size; however, each one can also be displayed at its original size, which is usually larger than a fixed-size thumbnail video. This tool can be enhanced so that it works with the remote tools, enabling the chairperson or organizer to better control the video presentation.

Vote-Counting Tool

Our system has a vote-counting tool that can be used for simple questionnaires and voting. For voting, the participants cast votes by pressing one of their mouse buttons, and the tool counts the number of button presses and pointer shapes. Appropriate settings for the hand-raising action enable the participants to confirm the results visually. The results can be displayed in the form of a pie chart (Figure 17) or a bar chart.

Screen Image Transmission

FocusShare enables a user to capture screen images at high resolution and transmit them to

Figure 15. Recording/replaying/ relaying tool

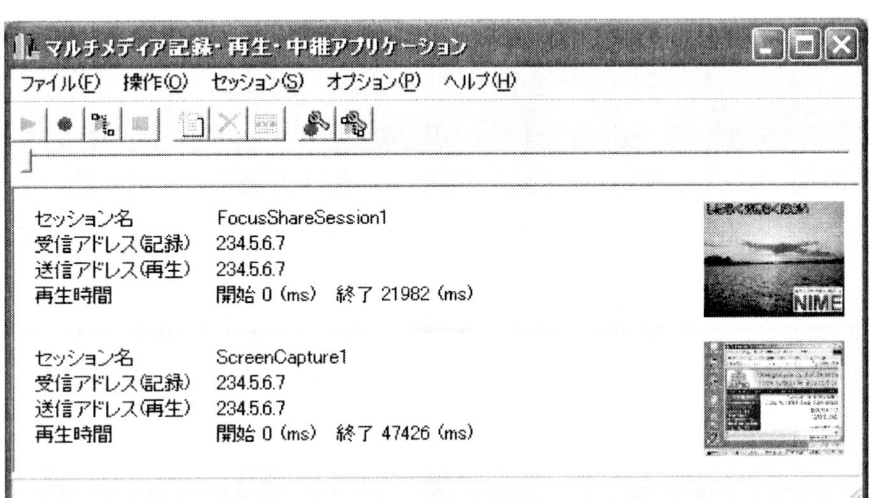

Figure 16. Multipoint viewer

Figure 17. Pie chart display of voting tool

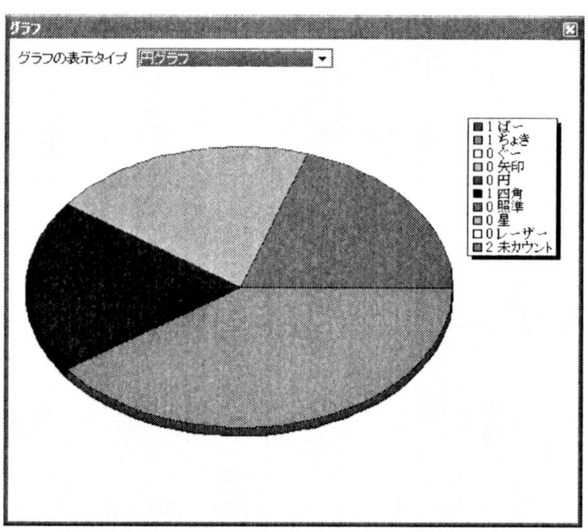

others. Dynamic images on the screen can be transmitted. If an appropriate (lossless) codec is used, the received images will be the same as the sent images. The frame rate for transmission can be specified.

This function can be used to transmit screen images showing presentation graphics, such as those in Microsoft PowerPoint, Apple Keynote, and Lotus Freelance. A screenshot of a PC running Windows XP is shown in Figure 18. The screen has a window displaying a captured Macintosh screen showing the Safari browser with a graphical annotation.

Sender/Receiver Status Monitor

The tools in our system can monitor and display the transmission status. A screenshot of a receiver monitor display is shown in Figure 19. When a network problem arises in a multipoint remote conference, it is often time-consuming to solve the problem. The monitoring functions are useful for determining the status of the network and diagnosing the problem. Its remote control tool enables the status monitored on a remote PC to be shown on the local PC as well.

Figure 18. Received PC screen (The receiver tool shows a captured Macintosh desktop screen with a Safari browser window open and graphical drawings.)

Insertion of Video and Audio Clips

The sender tool lets users insert video and audio clips into transmissions. This function can be used to insert instructional videos, background music (BGM), and other clips.

When a video clip is selected, the specified clip is transmitted instead of the feed from the default video source, which is usually a camera or a screen capture module. After the video clip has been transmitted, the sender returns to the previously specified video source.

When an audio clip is selected, the sound signal is transmitted. Users can mix an audio clip with the captured audio feed or play the clip by itself. The clip can also be replayed. Mixing a repeating audio clip with a captured audio feed can be useful for combining audio feeds with BGM.

Captions

Users can easily add captions to videos. Captions are particularly useful when multiple videos are used because they help distinguish one video from another. A caption of up to 30 double-byte characters can be specified for each video. The specified caption is then transmitted from the sender to the receiver, where it appears overlaid

Figure 19. Receiver status monitor

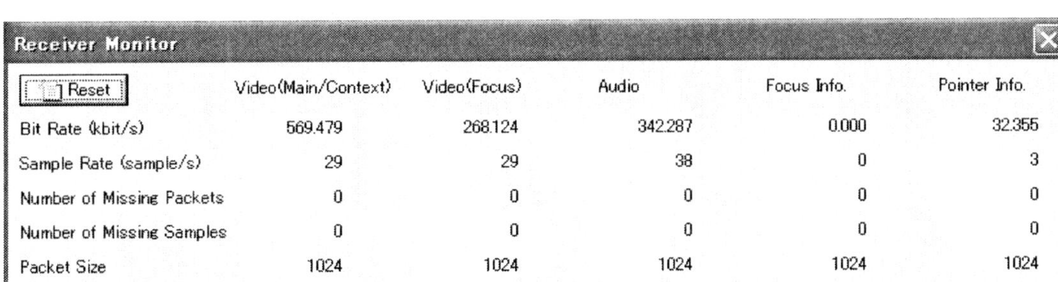

Reset	Video(Main/Context)	Video(Focus)	Audio	Focus Info.	Pointer Info.
Bit Rate (kbit/s)	569.479	268.124	342.287	0.000	32.355
Sample Rate (sample/s)	29	29	38	0	3
Number of Missing Packets	0	0	0	0	0
Number of Missing Samples	0	0	0	0	0
Packet Size	1024	1024	1024	1024	1024

in the video window on the receiver. It is usually displayed at the bottom-center of the window. An example of a video caption on a receiver is shown in Figure 20. Although the caption hides part of the video, the user can turn it on and off.

History

All the tools have history functions to simplify software operations. Recent operations are saved in the tool history, which is listed in the menus. Users can choose menu items to repeat previous operations. This makes it easier to repeat operations. For example, if a user wants to change video captions, he/she can easily do so by selecting an operation history item.

Internationalization

The tools have a language configuration file enabling user interfaces to be displayed in various languages. The file can be used to customize the way menus are displayed in the selected language. Moreover, the tools provide built-in support for English and Japanese. An example display in Japanese is shown in Figure 15.

EXPERIENCE OF USE

Several experiments on the use of our system demonstrated its effectiveness for both multipoint and point-to-point conferencing.

In one experiment, four international institutes (the Institut Teknologi Bandung in Indonesia, the University of the South Pacific at Suva in Fiji, Chiang Mai University in Thailand, and the National Institute of Multimedia Education in Japan) conducted a multipoint conference using satellite communications (Osawa, Shibuya et al., 2005). This experiment demonstrated that the system worked for multipoint conferencing.

In another experiment, distance education between an indoor room and an outdoor farm was conducted using three-dimensional videos (Osawa, Asai et al., 2005). The tools were used to send multiple video streams for an experimental lecture using stereoscopic videos. The experiment showed that the system could be used for a point-to-point conference using multiple video streams.

Figure 20. Video with caption

EVALUATION OF ATTENTION-SHARING TECHNIQUES

After our previous study (Osawa and Asai, 2008), we conducted further evaluations of the attention-sharing techniques, which are unique to FocusShare. The study and analysis described below are based on both the previous and new results. Ninety-nine university students (49 male, 50 female) participated in total.

After listening to an explanation of the experimental procedures, participants watched a short demonstration of how to use the system. Each participant was given a complete system manual, but since it had descriptions of all the functions and required a long time to read, participants were also provided a brief guide covering the areas relevant to the experiment. Moreover, an assistant helped each participant use the system and follow the experimental procedure. After each participant understood the experimental procedure, system usage, and evaluation form, he/she used the system in order to evaluate it.

As shown in Figure 21, two notebook-type personal computers (IBM ThinkPad A31p) were used: one as the sender and the other as the receiver. They were connected by a network-switching hub. There was no other traffic in the network. A live video feed from a video camcorder was used as the input signal for the sender tool. The input resolution was 720×480 pixels. The received video was displayed on a maximized window of the receiver.

After using the system, each participant completed an evaluation form about their experience. They rated each statement on a scale of 1 (strongly disagree) to 5 (strongly agree). The participants could also make free comments about their experience.

Attention-Sharing Display Using Video Processing Techniques

Participants first evaluated the attention-sharing display techniques using video processing. The evaluation statements are listed in Table 1.

We had previously conducted an experiment (Osawa & Asai, 2006) in which 15 participants subjectively evaluated the use of this system from the viewpoints of both a lecturer at a sending site and a student at a receiving site. The objective was to identify any differences in use between the sending and receiving sites. We used the same statements as listed in Table 1. The participants evaluated its use as about the same—the correlation coefficients between the two sites were positive except for Statement *C* (intelligibly) for partial zooming—and 52 of 60 coefficients were larger than 0.3. These previous results (Figure 22) showed that answers for either one site or the other were sufficient for evaluating the attention-sharing display techniques. Therefore, since the participants in the current experiments were students, we asked them to rate the statements from the viewpoint of only a student at a receiv-

Figure 21. Configuration for experimental evaluation

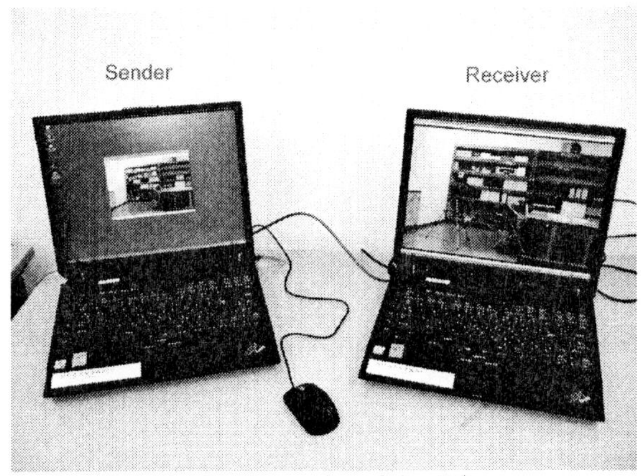

(a) Sending and receiving PCs

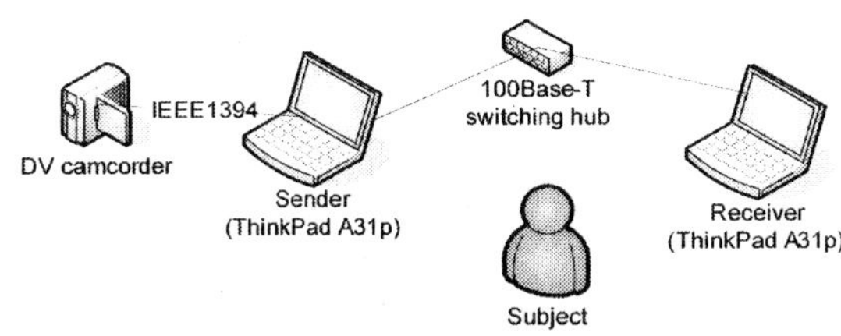

(b) Schematic layout

Table 1. Statements about attention-sharing display techniques using video processing

A	The ROI can be indicated quickly.
B	The ROI can be indicated precisely.
C	The ROI can be indicated intelligibly.
D	The ROI surroundings can be indicated.
E	An overview can be shown.
F	The technique is good from a general viewpoint.
G	Using the technique is less fatiguing than using a conventional system without it.
H	Your experience with the technique was satisfactory.
I	You would like to use the technique again.
J	Your experience with the technique was interesting.

ing site. Understanding the students' perspective is particularly important for enhancing distance education.

The average ratings for the current experiments are shown in Figure 23. This and the following data and figures are based on the results of experiments with 99 participants. The ratings for Statements *A*, *B*, and *C* indicate that the participants preferred the attention-sharing techniques used in the system over ordinary video without attention-sharing techniques (without an ROI) when they wanted to indicate a region of interest. The rating for Statement *F* indicates that linear zooming was the most preferred technique. The ratings for all the statements indicate that nonlinear zooming was not liked as much as the other zooming techniques nor as much as ordinary video without ROI.

Although nonlinear zooming is considered to be a smart and effective technique for Focus+Context visualization in information visualization, the ratings in our experiments indicated that it was not liked for video communication of actual scenes. This is probably because actual scenes have natural dimensions, and any distortion would be perceived as unnatural. The data for information visualization, on the other hand, does not have natural dimensions, so distortion would not affect the user's experience.

Figure 23 also shows that the technique receiving the highest score varied among the statements.

Figure 22. Correlation between ratings at sender and at receiver in previous experiment

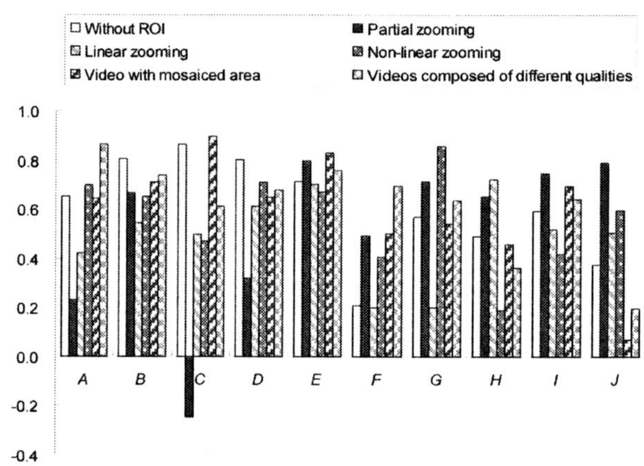

Figure 23. Average ratings for attention-sharing techniques using video processing

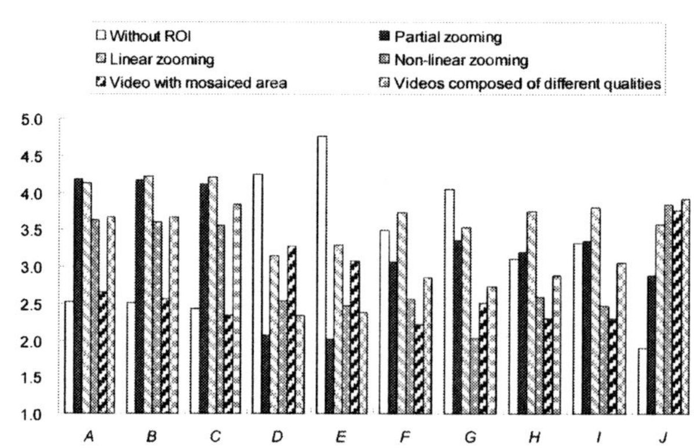

This indicates that various attention-sharing techniques are needed to satisfy the various user demands. Since our system supports various attention-sharing techniques, it better satisfies user demands than conventional video conferencing systems.

Telepointers and Graphical Annotations

The participants then evaluated the use of telepointers and graphical annotations as a means of indicating a point of interest (POI). They comparatively evaluated video conferences without telepointers or graphical annotations, with telepointers only, and with both telepointers and graphical annotations.

The evaluation statements about telepointers and graphical annotations are listed in Table 2, and the average ratings are shown in Figure 24. ANOVA (analysis of variance) analysis revealed significant differences between the ratings for no telepointers or graphical annotations, that is, telepointers only, and for both telepointers and graphical annotations for all statements. For example, for Statement *N*, $F(2,294) = 108.4$ ($p<0.00001$), and for Statement *O*, $F(2,294)=92.5$ ($p<0.00001$). These results indicate that telepointers are useful for showing a POI and that graphical annotations enhance the subjective evaluation.

Figure 24. Average ratings for telepointers and graphical annotations (with standard deviation bars)

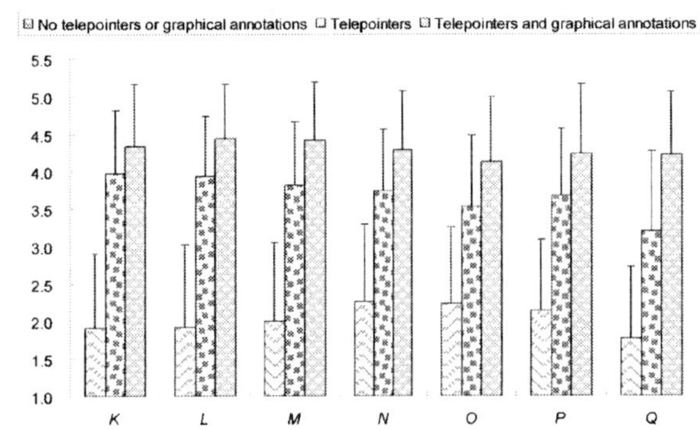

Preferred Combinations of Video Processing and Pointing

We then asked the participants to evaluate preferred combinations of video processing and pointing. The techniques and combinations evaluated are listed in Table 3. The average ratings are shown in Figure 25.

Linear zooming was the preferred technique. This is consistent with the results in Figure 23. Moreover, free choice of all techniques, i.e., *g*, was rated higher than the individual techniques. This is not surprising because people usually like freedom of choice.

Table 2. Statements about telepointers and graphical annotations

K	The POI can be indicated quickly.
L	The POI can be indicated precisely.
M	The POI can be indicated intelligibly.
N	The technique is good from a general viewpoint.
O	Your experience with the technique was satisfactory.
P	You would like to use the technique again.
Q	Your experience with the technique was interesting.

Table 3. Attention-sharing techniques and various combinations

a	Without ROI
b	Partial zooming
c	Linear zooming
d	Nonlinear zooming
e	Video with mosaiced area
f	Videos composed of different qualities
g	*a* to *f*
h	*a* plus pointing
i	*g* plus pointing

Figure 25. Average ratings for attention-sharing techniques and combinations (with standard deviation bars)

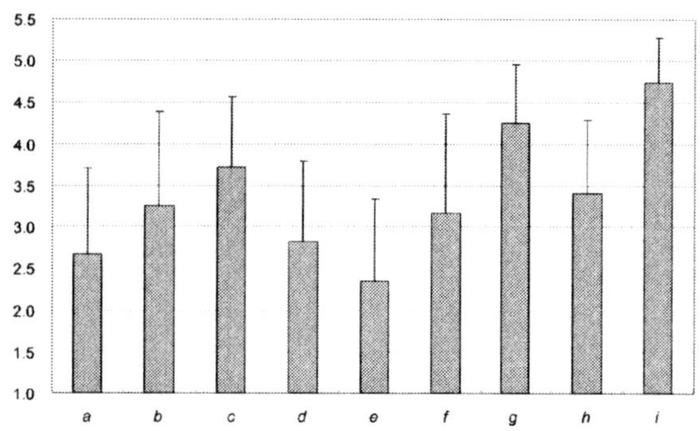

Figure 26. Average ratings for conventional video conferencing and FocusShare (with standard deviation bars)

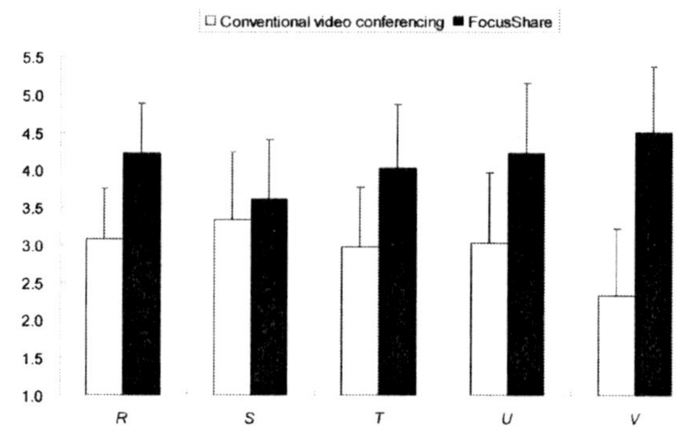

The ratings for *h* and *i* were higher than those for *a* and *g*, respectively. The rating for *i* was the highest. That is, free choice of all techniques plus using video processing and pointing was appreciated the most by the participants.

Overall Comparison of Conventional Video Conferencing and FocusShare

The participants also comparatively evaluated FocusShare and conventional video conferencing without multiple telepointers and attention-sharing functions. The evaluation statements are listed in Table 4 and the average ratings are plotted in Figure 26.

The differences between the mean ratings were significant ($p<0.01$ for the paired t-test except for Statement *S* and $p<0.05$ for the paired t-test for Statement *S*). These results demonstrate that our system was evaluated more positively than conventional video conferencing systems. The difference between them with respect to usability, i.e., Statement *S*, was also statistically significant at $p<0.05$, although the significance level was higher than those for other statements. This means that although FocusShare has more functionality than conventional systems, it is no more difficult to use. In other words, FocusShare is useful without being burdensome.

Table 4. Statements about overall system evaluation

R	The system is good from a general viewpoint.
S	The system is easy to use.
T	You are satisfied with the system.
U	You want to use the system.
V	The system is interesting.

CONCLUSION

We have developed a multipoint, multimedia conferencing system called FocusShare that enables real-time collaboration between multiple sites. It supports group-awareness and attention-sharing to enable efficient and effective remote collaboration. Our evaluations revealed that its attention-sharing techniques are useful in various situations. FocusShare was preferred over conventional video conferencing systems, which do not have group-awareness and attention-sharing support. It includes various useful tools and remote management functions for distance education and remote collaborative work. Moreover, it can be easily adapted to various situations. FocusShare can thus assist in advancing synchronous distance education and collaborative learning.

ACKNOWLEDGMENT

We are grateful to Norio Takase for helping us develop the FocusShare tool. This research was partially supported by Grant-in-Aid for Scientific Research (17300281 and 20300280) in Japan.

REFERENCES

Adams, J., Rogers, B. S., Hayne, S. C., Mark, G., Nash, J., & Leifer, L. J. (2005). The effect of a telepointer on student performance and preference. *Comparative Education, 44*(1), 35–51. doi:10.1016/j.compedu.2003.11.002

Alkit Communications (n.d.). Alkit Confero. Retrieved January 12, 2009, from w2.alkit.se/confero/

Beavers, J., Chou, T., Hinrichs, R., Moffatt, C., Pahud, M., & Eaton, J. V. (2004). *The Learning Experience Project: Enabling Collaborative Learning with ConferenceXP*. MSR-TR-2004-42, Microsoft Research. Retrieved January 12, 2009, from ftp.research.microsoft.com/pub/tr/TR-2004-42.pdf

Card, S. K., Mackinlay, J., & Shneiderman, B. (1999). *Readings in Information Visualization - Using Vision to Think*. Morgan Kaufmann.

Childers, L., Disz, T., Olson, R., Papka, M. E., Stevens, R., & Udeshi, T. (2000) Access Grid: Immersive Group-to-Group Collaborative Visualization. *Immersive Projection Technology*. Ames, Iowa.

Gutwin, C., & Penner, R. (2002). Improving interpretation of remote gestures with telepointer traces. In *Proc. of 2002 ACM Conf. on Comp. Supported Cooperative Work* (pp. 49-57).

ITU-T(1996). Recommendation T.120, Data protocols for multimedia conferencing.

ITU-T(2003). Recommendation H.239, Role management and additional media channels for H.300-series terminals.

ITU-T(2007). Recommendation H.323, Packet-based multimedia communications systems, Series H: Audiovisual and multimedia systems, infrastructure of audiovisual services – Systems and terminal equipment for audiovisual services.

Johanson, M. (2001). Stereoscopic video transmission over the Internet. In *Proceedings of the Second IEEE Workshop on Internet Applications* (pp. 12-19).

Microsoft (n.d.) DirectShow. Retrieved January 12, 2009, from msdn2.microsoft.com/en-us/library/ms783323.aspx

Osawa, N. (2004). Multipoint remote focus sharing tool: FocusShare. *8th IASTED Int. Conf. on Internet & Multimedia Sys. & Apps. (IMSA 2004)* (pp. 379-384).

Osawa, N., & Asai, K. (2006) Multimedia conference system supporting group awareness and remote management. *12th International Conference on Distributed Multimedia Systems (DMS2006)* (pp. 65-72).

Osawa, N., & Asai, K. (2008). Multipoint Multimedia Conferencing System with Group Awareness Support and Remote Management. *International Journal of Distance Education Technologies, 6*(3), 23–44.

Osawa, N., Asai, K., Shibuya, T., Noda, K., Tsukagoshi, S., Noma, Y., & Ando, A. (2005). Three-dimensional video distance education system between indoor and outdoor environments. *6th International Conference on Information Technology Based Higher Education and Training (ITHET2005)*, F2C/13-18, CD-ROM.

Osawa, N., Shibuya, T., Yuki, K., Kondo, K., Sastrokusumo, U., Komolmis, T., & Kuroiwa, H. (2005) Multipoint conferencing through a satellite IP network. *8th IASTED Int. Conf. on Comp. and Adv. Tech. in Educ. (CATE 2005)* (pp. 41-46).

Sandras, D. (2001). *Ekiga*. Retrieved January 12, 2009, from ekiga.org/

Summers, B. (1998). *Official Microsoft Netmeeting 2.1 Book*. Microsoft Press. Retrieved from http://www.microsoft.com/windows/netmeeting/

Chapter 10
Enhanced Speech-Enabled Tools for Intelligent and Mobile E-Learning Applications

S- A. Selouani
Université de Moncton, Canada

T-H. Lê
Université de Moncton, Canada

Y. Benahmed
Université de Moncton, Canada

D. O'Shaughnessy
Institut National de Recherche Scientifique-Énergie-Matériaux-Télécommunications, Canada

ABSTRACT

Web-based learning is rapidly becoming the preferred way to quickly, efficiently, and economically create and deliver training or educational content through various communication media. This chapter presents systems that use speech technology to emulate the one-on-one interaction a student can get from a virtual instructor. A Web-based learning tool, the Learn IN Context (LINC+) system, designed and used in a real mixed-mode learning context for a computer (C++ language) programming course taught at the Université de Moncton (Canada) is described here. It integrates an Internet Voice Searching and Navigating (IVSN) system that helps learners to search and navigate both the web and their desktop environment through voice commands and dictation. LINC+ also incorporates an Automatic User Profile Building and Training (AUPB&T) module that allows users to increase speech recognition performance without having to go through the long and fastidious manual training process. New Automated Service Agents based on the Artificial Intelligence Markup Language (AIML) are used to provide naturalness to the dialogs between users and machines. The portability of the e-learning system across a mobile platform is also investigated. The findings show that when the learning material is delivered in the form of a collaborative and voice-enabled presentation, the majority of learners seem to be satisfied with this new media, and confirm that it does not negatively affect their cognitive load.

DOI: 10.4018/978-1-60566-934-2.ch010

INTRODUCTION

In the context of rapidly growing network applications, an abiding vision consists of providing computer-based media support where no sophisticated training is required. Among these applications, e-learning systems are rapidly gaining in popularity. In fact, easier-to-use development tools, lower costs, availability of broadband channels and potentially higher returns, in the form of better learner productivity, have made e-learning technology attractive to a wider variety of institutional and individual users. Numerous studies, including those of Najjar (1996) and Alty (2002), confirm that the type of computer-based media incorporated in e-learning materials can have a significant impact on the amount of information retained, understood, and recalled by learners. Recently mobile learning (m-learning) has emerged as a promising means to reach more prospective learners. M-learning refers to the use of mobile and handheld IT devices, such as cellular telephones, Personal Digital Assistants (PDAs), and laptops, in teaching and learning. As computers and the internet become essential educational tools, the portability of e-learning content across technologies and platforms becomes a critical issue. This portability has to be investigated in terms of benefits or disadvantages for the learning process. Jones et al. (2006) gave six reasons why mobile learning might be motivating: control over goals, ownership, learning-in-context, continuity between contexts, fun and communication.

Several web-based techniques are used to develop online Collaborative Learning (CL) systems. These systems may integrate a form of chat window or forum through a public or private communication channel. To some extent, these features switch the system to an interactive and communication system, which may be separated from the underlying learning context. This justifies the development of the proposed "in context" system described below. Moreover, to design an effective e-Learning tool for CL, we must avoid some common issues arising from applying or developing them. For example: (1) teachers fear to apply them in the classroom because of the apparent loss of control in the classroom; (2) students resist collaborating because of the lack of familiarity with CL techniques and class management; (3) students are accustomed to working competitively, not cooperatively (Bosworth, 1994). These issues motivated us to develop a Web-based learning tool called Learn IN Context (LINC).

The ideal user environment has not yet been found, but individual interface technologies are sufficiently advanced to allow the design of systems capable of making a positive impact on the e-learning experience. Central to such systems is a conversational interaction using speech recognition and text-to-speech synthesis. Deng (2004) states that, in recent years, Automatic Speech Recognition (ASR) and Text-To-Speech (TTS) have become sufficiently mature technologies. Therefore, this allows their inclusion as effective modalities in both telephony and other multimodal interfaces and platforms. New protocols, such as Media Resource Control Protocol (MRCP) (IETF, 2006), are providing a key enabling technology that facilitates the integration of speech technologies into network equipment and alleviates their adoption in many distributed and mobile applications. MRCP leverages IP telephony and Web technologies to provide an open standard and a versatile interface to speech engines that could open new horizons for e-learning applications.

In this chapter, we propose to include such technologies in a virtual laboratory dedicated to the mixed-mode learning of C++ language programming. This mode combines face-to-face and distance approaches to education. In this context, an instructor meets with students in the classroom, and a resource base of content material is made available to students through the web.

This chapter is further organized as follows. Section 2 is concerned with both TTS and ASR background. An overview on the relevance of including multimedia files into an e-learning environment is given in section 3. Section 4 describes the main components and features of the LINC platform and its speech-enabled enhanced versions: LINC+ and LINC Desktop. This section also describes the spoken query system for navigating and searching, the AIML-based method to enhance the dialog quality, the mobile platform we used to provide more accessibility options to learners, and the user profile and automatic training system. Section 5 presents the results of experiments carried out to evaluate how learners deal with the LINC (voiceless) platform, and reports objective and subjective evaluations of the ASR and TTS modules of LINC+. Finally, in Section 6 we conclude and discuss future perspectives of this work.

SPEECH TECHNOLOGY BACKGROUND

The general architecture of a TTS system has three components: text/linguistic analysis, prosodic generation and synthetic speech generation. Text analysis aims to analyze the input text. It involves orthographic/phonetic transcription, which performs the conversion of text letters and symbols into phonemes. At this first level, linguistic information is also extracted through the use of morphologic and syntactic analyzers. The linguistic features are used by the prosodic generator in order to obtain as much naturalness as possible with synthetic speech. Prosodic features include pitch contours, energy contours, and duration. These parameters are closely related to speech style, where variations in intonation, pause rhythm, stress and accent, are observed. Finally, speech synthesis can be performed through three approaches: concatenative synthesis, formant synthesis, and articulatory synthesis, according to Charpentier (1986), Grau (1993), and Sproat (1995).

Nowadays, most TTS systems use concatenative synthesis, which is based on the concatenation of recorded speech units. The naturalness and intelligibility of synthetic speech depend strongly on the selected speech units. Units such as diphone, syllable, triphone and polyphone are usually adopted by TTS systems. These units are preferred to phonemic units since they are longer than phonemes. This avoids the problem of managing coarticulation effects. However, during synthesis, when such units are concatenated back together, it is important to reduce the spectral discontinuity and distortion. Applications using a TTS module are numerous and quite diversified. They range from talking document browsers, to personal computer-based agents, to voice-mail and unified messaging systems, and to new telephone directory services. New TTS-based architectures allow developers to create natural language dialogue systems that combine TTS with natural language speech recognition.

Speech recognition has also made enormous progress over the past 20 years. Advances in both computing devices and algorithm development have facilitated these historical changes. In general, ASR can be viewed as successive transformations of the acoustic micro-structure of the speech signal into its implicit phonetic macro-structure. The main objective of any ASR system is to achieve the mapping between these two structures. To reach this goal, it is necessary to suitably describe the phonetic macro-structure, which is usually hidden behind the general knowledge of phonetic science, as studied by Allen (1994) and O'Shaughnessy (2001). One of the interesting challenges that ASR faces is building language-independent systems. Thus, according to Deng (2004), it is necessary to unify acoustic processing and to adapt the architecture of the ASR system to cover the broadest range of languages and situations. Modern configurations for ASR are mostly software architectures that generate a sequence of word hypotheses validated by a language model from an acoustic signal. The most popular and effective algorithm implemented in these architectures is based on Hidden Markov

Models (HMMs), which belong to the class of statistical methods (Jelinek, 1997). Other approaches have been developed, but due to the complexity of their usability, they are still considered as research and development tools. Among these techniques, we can cite the one using hybrid neural networks and HMMs (Bourlard, 1994).

Currently, the challenges for ASR are the following: the use of robust acoustic features and models in noisy and changing environments; the use of multiple word pronunciations and efficient constraints allowing one to deal with a very large vocabulary; the use of multiple and exhaustive language models capable of representing various types of situations; the use of complex methods for extracting conceptual representations and various types of semantic and pragmatic knowledge from corpora. Most ASR research has shifted to conversational and natural speech. The ultimate goal consists of making ASR indistinguishable from the human understanding system.

Speech recognition technology is already capable of delivering a low-error performance for many practical applications. For instance, we can already see, in certain cars, interfaces that use speech recognition in order to control useful functions. Speech recognition is also used for telecommunication directory assistance. For Personal Computer (PC) users, Microsoft offers an improved speech recognition engine in its Windows Vista operating system (Brown, 2006). It is now possible to control the system using speech commands. However, its biggest problem is that users need to learn a fixed set of commands. Mac OS X also provides a basic speech recognition engine. However, to use it, users must create macros for each program, which can become quite tedious.

In order to counter these limitations, natural language processing techniques present an interesting solution. One such technique is proposed by the Artificial Intelligence Markup Language (AIML), an XML based language. It was developed by Wallace (2005) to create chat bots rapidly and efficiently. It is a simple and flexible pattern matching language. One of its main advantages is reductionism through recursion. That is, multiple inputs can be reduced to a single general pattern. Knowledge in AIML consists of categories. Categories are then described using patterns and templates; the pattern corresponds to the user input. They can be enriched by the use of wildcards that can be theoretically used to match an infinite number of inputs. The template represents the system's response. It can be used to refer to previous input or other categories.

The e-learning system that we present in this chapter allows the use of ASR as another option for text input. It is often assumed that dictation software will insert correct grammar and punctuation automatically. Unfortunately, this is not always the case as it may mistakenly transpose homonyms, i.e., wrong words that sound similar to the correct ones. Furthermore, dictating is a skill in its own right, and perfect results may not necessarily be achieved. However, with the advent of new natural language processing software, we are able to allow users to control their environment using mostly natural language.

USING MULTIMEDIA FILES IN AN E-LEARNING ENVIRONMENT

E-learning content can be distributed in various ways. When the content is made available through the web, it is accessible by a large population. For Kruse (2002a), "the benefits of Web-based training stem from the fact that access to the content is easy and requires no distribution of physical materials." Nevertheless, it can be difficult for people with disabilities to access part of the content. For instance, it is difficult for someone with weak vision to read smaller text. Therefore, providing an audible content to such users can be quite helpful. The content could be recorded in audio files or it could be automatically generated by a voice synthesis system and later played on demand. One foreseen problem is that large audio files are slow to download with a low bandwidth connection. The potential solution is to use a speech synthesizer on the client's computer for reading the text; therefore, no audio data is actually transferred and hence slower bandwidth would suffice. Another advantage of this technique is that there is no need to pay a voice talent to record the text every time the lesson content is updated. One disadvantage is that users wishing to access the audio capability must install the speech synthesizer on their computers. Another problem is the lesser quality of speech generated by a synthesizer. Wald (2005) states that "Although speech synthesis can provide access to some text based materials for blind, visually impaired or dyslexic learners, it can be difficult and unpleasant to listen to for long periods" (p. 4). Another possibility is to create audio files with a speech synthesizer and hence, there is no more need for a voice talent. This technique still faces the problems of low-bandwidth connections and quality of speech.

Adding speech recognition to an e-learning environment is another way of increasing accessibility. Wald (2005) says that "automatic speech recognition can enhance the quality of learning and teaching and help ensure e-learning is accessible to all" (p. 1). Traditionally, users interact with software through the mouse and keyboard. While this technique works well for many, it is difficult to use those instruments for someone who is quadriplegic or who has arthritis. With speech recognition, the user interacts with the software by speaking, thus improving accessibility. Even those without any disabilities might enjoy the speech recognition aspect. The usability of the user interface is important for the success of the e-learning environment. "The success of any training program is largely dependent on the student's own motivation and attitude. If a poorly designed interface has one feeling lost, confused, or frustrated, it will become a barrier to effective learning and information retention," according to Kruse (2002b). Speech recognition can simplify the usage of the system, making everybody more satisfied. It could also be used if the e-learning content includes video with people speaking. Here also, Wald (2005) proposes an additional advantage: "speech recognition offers the potential to provide automatic live verbatim captioning for deaf and hard of hearing students." Adding audio files or speech synthesis and speech recognition to an e-learning environment can improve accessibility to the content for people with disabilities. Moreover, any user who feels tired by visual cognitive overload due to onscreen reading may be pleased with this solution. It is possible that some of the users will not be interested in these capabilities. However, such users will not be negatively affected.

SPEECH-ENABLED VIRTUAL LABORATORY TO LEARN PROGRAMMING LANGUAGE

The Learn IN Context (LINC) Web-based learning environment was effectively used as a virtual laboratory in the C++ language courses in the fall 2004 trimester at Université de Moncton. It is a mixed-mode learning tool, both in class and on line at the same time (Lê, 2005a and 2005b). LINC+ is its new version with a vocal user interface. LINC^d is the portable client application of LINC+, designed to be installed on the user computer. In the following subsections, we describe the LINC system and the vocal features added to the LINC+/LINC^d version. As defined by Karweit (2000), and if contextualized in the computer science domain, the LINC Web-based Tool Software is considered as a Virtual Laboratory (VL). It is developed according to the main objectives of a VL. These objectives consist of simulating engineering and science laboratory projects on a computer to offer experiment-oriented problems without the overhead costs incurred when maintaining a full laboratory.

The New LINC+ Vocalized Virtual Laboratory

The system has three components with various functionalities and interfaces. The first component is a multi-user online authoring system. It allows the team members (instructional designers) to collectively create the lesson's contents that include demonstrations (multimedia files) and corresponding documents (a URL or documents preloaded on the server). This component is standalone software. It allows easy structuring of the lessons in a task-oriented fashion and makes allowance for saving them in graphical knowledge networks (XML files). Each network (Figure 1) includes several connected nodes, which can be selected (clicked) and expanded into a text frame with several slots. The last slot is special and is reserved for stimulating questions. A good instructional designer chooses a suitable question for stimulating learner reflection about the underlying subject matter. The second component is the Learning Management System, the platform in which the course content, as well as associated files (teacher's photo, multimedia files), are assembled before online distribution. The third component is the software that generates the Web pages from every text frame created by the first component. Its interface is a standard Web page having the index of the actual lesson on the left side of the screen. This corresponds to the Knowledge Network illustrated in Figure 1. The topic's content displayed on the right corresponds to the text frame. In Figure 2, one can see the hyperlinks for "Reference" and "Demo" below the instructor's photo used to display the referenced document and to activate the multimedia demonstration (video clip, Flash file, etc.). With the addition of a synthesized voice and a facility for speech recognition to the LINC environment, the learner can listen to a voice reading the Web page content. Furthermore, he can navigate within this learning environment by using his/her own voice instead of using a mouse. We call this new environment with a vocal interface LINC+. After accessing LINC+'s home page, a simple click allows the users to see a list of courses. Another click allows them to choose a course. After this click, a login window will be displayed asking the user for a username and a password. The system can recognize two types of users: a professor and a student.

Various vocal commands are available depending on the type of user. After logging in and choosing a lesson, users have access to the complete functionalities of the vocal interface. Figure 3 is labelled with sections from A to F. By clicking on one of the speaker icons, the text displayed in the corresponding section will be read by the TTS. Section A contains the Links list (lesson's topics); Section B, the page's header; Section C, the Situation; Section D, the Actions; Section E, the Comments (not shown in Figure 3); and Section F contains all the content sections (C, D, and E). Some words, such as «Introduction» in the Actions section, which are light blue, are hotspots. If the user passes the cursor over this word, a tool tip will appear with a supplementary content in a yellow window (for a concept explanation or a term definition). Clicking on the word will cause the content to be read. It is also possible to interact with the site by launching a vocal command. To enable this facility of speech recognition, the user must first click on the microphone icon (on the right in the first yellow field). This microphone button is a toggle. Clicking on the microphone icon again will disable it. A small tooltip appears to show if this facility is enabled.

LINC Desktop

LINC Desktop (LINC^d) is a small portable client application (less than 1 MB) that can be installed on a teacher's or a student's computer. It can be used to interact with the LINC system through a voice interface. The only requirement is that the user needs to have Speech Application Programming Interface (SAPI) 5.1 compatible TTS

Figure 1. Example of a knowledge network

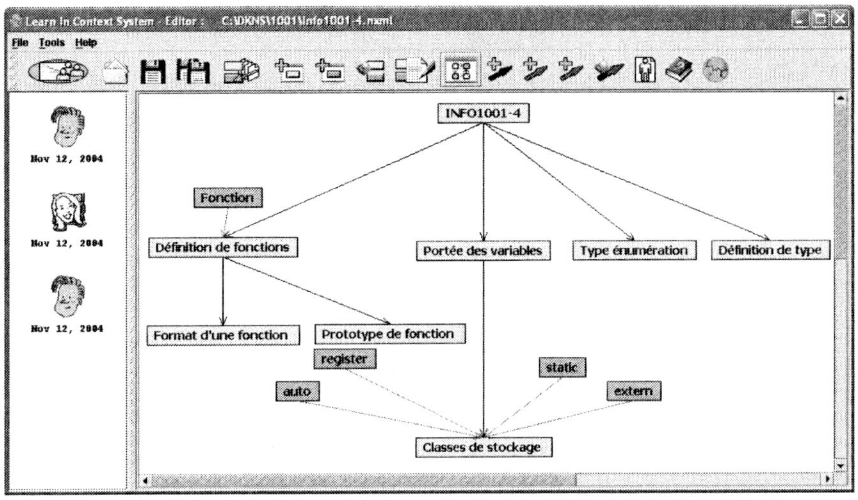

Figure 2. The LINC Learner's Interface

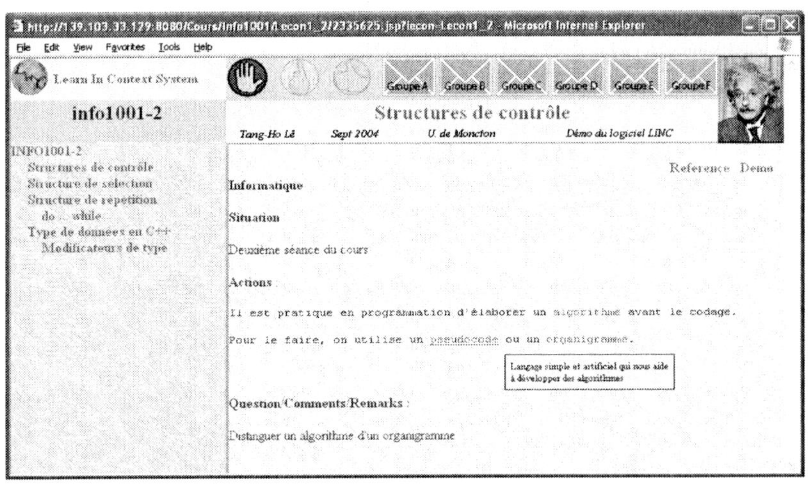

and recognition engine (Microsoft, 2006). It is especially useful for visually impaired users as the application makes use of speech recognition, text reading, and command feedback. The user is able to log in by using voice commands only, to post to the forums using dictation, as well as to navigate the course through voice commands.

Main Module of LINC[d]

The main module processes the events and messages issued from the grammar, browser and TTS engine modules. It also tells the browser engine to go to a certain page, or that it has to pass its HTML code to the parser. It can change the grammar according to the users' need. It is also responsible for calling the user profile application (described in the next section) on its first run, or when the user requests it. In order

Figure 3. The LINC+ Vocal Interface

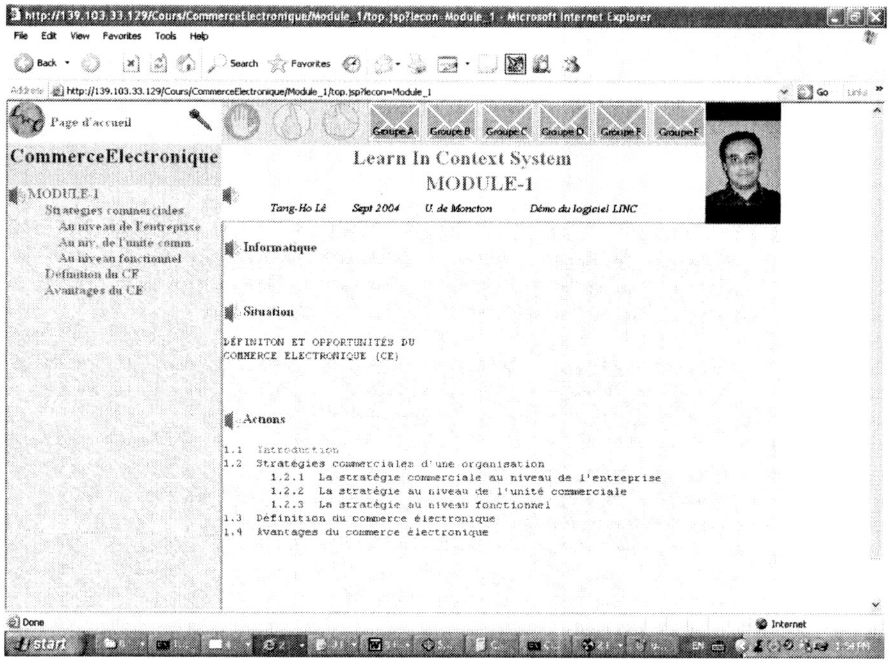

to help visually impaired users to know what the system is doing, a voice feedback is included. It tells the user which command it understood, as well as recognized search keywords. As a result, if the user wants to search for "university" and the system understands "universally" the user will be able to know that a recognition error occurred and he will be able to correct it.

Browser Engine and LINC[d] Parser Modules

The browser engine module is responsible for fetching and displaying web pages. It also tells the main module when it is ready to have its text parsed. The LINC[d] parser module is a custom algorithm made especially to analyze LINC[d]'s pages and to extract the relevant text as well as to post the username, password and comments to the forum discussions.

TTS, ASR and Grammar Modules

The TTS engine module receives text either from the main module or from the HTML parser module. Once it has received its text, it blocks the recognition engine to avoid false command recognition, and reads the text out loud to the user. The recognition engine module feeds the recognized utterances (with various hypotheses) to the grammar module for processing.

The grammar module contains eight different XML grammars similar to the one shown in Figure 4. In order to facilitate the transition from LINC+ to LINC Desktop, most of the commands available from LINC+ apply to LINC Desktop. Commands such as "go to this link" (the link pointed by the cursor), "read this link" (the link that the cursor is actually on), and "read this tooltip" (the tooltip below the cursor of the mouse) were dropped since visually impaired users cannot see the cursor. We instead replaced those with "enumerate links" and "read link *n*". For this purpose the following eight grammars are provided. The first one is used to select the course. The second one is used for logging into LINC. The third one is used to select the lesson. The fourth one is used to enumerate and select the lesson's topics, to navigate to the next or previous lesson's topic, to read the content of the lesson's topic, as well as to post to the group's forums.

The fifth one is available for only the teacher and is used to change the state of the discussion (red, yellow and green). The sixth one is used for dictation when students want to post messages in their group's discussion forum. Finally, the seventh and the last ones are used for spelling numbers and letters respectively.

Figure 4. LINC[d] XML login information grammar

```
<GRAMMAR LANGID="409">
    <DEFINE>
        <ID NAME="Lecon" VAL="1"/>
    </DEFINE>
    <RULE NAME="stop" ID="1" TOPLEVEL="ACTIVE">
        <P>-stop</P>
    </RULE>
    <RULE NAME="SpellIt" ID="2" TOPLEVEL="ACTIVE">
        <P>spell it</P>
        <L PROPNAME="letterOrNumber" PROPID="lor">
            <P>letters</P>
            <P>numbers</P>
        </L>
    </RULE>
    <RULE NAME="backspace" ID="3" TOPLEVEL="ACTIVE">
        <P>backspace</P>
    </RULE>
    <RULE NAME="clear" ID="4" TOPLEVEL="ACTIVE">
        <P>clear</P>
    </RULE>
</GRAMMAR>
```

Figure 5. Example of AIML categories

```
<category>
        <pattern>GO TO TOPIC  * </pattern>
        <template>
                GO_TOPIC  <star/>
        </template>
</category>
<category>
        <pattern>* TO SEE TOPIC *</pattern>
        <template>
                <srai>
                GO TO TOPIC  <star index="2"/>
                </srai>
        </template>
</category>
```

Interaction Using Natural Language Processing

Natural language interaction requires less cognitive load than interactions through a set of fixed commands because it is the natural way used by humans to communicate. With this in mind, we propose an improvement to the LINK[d] platforms that allows the user to interact using natural language processing. This is accomplished by integrating an Artificial Intelligence Markup Language bot to the system. For our system, we implemented Program# (Tollervey 2006). It can process over 30000 categories in under one second. The knowledge base consists of approximately 100 categories covering general and specialized topics of interaction. This is used to complement the fixed grammar. The AIML framework is used to design "intelligent" chat bots (ALICE, 2005). It is an XML compliant language. It was designed to create chat bots rapidly and efficiently. Its primary design feature is minimalism. It is essentially a pattern matching system that maps well with Case-Base Reasoning. In AIML, botmasters effectively create categories that consist of a pattern, the user input, a template, and the Bot's answer. The AIML parser then tries to match what the user said to the most likely pattern and outputs the corresponding answer. Additionally, patterns can include wildcards that are especially useful for our application. Moreover, the language supports recursion, which enables it to answer based on previous input. Figure 5 presents an example of an AIML category.

The first category represents the generic pattern to be matched and contains the *pattern*, *template* and *star* tags. The "*" in the *pattern* represents a wildcard, and will match any input. In the *template* tag, the *star* tag represents the wildcard from the *pattern* and indicates that it will be returned in the output. For example the input "Go to topic basics of object oriented programming" would output "GO_TOPIC basics of object oriented programming".

The second category also makes use of the tag *srai*. The *srai* redirects the input to another *pattern*, in this case, the "GO TO TOPIC *" *pattern*. The *star* tag with the *index* attribute set to "2" indicates that the second wildcard should be returned.

Speech-Enabled Mobile Platform

Recently mobile devices are becoming more popular and more powerful than ever. The size and portability of mobile devices make them particularly effective for users with disabilities. The features usually included in mobile devices are useful for learners with learning difficulties. For instance, PDAs often also include thesauruses that provide handy reference tools for this category of learners. Mobile devices can also be easily transported with wheelchairs. However, there are some limitations and disadvantages. For instance, the small buttons can be difficult to manipulate for people who are lacking manual dexterity. The stylus pens are often small and options for keyboard or mouse access are limited. The small screen size is also a disadvantage. Therefore, the use of speech technology constitutes an alternative to counter the interaction limitations of mobile devices. It is now becoming computationally feasible to integrate real-time continuous speech recognition in mobile applications. With this in mind, we propose a mobile adaptation of the LINK[d] platform which would allow students on the go to access in a timely fashion their course content. The ability to use speech interaction rather than tediously typing on the small and often limited keyboards of mobile phones is one obvious advantage.

One such recognition engine is CMU's PocketSphinx (Huggins-Daines, 2006). It is a light-weight real-time continuous speech recognition engine optimized for mobile devices. Platform speed is critical and often affects the choice of a speech recognition system. Various programming interfaces and systems have been developed around the SPHINX recognizers' family. There are currently used by researchers in many applications such as spoken dialog systems and computer-assisted learning. In our case, as illustrated in Figure 6, the SPHINX-II recognizer is used because it is faster than other SPHINX recognizers.

Figure 6. Improved speech accessibility through mobile platform using PocketSphinx recognizer

Internet Voice Searching and Navigating (IVSN) System

IVSN is a system made especially for navigating and searching the web using voice commands exclusively. The major appeal of IVSN is that users can search the web using dictation. In addition to this, if the users want to search for a word which is not in the lexicon, and if there is no need to add it to the system vocabulary, they can always revert to the spelling mode. This is also particularly useful for navigation purposes, as the users can spell out the URLs of web pages that they want to navigate

Figure 7. The IVSN system diagram

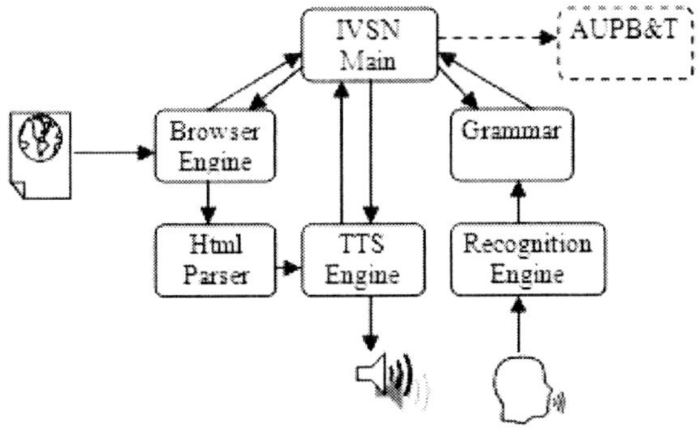

to. IVSN can change the grammar according to the user's needs. Furthermore, an AIML module was integrated in order to improve user interaction with the system. As Figure 7 shows, the system is built in a modular fashion.

Figure 8. The AUPB&T system diagram

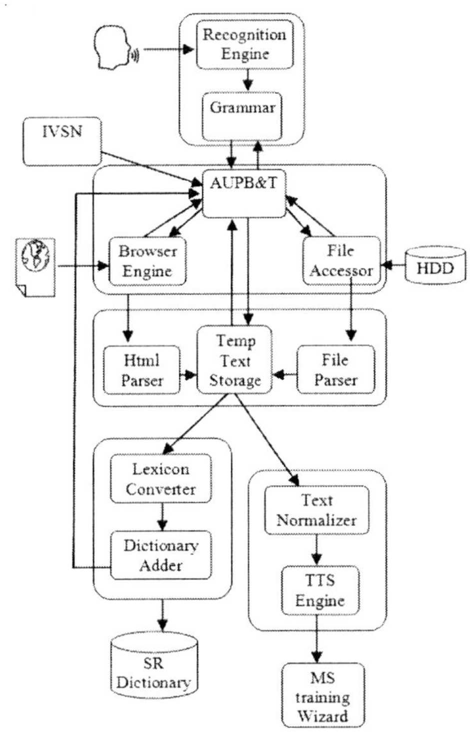

Automatic User Profile Building and Training System (AUPB&T)

Due to the general vocabulary provided by recognition engines, we needed to find a way to expand the vocabulary to suit the individual needs of users and tailor it to their day-to-day vocabulary, be it science, art, literature, etc. To get around this problem, we built an Automatic User Profile Building and Training (AUPB&T) system. The system adds the words found in documents and/or URLS given by the user, and then initiates an automatic training session where the user does not need to talk to the system, since a natural synthesized voice is used instead. Of course, to accommodate visually impaired users, we provide a means to control the system using voice commands. As Figure 8 shows, the system is built in a modular fashion to make it more manageable and to facilitate the addition of functionalities.

The main module of AUPB&T controls the fetching of the documents through the web browser engine and the file accessor engine. Once the documents are opened, the two engines pass them to their respective parsers. The main module is also in charge of telling the parser module that it can pass its text to the lexicon module. Then, the words contained in the parsed text are added to the trainer module dictionary.

The voice control module is used to tell the main module which documents should be opened, and from where to get the web documents. Two grammars are required for this task. The first one is the command grammar, which has all the necessary vocabulary to control the application. The second one is the spelling grammar, used to spell out the paths and URLs of the documents needed for profile building and training.

The parser module contains two engines and a temporary storage area. The first engine is a HTML parser used to filter out garbage text. The second one is used to open raw text documents as well as Microsoft Word documents. Once the parsing is done, the documents are appended to the storage area for later processing. The lexicon module is used to convert the text coming from the parser module to their phonetic representation. Finally, each word is added to the speech recognition's engine with its corresponding phonetic code.

The trainer module is used to automatically train the speech recognition engine. The text stored in the parser module is passed to the trainer module. This later normalizes the text and opens a training session. Once the training session is opened, the text is passed to the TTS engine in order to be read until the training session is over. A complete description of the method is given in (Benahmed & Selouani, 2006).

EXPERIMENTS AND RESULTS

In order to evaluate the efficiency of the LINC, LINC+, and LINC^d platforms, IVSN and the AUPB&T systems, we carry out a series of evaluations. The goal of the LINC and LINC+ evaluation is to determine how learners deal with these platforms. For the AUPB&T system, the goal of the evaluation is to determine how efficient it would prove in enhancing speech recognition performance. We have used the LINC, LINC+, and LINC^d e-Learning tool in a trimester programming course at Université de Moncton.

LINC Evaluation

The course is given to thirty-six undergraduate students. At each meeting in the classroom, we access the Web site and show the Web pages on a big screen. After class, the students are encouraged to use LINC at home or in a laboratory to review lessons and to collaborate with the group's members to answer questions by using LINC's forum. There are six groups with six students per group. We consider LINC as a new pedagogical resource that allows us to enhance learning in the classroom. With this tool, we offer students more opportunities to exchange their opinions on a subject matter. They can do that comfortably at home and at times convenient to them.

We adopt a method similar to the problem-based learning approach by elaborating the appropriate questions for each lesson, and encouraging students to answer these questions. If a group has a right answer, all members in this group will benefit from the same bonus. In this way, and at the same time, we create an atmosphere of competition between the groups. In the first two weeks, because of shyness (most of the students had not met each other before the course), not many students participated within the forum. From the third week on, we announced a specific bonus for each question. The participation rate increased day by day, from 30% to 70%. Comparing this with the past trimesters, we observed a relative improvement in learning. What is more evident is that the appointments we normally have with students are reduced, because they can now directly post their questions on the forum to other group members. By following the forum, we also measure the real knowledge level of students. In addition, through the student messages, we can easily detect misconceptions or misunderstandings, and proceed to clarify them at the next meeting. Here, we give a concrete example, extracted from the forum with our commentaries in parentheses:

The question was: "What will happen if you exceed the limit of a character array in copying a string to this array?"

- **Group A: Student X:** If a string's length is greater than a character array's length where it should be memorized, the overflowed string will overwrite the data in the memory addresses following the array.
- **Student Y** adds: I agree. So we have to ensure that the array's length is long enough to contain the whole string. (*This is a good advice for programmers*).
- **Group C:** If we go over the limit of an array, it will cause the system to "freeze". When we go over the limit of an array, the

"buffer" will be saturated and all the data remaining in it will be corrupted. (*This is wrong! He has a misconception about the data buffer*).

- **Group D:**I think that if the limit of a character array is exceeded, it will cause a loss of data; the data exceeding the limit will be lost. (*This is wrong*!). Later this student adds: I just tried to exceed the limit, and all the characters are still displaying. Maybe the array which is supposed to contain the information is not displaying, and C++ displays an array that was supposed to be copied. For example, strcpy(*a, b*), if the length of *b* is greater than the length of *a*, there will be no copy and *b* will be displayed. (*This is wrong! But he has tried to program, a necessary and good behavior*).
- **Student T corrects it:**The danger is that if we exceed the limit of the source, these memory locations will contain data copied outside the reserved addresses; even worse, this string will overwrite the data which can be mandatory to other programs or to the operating system and, sometimes, it can cause an execution error. (*This is a good explanation, although it suggests a lack of knowledge about the data location of the operating system*).

LINC+ and LINC^d Evaluation

The evaluation of LINC+ and LINC^d involved both speech recognition and speech synthesis with a total of fifty experiments. Twenty people were asked to test the speech recognition system, while thirty subjects were recruited to test the quality of the speech synthesis for a number of voices. The participants were mainly students and professors at our university who had never been involved in the project development. All participants were from a multicultural background. In order to collect data for testing speech recognition, a number of web navigation commands, usually used for the LINC system, were tested. Each of the twenty test subjects would try each command three times in order to see how many attempts would be successful, and hence obtain a total of sixty trials per command.

As for the evaluation of speech synthesis, a simple program was provided in order to permit users to control the repetition of each sentence until they understood it. The program calculated the time (in seconds) needed to understand each sentence, as well as the number of times each of them had to be repeated before it was understood. Thirteen meaningful sentences were used for this test. About half of the sentences were made of commonly used words, while the other half used scientific terms. The choice of scientific terms was intended to avoid the easy guess of a misunderstood word by a listener. Four voices were used for this testing session. Two voices (Pierre and Veronique) from the Lernout and Hauspie (L&H) TTS 3000 speech synthesizer (L&H TTS, 2006) as well as two voices (Jacques and Jacqueline) from the IBM ViaVoice Outloud speech synthesizer (IBM Viavoice, 2007) were used for comparison purposes. Fifty percent (50%) of the participants tested only one voice and 50% tested two voices.

We decided to limit the experiments to approximately ten minutes per participant in order to easily recruit participants. For the first twenty participants, the evaluation began with speech recognition followed by speech synthesis. The procedure was explained to the subjects before performing the commands three times. We noted how many times the system recognized the commands. For the synthesis evaluation, the first half of the participants tested the Veronique voice, while the other half tested the Jacques voice. Twenty people were considered enough for the evaluation of the speech recognition engine. Additional participants were recruited to compare voices in the context of informal discussions. We created a new set of sentences, and ten new participants evaluated both the Pierre and Jacqueline voices.

Table 1. Evaluation of TTS systems and synthetic voices involved in LINC+ and LINC[d]

Voice synthesizer	Average number of repetitions	Standard deviation	Average time in seconds	Standard deviation
L&H TTS 3000				
Veronique	1.607	0.731	5.883	7.828
Pierre	1.623	0.844	3.809	4.641
IBM ViaVoice				
Jacques	1.323	1.323	1.636	18.609
Jacqueline	1.415	0.429	3.107	4.639

The French sentences used for this test varied in length and in complexity.

For each participant, the percentage of word recognition rate per command and for all commands was calculated, as well as the standard deviations. During the experiment, we realized that the total success rate was better for men (74%) than for women (62%). The recognizer reached an average correct recognition rate of 69.99%.

The testing program used for speech synthesis calculated the time (in seconds) needed by the participant to understand a sentence as well as how often the sentence had to be repeated. The average and standard deviation were calculated for those data. Table 1 summarizes the results for each voice. Veronique and Pierre performed similarly. Veronique had slightly fewer repetitions on average, but with Pierre, participants took less time to determine whether they had understood or not. The results showed that the IBM ViaVoice Outloud engine performed better than the L&H TTS 3000 engine, both in number of repetitions and time of completion. For the two ViaVoice Outloud voices, Jacques yielded better results than Jacqueline.

AIMLComparative Evaluation

To evaluate the improvements that AIML brings over conventional command-based interaction, we propose the following scenario: A students wants to go to lesson four, see the contents of the class inheritance topic and check whether or not there are new answers in the group forum.

Using Fixed Grammar

User: Go to lesson 4
User: Go to topic class inheritance
User: Show forum

Using AIML

User: I want to see chapter 4

Or

User: Show me lesson 4
System(*internal*): GO_LESSON 4
User: Show me the class inheritance topic
System(*internal*): GO_TOPIC class inheritance
User: Are there any new answers in the forum since yesterday
System(*internal*): NEW_ANS_SINCE yesterday

As can be seen by this example, AIML provides more naturalness to student interaction. They are essentially able to query the system like they would a person.

IVSN and AUPB&T Evaluations

To evaluate the IVSN and the AUPB&T systems, we used two separate machines. The first one is the baseline system. It did not receive any training, and was used to establish the "no training" performance of the system. The second system was trained by using the AUPB&T technique. The free SAPI 5.1 compatible Microsoft English (U.S.) v6.1 recognition engine is used throughout all experiments. For the training, we used a document containing 1338 words that cover several subject matters. For the test, we used a document composed of 1909 words, from which 25% came from the training document. Figure 9 shows an excerpt from the test document. We evaluated the systems by using three speakers. The first two speakers were Ray and Julia, artificial voices. The third (young male) speaker, referred to as β, is a human speaker who did not participate in the training process. To insure a consistent set of results with β, we recorded him reading the test document. We also refrained from normalizing the volume of the wave file in order to reproduce a normal usage scenario.

In addition to correct word recognition rate, the three following measures were used to evaluate the speech recognition performance of our systems. The omission count is the number of words from the original text that were not recognized. The insertion count is the difference between the number of words in the recognized text and the number of words in the original text. The position count is the number of words in the recognized text that do not appear in the same order as in the original text. The text was tested three times with the same voice. The first phase of the experiment consisted of reading the multi-subject document by using the three voices on the baseline system. The average recognition rate was 84% for all speakers (virtual and real). The second phase of the experiment consisted of doing one AUPB&T session through the use of both Ray and Julia virtual voices. The multi-subject document was used for the test.

As shown in Figure 10, the recognition rate increased to reach an average of 94%, This represents an improvement of 10% for both Ray and Julia, the virtual speakers. Finally, to test the effectiveness of the system for a regular and unknown human user, the β speaker read the multi-subject document to a system using Ray's trained profile. This yielded the following results: 356 omission, 89 insertion and 16 position errors. This corresponds to 82% recognition rate which represents an improvement of 2%. This result suggests that we can improve the recognition rate without having to resort to a fastidious training session performed by a human speaker.

Figure 9. Excerpt from the multi-subject test document, in this case an excerpt from Shakespeare's Hamlet

Be not too tame neither, but let your own discretion be your tutor: suit the action to the word, the word to the action; with this special o'erstep not the modesty of nature: for any thing so overdone is from the purpose of playing, whose end, both at the
first and now, was and is, to hold, as 'twere, the mirror up to nature; to show virtue her own feature, scorn her own image, and the very age and body of the time his form and pressure. Now this overdone, or come tardy off, though it make the unskillful laugh, cannot but make the judicious grieve; the censure of the which one must in your allowance o'erweigh a whole theatre of others. ...

Figure 10. Comparative results of the recognizer without training (NT) and with a one-pass use (T_1) of the AUPB&T system in the context of a multi-subject spoken query

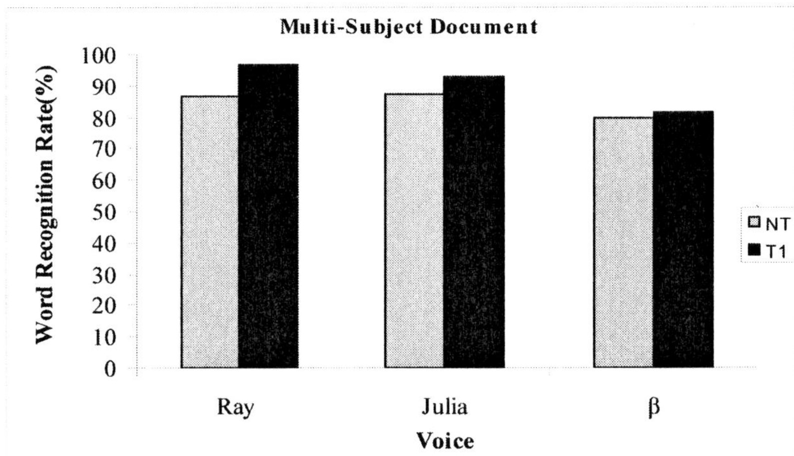

Impact of Speech-Enabled Virtual Laboratory on Student Achievement

As outlined in (Su et al, 2005) both instructors and learners of the virtual laboratory perceive interaction as an important aspect of successful learning. Our tool is intended to provide a collaborative workplace to encourage interactions among learners by the means of the Forum. As such, this environment enables learners to exchange their knowledge and their way of thinking, and to refine the knowledge acquired via lectures. To evaluate this knowledge, we followed a protocol similar to the one described in (Lawson & Stackpole, 2006). We compared the students' scores over two years. In the first year, the students followed the C++ course in a traditional classroom. In the second year, LINC+ and $LINC^d$ was implemented and used by students for their learning. At the end of the second year, the average score was 72.84/100 compared to 71.31/100 for the previous year where the LINC+ and $LINC^d$ had not been used. Even if an improvement is obtained, we need to test the tool with other online and traditional laboratory groups. This is essential to prove if the tool we proposed reinforces meaningful knowledge and skills in C++ programming.

We had also distributed a questionnaire with ten (10) questions to collect students' evaluation of this tool. The average score, compiled from 20 respondents, for the evaluation of this software tool reached 8.82/10. We found that there was satisfaction from almost all the students. With this result as well as the evident advantage for the instructor, we believe that the LINC+ and $LINC^d$ software are very useful for both learners (to improve their learning) and teachers (to discover the student's knowledge level). Table 2 gives the overall score for each question. Note that the best score is obtained when ergonomic and interaction issues are considered. It appears that these aspects are the strengths of the system. The lowest score is the one regarding the competition among groups, which is relatively less important than we expected. The average satisfaction rating was determined using a scale ranging from 0 "very dissatisfied" to 10 "very satisfied."

Table 2. Average scores of LINC+ and LINC^d evaluation using a scale ranging from 0 to 10 and a questionnaire submitted to 20 learners

Questions	Evaluation (form 0 to 10)
Do you find it easy and comfortable to use LINC+ outside the classroom?	8.88
Is LINC+ user-friendly ?	8.83
Has this tool permitted you to develop your knowledge cooperatively?	8.35
Is the division of the virtual classroom in small groups suitable and advantageous?	7.83
Do you feel that that there is competition between the groups?	7.00
Is the Forum interesting and useful for your learning?	8.06
Has your knowledge of C++ improved by using LINC+?	7.66
Were the questions asked in the Forum adequate and essential?	8.27
How would you evaluate the quality of the multimedia content and the speech tools?	8.72
Do you feel that your learning style has become more efficient by using this system?	8.00
Was the help and the monitoring by the professor in the Forum essential?	8.37
Overall, how would you rate this system?	8.82

CONCLUSION

In this chapter, we have presented a virtual laboratory system, which provides an augmented interaction modality by incorporating speech technology in a mixed-mode learning of the C++ programming language. The major finding of our work indicates that when learning material is delivered in the form of a speech-based presentation (LINC+ and LINC^d), the majority of learners seem to be satisfied with this new media, and suggests, as it is shown by the evaluation results, that their learning style was improved. The IVSN system easily allows for searching and surfing the Web through voice commands and dictation. The feedback system also plays an important role in improving the whole experience as it allows the user to know exactly what the system is doing. It also plays a role in the dictation and spelling mode as it gives users the ability to detect any recognition errors that might occur. Besides this, we noticed two main advantages by incorporating the AUPB&T system. The first one is the ability to improve speech recognition without having to spend time reading texts. The second one consists of using the user's documents to launch the training session. This, in fact, results in a tailored user profile. Learners who do not have the ability or the patience to deal with the manual training process (reading the training texts) should find it especially attractive. The proposed tool does not require sophisticated technical skills or a significant amount of time to learn how to use it effectively.

Traditional e-learning suffers from a "boredom" factor. The introduction of conversational technology constitutes a solution to improve retention rates. However, in incorporating speech technology into a virtual learning environment, there are many technological challenges. The ASR must be sufficiently robust and flexible, whatever the acoustical environment. In some situations, the TTS module must be bilingual, since in many technology-oriented courses, French and English are used interchangeably. Learners are faced with the task of reviewing their overall learning strategy in light of the opportunities provided by speech technology. To enrich the learning experience, we have introduced a mobile learning application that uses adapted speech technology and natural language processing module. It is expected that mobile learning could be an efficient incitation factor for involving disaffected young people to engage in learning, where more traditional methods have failed. In fact, as mobile phones combine features such as cameras, video and MP3 players with our natural speech-enabled interface, the world of learning becomes more flexible and more exciting for learners. Cobb (1997), Beacham (2002) and others have debated over the years regarding which modality or combinations of modalities to use. This debate as well as the problem of the cognition load will be the focus of our future work, because we believe that it is important to achieve an effective balance between the three basic elements of e-learning, namely content, technology and services. Speech technologies can drastically enhance a student's ability to access e-learning, but it is vital to match the right tools with both the user and the tasks to be undertaken.

REFERENCES

Allen, J. B. (1994). How do humans process and recognize speech? *IEEE Transactions on Speech and Audio Processing, 2*(4), 567–577. doi:10.1109/89.326615

Alty, J. L. (2002). Dual coding theory and education: Some media experiments to examine the effects of different media on learning. In *Proceedings of EDMEDIA2002: World Conference on Educational Multimedia, Hypermedia & Telecommunications* (pp. 42-47). Denver, Colorado, USA.

Beacham, N., Elliott, A., Alty, J., & Al-Sharrah, A. (2002). Media combinations and learning styles: A dual coding theory approach. In *Proceedings of EDMEDIA2002: World Conference on Educational Multimedia, Hypermedia & Telecommunications* (pp. 111-116). Denver, Colorado, USA.

Benahmed, Y., & Selouani, S.-A. (2006). Robust self-training system for spoken query information retrieval using pitch range variations. *IEEE Canadian Conference on Electrical & Computer Engineering* (pp. 949-952). Ottawa, Canada.

Bosworth, K. (1994). Developing collaborative skills in college students. *New Directions for Teaching and Learning, 59*, 25–31. doi:10.1002/tl.37219945905

Bourlard, H., & Morgan, N. (1994). *Connectionist speech recognition: A hybrid approach*. Kluwer Publisher.

Brown, R. (2006). Exploring new speech recognition and synthesis APIs in Windows Vista. *MSDN magazine*. Retrieved January 30, 2009 from http://msdn.microsoft.com/en-us/magazine/cc163663.aspx

Charpentier, F. J., & Stella, M. G. (1986). Diphone synthesis using an overlap-add technique for speech waveforms concatenation. In *Proceedings of International Conference on Acoustics, Speech and Signal Processing* (pp. 2015-2018). Tokyo, Japan.

Cobb, T. (1997). Cognitive efficiency: towards a revised theory of media. *Educational Technology Research and Development, 45*(4), 21–35. doi:10.1007/BF02299681

Deng, L., & Huang, X. (2004). Challenges in adopting speech recognition. *Communications of the ACM, 47*(1), 69–75. doi:10.1145/962081.962108

Grau, S., d'Alessandro, C., & Richard, G. (1993). A speech formant synthesizer based on harmonic + random formant-waveforms representation. In [Berlin, Germany.]. *Proceedings of Eurospeech, 93*, 1697–1700.

Huggins-Daines, D., Kumar, M., Chan, A., Black, A. W., Ravishankar, M., & Rudnicky, A. I. (2006). PocketSphinx: A free, real-time continuous speech recognition system for hand-held devices. In *Proc. of ICASSP, Toulouse, France*.

IETF. The Internet Engineering Task Force (2006). *A Media Resource Control Protocol (MRCP, RFC number 4463*. Jelinek, F. (1997). *Statistical Methods for Speech Recognition*. MIT Press.

Jones, A. Issroff., K., Scanlon, E., Clough, G. & McAndrew, P. (2006). *Using mobile devices for learning in informal settings: Is it motivating?* Paper presented at IADIS International conference Mobile Learning. July 14-16, Dublin.

Karweit, M. (2000). *Virtual engineering/science laboratory course*. Retrieved May 12, 2007 from http://www.jhu.edu/~virtlab/virtlab.html

Kruse, K. (2002a). *Using the Web for learning: advantages and disadvantages*. Retrieved May 12, 2007 from http://www.e-learningguru.com/articles/art1_9.htm

Kruse, K. (2002b). *E-learning and the neglect of user interface design*. Retrieved May 12, 2007 from http://www.e-learningguru.com/articles/art4_1.htm, retrieved May 12, 2007. L&H TTS3000. (2006). *Nuance: trademark*. Retrieved February 6, 2007 from http://www.nuance.com

Lawson, E. A., & Stackpole W. (2006). Does a virtual networking laboratory result in similar student achievement and satisfaction? In *Proceedings of the 7th conference on Information technology education*. 105-114, Minneapolis, Minnesota, USA.

Lê, T. -.H. & Roy, J. (2005-b). Integrating e-learning and classroom learning. In *Proceedings of CCCT-05, The 3rd International Conference on Computing, Communications and Control Technologies* (Vol. I, pp. 238-243). Austin, TX, USA.

Lê, T.-H., & Roy, J. (2005-a). LINC: A WEB-based learning tool for mixed-mode learning. *The 7th International Conference on Enterprise Information Systems*. (Vol. 5, pp. 154-160). Miami, Florida, USA.

Microsoft Corporation. (2006). *Microsoft English (U.S.) v6.1 Recognizer*. Retrieved June 10, 2006 from http://www.microsoft.com/speech/download/sdk51

Najjar, L. J. (1996). Multimedia information and learning. *Journal of Educational Multimedia and Hypermedia*, *5*(1), 129–150.

O'Shaughnessy, D. (2000). *Speech communication: human and machine*. IEEE Press.

Sproat, R. W. (1995). Text-to-speech synthesis. *AT&T Technical Journal*, *74*, 35–44.

Su, B. (2005). The importance of interaction in Web-based education: A program-level case study of online MBA courses. *Journal of Interactive Online Learning*, *4*(1), 1–19.

Tollervey, N. H. (2006). Program# - An AIML Chatterbot in C#. Retrieved January 30, 2009 from http://ntoll.org/article/program-20. Northamptonshire, United Kingdom.

Viavoice Outloud, I. B. M. (2007). Text-to-speech downloadable for many languages. Retrieved May 12, 2007 from http://www-306.ibm.com/software/voice/viavoice/dev/msagent.html

Wald, M. (2005). SpeechText: Enhancing learning and teaching by using automatic speech recognition to create accessible synchronised multimedia. Retrieved June 10, 2006 from http://eprints.ecs.soton.ac.uk/10723/01/mwaldedmediaproceedings.doc

Wallace, R. (2005). Artificial intelligence markup language (AIML) Version 1.0.1. *AI Foundation*. Retrieved January 30, 2009, from http://alicebot.org/TR/2005/WD-aiml

Chapter 11
WEBCAP:
Web Scheduler for Distance Learning Multimedia Documents with Web Workload Considerations

Sami Habib
Kuwait University, Kuwait

Maytham Safar
Kuwait University, Kuwait

ABSTRACT

In many web applications, such as the distance learning, the frequency of refreshing multimedia web documents places a heavy burden on the WWW resources. Moreover, the updated web documents may encounter inordinate delays, which make it difficult to retrieve web documents in time. Here, we present an Internet tool called WEBCAP that can schedule the retrieval of multimedia web documents in time while considering the workloads on the WWW resources by applying capacity planning techniques. We have modeled a multimedia web document as a 4-level hierarchy (object, operation, timing, and precedence.) The transformations between levels are performed automatically, followed by the application of Bellman-Ford's algorithm on the precedence graph to schedule all operations (fetch, transmit, process, and render) while satisfying the in time retrieval and all workload resources constraints. Our results demonstrate how effective WEBCAP is in scheduling the refreshing of multimedia web documents.

INTRODUCTION

Distance learning is the largest growing sector of the 1-to-12 and higher education in the world today. It defines a new way of interacting teaching that uses latest technologies to deliver the materials to remote students (usually off-campus). With the introduction of the Internet and the World Wide Web (WWW), the possibilities and the participation in distance learning have taken a large leap forward. Hence, the geographical boundaries and scheduling conflicts are not the obstacles to learning, which might have been in the past. This is usually accomplished by augmenting Internet applications and Web technology into a traditional classroom setting, which has created new challenges regarding material delivery, especially through the Internet. Because of the nature of the Internet as a distributed information system, heterogeneity, large frequent changes, and non-uniformity of information access, the growth of the Internet in terms of increasing resources cannot be sustained in keeping up with users' demands. The solution lies in sharing the limited Internet resources (servers and networks) among the users wisely.

The periodical refreshing multimedia (PRM) allows users to frequently access the latest information. PRM consists of various information objects such as a text, still image, audio, video, animation and mixes of all these objects. PRM may involve presentation of static and dynamic objects, which require specific order and timing. Thus, PRM imposes stringent and diverse constraints on the resources of the Web caching architecture such as the requirements of larger storage capacity, higher network bandwidth and higher transfer time. For example, the collected satellite images of past hurricanes and their visualizations can be used in educating how these violent weather fronts form and function, as well as their effects on the natural and human landscapes. In addition, the material collected can be used in class as a part of a tool for teaching Geosciences with Visualizations. For example, the tool could help in visualizing the Earth, its processes, and its evolution through time as a fundamental aspect of geosciences. Research sheds light on why teaching with visualizations is effective. Visualization has the power and ability to clarify relationships rather than reproducing exactly the natural world.

Geoscientists use a wide variety of tools to assist them in creating their own mental images. For example, multi-layered visualizations of geographically referenced data are usually created as animations to look at changes in data, model output through time, and to analyze the relationships between different variables. With new access to online data and new technologies for visualizing data, it is becoming increasingly important to analyze the relationships between the animated objects and system/network load in order to design a powerful tool for teaching geosciences. Our proposed system can measure the effectiveness of online visualizations in teaching, and can provide a hint on what resources are needed to increase the capability of teaching with visualizations in the geosciences.

In general, the Web caching architecture has to provide both network transparency and object availability so that clients can access these objects locally or remotely as if they were on the same site. To deliver the requested PRM from remote servers to users in time, while placing the least demands on the servers and networks is a challenging optimization (scheduling) problem due to the unpredictably of the execution time of server, and network involved in retrieving the PRM.

Due to the explosive and ever growing size of the Web, distributed Web caching has received considerable attention. The main goal of caches is to move the frequently accessed information closer to the users. Caching systems should improve performance for end users, network operators, and content providers. Caching can be recognized as an effective way to: speed up Web access, reduce latency perceived by the users, reduce network traffic, reduce server load, and improve response time to the users. Since the Web is huge in size, most caching techniques used a distributed cache system rather than a centralized cache system. In a centralized caching system, requesting direction would be efficient and maintaining the consistency of data is cheaper. However, the main bottleneck will be the communication with the central resource. On the other hand, distributed caching system increases the processing power by storing information on many servers. Moreover, it strives to store data close to users.

In this article, we present a novel Internet tool (WEBCAP) that has been collectively envisioned on the authors' work (Habib, 1997; 2005; Safar, 2000; 2002). The WEBCAP performs the following tasks:

- extracting information objects from the PRM documents
- modeling the extracted objects into an object flow graph (OFG)
- transforming the OFG into an operation flow graph (OPFG)
- transforming the OPFG into a timing flow graph (TFG)
- transforming the TFG into a precedence flow graph (PFG)
- finding a feasible schedule to all operations within PFG

We have structured WEBCAP to perform the six tasks in a sequential order, but we have included a number of feedback loops to relax any graph representation so we can achieve a feasible schedule. The main objective of the WEBCAP research as described here is to ***guide*** the distributed systems designer/manager to schedule or tune her/his resources for optimal or near optimal performance, subject to minimizing the cost of document retrieval while satisfying the in time constraints.

RELATED WORK

We are dealing with a multidisciplinary research, which involves the WWW authoring tools, multimedia document representation, data caching, scheduling, WWW resource management, and capacity planning. We have carried out an extensive survey, and to our knowledge there is no work that combines all the above topics yet. In this section, we summarize our survey.

The related issues to cache design were discussed and described in Safar (2002). Many caching techniques have been proposed in the literature (Wessels, 1995; Wang, 1997; Xu, 2004). Even though they have differed in their design approaches, they all have the same common design principles, which are keeping the cache data close to clients, sharing data among many caches, reducing network bandwidth demand, minimizing the number of servers accessed to get data, and not slowing down the system on cache miss.

To our knowledge, most of the published related work is limited only on object scheduling without considering the operation scheduling within the Web system (Courtiat, 2000; Xu, 2004). There are some early studies that attempted to model the caching of a multimedia Web document in forms of scheduling the nodes within an object flow graph (OFG) (Habib, 1997; Candan, 1998). An OFG is a directed acyclic graph, where a node represents an information object and an edge represents the order of flow between two objects. However, these early works have not attempted to schedule the periodical refreshing multimedia (PRM) with workload considerations.

Current multimedia presentation systems use different technologies (e.g., JAVA, ASP, JSP, XML) to support multi-level presentation requirements (Deliyannis, 2002). In such systems, the relations between different objects are described through a navigational graph. In the navigational graph each multimedia object is presented at one level and has a sequential dependency with the objects at the other levels. The work in Webster (2002) introduced presentation and interaction paradigms using commercially available multimedia environment MMS (e.g., Macromedia Director). The underlying graph structures of MMSs were used to organize/specify the relation between objects. The advantage of this system is that it features advanced interaction over the WWW, and dynamic editing and rendering of media objects. To describe data relationships between different media objects in a MMS system, the graphs describing the MMS structure use internal/external links to connect them. The internal links relate objects in a single MMS level, while external links describe data relationships between multiple MMS. Network dependencies (e.g., connection speed/bandwidth) and multimedia object dependencies (e.g., object size, render time) were not taken into consideration when implementing this system. This would affect the system usability for real applications.

A system named WIP (Knowledge-based Presentation of Information) was developed to generate coordinated presentations from several presentation goals provided by a presentation planner (Andre, 1993). Directed acyclic graph (DAG) was used to reflect the propositional contents of the potential document parts, as well as the relationships between them. The drawback of the WIP system is that it generates the material to be presented as animation sequences (sequential relationship between objects).

A system named PPP (Personalized Plan-based Presenter) was developed based on WIP that addresses the temporal relations between different multimedia objects (Andre, 1996). PPP designs multimedia material, and plans a presentation act and considers the temporal relations between objects. PPP considers multimedia object dependencies; however, since the presentation is not delivered through the Web, it does not consider network dependencies.

A multimedia distance learning system (WebWisdom) was developed that has an integrated set of tools supporting academic and corporate courseware storage, management, and delivery (Walczak, 2002). The system was used for several application areas (Beca, 1997; 1997b; Podgorny, 1998; Walczak, 2001). One of the major components of the system is the dynamic Web interface (Wiza, 2000; Cellary, 2001). It allows the retrieval of the data objects (e.g., images, audio, and videos) from the database and displays them in the form of Web pages in the client browser. The objects in this system are organized in a hierarchical matter, where each hierarchy represents a set of slides to be presented to the end user (PowerPoint-like), thus, imposing a sequential relation between the objects. Furthermore, the system does not consider the network dependencies and assumes that all data objects are available and will be delivered to the client's browser in time. In our work, we assume that a level might have more than one object, and we might have temporal dependencies between objects at the same or different levels.

Hierarchical Representation of Multimedia Documents

Many Web applications use heterogeneous objects in their Web presentation contents. An object can be a text, image, audio, video, animation or mixture of objects. An example of a periodical refreshing multimedia (PRM) document is depicted in Figure 1, which illustrates one of the Cable News Network's (CNN) weather news (CNN, 2004). This piece of weather news was tracking a hurricane movement in the Atlantic Ocean. In the next subsections, we demonstrate the transformation process that is automatically implemented within WEBCAP.

Object Flow Graph

The object flow graph (OFG), as shown in Figure 2, is a graphical representation of a Web multimedia document as illustrated in Figure 1. In

Figure 1. A typical periodical refreshing multimedia document

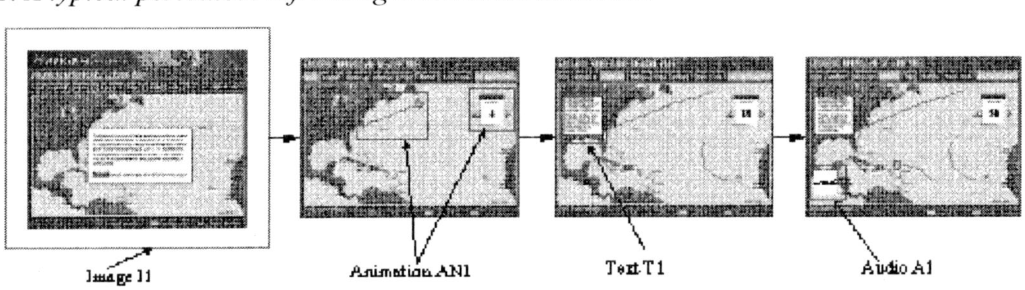

Figure 2. An object flow graph consisting of four heterogeneous objects (image, animation, text, and audio)

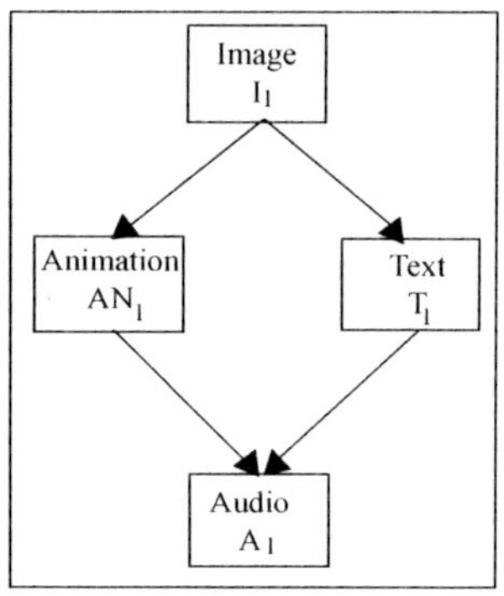

Figure 3. Allen's seven temporal properties

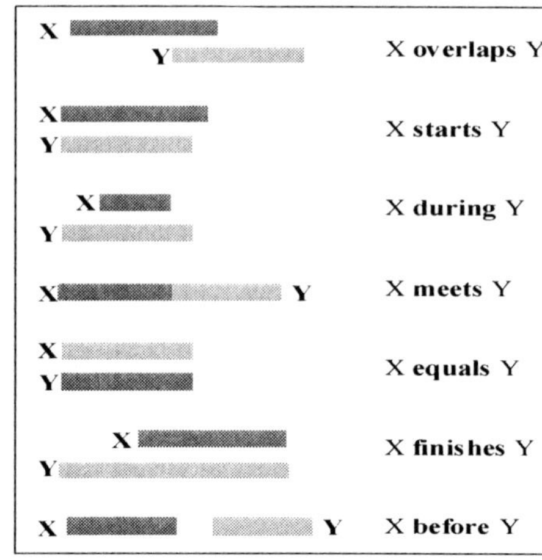

other words, the mapping of the Web multimedia document (real example) into a graph offers a fine grain representation of the relations between the objects. A node and edge in the object flow graph represent an object and a flow between two objects respectively. The rendering of the four heterogeneous objects: image (I1), animation (AN1), text (T1), and audio (A1) should follow the following five constraints:

1. image (I1) meets with animation (AN1),
2. image (I1) occurs before text (T1),
3. animation (AN1) overlaps with audio (A1),
4. text (T1) occurs during animation (AN1), and
5. text (T1) occurs before audio (A1).

These constraints ensure a correct order of presentation for all objects involved in the document. The relationships between the objects are formulated based on Allen's seven temporal relations (Allen, 1983), as shown in Figure 3. Allen's temporal properties include: overlap, start, during, meet, equal, finish, and before. Some of Allen's temporal properties are known to be commutative, such as start, equal and finish. The graphical representations of all Allen's temporal properties are included during the transformation from the timing flow graph to the precedence flow graph.

Operation Flow Graph

The operation flow graph (OPFG) depicts all operations (fetch, transmit, process, render) that are involved in fetching an object from a server, transmitting an object from a server to client through a network, processing an object at a client, and rendering an object at a client. Figure 4 illustrates the operation flow graph for the object flow graph depicted in Figure 2. The operation flow graph shows all the Web resources that are involved in storing, transmitting, and accessing a Web multimedia document. The structure complexity of OPFG is four times the structure complexity of OFG with respect to the number of nodes in each graph. Our algorithm assumes that there are two extra dummy nodes: starting and ending. The starting is connected to all fetch operations, and all rendering operations are connected to the ending node. Usages of the starting and ending nodes are to facilitate the execution and termination of the algorithm respectively.

Figure 4. An operation flow graph consisting of 4 fetching nodes, 4 transmission nodes, 4 processing nodes, and 4 rendering nodes

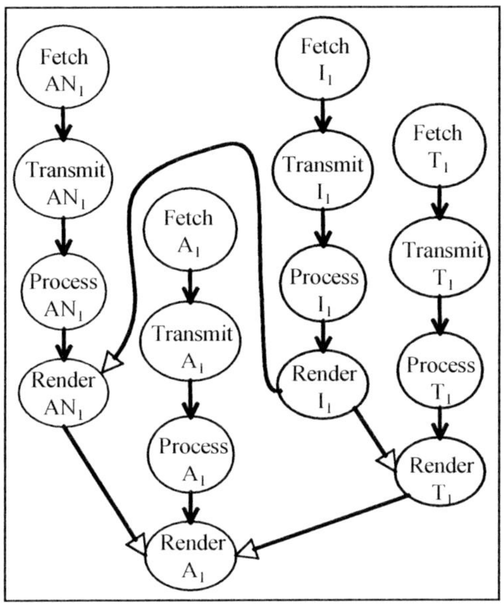

Timing Flow Graph

The timing flow graph (TFG) includes all starting and ending times for all operations within the OPFG. Thus, each operation node is divided into two nodes, where the first node represents the starting time and the second node represents the ending time. Figure 5 illustrates the transformation from the operation flow graph (as shown in Figure 4) into the timing flow graph.

The connection between the starting and ending nodes of the same operation indicates the total execution time of that operation. The structure complexity of TFG is eight times the structure complexity of OFG and four times the structure complexity of OPFG with respect to the number of nodes in each graph. To reduce the structure complexity of the TFG, we have embedded a procedure within WEBCAP to combine a certain two nodes together into a single node without losing any information. For example, the reduction procedure combines the ending time of the fetch operation with the starting time of the transmission operation. Such reduction reduces the structure complexity of TFG to five times the structure complexity of OFG rather than eight times. Also, the reduced TFG will be traversed faster especially when WEBCAP is trying to determine a feasible schedule.

Precedence Flow Graph

The precedence flow graph (PFG) is similar to the timing flow graph as shown in Figure 5, but PFG contains all the rendering constraints. The rendering constraints ensure a smooth and in-time presentation between the objects at the client side. These constraints are placed between the rendering operations using Allen's temporal properties, as shown in Figure 5. The structure complexity of the PFG is the same as TFG with respect to the number of nodes, except a few edges are added to set Allen's temporal properties.

We used the following three notations, which are governing the graphical representation of the nodes and the links between them. We assume that each node in the graph represents either a start or end time for the render operation of an object, and that each link/edge represents the temporal relation between two nodes. We will use the defined notations to encode Allen's temporal relations. Figure 6 illustrates the three notations assuming that T_1 and T_2 are the start/end time of two nodes. Then our notations for the edge directions, value and signs are as follows:

- If T_1 is larger than T_2 (i.e., T_1 starts after T_2), then we say that $T_1 - T_2 \geq +\delta$ and is represented by one edge from T_1 to T_2 with $-\delta$ value.
- If T_1 is smaller than T_2 (i.e., T_1 starts before T_2), then we say that $T_1 - T_2 \leq +\delta$ and is represented by one edge from T_2 to T_1 with $+\delta$ value.
- If the difference between T_1 and T_2 is a certain amount of time, then we say that $T_1 - T_2 = \pm\delta$ and is represented by two edges, one from

Figure 5. Timing and precedence flow graph

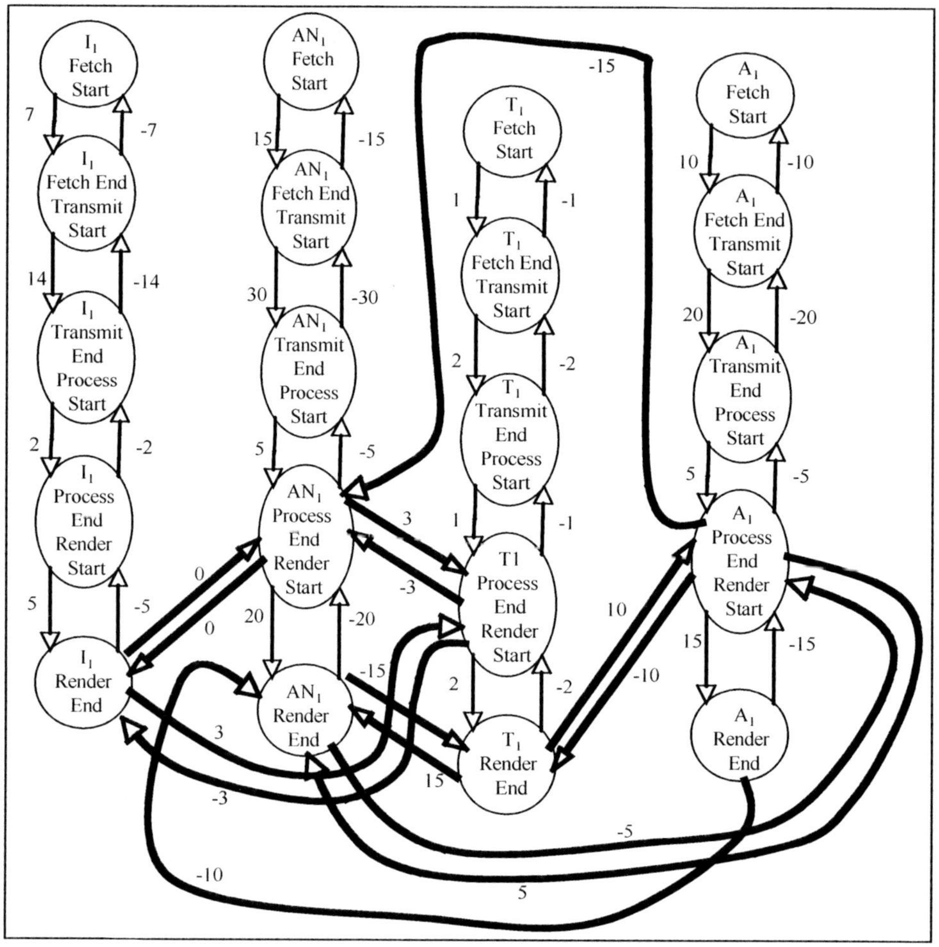

T_1 to T_2 with $-\delta$ value and another from T_2 to T_1 with $+\delta$.

In the next subsections, we have examined and illustrated how to encode all Allen's temporal properties graphically.

Overlap Property

An *overlap* property between the rendering operations of objects A and B insures the following properties: 1) A starts rendering before B; 2) B starts rendering at a certain period of time after the rendering of A and not at the same time; 3) the rendering of B should start before the end of rendering of A, and not at the exact end time of rendering A; 4) the rendering of B should end after the end of rendering of A, and not at the exact end time of rendering A . In Figure 7: δ_1 represents the rendering time for A;

Figure 6. Graphical representation notations

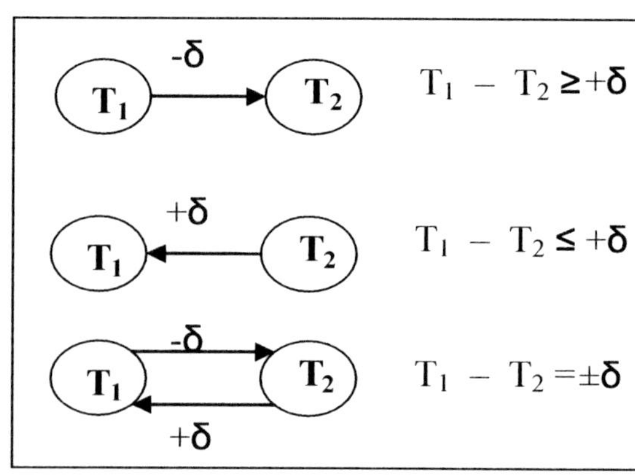

δ_2 represents the rendering time for B; δ_{o2} insures properties 1) and 2); δ_{o1} insures property 3); and δ_{o3} insures property 4).

Start Property

A *start* property between the rendering operations of objects A and B insures the following properties: 1) A and B start rendering simultaneously at the same time; 2) the rendering of B should end after the end of rendering of A, and not at the exact end time of rendering A. In Figure 8: δ_1 represents the rendering time for A; δ_2 represents the rendering time for B; 0 link between the start of A and the start of B insures property 1); δ_s insures property 2).

During Property

A *during* property between the rendering operations of objects A and B insures the following properties: 1) A starts rendering at a certain period of time after the rendering of B and not at the same time; 2) the rendering of A should end at a certain period before the end of rendering of B, and not at the exact end time of rendering B. In Figure 9: δ_1 represents the rendering time for A; δ_2 represents the rendering time for B; δ_{D1} insures property 1); δ_{D2} insures property 2).

Meet Property

A *meet* property between the rendering operations of objects A and B insures the following properties: 1) B starts rendering exactly at the end of rendering object A. In Figure 10: δ_1 represents the rendering time for A; δ_2 represents the rendering time for B; 0 link between the end of rendering of A and the start of rendering of B insures property 1).

Equal Property

An *equal* property between the rendering operations of objects A and B insures the following properties: 1) A starts rendering exactly at the start of rendering object B; 2) A ends rendering exactly at the end of rendering object B. In Figure 11: δ_1 represents the rendering time for A; δ_2 represents the rendering time for B; 0 link between the start of rendering of A and the start of rendering of B insures property 1); 0 link between the end of rendering of A and the end of rendering of B insures property 2).

Finish Property

A *finish* property between the rendering operations of objects A and B insures the following properties: 1) the rendering of A should start after the start of rendering of B, and not at the exact end time of rendering B; 2) A and B end rendering simultaneously at the same time. In Figure 12: δ_1 represents the rendering time for A; δ_2 represents the rendering time for B; δ_F insures property 1); 0 link between the end of A and the end of B insures property 2).

Before Property

A *before* property between the rendering operations of objects A and B insures the following properties: 1) the rendering of B should start at a certain period after the end of rendering of A, and not at the exact end time of rendering A. In Figure 13: δ_1 represents the rendering time for A; δ_2 represents the rendering time for B; δ_B insures property 1).

WEBCAP TOOL

The WEBCAP consists of four modules as shown in Figure 14. The object extractor (OE) is an automating process of identifying the precedence

Figure 7. The graphical and mathematical representation of the OVERLAP property

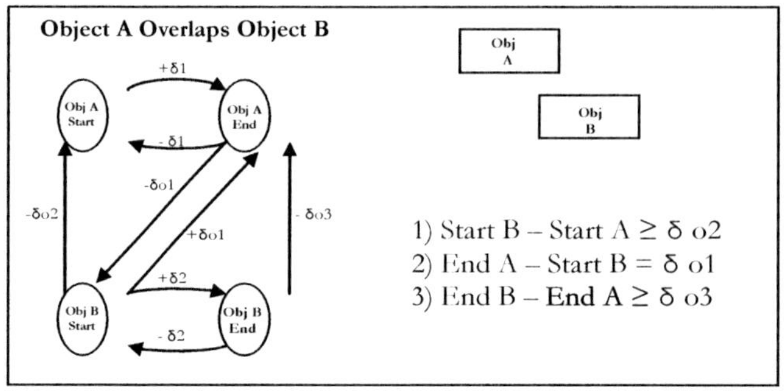

Figure 8. The graphical and mathematical representation of the START property

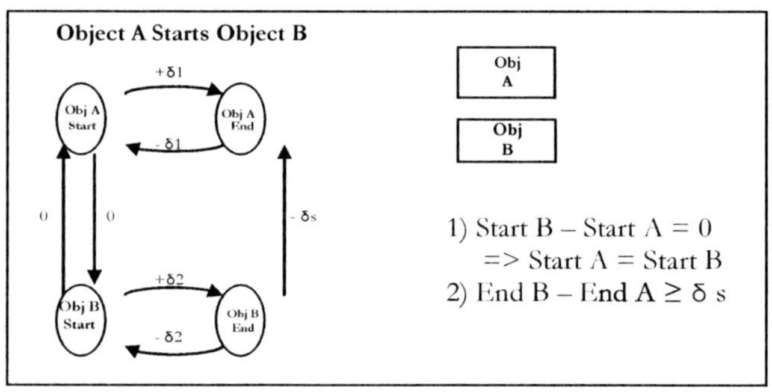

Figure 9. The graphical and mathematical representation of the DURING property

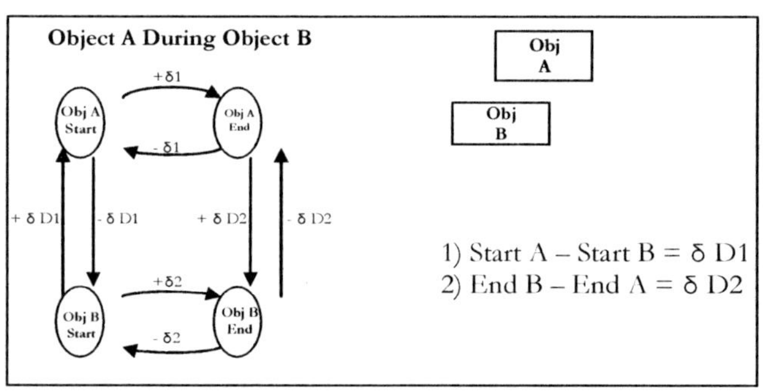

Figure 10. The graphical and mathematical representation of the MEET property

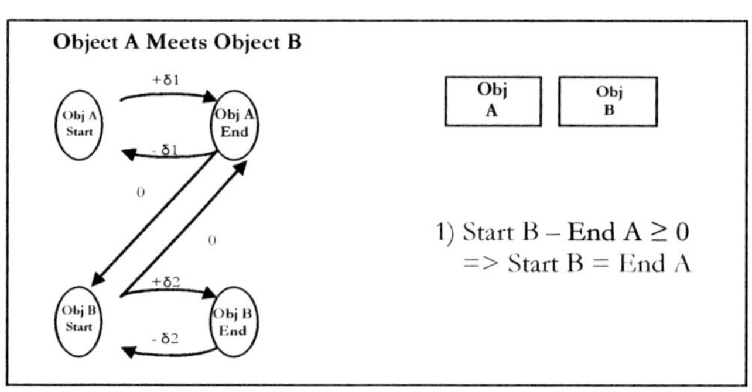

Figure 11. The graphical and mathematical representation of the EQUAL property

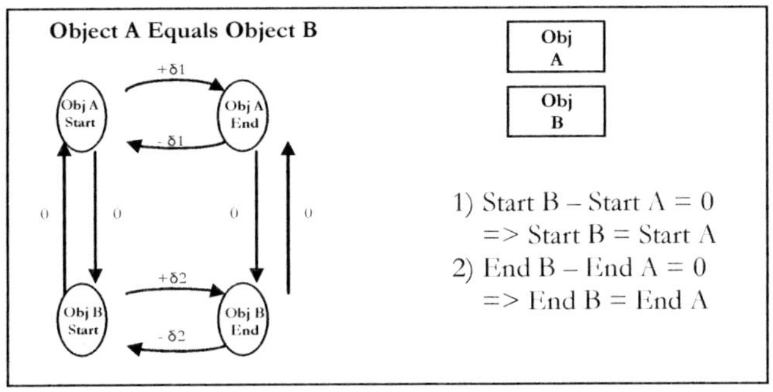

Figure 12. The graphical and mathematical representation of the FINISH property

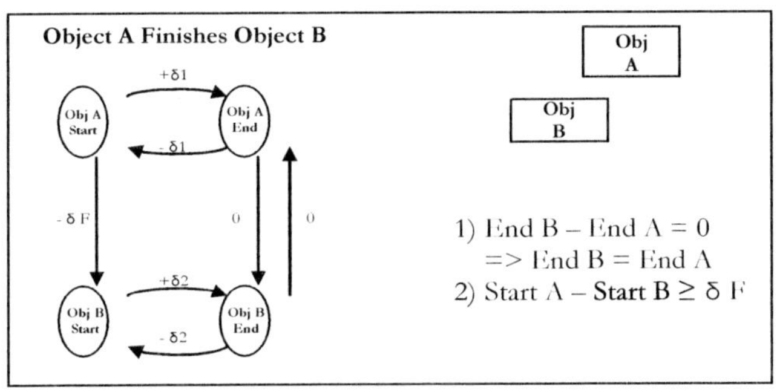

Figure 13. The graphical and mathematical representation of the BEFORE property

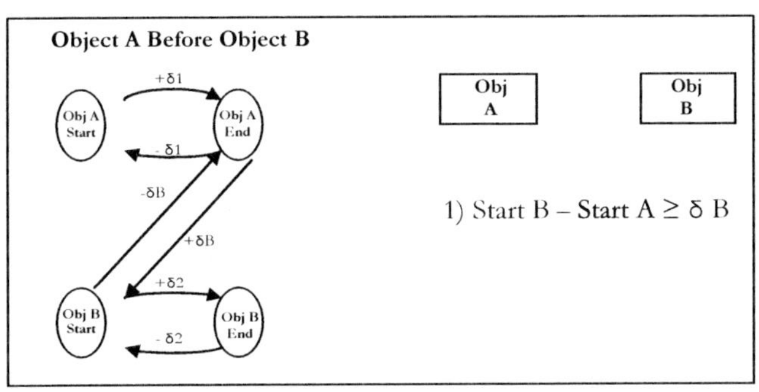

relations among the objects inside Web documents of different contents. For example, with static Web page content, some use of *regular expressions* (e.g., XPath expressions), special *mark up tags*, or *HTTP headers* could be required to provide minimal hints that help to decide the precedence relations between the objects. While with dynamically generated Web page content, RSS libraries can help in deciding the precedence relations between the objects in the Web page. Finally, with RSS or XML feed content, the process of identifying the precedence relations among the objects in a feed can be automated by adding new RSS Modules (IBM), where namespaces are used to describe a space for our own extensions.

The object representer (OR) performs all graph transformations, where in the first transformation a multimedia document is modeled as an *object*

Figure 14. An overview of the WEBCAP tool

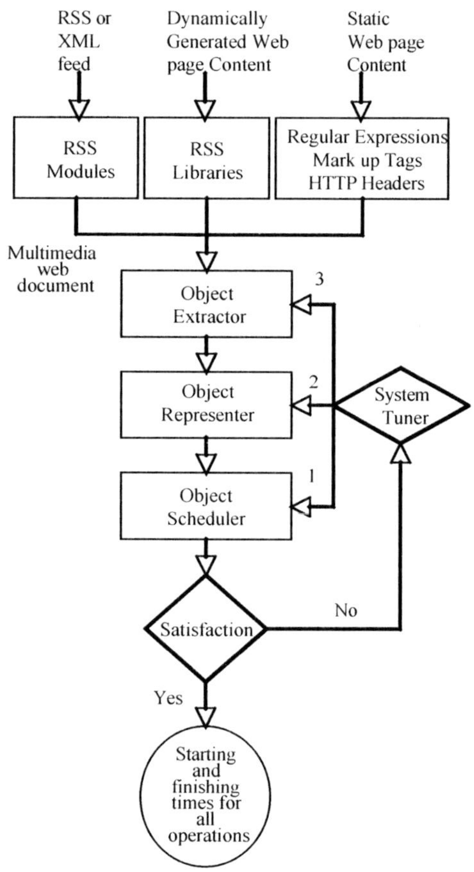

flow graph (OFG). The node in OFG represents a multimedia object such as a text, still image, audio, animation or video. The edge in OFG represents the precedence among objects. In the second transformation, the object flow graph is mapped into an operating flow graph (OPFG) including all operations (fetch, transmit, process, and render) that are needed to fetch an object from the server, transmit it through the network, and process and render it at the user side. In the third transformation, the operation flow graph is mapped in a timing flow graph (TFG) including all the starting and finishing times of all operations. In the fourth transformation, all the precedence relationships among the objects are mapped into the timing flow graph using Allen's temporal properties (Allen, 1983), which are depicted in Figure 3.

The object scheduler (OS) takes the precedence flow graph (PFG) as an input and also the latest status of the workload on the servers and networks, then determines the optimal starting and finishing times for all operations, subject to the available resources while maintaining all precedence relations among the objects. If the object scheduler fails to satisfy the precedence relations or exceed the available resources, then the system tuner (ST) is invoked to either re-manage system resources (Figure 14, loop 1), reconfigure document representation (Figure 14, loop 2) or relax precedence relations (Figure 14, loop 3).

Experimental Results

The WEBCAP was implemented in C++ on SUN Blade 100. Here we present the results for three experiments based on the CNN weather news example (CNN, 2004). Our example comprises four objects: image, animation, text and audio as shown in Figure 2, and Table 1 describes all operations on all the objects with their execution times.

In the first experiment, we ran WEBCAP with an ideal situation, where all the server and network resources are available with very light workload. Also, we have not forced a constraint on the length of the presentation of the entire PRM document (the starting time and ending time are not set). The goal was to insure that all five rendering temporal constraints were satisfied. WEBCAP found a feasible schedule and it is illustrated in a form of timing diagram, as shown in Figure 15. To satisfy all five rendering temporal constraints, the animation object had to be fetched and transmitted before the image object, even though it had to be rendered first. In the ideal situation, the presentation's length (rendering time only) should start at 45 seconds and end at 80 seconds.

The second experiment is similar to the first experiment except that the workload on the server had been increased during the fetching of the

Table 1. Execution times for all operations involved in refreshing Web document

Objects\Operations	Fetch Time, seconds	Transmit Time, seconds	Process Time, seconds	Render Time, seconds
Image (I_1)	7	14	2	5
Animation (AN_1)	15	30	5	20
Text (T_1)	1	2	1	2
Audio (A_1)	10	20	5	15

animation object. In an ideal situation, the fetching time of the animation object would take 15 seconds; however, during the heavy workload on the server, it took 65 seconds. WEBCAP found a feasible schedule and it is illustrated in Figure 16. Due to the heavy workload on the server, the entire schedule was shifted by 50 seconds as illustrated in the timing diagram. The shift in the schedule had not violated any of the five rendering temporal constraints. However, the rendering had to be delayed until 95 rather than 45 in the ideal situation.

The third experiment is similar to the first experiment except that the workload on the network had been increased during the transmission of the image and animation objects. In an ideal situation, the transmission time of the animation and image objects would take 30 and 14 seconds, respectively. However, during the heavy workload on the network, they took 90 and 74 seconds, respectively. WEBCAP found a feasible schedule and it is illustrated in Figure 17. Due to the heavy workload on the network, the entire schedule was shifted by 60 seconds as illustrated in the timing diagram. The shift in the schedule had not violated any of the five rendering temporal constraints. However, the rendering had to be delayed until 105 rather than 45 in the ideal situation. To satisfy all five rendering temporal constraints, the animation object had to be fetched 75 seconds before the image object, even though it had to be rendered first.

Knowing the amount of delays in advance, it may hold the user not to refresh the PRM document now and wait for a later time. The halting action by the user can reduce the frustration of the user for not waiting longer to retrieve the PRM document, and it can reduce the load on the network. This is the main advantage of embedding WEBCAP within an Internet browser that can estimate/predict the delays in refreshing multimedia documents before the actual retrieval.

Figure 15. A timing diagram for an ideal experiment where the workload on server and network are light and no constraint on the presentation's length

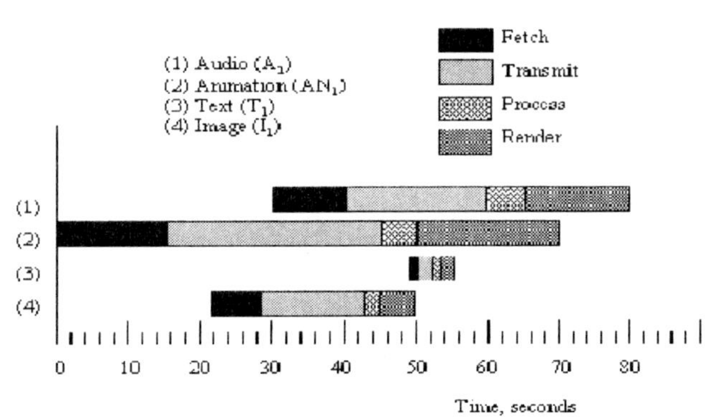

Figure 16. A timing diagram for the second case, where the workload on server is heavy

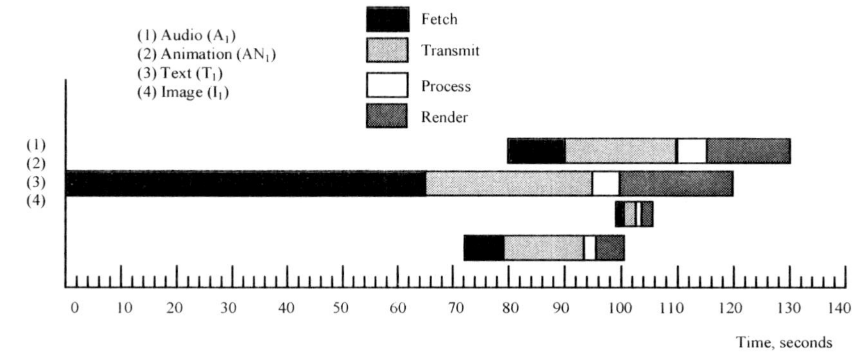

Figure 17. A timing diagram for the third case, where the workload on network is heavy

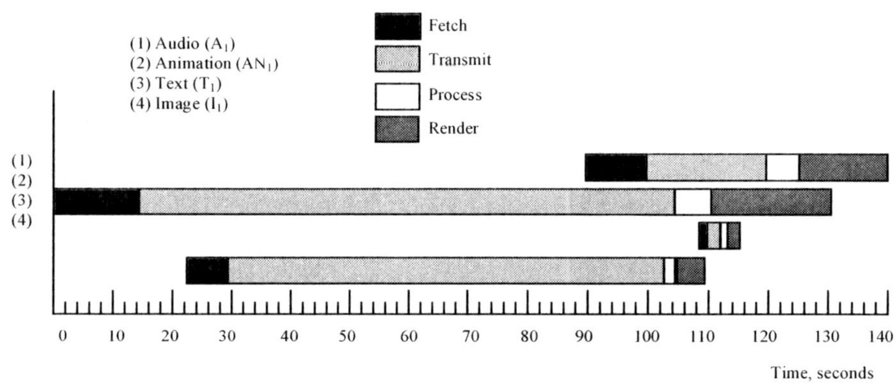

In the fourth experiment, we ran WEBCAP with the same inputs as in the first experiment except that we increased the rendering time of the animation object from 20 to 50. This increase made it impossible for WEBCAP to find a feasible schedule and at the same time satisfy all five rendering temporal constraints. The rendering constraint between the text object and audio object, which is "*a text object renders **before** audio object at exactly 10 seconds,*" could not be satisfied.

CONCLUSION

We have introduced an ongoing project called WEBCAP that schedules a periodical refreshing multimedia (PRM) document while considering the presentation and Web constraints. The internal structure of WEBCAP is based on three transformations (object → operation → timing → precedence) that allow the retrieving algorithm to manipulate the Web multimedia document in three different ways. The *object transformation* can be used in editing the overall structure of a multimedia document. The *operation transformation* can be used to reconfigure or redesign Web resources for real-time multimedia document retrieval while satisfying all users and Web constraints. The *timing transformation* can be used to examine the retrieval of objects under non-deterministic execution times. Currently, we are working on embedding WEBCAP in an Internet browser, and we are using WEBCAP to examine Web infrastructure for more real-time applications, such as distance learning, e-learning and tele-medicine.

ACKNOWLEDGMENT

The authors would like to acknowledge the support of Kuwait University, Research Grant No. EO 05/04.

REFERENCES

Allen, J. (1983). Maintaining knowledge about temporal intervals. *Communications of the ACM, 26*(11), 832-843.

André, E., Finkler, W., Graf, W., Rist, T., Schauder, A., & Wahlster, W. (1993). WIP: The automatic synthesis of multimodal presentations. *Intelligent Multimedia Interfaces,* 75-93, AAAI Press.

André, E., Müller, J., & Rist, T. (1996). The PPP persona: A multipurpose animated presentation agent. *Advanced Visual Interfaces,* 245-247, ACM Press.

Beca, L., Cheng, G., Fox, G., Jurga, T., Olszewski, K., Podgorny, M., et al. (1997). Web technologies for collaborative visualization and simulation. *Proceedings of the 8th SIAM Conference on Parallel Processing.* Minneapolis, MN.

Beca, L., Cheng, G., Fox, G., Jurga, T., Olszewski, K., Podgorny, M., et al. (1997b). Java enabling collaborative education healthcare and computing. *Concurrency: Practice and Experience, 9,* 521-534.

Candan, K., Prabhakaran, B., & Subrahmanian, V. (1998). Collaborative multimedia documents: Authoring and presentation. *International Journal of Intelligent Systems, 13,* 1059-1111.

Cellary, W., Walczak, K., Wieczerzycki, W., & Wiza, W. (2001). DIPS - A dynamic system for Web-based business process reengineering. *Proceedings of 7th International Conference on Reengineering Technologies for Information Systems ReTIS, Data and Document Reengineering for the Web* (pp. 33-47). Lyon, France.

CNN. (2004). *http://www.cnn.com/ SPECIALS/2004/hurricanes/interactive/hurricane.paths/index.html.*

Courtiat, J., Santos, C., Lohr, C., & Outtaj, B. (2000). Experience with RT-LOTOS, a temporal extension of the LOTOS formal description technique. *Computer Communications, 23*(12), 1104-1123.

Deliyannis, I. (2002). *Interactive multimedia systems for science and rheology.* Doctoral Thesis, University of Swansea.

Habib, S., Ravikumar, C., & Parker, A. (1997). Storage allocation and scheduling problems in Web caching applications. *Proceedings of National Laboratory for Applied Network Research (NLANR) Web Cache Workshop.* Boulder, CO.

Habib, S., & Safar, M. (2005). WEBCAP: A capacity planning tool for Web resource management. *Proceedings of the International World Wide Web Conference (WWW2005)* (pp. 918-919). Chiba, Japan.

IBM Developer Works. http://www-106.ibm.com/developerworks/

Podgorny, M., Walczak, K., Warner, D., & Fox, G. (1998). Internet groupware technologies - Past, present, and future. *Proceedings of the International Conference on Business Information Systems.* Poznan, Poland.

Safar, M. (2000). *Efficient MBC-based shape retrieval and spatial querying.* Doctoral Dissertation, University of Southern California. Los Angeles, CA.

Safar, M. (2002). Classification of Web caching systems. *Proceedings of IADIS International Conference on WWW/Internet.* Lisbon, Portugal.

Walczak, K., Wiza, W., & Podgorny, M. (2001). WebWisdom - Database support for distance learning systems. *Proceedings of 3rd International Conference on Information Integration and Web-based Applications and Services* (pp. 289-299). Linz, Austria.

Walczak, K., Wiza, W., & Podgorny, M. (2002). Managing multimedia educational contents in databases. *Proceedings of the IADIS International Conference on Information Society WWW/Internet* (pp. 152-159). Lisboa, Portugal.

Wang, Z., & Crowcroft, J. (1997). Cachemesh: A distributed cache system for the World Wide Web. *Proceedings of the 2nd National Laboratory for Applied Network Research (NLANR) Web Cache Workshop.* Boulder, CO.

Webster, M., & Deliyannis, I. (2002). WWW delivery of graph-based multi-level multimedia systems: Interaction over scientific industrial and educational. *Proceedings of the IADIS International Conference on Information Society WWW/Internet* (pp. 607-612). Lisboa, Portugal.

Wessels, D. (1995). Intelligent caching for World Wide Web objects. *Proceedings of INET-1995 Conference.*

Wiza, W., & Walczak, K. (2000). Dynamic Web systems based on XML and database technologies. *Proceedings of 4th Business Information Systems Conference* (pp. 229-241). Poznan, Poland: Springer-Verlag.

Xu, J., Lee, W., & Liu, J. (2004). Scheduling Web requests in broadcast environments. *Proceedings of the 13th International World Wide Web Conference* (pp. 280-281).

This work was previously published in International Journal of Distance Education Technologies, Vol. 6, Issue 1, edited by S. Chang; T. Shih, pp. 32-48, copyright 2008 by IGI Publishing (an imprint of IGI Global).

Chapter 12
Quasi-Facial Communication for Online Learning Using 3D Modeling Techniques

Yushun Wang
Zhejiang University, China

Yueting Zhuang
Zhejiang University, China

ABSTRACT

Online interaction with 3D facial animation is an alternative way of face-to-face communication for distance education. 3D facial modeling is essential for virtual educational environments establishment. This article presents a novel 3D facial modeling solution that facilitates quasi-facial communication for online learning. Our algorithm builds 3D facial models from a single image, with support of a 3D face database. First from the image, we extract a set of feature points, which are then used to automatically estimate the head pose parameters using the 3D mean face in our database as a reference model. After the pose recovery, a similarity measurement function is proposed to locate the neighborhood for the given image in the 3D face database. The scope of neighborhood can be determined adaptively using our cross-validation algorithm. Furthermore, the individual 3D shape is synthesized by neighborhood interpolation. Texture mapping is achieved based on feature points. The experimental results show that our algorithm can robustly produce 3D facial models from images captured in various scenarios to enhance the lifelikeness in distant learning.

INTRODUCTION

In traditional education, face-to-face communication is natural among students and teachers. The situation in virtual education (Chang, 2002) and e-learning (Zhuang & Liu, 2002) is different, where facial interaction is not commonly used. Students using a computer-based learning system are likely to study alone with relatively little classmate support (Ou et al., 2000).

Online interaction with facial animation over the network is an alternative way of face-to-face communication. 3D facial modeling is essential for building interactive virtual educational environments. In general, the use of facial modeling techniques in distance education mainly has three practical requirements. First, the method should be easily applied to new individuals. Second, it should require no exorbitant equipments and computation cost. Third, the results should be robust and realistic.

RELATED WORK

The pioneering work of facial modeling for animation was done by Parke (1972). Currently, there are several main streams of available solutions:

- **Modeling by 3D scanners:** Special equipments like 3D scanners can be used to capture the 3D shape of human heads. The data produced often need a lot of post-processing in order to reduce noise and fill the holes. Besides, in order to animate 3D scanned models, the shape must also be combined with an animation structure, which can not be produced by the scanning process directly.
- **Physical-based modeling:** (Terzopoulos & Waters, 1990; Kahler et al., 2002; Sifakis et al., 2005) One of the approaches to facial modeling is to approximate the anatomical structures of the face, that is, skull, muscles and skin. The animation from physical models reflects the underlying tissue stresses. Due to the complex topology of human faces, it requires tedious tuning to model a new individual's face.
- **Feature-points-based modeling:** (Pighin et al., 1998; Lee & Magnenat-Thalmann, 2000) Starting with several images or a 3D scan of a new individual, the generic model is deformed by the extracted facial feature points. Images are ubiquitous nowadays and a good source for facial modeling. In order to recover the 3D information, it needs orthogonal pair or more uncalibrated images.
- **Example-based modeling:** Blanz and Vetter (1999) propose a method named morphable model, which builds new faces by a linear combination of examples. Their work can be applied to reanimating faces in images and videos (Blanz, 2003; Vlasic et al., 2005). Supported by the examples, the input constraints can be released to only one image of the individual to generate plausible 3D results. The convergence process takes nearly an hour on SGI workstation, which limits its applications.

OUR APPROACH

The example-based approaches work well when there are a small number of examples. The iteration process converges and gets reasonable synthetic shapes and textures. However, as the number of examples increases, the structure of the 3D face space becomes more complicated and the global Euclidean distance measurement becomes invalid. The iterative optimization algorithms such as gradient descent need a lot of time to converge and easily get lost or trapped in local minimums. On the other side, in order to span a complete range of facial shapes, a large set of examples needs to be built. Due to the development of 3D scanners and the demand of realistic facial modeling and animation, the number of examples may increase dramatically. For instance, the facial animations of Gollum in the feature film The Two Towers employed 675 example shapes (Fordham, 2003).

In order to solve this problem, we introduce nonlinear learning algorithm from dimension reductions (Roweis & Saul, 2000), which maps its inputs into a single global coordinate system of lower dimensionality, and its optimizations—though capable of generating highly nonlinear embeddings—do not involve local minima. The

Figure 1. 3D faces lie on a high dimensional manifold, where each 3D face can be reconstructed by its neighbors. The properly selected neighborhood will preserve the most salient features of the reconstructed 3D shape.

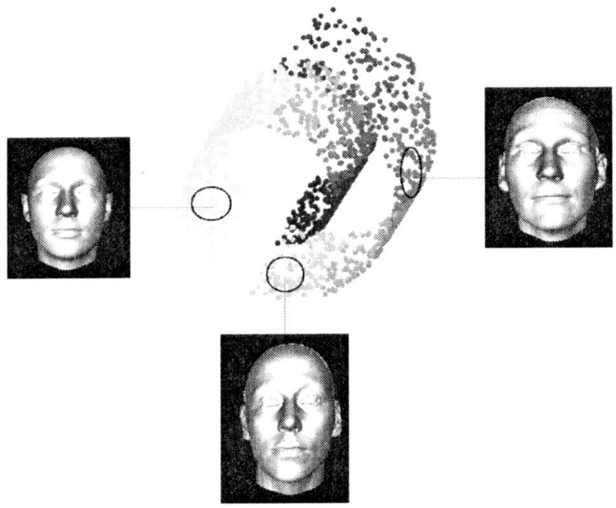

idea is based on simple geometric intuitions that the data points can be locally interpolated by its neighbors on a small piece of manifold patch. An n dimensional manifold is a topological space that is locally Euclidean (i.e., around every point, there is a neighborhood that is topologically the same as the open unit ball in R^n). The intuition is that if we can find the neighbors in the 3D face space for the given image, the synthesis process could be accelerated, as shown in Figure 1.

Based on the analysis above, we present a fast and efficient methodology to exploit a single photograph to get an animatable face model in a virtual world. The approach falls into the category of example-based modeling, but also we extend this method by exploring the nonlinearity of 3D faces. Our algorithm efficiently finds the neighborhood for a given image in the 3D face space and synthesizes new faces using neighborhood interpolation.

Algorithm Overview

As shown in Figure 2, our system takes a single image as input, and outputs a textured 3D face. Our algorithm can be summarized into five steps. The first three steps directly relate to the nonlinear analysis, that is, locally embedding of the 3D face space, which provide a foundation for neighborhood interpolation. The latter two steps are about the synthesis of new faces:

- **Step 1:** Given a frontal face image, a set of pre-defined feature points is extracted;
- **Step 2:** Based on the feature points and a reference model, the head pose in the image is recovered automatically;
- **Step 3:** The image finds its neighbors in the space of 3D faces by our similarity measurement;
- **Step 4:** The 3D shape for the image is constructed by the neighborhood-based optimization;
- **Step 5:** Texture coordinates are generated on the basis of the feature points to produce texture mapping of the model.

The rest of the article is organized as follows. In the next section, we describe the locally embedding analysis of 3D face space. Then the

Figure 2. Overview of our 3D facial modeling system, which takes a single image as an input and gives a 3D textured model as output

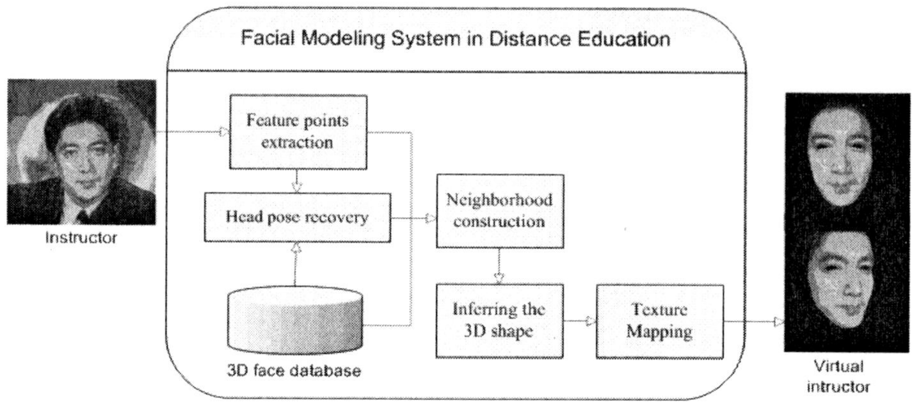

neighborhood interpolation algorithm for the synthesis of new faces is presented, followed by the experimental results. Finally, we conclude this article and discuss some ideas for future work.

LOCALITY OF 3D FACE SPACE

In order to find the right position in the space of 3D faces for a given 2D image, a similarity measurement is needed. We employ the feature points on both images and face models as the input parameters for similarity measurement after an automatic head pose recovery.

Definition of Feature Points

MPEG-4 employs 84 feature points (Facial Definition Parameters, FDP) (Ostermann, 1998) to define a head model. For creating a standard conforming face, the set of facial definition points used in our article are derived from the MPEG-4 FDP. We exploit 58 feature points, as shown in Figure 3, to define the frontal facial features. The feature points of a given image can be extracted manually or automatically.

The 3D models used in this article are complete models with necks and ears besides the facial mesh. They are all preprocessed and in correspondence. The definition of the feature vertices on a reference model will also be made on other examples from their correspondence. The feature points define a bounding box in which the part of mesh is our volume of interest from the facial animation point of view. During the operations of facial modeling and texture mapping, only the mesh in the bounding box is rendered.

Figure 3. Standard-conforming feature points definition

Head Pose Recovery

The head pose of the image needs to be determined before calculating similarity. Various methods have been reported in the scenario of

Figure 4. Feature points used to estimate the head pose of the image (right) with a 3D face example (left)

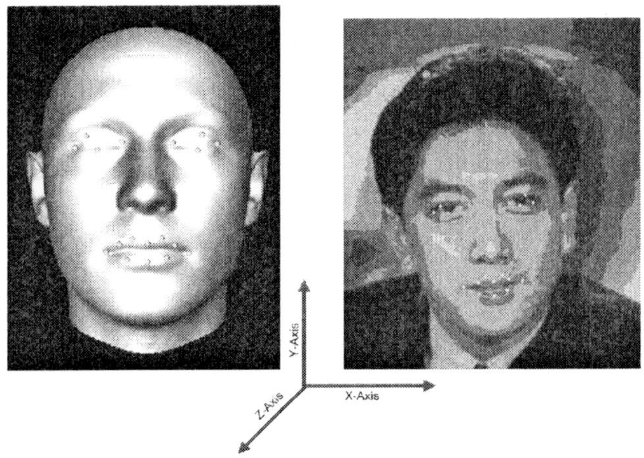

image sequences (Zhu & Ji, 2004) or range data (Malassiotis & Strintzis, 2005). This article proposes an efficient solution for pose recovery, which has three characteristics. First, with support of a 3D face example, we can recover the pose parameters from a single fronto-parallel image. The reference model employed here is the 3D mean face in our database for its generality. Second, similarity transformation parameters are used, that is, the parameters to be estimated are rotation $\boldsymbol{R}$, translation $\boldsymbol{t}$, and scaling s. Third, using least squares estimation, the similarity transformation parameters can be calculated efficiently by matrix operations.

Our system chooses the feature points on eyes and mouth to estimate pose, for they are nearly on a plane. These 2D feature points on fronto-parallel images can be thought as on *xoy* plane in the 3D space. Then the problem of pose estimation is translated to the problem of similarity transformation parameters estimation between two point patterns, as shown in Figure 4. We use least squares estimation to minimize a cost function:

$$C(R,t,s) = \frac{1}{n}\sum_{i=1}^{n}\left\| p_i - (sRv_i + t)\right\|^2 \qquad (1)$$

Figure 5. Estimated head pose parameters applied to the 3D face example

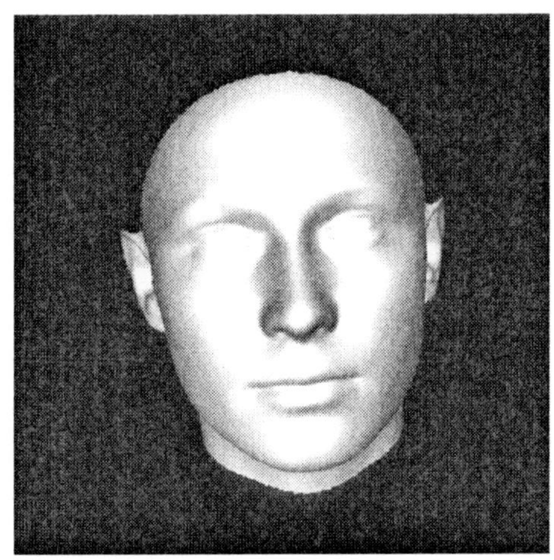

where $\{p_i = (x_i, y_i, 0)\}$ is a set of feature points on image, $\{v_i = (x_i, y_i, z_i)\}$ is a set of feature vertices on the 3D model, R: rotation, t: translation:, and s: scaling are the 3D similarity transformation parameters, n is the number of feature points and vertices. Minimizing the cost function in Equation 1 will give the transformation parameters.

The estimated transformation parameters for Figure 4 are calculated and applied to the 3D model, as shown in Figure 5.

Neighborhood Construction

After the head pose estimation, the distance between the image and the 3D examples can be written as:

$$D(I, M_j) = \sqrt{\sum_{i=1}^{n} \left\| p_i - proj_{xoy}(sRv_i + t) \right\|^2} \qquad (2)$$

where I is the input image, M_j is the jth example in 3D face space, and $proj_{xoy}$ is a mapping function to choose (x, y) from (x, y, z).

Once the distance function is determined, the only problem in the manifold analysis is how to choose the boundary of neighborhood. K nearest neighbors (k-NN) and ε-neighborhood: $N_\varepsilon(I) = \{M_j \mid D(I, M_j) \leq \varepsilon\}$ are two strategies for selecting the size of local neighborhood. Our system combines k-NN and cross-validation to analyze and determine the value of k adaptively. We keep some 3D examples outside the database for cross-validation. As shown in Figure 6, the image on the left is input to our system for 3D reconstruction. The reconstruction result is compared with the real 3D data and gets a validation error. By testing the relationship between the error and the value of k, the optimum value of k is determined adaptively, as shown in Figure 7. The reconstruction error falls to its minimum where the neighbors represent most of the given example's salient features. As

Figure 6. Extra image and 3D shape of an individual who is not in the database for cross-validation

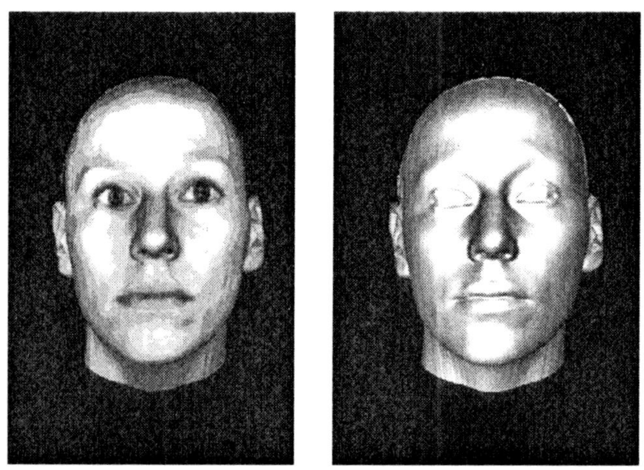

Figure 7. The cross-validation result to choose k adaptively

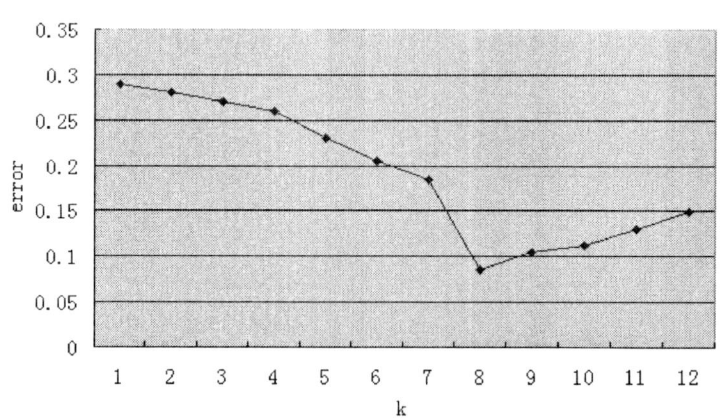

the number of k exceeds some value, the salient features tend to be smoothed out by averaging too many examples. Several such validation examples may be processed and the value of k is chosen by averaging these validation optimums. The properly selected neighborhood will preserve the most salient depth features of the individuals. This idea could also be applied to ε-neighborhood, where the value of ε can be chosen via validation by extra examples.

SYNTHESIS OF NEW FACES

Once the neighborhood for a given image is found, optimization techniques can be used to infer the 3D shape.

Inferring 3D Shapes by Neighborhood Interpolation

We construct a function that maps the 2D pixel positions $P = \{p_i\}$ to the 3D vertex coordinates $V = \{v_i\}$. Constructing such a function can be regarded as an interpolation or approximation problem, which solves a problem of approximating a continuous multivariate function $f(\bar{x})$ by an approximate function $F(\bar{x}, \bar{c})$ with an appropriate choice of parameter set $\bar{c}$ where $\bar{x}$ and $\bar{c}$ are real vectors ($\bar{x} = x_1, x_2, ..., x_n$ and $\bar{c} = c_1, c_2, ..., c_k$).

The family of radial basis functions (RBF) is well known for its power to approximate high dimensional smooth surfaces and it is often used in model fitting [9]. The network of RBF to infer the 3D shape of a given image is:

$$v_j = \sum_{i=1}^{k} c_{ji}\phi(D(I, M_i)) \tag{3}$$

where I is the input image represented by feature points, M_i is the ith 3D model in its neighborhood, $D(I, M_i)$ is the distance function described in Equation 2, k is the number of k-NN neighbors, c_{ji} denotes the parameters to be learned , j represents the jth element in the output vector, $\phi(r)$ is radially symmetric basis functions. Examples of basis functions are Gaussian functions $\phi(r) = e^{-(\frac{r}{c})^2}$, multi-quadrics $\phi(r) = \sqrt{(r^2 + c^2)}$ and thin plate splines $\phi(r) = r^2 \log r$ with a linear term added. Plugging the Hardy basis function into Equation 3 results in:

$$v_j = F_j(I) = \sum_{i=1}^{k} c_{ji}\sqrt{D(I, M_i)^2 + s_i^2} \tag{4}$$

where $s_i = \min(D(I, M_i))$ is the stiffness coefficient for balancing the scope of neighborhood.

Substituting the k pairs of neighborhood training data $(\bar{p}, \bar{v})$ into Equation 4 results in a linear system of k equations, where $\bar{p}$ is the vector concatenating all the elements of $proj_{xoy} = (sRv_i + t)$ and $\bar{v}$ is the vector concatenating all the elements of vertex coordinates on the ith 3D model. Solving the linear system yields:

$$\bar{c} = H^{-1}\bar{v} \tag{5}$$

$$\bar{c} = (H + \lambda I)^{-1}\bar{v} \tag{6}$$

where $\lambda = 0.01$ is a small disturbing factor determined empirically to decrease the impact of noise and I here is the identity matrix.

Texture Coordinates Extraction

Based on the feature points of the image, the texture coordinates can be interpolated to get texture mapping. Given a set of corresponding feature vertices on the 3D model and texture coordinates, the in-between vertices can get their texture coordinates via scattered data interpolation. We use the method similar to one in the previous subsection, except that the input of the RBF system is the 3D vertex and the output is the corresponding texture coordinates.

$$t = F(v) = \sum_{i=1}^{n} c_i\,\phi(\|v - v_i\|) \tag{7}$$

where v is the input 3D vertex, v_i is the ith feature vertex, t is the texture coordinates.

EXPERIMENTS

The 3D face database was provided by the Max-Planck Institute for Biological Cybernetics in Tuebingen, Germany. The 3D scanned faces in the database provide a good start point for our supportive database. We have aligned all the 3D models with an animatable model and reduced its vertex density. The eyes and mouth areas were excided for animation purpose. Besides, we added extra examples to the database by face modeling software. After that, the database consists of 200 heads each with 6K vertices.

In order to test our techniques, we have implemented a prototype system using Visual C++ and Matlab. We have tested our system by modeling a traditional Beijing opera face painting (Figure 8). We also applied our method to paintings such as Mona Lisa by Leonardo (Figure 9). We reconstructed the face models from color images taken by us (Figure 10), black and white images from Cohn-Kanade (Kanade et al., 2000) facial expression database (Figure 11) or images taken under arbitrary unknown conditions (Figure 12). We manually marked the feature points and the system takes approximately one second to reconstruct the 3D model with texture mapping. Although reconstructing the true 3D shape and texture from a single image is an under-determined problem, 3D face models built by our system look

Figure 8. The 3D modeling of a traditional Beijing opera face painting

Figure 9. The 3D modeling of Mona Lisa

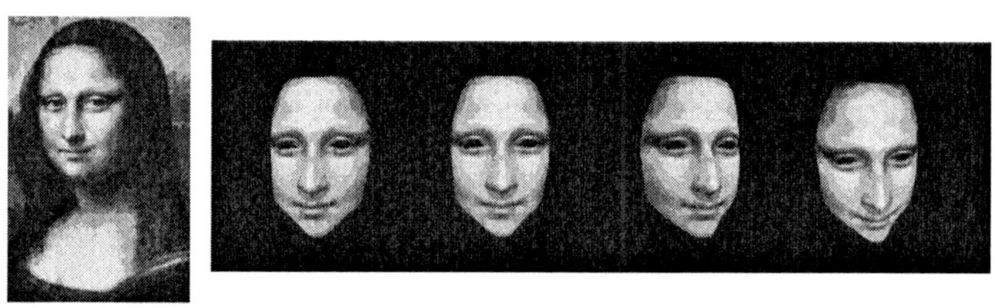

Figure 10. An example of 3D modeling of image taken by the authors

Figure 11. 3D modeling of a black and white image from an open face database

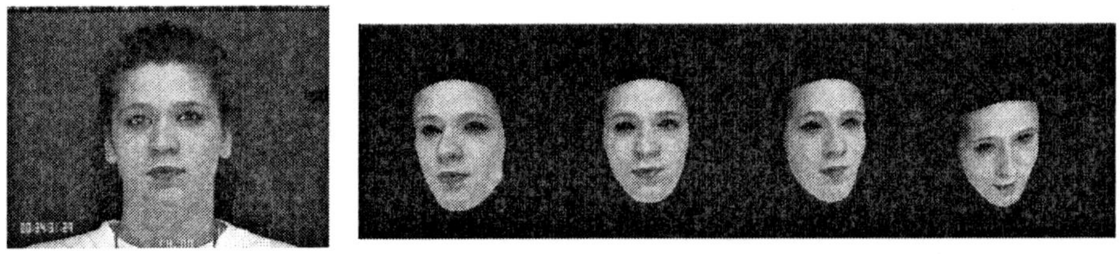

Figure 12. Another facial modeling example

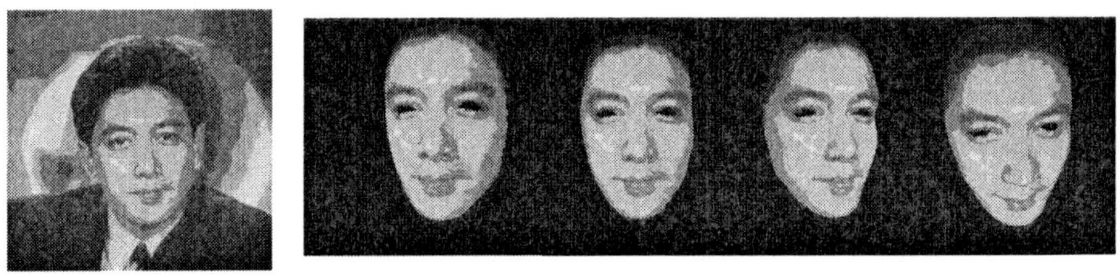

Figure 13. Quasi-facial online learning system

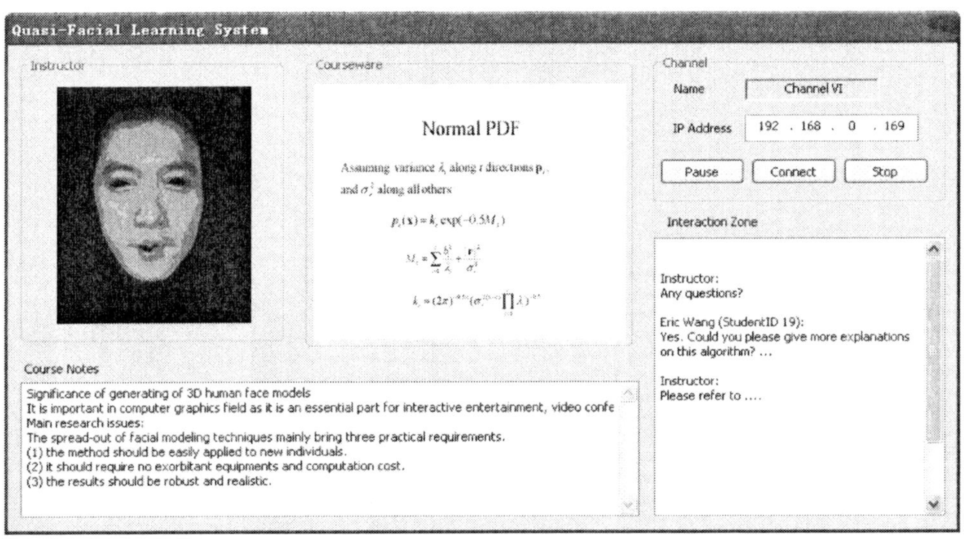

vivid from the frontal viewpoint and natural from other viewpoints.

Besides, we have implemented a prototype of the quasi-facial online learning system over college intranet, as shown in Figure 13. The 3D modeling techniques facilitate the quasi face-to-face communications. The virtual instructor can perform facial expressions and oral communications, which will be supportive for an effective distant learning atmosphere.

CONCLUSION AND FUTURE WORK

This article proposes a novel approach to 3D facial modeling from a single image. In this algorithm, we measure the distance between the input image and the 3D models after estimating similarity transformation. Neighborhood interpolation is used to find the optimum of the 3D shape to preserve salient features. Furthermore, the image is mapped onto the synthesized model as texture.

Vivid 3D models and animation can be produced from a single image through our system.

Our algorithm only needs matrix operations instead of an iterative process to find optimums. Therefore, it is efficient for many applications, such as teleconference, digital entertainment and video encoding. The application in distance learning is very encouraging for supporting a vivid online learning environment.

There are several directions of improvement in the future. The inner properties of the face space need to be further explored in order to synthesize new faces efficiently and accurately. Currently, the texture mapping just exploits the colors on the image that reflect the lighting conditions under which it was taken. Relighting techniques should be developed for integrating our facial model with the virtual environment. Furthermore, the wrinkles and detailed textures have not been properly tackled in the existing techniques. These problems ought to be considered in future work.

ACKNOWLEDGMENT

This work is supported by the National Natural Science Foundation of China (No.60525108, No.60533090), 973 Program (2002CB312101), Science and Technology Project of Zhejiang Province (2005C13032, 2005C11001-05). Yushun Wang would like to thank Ming Zhao and Feng Liu for suggestions on revising the article.

REFERENCE

Blanz, V., & Vetter, T. (1999). A morphable model for the synthesis of 3D faces. *Proceedings of The Siggraph 99 conference* (pp. 187-194). New York: ACM Press.

Blanz, V., Basso, C., Poggio, T., & Vetter. T. (2003). Reanimating faces in images and video. *Computer Graphics Forum, 22(3), EUROGRAPHICS 2003* (pp. 641-650). Granada, Spain.

Chang, S.-K. (2002). A growing book for distance learning. *Proceedings of the First International Conference on Advances in Web-Based Learning (ICWL'02)* (pp. 3-18). Hong Kong, China.

Fordham, J. (2003). Middle earth strikes back. *Cinefex, 92,* 71-142.

Kahler, K., Haber, J., Yamauchi, H., & Seidel, H.-P. (2002). Head shop: Generating animated head models with anatomical structure. Proceedings of The ACM SIGGRAPH Symposium on Computer Animation (pp. 55-64).

Kanade, T., Cohn, J., & Tian Y. (2000). Comprehensive database for facial expression analysis. *Proceedings of FG* (pp. 46-53).

Lee, W., & Magnenat-Thalmann, N. (2000). Fast head modeling for animation. *Journal of Image and Vision Computing, 18*(4), 355-364. Elsevier Science.

Malassiotis, S., & Strintzis, M. (2005) Robust real-time 3D head pose estimation from range data. *Pattern Recognition, 38*(8), 1153-1165.

Ostermann, J. (1998). Animation of synthetic faces in MPEG-4. *Computer Animation,* 49-51.

Ou, K.-L., Chen, G.-D., Liu, C.-C., &Liu, B.-J. (2000). Instructional instruments for Web group learning systems: The grouping, intervention, and strategy. *Proceedings of the 5th annual SIGCSE/SIGCUE ITiCSE conference on Innovation and technology in computer science education* (pp. 69-72). Helsinki, Finland.

Parke, F. (1972). Computer-generated animation of faces. *Proceedings of the ACM annual conference.*

Pighin, F., Hecker, J., Lischinski, D., Szeliski, R., & Salesin, D. (1998). Synthesizing realistic facial expressions from photographs. *Siggraph proceedings* (pp. 75-84).

Roweis, S., & Saul. L. (2000). Nonlinear dimensionality reduction by locally linear embedding. *Science, 290,* 2323-2326.

Sifakis, E., Neverov, I., & Fedkiw, R. (2005). Automatic determination of facial muscle activations from sparse motion capture marker data. *SIGGRAPH 2005, ACM TOG 24* (pp. 417-425).

Terzopoulos, D., & Waters, K. (1990). Physically-based facial modelling, analysis, and animation. *Journal of Visualization and Computer Animation, 1*(2), 73-80.

Vlasic, D., Brand, M., Pfister, H., & Popovic, J. (2005). Face transfer with multi-linear models. *ACM Transactions on Graphics (TOG),* 24(3), 426-433.

Zhu, Z., & Ji, Q. (2004). Real-time 3D face pose tracking from an uncalibrated camera. *Conference on Computer Vision and Pattern Recognition Workshop (CVPRW'04), 5,* 73.

Zhuang, Y., & Liu, X. (2002). Multimedia knowledge exploitation for e-Learning: Some enabling techniques. *Proceedings of the First International Conference on Advances in Web-Based Learning (ICWL'02), LNCS 2436* (pp. 411-422). Hong Kong, China.

This work was previously published in International Journal of Distance Education Technologies, Vol. 6, Issue 1, edited by S. Chang; T. Shih, pp. 67-78, copyright 2008 by IGI Publishing (an imprint of IGI Global).

Chapter 13
Enhancing Skills of Application Software via Web-Enabled Problem-Based Learning and Self-Regulated Learning: An Exploratory Study

Pei-Di Shen
Ming Chuan University, Taiwan

Tsang-Hsiung Lee
National Chengchi University, Taiwan

Chia-Wen Tsai
Ming Chuan University, Taiwan

ABSTRACT

The computer software education in vocational schools in Taiwan can hardly be deemed as effective. To increase students' learning motivation and develop practical skills, innovative learning designs such as problem-based learning(PBL) and self-regulated learning (SRL) are on trial in this specific context. We conducted a series of quasi-experiments to examine effects of these designs mediated by a web-based learning environment. Two classes of 106 freshmen in a semester course at Institute of Technology in Taiwan were chosen for this empirical study. Result sreveal that effects of web-enabled PBL, web-enabled SRL, and their combinations, on students' skills of application software have significant differences. The implications of this study are also discussed.

INTRODUCTION

Professionals with a vocational degree represent a major portion of the work force in Taiwan. Vocational education is highly competitive in that it must attract enough student enrollments in the face of a continually decreasing birthrate and a rapidly increasing number of schools. Students in these schools tend to have lower levels of academic achievement. They spend more time on part-time jobs and do not get involved in their schoolwork adequately. They also care less about their grades. Teaching in such a context, particularly teaching the curriculum of application software, is a great challenge to most educators.

No one doubts the guiding principles of practical applications in the vocational education in Taiwan (Tai, Chen, & Lai, 2003). However, most teaching and learning efforts in this area have been devoted to helping students pass written tests, and, thus, receiving awards or official certificates. Schools, facing the high pressure of market competition, often emphasize the proportion of students awarded such certificates before they graduate instead of quality education. This materialistic aim puts students' attention less on mastering application software and more on preparing for tests through memorization. Consequently, a student who has passed the examination may still be unable to apply what was learned in school, and worse, lack motivation to learn more in the future.

The courses in application software traditionally emphasize memorization by applying short, disjointed, lack-of-context examples. There is a wide gap between what is learned in school and what is required in the workplace (Wu, 2000). In this regard, the computer software education in vocational schools in Taiwan can hardly be deemed as effective. In order to increase students' learning motivation and develop practical skills, problem-based learning (PBL) is considered to be the most appropriate. PBL uses real-world, simulated, contextualized problems in practice to motivate, focus, and initiate content learning and skill development (Boud & Feletti, 1991; Bruer, 1993; Williams, 1993). We believe that PBL could help low-academic-achievement students to develop practical skills of application software through online courses.

Web-based instruction seems to be an ideal learning environment because students can access an almost-unlimited amount of information and apply it in multiple ways (Kauffman, 2004). However, implementing e-learning for low-academic-achievement students inevitably runs high risks. For instance, Internet addiction is quite common among low-academic-achievement students. When students enter the traditional classroom, they are used to logging on to MSN Web Messenger and checking their e-mail first. Many students like to chat with each other frequently via MSN Web Messenger, even though they are in the same classroom. They might browse shopping Web sites, even while a teacher is lecturing in the classroom. Thus, the teacher has to disconnect the network several times in his classroom to focus students' attention. It is even more difficult for students to concentrate on online learning because of this addiction to the Internet and a lack of on-the-spot teacher monitoring. To respond to this challenge, we propose an approach that can help students regulate their learning in a better way.

Success in online courses often depends on students' abilities to successfully direct their own learning efforts (Cennamo, Ross, & Rogers, 2002). It is very critical to develop students' self-regulation of learning before providing online courses to them. In web-based learning environments, physical absence of an instructor and increased responsibility of learners to effectively engage in learning tasks may present difficulties, particularly those with low self-regulatory skills (Dabbagh & Kitsantas, 2005). Student motivation may benefit from Web-based instruction with self-regulated learning (SRL) strategies. Students in the online environment, equipped with SRL competence, become more responsible for their learning and more intrinsically orientated (Chang, 2005). So self-regulation is important, particularly while learning in World-Wide-Web-supported environments (Winnips, 2000).

Although researchers have consistently shown that self-regulation helps high achievers reach their potential (Risemberg & Zimmerman, 1992), it also makes a difference between failure and success for low achievers (Borkowski & Thorpe, 1994). However, there has been relatively little empirical research on students' SRL with such complex technology-based learning environments (Azevedo & Cromley, 2004). Therefore, this study applies SRL in this study to help vocational school students (particularly the low achievers) concentrate on their learning, leave time for learning after their part-time jobs, and furthermore, take responsibility for their learning.

There are few studies that have discussed effective online teaching methods for low academic achievers. In this area, the restructuring and translation of traditional computer software courses into e-learning has seldom been documented. Thus, this study redesigns a course in application software to integrate innovative teaching methods and learning technologies to help students learn and apply what they have learned. This study specifically explores potential effects of Web-based PBL and SRL on the development of low-academic-achievement students' skills in using packaged software.

AUTHENTIC ASSESSMENT

The traditional teaching approach regarded learners as passive recipients of information. Memorization of the content lectured by the teacher was the main goal of the instructional process. The assessment approach that accompanied this instructional approach was mainly operationalized by the so-called objective test, often standardized and with a true/false or a multiple-choice item format. Such assessments mostly do not seem to assess higher-order cognitive skills, such as problem solving, critical thinking, and reasoning (Segers, Dochy, & De Corte, 1999).

However, the objective tests are often given, even in computer software education. They could not evaluate students' practical skills, but also limit the potential application. Two innovative and practical teaching methods are applied in this study, so the traditional measurement is not appropriate to assess students' learning, particular in computer software education. More appropriate assessment methods for PBL would include reports, practical examinations, construction of concept maps, peer assessment, or oral presentations (Sonmez & Lee, 2003). In this regard, we measure students' skills of application software according to the correctness and completeness of their problem solving and artistry of their design instead of the memorization. The way we assess students' improvement in skills of application software is described in the "Measures" section.

PROBLEM-BASED LEARNING

Problem-based learning (PBL) is a teaching method that may engage students in authentic learning activities by using challenging problems in practice as a starting point, stimulus, and focus for learning (Barrows & Tamblyn, 1980; Boud, 1985; Barrows, 1985, 1986; Walton & Matthews, 1989; Boud & Feletti, 1991). PBL promotes student learning based on the need to solve problems. It not only emphasizes the learning in the subject area, but also provides opportunities for students to practice and apply knowledge and learned skills.

Davis and Harden (1999) indicate that PBL is one of the most effective teaching methods in recent 30 years. The probable reason is that the learning environment of PBL includes all kinds of factors currently known which can improve efficiency of learning, such as activity, cooperation, feedback, adaptability, and accountability.

Albanese and Mitchell (1993) reveal that PBL helps students more in knowledge construction and reasoning skills compared with the traditional teaching approach. PBL may help students achieve learning goals, such as professional reasoning; integration of scientific, academic, and professional knowledge; and lifelong learning skills (Dunlap, 2005).

Many Researchers examine PBL's positive impact on knowledge and skill acquisition and transfer, problem solving, attitudes and opinions about courses and programs, measures of performance, and self-directed learning (Norman & Schmidt, 1992; Albanese & Mitchell, 1993; Berkson, 1993; Vernon & Blake, 1993; Colliver, 2000; Davies, 2000). Furthermore, Polanco, Calderón, and Delgado (2004) point out that students in PBL groups attain significantly higher scores than students in a course from a control group composed of physics, mathematics and computer science.

In the domain of Information Science, Greening, Kay, Kingston, and Crawford (1996) consider that upper-level university students should have developed many key competencies. However, during teaching, they actually find many third-year students not having acquired necessary competencies from information science curriculum. PBL, as an alternative teaching method, demonstrates that it helps to improve students' key competencies. Yip (2001) points out that PBL can enhance competencies, both in professional and information systems education.

PBL is a flexible approach. It has demonstrated its working well with both small teams and large groups. However there might be disagreement whether PBL will be as effective, or even possible, for online learning. In this regard, Chanlin and Chan (2004) examine the effects of PBL in a Web-based approach. Results reveal that students in the PBL treatment group perform better than those from the control group. Therefore, it can be summarized that, in a Web-enabled learning environment, the effects of problem-based learning on students' skills of application software are positive, and higher than those without PBL.

SELF-REGULATED LEARNING

Zimmerman and Schunk (1989) define SRL in terms of self-generated thoughts, feelings, and actions, which are systematically oriented towards attainment of students' own goals. SRL is also defined as a learner's intentional efforts to manage and direct complex learning activities and is composed of three primary components, namely cognitive strategy use, meta-cognitive processing, and motivational beliefs (Kauffman, 2004).

Yang (1993) finds that students who are high self-regulatory skill users, as measured by a preexisting index, score significantly higher than their counterparts, low self-regulatory skill users, regardless of the level of control. Characteristics attributed to self-regulated persons coincide with those attributed to high-performance, high-capacity students, as opposed to those with low performance (or learning disabilities), who show a deficit in these variables (Roces & González Torres, 1998; Zimmerman, 1998; Reyero & Tourón, 2003).

Zimmerman and Martinez-Pons (1986) point out that students' frequency of self-regulated strategy use predicts a substantial amount of variance in their achievement test scores. Nota, Soresi, and Zimmerman (2004) indicate that the cognitive self-regulation strategy of organizing and transforming proves to be a significant predictor of the students' course grades in mathematics and technical subjects of high school, their subsequent average course grades, and examinations passed at the university.

As for the effects of SRL on computer software, Bielaczyc, Pirolli, and Brown (1995) incorporate self-explanation and self-regulation strategies in the attainment of the cognitive skill of computer programming. They find that their treatment group, which incorporates the self-regulation strategies of self-monitoring and clarifying comprehension failures in conjunction with self-explanation strategies, outperforms a control group that did not have the benefit of instruction in these strategies. Their study implies that, in addition to knowledge acquisition strategies, students benefit from the incorporation of strategies which allow them to plan, monitor, and evaluate their understanding and strategy use (Bielaczyc, Pirolli, & Brown, 1995). In a similar vein, this study provides us an insight that SRL is appropriate to be applied in computer software education.

Researchers have consistently shown that self-regulation helps high achievers reach their potential (Risemberg & Zimmerman, 1992). It also makes a difference between failure and success for low achievers (Borkowski & Thorpe, 1994). Young (1996) identifies that low self-regulatory skill users are found to perform significantly lower in computer-based instruction that applied learner control of the sequencing. It is believed that SRL is effective to the low achievers, not only through face-to-face instruction, but also in computer-based or technology-based instruction. Learners who report more extensive use of SRL strategies show higher academic achievement than learners who use self-regulated learning strategies less often (Zimmerman & Martinez-Pons, 1986). In the same study, students' achievement could be predicted with 93% accuracy from reported use of SRL strategies.

Web-enabled learning environment is an interactive network system consisting of a variety of functions to support a virtual classroom to enhance the quality of teaching and learning activities (Poon, Low, & Yong, 2004). Students can access information at their convenience, are free to work at their own pace, and can revisit information that they find confusing and/or interesting (Lehman, Kauffman, White, Horn, & Bruning, 2001). Nevertheless, providing students with opportunities to integrate their knowledge through Web-enabled instruction may not be effective if they lack the skills needed to regulate their learning. Thus, strategies that prepare students for the rigors of learning at a distance and increase the probability of retention and success must be put into practice (Chang, 2005). Winnips (2000) suggests that self-regulation is particularly important when learning in World-Wide-Web-supported environments. In other words, it is even more critical for students to transform into self-regulated learners in Web-enabled learning. Previous studies have established that self-regulated skills can help foster learning from any instructional method (Weinstein, 1989; Zimmerman, 1990; Lindner & Harris, 1993; Ertmer, Newby, & MacDougall, 1996). To sum up, in the Web-enabled learning environment, effects of self-regulated learning on students' skills of application software are positive and performance higher than those without SRL.

PROBLEM-BASED LEARNING AND SELF-REGULATED LEARNING

In PBL, students work in collaborative groups to identify what they need to learn in order to solve problems. They engage in self-directed learning (SDL), apply knowledge they acquire to the problems, and reflect on what they have learned and the effectiveness of the strategies they have employed. That is, PBL is well-suited to help students become active learners as it situates learning in real-world problems and makes students responsible for their learning (Hmelo-Silver, 2004). PBL helps prepare students for lifelong learning by developing students' ability for self-directed learning and their meta-cognitive awareness (Dunlap, 2005).

PBL is a task-based approach that teachers can apply to support development of SRL. If PBL activities are designed carefully with teachers who provide appropriate modeling and scaffolding, they facilitate and necessitate SRL. PBL provides opportunities for self-directed learning by offering students choice, control of what to work on, how to work, and what products to generate. PBL facilitates SRL because it places responsibility on the students to discover information, to coordinate actions and people, to monitor understanding, and to reach goals (Paris & Paris, 2001).

Hmelo-Silver (2004) points out that students' approaches to learn from problems are different qualitatively because of their degree of self-regulation. Ertmer et al. (1996) conducts a qualitative study of how veterinary students learned from problems. Low self-regulated learners have difficulty in adapting to the kind of learning required in problem-based instruction. They fluctuate according to their perception of the value of learning from problems. High self-regulated students value learning from problems and tend to focus on the problem analysis and reflection process. In contrast, low self-regulated students tend to focus on fact acquisition. Furthermore, the results of Ertmer et al. suggest that low self-regulated students may have difficulty in dealing with SRL demands of a PBL curriculum.

Combined training with self-regulatory and problem-solving strategies is effective for enhancing self-regulatory competences in solving mathematical problems (Perels, Gürtler, & Schmitz, 2005). However, there are very few studies that discuss the effects of PBL and SRL simultaneously, particularly through teaching Web sites. According to the literature reviewed , it is believed that the learning effect will be even stronger when teachers arouse students' interest, lead them to apply their skills and knowledge to solve problems, and encourage them to self-regulate their learning.

In this research, we hypothesize that students focusing on the aspects of problem-based learning variant with self-regulated learning would gain more development on the skills of application software than students studying the task without these co-existing treatments. We also hypothesize that learning effects of PBL and non-SRL group or non-PBL and SRL group are better than non-PBL and non-SRL group. That is, highest increase of development in skills of applying packaged software is expected in conditions wherein students are confronted with the situation of simulated problems and with self-regulated or self-directed learning style without teachers' pressure. Therefore, we propose the following: in a Web-enabled learning environment, the effects of PBL and SRL intervention on students' skills of application software are positive, and higher, than those without the combined intervention.

METHODS

Participants

Participants in this study are 106 fresh students taking a compulsory course of 'Packaged Software and Application' in an institute of technology in Taiwan. None of them major in the field of information or computer technology. However, in an institution for technological/vocational education, practical applications of technology are guiding principles (Tai, et al, 2003). Students are expected to spend more time and efforts in mastering a variety of technological skills, as compared to those in universities in Taiwan.

Course Setting

The course under study is a semester-long, two-credit-hour class, targeted at first-year college students from different majors. Students solve a series of authentic tasks by applying Microsoft Office (including Word, Excel, and PowerPoint).

Experimental Design and Procedure

In this study we explore whether students in the "Packaged Software and Application" course enhance their skills of application software via e-learning. Based on feedback from earlier research, we have re-designed the course and conducted a series of quasi-experiments to examine the effects of web-enabled PBL, SRL, and their combinations.

The experimental design is a 2 (PBL vs. non-PBL) × 2 (SRL vs. non-SRL) factorial pretest-post-test design (see Figure 1). Students from four groups solve the same task but in different learning conditions. Participants are randomly assigned to one of the four experimental conditions in such a way that each condition contains 24 to 30 students. The PBL and SRL group (C1, n=30), PBL and non-SRL group (C2, n=25), non-PBL and SRL group (C3, n=24) are experimental groups, while non-PBL and non-SRL group (C4, n=27) is the control group. The sample size in this study is large enough to be tested in statistics.

The course design in the present study consists of three subsequent modules: the Word module, the Excel module, and the PowerPoint module. A skill test is administered after the completion of each module. The first test is held during mid-term examination (eighth week). The second test is held in the 13th week and the final one in the 16th week. A schedule of teaching of modules and skill tests is depicted in Figure 2.

In the beginning of a course, students are encouraged to adapt and learn via a course Web site. Teaching during this period is through a traditional classroom. A teacher records every session of the lecture first and then converts these lectures into a HTML file with flash, video, and voice. These HTML files are then loaded into the course Web site. Students can preview and review the course sessions on this course Web site. After three weeks, most of the coursework is moved onto the Web site. We help students to adapt to learning through the net and try lessen down a feeling of isolation. Within these three weeks, we adjust students' learning gradually and smoothly.

Figure 1. Expected effects of variation in instructional methods

	PBL	non-PBL
SRL	The most significant effect (C1 Group)	Medium effect (C3 Group)
non-SRL	Medium effect (C2 Group)	No difference (C4 Group)

PBL Treatment

A teacher creates interesting, challenging, and authentic problem situations. In the first Word module, students are required to apply for a job as Marketing Assistant in an online-game company. They are required to design and then build autobiographies and resumes by applying skills of application software that they have just learned. In the Excel module, students play roles as if they are employed by this same software company, and a marketing manager asks them to compare expenses resulting from different distribution channels. They have to survey and then complete a worksheet with some graphs to contrast differences between channels. Additionally, they must come up with a recommendation regarding the best combination of channels. In the last module of PowerPoint, they are promoted as Marketing Managers of higher rank. They are asked to develop a business proposal for a new online game. They have to present this proposal with visual aids to convince the managing director to enter in to a market. Therefore, a persuasive PowerPoint presentation is built at this stage.

A teacher demonstrates first how they could approach the situation and solve the problem with the help of a Web-based multimedia application. In addition to the teaching of skills of application

Figure 2. Schedule of three modules and skill tests

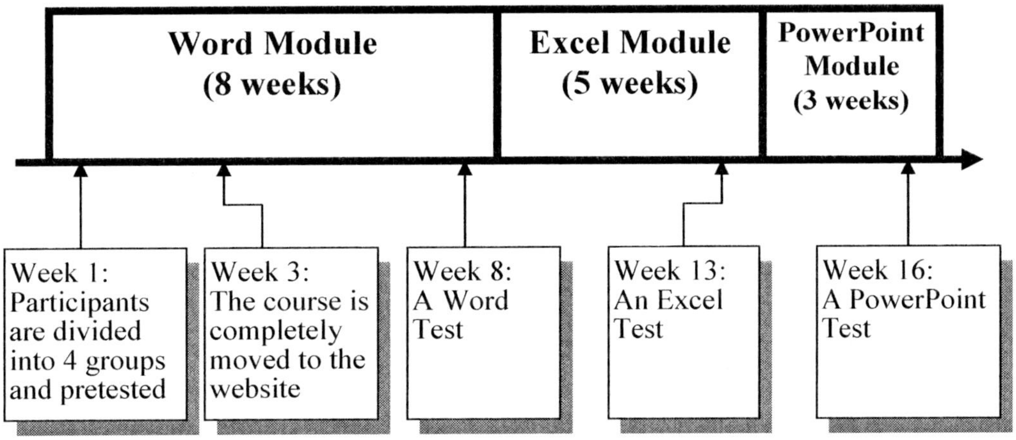

software, similar situations and related applications are also discussed in the class. Latter, the teacher guides students in constructing their own models of problem-solving.

SRL Treatment

There is a SRL group in each class. Two SRL groups from the PBL class and non-PBL class are gathered in a classroom and a two-hour lecture is delivered discussing how to manage study time and regulate their learning. The lecture is given in an after-school course. Content of this SRL course is composed of following four processes addressed by Zimmerman, Bonner and Kovach (1996), that is,

- Self-evaluation and monitoring,
- Goal-setting and strategy planning,
- Strategy implementation and monitoring
- Monitoring of the outcome of strategy.

Students are taught how to implement these four processes to become more regulated learners.

In addition to the two-hour lecture, students in SRL groups are required to prepare and read the textbook regularly before classes, and to review or practice the skills of application software they have learned after school. They are also required to record their learning behavior every week. Data is recorded on the course Web site instead of their notebooks in order to prevent falsification of records. A teacher cursorily examines students' records.

Treatments in four groups are illustrated and compared in Table 1.

Measures

To examine levels of change manipulated by variations in experimental conditions, we first measured students' skills of application software as a baseline before they entered the class. In the first week, students complete three Word documents as a pretest. We choose Microsoft Word for the pretest because almost every student in Taiwan learns Word before he learns any other software package.

The pretest grades show that computer skills of almost all are low. None of the participants are able to answer any of the pretest questions correctly. This confirms that all participants in the four groups had a little knowledge or a skill of software package. The difference in students' skills of application software at the beginning

Table 1. Teaching and learning activities in different experimental groups

Group	Teaching Activities	Learning Activities
C1	A teacher... • demonstrates how to solve authentic problems and discusses its potential applications. • teaches SRL skills and urges students to study regularly.	Students... • take on authentic tasks and learn by problem solving. • practice SRL and record learning behaviors every week.
C2	Teaching activities are the same as C1 but without SRL lectures.	Students experience authentic situations and solve the problems without extra requirements of SRL.
C3	A teacher... • converts his traditional way of teaching without any modification into an online format. • teaches SRL skills and urges students to study regularly.	Students... • receive traditional computer software course through internet. •practice SRL and record learning behaviors every week.
C4	Teaching activities are the same as C3 but without SRL lectures.	Students experience traditional style of teaching and do not deal with extra requirements of SRL, although teaching is conducted via Internet.

stage among the four groups was not statistically significant. Therefore, we assume that the students have equal or no computer skills before they take this course. In addition, none of them had any experience in taking a Web-based course. We then evenly and randomly divided the students into the four experimental groups.

Later, skill tests are administered at the end of each module. In this study, we applied two practical and authentic teaching methods. It is very important to measure students' practical skills in problem solving rather than the memorization. In this regard, the lecturer simulated practical problems for students to solve to evaluate their enhancement of skills of application software. For example, students are required to complete a worksheet with some graphs and tables to compare the market share with all competitors. They have to apply several functions to compute the numerals and sort them. Students' grades come from their correctness and completeness of problem solving, and the artistry of their designs. Students will get high grades if they completely solve the problems with exquisite designing.

Before testing, students are assigned random seats. All students are tested at the same time. Every test consists of five to seven questions. A teacher grades and records the results immediately after each test. A surrogate representing skills in application software is averaged from the scores of these three tests. Finally, the enhancement of skills in application software of a module is the result of one's grade minus pretest grade. We test differences in the enhancement of the skills of application software under different conditions.

Results

To examine levels of change manipulated by variants in experimental conditions, we first measured students' skills using application software as a baseline. The pretest confirmed that all participants from four groups had a little or no knowledge and skills in packaged software. The difference in students' skills of application software at the beginning stage among four groups was not statistically significant. In addition, none of them had any experience in taking a Web-based course. We then randomly divided the students into four experimental groups.

Independent sample t-test was used to compare improvement of grades between PBL and non-PBL teaching methods. As shown in Table 2, the improvement in students' grades for Word, Excel

Table 2. Independent samples t-test: Improvement of grades

		N	Mean	S. D.	F	t-value	df	P
Word	PBL	55	64.29	11.063	2.604	3.147	104	.002**
	non-PBL	51	56.84	13.269				
Excel	PBL	55	64.98	17.948	24.992	3.809	104	<.001**
	non-PBL	51	46.43	30.943				
PowerPoint	PBL	55	72.00	11.617	.029	2.186	104	.031**
	non-PBL	51	66.98	12.016				
Average	PBL	55	67.09	9.779	5.430	4.722	104	<.001**
	non-PBL	51	56.75	12.673				

**$P < 0.05$; *$P < 0.1$

Table 3. Independent samples t-test: The improvement of grades

		N	Mean	S. D.	F	t-value	df	P
Word	SRL	54	63.11	11.647	.102	2.018	104	.046**
	non-SRL	52	58.21	13.325				
Excel	SRL	54	62.37	23.770	2.483	2.554	104	.012**
	non-SRL	52	49.50	28.021				
PowerPoint	SRL	54	72.54	12.462	.222	2.649	104	.009**
	non-SRL	52	66.52	10.831				
Average	SRL	54	66.01	11.305	.769	3.473	104	.001**
	non-SRL	52	58.08	12.195				

**$P < 0.05$; *$P < 0.1$

and PowerPoint modules in PBL class (67.09) was on an average higher than that in the non-PBL class (56.75). This is also true if one takes the test scores of each module into account separately. Therefore, effects of Web-based PBL on students' skills of application software are positive, and higher than those who do not receive PBL.

Results from Table 3 show that the average grade for Word, Excel and PowerPoint modules in SRL group (66.01) is higher than that in the non-SRL group (58.08). This is also true if one takes test scores of each module into account separately. Thus, the effects of web-based SRL on students' skills in using application software are positive, and higher than those without SRL intervention.

Finally, data from Table 4 shows that combination of PBL and SRL intervention a group results in the highest grades among four groups. The improvement of skills using application software in C1 is significantly higher than C3 and C4, and also higher than C2, though insignificant. Therefore, we conclude that the effects of Web-based PBL and SRL intervention on students' skills in using application software are positive, and higher than those who do not receive PBL or/and SRL.

For those teachers who wish to stick to traditional methods of teaching, directly transforming their teaching material into electronic form may not be a fruitful approach. Students from the controlled group (C4) received lowest grades among four groups, and differences in grades among them are significant (see Table 4). It is suggested that teachers should redesign their courses and then adopt new instructional methods and technologies to fully exploit benefits of deploying Web-based learning environments.

DISCUSSION

This study provides valuable insights and sheds some lights on new, effective practices that can be used by schools (particularly vocational schools), scholars, and teachers planning to implement or presently engaged in implementing e-learning environments. The implications of this study consist of three-fold:

Firstly, the PBL teaching method was found to play a consistently positive role in enhancing students' skills of using application software (see Table 2). There are significant differences between PBL and non-PBL classes, either in case of individual module tests or in an average of the three module tests. It was demonstrated that PBL is good for computer software education in general and e-learning in particular. Teachers could redesign their courses by simulating meaningful and interesting business situations, and, thus, engaging students' imaginations and interest to solve challenging problems.

Secondly, evidence also supports that the second teaching method based on SRL also enhances students' skills of using application software (see Table 3). There are significant differences between SRL and non-SRL groups on three tests and in average. Interestingly, as we focused on the variation of P-value related to each module, it became clear that the effects of SRL increased over time. This suggests that the effects of SRL among low achievers can be significantly improved, even by a limited amount of intervention, such as two-hour lecture regarding SRL at the beginning of teaching program and later by students' monitoring their own learning.

Finally, this study found some support for the effectiveness of a combination of instructional methods. As shown in Table 4, results show that the effects of a combination of PBL and SRL intervention on students' skills of application software are positive and higher than those who do not receive PBL or/and SRL, although the

Table 4. One-way ANOVA (Analysis of Variance): Average of the improvement of grades.

Dependent Variable		(I) Group	(J) Group	Mean Difference (I-J)	Std. Error	Sig.
Average	Scheffe	1	2	5.862	2.910	.262
			3	8.436(*)	2.943	.047
			4	17.064(*)	2.851	.000
		2	1	-5.862	2.910	.262
			3	2.574	3.071	.872
			4	11.202(*)	2.983	.004
		3	1	-8.436(*)	2.943	.047
			2	-2.574	3.071	.872
			4	8.628(*)	3.015	.048
		4	1	-17.064(*)	2.851	.000
			2	-11.202(*)	2.983	.004
			3	-8.628(*)	3.015	.048

* The mean difference is significant at the .05 level.

difference between C1 and C2 is not statistically significant.

This study contributes to e-learning practices in three different ways: (a) this study specifies how teachers can engage students in improving learning under authentic conditions. At the same time, teachers help students to regulate their learning by applying PBL and SRL instructional methods in a Web-based learning environment; (b) this study is one of the first attempts to explore learning effects of various combinations of PBL, SRL, and Web-based learning; and (c) this empirical study provides evidence that skills of low academic achievers, for using application software can be improved through e-learning.

Teachers face tremendous challenges in implementing e-learning among relatively low academic achievers. For example, Internet addiction is common, and it is not immediately clear how to focus students' attention and improve their learning in a Web-based environment without teachers' on-the-spot monitoring. This study proposes an effective approach in this kind of e-learning environment.

REFERENCES

Albanese, M. A., & Mitchell, S. (1993). Problem-based learning: A review of literature on its outcomes and implementation issues. *Academic Medicine, 68*(1), 52–81.

Azevedo, R., & Cromley, J.G. (2004). Does training on self-regulated learning facilitate students' learning with hypermedia? *Journal of Educational Psychology, 96*(3), 523-535.

Barrows, H. (1985). *How to design a problem-based curriculum for the preclinical years.* New York: Springer.

Barrows, H. (1986). A taxonomy of problem-based learning methods. *Medical Education, 20*(6), 481-486.

Barrows, H., & Tamblyn, R. (1980). *Problem-based learning.* New York: Springer.

Berkson, L. (1993). Problem-based learning: Have the expectations been met? *Academic Medicine, 68*(1), 79-88.

Bielaczyc K, Pirolli P., & Brown A. (1995). Training in self-explanation and self-regulation strategies: investigating the effects of knowledge acquisition activities on problem solving. *Cognition and Instruction, 13*(2), 221–252.

Borkowski, J. G., & Thorpe, P. K. (1994). Self-regulation and motivation: A life-span perspective on underachievement. In D. H. Schunk & B. J. Zimmerman (Eds.), *Self-regulation of learning and performance* (pp. 45-73). Hillsdale, NJ: Lawrence Erlbaum Associates.

Boud, D. J. (1985). Problem-based learning in perspective. In D. J. Boud, (Ed.), *Problem-based learning in education for the professions* (pp. 13-18). Sydney: Higher Education Research and Development Society of Australasia.

Boud, D., & Feletti, G. (1991). *The challenge of problem based learning.* London: Kogan Page.

Bruer, J. T. (1993). *Schools for thought: A science of learning in the classroom.* Cambridge, MA: MIT Press.

Cennamo, K. S., Ross, J. D., & Rogers, C. S. (2002). Evolution of a Web-enhanced course: Incorporating strategies for self-regulation. *Educause Quarterly, 25*(1), 28-33.

Chang, M. M. (2005). Applying self-regulated learning strategies in a Web-based instruction - An investigation of motivation perception. *Computer Assisted Language Learning, 18*(3), 217-230.

Chanlin, L. J., & Chan, K. C. (2004). Assessment of PBL design approach in a dietetic Web-based instruction. *Journal of Educational Computing Research, 31*(4), 437-452.

Colliver J. A. (2000). Effectiveness of problem-based learning curricula: Research and theory. *Academic Medicine*, *75*(3), 259-266.

Dabbagh, N., & Kitsantas, K. (2005). Using Web-based pedagogical tools as scaffolds for self-regulated learning. *Instructional Science*, *33*(5–6), 513–540.

Davies, P. (2000). Approaches to evidence-based teaching. *Medical Teacher*, *22*(1), 14-21.

Davis, M. H., & Harden, R. M. (1999). Problem-based learning: A practical guide. *AMEE Education Guide*, 15, http://www.amee.org/index.asp?tm=43

Dunlap, J. C. (2005). Changes in students' use of lifelong learning skill during a problem-based learning project. *Performance Improvement Quarterly*, *18*(1), 5-33.

Ertmer, P. A., Newby, T. J., & MacDougall, M. (1996). Students' approaches to learning from case-based instruction: The role of reflective self-regulation. *American Educational Research Journal*, *33*(3), 719-752.

Greening, T., Kay, J., Kingston, J. H., & Crawford, K. (1996). Results of a PBL trial in first-year computer science. *The 2nd Australasian Conference on Computer Science Education* (pp. 201-206). New York: ACM Press.

Hmelo-Silver, C. E. (2004). Problem-based learning: What and how do students learn? *Educational Psychology Review, 16*(3), 235-266.

Kauffman, D. F. (2004). Self-regulated learning in Web-based environments: Instructional tools designed to facilitate cognitive strategy use, metacognitive processing, and motivational beliefs. *Journal of Educational Computing Research*, *30*(1 & 2), 139-161.

Lehman, S., Kauffman, D., White, M., Horn, C., & Bruning, R. (2001). Teacher interaction: Motivating at-risk students in Web-based high school courses. *Journal of Research on Computing in Education*, *33*(5), http://www.iste.org/inhouse/publications/jrte/33/5/lehman-s.cfm?Section=JRTE_33_5

Lindner, R. W., & Harris, B. (1993). Teaching self-regulated learning strategies. In M.R. Simonson & K. Abu-Omar, (Eds.), *Proceedings of selected research and development presentations at the annual conference of the Association for Educational Communications and Technology* (pp. 641–654). Ames, IA: Instructional Resources Center, Iowa State University.

Norman, G.., & Schmidt, H. (1992). The psychological basis of problem-based learning. *Academic Medicine*, *67*(9), 557-565.

Nota, L., Soresi, S., & Zimmerman, B. J. (2004). Self-regulation and academic achievement and resilience: A longitudinal study. *International Journal of Educational Research*, *41*(3), 198–251.

Paris, S. G.., & Paris, A. H. (2001). Classroom applications of research in self-regulated learning. *Educational Psychologist*, *36*(2), 89-101.

Perels, F., Gürtler, T., & Schmitz, B. (2005). Training of self-regulatory and problem-solving competence. *Learning and Instruction*, *15*(2), 123-139.

Polanco, R., Calderón, P., & Delgado, F. (2004). Effects of a problem-based learning program on engineering students' academic achievements in a Mexican university. *Innovations in Education & Teaching International*, *41*(2), 145-155.

Poon, W. C., Low, K. L. T., & Yong, D. G. F. (2004). A study of Web-based learning (WBL) environment in Malaysia. *The International Journal of Educational Management*, *18*(6), 374–385.

Reyero, M., & Tourón, J. (2003). *El desarrollo del talento: La aceleración como estrategia educativa* [*The development of talent: Acceleration as an educational strategy*]. A Coruña: Netbiblo.

Risemberg, R., & Zimmerman B. J. (1992). Self-regulated learning in gifted students. *Roeper Review, 15*(2), 98-101.

Roces, C., & González Torres, M. C. (1998). Capacidad de autorregulación del aprendizaje [*Ability to self-regulate learning*]. In J. A. González Pienda & J. C. Núñez (Eds.), *Dificultadesde aprendizaje escolar* (pp. 239-259). Madrid: Pirámide/Psicología.

Segers, M., Dochy, F., & De Corte, E. (1999). Assessment practices and students' knowledge profiles in a problem-based curriculum. *Learning Environments Research, 2*(2), 191–213.

Sonmez, D., & Lee, H. (2003). Problem-based learning in science, http://www.eric.ed.gov/ERICWebPortal/recordDetail?accno=ED482724

Tai, C. F., Chen, R. J., & Lai, J. L. (2003). How technological and vocational education can prosper in the 21st century? *IEEE Circuits & Devices Magazine, 19*(2), 15-51.

Vernon, D., & Blake, R. (1993). Does problem-based learning work? A meta-analysis of evaluative research. *Academic Medicine, 68*(7), 550-563.

Walton, H., & Matthews, M. (1989). Essentials of problem-based learning. *Medical Education, 23*(6), 542-558.

Weinstein, C. (1989). Teacher education students' preconceptions of teaching. *Journal of Teacher Education, 40*(2), 53-60.

Williams, S. M. (1993). Putting case-based learning into context: Examples from legal, business, and medical education. *Journal of Learning Sciences, 2*(4), 367-427.

Winnips, K. (2000). *Scaffolding-by-design: A model for WWW-based learner support*, Enschede: University of Twente Press.

Wu, T. Y. (2000). Integrative curriculum planning in technological and vocational education in Taiwan, Republic of China. http://www.eric.ed.gov/ERICWebPortal/recordDetail?accno=ED450230

Yang, Y. (1993). The effects of self-regulatory skills and type of instructional control on learning from computer-based instruction. *International Journal of Instructional Media, 20*(3), 225-241.

Yip, W. (2001). Utilisation of the problem-based learning approach facilitated by information technology to teach information on systems development. http://citeseer.ist.psu.edu/535807.html

Young, J. D. (1996). The effect of self-regulated learning strategies on performance in learner controlled computer-based instruction. *Educational Technology Research and Development, 44*(2), 17-27.

Zimmerman, B. J. (1990). Self-regulated learning and academic achievement: An overview. *Educational Psychologist, 25*(1), 3-17.

Zimmerman, B. J. (1998). Developing self-regulation cycles of academic regulation: An analysis of exemplary instructional model. In D. H. Schunk & B. J. Zimmerman (Eds.), *Self-regulated learning: From teaching to self-reflective practice* (pp. 1-19). New York: Guilford.

Zimmerman, B. J., Bonner, S., & Kovach, R. (1996). *Developing self-regulated learners: Beyond achievement to self-efficacy.* Washington, DC: American Psychological Association.

Zimmerman, B. J., & Martinez-Pons, M. (1986). Development of a structured interview for assessing student use of self-regulated learning strategies. *American Educational Research Journal, 23*(4), 614-628.

Zimmerman, B. J., & Schunk, D. H. (1989). *Self-regulated learning and academic achievement: Theory, research, and practice*. New York: Springer-Veri

This work was previously published in International Journal of Distance Education Technologies, Vol. 6, Issue 3, edited by Q. Jin, pp. 69-84, copyright 2008 by IGI Publishing (an imprint of IGI Global).

Chapter 14
Constructivist Learning Through Computer Gaming

Morris S. Y. Jong
Centre for the Advancement of Information Technology in Education, The Chinese University of Hong Kong, Hong Kong

Junjie Shang
Graduate School of Education, Peking University, Beijing, China

Fong-lok Lee
Centre for the Advancement of Information Technology in Education, The Chinese University of Hong Kong, Hong Kong

Jimmy H. M. Lee
Centre for the Advancement of Information Technology in Education, The Chinese University of Hong Kong, Hong Kong

ABSTRACT

Apart from the ability of computer games to make learning more interesting, a number of researchers and educators have been exploring other educational potentials of computer games. In parallel with the advancement of computer and information technology and the advocacy of constructivism in education, the issue of harnessing computer games to create new constructivist learning opportunities has received attention in both education and game research domains. This chapter is aimed at giving an introduction to computer game-based learning. Besides discussing computer games' intrinsic educational traits favouring constructivist learning from different perspectives, the authors also review a number of instances of two recent foci in the game-based learning domain. The first one is education in games that involves the adoption of existing recreational games in the commercial market for educational use. The second is games in education that entails designing and developing educational games articulated with different constructivist learning paradigms or pedagogical approaches.

DOI: 10.4018/978-1-60566-934-2.ch014

INTRODUCTION

Computer games have become an important part of the leisure lives of young generation (Kirriemuir & McFarlane, 2004; Newman, 2004). This attention has been one of the common premises of various research on harnessing games[1] in education for these decades (e.g., Adam, 1998; Betz, 1995; Bowman, 1982; Buckingham & Burn, 2007; Cameron, 2008; Egenfeldt-Nielsen, 2007; Gredler, 2004; Jong, Shang, Lee & Lee, 2006, 2007; Lee, Lee & Lau, 2006; Malone, 1980, 1981; Mason & Moutahir, 2006; Squire, 2003, 2005; Shaffer, 2006).

Along with the advancement of multimedia, gaming, and Internet technology, as well as the pervasive promotion of student-centredness in education, the focus of game-based learning has been shifting from its original purpose of "sugaring" the process of learning onto today's purpose of offering students constructivist learning experiences. A number of contemporary game-based learning researchers have been endeavouring to investigate how to employ the intrinsic educational traits of games for exploiting new constructivist learning environments. In general, their work can be categorized into two main research foci, namely, (1) *education in games*, and (2) *games in education*. The former adopts existing recreational games in the commercial market for educational use, while the latter designs and develops educational games articulated with different constructivist learning paradigms or pedagogical approaches.

In this chapter, firstly, we discuss what and how the intrinsic traits of games can promote constructivist learning. After that, we review a number of instances of the recent research foci in the game-based learning domain. Further, we give an introduction to our recent game-in-education work, before our concluding remarks are given.

INTRINSIC EDUCATIONAL TRAITS OF GAMES

The discussion of utilizing games for learning and teaching has started since the widespread popularity of Pac-Man in the early 1980s (Squire, 2003). Without doubt, the "games" discussed in most of today's game-based learning research are quite different from the ones that were used in education in the last few decades. The differences are not only in games' technical enhancement (e.g., more sophisticated 3D user interfaces, dynamic synchronous players' interaction, etc.) brought by the advancement of technology, but also their underpinning learning philosophy, shifting from behaviourism (Rachlin, 1991; Skinner, 1938) to constructivism (Bruner, 1960; Papert, 1993; Piaget, 1964, 1970). In direct contrast to behaviourist education, constructivist education emphasizes that students should construct knowledge on their own. Students' learning is not imposed simply by conditioning and reinforcement, but rather a cognitive and socio-cultural interaction in an engaging and authentic learning environment (Otting & Zwaal, 2007).

Initiating and sustaining students' learning motives through gaming has been one of the significant research areas of game-based learning (e.g., Bowman, 1982; Cordova & Lepper, 1996; Malone, 1980, 1981; Martens, Gulikers & Bastiaens, 2004). More recently, researchers in the domain (e.g., Aylett, 2005; Gee, 2003, 2005; Kirriemuir & McFarlane, 2004; Mason & Moutahir, 2006; Prensky, 2001, 2006; Shaffer, 2006; Squire, 2005) have also argued that the underlying cognitive and socio-cultural features of games can offer various "educative" opportunities to students. In the following, we will discuss games' intrinsic educational traits that promote constructivist learning from the *motivational*, *cognitive* and *socio-cultural* perspectives.

Motivational Perspective

Constructivist learning theorists (e.g., Papert, 1993; Piaget, 1964, 1970) realize that game-like activities can foster students' deep learning. It is because, in those activities, students are willing to spend more time and effort on learning. They also feel better about what they learn, and will try to apply the acquired knowledge and skills in the future.

There have been a number of game-based learning studies focusing on investigating what, why, and how gaming can make students more motivated during the process of learning. Based on a series of surveys, observations and interviews with gamers, Malone (1980, 1981) put forward a motivation theory, which asserts that *challenge*, *fantasy*, *control*, *curiosity*, *cooperation*, *recognition*, and *competition* are the most significant elements that make gaming fun and engaging, and sustain gamers' continual motives. Malone advocated that schools should try to integrate gaming elements into curricula so as to arouse students' intrinsic motives in learning. Apart from that, Bowman (1982) tied his study on learning through gaming with Csikszentmihalyi's (1975, 1990) psychological conception of *flow*. Flow is a state of experience of "*intense concentration and enjoyment*." Under the flow state, a person will engage in a complex, goal-directed challenge not for external rewards, but simply for the exhilaration of dealing with the challenge. Bowman believed that learning through gaming is a spontaneous way to bring students to the flow state of learning. Although Bowman's work was done more than two decades ago, recent empirical evidence (e.g., DeLisi & Wolford, 2002) still accords with his assertion.

Fun and enjoyment are essential elements in the process of learning as students can be more relaxed and motivated to learn (Bisson & Luncker, 1996; Cordova & Lepper, 1996). Gamers always undergo hard but engaging, challenging but pleasurable, and risk-taking but rewarding experiences in gaming (Prensky, 2001). All these are the experiences of fun and enjoyment. From both theoretical and empirical points of view, it is expected that students are more motivated to participate in educational activities if these activities take place in a form of gaming.

Cognitive Perspective

The traditional school curricula are often fragmented into small and unconnected pieces (Papert, 1993). The original intention is for making learning easier, but this usually ends up neglecting the rationale behind the knowledge itself, creating unrealistic learning contexts, and rendering the whole learning process boring. Without chunking or turning learning content into a series of split-screens, a well-designed game does well in presenting near real-life context for students to acquire knowledge and skills unintentionally rather than deliberately (Gee 2003). This sort of learning experience coincides with Lave and Wenger's (1991) conception of *situated learning*.

When discussing games' educational potential from the cognitive perspective, we should first classify today's games into *mini-games* or *complex-games* (Prensky, 2006). In general, playing mini-games takes around several minutes to an hour. Usually, these games contain simple challenges and content, with neither ethical dilemma nor human gamers' interaction. In contrast to mini-games, complex-games require gamers' dozens of hours (or even more) of concentrated attention to master. Most tasks therein are generative and open-ended without prescribed gaming strategies. Gamers engaged in complex gaming cannot be passive (Antonacci & Modaress, 2008). They have to analyze the perceived information and context in the games proactively, and then apply their existing knowledge and skills to formulate strategies, make decisions, and then examine results. It is also necessary for them to acquire new and multiple skills, and interact (compete, cooperate or collaborate) with other human gamers or NPCs (non-player characters) inside the games (Gee, 2003; Mason & Moutahir, 2006).

Complex games offer the prospect of user-defined learning environments (Halverson, 2005) in which individuals can try out and get feedback on their assumptions and strategies. This is a new cognitive way for learners to acquire knowledge and skills in a constructivist fashion (Shaffer, Squire, Halverson & Gee, 2005).

Socio-Cultural Perspective

How to educate students is not seen as how to build representations in each of their heads, but how to engage them in social practices (Lave & Wenger, 1991). Knowledge itself arises from social needs, fulfills social functions, and is tied inherently with cultural conditions (Cole, 1996). Thus, learning is not just a process of mastering facts, or even doing complex tasks, but rather, participating in socio-cultural practices. This requires learners to develop their own identity in relation to others.

Most of today's gaming activities are situated socially and culturally (Gee, 2003), entwining practice, participation, community, and identity (Wenger, 1998). The gamer generation prefers human competitors and/or collaborators rather than purely artificial intelligence (AI) (Prensky, 2001). Gamers meet online and form teams to discuss challenges, complete quests, and solve puzzles. Moreover, nearly every prevalent game does not simply appear alone as a game itself, but exists logically as a *game system* (Prensky, 2006). In each of these systems, besides a complex game concatenating with a built-in real-time chat console, it also entails gamers' self-initiated components, such as online discussion forums, fans' sites, blogs, etc. All these components enable and encourage individuals to share, discuss, evaluate and apply the community knowledge co-constructed by the community members.

In didactic schooling approaches, learning takes place through teaching and testing (Gee, 2005), and students can merely gain standardized learning experiences (Halverson, 2005). Compared to those traditional approaches, game-based learning can create a more social and cultural world that helps individuals learn by integrating thinking and social interactions (Shaffer et al., 2005). Moreover, the whole learning process does not necessarily need to be face-to-face and take place at school.

CONTEMPORARY GAME-BASED LEARNING STRATEGIES

When the idea of "learning through gaming" was first introduced into education, most of the so-called "educational games" were designed mainly based on the drill-and-practice learning principle (Egenfeldt-Nielsen, 2007). Usually, those games had a clear reward structure that was used as a way to push students' learning forwards. It was assumed that students could be put in front of computers, and then learned the designated content and skills through drills and practice, without teachers' help or involvement. For example, in *Math Blaster!*[2], students have to shoot down the right answer to the mathematics question shown on the screen. On each success, the player's balloon will move towards a needle. A student who can pop his/her balloon eventually will win the game.

Squire (2003) observed that drill-and practice games are still popular in today's education. It is because they can be integrated easily into ordinary school curricula as enrichment exercises for students to reinforce their exiting knowledge or skills during their independent study time. However, a number of educators and researchers (e.g., Card, 1995; Gredler, 2004; Kirriemuir & McFarlane, 2004; Papert, 1993; Prensky, 2001) have been criticizing that drill-and-practice games lack integration of learning experience into gaming experience, and promote rote memorization. "Parrot-like" learning will result in weak transfer and application of knowledge and skills (Gee, 2003; Jonassen & Howland, 2003).

Contemporary game-based learning researchers (e.g., Adam, 1998; Aylett, 2005; Cameron, 2008; Gee, 2003, 2005; Ip, Luk, Cheung, Lee & Lee, 2007; Johnson, 2005; Jong et al., 2006, 2007; Lee et al., 2006; Shaffer, 2006; Squire 2005) believe learning through gaming can be much more than drilling and practicing. The ability of today's games to sustain spontaneous gamers' engagement, offer gamers near real-life experiences, and exploit proactive gamers' communities makes gaming another possible means to realize constructivist education. In the following, we will review and discuss a number of constructivist game-based learning instances in the domain. In general, they can be categorized into two research foci, namely, *education in games*, and *games in education*.

Education in Games

Gee (2003) has been advocating the exploration of the possibility of adopting recreational games in the commercial market for educational use. He argued that many bestselling recreational games (e.g., *Full Spectrum Warrior*[3]) are already state-of-the-art learning games as they are hard but fun, time-consuming but enjoyable, and complex but "learnable." As an education-in-game proponent, Adam (1998) adopted a prevalent recreational game, SimCtiy 2000[4], into a university-level introductory urban geography class for the students to acquire urban planning concepts through playing the game in a self-directed manner. SimCity 2000 is a "city-building" simulation game. The game cannot only approximate near real-world conditions and phenomena of designing and building a city, but can also demonstrate the potentially successful or disastrous consequences of complex decision making in urban planning. Prior to the adoption, Adam analyzed SimCity 2000, and set up a number of learning objectives related to urban planning that they expected students could achieve after playing the game. Further, he conducted a number of learning experiments to verify quantitatively whether those gaming experiences would yield the expected students' learning outcomes. The research results revealed that, in terms of students' knowledge acquisition (urban planning concepts) and their perceptions of "learning through gaming," the game-based learning adoption in Adam's study yielded positive outcomes.

Another education-in-game proponent, Squire (2005), investigated the possibility of integrating another prevalent recreational game, *Civilization III*[5], into a US high-school classroom for teaching the formal world-history curriculum. Civilization III allows players to lead a civilization from 4000 BC to the present, with a mission to compete for political, scientific, military, cultural, and economic victories. In this game, each player has to seek geographical resources, manage economics, plan the growth of his/her own civilization, and engage in diplomacy with other players competitively and collaboratively. In the study, although Squire concluded that the students could develop more understanding and interest in historical knowledge, he remarked that it was difficult to align the "educative" content in the game with what was required in the subject curriculum. In fact, this remark, to a certain extent, coincided with some other similar arguments made by other game-based learning researchers. Mishra and Foster (2007) realized that it is hard to integrate existing recreational games into existing school curricula, as those games are designed originally for entertainment purpose, rather than education purpose. It is difficult for teachers to identify what and how a particular part of a recreational game is relevant to a particular part of a subject curriculum. On top of that, the authenticity and accuracy of the "educative" content of recreational games are another cause for concern over the integration of recreational games into formal schooling (Kirriemuir & McFarlane, 2004).

More recently, there has been literature (e.g., Gee, 2005; Prensky, 2006; Reese, 2007; Salen, 2007), from a more theoretical perspective, discussing recreational games' potential for preparing youngsters to become the skilled workforce in the twenty-first century. Nevertheless, some critics (e.g., Egenfeldt-Nielsen, 2007; Mishra & Foster, 2007) have been arguing that those claims lack empirical evidence, and most ideas therein still remain philosophical arguments.

Games in Education

Instead of adopting existing recreational games in the commercial market, a number of game-based learning researchers design and develop educational games articulated with different constructivist learning paradigms. For example, *distributed authentic professionalism* (Gee, 2005) is the underlying learning paradigm of Shaffer's (2006) educational games. Distributed authentic professionalism refers to the distribution of authentic professional expertise between NPCs (non-player characters) and gamers' avatars while gamers are engaged in specific activities during gaming. Professional knowledge and practice are embodied through the interactions between NPCs and gamers. Thus, gamers can gain first-hand experiences on how members of these professions think, behave, and solve problems. The whole cognitive process is situated both socially and culturally. Shaffer (2006) gave a more detailed account of Gee's (2005) idea of distributed authentic professionalism. He realized that members of a profession have an *epistemic frame*—a particular way of thinking and working, i.e., a grammar of a particular culture. In other words, epistemic frames are the conventions of participation that learners become internalized and acculturated. Thus, developing students to be members of a particular profession is a matter of equipping them with a right epistemic frame. To accomplish this, Shaffer and his colleagues developed a number of *epistemic games* which allow students to participate in simulations of various professional communities that they might someday inhabit. The communities include, for example, biomechanical engineers in **Digital Zoo**[6], ecological thinkers in **Urban Science**[7] journalists in **Journalism.Net**[8], etc.

Lee et al. (2006) proposed a constructivist learning paradigm for designing educational games, namely, *Folklore-based learning.* This paradigm suggests that learning takes place in an interactive adventure highlighted by problem-solving tasks which are situated in a folklore-based story plot. It is not only aimed at enabling students to learn in an authentic environment, but also offering interesting story episodes as a motivating agent for less initiated students. As prototype work, Lee et al. developed a game to realize this learning paradigm, namely, *Tong Pak Fu and Chou Heung*[9], based on the topic of probability in Mathematics education. This game is composed of several gaming stages, from sample space construction in the first stage, to simple probability, to conditional probability, and eventually to the *Monty Hall Problem* (Fowler, 1996) in the last stage. In each stage, students are presented a problematic scenario and required to solve the problems therein in order to proceed to the next stage.

Emergent narrative is the underlying constructivist learning paradigm of Aylett's (2005) narrative games. This paradigm suggests learning through role-playing in an improvised, rather than scripted digital story. The plot of the story in a narrative game emerges from the interactions between players' avatars and NPCs therein. If necessary, a teacher can participate in the game to intervene the emerging story so as to facilitate his/her students' learning. FearNot! (Aylett, Figuieredo, Louchart, Dias & Paiva, 2006) is an instance of narrative games. It was designed to educate children against bullying behaviour at school. Students in this game act as counselors to give advice to victims (the NPCs in the game) who are being bullied at school. Their advice will influence the proceedings about the victims in the next episode. Thus, students can observe the consequence of the actions taken by the victims in accordance with their prior advice. This game offers a safe environment for students to witness bullying incidences and reflect on how they have to cope with these incidences in real life.

4. OUR GAME-IN-EDUCATION WORK

In this section, we will introduce two pieces of our recent game-in-education work. The first one is *Learning Villages*[10] (Ip et al., 2007; Jong, Tse, Zhou, Chen, Lee and Lee, 2008)—a massively multi-player online game to support collaborative learning. The second is *Virtual Interactive Student-Oriented Learning Environment* (Jong et al., 2006, 2007)—a constructivist pedagogical approach to game-based learning.

Learning Villages

CSCL (Computer-Supported Collaborate Learning) refers to the process of a group of students engaging in discussing their perspectives on a problem with the goal of knowledge acquisition through a computer-based communicative platform (Weinberger & Fischer, 2005). Success of a group is attributed to all group members rather than merely the group leader (Scardamalia & Bereiter, 2003). Each member is responsible for knowing what needs to be known, and ensuring others to know the same.

Learning Villages *(LV)* is a game-based CSCL platform that operates in a form of massively multi-player online gaming, in which each student can design his/her own virtual character (an avatar) to participate in this virtual world. There are various entertaining elements in LV. For example, students can earn the *passion value* and upgrade their own *symbolic status* through playing a range of mini-games. Furthermore, there are various "hangout places" for students to meet one another. The interactions include real-time chat, making funny gestures and showing funny emotional icons to draw others' attention, etc. Figure 1 shows one of the hangout places in LV. Besides the entertainment, LV facilitates students' 2-tier issue-based discussion for collaborative learning. The first-tier is "village-level discussion," while the second-tier is "house-level discussion."

Both levels of discussion can take place concurrently. Each *village* in LV represents a discussion issue. A student can create a village, taking the role of *Chieftain* by initiating an issue for discussion. Any other students in LV who are interested in that issue, can become *Villagers* by building *houses* in that village. They can use houses to elaborate, for example, their perspectives, arguments or some related concepts with respect to the issue. In addition, students can build *roads* between the houses to interconnect different perspectives, arguments or concepts delineated in the village. They can make use of different types of roads, namely, *Explanation*, *Evidence*, *Problem*, *My Reply*, *Solve This First*, *Another View*, *Compare With*, and *Others* to reflect the different relationships between the elaborations represented by those houses. This is called village-level *(the first-tier)* discussion. An example is shown in Figure 2.

In the village, every house is "enterable," and it functions as an individual forum to facilitate discussion on a specific perspective, argument or concept raised in the village-level discussion. In LV, the term "*postings*" is used to represent the discussion threads inside houses (see Figure 3). This is called house-level *(the second-tier)* discussion. The more postings there are in a house, the larger its size and the higher its modernity level will be. The advantage of the 2-tier design in LV is that, major perspectives, arguments and related concepts, as well as their relationships with respect to a discussion issue can be arranged neatly in the form of mind mapping at the village level. However, it is still handy for students to review the details of a particular perspective, argument, or concept discussed at the house level.

Figure 1. A hangout place in LV

Figure 2. Village-level discussion

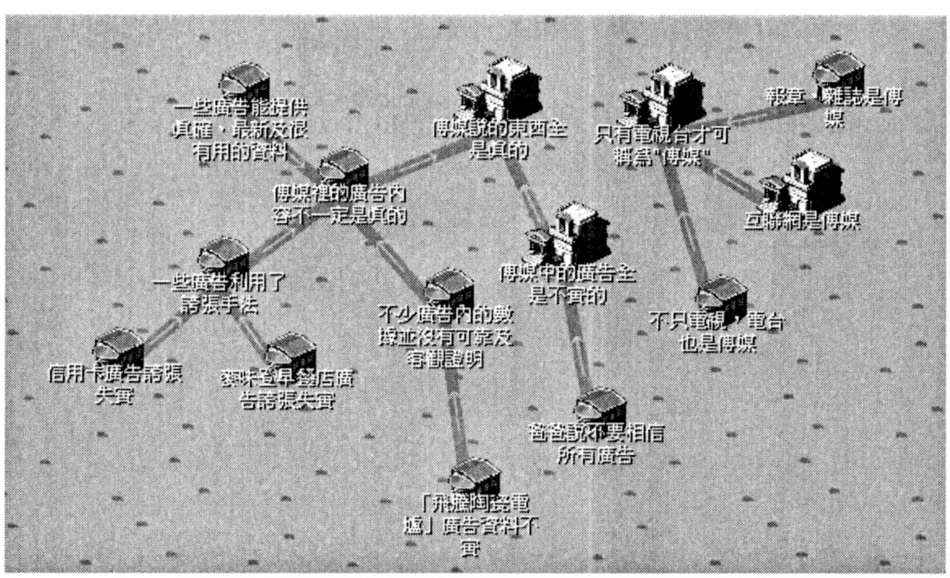

Figure 3. House-level discussion

In order to encourage students to participate in quality issue-based discussions, the invest-and-reward mechanism is one of the strategies adopted in LV for the purpose. Every time when a student creates a village, or builds a house in villages created by others, he or she has to pay "donuts" *(the virtual money in LV)*. Nevertheless, when the number of quality houses and postings in the villages *(that he or she has "invested" in)* reaches a certain amount, the village will be upgraded by either the LV system administrator or their learning facilitators *(usually their teachers)*. Benefits brought about by the upgrade include donut reward, higher social status conferment for enjoying extra privileges in LV, etc.

Virtual Interactive Student-Oriented Learning Environment

Virtual Interactive Student-Oriented Learning Environment *(VISOLE)* is a constructivist pedagogical approach to empower game-based learning. This approach encompasses the creation of a near real-life online interactive world modeled upon a set of multi-disciplinary domains, in which each student plays a role in this "virtual world" and shapes its development. In VISOLE, we adopt a game-pedagogy co-design strategy in which we emphasize the importance of teachers and their roles therein. Upon the theoretical foundation[11] of *intrinsic motivation* (Malone, 1980, 1981), *situated learning* (Lave & Wenger, 1991), *scaffolding* (Vygotsky, 1978), and *debriefing* (Thiagarajan, 1998), VISOLE is framed into three operable pedagogical phases, namely *Multi-disciplinary Scaffolding* (Phase 1*), Game-based Situated Learning* (Phase 2), and *Reflection and Debriefing* (Phase 3), as diagrammatically shown in Figure 4. Please note that Phase 2 and Phase 3 take place in an interlacing fashion, but Phase 2 starts a bit earlier than Phase 3.

- **Phase 1: Multi-disciplinary scaffolding.** VISOLE teachers act as cognitive coaches to activate VISOLE students' learning motive, and assist them in gaining some preliminary

Figure 4. Three pedagogical phases of VISOLE

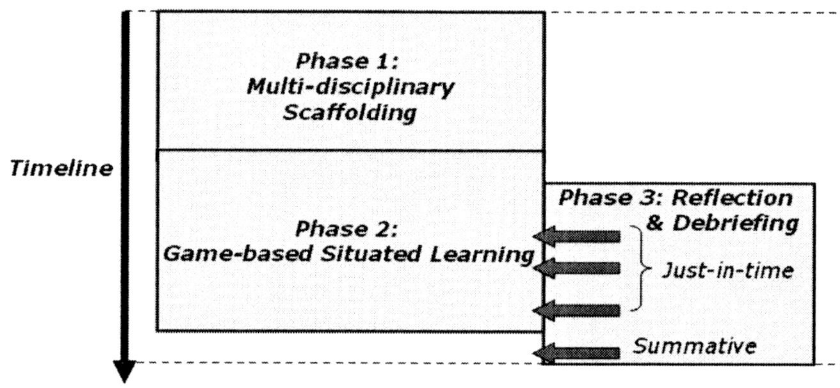

high-level abstract knowledge (prior knowledge) based upon a selected multi-disciplinary framework. In this phase, students are equipped with "just enough" knowledge, and given only some initial "knowledge pointers." They have to acquire the necessitated knowledge and skills on their own in the next learning phase, not only from the designated learning resources but also a wider repertoire of non-designated learning resources, such as the Internet.

- **Phase 2: Game-based situated learning**. This phase deploys an online multi-player interactive game portraying a virtual world. The scenarios therein become the dominant motivator driving students to go on to pursue the inter-related understandings of the multi-disciplinary abstractions encountered in Phase 1. The game encompasses the creation of a virtual interactive world in which each student plays a role to shape the development of this world for a period of time. The missions, tasks and problems therein are generative, and there is no prescribed solution. Since every single action can affect the whole virtual world, students have to take account of the overall effects associated with their strategies and decisions on others contextually and socioculturally. "Being situated" in this virtual world, not only do students have to acquire the subject-specific knowledge in a multidisciplinary fashion, but they also need the generic skills of problem analysis, strategy composition, decision making, etc.
- **Phase 3: Reflection and debriefing.** This phase interlaces with the activities in Phase 2. After each gaming session, students are required to write their own reflective journal to internalize their learning experience in the virtual world in a just-in-time fashion. Moreover, at the end of this phase, they are required to write their own report in a summative fashion to reflect on their overall learning experience. In addition, teachers monitor closely the progress of students' development of the virtual world at the backend, and look for and try to act on "debriefable" moments to "lift" students out of particular situations in the game. Respectively during the course and at the end of this phase, teachers extract problematic and critical scenarios arising in the virtual world, and then conduct just-in-time and summative case studies with their students in face-to-face debriefing classes.

FARMTASIA (Cheung, Jong, Lee, Lee, Luk, Shang & Wong, 2008) is the first online game following the pedagogical paradigm of VISOLE. It involves the subject areas of geography (natural environment and hazards, as well as environmental problems), biology, economics (including government, and production system) and technology. The "virtual world" of FARMTASIA consists of interacting farming systems, covering the domains of cultivation, horticulture, and pasturage. In the game, every student acts as a *farm manager* to run a farm which is composed of a cropland, an orchard, and a rangeland. Each student competes for *financial gain* and *reputation* with three other farm managers who are also at the same time running their own farm somewhere nearby in the same virtual world. Throughout the gaming period, students have to formulate various investment and operational strategies to yield both quality and abundant farm products to the market for making profit. Nevertheless, the richest may not be the final winner. Students' final reputation in the virtual world is another crucial judging criterion, which is determined by their practices on sustainable development and environmental protection. "Wise Genie," who is one of the game characters, will appear in the virtual world for giving advice or hints to students in some critical moments.

In order to enable teachers to review students' performance in the game, a "record-and-replay" system is implemented in FARMTASIA. While students run their own farm in the virtual world, the system logs their every single gaming action. Teachers can make use of the teacher console to re-transform the logging stored in the game server into students' gaming proceedings, and then replay the proceedings in a form of "video" playback. With the record-and-replay system, teachers can look for and extract interesting, problematic, or critical scenarios taking place in the virtual world to conduct just-in-time and summative case studies with their students. Since all these scenarios come from students' actual gaming experiences, it is easier for them to recognize, empathize, and understand the constructive and destructive occurrences therein, and the corresponding enhancement and corrective actions.

5. CONCLUSION

In this chapter, we have introduced briefly the background of game-based learning, from the early 1980s' drill-and-practice learning paradigm to the recent constructivist learning paradigm, and from its original purpose of "sugaring the pills" to today's purpose of sustaining learners' intrinsic engagement and exploiting cognitive and sociocultural learning environments. Besides elaborating on a number of intrinsic educational traits of today's games that favor constructivist learning, we have also reviewed two recent research foci in the game-based learning domain, namely, education in games, and games in education.

Education-in-game researchers (e.g., Adam, 1998; Gee, 2003; Squire, 2005) have focused on investigating the possibility of a direct transformation of entertainment into edutainment. Nevertheless, some game-based learning commentators (e.g., Rice, 2007) realize that the education-in-game approach is more suitable to support students' after school informal learning, rather than formal schooling. On the other hand, instead of adopting existing recreational games in the commercial market, game-in-education researchers (e.g., Aylett, 2005; Ip et al., 2007; Jong et al., 2006, 2007; Lee et al., 2006; Shaffer, 2006) have focused on designing and developing educational games articulated with different constructivist learning paradigms or pedagogical approaches.

We have no intention to argue that all learning should be via gaming. However, we believe that game-based learning could be an integral part of our education systems allowing a variety of contemporary pedagogical approaches to coexist and interplay. Some researchers argued that today's educational environment is still not flexible

Figure 5. The gaming interface of FARMTASIA (A) Cropland, (B) Orchard, (C) Rangeland, & (D) Wise Genie

enough to accommodate game-based learning in place (e.g., Squire, 2005), and the real integration of games into formal schooling has not yet been explored systematically (e.g., Halverson, 2005). Apart from discussing how to design and develop the best games for the educational use, the actual adoption, implementation, and evaluation of game-based learning within school and institution settings are issues which need to be addressed.

We hope our discussion in this chapter can generate a flash of inspiration for game-based learning researchers, educators, school teachers, game designers, as well as game companies, when reflecting on the questions of what, why, how, and when gaming can be educational. More mature and comprehensive frameworks for the educational use of games (*either the education-in-games approach or games-in-education approach)* will emerge soon, provided that we continue to pursue open discussion and conversation within multiple fields and disciplines.

REFERENCES

Adams, P. C. (1998). Teaching and learning with SimCity 2000. *The Journal of Geography*, *97*, 47–55. doi:10.1080/00221349808978827

Antonacci, D., & Modaress, N. (2008). Envisioning educational possibilities of user-created virtual worlds. *AACE Journal*, *16*(2), 115–126.

Aylett, R. (2005). And they both lived happily ever after? Digital stories and learning. In G. Dettori, T. Giannetti, A. Paiva, & A. Vaz (Eds.), *Technology-mediated narrative environments for learning*. Amsterdam: Sense Publishers. Retrieved January 15, 2009, from http://www.macs.hw.ac.uk/~ruth/Papers/narrative/Kal-Lisbon.pdf

Aylett, R., Figuieredo, R., Louchart, S., Dias, J., & Paiva, A. (2006). Making it up as you go along - improvising stories for pedagogical purposes. In J. Gratch, M. Young, R. Aylett, D. Ballin, & P. Olivier (Eds.), *Proceedings of the 6th International Conference IVA 2006* (pp. 307-315).

Betz, J. A. (1995). Computer games: Increase learning in an interactive multidisciplinary environment. *Journal of Educational Technology Systems, 24*(2), 195–205. doi:10.2190/119M-BRMU-J8HC-XM6F

Bisson, C., & Lunckner, J. (1996). Fun in learning: The pedagogical role of fun in adventure education. *Journal of Experimental Education, 9*(2), 109–110.

Bowman, R. F. (1982). A Pac-Man theory of motivation. Tactical implications for classroom instruction. *Educational Technology, 22*(9), 14–17.

Bruner, J. S. (1960). *The process of education*. Cambridge: Harvard University Press.

Buckingham, D., & Burn, A. (2007). Game literacy in theory and practice. *Journal of Educational Multimedia and Hypermedia, 16*(3), 323–349.

Cameron, B. (2008). Gaming, cognitive style, and feedback in the achievement of learning objectives. In T. T. Kidd, & H. Song (Eds), *Handbook of research on instructional systems and technology* (pp. 416-448). Hershey, PA: Information Science Reference.

Card, O. S. (1995*). What are computers doing at school*. Windows Sources.

Cheung, K. K. F., Jong, M. S. Y., Lee, F. L., Lee, J. H. M., Luk, E. T. H., Shang, J. J., & Wong, M. K. H. (2008). FARMTASIA: An online game-based learning environment based on the VISOLE pedagogy. *Virtual Reality (Waltham Cross), 12*(1), 17–25. doi:10.1007/s10055-008-0084-z

Cole, M. (1996). *Cultural psychology: A once and future discipline*. Cambridge, MA: The Harvard University Press.

Cordova, D. I., & Lepper, M. R. (1996). Intrinsic motivation and the process of learning: Beneficial effects of contextualization, personalization, and choice. *Journal of Educational Psychology, 88*, 715–730. doi:10.1037/0022-0663.88.4.715

Csikszentmihalyi, M. (1975). *Beyond boredom and anxiety.* San Francisco: Jossey-Bass.

Csikszentmihalyi, M. (1990). *Flow: The psychology of optimal experience*. New York: Harper & Row.

DeLisi, R., & Wolford, J. L. (2002). Improving children's mental rotation accuracy with computer game playing. *The Journal of Genetic Psychology, 163*(3), 272–282.

Egenfeldt-Nielsen, S. (2007). Third generation educational use of computer games. *Journal of Educational Multimedia and Hypermedia, 16*(3), 263–281.

Fowler, G. (1996). *Monty Hall (let's make a deal) Problem*. Retrieved January 15, 2009, from http://www.nadn.navy.mil/MathDept/courses/pre97/sm230/MONTYHAL.HTM

Gee, J. P. (2005). *What would be a state of the art instructional video game look like?* Retrieved January 15, 2009, from http://www.innovateonline.info/index.php?view=article&id=80

Gee. J. P. (2003). *What video games have to teach us about learning and literacy*. New York: Palgrave Macmillan.

Gredler, M. (2004). Game and simulations and their relationships to learning. In D. Jonassen (Ed.), *Handbook of Research on Educational Communications and Technology* (2nd ed., pp. 571-581). New Jersey: Lawrence Erlbaum Associates.

Halverson, R. (2005). What can K-12 school leaders learn from video games and gaming? *Innovate, 1*(6). Retrieved January 15, 2009, from http://www.innovateonline.info/index.php?view=article&id=81

Ip, C. W. H., Luk, E. T. H., Cheung, K. K. F., Lee, J. H. M., & Lee, F. L. (2007). A game-based computer supported collaborative learning environment: Learning Villages (LV). In *Proceedings of the 11th Annual Global Chinese Conference on Computers in Education* (pp. 289-292). 26-30 May, Guangzhou, China.

Johnson, S. (2005). *Everything bad is good fro you*. New York: Penguin.

Jonassen, D. H., & Howland, J. (2003). *Learning to solve problems with technology: A constructivist perspective*. Upper Saddle River, N.J.: Merrill Prentice Hall.

Jong, M. S. Y., Shang, J. J., Lee, F. L., & Lee, J. H. M. (2006). A new vision for empowering learning and teaching with IT: The VISOLE approach. In *Proceedings of the Hong Kong International IT in Education Conference 2006: Capacity Building for Learning through IT* (pp. 18-25). 6-8 February, HKSAR, China.

Jong, M. S. Y., Shang, J. J., Lee, F. L., & Lee, J. H. M. (2007). *An exploratory study on VISOLE—A new game-based constructivist online learning paradigm*. Paper presented at American Educational Research Association Annual Convention 2007 (AERA 2007). Chicago, IL.

Jong, M. S. Y., Tse, A. W. C., Zhou, Y. Z., Chen, W. Q., Lee, F. L., & Lee, J. H. M. (2008). Using posting templates for enhancing students' argumentative elaborations in Learning Villages. In *Proceedings of the 2nd IEEE International Conference on Digital Game and Intelligent Toy Enhanced Learning (DIGITEL 2008)* (pp. 180-187). Banff, Canada. Los Alamitos, CA: IEEE Computer Society.

Kirriemuir, J., & McFarlane, A. (2004). *Literature review in games and learning* (No. 8). Bristol, UK: Futurelab.

Lave, J., & Wenger, E. (1991). *Situated learning: Legitimate peripheral participation*. Cambridge, UK: Cambridge University Press.

Lee, J. H. M., Lee, F. L., & Lau, T. S. (2006). Folklore-based learning on the web—pedagogy, case study, and evaluation. *Journal of Educational Computing Research, 34*(1), 1–27. doi:10.2190/3HFM-D9NQ-G7Y7-QC1G

Malone, T. W. (1980). *What makes things fun to learn? A study of intrinsically motivating computer games*. Palo Alto: Xerox.

Malone, T. W. (1981). Toward a theory of intrinsically motivating instruction. *Cognitive Science, 4*, 333–369.

Martens, R. L., Gulikers, J., & Bastiaens, T. (2004). The impact of intrinsic motivation on e-learning in authentic computer tasks. *Journal of Computer Assisted Learning, 20*, 368–376. doi:10.1111/j.1365-2729.2004.00096.x

Mason, H., & Moutahir, M. (2006). Multidisciplinary experiential education in Second Life: A global approach. In J. Kemp, & D., Livingstone (Eds.), In *Proceedings of the Second Life Education Workshop at the Second Life Community Convention* (pp. 30-34), San Francisco.

Mishra, P., & Foster, A. N. (2007). The claims of games: A comprehensive review and directions for future research. In [San Antonio, Texas.]. *Proceedings of Society for Information Technology and Teacher Education Interactional Conference, 2007*, 2227–2232.

Newman, J. (2004). *Videogames*. London: Routledge.

Otting, H., & Zwaal, W. (2007). The identification of constructivist pedagogy in different learning environments. In M. K. McCuddy, H. van-den-Bosch, W. B., Martz, A. V. Alexei, & K. O. Morseb (Eds.), *The challenges of educating people to lead in a challenging world* (pp. 171-196). Netherlands: Springer.

Papert, S. (1993). *The children's machine: Rethinking school in the age of the compu*ters. New York: Basis Books.

Piaget, J. (1964). Development and learning. *Journal of Research in Science Teaching, 2*, 176–186. doi:10.1002/tea.3660020306

Piaget, J. (1970). *Science of education and psychology of the child*. New York: Oxford University Press.

Prensky, M. (2001). *Digital game-based learning*. New York: McGraw Hill.

Prensky, M. (2006). *Don't bother me mom – I'm learning*. St. Paul, MN: Paragon House.

Rachlin, H. (1991) *Introduction to modern behaviorism* (3rd ed.). New York: Freeman.

Reese, D. D. (2007). First step and beyond: Serious games as preparing for future. *Journal of Educational Multimedia and Hypermedia, 16*(3), 383–300.

Rice, J. W. (2007). New media resistance: Barriers to implementation of computer video games in the classroom. *Journal of Educational Multimedia and Hypermedia, 16*(3), 249–261.

Salen, K. (2007). Gaming literacies: A game design study in action. *Journal of Educational Multimedia and Hypermedia, 16*(3), 301–322.

Scardamalia, M., & Bereiter, C. (2003). Knowledge building. *Encyclopedia of education* (pp. 1370-1373). New York: Macmillan Reference.

Shaffer, D. W. (2006). *How computer games help children to learn*. New York: Palgrave Macmillan.

Shaffer, D. W., Squire, K. R., Halverson, R., & Gee, J. P. (2005)... *Phi Delta Kappan, 87*(2), 104–111.

Skinner, B. F. (1938). *The behavior of organisms*. New York: Appleton-Century-Crofts.

Squire, K. R. (2003). Video games in education. *International Journal of Intelligent Games & Simulation, 2*(1). Retrieved January 15, 2009, from www.cyberfest.us/Education/Video_Games_in_Education-MIT_Study.pdf

Squire, K. R. (2005). Changing the game: What happens when video games enter the classroom? *Innovate, 1*(6). Retrieved January 15, 2009, from http://www.innovateonline.info/index.php?view=article&id=82

Thiagarajan, S. (1998). The myths and realities of simulations in performance technology. *Educational Technology*, 35–41.

Vygotsky, L. (1978). *Mind and society*. Cambridge: MIT Press.

Weinberger, A., & Fischer, F. (2005). A framework to analyze argumentative knowledge construction in computer-supported collaborative learning . *Computers & Education, 46*, 71–95. doi:10.1016/j.compedu.2005.04.003

Wenger, E. (1998). *Communities of practice: Learning, meaning, and identity*. UK: Cambridge University Press.

ENDNOTES

1 Unless otherwise specified, the terms "game(s)" and "gaming" refer to "computer game(s)" and "computer gaming."

[2] *Math Blaster* is an educational game for children aged 6-9 to assist them in learning the criteria for Key Stage 1 and 2 mathematics skills. http://www.smartkidssoftware.com/nddav31.htm (Retrieved on January 15, 2009)

[3] http://www.fullspectrumwarrior.com/ (Retrieved on January 15, 2009)

[4] http://www.sc3000.com/sc2000/ (Retrieved on January 15, 2009)

[5] http://www.civ3.com/ (Retrieved on January 15, 2009)

[6] http://epistemicgames.org/eg/?cat=15 (Retrieved on January 15, 2009)

[7] http://epistemicgames.org/eg/?cat=14 (Retrieved on January 15, 2009)

[8] http://epistemicgames.org/eg/?category_name=journalism-game (Retrieved on January 15, 2009)

[9] http://www.cse.cuhk.edu.hk/~mhp/ (Retrieved on January 15, 2009)

[10] http://www.learningvillages.com (Retrieved on January 15, 2009)

[11] For the details of the theoretical foundation of VISOLE, please refer to the work of Jong et al. (2006, 2007).

Chapter 15
Stimulating Learners Motivation in a Web-Based E-Learning System

Keita Matsuo
Fukuoka Institute of Technology, Japan

Leonard Barolli
Fukuoka Institute of Technology, Japan

Fatos Xhafa
Polytechnic University of Catalonia, Spain

Akio Koyama
Yamagata University, Japan

Arjan Durresi
Indiana University Purdue University at Indianapolis, USA

ABSTRACT

The authors of this chapter designed and implemented new functions such as: a new ranking function, automatic interface change function, vibration function, room light control function and sound emission function in order to improve the performance of their Web-based e-learning system. By using these new functions, the proposed e-learning system can increase learner's efficiency by stimulating learner's motivation. The experimental results showed that the implemented system has better performance than previous systems.

INTRODUCTION

Distance learning is an alternative approach to provide qualified education and generate revenues. This approach is beneficial for both the students and the universities because many students that are unable to take face-to-face classes can study and get their degrees and also the universities can reduce the educational cost. During last decade, due to the opportunities provided by the Internet, more and more people are taking advantage of distance learning courses and enormous research efforts have

DOI: 10.4018/978-1-60566-934-2.ch015

been dedicated to the development of distance learning systems. Also, many large projects such as Arizona Regents University, Blackboard and WebCT, CALAT Project (1998), CALsurf(2000), California Virtual University, Globewide Network Academy, IU Online and Distance Education, Kentucky Virtual Campus, MindEdge (Online Education), Michigan State University (Virtual University), Ohio Learning Network, Oregon's One-Stop for Distance Education, Pennsylvania State University (World Campus), The Open University, The University of the Air, University of Florida Distance Learning, University of Illinois Online, University of Wisconsin-Platteville Distance Learning Center, WIDE University (1997), WebCAI (1999) have been established. However, in these systems the e-learning completion rate is low. One of the reasons is the low study desire when the learner studies learning materials. Therefore, it is very important to stimulate learner's motivation during the study.

There are several Web-based e-learning systems that consider the learner's capability and understanding (Kuwabara et al., 2000; Tamaki et al., 2000; Katayama et al., 1999; Nakabayashi et al., 1999). In Kuwabara et al. (2000) and Tamaki et al. (2000), the authors present the MESIA system. The system is able to keep the teacher operating cost low and to offer fine education by the cooperation of Computer Assisted Instruction (CAI) and teacher. The system is able to recognize the learners who need assistance, but its main purpose is to support the teacher, not the learners. In (Koyama et al., 2001; 2002) and (Barolli et al., 2004; 2005), we proposed and evaluated an agent based distance learning system to deliver appropriate studying materials to learners.

In order to offer a suitable and efficient study for learners, in our previous work (Barolli et al., 2006), we proposed a Web-based distance learning system in order to increase learner's efficiency. The proposed system has three subsystems: learning subsystem, learner supporting subsystem and teacher supporting subsystem.

The purpose of this system is to increase the e-learning completion rate by stimulate learner' motivation. We evaluated this system by several experiments and surveys and have shown that our previous system by using learner's study history, encourage function, ranking function, and self-determination of the study materials can increase the learning efficiency. However, the previous system needed some other functions to improve the performance. For this reason, we designed and implemented new functions in our system such as: interface changing function, new ranking function and learner's learning situation checking function.

This chapter is organized as follows. Firstly, we introduce the previous system structure. Next, we present the design and implementation of new functions. In following, we evaluate the proposed system. After that, we discuss and compare the functions of the proposed system with other e-learning systems. Finally, we give some conclusions and future work.

SYSTEM STRUCTUTE

The system structure is shown in Figure 1. The proposed system has three subsystems: learning subsystem, learner supporting subsystem and teacher supporting subsystem. The learning subsystem includes the studying materials, examination exercises, and some functions to stimulate learner's motivation. The learner supporting subsystem supports the learners when they have problems during the study. In this subsystem are implemented some interaction functions. The teacher supporting subsystem has some function to get the learning situation of learners and to give hints from the teacher to improve the learning efficiency.

Figure 1. System structure

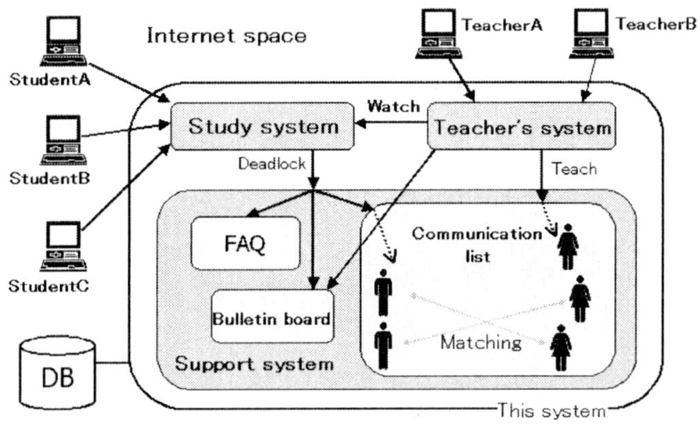

Learning Subsystem

At the beginning, the learner by using the login and password enters the system. Next, he/she reads the text and if understands the text information starts to do the exercises. Then, the obtained results and ranking are shown in the computer display. After that, the learner decides the next items to study and the learning procedure is repeated again. If the learner does not understand some parts of the text, he/she moves to the learner support subsystem. After he/she understands the text, it goes back to the learning subsystem.

Teacher Supporting Subsystem

In this subsystem, the person who is registered as a teacher can enter the system by using the registered login and password. By using this subsystem, the teacher is able to judge the learning situation of the learners. The teacher can check the following items.

- The learners who are using the system.
- The items which are finished.
- The learner study situation (is the learner using the learner supporting system or not).
- The FAQ of the learner support subsystem.
- The Bulletin Board (BB) of the learner support subsystem

If the teacher finds that a student is using the learner support subsystem, the teacher can communicate with the learner by e-mail. It is also possible to communicate with the learner by using Window Messenger (WM). By these communications, the teacher can help the learner if he has problems during the study. By using WM, it is possible to have voice chat or video chat, while BB is used to explain the content that the learners do not understand.

Learner Supporting Subsystem

The learner supporting system is used to help the learners when they have problems during the study. This subsystem includes:

- FAQ,
- BB,
- The list of persons who can communicate together.

The learner can investigates by FAQ whether there are answers of previous questions related with the content that the learner is studying or not. If there are not answers, the learner waits until the answer is shown in the BB. If the learner needs the answer in real time he enters in the member list. Then, the present learner can select a member who answered the questions in the previous test and communicate with him.

Interactive Functions

The proposed system has the following communication modes.

- Communication between students
- Communication between the student and teacher (question mode)
- Communication between the teacher and student (explanation)

Design and Implementation of New Functions

Here, we present the design and implementation of new functions for our system. The page output is generated by using JSP. For the system logic, we use Java and Java Servlet. For the system database is used Postgresql. The system works in the following way. At the beginning, the learner enters the study room. Next, the learner starts to study the learning materials. The teacher checks the learning situation and based on that decides how to support the learner. By using WM it is possible to have voice chat or video chat.

Also, because the FAQ and learner support subsystem are linked in this page, they can be referred if are needed. The BB can be used by teacher to explain the content that the learners do not understand. If the learner understands the problem he asked the teacher, he goes back to the learning phase and starts again learning process. The e-learning flow is shown in Figure 2. In order to check whether the learner is in the room or not we implemented a RFID system as shown in Figure 3. The implemented system interface is shown in Figure 4. We will present in the following its new implemented functions.

Figure 2. E-learning flow

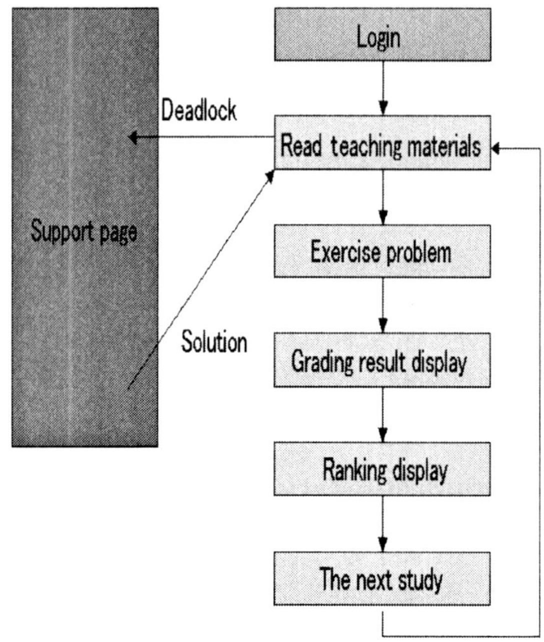

Figure 3. RFID checking system

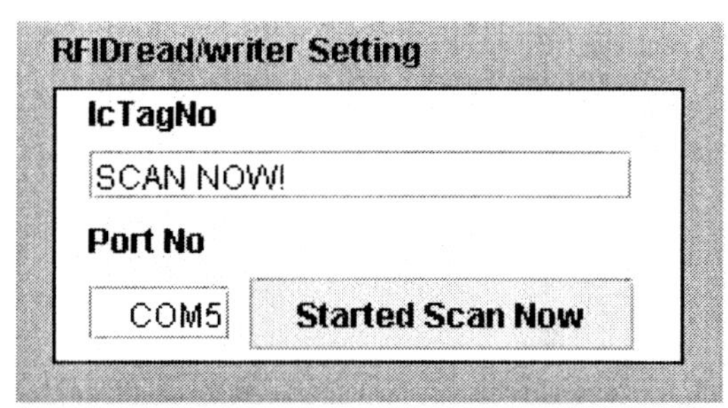

Visible Motivation Function

In the previous procedure of the learning, it is very difficult to check the student's learning situation. For this reason we designed and implemented a new function. If a learner does not use the computer keyboard or the mouse for more than 20 minutes, it is assumed that he has lost concentration, for this reason the system sends the first alert (Figure 5) and changes the display color in yellow. If the learner still does not use the keyboard or mouse,

Figure 4. System interface

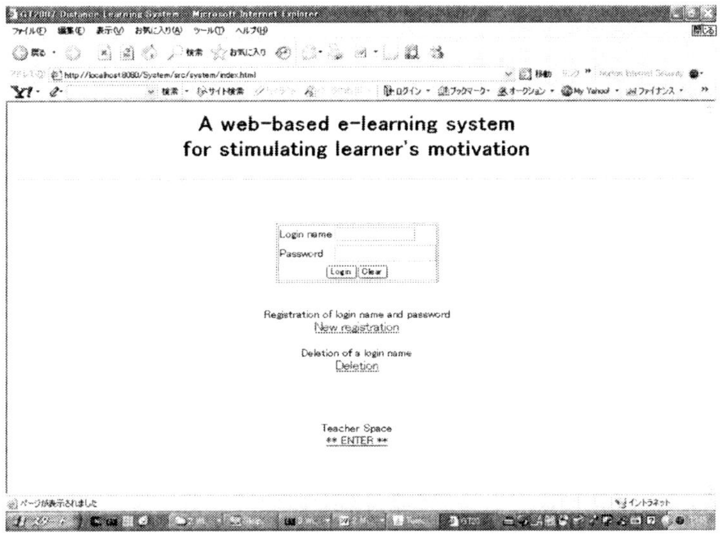

after 10 seconds, the system sends the second alert (Figure 6) and the display is changed in red color. The present learning situation of the learner is checked by the teacher using his Web site as shown in Figure 7. In the left frame of the page are shown the students who are using the system, their ID, learning situation, SOS (students that have problems with learning materials) and Alert.

Sound Emission Functions

In the case when the learner does not change his behavior, the system emits a relaxing sound to change the mood of learner. Another function is implemented using the cellular phone. We used the sound function of cellular phone to send some music to the learner.

Vibration Functions

In the case when the learner still does not react we considered the vibration function. We realized this function by using the vibration function of the cellular phone. Another implementation was carried out using a motor in the chair. We can control the motor of the chair by our implemented system as shown in Figure 8. By changing the angle of the motor, the system can change the learner mood.

Room Light Control Function

In our system, we also implemented the room light control function. By this function, we can change the room brightness and stimulate learners to increase the learning efficiency. The snapshot of system is shown in Figure 9.

Smell Function

With this function the system changes the smell of the room based on the learner's taste (learner's favorite smell), so the mood of the learners can be changed.

Ranking Function

In the previous system, we used a ranking function that displayed the results of a learner that had average results more than a predefined value. However, this may cause problems if learners have not good results. In proposed system, we

Figure 5. First alert

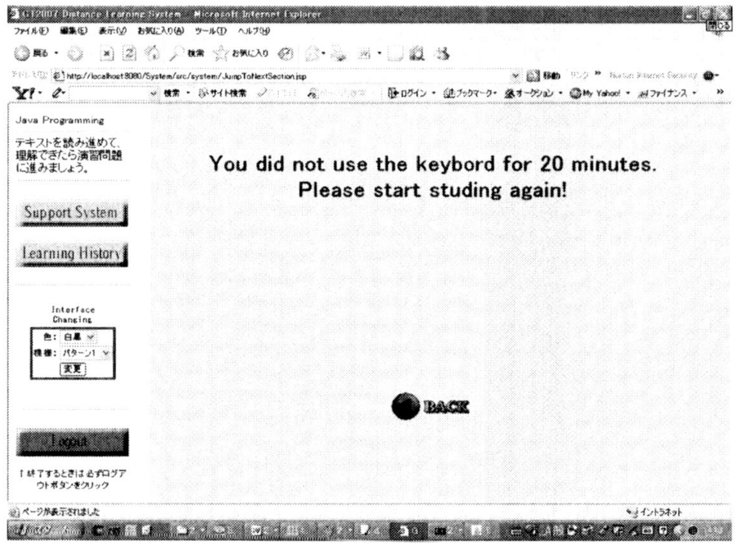

Figure 6. Second alert

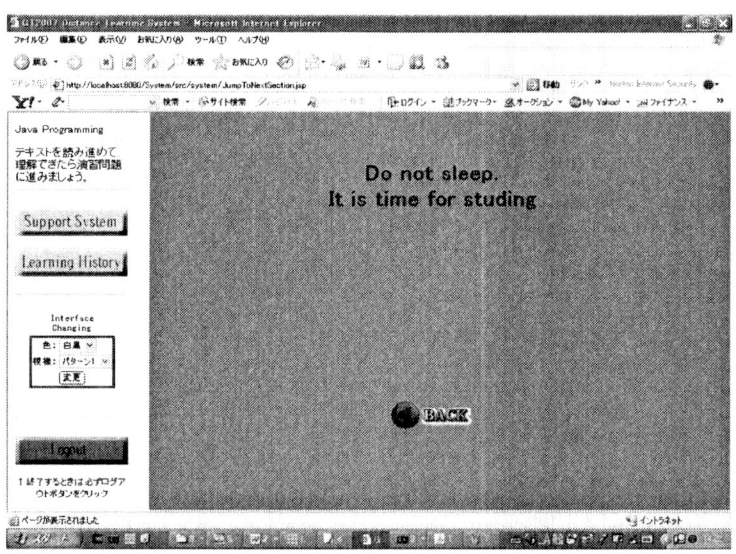

implemented a new ranking function as shown in Figure 10.

The ranking method is as follows. We divide the learners in different ranks such as A (90 to 100 points), B (80 to 89 points), C (70 to 79 points), D (60 to 69 points) and E (0 to 59 points). If a learner is ranked in A or B rank, the system shows the other learners who have 10 points more and 5 points less than the present learner. If the learner is ranked in C or D rank, the system shows the other learners that have 5 points more and 5 points less than the present learner. Otherwise, if the learner is ranked in E rank, the system does not display the results. Also, if a learner wants to check his studying situation and history, the system can

Figure 7. Teacher page

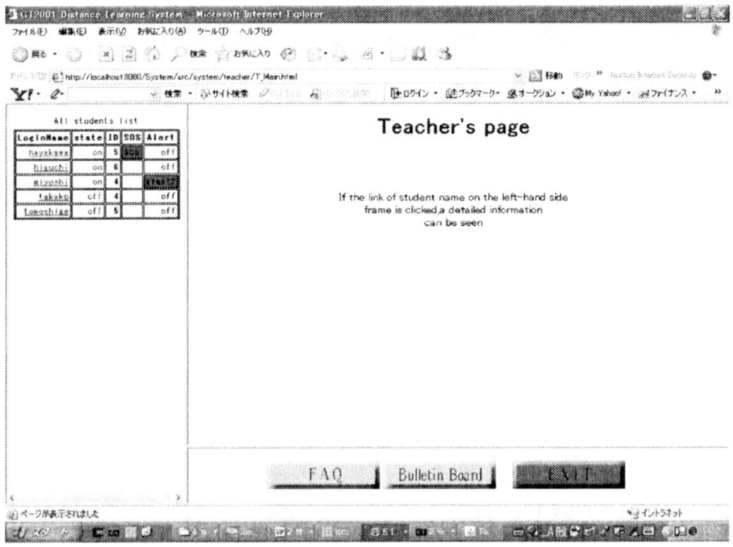

Figure 8. Chair motor control

Figure 9. Room light control

show the ranking level for each item as shown in Figure 11.

SYSTEM EVALUATION

For experiments we implemented some stimulation devices. The snapshot of RFID and USB experimental devices is shown in Figure 12. IC tag is recognized by the RFID reader and LEDs connected to the RFID reader by USB will start to blink. Our system identifies the learners by RFID. Also, we controlled USB, RS232C, Motor and RFID by implementing a Java program. The functions and interfaces of our proposed system are shown in Figure 13.

The proposed system can detect the learner's movement by using hand and body sensors. In our experiments, we used one hand sensor and two body sensors. The hand sensor detects the

Figure 10. Ranking function

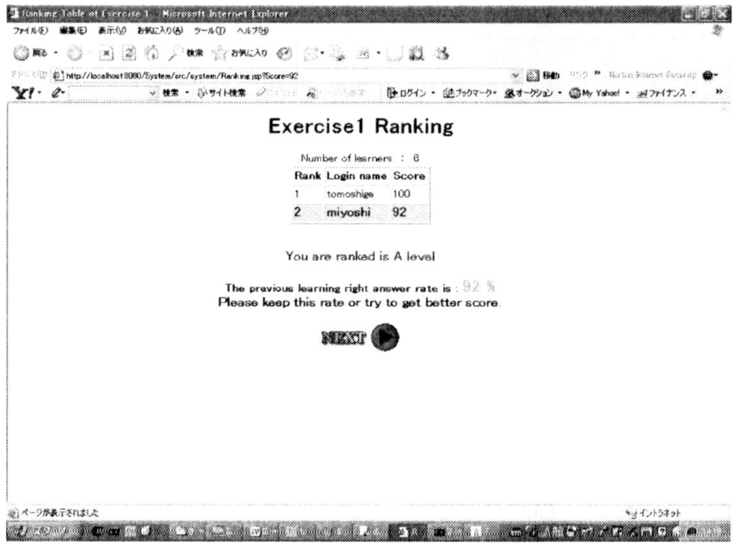

Figure 11. Learning history

Login name	miyoshi
FullName	三好貴子
Furigana	ミヨシタカコ
Mail Address (PC)	s04b2046@ws.ipc.fit.ac.jp
Mail Address (Cellphone)	s04b2046@ws.ipc.fit.ac.jp
Present situation	SOS(§4)

No	学習項目	SS	状況	Score	Rank	最終アクセス日時
0	Introduction	20	学習済	87	B	
1	Web and Java language	70	学習済	92	A	
2	Object-Oriented Programming	50	学習済	99	A	
3	Java Programming 1	100	学習済	90	A	
4	Java Programming 2	100	学習済	76	C	
5	Java Programming 3	100	学習済	100	A	
6	Java Programming 4	100	学習済	63	D	
7	Java Programming 5	100	未学習	---	---	
8	Java Programming 6	100	未学習	---	---	
9	Java Programming 7	100	未学習	---	---	
10	Java Programming 8	100	未学習	---	---	
11	Java Programming 9	100	未学習	---	---	

CLOSE

Figure 12. RFID and USB devices

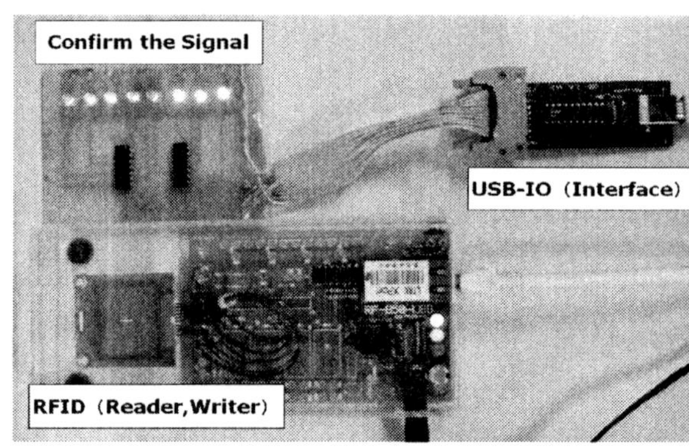

hand motions of the learner, while the body sensors are used for detecting the body movements of the learner. By combining Web and sensor technologies, the proposed system not only can monitor and control the learners' in the internet but also can stimulate and increase the learners' motivation. The combination of Web and sensor technologies is shown in a schematic way in Figure 14 and "Hand Sensor" and "Body Sensors" are shown in Figure 15.

The measurement data for learners' body and hand movements are shown in Table 1. We got these data after observing two learners studying for 40 hours. After a sensor reacts, the interval time will be reset to zero. For the "All Sensors", we make the record of data whenever we get a reaction from either "Hand Sensor" or "Body Sensors".

We consider where is the point of effective stimulation for learners from the sensing rate values. We pay attention to the reaction frequency

Figure 13. Functions and interfaces

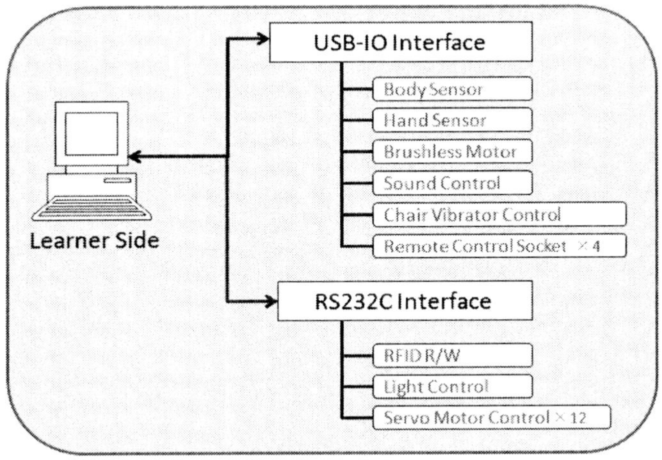

Figure 14. Combination of Web and sensors technologies

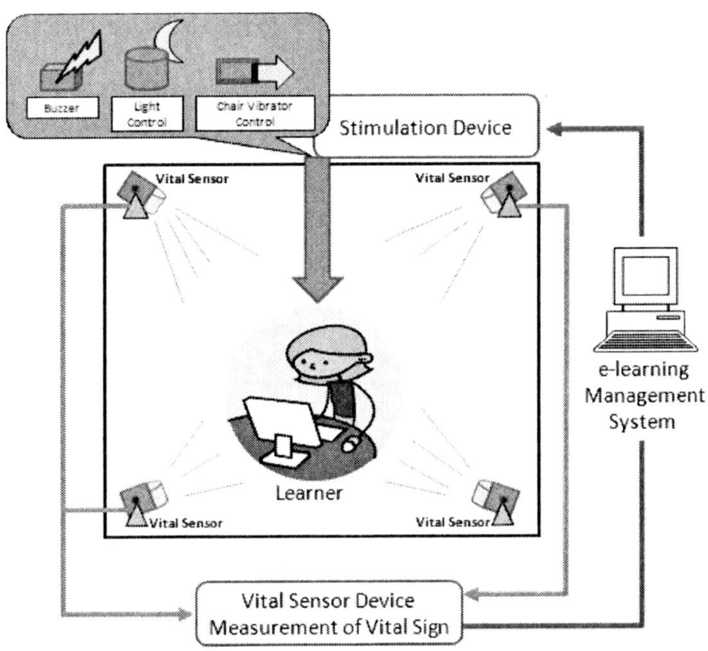

of each sensor. The interval of sensors response is very active at about 20 to 30 seconds, but it gets less active after 30 seconds. This shows that the learners make certain actions every 30 seconds while they are studying. After 80 seconds, there is almost no reaction for the sensors.

Especially, when we see the response time for "All Sensors" this is very clearly. In Table 2 are shown values of reaction number for "All Sensors". We can see from Table 1 that the learner's body moves more than learner's hand (mouse). We show in Table 3 the sensor response range and the average value of response time. Moreover,

Figure 15. Hand and body sensors

we can obtain the stimulation point by using the regression analysis.

We used the least square method for obtaining the regression line. The regression line can be expressed by Equation (1).

$$y = \beta_0 + \beta_1 x \tag{1}$$

In order to construct the regression line, we should calculate β_0 and β_1 values, but they are very difficult to be calculated. For this reason, we will find the expectation values: $\hat{\beta}_0, \hat{\beta}_1$. First, we find the relation between β_0 and β_1 shown by Equation (2).

$$l(\beta_0, \beta_1) = \sum_{i=1}^{n} (y_i - (\beta_0 + \beta_1 x))^2 \tag{2}$$

The Equation (2) should fulfill the condition of Equation (3).

$$_{\beta_0} \min_{\beta_1} l(\beta_0, \beta_1) \tag{3}$$

Then, the $\hat{\beta}_0, \hat{\beta}_1$ values can be calculated by Equations (4) and (5).

$$\hat{\beta}_1 = \frac{\sum (x_i - \bar{x})(y_i - \bar{y})}{\sum (x_i - \bar{x})^2} \tag{4}$$

$$\hat{\beta}_0 = \bar{y} - \hat{\beta}_1 \bar{x} \tag{5}$$

Table 1. Learner's body and hand movement

Response Range	Hand Sensor Sensing Rate	Body Sensors Sensing Rate	All Sensors Sensing Rate
0s-10s	27.31	45.60	62.39
10s-20s	30.63	37.61	26.55
20s-30s	15.27	7.94	5.47
30s-40s	8.52	3.20	2.23
40s-50s	5.90	1.43	1.04
50s-60s	3.95	1.11	0.77
60s-70s	2.65	0.64	0.41
70s-80s	1.67	0.58	0.27
80s-90s	1.13	0.29	0.20
90s-100s	1.09	0.29	0.23
100s-110s	0.61	0.26	0.09
110s-120s	0.27	0.26	0.07
120s-130s	0.24	0.24	0.14
130s-140s	0.40	0.21	0.05
140s-150s	0.24	0.19	0.07
150s-160s	0.12	0.13	0.02

Table 2. Reaction number for "All Sensors"

Response Range	All Sensors Reaction Number	Average of Appearance Time (min)
0s-10s	2747	0.9
10s-20s	1169	2.1
20s-30s	241	10.0
30s-40s	98	24.5
40s-50s	46	52.2
50s-60s	34	70.6
60s-70s	18	133.3
70s-80s	12	200.0
80s-90s	9	266.7
90s-100s	10	240.0
100s-110s	4	600.0
110s-120s	3	800.0
120s-130s	6	400.0
130s-140s	2	1200.0
140s-150s	3	800.0
150s-160s	1	2400.0
Total of Data	4403	

Table 3. Regression line

i	Response Range Middle Value [sec] (*X*)	Average Response Time [min] (*Y*)	Deflection Value (*X*)	Deflection Value (*Y*)	Product of Deflections	Value of Regression Line
1	5	0.9	-15	-8.5	127.1	-2.47
2	15	2.1	-5	-7.3	36.5	5.41
3	25	10.0	5	0.6	3.1	13.28
4	35	24.5	15	15.1	227.2	21.16

The experimental values and regression line are shown in Figure 16. It is proved that in general the people concentration is about 20 minutes. By checking the values of Figure 16, we see that when the response range is about 35 seconds, the value of regression line is about 21.16 minutes. The calculation is done considering that the total experimental time is 40 hours. This value is very close with the region of human concentration (20 minutes). For this reason, we consider that is better to stimulate the learners after 20 minutes in the design of our proposed system.

We considered that is an effective way to stimulate the learner after 35 seconds, 55 seconds and 80 seconds as shown in Figure 17. According to the results of the experiment, we decided that if the learners don't move for 35 seconds, we would give them a slight stimulation by light, and then after about 55 seconds from the start give them a sound stimulation and then start vibrate their chair after about 80 seconds. We will also give the smell stimulation to learners if they do not respond after more than 100 seconds.

Figure 16. Experimental values and regression line

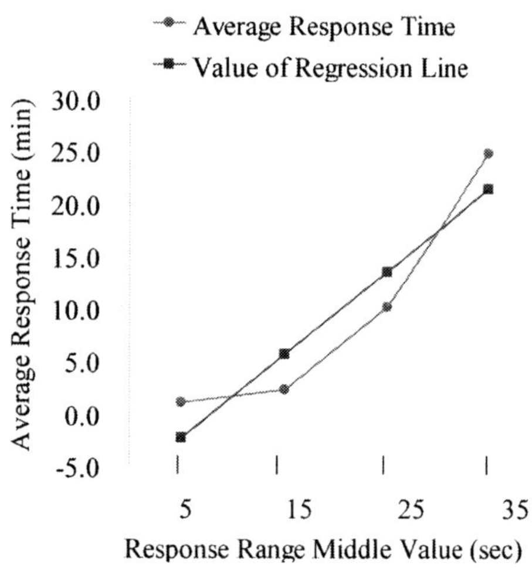

Figure 17. Flow chart of learner stimulation

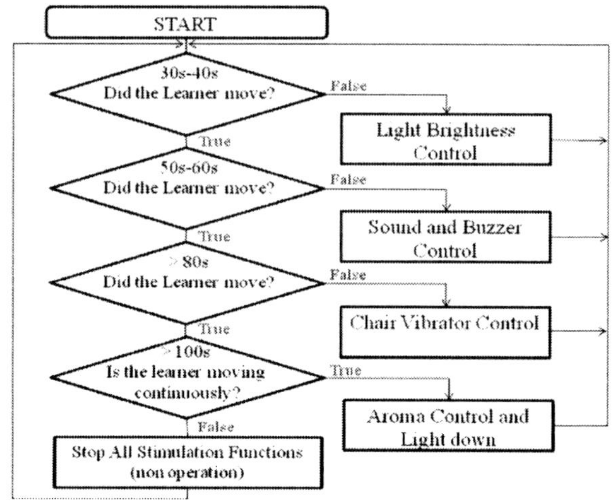

In order to evaluate the proposed system, 10 learners used the system and after that we made a questionnaire and asked the learners how it was the system performance and especially how the system stimulated the learner's volition? The questionnaire content is shown in Table 4 and the questionnaire results are shown in Table 5.

In the questionnaire, the learners answer the questions by using a five-grade system from 1 to 5. Only Q2 is a threefold choice (Table 4). The performance evaluation is better when the evaluation number is higher. When a learner evaluates with 5, it means that the system had very good performance. The values shown in Table 5 are the average values collected from 10 learners.

Considering the questionnaire results, we conclude that proposed system is an effective system for keeping the learner's motivation. The "Vibration function" and "Movement" of Q2 has the highest result. These results proved that by giving a directly physical stimulation to learners, the proposed system has a better efficiency than just using the computer display of the previous system. Especially, for the answer of Q2, the evaluation rate is 80% for the question: How you evaluate the directly stimulation to learners? This result also corresponds with the results of Q1. Therefore, we think that the proposed system is more effective than the previous system. Also, the implementation of RFID has a high evaluation value. We think that we can develop even more effective functions using RFID. However, the evaluation of smell function was low. This is because the learners have different smell tastes. But, we think that by selecting an appropriate taste for each learner, the evaluation for this function will be improved.

COMPARISON EVALUATION OF E-LEARNING SYSTEMS

We compare the functions of the proposed system with MESIA system and our previous system as shown in Table 6. In the proposed system the same with previous system the BB is used to give the hints by teacher, but in MESIA the hints are used to advice the learners on wrong answers and HELP/MORE for guiding learners to correct answers. As test function, MESIA uses a short test, while in our previous system and the proposed system the learner repeats the exercises until he passes the test. For teacher-student interaction, MESIA uses messages, while in our previous system and the

Table 4. Questionnaire content

Question Number	Question Content
Q1	*How much did the "Sound, Light Control, Chair Vibration and Smell function" keep your learning motivation?*
Q2	*How do you evaluate the stimulation by visual, sound and learner's body movement? Which one do you think is more effective? [visual and sound, vibration and movement, both]*
Q3	*How do you evaluate RFID control and management function?*
Q4	*How do you evaluate the e-mail attention function when the learner is not in the room?*

Table 5. Questionnaire results

Question Number	Performance Results
Q1	Sound 4.4 / Light 3.1 / Vibration 4.5 / Smell 2.7
Q2	Visual, Sound 10% / Movement 80% / Others 10%
Q3	4.9
Q4	4.3

Table 6. Comparison of functions for different systems

Functions	MESIA	Previous System	Proposed System
Hints	○	○	○
Tests	○	○	○
Teacher Student Interaction	○	○	○
Students Questions	○	○	○
Network Environment	○	○	○
Synchronous Learning	○	○	○
Asynchronous Learning	×	○	○
Ranking Function	×	Δ	○
Interface Change Function	×	Δ	○
Vibration Function	×	×	○
Sound Emission Function	×	×	○
Room Light Control Function	×	×	○
Smell Function	×	×	○

proposed system is used e-mail. In the case when a learner wants to ask the teacher a question, in MESIA is used an online message or video meeting. While, in our previous system and proposed system, the teacher answers the student's question by e-mail or using WM.

The MESIA is used in the Intranet environment, while the previous system and proposed system are Web-based application and can be used in Internet environment.

In order to have an efficient study, in MESIA the student and the teacher use a synchronous interaction. The previous and proposed system can be used for synchronous and asynchronous learning. MESIA does not have a function to stimulate the learner's motivation, while in our previous system has the display of learner's study history, change of interface color in manual way, encourage function, ranking function, and self-determination of the study materials. Our proposed system has all these functions. We also implemented the following functions: a new ranking function, the automatic interface change function, the vibration function, the room light control function and sound emission function.

CONCLUSION

We designed and implemented new functions such as: a new ranking function, automatic interface change function, vibration function, room light control function and sound emission function in order to improve the performance of our Web-based e-learning system. By using these new functions, the proposed e-learning system can increase learner's efficiency by stimulating learner's motivation. The experimental results showed that the implemented system has better performance than previous systems.

In the future, we want to evaluate the proposed system and its new functions in a real environment. We also want to deal with following problems: learner's privacy, system security, and improving the encouraging function by using not only text but also the animations.

REFERENCES

Arizona Regents University. (n.d.). Retrieved from http://www.azun.net/

Barolli, L., & Koyama, A. (2004). A distance learning system for delivering appropriate studying materials and stimulating learner volition. *Journal of Distance Education Technologies*, *2*(1), 1–17.

Barolli, L., Koyama, A., Durresi, A., & De Marco, G. (2006). A Web-based e-learning system for increasing study efficiency by stimulating learner motivation. *Journal of Information Systems Frontiers*, *8*(4), 297–306. doi:10.1007/s10796-006-9004-5

Barolli, L., & Koyama, K. (2005). A Web-based distance learning system using cooperative. In C. Howard, J. Boettcher, L. Justice & K. Schenk (Eds.), *Encyclopedia of distance learning* (pp. 430-439).Hershey, PA: Information Science Reference.

Blackboard and WebCT. (n.d.). Retrieved from http://www.black board. com/webct

CALAT Project. (1998). *Nippon Telegraph and Telephone Corporation*. Retrieved from http:// www. calat.com/.

California Virtual University. (n.d.). Retrieved from http://www.california.edu/.

CALsurf. (2000). NTT Software Corporation. Retrieved from http://webbase.ntts.co.jp/

Campus, K. V. (n.d.). Retrieved from http://www. kcvu.org/

Canadian Virtual University. (n.d.). Retrieved from http://www.cvu-uvc.ca/.

Globewide Network Academy. (n.d.). Retrieved from http://www.gnacademy.org/.

Indiana University. IU Online and Distance Education. (n.d.). Retrieved from http://www.iu.edu/~iuonline/index.html.

Katayama, K., & Kambayashi, Y. (1999). Support of distance lectures using active database. *Trans. of IEICE, D-I, 82*(1), 247–255.

Koyama, A., Barolli, L., Cheng, Z., & Shiratori, N. (2002). An agent-based personalized distance learning system for delivering appropriate studying materials to learners. (. *LNCS, 2343*, 3–16.

Koyama, A., Barolli, L., Tsuda, A., & Cheng, Z. (2001). An agent-based personalized distance learning system. In *Proceedings of ICOIN-15* (pp. 895-899).

Kuwabara, T., Tamaki, M., Yamada, K., Nakamura, Y., Mistunaga, Y., Konishi, N. & Amano, K. (2000). Support functions for stalled students and their effect in a multi-media assisted education system with individual advance (MESIA). *Transactions of IEICE, J83-D-I, 83*(9) 1013-1024.

Michigan State University. Virtual University. (n.d.). Retrieved from http://www.vu.msu.edu/site/

MindEdge. Online Education. (n.d.). Retrieved from http://www.newpromise.com/

Nakabayashi, K., Koike, Y., Maruyama, M., Touhei, H., Fukuhara, Y., & Nakamura, Y. (1999). CALCAT: An Intelligent CAI System Using WWW. *Trans. of IEICE, D-II, 80*(4), 906–914.

Ohio Learning Network. (n.d.). Retrieved from http://www. oln.org/

Oregon's One-Stop for Distance Education. (2008). Retrieved from http://oregonone.org/

Pennsylvania State University. "World Campus" (2008). Retrieved from http://www.worldcampus.psu.edu/

Tamaki, M., Kuwabara, T., Yamada, K., Nakamura, Y., Mistunaga, Y., Konishi, N., & Amano, K. (2000). Multimedia Assisted Education System with Individual Student Advance. *IPSJ Journal, 41*(8), 2351–2362.

The Open University. (2008). Retrieved from http://www.open.ac.uk/

The University of The Air. (1984). Retrieved from http://www.u-air.ac.jp/

University of Florida Distance Learning. (2008). Retrieved from http://www.distancelearning.ufl.edu/.

University of Illinois Online. (2008). Retrieved from http://www.online.uillinois.edu/.

University of Wisconsin-Platteville Distance Learning Center. (2008). Retrieved from http://www.uwplatt. edu/disted/.

WebCAI Courseware System. (1999). Retrieved from Nihon University, http://iclab.ce.nihon-u.ac.jp/~webcai/.

WIDE University, School of Internet. (1997). Retrieved from http://www.sfc.wide.ad.jp/soi/contents.html.

KEY TERMS AND DEFINITIONS

Computer Interface: The term Computer Interface refers to the way a person experiences the computer, its application programs, hardware components, output devices and functionality.

Distance Learning: Teaching and learning situations in which the instructor and learner (or learners) are geographically separated, and therefore, rely on electronic devices and print material for instructional delivery.

Learning Motivation: There are two types of learning motivation: the internal and external. The former has to do with the learner's spontaneity and interest, the latter one arises from external factors such as competition with the others, rewards, and penalties.

Multimedia: The use of computers to present text, graphics, video, animation, and sound in an integrated way.

Radio-Frequency Identification (RFID): RFID is the use of an object (typically referred to as an RFID tag) applied to or incorporated into a product, animal, or person for the purpose of identification and tracking using radio waves. Some tags can be read from several meters away and beyond the line of sight of the reader.

Regression Line: A regression line is a line drawn through scatter-plot of two variables. The line is chosen so that it comes as close to the points as possible.

Stimulation Function: Stimulation functions are functions that increase the learner's motivation and thus increasing learning efficiency.

WWW: Computer network consisting of a collection of internet sites that offer text, graphics, sound and animation resources through the hypertext transfer protocol.

Chapter 16
Using a User-Interactive QA System for Personalized E-Learning

Dawei Hu
University of Science and Technology of China, China

Wei Chen
City University of Hong Kong, China

Qingtian Zeng
Shandong University of Science and Technology, China

Tianyong Hao
City University of Hong Kong, China

Feng Min
City University of Hong Kong, China

Liu Wenyin
City University of Hong Kong, China

ABSTRACT

A personalized e-learning framework based on a user-interactive question-answering (QA) system is proposed, in which a user-modeling approach is used to capture personal information of students and a personalized answer extraction algorithm is proposed for personalized automatic answering. In our approach, a topic ontology (or concept hierarchy) of course content defined by an instructor is used for the system to generate the corresponding structure of boards for holding relevant questions. Students can interactively post questions, and also browse, select, and answer others' questions in their interested boards. A knowledge base is accumulated using historical question/answer (Q/A) pairs for knowledge reuse. The students' log data are used to build an association space to compute the interest and authority of the students for each board and each topic. The personal information of students can help instructors design suitable teaching materials to enhance instruction efficiency, be used to implement the personalized automatic answering and distribute unsolved questions to relevant students to enhance the learning efficiency. The experiment results show the efficacy of our user-modeling approach.

INTRODUCTION

Traditional educational approaches are usually teacher-centric, not student-centric, since they do not sufficiently take into account the differences of characteristics among different students (Angehrn et al., 2001). In order to enhance student-centric learning and instruction efficiency, instructors should know the implicit requirements of students so as to prepare and design their teaching materials. As a result, personalized support for learners becomes more and more important and, consequently, many researchers start to focus on this topic to increase the performance of the learning systems (Henze et al., 2004; Dolog et al., 2004). Moreover, knowledge accumulation and knowledge reuse are also important in collaborative e-learning (Millard et al., 2006), because they can be used to reduce the workload of the instructors and to enhance the learning efficiency. Up to now, Web-based learning has been regarded as an appropriate auxiliary method of traditional teaching methods to achieve higher learning quality, especially when e-learning takes place in open and dynamic learning and information networks. The advantage of Web-based learning is that the historical knowledge and the behavior and habit of the learners in different courses can be easily recorded for analysis. However, it is usually difficult to implement such an e-learning system, which can efficiently capture the students' model about the course content, such as knowledge background, interest, authority, and so on.

In this article, we propose a personalized e-learning framework using the *BuyAns* (BuyAns, 2005-2007; Wenyin, 2006) environment, which is a Web-based user-interactive question-answering (QA) system for users (or students) to interactively post and browse questions and answers. In *BuyAns*, users exchange their knowledge by posting their questions on related boards and browsing finding interesting/favorite questions to answer. The system records all the Q/A pairs and the historical activities all users, including browsing records, questions and answers.

The main processes of our framework are as follows: when a new question comes, the system first tries to automatically find the suitable answer from the knowledge base. If the answer is found, the question is then distributed to suitable users. With the help of *BuyAns*, two main improvements can be done in our e-learning framework. Firstly, all of those historical data contain a tremendous amount of information about users' personal information, such as interests, authorities, and so on. If the students' interests and authorities about the course content are known, *BuyAns* can automatically and properly distribute relevant questions and answers to relevant students. Students' interests and authorities can also be used to help instructors organize and design their teaching materials (Huang & Wenyin, 2005). Consequently, collaborative learning between students and instructors can be enhanced. Secondly, all the historical Q/A pairs can be accumulated to answer new questions automatically. Hence, the echo speed for answering new questions can be increased. Additionally, the personal information of the asker can be used to estimate whether the answer can meet his requirement.

In order to obtain the personal information of the users, we propose a method to calculate users' interest and authority about the course content. The capturing process is easy to implement, since only a topic ontology (or concept hierarchy) for the course content needs to be defined by the instructor. After the topic ontology is defined, the corresponding board structure can be generated to allow students to interactively post questions and answer others' questions.The topic ontology consists of topics, which belong to categories, and categories. With the accumulation of the historical data, we can build the association relations between Q/A pairs and the topic ontology. Based on the association relations the students' interest and authority on the topic ontology can be computed. Experiment results show that the users' model generated by our method reveals the students' true background (interest and authority). Meanwhile, in order to implement the personalized automatic answering to reuse the historical knowledge, we propose an answer extraction algorithm in which a novel answer evaluation algorithm is used to estimate the correctness of the answers extracted from the knowledge base for a new question (Hao et al., 2007).

The remainder of the article is organized as follows: Related work is presented, then the system architecture of *BuyAns* is shown. The personalized e-learning methods are then described; then the experiments and the analysis of the results are shown. Finally, concluding remarks including potential applications and future work are presented.

RELATED WORK

There are lots of research reports on personalized intelligent tutoring systems, focusing on knowledge reuse and personal information analysis, such as user authority analysis and user interest analysis (Angehrn et al., 2001; Guetl et al., 2005; Millard et al., 2006; Brusilovsky & Nijhawan, 2002).

To reuse acquired knowledge in a QA system, the historical information of Q/A pairs should be stored and an answer extraction algorithm is needed to find the suitable answer to a newly asked question. Brusilovsky and Nijhawan (2002) propose a method to manually collect and reuse a distributed historical educational repository. Along with the process of knowledge accumulation, the size of knowledge base will soon become too large to be analyzed manually. As a result, Wang et al. (2006) propose an automatic answering method which uses repository-based QA system to search the suitable answer in the knowledge repository. If some user asks a new question, the most similar questions are first found from the historical Q/A repository and their answers are then returned to the user. This method is efficient except that it does not take into account the quality of each answer and the interest of the asker. However, the quality of the answers to those historical questions is also very important to be considered in the automatic answering system, and the interest of the asker determines which answer is preferred if many answers are extracted. Therefore, we propose a novel answer evaluation algorithm for personalized automatic answering which combines the user's personal information, the weight of the historical questions, and the quality of the answers to the historical questions.

In personal information analysis, machine learning is usually used to construct a student's model for an intelligent tutoring system (Beck & Woolf, 2000), which can learn on a per student basis how long it takes for an individual student to solve a problem presented by the tutor. The model of relative problem difficulty is learned within a "two-phase" learning algorithm. In that method, data from the entire student population are used to train a neural network at first. The system learns how to modify the output of the neural network to better fit each individual student's performance. A learning agent is constructed to model students' behavior for a mathematics tutor in Beck & Woolf (1998), which determines how likely the student is to answer a question correctly and how long the student will spend to generate that response. The traces from previous users of the system are used to train the machine learning agent. This model is very accurate on predicting the time that a student needs to generate a response and is somewhat accurate on predicting the likelihood the student's response was correct.

With the development and applications of Web technologies, modeling users' behavior from the Web logs has also been an active research area (Kim & Chan, 2003; Sugiyama et al., 2004; Grčar et al., 2005; Pazzani & Billsus, 1997). The generalized method is to construct users' profiles from their interest-focused browsing histories.

A tree-like hierarchy of interests is proposed in (Kim & Chan, 2003), with the root node being the general interest of a user and leaves representing the domains that the user is interested in. The user-interest hierarchies are built using a form of hierarchical clustering on a set of Web pages visited by the user. A user profile is used to analyze the user's browsing history and applied-for modified collaborative filtering techniques in Sugiyama et al. (2004). A naive Bayesian classifier is used for learning and revising user profiles and hence determining which Web sites on a given topic would be interesting to a user (Pazzani & Billsus, 1997). It can also incrementally learn profiles from user feedback on the interestingness of Web sites. Recently, user profiling for interest-focused browsing history has been proposed in Grčar et al. (2005), which presents a system incorporated into the Internet explorer to maintain a dynamic user profile in a form of automatically-constructed topic ontology. A subset of previously visited Web pages is associated with a corresponding topic in the ontology. By selecting a topic, users can view the set of associated pages and choose to navigate to the page of their interest. These existing approaches aim to mine a user's model from a large-scale accumulated data set or a large training set. It usually takes a long time to accumulate sufficient data and the training method is usually complicated. In fact, the model about an individual including interest and authority may change after a long time. Hence, the existing methods for mining students' models are not adaptive for student-centric instruction in the traditional classes. Hence, we propose a method to capture students' interests and authorities about course content from the historical data accumulated in *BuyAns*.

In order to facilitate understanding our e-learning framework, we will briefly introduce the *BuyAns* system in the next section.

BUYANS: A USER-INTERACTIVE QA SYSTEM

In this section, we briefly introduce the system architecture and some main features of *BuyAns*. Figure 1 shows the system architecture of BuyAns (BuyAns, 2005-2007; Wenyin, 2006), which contains the User Interface for users to interactively post and browse Q/A; the Content Analyzer; the Search module; the Answer Clustering and Quality Assessment module (enabling users to annotate the quality of each answer); the User Management module; the Pattern Database; the Current Q/A Database (storing all unsolved questions and their current answers arranged in different boards/categories); the Accumulated Q/A Database (for historical questions with correct answers); and the Knowledge Base.

A typical user scenario is as follows: a user uses a pattern (or not) to post a question (with an amount of money offered) for correct answer(s) using the User Interface. The Content Analyzer accepts the question and distributes it into the corresponding board in the Current Q/A Database. The user can also manually select a suitable board to host this question. At the same time, it also automatically sends this question to the Search module, which first tries to obtain an answer from the Knowledge Base by searching and inference, and, if it fails, tries to search for similar questions in the Accumulated Q/A Database and returns their associated correct answers. Those answers will be automatically associated with the newly-asked question and displayed in the corresponding board. All other users can visit the board and see this question, and, if they want, can manually post their answers to this question, using the suitable pattern or not. Additionally, the question can be automatically distributed to the suitable user for answering based on his or her personal information, such as the interest and authority. The asker can browse all the answers (both automatically found by the Search module and manually posted by other users) to his or her question and select

Figure 1. System architecture of BuyAns

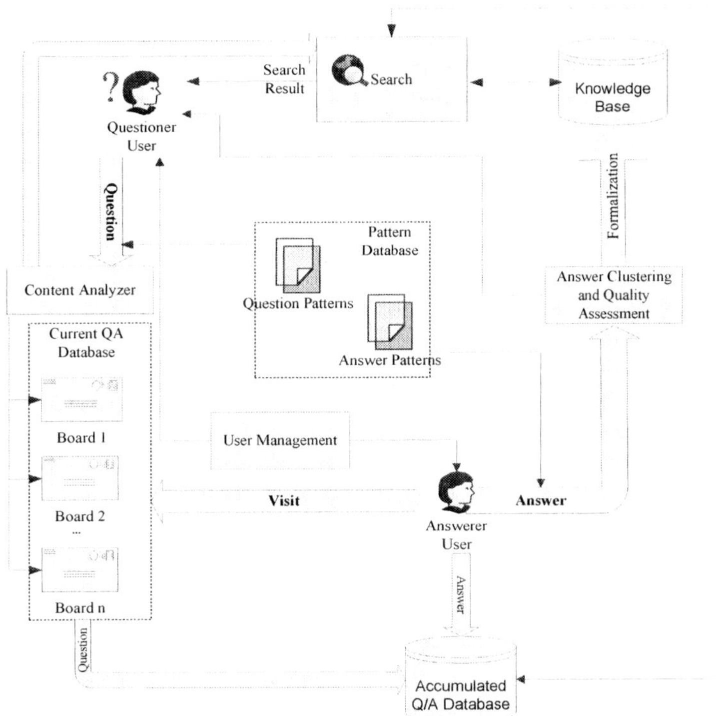

the first/earliest correct answer (or several correct answers) as the final correct answer based on his or her judgment. If there is no dispute, the money offered by the asker will be paid to the correct answerer(s) after deducting a corresponding commission fee for the system. If the correct answer selected was found automatically in the Accumulated Q/A Database, its previous provider can still earn the offered money though the commission fee to the system may be higher. The Answer Clustering and Quality Assessment module helps group similar/relevant answers into several groups and provides an overall quality for each answer and each group based on the capability, reputation, and timeliness of the answer and the group. The clustering and fusion result can greatly facilitate the asker to browse the answers and select the correct answer quickly. The question and its correct answer(s) selected by the asker are associated and stored in the Accumulated Q/A Database as a pair. Hopefully, those high quality Q/A pairs are converted and formalized into formal knowledge and stored in the Knowledge Base for future auto-answering.

The User Management module is responsible for computing and managing users' models, including their interests, authorities (capabilities and experiences), reputations, and financial transactions. It also includes functions of facilitating dispute settlement between askers and answers.

In the next section, we will firstly present our e-learning framework and then describe the capturing method of students' models about course content using *BuyAns*. Finally, we will introduce the knowledge reuse method on the basis of the knowledge base.

Personalized E-Learning Using Buyans

In our personalized e-learning framework, the QA system, *BuyAns*, is used as a component which

Figure 2. The personalized e-learning framework based on BuyAns

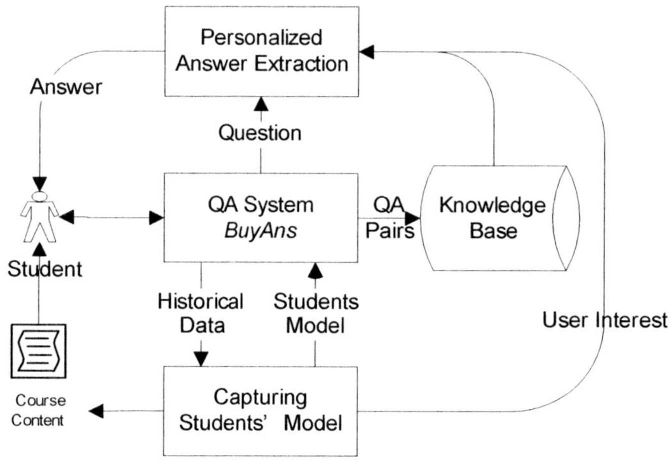

provides all the QA functionalities and all the collected content, including the historical data, such as Q/A pairs and the user log of activities, e.g., browsing, asking and answering. The personalized e-learning framework is shown in Figure 2.

Buyans is the key component of our e-Learning framework, in which students post, browse, and answer questions. The historical Q/A pairs are stored in the knowledge base and the historical activities data are used to capture the personal information of the students. With the help of the personal information, instructors can design suitable course contents for different students. Moreover, for each new question posted, the personalized answer extraction module tries to find the suitable answer from the knowledge base according to the asker's interest. If there is no suitable answer in the knowledge base, *BuyAns* can distribute the question to a suitable user for answering based on his authority and interest. Next, we will introduce two key techniques in our framework: the students' model capturing method and knowledge reuse method.

Capturing Students' Model on Course Content

The Accumulated Q/A Database is an import component of BuyAns which stores all the Q/A pairs from different users. The Accumulated Q/A Database, as well as the user log of other activities, e.g., browsing, asking, and answering, are used as users' historical data to capture students' interests and authorities about course content in this article.

Framework of the Capturing Process

Figure 3 presents the framework of the capturing process. The whole process includes the following main steps:

1. Topic ontology (or concept hierarchy) definition: The topic ontology represents the structure of the course content and is defined by the instructor with suitable granularity and scale.
2. User-interactive QA process: Based on the defined topic ontology, the system can generate the corresponding board structure in *BuyAns*. Within their favorite boards, students can post their urgent questions about the corresponding topic and browse and select to answer others' questions. The *BuyAns* system can record and accumulate students' activities of browsing, posting and answering as historical data.

Figure 3. Framework of capturing students' model about course content

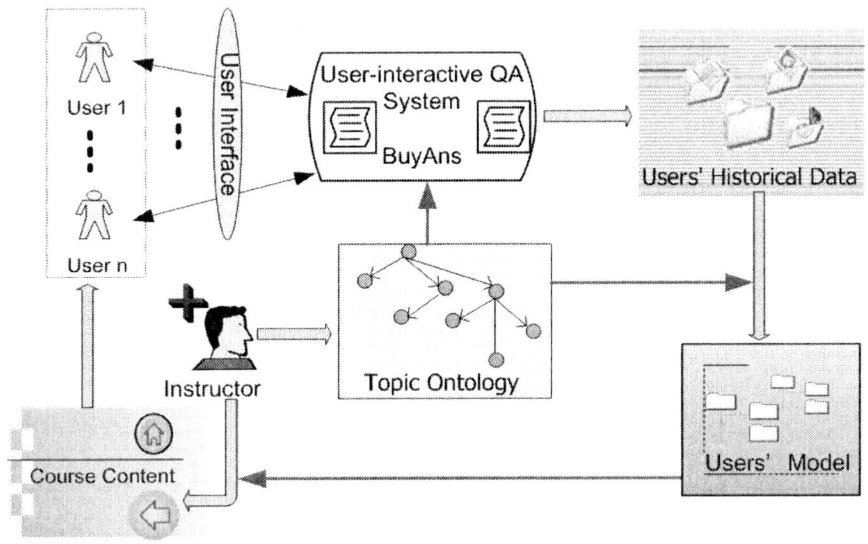

3. User modeling: With the accumulated historical data, the system builds the association relations between the Q/A pairs and the topic ontology. Based on the association relations, it computes the students' interest and authority about the topic ontology.

With the visualized information of the students' model about the topic ontology defined, the instructors can adjust or redesign their course contents to satisfy the students' requirements. Next, we will introduce the related technologies within the capturing process, including topic ontology, association space between topics and historical data, and the methods to compute the students' model.

Topic Ontology

Before capturing the students' model, it is necessary to define the related topic ontology (or concept hierarchy), which presents the outline, or skeleton, about the course content. Firstly, we propose the formal definition of topic ontology.

Definition 1*: a topic ontology is defined as a directed, tree-like graph TopicOnto = <TS,R>, where:*

1. *The set of nodes* $TS = \{term_1, term_2, ...term_n\}$ *represents a set of terms.*
2. *The set of edges* $R \subseteq (TS \times TS)$ *represents the binary relations on the set TS. If two terms satisfy one of Is_A, Part_Of, and Component_Of relations, then there is a direct edge between them.*

In the topic ontology, a term can be the name of a chapter, a section, or a key concept in the course content, which is decided by the instructor. We do not consider all kinds of relations among the terms. Three kinds of well-known relations between terms in ontology, namely, *Is_A*, *Part_Of*, and *Component_Of* relations (Noy & McGuinness, 2001), have been considered since they are the most important to capture users' model about course content. If $term_1$ and $term_2$ satisfy *Is_A* ($term_2$, $term_1$), *Part_Of*($term_2$, $term_1$), and *Component_Of*($term_2$, $term_1$), it means that $term_2$ is a (part of, or component of) $term_1$

Figure 4. Sketch map of an association space

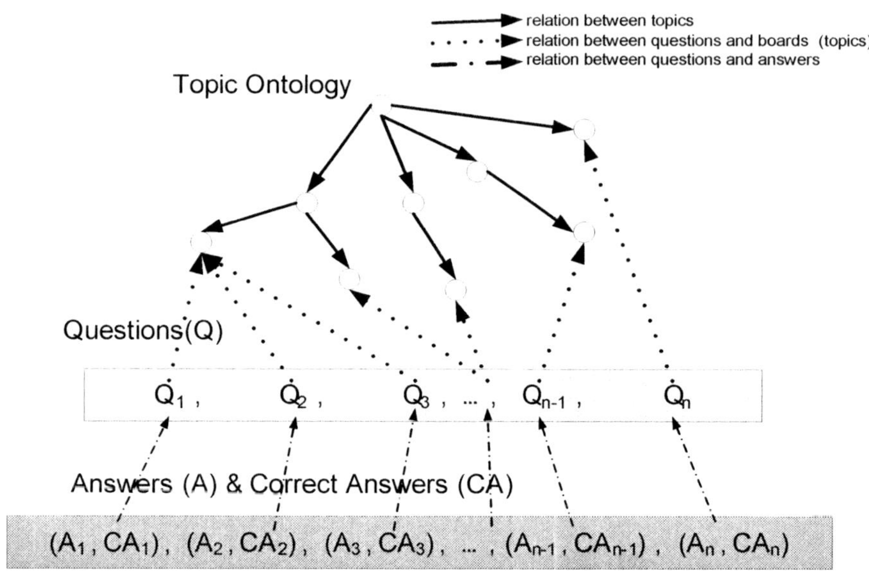

and there is a direct edge from $term_1$ to $term_2$. A node is named as a *leaf* if its out-degree is zero. For example, "Software Design", "Designing for Change", and "Code Review" are three terms in software engineering. The relation between these terms should be Part_Of("Designing for Change", "Software Design") and Part_Of("Code Review", "Software Design"), since "Designing for Change" and "Code Review" are two sub-concepts of "Software Design". The scale of the topic ontology is decided by the term set, which is defined by the instructor based on the course content. To capture the students' model about the course content, each of the leaves of the topic ontology is regarded as a *board* in the *BuyAns* system and each of the non-leaves of the topic ontology is regarded as a *category* in the *BuyAns* system. Students can interactively post and browse Q/A within the corresponding boards.

Association Space

We build the Q/A space from the historical data to describe the relations between questions and answers. The association space is defined and used to represent the relations between Q/A space and the topic ontology.

***Definition 2**: A Q/A space is a five-tuple QASpace* $= <QS, AS, f_B, f_A, f_{CA}>$, *where:*

1. *QS is the set of questions.*
2. *AS is the set of answers.*
3. $f_B : QS \rightarrow Z$ *is a function from QS to Z, where Z is the integer set.* $\forall Q \in QS, f_B(Q)$ *is the browsing frequency (or, the number of times being browsed) of question Q and* $f_B(Q)$ *is nonnegative.*
4. $f_B : QS \rightarrow AS$ *is a function from QS to AS. For each question* $Q \in QS$, $f_A(Q)$ *is the set of answers of Q.*
5. $f_{CA} : QS \rightarrow AS$. *For each question* $Q \in QS$, $f_{CA} : (Q)$ *is the set of correct answers of Q.*

In Definition 2, it is obvious that $f_{CA}(Q) \subseteq f_A(Q)$.

We can use a directed graph to represent the relations between *QS* and *AS*. *QS* and *AS* are represented by different nodes, and there are directed edges from answers to question Q if $|f_A(Q)| \geq AS$. We illustrate the graphic representation in Figure 4.

Based on the functions f_B, f_A, and f_{CA} on QS, we give a classification of all the questions.

Definition 3: *Let QASpace = <QS, AS, f_B, f_A, f_{CA}>be a Q/A space. $\forall Q \in QS$.*

1. *Q is a hot question if $f_B(Q) \geq \delta$, where δ is a threshold.*
2. *Q is a closed question if $|f_A(Q)| \geq 1$.*

Obviously, a hot question should be attractive to many students' interests and be frequently browsed, while a closed question must have at least one correct answer. Different kinds of questions play different roles in capturing the users' model about the course content. The hot questions are used to compute the interest of a class of students about the topic ontology. The threshold δ for hot questions is used to filter out unrelated or useless questions in the historical data. We assume that if the browsing frequency of a question is smaller than δ, this question is not an interesting one for the students and therefore it does not contribute to the interest model of the students. The value of δ can be adjusted by the system administrator. The closed questions are used to compute the authority of a class of students about the topic ontology. If a question is closed with correct answers, it means that the students have probably mastered the related knowledge about the question.

Given the topic ontology, we can build the association space to represent the relations between the historical data and the related topics. The formal definition of the association space is presented in Definition 4.

Definition 4: *An association space between the Q/A space QASpace = <QS, AS, f_B, f_A, f_{CA}> and the topic ontology TopicOnto = <TS,R> is a three-tuple ASpace = <QASpace, TopicOnto, R_{AT}>, where R_{AT} is the relation between QS and TS. If question Q is posted on the board corresponding to T, then $(Q,T) \in R_{AT}$.*

We can use a directed graph to represent the association space between the Q/A space and the topic ontology. Figure 4 shows a sketch map of an association space.

Capturing Method

The association space between the Q/A space and the topic ontology indicates the relations between the historical data (browsing activities, questions, answers, and correct answers) and the topic ontology. For each student, we can build his/her own association space between the Q/A space and the topic ontology to obtain his/her interest and authority. We can also capture the model about all the students in a class as an entire object using all the historical data accumulated for all the students. Next, we present the capturing method using the historical data for all the students in an entire class.

First, we compute the interest and authority of students about every question, which are determined by the related parameters of each question including the browsing frequency, number of answers and number of correct answers.

Definition 5: *Let ASpace = <QASpace, TopicOnto, R_{AT}> be the association space between the Q/A space and the topic ontology, where QASpace = <QS, AS, f_B, f_A, f_{CA}> is the Q/A space of all students. For any question $Q \in QS$, equation (1), shown in Box 1, is the interest of the students about the question Q, where δ is a threshold, $Mean_B$ and $Mean_A$ are respectively the mean of $f_B(Q)$ and $|f_A(Q)|$ of all questions, and θ is a linear transformation parameter determined by the system administrator to adjust the slope of the arctan function. $f_B(Q) \leq \delta$ means that Q is not a hot question. Equation (2), shown in Box 1, is the authority of students about the question Q.*

Box 1.

$$Interest(Q)=\begin{cases}0 & f_B(Q)\le\delta\\ \dfrac{\arctan(\dfrac{f_B(Q)-Mean_B+|f_A(Q)|-Mean_A}{\theta})}{\pi}+\dfrac{1}{2} & Otherwise\end{cases} \quad (1)$$

$$Authority(Q)=\begin{cases}0 & |f_{CA}(Q)|=0\\ \dfrac{\pi-2\arctan(\dfrac{|f_A(Q)|}{\beta\,|f_{CA}(Q)|})}{\pi} & Otherwise\end{cases} \quad (2)$$

$$Weight_j(term)=\frac{\sum_{i=1}^{n}Weight_j(Son_i)}{n}\times\log_{10}n \quad (3)$$

In Definition 5, we can see that the interest of the students about a question Q is mainly determined by the browsing frequency $f_B(Q)$ and the number of answer $|f_A(Q)|$. The larger $f_B(Q)$ and $|f_A(Q)|$ are, the more interest the students have about the question. The authority of the students about one question Q is mainly determined by the ratio of

$$\frac{|f_{CA}(Q)|}{|f_A(Q)|}.$$

A larger value means higher authority of the students about the question.

Definition 6: *$ASpace = <QASpace, TopicOnto, R_{AT}>$ be the association space between the Q/A space and the topic ontology, where $QASpace = <QS, AS, f_B, f_A, f_{CA}>$ is the Q/A space of all the students, and $TopicOnto = <TS,R>$ is the topic ontology about the course content. For each term term $\in TS$, $(j = 1,2)$, Equation (3), shown in Box 1, is the interest or authority of the students about term, and $Son_i (1 \le i \le n)$ is the son (term or question) of term term. For each term term $\in TS$, we denote that Interest(term) = $Weight_1$(term) and Authority(term) = $Weight_2$(term), respectively.*

With Definition 6, the interest and authority on each leaf term in the topic ontology are computed respectively by the interest and authority of all the questions on the corresponding board, where a question is also named as a son of the term if the question is in the corresponding board of the term. The interest and authority on each non-leaf term are computed respectively from the corresponding interest and authority of its sons. Figure 5 lists the steps of the method to compute students' model based on the topic ontology.

Knowledge Reuse

To efficiently reuse the historical knowledge for automatic answering in e-learning, we accumulate each Q/A pair whose question is asked by the students in *BuyAns* to construct our knowledge base. Meanwhile, an personalized answer extraction method is proposed to automatically extract the suitable answer from the knowledge base for a newly asked question. Our personalized answer extraction method combines the weight of the historical question, the quality of the answer to the historical question and the personal information of the user. Next, we will describe the structure of our knowledge base and the answer extraction method.

Figure 5. Steps of the method to compute students' model based on the topic ontology

INPUT: Topic ontology
OUTPUT: Student's model about the topic ontology
Step 1: define the topic ontology $TopicOnto = \langle TS, R\rangle$ by the instructor
Step 2: generate the board structure of *BuyAns* based on the topic ontology $TopicOnto = \langle TS, R\rangle$
Step 3: construct Q/A space $QASpace = \langle QS, AS, f_B, f_A, f_{CA}\rangle$ of all the students by asking them to ask and answer question in the corresponding board and to close their own questions if a correct answer is found
Step 4: classify all the questions into the hot and closed questions based on functions f_B, f_A, and f_{CA}
Step 5:construct the association space $AS = \langle QASpace, TopicOnto, R_{AT}\rangle$ between the Q/A space and the topic ontology
Step 6: compute the students' interest and authority about each question in the Q/A space $QASpace = \langle QS, AS, f_B, f_A, f_{CA}\rangle$
Step 7: compute the students' interest and authoristy about each term in the topic ontology bases on $ASpace = \langle QASpace, TopicOnto, R_{AT}\rangle$
Step 8: output *(term, Interest)* and *(term, Authority)* for all term $term \in TS$

Knowledge Base

When a question is answered by some users and one of those answers is chosen as the correct answer by the asker, a correct Q/A pair is accumulated into the knowledge base for e-learning. The use table structures of our knowledge base are shown in Figure 6, in which two tables are used to store the historical Q/A data. In the QA pair table, each record stores one Q/A pair. The "Question" field stores the text of the question and the "Answer" field stores the correct answer to the question which is chosen by the asker. The "PID" stores the ID of the pattern which matches the question and "Board" stores the board which the question is posted in. "Quality" stores the the quality of each answer which can be obtained from *BuyAns*. The value of answer quality is between 0 and 1. The quality of an answer is determined by its post time and its provider's reputation and authority. In the pattern base, each record represents one pattern. The "Pattern" field stores a pattern and the "PID" field stores its unique ID.

The pattern's definition follows the definition of semantic pattern in Hao et al (2007). A pattern consists of question target which is used to represent the target of question, question type which is used to represent the type of question (e.g. what and when), concept which is used to label meaningful nouns in the question and event which is used to represent something happening or any specific behavior. For example, a pattern is shown in Figure 7. The question target, "Entity\Color", indicates that the question is asked about a color. The two concepts, "Abstraction\Property" and "Physical_Entity\Plant", are two meaningful words. Moreover, the question type is "What".

On the basis of this knowledge base, we implement automatic answering using the following personalized answer extraction algorithm.

Personalized Answer Extraction

We use an approach called Pattern Matching and Answer Evaluation (PMAAE) to extract answers from the knowledge base. The reason why we use pattern matching is that the weight of each part in the question can be precisely estimated

Figure 6. Knowledge base structure

Q/A pair Table

Question	PID	Answer	Quality	Board
What food is not so good to heart-attack patients?	45	high sodium, high fat	0.08	Health
What is the symptom of Anemia ?	2	fatigue, shortness of breath, and malaise	0.25	Health
…	…	…	…	…

Pattern Table

ID	Pattern
1	<Q> Who </Q> is [Entity\Person] ?
2	<Q> What </Q> is [Abstraction\Property]?
…	…

Figure 7. Example of our pattern

<Type:What> is the [Abstraction\Property] of [Physical_Entity\Plant]?
<Target:Entity\Color>

Figure 8. Main steps of answer extraction

Input: *A given question X*
PMAAE processing:
Step1: Pattern matching from the pattern table
1) *Analyze the question type*
2) *Analyze keywords (nouns and verbs)*
3) *Obtain the main structure*
4) *Retrieve similar patterns*
Step2: Data (Q/A pair) retrieval from the QA database
Step 3: Answer evaluation (for each pair of question and answer)
1) *Calculate the matched parts*
2) *Calculate the weight of different parts of question.*
3) *Calculate the interest score*
4) *Calculate the answer score*
Output: *Top Y highest score of answers*

on the basis of the pattern annotation (Hao, et al., 2007). The main steps of this approach are shown in Figure 8.

From the algorithm, we can see that for a new question *Q*, this method firstly finds similar patterns by matching the main structure of the question from the pattern base. The IDs of those patterns are then collected to construct an ID set *IDS* and any Q/A pair in the Q/A pair base whose PID belongs to *IDS* will be retrieved to obtain a Q/A

Box 2.

$$Weight\ (Q_i^T) = \alpha \times Match(T) \times \frac{1}{|M|} (0 \le \alpha \le 1) \quad (6)$$

$$Weight\ (Q_i^Y) = \beta \times Match(Y) \times \frac{1}{|M|} (0 \le \beta \le 1) \quad (7)$$

$$Weight\ (Q_i^C) = \delta \times \sum_{i=1}^{M-2} (Match(C_i) \times \frac{1}{|M|})(1 \le M, 0 \le \delta \le 1) \quad (8)$$

$$Interest(U(Q), B(Q_i)) = \chi \times Interest(B(Q_i)) \times \frac{1}{|M|} (0 \le \chi \le 1) \quad (9)$$

pair set *QAS*. With the help of pattern, a question Q_i can be divided into Q_i^T, Q_i^Y and Q_i^C. Q_i^T means the question target of Q_i, Q_i^Y means the question type of Q_i and Q_i^C means the concept and event of Q_i. At last, we propose an answer evaluation algorithm to calculate the score of each answer and return the top answers to the users.

The answer quality assessment algorithm is mainly used to evaluate the answer scores according to the weight of questions, the quality of answers and the asker's interest. The higher the score, the better the answer. The quality of answer is calculated in *BuyAns*. Given a Q/A pair set $QAS = \{\{Q_1, A_1\}, \{Q_2, A_2\} \ldots \{Q_i, A_i\} \ldots \{Q_n, A_n\}\}$, $\{Q_i, A_i\}$ means the *i-th* Q/A pair. *N* means the number of Q/A pairs, $B(Q_i)$ means the board which Q_i is posted in and $U(Q_i)$ means the asker of Q_i. We can calculate the score for each $A_i (1 \le i \le n)$ using the following formula:

$$Score(A_i) = WeightQ_i * Quality\ (A_i), \quad (4)$$

where $Weight\ (Q_i)$ is the weight of Q_i and $Quality\ (A_i)$ is the quality of A_i. $Weight\ (Q_i)$ can be calculated using the following formula:

$$Weight\ Q_i = Weight\ Q_i^T + Weight\ Q_i^Y + Weight\ Q_i^C + Interest(U(Q), B(Q_i)), \quad (5)$$

where, $Weight\ Q_i^T$ means the weight of Q_i^T, $Weight\ Q_i^Y$ means the weight of Q_i^Y, $Weight\ Q_i^C$ means weight of Q_i^C and $Interest(U(Q), B(Q_i))$ means how interested the new question asker is in $B(Q_i)$. The Q_i^T, Q_i^Y, Q_i^C can be obtained through matching Q_i with its pattern. Assume the total number of all components of the pattern is *M*, i.e., $M = |T| + |Y| + |C| + 1$ where $|T|$ means the number of Q_i^T, $|Y|$ means the number of Q_i^Y and $|C|$ means the number of Q_i^C. The weight of each component and the interest value is calculated in Equations(6), (7), (8), and (9), shown in Box 2, where *Match(T)* represents whether the question target is matched or not, which has two values, 0 means NOT matched, and 1 means matched, α represents the importance of matching the question target. *Match(Y), Match(C),* β, δ and χ are similarly defined. $Interest(B(Q_i))$ is the interest value of the asker about term $B(Q_i)$, which is calculated by users' model capturing module. We adjust those parameters to appropriate values according to a series of experiments.

For example, given the question "What is the color of rose?", its question pattern is "<Target:Entity\Color> <Type:What> is the [Abstraction\Property] of [Physical_Entity\Plant]?". The interest value between the asker and "biology" is 0.8. We acquire all the historical Q/A pairs that use this pattern. For each pair of question and its

Figure 9. The topic ontology for the experiments

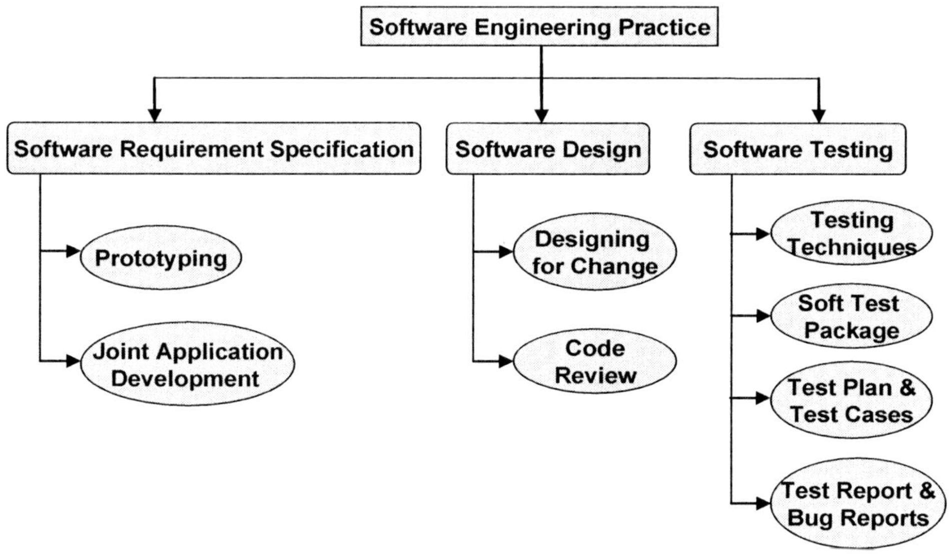

corresponding answer, the system calculates its weight to obtain the score of the answer.

For a question Q_i, "What is the shape of rose?" which is posted in the board of "biology", the number of concepts in its question pattern is 2. Hence, *M = 1 (question type) + 1 (question target) +2 + 1 = 5*. Assume α=0.77, β=0.36, δ=0.84, χ= 0.3, *Interest(biology)* and the original quality of answer is 0.7 (obtained from *BuyAns*), we can obtain the following:

$Weight\ (Q_i\_T) = 0.77 * 0 = 0$
$Weight\ (Q_i\_Y) = 0.36 / 5 = 0.072$
$Weight\ (Q_i\_C) = 0.84 * (0+1/5) = 0.168$
$Interest(U(Q), biology) = 0.3 * 0.8 * 1/5 = 0.048$
$Weight\ (A_i) = 0+0.072+0.168 + 0.048 = 0.288$
$Score\ (A_i) = 0.288 * 0.7 = 0.20$

Finally, we obtain 0.20 as the score of this answer for the historical question Q_i is. If the value is the highest, we consider this answer as the best one for the user's question.

EXPERIMENTS

We have done experiments in *BuyAns* to evaluate the proposed user model capturing method using course CS3343, "Software Engineering Practice" at City University of Hong Kong.

Before the experiments, we first define a topic ontology shown in Figure 9. The topic ontology contains three sections of the course, which are Software Requirement Specification (including two topics: Joint Application Development and Prototyping), Software Design (including two topics: Designing for Change and Code Review) and Software Testing (including four topics: Testing Techniques, Soft Test Package, Test Plan & Test Cases and Test Report & Bug Reports).

There are 12 terms in the defined topic ontology, four of them (Software Engineering, Software Requirement Specification, Software Design and Software Testing) are non-leaf nodes, and other eight are leaf nodes. Hence, eight corresponding boards are generated on *BuyAns*.

After these preparations, all of the students registered in the course are encouraged to post at least 5 urgent questions in their favorite boards. They are then asked to browse all the questions

Table 1. Statistic information about each board

Board Name (Leaf-terms)	Number of Questions	Number of Hot Questions	Number of Answers	Number of Closed Questions
Prototyping	19	19	22	13
Joint Application Development	39	39	28	21
Designing for Change	34	34	24	17
Code Review	24	24	23	16
Testing Techniques	43	43	24	31
Soft Test Package	9	9	8	8
Test Plan & Test Cases	13	13	10	6
Test Report & Bug Reports	14	14	7	8

and select at least 5 favorite questions to answer. They are also asked to pay more attention to their own questions. They should close their questions if at least one correct answer is found based on their judgment. Otherwise, they will be complained by others.

After the scale of the historical data is sufficient for the experiments (the data used for experiments are shown in Table 1, where the threshold for the hot question is $\delta = 3$), we can easily obtain the statistic information of the topic ontology (the information of the leaf node can be directly obtained based on Table 1 and the information of the non-leaf node can be calculated through adding the numbers of its children nodes). Having these statistic information, the association space between the Q/A space and topic ontology is built, from which, the model of all the students in the class about the topic ontology is computed. The interest and authority of the students of CS3343 about the topic ontology in Figure 9 are shown in Table 2, and their histograms are shown in Figure 10 and Figure 11, respectively.

To evaluate the reliability of the model computed by the proposed method, we conduct an e-survey through *BuyAns* to collect the students' real model by the feedback. Participants are limited to the registered students of CS3343 who attended the experiment. Each participant is required to provide their true opinions about the survey questions. The user interface and the e-survey questions about the students' interest

Figure 10. The interest of the students about the topic ontology

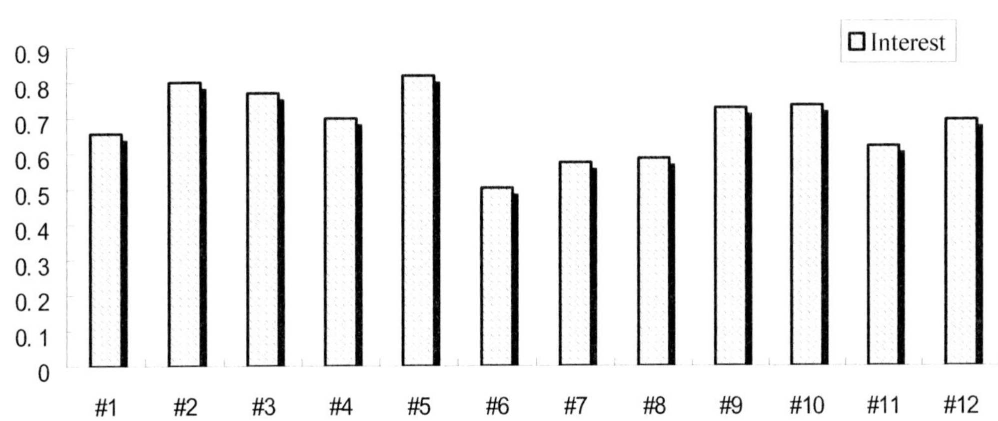

Figure 11. The authority of the students about the topic ontology

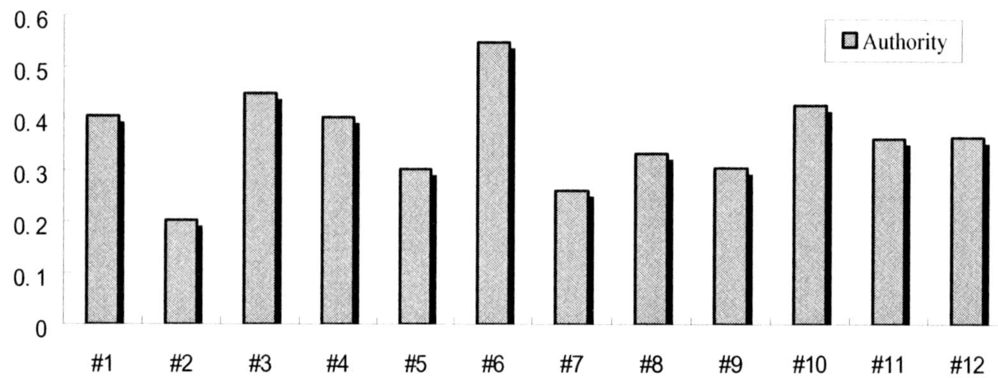

Table 2. The users' model about the topic ontology

#	Term	Interest	Authority
#1	Prototyping	0.656824829	0.404350536
#2	Joint Application Development	0.800441521	0.202653753
#3	Designing for Change	0.769930287	0.448449328
#4	Code Review	0.699843435	0.402084560
#5	Testing Techniques	0.819143459	0.301959706
#6	Soft Test Package	0.503029648	0.547475421
#7	Test Plan & Test Cases	0.575045662	0.260217096
#8	Test Report & Bug Reports	0.585603818	0.331952878
#9	Software Requirement Specification	0.728633175	0.303502145
#10	Software Design	0.734886861	0.425266944
#11	Software Testing	0.620705647	0.360401275
#12	Software Engineering Practice	0.694741894	0.363056788

Figure 12. The interface of e-survey

Table 3. The e-survey result about the interest of each topic

#	Term	Number
#1	Prototyping	13
#2	Joint Application Development	24
#3	Designing for Change	8
#4	Code Review	19
#5	Testing Techniques	21
#6	Soft Test Package	6
#7	Test Plan & Test Cases	18
#8	Test Report & Bug Reports	21

Figure 13. The comparison between the computation result and the E-survey result

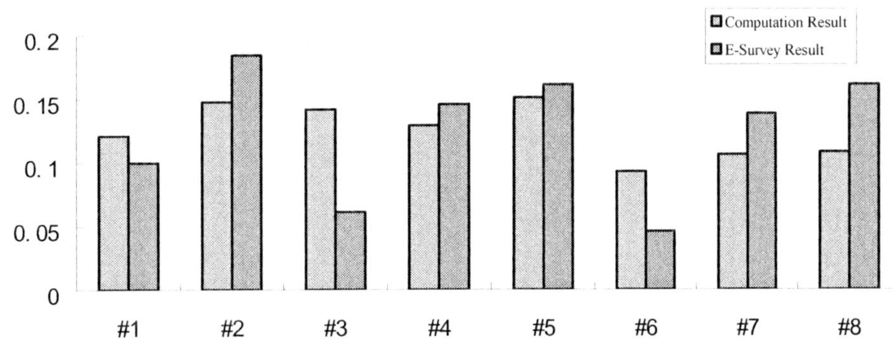

of the eight leaf terms in the topic ontology are shown in Figure 12. In the e-survey process, all the students are asked to select their favorite topics from the eight terms.

The feedback data on the interest about the eight leaf terms collected from the students of CS3343 are shown in Table 3.

In order to compare the computation result and the e-survey result, we compute the interest percentage of each topic in all eight topics. The comparison between the computed users' model and the e-survey result is shown in Figure 13. With the histogram in Figure 13, we can see that the difference between the computed users' model and the e-survey result for most of the eight leaf terms within the topic ontology is not big. Hence, the proposed method can be used to find the true interest of the students.

The authority result is not as easy as the interest result to be evaluated. The computed authority of the students about one topic is the evaluation of their historical behaviors about the topic. For the students themselves, it is difficult for them to know their own real authority about one topic, since they only compare their authority among several topics. One method to evaluate the reliability of the authority model is role-based multi-agent simulation, which has been used to evaluate the reputation model in *BuyAns* (Chen et al., 2007). We can define different agents to complete questioning and answering actions in the simulation system, acted as students with high, middle or low authority in the *BuyAns* system. The reliability of the authority model can be verified by the consistency of computed authority and predefined roles of all the agents. More discussion about the role-based multi-agent simulation to evaluate the reliability of the users' model can be found in Chen et al. (2007).

CONCLUSION

In this article, we proposed a personalized e-learning framework based on a user-interactive QA system, *BuyAns*. Two key techniques, which are users' model capturing method and personalized answer extraction method, are used to enhance its efficacy. The user historical logs obtained from *BuyAns* are used to capture the users' model, which can efficiently and properly be used in personalized automatic answering, distributing unsolved questions to relevant students to enhance the learning efficiency, and helping instructors design suitable teaching materials to enhance instruction efficiency. The experiments show good quality of the users' models we captured.

Once the students' interest and authority models and the automatic answering mechanism are proposed, there are many potential applications within *BuyAns* for adaptive teaching and collaborative learning. Some of them are listed as follows:

1. **Course Content Design.** At the beginning of a semester, an instructor can use this method to capture the students' model and then design or reorganize the teaching materials to satisfy the real requirements of the students to enhance the student-centric instruction efficiency based on their interest and authority. During the semester, the instructor can also check the instruction effectiveness using the same methods.
2. **Question Recommendation.** When a new question is asked in *BuyAns*, it can be automatically sent to the students with interest and especially with high authority.
3. **Learning from Q/A pairs.** After a correct answer is posted and chosen, the *BuyAns* system can send it with its question to the students with low-authority. The students can learn from the question and its corresponding answer to enhance their learning.

ACKNOWLEDGMENT

The work described in this article was fully supported by a grant from City University of Hong Kong (Project No. 7002137), the China Semantic Grid Research Plan (National Grand Fundamental Research 973 Program, Project no. 2003CB317002), and Natural Science Foundation of China (Project No.60603090). The author thanks the students enrolled in the CS3343 course at the City University of Hong Kong for their efforts in using and evaluating the system.

REFERENCES

Angehrn, A. A., Nabeth, T., & Roda, C. (2001). *Towards Personalized, Socially Aware and Active e-Learning Systems*. CALT White Paper, http://www.calt.insead.edu/Publication/albert.shtm.

Beck, J., & Woolf, B. P. (1998). Using a learning agent with a student model, intelligence tutoring system. *Proceedings of 4th International Conference (ITS'98)*, 6-15.

Beck, J., & Woolf, B. P. (2000). High-level student modeling with machine learning. *Proceedings of 5th International Conference Intelligent Tutoring Systems*, 584-593.

Brusilovsky, P., & Nijhawan, H. (2002). A framework for adaptive e-learning based on distributed re-usable learning activities. *Proceedings of the 7th World Conference on E-Learning in Corporate, Government, Healthcare, & Higher Education (E-Learn'02) Canada*, 154-161.

BuyAns (2007). Retrieved from http://www.buyans.com/

Chen, W., Zeng, Q., & Wenyin, L. (2007). A user reputation model for a user-interactive question answering system.

Dolog, P., Henze, N., Nejdl, W., & Sintek, M. (2004). Personalization in distributed e-learning environments. *Proceedings of the 13th International World Wide Web Conference (WWW'04)*, NewYork.

Grčar, M., Mladenić, D., & Grobelnik, M. (2005). User profiling for interest-focused browsing history. *Workshop on End User Aspects of the Semantic Web (ESWC'05).*

Guetl C., Dreher, H., & Williams, R. (2005), E-TESTER: A computer-based tool for auto-generated question and answer assessment. *Proceedings of 10th World Conference on E-Learning in Corporate, Government, Healthcare, & Higher Education (E-Learn'05),* Canada.

Hao, T., Hu, D., Wenyin, L., & Zeng, Q. (2007). Semantic patterns for user-interactive question answering. *Journal of Concurrency and Computation: Practice and Experience, 20*(1).

Henze, N., Dolog, P., & Nejdl, W. (2004). Reasoning and ontologies for personalized e-learning. *Journal of Educational Technology & Society, 7*(4).

Huang, G. L., & Wenyin L. (2005). Using Web based answer hunting system to promote collaborative learning. *Proceedings of International Conference on Web Learning (ICWL'05),* 387-396.

Kim, H. R., & Chan, P. K. (2003). Learning implicit user interest hierarchy for context in personalization. *Proceedings of 8th International Conference on Intelligent User Interfaces (IUI'03),* Miami, FL: 101-108.

Millard, D., Tao, F., Doody, K., Woukeu, A., & Davis H. (2006). The knowledge life cycle for e-learning. *Journal of Continuing Engineering Education and Lifelong Learning: Special Issue on Application of Semantic Web Technologies in E-learning, 16*(1/2), 110-121.

Noy, N. F., & McGuinness, D. L. (2001). *Ontology Development 101: A Guide to Creating Your First Ontology.* Stanford Knowledge Systems Laboratory Technical Report (KSL-01-05).

Pazzani, M. J., & Billsus, D. (1997). Learning and revising user profiles: The identification of interesting Web sites. *Journal of Machine Learning, 27*(3), 313-331.

Sugiyama, K., Hatano, K., & Yoshikawa, M. (2004). Adaptive web search based on user profile construction without any effort from users. *Proceedings of the 13th International Conference on the World Wide Web(WWW'04),* NewYork.

Wang, C. C., Huang, J. C., Shih, T. K., & Lin, H. W. (2006). A repository-based question answering system for collaborative e-learning. *Journal of Computers: Special issue on E-Learning, 17*(3).

Wenyin, L. (2006). BuyAns—An incentive & collaborative platform for knowledge acquisition. *Proceedings of 2nd International Conference on Semantics, Knowledge and Grid (SKG'06),* GuiLin

This work was previously published in International Journal of Distance Education Technologies, Vol. 6, Issue 3, edited by Q. Jin, pp. 1-22, copyright 2008 by IGI Publishing (an imprint of IGI Global).

Chapter 17
Distance-Learning for Advanced Military Education: Using Wargame Simulation Course as an Example

Huan-Chao Keh
Tamkang University, Taiwan

Kuei-Min Wang
Shih Chien University, Taiwan

Shu-Shen Wai
Tamkang University, Taiwan

Jiung-yao Huang
National Taipei University, Taiwan

Lin Hui
Tamkang University, Taiwan

Ji-Jen Wu
Tamkang University, Taiwan

ABSTRACT

Distance learning in advanced military education can assist officers around the world to become more skilled and qualified for future challenges. Through well-chosen technology, the efficiency of distance-learning can be improved significantly. In this paper we present the architecture of Advanced Military Education – Distance Learning (AME-DL) prototype for advanced military distance-learning, it combines advanced e-learning tool, simulation technology, and Web technology to provide a set of military learning and training subjects that can be accessed easily anywhere, anytime through a Web browser. The major goal of AME-DL is to provide a common standard framework for military training program, and the major contribution for such a prototype is to reduce training cost while providing high quality learning experience.

INTRODUCTION

During the past several decades, the proliferation of the technological advancements has led to numerous educational institutions to choose Distance-Learning (DL) as an alternative approach to provide qualified education and to generate revenues. DL is beneficial for both the students and educational institutions because it meets the needs of most students and reduces the cost of educational institutions. Furthermore, such a program is even more applicable for military personnel since the major issue in military training is the territorial dispersion of military personnel which enforces officers to be gathered in training camps to attend the lessons. As a result, DL is the most desirable solution for military officers who have to be available to deploy anytime and anywhere.

The general public, however, often views DL as a byproduct of the technology evolution and equates the success of DL with computer technology such as audio/video streaming and collaboration groupware. They fail to realize that DL is more than a set of computer hardware; instead it is a whole package with multiple factors. In order to fully understand the concept of DL and to design a successful curriculum, we first need to define the term "Distance-Learning." The American Council on Education characterizes DL as "separation of place and/or time between instructor and learner, among learners, and/or between learners and learning resources" (Mitelstedt, 2001). This definition has nothing that can be constructed to make DL synonymous with technology. Thus, we can see that DL requires much more than just a fast Internet connection and a few sets of compact discs. The central focus of a successful DL program should be on the development and continuous evaluation of a total package that integrates instructor training, facility design, support staff contribution, courseware development, and student expectation. Technology can acted as the central vital vassal that links all the factors together to reduce development cost, and to achieve the goal of providing quality education to military personnel anywhere and anytime.

DL has gained acceptance in the United States military for its capacity in saving training cost as well as reducing the time a military staff spends away from his/her unit, and for its efficiency in increasing training readiness. In November 1997, the Department of Defense (DoD) and the White House Office of Science and Technology Policy launched the Advanced Distributed Learning initiative. This initiative was designed to create an environment for dynamic and cost effective learning software in order to meet the education and training needs of the military in the 21st century. The Department of Defense's vision is to "ensure that DoD personnel have access to the highest quality education and training that fan be tailored to their needs and delivered cost effectively, anytime and anywhere" (Carol, 2000). The strategy is to study and utilize emerging network-based technologies to create common standards that will enable reusability and interoperability of learning content, for example, reusability between applications and platforms in order to lower development costs. Another major goal of Advanced Distributed Learning initiative is to promote widespread collaboration that can satisfy common needs, enhance existing product development cycle, and establish a corresponding implementation process (Mitelstedt, 2001).

This article will first describe the current situation of military advanced education; then introduce the proposed AME-DL prototype, which is based on Microsoft Office SharePoint Server (MOSS) 2007. All the technological terminologies and underline concepts will be summarized in this article for the audience to become familiar with this network infrastructure. It will explain the merits that AME-DL can bring and how training officers, course administrators, and so on can customize military training classes utilizing this infrastructure. It will also provide recommendations to Ministry of National Defense as to the direction it must pursue in order to maintain a high quality DL program.

TRADITIONAL ADVANCED EDUCATION IN THE MILITARY-OVERVIEW

The advanced military education is mainly administrated by Staff College and War College; two choices are available for the military officers who desire to expand their professional knowledge and to obtain higher career opportunity through the extended education. Taking the War College as an example, the first option offered for military line officers is the traditional residential education. It is a one year program with a total onsite class time of 1012 hours for each enrollment. The second option is through the correspondence course. This program, on the other hand, is a two year program which only requires students to attend classes on campus for 232 hours in total. The remaining 780 hours of courses are conducted through correspondence education with occasional face to face meetings.

Most of correspondence course attendees are active line officers who can only study during their spare time. The assumption is that the learners are self-directed and self-sufficient. These officers often face a common problem. When they have questions that they need to ask for advices, they will have to wait until the next onsite meeting. The effectiveness and efficiency of the training is greatly reduced because of this asynchronous method of study. As a result, correspondence course attendees will most likely spend even more time to advance to the next grade level. For instance, at the end of the semester, each student is asked to set up a joint operation war game as a measurement of his/her learning performance competency. Since the attendee of the one year residential education can received full time education and support from faculty and staff throughout the program, they have a comprehensive knowledge of principles of war, military operation, and war tactics. On the other hand, the attendees of the vocational correspondence courses only have limited class time and interaction with faculties. As a result, compare to of the later, the line officers of the one year residential education react better towards various combat situations with more precise scenario design and data analysis.

Knowing this issue, educational authority has been trying to design and implement a balanced training program that will improve the quality of education while not affecting mission deployments. Obviously, simply increasing onsite meeting time would not solve this problem.

Due to revolutionary evolvement in computer technology and the proliferation of World Wide Web in the recent years, online distance learning has become a promising medium in the education field. Currently, there are more than 60 colleges and universities offering online distance learning degrees with a total of more than 500 courses in Taiwan. In May 2005, the Ministry of Education issued a "General Guide for Distance Learning in Postsecondary Education." This guideline approves the use of distance learning for the academic terms and allows universities to credit students with online course units up to 1/3 of the total units required for their graduation. This guideline also encourages schools to offer online distance learning degree for vocational adults as the life-long learning program (University Distance Learning Network, 2005). However, since the course subjects and teaching material for the military education is highly specialized, online distance learning is still in a conceptual stage.

Due to the change in the international and sociopolitical milieu, the number of military personnel is reduced each year. Consequently, how to maintain a war ready arm force while improve the quality of soldiers has become the most critical issue for the military educational authority. As mentioned above, the correspondence education is an asynchronous teaching method and is not as efficient and complete as the resident education.

Obviously, the military needs to construct a more innovative teaching methodology. By fully explore the Internet and World Wide Web technologies, advanced military education through the distance learning can become a powerful instrument to narrow down the performance disparity between these two groups of learners. Distance learning can break time and space barriers created by the legacy vocational training program.

The following section present an online distance learning prototype system for Advanced Military Education-Distance Learning (AME-DL) proposed in this article. This prototype system is based on widely accessible and matured commercial technological platform. This prototype is adjusted and tailored based on the unique requirements of military education and can be used as a constructive reference for the military to implement distance learning in the near future.

TECHNOLOGY OVERVIEW FOR WEB BASED DISTANCE-LEARNING

Currently, there are still many debates on what learning reference model and standard should be implemented as the foundation to build a digital distance learning program upon. One of the most influential reference models is the SCORM2004(Sharable Content Object Reference Model) (Mackenzie, 2004), which is based on U.S.A. DoD's Strategic Plan for Advanced Distributed Learning (ADL) mentioned above. SCORM at a high-level is a collection of specifications and standards that are used to characterize the major principles of ADL. SCORM applies current developments in the training technology through the use of a specific content model to ensure consistent training implementation across the e-learning community. The AMD-DL prototype is designed based on SCORM2004 because it reflects on the major implications of ADL. There are six major objectives of SCORM:

- **Interoperability:** The ability to take instructional components developed in one location with one set of tools or platform and the ability to apply them in another location with a different set of tools or platform.
- **Accessibility:** The ability to locate and access training instructional components from one location and deliver them to several other locations.
- **Reusability:** The flexibility to incorporate instructional components in different applications and contexts.
- **Durability:** The ability to withstand technological changes without costly redesign, reconfiguration or re-programming.
- **Maintainability:** The ability to withstand content growth and changes without costly redesign, reconfiguration or re-programming.
- **Adaptability:** The ability to tailor instruction to fit individual and organizational needs.
    - SCORM defines communications between client side content and host system (Learning Management System-LMS). Learning Management System is a term used to describe software tools designed to manager user learning interventions. Learning Management Systems are not just training records management and reporting. Learning Management System offers a wide range of functionalities such as training workflow, the provision of online learning, online assessment, management of Continuous Professional Education, collaborative, and training resource management. In other words, how learning content is transferred into an LMS system, how this content is presented to learners, and how the learner's progress within that content is communicated. To summarize, SCORM is a suite of techni-

cal standards that enable web-based learning systems to find, import, share, reuse, and export learning content in a standardized way.

In our research, we evaluate Microsoft Learning Gateway (Microsoft, 2007) and find that this software package can be used in our AME-DL (Advanced Military Education-Distance Learning) prototype. The Learning Gateway portal framework takes existing applications and resources of an institution and delivers them via secure, customized personal Web portals. It is a scalable learning platform providing services via a Web browser from anywhere and anytime. From one customized home page, each individual can immediately access the applications, files, e-mails, timetables, planners, diary notes, assessments, progress remarks, administration software, and other resources as needed. Students can organize assignments and lecture notes using OneNote, which is one of the Learning Gateway's many building blocks. They can also immediately access educational resources, check academic results, course requirements, and billing details for a complete snapshot of their status. Scholars can collaborate with colleagues overseas, publish articles and resources and enter marks which are instantly recorded on the student's portal site for them to view. Microsoft Learning Gateway allows trainees, trainers, and administrators to communicate with each other without time and geographical barriers. Based on Microsoft Learning Gateway Solution, we have designed the AME-DL prototype.

AME-DL PROTOTYPE ARCHITECTURE AND FUNCTIONAL CAPABILITIES

The proposed AME-DL prototype architecture is designed to achieve the learning objectives for the military education and provides a low-cost, customizable, interoperable and accessible training environment. Furthermore, the AME-DL architecture includes distributed networks, interconnected databases, dynamic modeling of real-time information, artificial intelligence and adaptive assessment features.

As illustrated in Figure1, the AME-DL architecture contains four primary parts, including Front-End Web Tier, Application Tier, Database Tier, and After Action Review Viewer (AAR Viewer). The brief description of each part is given as follows:

- **Front-end Web tier:** It contains all user interfaces, such as training course interface, collaboration interface and customized personal interface. The front-end user interface is built upon many Web page modules and helps all users customize their Web interface.
- **Application tier:** The application tier is the core of AME-DL architecture and all tasks (i.e., parameter updating/querying, database updating, assumption editing, and scenario designing) are accomplished in this tier. As shown in Figure 1, the application tier is constructed by Microsoft Office SharePoint Server (MOSS) 2007, Windows SharePoint Service (WSS) 3.0, SharePoint Learning Kit (SLK), parameter manager, assumption manager, scenario manager, ECM, model agent, Business Intelligence (BI), and Virtual Path Provider. Each function module is described as follows.
    - **Microsoft Office SharePoint Server (MOSS) 2007:** It is an integrated suite of applications and provides a single platform to help users manage all Web site applications in AME-DL architecture. With the help of MOSS 2007, diverse learning needs, such as training content and process management can be fulfilled for the instructors and trainees to make better decisions.

Figure 1. AME-DL prototype architecture

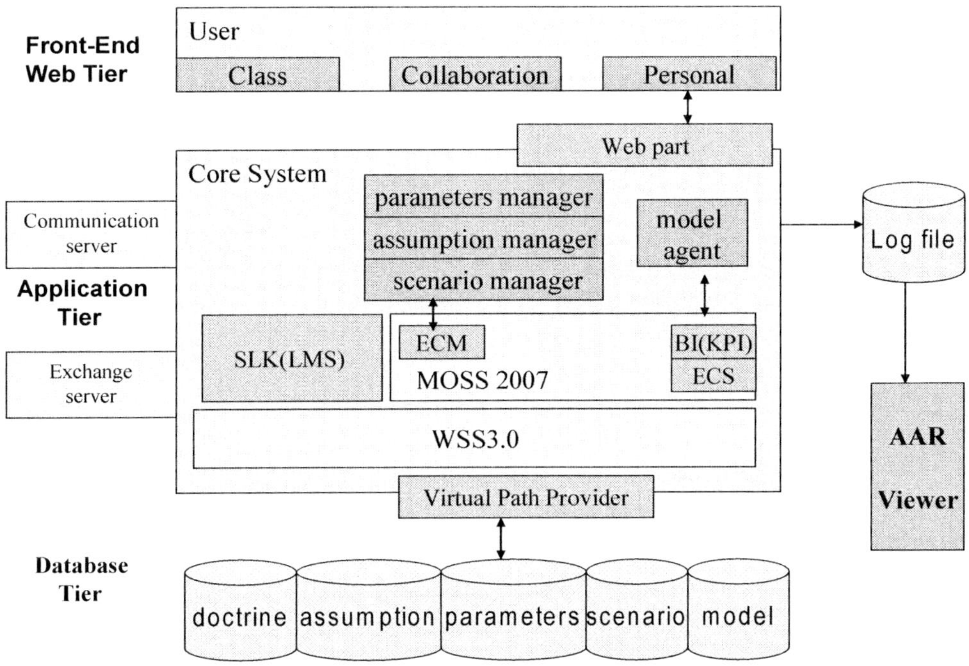

- **Windows SharePoint Service (WSS) 3.0:** It creates sites and Web pages in AME-DL and provides document libraries to store and share all learning knowledge between trainees.
- **Sharepoint learning kit (SLK):** In AME-DL architecture, SLK helps teachers create assignments from the documents in the SharePoint Document Library. When SLK is integrated with MOSS 2007, SCORM 2004 (the most widely accepted worldwide standard for e-learning) can be supported to allow users to manage the content, and to track documents in SharePoint document libraries. Note that we can replace the SharePoint Learning Kit with any other Learning Management System (LMS) and integrate it with the SharePoint Server in the AME-DL architecture.

Based on above function modules (i.e., MOSS, WSS, and SLK), parameters manager, assumption manager and scenario manager can be built accordingly:

- **Enterprise content management (ECM):** In AME-DL architecture, ECM refers to the technologies used to capture, manage, store, preserve, and deliver all content and documents in an organization. ECM is divided into two parts, one mainly handling document definition, creation, authorization, and publishing while the second module prints out bar code labels for documentation identification, certification and document library maintenance.
- **Business intelligence (BI):** Business intelligence can be used as a platform for building dashboard-style applications that provide upper-level management with up-to-date data that reflects the health of a business and flags potential problems in a timely matter. Taking "Report Center" Web site as an example, it mainly stores SQL server

information, including SQL server reporting service, SQL server analysis report and excel service.

- **Excel calculation service (ECS):** In ECS, all users can show and share an Excel spreadsheet with embedded program on a browser and then they can load, calculate, and render Excel workbooks on server. In addition, it also provides Excel snapshot file downloading, Excel web page component analysis and user-defined calculating functions.
- **Model repository:** Model repository contains various simulation models for training officers to choose from based on different mission objectives.
- **Model agent:** Model agent is the remote interface to execute simulations. In AME-DL prototype, there are three types of executable simulation models. The first is the spreadsheet model. Training users can perform spreadsheet simulations constructed by Excel Calculation Service (ECS) on servers through the Web browser. The second model is the standalone model. Standalone models consist of simple warfare simulations such as sub vs. sub, and so on. Trainees can choose appropriate models and parameters to generate results and perform analysis. The last category is the multi-person interactive model. This model is originated from collective war games done in war-game center. Under this model, each training user can act as his/her own federate and join a federation at the same time online utilizing high level architecture (HLA) collaboratively to perform a large scale wargame.
- **Parameter, assumption and scenario managers:** Architecture, parameter, assumption, and scenario managers are three customized management units that are responsible for editing and managing assumption, parameter, and scenario databases. These three units are carried out by the ECM functionality in MOSS 2007.
- **Virtual path provider:** In AME-DL architecture, Virtual Path Provider provides a set of methods that enable a web application to retrieve resources from a virtual file system in which all files and directories are managed by a data store rather than the file system provided by the server's operating system. For example, users can utilize a virtual file system to store content in a SQL server.
- **Web page module:** Web page modules are pre-designed and pre-defined functional modules. Through these modules, users can customize the content of a Web page layout by adding, editing and removing modules, and all these settings will be stored in his/her profile on the MOSS server (Ryan & Tschudi-Sutton, 2006).

• **Database Tier:** Four different databases are included in this tier. All users can query and acquire data and information they desired from these databases. The functionality of each database is demonstrated as follows.

- **Doctrine database:** Doctrine database stores all the doctrines which the military defined for military operations and training. For instance, principles of war, military operation, war tactics, and engage rules are all stored in the doctrine database. Through the World Wide Web, all of the digitalized doctrines can be accessed and queried by the training users easily and quickly.
- **Assumption database:** Assumption database provides the most fundamental statistical data for wargame

simulations. It sets the basic assumptions such as the initial armed force size and logistical capacity for the red team and blue team for the trainees to create and move forward into his/her operational tactic plan.

- **Parameter database:** In order to design a computer-aided wargame scenario, the first task is to quantify and correlate all available intangible resources such as solider weaponry competency into useful information. Data collected from operational military exercise and statistical calculations become different parameters that can be applied and manipulate in a scenario. Accurate simulation results are based on well-chosen parameter settings. By offering the training users a preset parameter database with various parameters, training users can minimize data collection time and improve the accuracy of simulation results
- **Scenario database:** Scenario setting is a major prerequisite before executing simulations. Based on a particular scenario, the major task is to apply an appropriate battle plan. Taking sea combat as an example, the properties of each frigate such as type, speed, course, and initial position all need to be taken into considerations. Sea environment information, such as day/night, wind speed direction, tide height, and time, also are important factors that need to be taken into accounts. The scenario database offers training users a space to store historical scenario settings for future trainees to utilize and adjust. This database can reduce scenario setting time consequently.

- **AAR Viewer:** AAR (After Action Review) Viewer is implemented as a separated application module from Model agent and it can read the log files generated from AME-DL based training. More importantly, AAR Viewer provides the ability to trace and review the detailed actions taken during the training process. From this review procedure, each user is able to evaluate all decisions made in the training, and more insights can be obtained to improve the training performance. Compared with the traditional e-learning system, AAR Viewer emphasizes heavily on the review and evaluation process, which is an important training procedure in the advanced military education.
- **Communication & Exchange Server:** The communication server in the AME-DL architecture provides instant messaging to all users and helps them to share their ideas and information instantly. Through this communication platform, users who are geographically separated can communicate with each other without interrupting their work on hand. In addition, exchange server provides Web-based e-mail accounts and calendaring to trainees.

FUNCTIONAL DESCRIPTION

Application server: Uses virtual path provider to link various database and builds parameter, scenario, data, and model mangers into WSS, SLK, and MOSS systems. These management modules are represented through the use of Web parts:

- **System administrator:** By utilizing MOSS, BCM, ECS, and SLK modules, system administrators are able to build and maintain parameter, scenario, data, and model managers in a digital learning platform based on a particular training content and system functionality.

- **Course manager:** By using class web part interface, the course administrator can input curriculum related data such as: semester length, orientation date, instructor profile, and so on.
- **Instructor:** Through class Web part and personal Web part interface, a training officer can key in course requirement, assignment guide, reading material, and so on. He/she can use ECS to apply appropriate assumption and scenario base on the course content. Through SLK the trainer also can assign students into different teams and monitor/control assignment their progresses as a course goes on. Finally, KPI can be used to measure students performance competencies, the well qualified assignments can become blueprints for future trainees.
- **Trainee/students:** Officers on training can use class and personal Web part to complete the following tasks:
  1. Applying suitable assumptions to meet course requirements.
  2. Choosing proper synopsis from model repository by using model agent, and to manipulate spreadsheet model based on different combating scenarios to satisfy and improve the accuracy of a simulation.
  3. Completing scenario simulation setting by applying appropriate assumptions into scenario manager.
  4. After scenario setting is done, extract data necessary for simulation through database.
  5. Once all the preparations are done, officers on training can use a browser to execute simulation and present simulation result to training officers. Since the simulation is done by officers on training through Internet, they can adjust applied data and repeat simulations until the result is consist and reliable.

Figure 2. AME-DL workflow

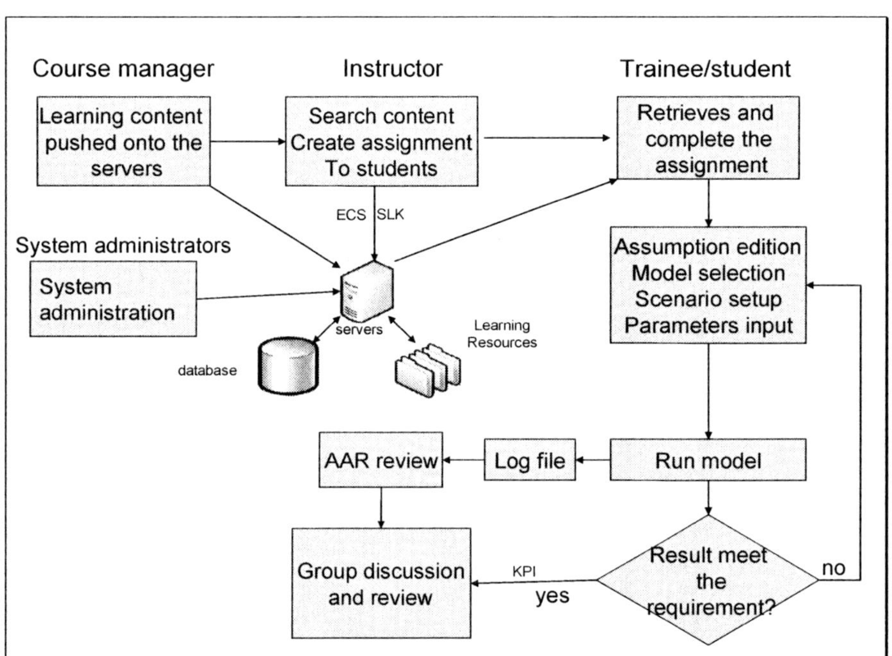

All the simulations that the officers on training have executed are saved into log files, training officers can use AAR viewer to supervise all the "action and decision making" that the trainees have done. The training officer then uses both KPI indicators and these log files as bases to create group discussion and reviews on collaboration Web part. Figure 2 illustrates the work flow of AME-DL prototype

CONCLUSION AND FUTURE WORK

In this article we have presented the architecture of AME-DL prototype for advance military distance-learning; it combines advanced e-learning tools, simulation technology, and Web technology to provide a set of military learning and training subjects that can be accessed easily anywhere, anytime through a Web browser. Although this article is a preliminary introduction attempt to implement a new educational infrastructure in military advanced education by using a commercial ready technological infrastructure, we can see that browser based Internet distance learning is a firm proposition that military education authority should definitely bear in mind. The next step is to expand this distance learning groundwork by incorporating war tactics and operations into plan. Once Internet based distance learning is fully deployed in military education and training, military officers will be able to improve and gain new skills through constant training anytime anywhere.

REFERENCES

Carol Gaddy, A. (2000). *Training through technology distance learning is more than hardware*. U.S. Army War College, Carlisle Barracks, PA.

Gord Mackenzie, G. (2004). *SCORM 2004: Primer*. McGill.

Microsoft. (2007). *Microsoft learning gateway refresh for SharePoint Server 2007 deployment guide*.

Mitelstedt, P.A. (2001). *Distance learning receives high marks*. U.S. War College, Carlisle Barracks, PA.

Ryan, B. and & Tschudi-Sutton, M. (2006). *7 development projects for Microsoft Office SharePoint Server 2007 and Windows SharePoint Services Version 3.0*. Washington: Microsoft Press.

University Distance Learning Network. (2005). University digital education development in Taiwan., Retrieved from http://dised.ntu.edu.tw/.

This work was previously published in International Journal of Distance Education Technologies, Vol. 6, Issue 4, edited by S. Chang & T. Shih, pp. 50-61, copyright 2008 by IGI Publishing (an imprint of IGI Global).

Chapter 18

Virtual On-Line Classroom for Mobile E-Learning over Next Generation Learning Environment

Tin-Yu Wu
Tamkang University, Taipei, Taiwan, ROC

ABSTRACT

This chapter develops an environment for mobile e-Learning with interactive courses, virtual online labs, interactive online tests, lab-exercise training platform and the identification of learning information by next generation tag on the 4th generation mobile communication system. What the Next Generation Learning Environment (NeGL) promotes is "Knowledge Economy" At present, inter-networking has become one of the most popular technologies in Mobile e-Learning for the Next Generation Networks (NGN) environment. This system uses various computer embedded devices to ubiquitously access multi-media information like smart phones and PDAs, and the most important feature is its greater available bandwidth. The future learning mode will include an immediate, virtual, interactive classroom with personal identification that enables learners to learn and interact. (Wu et al. 2008)

INTRODUCTION

The development of new approaches and technologies to support distance learning are undergoing now. Web-based and mobile asynchronous learning environments and virtual classrooms via the Internet have been adopted widely in particular. For the time being, the current trend of e-Learning is the static information as an instructional delivery method. Learners using these kinds of conventional learning methods are only able to browse through the mass static information and this is passive learning by reading online.

In the last decade, technologies enabling e-Learning have made the learning locations much more flexible and wireless communication technologies further increase the options for learning locations. Advances in wireless communication technologies have provided the opportunity for educators to create innovative educational models. With the aid of wireless communication technology, educational practice can be embedded into mobile

DOI: 10.4018/978-1-60566-934-2.ch018

life without wired-based communication. With the more mobile, portable and individualized trend in educational media, the learning form is being modified in spectacular ways. (Gang et al. 2005)

In the third generation cellular system (3G) environment (like Universal Mobile Telecommunications System, UMTS), the data rate reaches 2Mbps while the user is standing and 384Kbps while the user is moving slowly. Multimedia streaming, video conferencing, and on-line interactive 3D games are expected to attract an increasing number of users. However, such bandwidth is not sufficient for these increasingly popular applications and would be the major challenge for wireless networks. The 3G bandwidth has great problems in interactive teaching. (Bos et al. 2001)

In the future, wireless network traffic is expected to be a mix of real-time traffic such as voice, music, multimedia teleconferencing, online games, and data traffic like web pages browsing, instant messaging, and file transfers. All of these applications will require widely varying and very diverse quality of service (QoS) guarantees for different types of offered traffic. (Dixit 2001)

The mobile devices have limited screen sizes, computation resources, bandwidth and interaction. The information often needs to be formatted, structured and translated before it can be displayed on the devices. Moreover, learners can use different devices to access learning servers no matter by fixed or mobile devices. The RuBee tag stores the personal's identification to support adaptability with respect to available bandwidth in the query processing. It can classify the different types of queries specific and adaptability module which maximizes information transferred. Within RuBee tag technology to provide mobile users with flexibility for using. (Wu et al. 2008)

For these reasons, a 4th generation improving mobile communication system is unquestionably necessary. The 4G system can support more bandwidth than other systems and its advantages include authentication, mobile management and quality of service (QoS). Nevertheless, how to implement future distance learning environments for the 4th generation mobile communication system is the question. In this chapter, we distinguish four kinds of interactive courses: virtual online labs, Interactive online test and lab-exercises training platform to deliver over the 4th generation mobile communication system. The 4th generation mobile communication system can use various computer embedded devices to ubiquitously access multimedia information, such as smart phones, PDA; and most importantly, it offers more bandwidth to supply ubiquitous learning environment. (Girish et al.2000)

These new functions can improve the latency and location limits during transmission. Our proposed Next Generation Learning Environment (NeGL) offers learners the opportunities to use all kinds of mobile nodes that can connect to an Internet learning equipment system for access using All-IP communication networks and the Sharable Content Object Reference Model (SCORM) is used to compose information. Hence, as you can imagine, the condition of the future learning mode will be an international, immediate and virtual interactive classroom that enables learners to learn and interact.

ENVIRONMENTS FOR MOBILE E-LEARNING

Wireless communications technologies have enabled many conveniences in our lives. Ubiquitous access to information anywhere and anytime will characterize the whole new kinds of information systems in the 21st century and these characteristics are being enabled by rapidly emerging wireless communications system, based on WiMAX, cellular networks, wireless LANs, etc. Additionally, technologies enabling e-Learning have increased the flexibility of the learning locations and wireless communication technologies further increase

Figure 1. The virtual on-line classroom over NGN

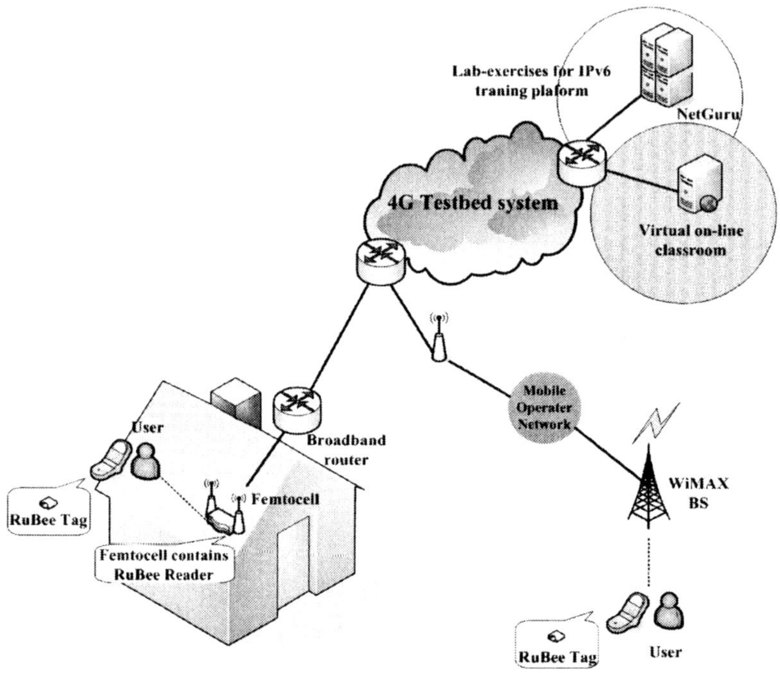

the options for these locations. Advancements in wireless communication technologies have recently provided the opportunity for educators to innovate educational models. With the trend of the Ubiquitous-Learning (U-Learning), the educational media are becoming more mobilized, portable and individualized, and the learning form is being modified spectacularly.

Several investigations have focused on how to support great service for mobile e-Learning. How many services will be able to fill the bill? This session introduces that mobile e-Learning environment possesses many unique characteristics as follows. (Tony et al. 2004)

- Better adaptation to individual needs
- Interactive knowledge acquisition
- Situational instructional activities
- Flexibility of location and time to learn
- Ubiquitous and responds to urgent learning need
- Efficiency due both to re-use and feedback
- Integrated instructional context. (Chao et al. 2004)

The mobile e-Learning system includes interactive courses, virtual online labs, interactive online test and lab-exercises training platform on the Next Generation Networks (NGN) system. As shown in Figure 1 the following sessions will present Interactive course system, Virtual online labs system, Interactive online test system, Lab-exercises training platform, Access Network and Core Network.

- **Interactive course system:** In the learning history, learners can only experience interactive learning in the classroom and what the e-Learning systems support is only one-way learning. To enable the learning anytime and anywhere, we therefore developed an interactive course system so that learners can choose which chapter they want to learn in the system and the learning method is no more limited by the environment.

- **Virtual online labs system:** Generally speaking, experiments must be conducted in a laboratory; learners are thereby limited to a specific learning area. To solve this problem, special equipments are required. By a flash program, we simulate laboratory experiments all the time. This virtual online lab platform supports step-by-step experimentation and learners are therefore not restricted in the laboratory.
- **Interactive online test system:** An online interactive test system is adopted to examine the teaching effect on learners. Via the test system, instructors can know how many learners are impacted and learners can obtain the learning effect on themselves.
- **Lab-exercises training platform:** Learners have more items for experimentation. NetSmooth Inc. developed a complete solution called NetGuru platform to tackle this issue. Learners can access the lab-exercises training platform via pre-arranged authorization.

Besides these platforms, a communication system is needed to take the learning data, and the Next Generation Networks (NGN) achieves the goal of Ubiquitous-Learning (U-Learning). This system can be divided into two parts: Access Network and Core Network.

- • **Access network:** The Next Generation Networks (NGN) will integrate all heterogeneous networks to achieve an ubiquitous access network. The wireless networks cover the scope from WMAN, WLAN to WPAN and the last mile technology especially. To provide enhanced services over the last mile, instead of wires, wireless network is preferred to connect a stationary terminal to the wireline network. Nowadays, Femtocell that under Macro-cell and Picocell, is a hot issue. The Femtocell can reduce the construction cost and improve the cover rate for 3G system. In addition, the FMC (Fixed Mobile Convergence) is the wide range of mobile services that converges elements of fixed communications infrastructure to complement the core mobile service. This encompasses a wide range of services; however, they generally have the core of allowing users or the network to take advantage of higher speed, cheaper local unlicensed access networks in local environments for lower value but high volume transactions. According to a new concept of FMC including wire and wireless communication technology, such

Figure 2. The home networks for Femtocell

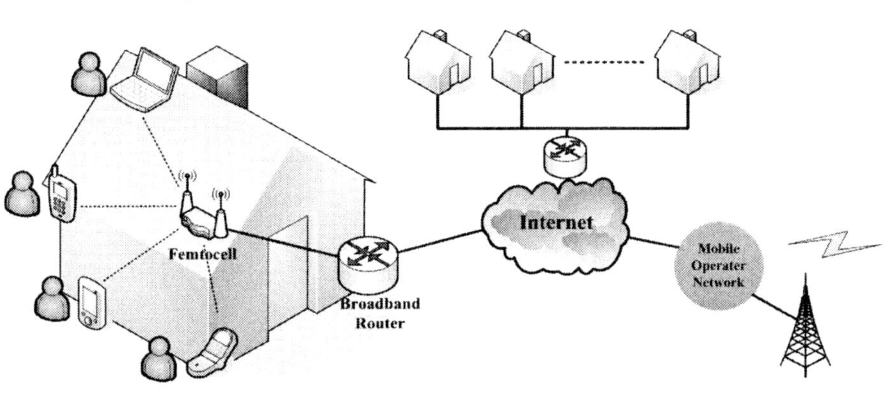

Figure 3. The ubiquitous-learning over the heterogeneous network

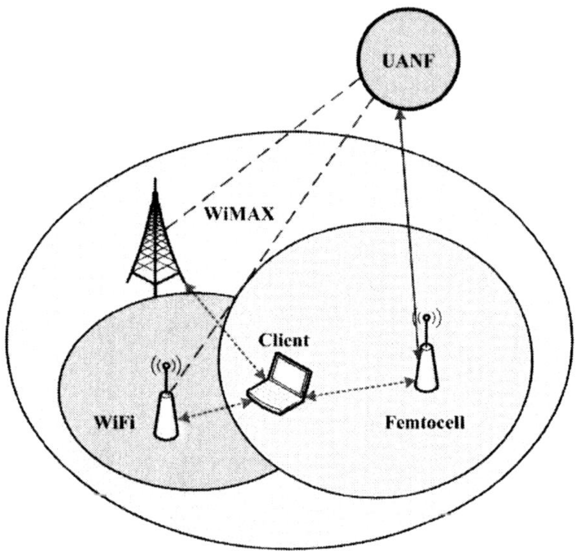

as ADSL, Fiber and WiMAX etc., learners have more choices, as shown in Figure 2 and 3.

- • **Core network:** The future education information will be mainly based on multimedia, Thus, to ensure the QoS, to have efficient network administration (authentication, authorization, accounting; AAA), to ensure the network security, and the integration of telecom and datacom with the arrival of All-IP era, this brand new network system will provide massive end to end multimedia services, and ensure QoS, security and AAA in the meantime.

This is the introduction of IMS (IP Multimedia Subsystem) proposed by 3GPP and 3GPP2 that will fulfill the purpose of end to end multimedia service. IMS has the following distinguishing features:, the parallel network structure based on SIP protocol; and to provide rich and dynamic combined services by separating control and data traffic. Therefore, IMS can archive the following requirements:

1. Establish IP multimedia conference
2. Support QoS mechanism
3. Support Packet switch and circuit switch exchange
4. Support roaming
5. Provide service provider an efficient service control to the end users
6. Support a none-standardized and prompt service creation

VIRTUAL ON-LINE CLASSROOM

In the field of virtual on-line classrooms, much effort is made all around the world. One of the most popular trends is the web-based virtual classroom via the Internet as an instructional delivery method. As the passive learning, traditional learning methods only allowed students to browse through mass static information. This session will introduce an interactive virtual classroom that includes interactive courses, virtual online labs, interactive online test and a lab-exercise training platform. The virtual on-line classroom interactive website: http://6book.niu.edu.tw/. (6BOOK)

Setting Up the Interactive Learning Course Website Platform

The Internet has uni-location and unlimited time features. Early on-line teaching materials included video lessons captured by DV, e-books and poster messages etc. and these materials were used via the Internet. However, these approaches belong to one-way learning and cannot attain learning anytime and anywhere. Therefore, with our proposed interactive course system as shown in Figure 5, learners can choose which chapter they want to learn and the system can repeat whatever learners want. This course is also provided with interactive online test with interactive capability so that learners can learn anytime and anywhere unlimitedly.

Figure 4. The interactive virtual on-line classroom website

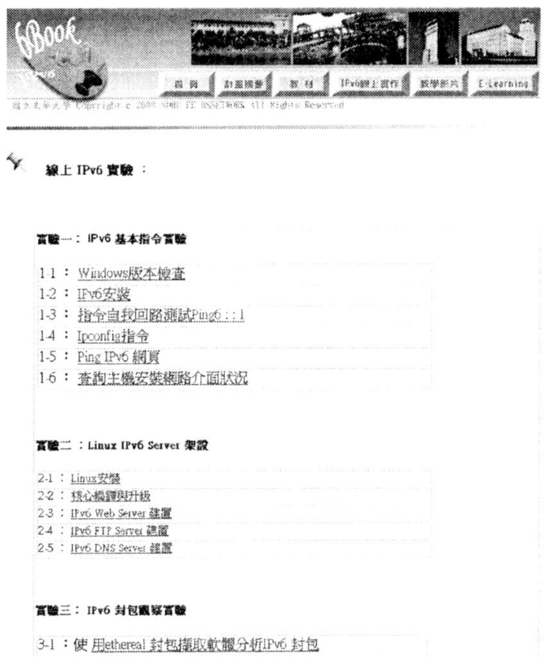

Learners not only select can the target chapters to learn or preview/review, but also can save all previous study processes. With the sliders with hints and oral explanations of the system, learners can control the learning speed at their own will and see the content clearly just like the classes are taking place (Shown in Figure 6).

Setting Up Virtual On-line Lab-Exercises

Usually, Lab-Exercises must be conducted in a laboratory and learners cannot perform experiments without a laboratory, but this reduces lots of opportunities to learn. Therefore, we used FLASH to produce a series of on-line lab-exercises that explain the lab-exercises from the beginning to the end and perform the exercises with detailed background voice and subtitles. For each exercise, detailed explanations will be given, including the experiment goals, steps and approaches that can help learners understand the background.

Most importantly, learners can control the speed of the lab-exercises by themselves. Relying on on-line lab-exercises, learners can perform lab exercises for an unlimited number of times and perform experiments anytime from anywhere. For instructors, they no longer have to spend time to prepare lab-exercises or setup equipments. If learners have any questions about the exercises, hyperlink to the text or to the website can be used

Figure 5. Interactive learning course website platform

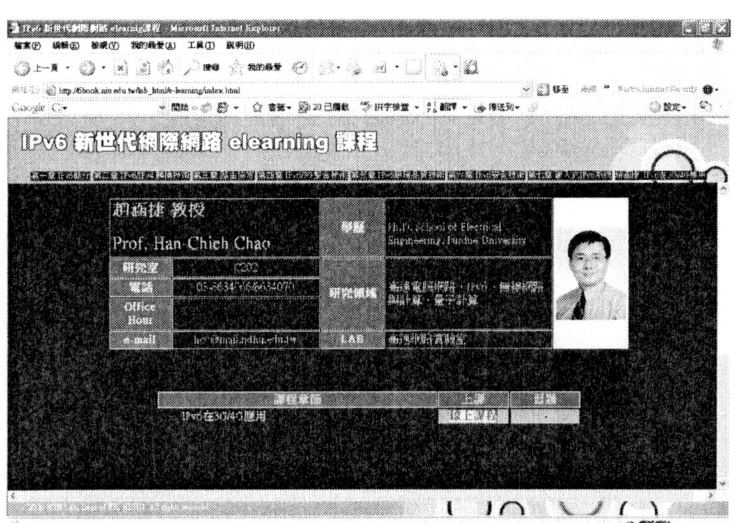

Figure 6. The teaching slides with voice on the platform

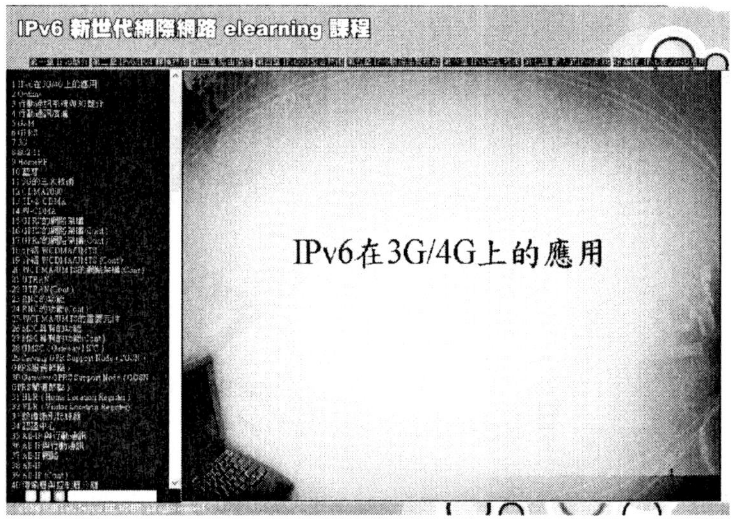

to find answers. This teaching platform covers both theory and lab exercises interactively.

Setting up on-line lab-exercises

The Virtual on-line lab-exercises and interactive learning website platform help learners study efficiently and identify the learning effect. We developed on-line interactive exercises for each chapter. These exercises identify the comprehension of each learner for the instructors who use these teaching materials and this system tutors learners who cannot completely comprehend the whole lessons. By practicing the exercises, learners can also know clearly which section of each chapter should be enhanced.

Lab-Exercises Training Platform

The lab-exercises training platform is set-up by using the NetSmooth Inc. test platform. This platform supports another solution with lab-exercises for learners. The proposed NetGuru platform helps instructors to conduct network courses easily with web-based tutorial courseware and

Figure 7. The virtual on-line lab-exercises

it also assists students to strengthen the concepts of network with hands-on lab experiences. The pragmatic lab-exercises for IPv6 training platform use a small-sized personal computer. (Chiang et al. 2005)

Figure 8. The on-line interactive exercises platform

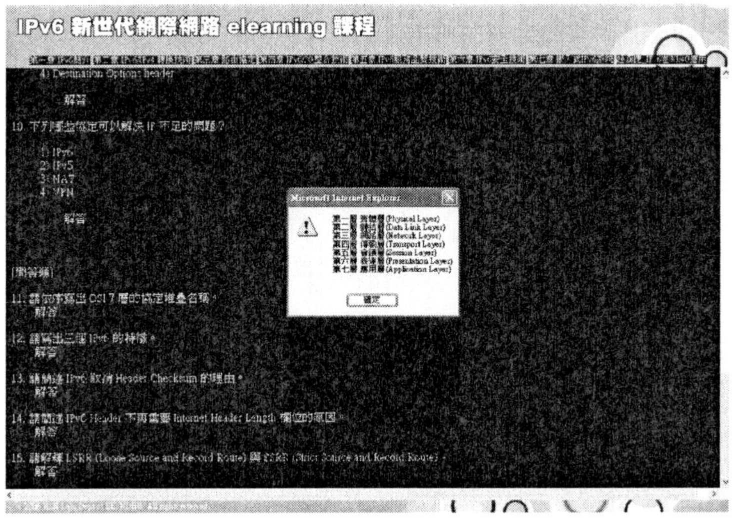

IDENTIFY LEARNING INFORMATION BY NEXT GENERATION TAG FOR MOBILE E-LEARNING

Mobile e-Learning is a new challenge for mobile devices which identification and learning information services. The mobile devices have limited screen sizes, computation resources, bandwidth and interaction; thus, the information often needs to be formatted, structured and translated before it can be displayed on the devices. In addition, one change of personal learning information is the usage of RFID (Radio Frequency Identification) tags.

In this session, instead of RFID, we use the next generation tag to deal with the identification of learning information. Since being adopted in WWII, the applications of RFID have become very extensive: RFID is applied to logistics and warehousing, medical treatment, cash card, easy card, entrance card, bank card and so on. RFID is useful but it has much limitations. For example, neighboring RFID tags easily interfere with one another; and storage environments might cause bad influence upon signal transmission. Furthermore, fatal problems of RFID include its passive attribute and inability to connect to Internet.

In 2007, IEEE innovated the new generation short-distance standard IEEE1902.1, RuBee., which will replace RFID as the latest Identification system. As an active tag, RuBee is able to connect to the Internet and can be used in harsh environments. RuBee functions with long wavelength within the rage of 10 to 50 ft and uses low-cost wireless tags. With networks of thousands of tags and operation at less than 450 kHz, RuBee is able to work in bad environment: near metals or water, or in electrical noises. One advantage of RuBee is that it can transmit data to the Internet directly, but RuBee transmission is low-speed so that it is not suitable to use on a large number of moving devices. Some advantages of RuBee tags are listed in the following. (Raj et al. 2007)

- Low power consumption
- Long battery life
- Normal operation near steel and water
- RuBee tags functions successfully in harsh environments
- RuBee tags have a network transceiver that actually transmits a data signal
- High security and privacy RuBee tags have many unique advantages in high security applications

- Controlled volumetric range

RuBee tag technology provides mobile users more flexibility; learners thus can use different devices to access learning server no matter by fixed or mobile devices. The RuBee tag can stores personal's identification to support adaptability with respect to available bandwidth in the query processing. It can classify the different types of queries specific and adaptability module which maximizes information transferred. (Yang et al. 2006)

4TH GENERATION TESTBED SYSTEM DESIGN ANALYSES

This chapter proposed a 4th generation mobile communication testbed system that can support greater bandwidth than other systems and its advantages include authentication, mobile management, and quality of service (QoS).

This session will introduce our 4th generation communication testbed system. We followed the specification defined in 3GPP to design our system that is composed of two main components: RAN (Radio Access Network) and Core-Network. RAN includes RNC and Node B, and the Core-Network includes SGSN (Serving GPRS Support Node), GGSN (Gateway GPRS Support Node), and HSS (Home Subscriber Server), as shown in Figure 9.

At RAN, Node B works like the access point of wireless network: providing the ability for UE (User Equipment) to connect to the core network through radio interface. Each RNC can work with single or multiple Node B to form a RNA, and RAN is then constituted by these RNS.

Figure 9. The cross-layer coordination plane

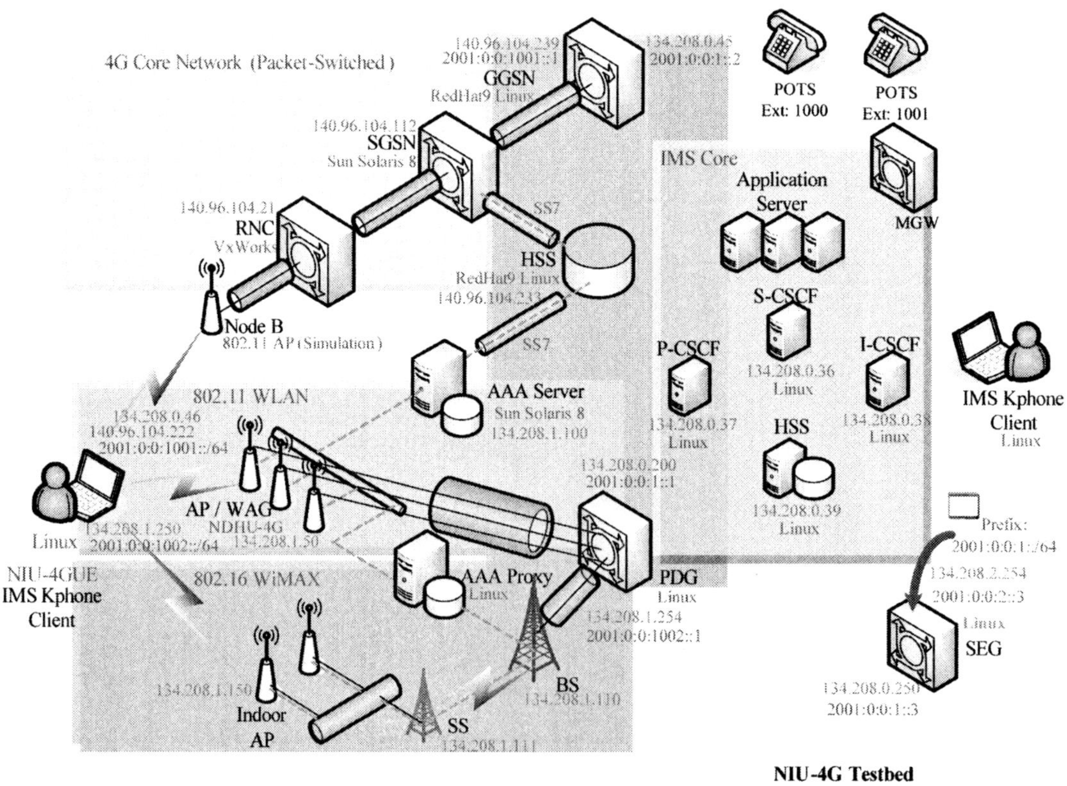

At the core network, SGSN is responsible for tasks such as connecting to the core network with single or multiple RAN, access control, location management, routing management etc. GGSN is an interface that is responsible for connecting core network and outer network, routing traveling packets, and mobility management. (Uskela 2001)

HSS is a data center that is responsible for recording the operations of the entire network and HLR is its main component. The function of HSS is to store users' identity, location and registered permitted services.

Since the radio frequency used by a 3GPP cellular phone is a licensed band, a legal license must be required. Therefore, we used 802.11g that belongs to the ISM band. Through broadcasting UDP packets to simulate the radio network and executing the protocol stack of the simulation program in UE according to the 3GPP standard, all generated packets are identical to packets generated by an actual 3GPP cell phone. UE enables us to acquire the flowchart of packets generated through the data exchange process between UE and the network. Figure 10 illustrates the entire system. (3GPP, 3GPP TS 23.228, 3GPP TS 23.234)

Interworking WLAN Domain

To achieve the inter-working between packet-switched core network domain and WLAN domain, the AAA (Authentication, Authorization and Accounting) server and the PDG (Packet Data Gateway) appeared in the 3GPP. The AAA server supports EAP-SIM or EAP-AKA authentication method. During the authentication, AAA server must request the relevant information of AuC from HSS to process the mutual authentication and authorization. AAA server is also responsible for collecting the information of charging.

802.16d WiMAX Network Domain

At present, we have deployed the 802.16d equipments as the Backhual in our testbed. This might be used by the operators as the solution to the last mile problem. We deployed these 802.16d equipments outdoors, and configured the point-to-multipoint authentication mechanism among its BS and SS. On the other side, the SS is deployed indoors and connected with Access Point equipped 802.1x authentication function. Before accessing the network resources, the UE would be verified

Figure 10. The 4th generation mobile communication testbed system

with AAA Server or AAA Proxy Server via SIM-based Authentication.

IP Multimedia Subsystem (IMS) Domain

In order to construct the IMS domain to provide extensible services in the testbed, we built the CSCFs servers on the Linux system platform based on the Open IMS Core. We also developed the IMS Kphone Client based on the Kphone for the IMS services. After registering to the IMS core with the AKAv1-MD5 mechanism, the UE can access the IMS services either through the packet-switched network, 802.11 WLAN or WiMAX. We installed the OpenSER SIP server as the IMS application server, and used group module of OpenSER to provide the presence service. The constructed IMS testbed can provide users functions including voice call, video call, presence service, and instant message.

CONCLUSION

The explosive development of the Internet and wireless communications has made personal communication more convenient. Mobile computing uses the Next Generation Learning Environment (NeGL) to set up learning systems. In this chapter, we proposed a mobile e-Learning system that includes interactive courses, virtual online labs, Interactive online testing, a lab-exercise training platform and identification of learning information by next generation tag via the 4th generation mobile communication system. This system offers learners opportunities to use all kinds of mobile nodes or anything that can connect to an Internet learning equipment system to be accessed using All-IP communication networks. For Sharable Content Object Reference Model (SCORM) to compose information the 4G uses a variety of computer embedded devices to ubiquitously access multimedia information, such as smart phones and PDA. Most importantly, more bandwidth is available. As you can imagine, the condition of the future learning mode will be an international, immediate and virtual interactive classroom that enables learners to learn and interact.

REFERENCES

6BOOK. (n.d.). Retrieved from http://6book.niu.edu.twf

Bos, L., & Leroy, S. (2001). Toward an All-IP-Based UMTS System Architecture. *IEEE Network*, *15*(1), 36–45. doi:10.1109/65.898820

Chan, T., Sharples, M., Vavoula, G., & Lonsdale, P. (2004). Educational Metadata for Mobile Learning. In *Proc. The 2nd IEEE International Workshop on Wireless and Mobile Technologies in Education 2004* (pp. 197-198).

Chao, H.-C., Wu, T.-Y., & Kao, M. T. C. (2005). Environments for mobile learning. In C. Howard, J. Boettcher, L. Justice, K. Schenk, P. Rogers, & G. Berg (Eds.), Encyclopedia of Distance Learning (pp. 853-856). Hershey, PA: Idea Group Reference.

Chiang, F.-Y., Liang, M.-H., Wu, T.-Y., & Chao, H.-C. (2005). *Pragmatic Lab-Exercises for IPv6 Training*. iCEER-2005, Tainan, Taiwan, March 1-5, 2005.

Dixit, S. S. (2001). Evolving to Seamless All-IP Wireless/Mobile Networks. *IEEE Communications Magazine*, *39*(12), 31–32. doi:10.1109/MCOM.2001.968809

3GPP. Third Generation Partnership Project (n.d.). Retrieved from http://www.3gpp.org

3GPP TS 23.228 V6.10.0 (2005-06). *IP multimedia subsystem*.

3GPP TS 23.234 V6.5.0 (2005-06). *3GPP system to Wireless Local Area Network (WLAN) interworking*.

Patel, G., & Dennett, S. (2000). The 3GPP and 3GPP2 Movements toward an All-IP Mobile Network. *IEEE Personal Communications*, *7*(4), 62–64. doi:10.1109/98.863998

Prithvi, R. (2007). IEEE Begins Wireless, Long-Wave Standard for Healthcare, Retail and Live-stock Visibility Networks; IEEE P1902.1 Standard to Offer Local Network Protocol for Thousands of Low-Cost Radio Tags Having a Long Battery Life. *2007 North American Supply Chain Visibility Solutions Technology Innovation of the Year Award*. Frost&Sullivan.

Uskela, S. (2001). All IP Architectures for Cellular Networks. In *Proceedings of Second International Conference on 3G Mobile Communication Technologies* (pp.180-185).

Wu, T.-Y., & Chao, H.-C. (2008). Mobile e-Learning for Next Generation Communication Environment. *International Journal of Distance Education Technologies*, *6*(4), 1–13.

Wu, T.-Y., Wu, J.-C., & Weng, W.-F. (2008, September 10-12). Improvement Security for RuBee Radio-WiMAX Mesh Networks. *The 5th International Conference on Mobile Technology, Application & Systems (Mobility Conference 2008), Ilan, Taiwan.*

Yang, S. J. H., & Chen, I. Y. L. (2006). Providing Context Aware Learning Services to Learners with Portable Devices. *Advanced Learning Technologies, 2006. Sixth International Conference on 5-7 July 2006* (pp. 840-842).

Zhao, G., & Yang, Z. (2005). Learning Resource Adaptation and Delivery Framework for Mobile Learning. *Frontiers in Education, 2005. FIE '05. Proceedings 35th Annual Conference*.

Chapter 19
A Methodology for Developing Learning Objects for Web Course Delivery

Karen Stauffer
Athabasca University, Canada

Fuhua Lin
Athabasca University, Canada

Marguerite Koole
Athabasca University, Canada

ABSTRACT

This article presents a methodology for developing learning objects for web-based courses using the IMS Learning Design (IMS LD) specification. We first investigated the IMS LD specification, determining how to use it with online courses and the student delivery model, and then applied this to a Unit of Learning (UOL) for online computer science courses. We developed an editor and runtime environment to apply the IMS LD to a UOL. We then explored the prospect for advancement of the basic IMS LD UOL. Finally, we discussed how to construct ontology-based software agents to use with the learning objects created with the IMS LD Units of Learning.

INTRODUCTION

There has been research effort directed far and wide towards defining learning objects, their standards, and building tools for developing web-based courses using learning objects with standards such as the IMS Learning Design (IMS LD) specification (Koper & Olivier, 2004; Paquette et al., 2005). However, at the time this research was undertaken, in early 2004, locating a runtime environment for learning objects that would work with these standards was a much more difficult task. In the beginning of the project, we needed to determine how to create learning objects, what the granularity of the learning objects should be, how to fit these learning objects together to form units in a course, and how to actually create learning object files using the IMS LD specification.

The need to create a runtime environment for the learning objects was the next facet to consider. Finally, because intelligent search and selection capabilities are possible with learning objects, the question of how to use agents and ontologies with learning objects was studied.

The goal of this research was, therefore, to develop a methodology for developing Extensible Markup Language- (XML) based learning objects for Web-based courses using the IMS LD specification and to design a runtime environment for these learning objects. The contributions of this project are the following: developing the means of creating Web-based courses using learning objects at various levels of granularity, developing the means of delivering courses online using learning objects, and initially exploring agents and learning objects using ontologies.

This chapter addresses the process of developing this methodology from the research stages through to the development and implementation of the IMS LD units of learning (UOL). As well, the final discussion looks at how the specification used for the learning objects can be extended by using intelligent agents and more advanced levels of the IMS LD.

LITERATURE REVIEW

One of the greatest strengths for institutions using learning objects lies in sharing and reducing redundancy in the distance learning development effort. There are a variety of standards based on XML that involve various organizations and aspects of learning objects. The standards for interoperability have been addressed by the Shareable Content Object Reference Model (SCORM) (http://www.adlnet.gov/scorm/). The IMS Global Learning Consortium, Inc. (IMS) (http://www.imsglobal.org/) and CanCore (http://www.cancore.ca) look after cataloguing learning objects for searches. Organizations such as the Multimedia Educational Resource for Learning and Online Teaching (MERLOT) (http://www.merlot.org/) and the Campus Alberta Repository of Educational Objects (CAREO) (http://www.careo.org/) address repository standards. Furthermore, the Learning Object Review Instrument (LORI) addresses learning objects evaluation to help users determine which ones are worthwhile and which ones are not (Nesbit & Li, 2004).

The IMS Learning Design specification was chosen for this project because it nicely addresses the issue of defining the learning object files in its simplest format at Level A of the specification. It also has the ability to expand to Levels B and C and offer many more interesting and interactive capabilities. Koper and Olivier (2004) describe the IMS LD UOL as containing the learning objects and services that are needed in the process of learning and teaching. At the time of the study, there were tools being developed to work with the IMS LD specification, with the most promising tools under development, specifically CopperCore (http://coppercore.sourceforge.net/) and Reusable Learning Object Authoring and Delivery (RELOAD) (http://www.reload.ac.uk/). These tools are now available in stable release from these websites.

As well, the IMS LD can be enhanced with the Learning Object Metadata (LOM), defined by the Institute of Electrical and Electronics Engineers (IEEE) (http://ltsc.ieee.org/wg12/20020612-Final-LOM-Draft.html), to enable expansion of the specification for more advanced methodology using the created learning objects. The IMS LD specification has future development potential in the integration of ontologies through the W3C Web Ontology Working Group (http://www.w3.org/TR/owl-features/). This would allow the use of software agents in supporting both developers and learners (Koper & Olivier, 2004; Richards, 2002). Finally, using ontologies could provide the model of the conceptual structures of learning objects and Web courseware authoring (Aroyo, Dicheva, & Cristea, 2002).

METHODOLOGY

Analysis and Design

The IMS LD specification describes a unit of study which defines the learning actions that satisfy any number of related learning objectives. The use of the IMS LD along with a runtime application is described as similar to HTML being recognized in a web browser (Tattersall et al., 2003). Also, the IMS LD describes how to structure the course materials to define the roles, methods, and resources of the UOL (McAndrew et al., 2004). McAndrew et al. (2004) suggested that a method to template the basic IMS LD implementation would be useful, in that replicating methods for the required instructional design model could be created. This is the model that has been used for this project.

Learning objects that make up a UOL can vary widely in granularity. A top level learning object would be the UOL itself (either a unit or section) with finer granularity learning objects being contained within the UOL. Consequently, due to varying levels of supplied context, the learning objects that make up an IMS LD UOL will differ in their usefulness as reusable resources.

The steps for getting started, recommended in IMS (2003), provide detailed guidelines for the analysis and design phases of the IMS LD development. These phases include the use case narrative, the Unified Modeling Language (UML) Activity Diagram, composition of XML document instance, and the required inclusion of resources using the IMS Content Packaging specification. The first step in the design of a learning design is the use case narrative (IMS, 2003).

Since there is only one role defined, that of the independent learner, the activities will not need to be sorted into separate role parts. The student can choose any, or all, of the activities related to the UOL. The activities that fall under the learning objectives are encapsulated so that learning activities that include learning objectives can themselves be considered learning objects (and, therefore, can be reused outside of this instance of the IMS LD). All learning activities consist of elements within the IMS LD XML document and describe the various course items defined in the instructional design model in computer science courses at Athabasca University. These course items consist of the commentary, learning objectives, readings, exercises, answers to exercises, key terms, and unit activities (defined here as simple learning objects). In terms of learning objects, the UOL is itself a learning object. The UOL contains other learning objects in the form of both simple learning objects and more complex learning objects composed of learning objectives encapsulated with related course items, such as readings, exercises, answers, and simple learning objects.

The learning activities are then incorporated into the learning structures. Any simple learning objects added are further defined inside the environment's container. The methods container defines how the learning structures are assigned to roles and acted out (IMS, 2003). This insures that the instructional design recommendations for computer science courses are being carried out at the content creation stage. The UML Activity Diagram for this is shown in Figure 1.

Creation of the XML Document

The next step involves creating the XML document based on the narrative and UML diagram. The method element contains the play, act, and role parts. The act elements are run sequentially, with the role parts run in parallel. If there is more than one play element, they are run in parallel (such as when a course is running in both distance learning or blended delivery). Role parts are the links to the activity-structure, activity, or environment. An activity-structure is assigned to a role at a specific point in the learning process (IMS, 2003). In the case of the computer science course development, the assignment is predetermined to

Figure 1. UML activity diagram

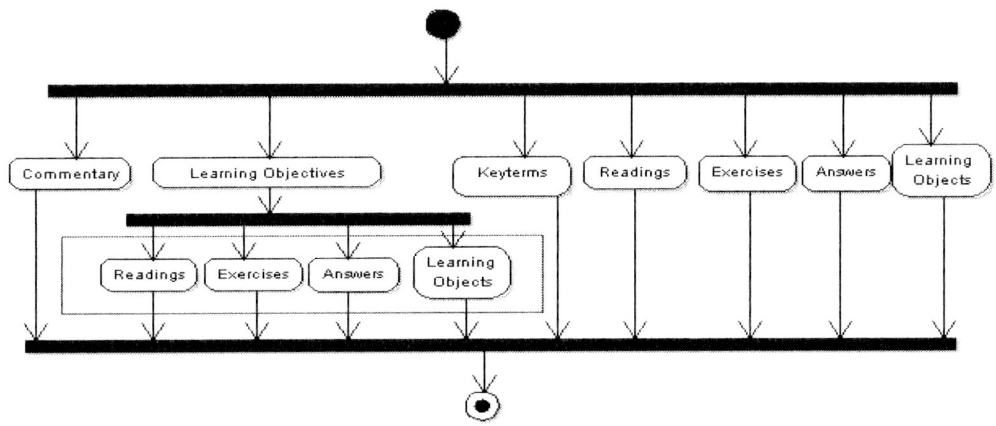

be the individual learner. The components of the learning design are reusable, and to foster this reuse, references are used extensively, instead of nesting elements together. In creating the XML document for the course units of learning, the fixed methodology of online delivery to individualized learners determined the process of the design. Since the roles and methods are based on the independent learner, this allowed a standard definition for all the developed learning design documents. The methods container contains the entire UOL as the play, with the single role of individualized learner. This will be consistent from one UOL to the next, and therefore formed our template for creation of the rest of the IMS LD. Creating a UOL involved using this template to first generate the title for the learning design, and then determining the activities, activity-structures, and environments contained in the component container of the LD. The activities that are performed are any of the commentaries, readings, exercises, answers to exercises, or activities in the form of learning objects.

Once the IMS LD document was defined, the actual physical files needed to be referenced. This was done by including the specification with the IMS Content Packaging Specification. These two specifications work together within a manifest file to incorporate both a complex objectives-based learning structure, as well as the inclusion of the usable content (Stauffer, 2005).

Learning activities containing learning objectives are generally self-contained references to the items required for that learning objective. These could include readings, exercises, exercise answers, and learning objects (activities), and are defined in the recommended instructional design at Athabasca University. Each learning activity that has learning objectives included is encapsulated so that it is potentially an individual learning object and can be displayed individually or reused. This has implications for future use of intelligent agents once the LOM metadata has been added. The lowest level learning objects are referenced as environment elements in the IMS LD. These learning objects will reside in the Digital Reading Room (http://library.athabascau.ca/drr) repository of the library of Athabasca University, which provides consistency and documentation of the learning objects, and improves their capability for reuse.

Development of the LMS Editor and Runtime Environment

The IMS LD editor that was created for this project is a form-based servlet that creates the

Figure 2. System design flowchart

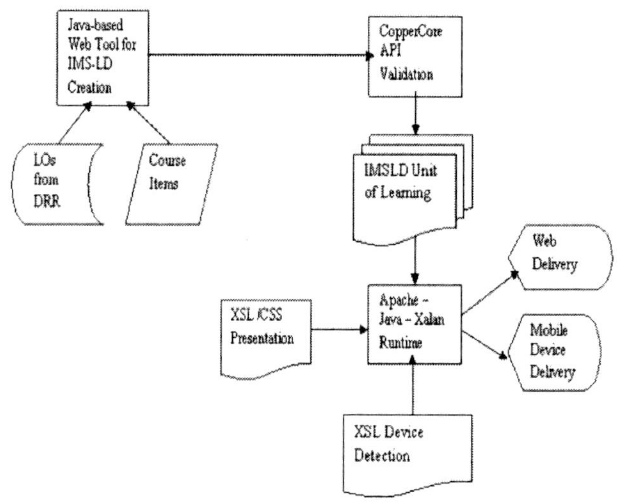

units of learning specific to Web-based courses. It was developed on a Linux platform using Apache/Tomcat Web services. The planning process overview of the system for the software project started with the design of the editor to create course files from course items and learning objects, and a runtime capable of displaying the files for the IMS LD UOLs. The UOL created by the editor can be validated with the CopperCore API to ensure that it meets the IMS LD specification standards. The UOL is then passed to the Web server where the presentation of the UOL is looked after by Cascading Stylesheets (CSS) and Extensible Stylesheet Language Transformation (XSLT) stylesheets. Device detection is done at this stage to determine the device requirements for the stylesheets. Figure 2 shows the system design flowchart of this process.

The editor was designed to be a simple, form-based editor that would allow the user to input the items that make up a Web-based course. Instructional design considerations regarding the unit commentary, learning objectives, exercises, answers to exercises, and activities-based learning objects were all incorporated in the design of the editor and the runtime. The user interface was meant to be intuitive and easy to use, while still allowing enough flexibility to adapt different learning approaches in the development tool.

Since each UOL describes either a unit or section and is developed separately by the editor, one UOL can be run independently from others. The physical files in a UOL include the *imsmanifest.xml* Java Server Pages (JSP) files and related Extensible HyperText Markup Language (XHTML) files for that UOL. Each UOL is contained within its own separate directory. A course directory is also created to list the course units, but this directory does not include an *imsmanifest.xml* file and does not in itself become a UOL. The entire UOL is contained within a directory structure that contains the *imsmanifest.xml* file and accompanying resource files. Once the UOL is created and validated, it is then passed to the JSP/XSLT-based runtime environment. The runtime enforces the instructional design recommendations for computer science courses at Athabasca University. The visual design aspects of the UOL are handled within the CSS and XSLT stylesheets. The use of CSS and XSLT for presentation used with Java and JSP creates a dynamic presentation of the course content that allows for device detection for stylesheet determination.

Figure 3. Design for CreateUOL (Presentation Layer) and detailed design for UOL (Content Layer)

```
String getRequest ()
{  start HTTPSession
   display Menu (course level) }
if Menu displayed {
  if (action request for course creation)
    display course creation Menu
  if (action request course edit)
    display Unit menu
  if (action request for new Unit)
   create new unit and display Unit Items menu
 if (action request for edit Unit)
   display Unit Items menu     }
```

```
String getRequest ()
{  start HTTPSession;  display Menu (Unit Items level)   }
if Menu displayed {
if (action request for add Item) display add Item menu
if (action request for save Item)  update item and display Unit Items menu
if (action request for update Item)   update item and display Unit Items menu
 if (action request for new Section)  create new section and display Section Items menu
if (action request for add Item) display add Item menu
if (action request for save Item)  update item and display Section Items menu
if (action request for update Item)   update item and display Section Items menu  }
```

The development of the editor was separated into two implementations: content and presentation. The presentation layer of the editor creates the directory and adds the files and titles to the UOL. The content layer then works directly on the XML development of the *imsmanifest.xml* file and the resource files associated with the UOL. Because of this partition, the detailed design of both modules then involved separating the methods required to build the unit and section directories into the presentation level and the methods required to create the XML/XHTML into the content layer (UOL Servlet). The basic outline of the detailed design model can be viewed in Figure 3.

Exploring Ontologies and Agents with the IMS LD

With the development of computer science courses using the IMS LD specification and the concurrent development of learning objects, the potential is open for further advancements, such as the use of intelligent agents. There are constantly new technologies emerging for IMS LD, and many of these can be used to advance the basic IMS LD UOL developed with this project. This is discussed further in the discussion portion of this chapter.

RESULTS

The IMS LD editor and runtime are based on instructional and visual design recommendations for computer science courses at Athabasca University. (In 2007, this system is in full implementation for development and delivery of the study-guide-portion of the computer science course materials in the School of Computing and Information Systems at Athabasca University.) The resulting UOL is not readily adaptable for use outside of Athabasca University because it was developed using the instructional design model that is specific to the computer science courses. The user is restricted to the documents allowed by the editor. However, because these documents are not restrictive in themselves as XHTML files, they can include any content type that is desired. There is also the ability to link to either outside learning objects or to upload other files locally, including HTML, graphics, program code, and other document formats. The display of other documents is handled by the browser and not the XSLT stylesheets.

The Editor

The actual editor is a simple, form-based web application. The user is given a series of menus for choosing a course to create or edit. The user then continues on to either create a new unit or

Figure 4. Screen shot of IMS LD editor

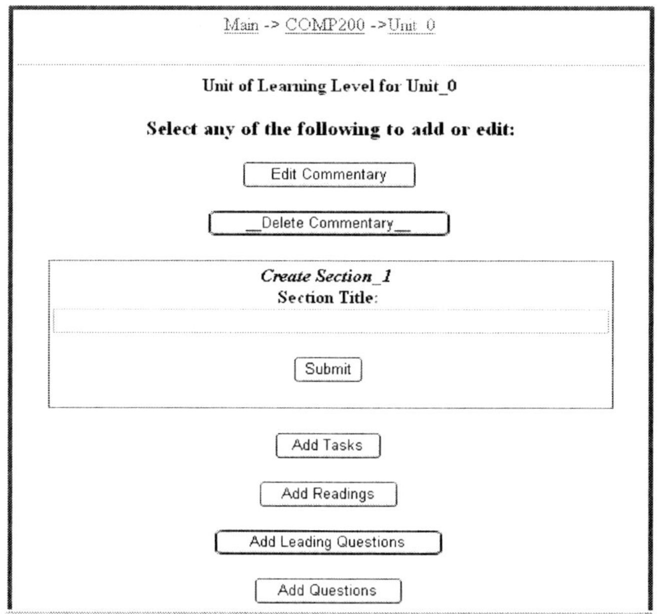

Figure 5. Screen shot view of runtime sample

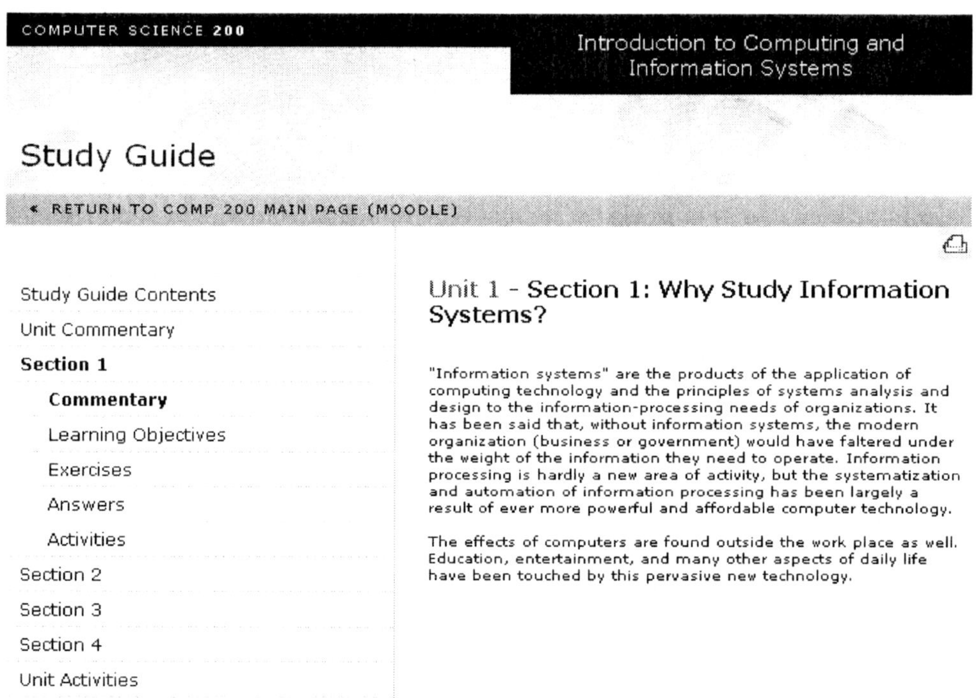

select a unit to edit. All of the previous steps are part of the presentation layer of the servlet. Once inside the Unit level, the user is interacting with a unique UOL, and therefore is working within the content layer. Figure 4 shows a screen shot of the content layer at the Unit level in the IMS LD editor developed.

An Example

Computer Science 200: Introduction to Computing and Information Systems is a course at Athabasca University in Canada that is designed as a program introduction for computer science courses. Students in this course use a combination of locally-installed course materials, including an online textbook, and links to external sites. A number of course enhancements, including applets and a software lab, are also part of the course materials. A working demonstration of the IMD LD editor is available at http://scis.athabascau.ca/servlet/Indse.createUOL. Figure 5 shows a screen shot of the runtime with Unit 1 – Section 1 learning objectives displayed.

DISCUSSIONS

There are constantly emerging new technologies for IMS LD and many of these can be used to advance the basic IMS LD UOLs developed with this project. The RELOAD editor can be used with the UOL files as a method to add Learning LOM to describe the various learning objects. The IMS LD has place holders specified at different levels for metadata addition using the LOM specification (IMS, 2003). This can occur from the top IMS LD element, down through to the lower level elements. In this way, the granularity of learning objects described by the LOM can include unit, section, learning-objectives-based and simple learning objects. Moreover, the LOM introduces nine categories of metadata and can be applied to each learning object in the IMS LD. In the case of computer science courses, it would be beneficial to determine the learning objects with the greatest potential for reuse and apply the LOM metadata to these. This could be an entire unit or section, a subset of learning objectives, or a single simple learning object.

Protégé OWL and Ontology Development

Qin (2003) created an ontology tool that represents the elements of the LOM and how they relate to each other (Qin & Hernandez, 2004). This tool also provides the full description of the classes and slots within each of the elements. The information derived from this documentation was valuable to this project, as it can be inserted into the Protégé Editor (http://protege.stanford.edu/) as the ontology representing the LOM.

The Protégé Editor also can be extended to include Java API plug-ins, specifically those to work in ontology development. The Ontology Bean Generator is one of these extensions. Its purpose is to create Java class files that can be used with the JAVA Agent DEvelopment Framework (JADE) environment (http://jade.tilab.com/). This requires adding the Ontology Bean Generator class and property files into the Protégé plug-in directory to load it into Protégé. Once in place, it can generate JADE-compliant Java classes that can be used in agent applications. The connection between the IMS LD UOL files and the ontology development using Protégé then becomes clear. The Ontology Bean Generator is used to create a group of Java class files that are JADE-compliant. The generated Java files can be used with a JADE agent application to supply the ontology information between the agent application and the IMS LD UOL files that have been enhanced with the LOM. The Java files created by the Protégé/Ontology Bean Generator can be compiled and used with the classes of a JADE-based agent application. Each class file represents an element of the LOM and has methods that represent the slots and relationships of each element class.

CONCLUSION AND FUTURE WORK

The use of the IMS LD to develop learning objects and UOLs for online courses has introduced some new possibilities for online course delivery. Enabling course creation using XML and IMS LD standards is a small step towards greater advancements in online learning systems. The course development process developed in this project separates the content of the course materials from the presentation, allowing the course materials the flexibility to be delivered to a variety of platforms and devices. Using the IMS LD specification, with shareable content in the form of learning objects, enhanced with the possibility of ontology-based agents, may well provide a much more individualized approach to learning.

The editor and runtime can be enhanced to enable the richer content structure of the more complex IMS LD levels. In this project, we focused on only the Level A of the IMS LD. Future developments at this level can be enhanced to allow grouped and collaborative learning roles that interact at specified points and with specified environments and services. Further enhancements involving the development of middleware applications composed of intelligent agents would enable interaction with the learning objects metadata for searching and collecting appropriate objects, as well as delivering learning objects to the learner based on content requests and specifications.

ACKNOWLEDGMENT

We thank Daniel Burgos, Fred de Vries, Rob Koper, Colin Tattersall, et al from the Open University of the Netherlands for their encouragement and great technical support.

REFERENCES

Aroyo, L., Dicheva, D., & Cristea, A. (2002, June). *Ontological support for Web courseware authoring.* Paper presented at ITS 2002, the Proceedings of the 6th International Conference on Intelligent Tutoring Systems, San Sebastian, Spain.

IMS Global Learning Consortium, Inc. (2003). *IMS Learning Design Best Practice and Implementation Guide.* Retrieved from http://www.imsproject.org/learningdesign/ldv1p0/imsld_bestv1p0.html

Koper, R., & Olivier, B. (2004). Representing the learning design of UOLs. *Educational Technology & Society, 7*(3), 97-111.

McAndrew, P., Woods, W., Little, A., Weller, M., Koper, R., & Vogten, H. (2004). *Implementing learning design to support Web-based learning.* Paper presented at The Tenth Australian World Wide Web Conference, Gold Coast, Australia.

Nesbit, J., & Li, J. (2004, July). *Web-based tools for learning object evaluation.* Paper presented at the International Conference on Education and Information Systems: Technologies and Applications, Orlando, FL.

Paquette, G., Marino, O., de la Teja, I., Léonard, J., Lundgren-Cayrol, K., & Contamines, J. (2005). Implementation and deployment of the IMS learning design specification. *Canadian Journal of Learning and Technology, 31*(2).

Qin, J., & Hernandez, N. (2004, May). *Ontological representation of learning objects: Building interoperable vocabulary and structures.* Paper presented at the Proceedings of the 13th international World Wide Web conference on Alternate track papers & posters, New York, NY.

Richards, G. (2002). Editorial: The challenges of the learning object paradigm. *Canadian Journal of Learning and Technology, 28*(3).

Stauffer, K. (2005). *XML, IMS LD, and learning object development for Web course delivery.* Unpublished master's thesis, Athabasca University, Athabasca, Alberta, Canada.

Tattersall, C., Manderveld, J., Hummel, H., Sloep, P., Koper, R., & de Vries, F. (2003). IMS Learning Design Frequently Asked Questions. *Educational Technology Expertise Centre.* Retrieved from http://dspace.learningnetworks.org/retrieve/206/IMS+Learning+Design+FAQ+1.0.pdf

This work was previously published in International Journal of Distance Education Technologies, Vol. 6, Issue 3, edited by Q. Jin, pp. 58-68, copyright 2008 by IGI Publishing (an imprint of IGI Global).

Chapter 20
A Chinese Interactive Feedback System for a Virtual Campus

Jui-Fa Chen
Tamkang University, Taiwan

Wei-Chuan Lin
Tak Ming College, Taiwan

Chih-Yu Jian
Tamkang University, Taiwan

Ching-Chung Hung
Tamkang University, Taiwan

ABSTRACT

Considering the popularity of the Internet, an automatic interactive feedback system for E-learning websites is becoming increasingly desirable. However, computers still have problems understanding natural languages, especially the Chinese language, firstly because the Chinese language has no space to segment lexical entries (its segmentation method is more difficult than that of English) and secondly because of the lack of a complete grammar in the Chinese language, making parsing more difficult and complicated. Building an automated Chinese feedback system for special application domains could solve these problems. This paper proposes an interactive feedback mechanism in a virtual campus that can parse, understand and respond to Chinese sentences. This mechanism utilizes a specific lexical database according to the particular application. In this way, a virtual campus website can implement a special application domain that chooses the proper response in a user friendly, accurate and timely manner.

INTRODUCTION

The easiest way to communicate to users is to talk to them in their natural language. Considering the popularity of the Internet, an automated interactive feedback system for e-learning Web sites is becoming increasingly desirable. However, it still is difficult for a computer to understand the meaning of some natural languages. At present a three-year old child can understand and respond to languages better than a computer can. To understand the natural language, a computer must be trained to understand a single sentence. Then, it would need to be trained to analyze longer sentences or paragraphs. In principle, there are at least two skills that a computer should be able to apply to a single sentence:

1. Defining the meaning of each word in the sentence.
2. Transforming the linear structure of a sentence into another structure that represents the meaning of that sentence.

The first step of processing a Chinese sentence is seeking the meaning of each lexicon in a dictionary. However, there can be many meanings for each lexicon, and the computer must have the ability to choose the right one. Even if that is accomplished, it is still difficult for the computer to process the Chinese sentence because there are no spaces used to segment the lexicon. Therefore, a segmentation method is needed before parsing the Chinese sentences.

The second step of understanding a Chinese sentence is transforming the segmented lexicons into a structure that can be understood by a computer. In general, the transformation procedure can be divided into three parts:

A. Syntactic analysis procedure: In this procedure, the input lexicon is transformed into a specific structure that represents the relationship between lexicons. However, not all the combinations of lexicons of a sentence are legal. The computer must eliminate the illegal combinations to ensure a correct performance.
B. Semantic analysis procedure: This procedure obtains the meaning of the sentence from the established structure. The obtained meaning is a unit of knowledge representation, which can be mapped to the corresponding object or event in the actual world.
C. Pragmatics analysis procedure: This procedure determines the real purpose of the sentences and gives the appropriate response to users.

The remainder of this paper is laid out as followed. The next section discusses the related works on syntax and semantic analysis, followed by a description of the proposed four subsystems of segmentation, syntactic analysis, semantic analysis, and the response subsystems. The next section provides some examples to show the implementation of the proposed method. Finally, there is conclusion and some future works.

REVIEW OF RELATED WORKS

Link Grammar Technology

Most sentences in a natural language are structured so that arcs that connect words may not cross each other. This phenomenon is called planarity in the link grammar system (Sleator & Temperley, 1991). A link grammar consists of a set of words and has a linking requirement. The linking requirements of each word are contained in a dictionary. To illustrate the linking requirements, Figure 1 shows a simple dictionary for the words "a," "the," "cat," "mouse," and "chased." The linking requirement of each word is represented by the Figure 1 above the word.

Each of the lettered boxes is a connector which is satisfied when it is "plugged into" a compat-

Figure 1. Words and connectors in the dictionary

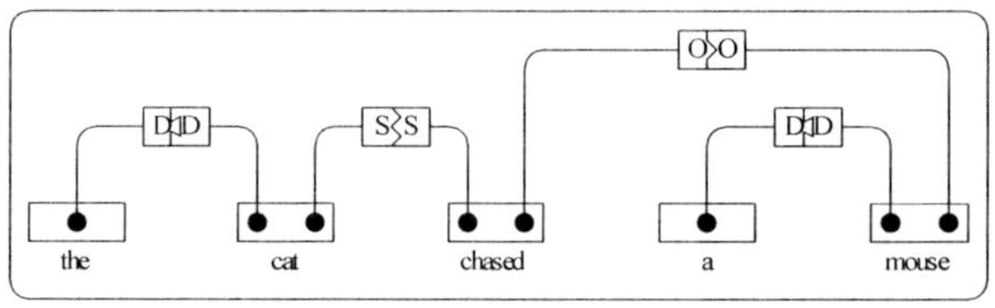

Figure 2. The simplified form of Figure 1

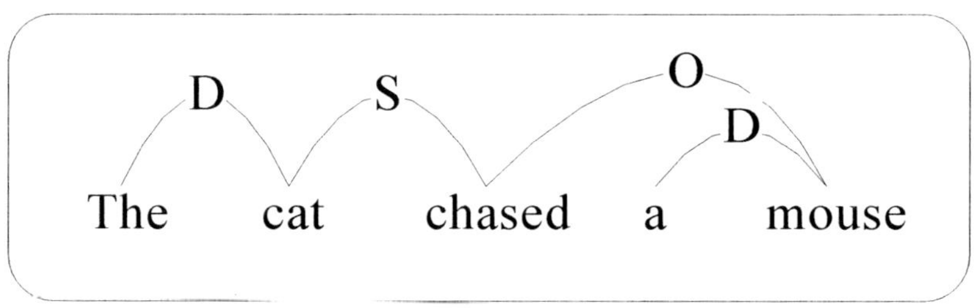

ible connector, as indicated by its shape. If the mating end of a connector is drawn facing to the right, then its mate must be to its right facing to the left. Exactly one of the connectors attached to a given black dot must be satisfied. Thus, the "cat" requires a D connector to its left and either an O connector to its left or an S connector to its right. Plugging a pair of connectors together corresponds to drawing a link between that pair of words.

Figure 2 is the simplified form of Figure 1 and shows that "the cat chased a mouse" is part of the language. Table 1 encodes the linking requirements of the example in Figure 2.

The link grammar dictionary consists of a collection of entries, each of which defines the linking requirements of one or more words. These requirements are specified by a formula of connectors combined by the binary associative operators & and or. Precedence is specified by parentheses. A connector is simply a character string ending in + or -.

Memory-Based Parsing System

Most methods of semantic analysis first recognize the verb of a sentence and then determine the correctness on the semantics of lexical entries around the verb. Memory-based parsing (Chung, & Moldovan, 1993, 1994a, 1994b; Kim & Moldovan, 1993) also begins with the restrictions of a verb to determine the correctness of subject and object. The memory-based parsing system consists of four modules:

Table 1. The words and linking requirements in a dictionary

Words	Formula
a the	D+
cat mouse	D- & (O- or S+)
Chased	S- & O+

- Concept sequence layer: Keeps the restrictions of the subject and object of each verb for both syntax and semantics.
- Syntactic layer: Keeps all parts of speech for comparing the syntactic restrictions.
- Semantic concept hierarchy: Defines the relationship of all nouns, and is used for verifying the semantic restrictions.
- Instance layer: Contains the lexical entries of a sentence typed by the user.

Figure 3. Part of knowledge base used for processing: "The Shining Path"

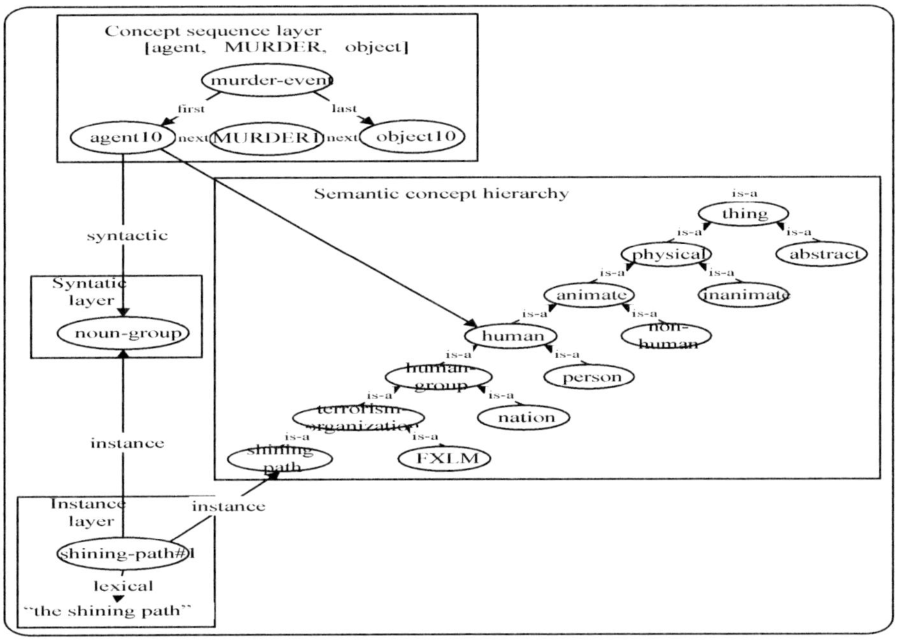

Figure 3 shows an example of a memory-based parsing with a concept sequence [agent, MURDER, object] for murder-event. At the top of the knowledge base is the concept sequence layer, which consists of concept sequence roots and elements. The semantic concept hierarchy and syntactic layer connect concept sequence elements with concept instances in the instance layer. Concept instances are produced from phrasal inputs and are connected to the corresponding syntactic category and semantic concept nodes. The result of parsing is represented by connecting instances of concept sequence roots and corresponding concepts in the instance layer.

THE PROPOSED SYSTEM

Overview

There are many learners in a virtual campus, and each learner has his or her own preference. Although the search goal can be found by a belief network, as considered in customization, using only the default category to analyze is insufficient. When a learner logs onto a virtual campus, if he or she is an existing learner, the system could load his learning profile to achieve the customization. If the learner is new, the system could administer a quiz to determine an initial learning profile. The flowchart is shown in Figure 4

The proposed Chinese interactive feedback system (Chen, Lin, & Jian, 2003a, 2003b, 2003c; Chen, Lin, Jian, & Hung, 2005) is divided into four sub-systems: the segmentation system, syntactic analysis system, semantic analysis system, and response system. Thus, learners can use Chinese sentences to interact with the virtual campus. When the learners input Chinese sentences, the segmentation system separates the learner's input sentences and gives the appropriate part of speech for each segmented lexical entry. The syntactic analysis system parses these segmented lexical entries to judge whether the sentence is legal and gives the syntactic part of each lexical entry. The semantic analysis system judges the correctness of the semantics and provides a semantic learning method based on the learner's habits. Finally, a

Figure 4. Flowchart of feedback system

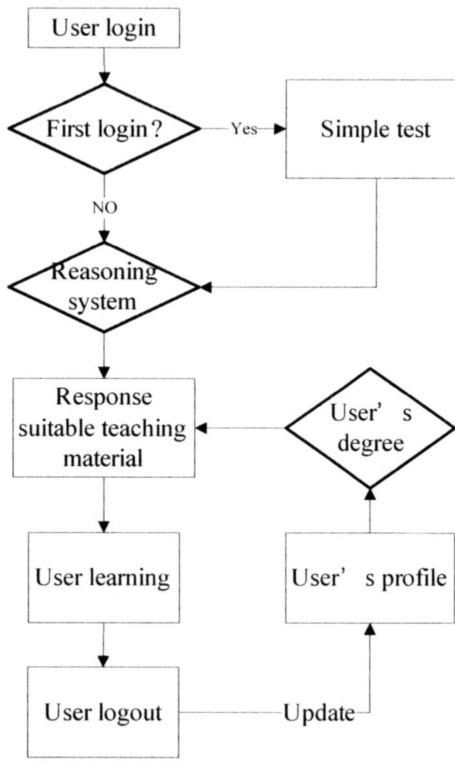

response system gives the learner the response result according to the encoding of the input sentence.

Segmentation System

One difference between the Chinese and English language is that the Chinese language has no obvious separation to segment the lexical entry. Therefore a segmentation method to parse the Chinese language is necessary. Figure 5 shows the architecture of the Segmentation System.

The segmentation system structure is divided into four sub-systems: the segmentation system, corpora-comparing system, keyword in context comparing system, and weighted calculation method (Chen, Lin, & Jian, 2003a). These sub-systems are explained as follows:

1. Segmentation: Segmentation separates the user's input sentences and compares the separated units with those obtained from the corpora-comparing system.
2. Corpora-comparing system: This system includes two steps: corpora-comparing and

Figure 5. The architecture of the segmentation system

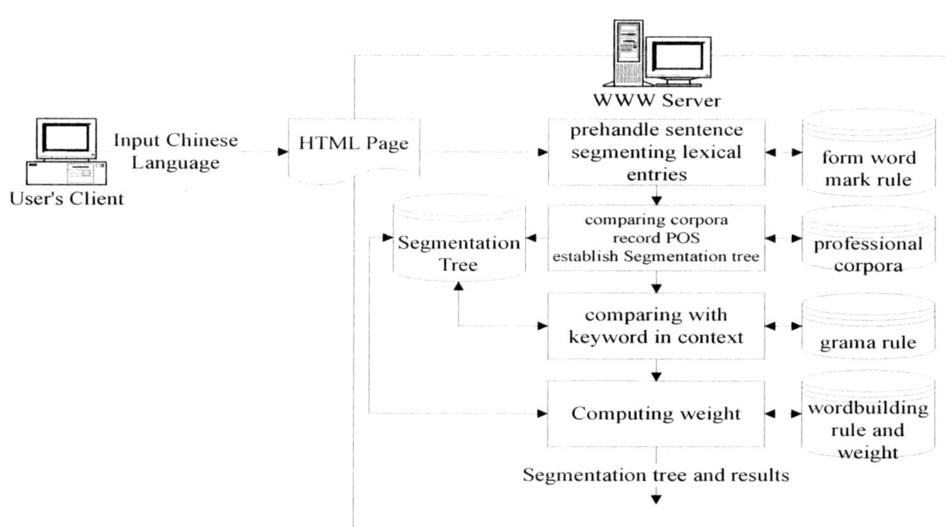

Figure 6. Segmentation system's flow chart

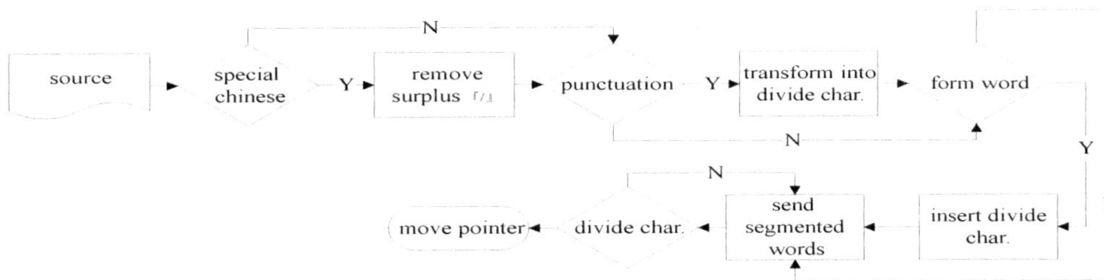

part-of-speech(POS) saving. It compares the receiving strings with those in the corpora and saves the results to build a segmentation tree.

3. Keyword in context comparing system: After building a segmentation tree, the system compares the POS with the keyword in context according to the grammar rules and deletes the improper segmentation tree. This mechanism is divided into the Unknown Word Judgment System and Context-proofreading System.
4. Weighted calculation system: Because there may be more than one kind of segmentation result, each result's weighted value is computed to find the most proper one. The segmentation result with the largest weighted value is the most suitable result.

Segmentation

There is no space between lexical entries in the Chinese language to help segmentation. Chinese characters are composed of two continuous bytes in representation. The system judges whether this word is Chinese code when segmenting sentences to put the pointer's displacement in the best place. However, in transmitting, some special Chinese words have a special 『\』 inserted after transmitting through the network browser. The system would remove the 『\』 prior to segmenting the sentences.

The main functions of the segmentation system are:

1. The consideration of special Chinese words in the user's input sentences serves to avoid punctuation-transferring mistakes
2. The transfer of punctuation in the user's input sentences serves to obtain the same dividing code. The system splits the continuous Chinese words and numbers them into strings and adds a dividing code both in front of and behind the strings. The system also adds a dividing code behind the empty word of the user's input sentence. In addition the system also splits the user's input sentence and compares the segmented lexical entries with the corpora-comparing system. Figure 6 shows the segmentation system process.

Most Chinese lexicons possess at most six characters. The segmentation length of a Chinese sentence should be limited to avoid segmenting a sentence into many impossible ways. For example, a sentence composed of n words should have 2^{n-1} possible segmentations. A maximum matching (Chen & Liu, 1992) mechanism is used to segment a sentence. Basically, the maximum matching method compares a string started at the kth character with a lexical database and finds out all possible segmentations. If $C(k)$, $C(k)\_C(k+1)$, $C(k)\_C(k+1)\_C(k+2)$ are stored in the lexical database, the maximum matching method would choose the longest word and continue with $C(k+3)$. Because the length of most of the Chinese lexicons do not exceed six characters, the maximum length of a word in a sentence is set to six characters.

Table 2. Corpora data structure

Numbers of words	Context	POS	Types	Word frequency

Figure 7. Unknown word judgment system process

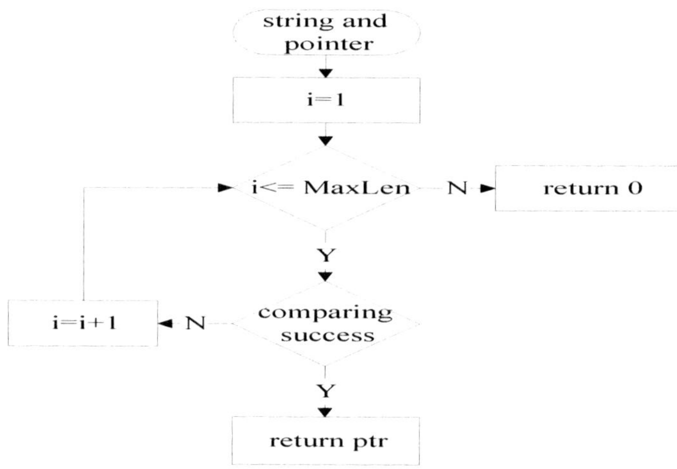

Corpora-Comparing System

After the segmentation system separates the sentences, it compares string length and context. The system records all matching POSs and adds the information of the lexical entries to a segmentation tree. If no POSs match, the system feeds back a false value and recalls the unknown word judgment sub-system to determine whether this word is an unknown word. If the lexical entry is determined by the system to be an unknown word, then the entry is saved into the segmentation tree. Because most new unknown words are proper names, the system often sets the POSs of these unknown words to be temporary nouns, and continues processing the following set of strings. If the system still cannot find the corresponding POS in the corpus database of one to six continuous words or cannot find the proper unknown word after processing by the unknown word judgment system, it views these six continuous words as an unknown word and adds the unknown word into the segmentation tree.

The corpora structure used in the system is shown in Table 2. The saved data format contains the numbers of words, context, POS, types, and word probability. They are explained as follows:

A. **Numbers of words:** To speed up the comparing of the corpora, the information of the numbers of lexical entries are recorded so that the system does not have to search the entire database, greatly improving the efficiency of the system.
B. **Context:** Refers to the recorded context of the lexical entry.
C. **POS:** Records the POS of the lexical entry. If the number of the POS is larger than one, the system separates the sentence with "," as a divided symbol.
D. **Types:** This paper is focused on mutual conversation segmentations in the basic computer concept domain. Therefore, the type is used to mark the kind of special domain database that is used for the lexical entry.

Figure 8. Segmentation tree structure

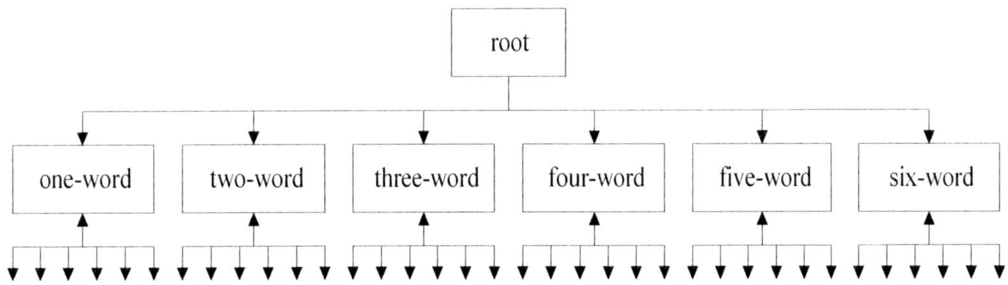

E. **Word frequency:** Shows how often the lexical entry has appeared in the equilibrium corpus database. The information is used primarily for weight calculation.

Unknown Word Judgment System

This system searches the segmented lexical entries for unknown words. After the system receives strings, it splits N continuous words continuously and compares them with the corpus database. If the proofreading is successful, the system feeds the first words of the lexical entry back to the position where the string engages. The system sets the string which is beyond the position of being an unknown word and saves it into a segmentation tree. If the system fails when compared, it feeds back 0 to show that this word is not an unknown word. Figure 7 shows the flow of the unknown word judgment system.

The Data Structure of the Segmentation Tree Node

The system adds the segmented lexical entry into the segmentation tree to speed up node searching. The segmentation tree structure can make data saving more flexible by increasing or decreasing segmentation nodes. The segmentation tree is a six node tree. The tree structure is shown in Figure 8. Every node in Figure 8 follows from zero to at most six sub-nodes which are added dynamically when compared with the corpora. The original input sentence connects the first node of the root to the following branches. In this way the system can dispose of space dynamically to save and display the segmentation results.

Every node of the segmentation tree is composed of the following node structure as shown in Figure 9. Each node records the information after the system searches the database which is convenient for the context-proofreading system and the weighted-calculating system.

The fields in Figure 9 are explained as follows:

A. **Context:** The context of the lexical entry.
B. **Length:** Records the length of the strings.
C. **Array of POS:** Records the POS of a lexical entry (up to six) with a pre-set value of an empty string.
D. **Result of database searching:** Records the searching result of this lexical entry. If the searching result is found from the corpus database, it is recorded as true. However, if it is an unknown word, it is recorded as false.
E. **Down-connection and up-connection:** Records the number of the upper or lower nodes, referring to the upward or downward lexical entry. If there is no up or down connection, it records 0. Because the system deals at most with six continuous words when segmenting sentences, the array size of the down-connecting is six and that of the up-connecting array is one.

Figure 9. Node data structure

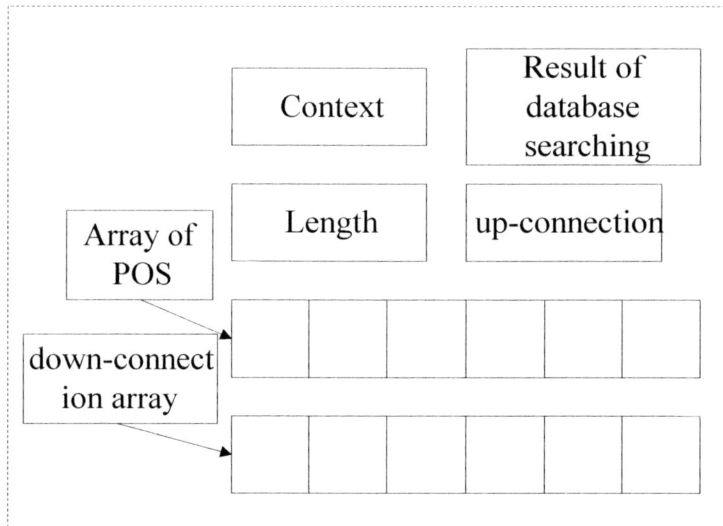

Context-Proofreading System

This system uses the segmentation tree built in the corpora-comparing system to evaluate the context according to the grammar recorded in the grammar principle database. This system deletes segmentation sub-trees which are not matched with the grammar and decides the POS which the lexical entry belongs to. When proceeding with the grammar proofreading, the system only compares the POS of the front lexical entry rather than proofreading the whole article so that the system can determine the POS of the lexical entry in the oral language conversation more correctly while increasing speed and flexibility of the judgment.

The main reason for adopting the method of judging the relationship of the grammar between the front and rear words is that grammar structure is usually not perfect in an oral language conversation. If the system uses only grammar rules it would find errors in determining the POS. In contrast, if the system checks only the relationship between the front and rear words, it would correctly determine the POS. The detailed procedure is shown in Figure 10.

Weighted-Calculation System

The weighted-calculation system is used to judge the correctness of segmentation results when there is more than one result after grammar analyzation, as a segmented Chinese sentence may have more than one suitable way for splitting. This system computes the weights according to the lexical entry building principle, with the segmentation result having the largest weight being the correct one. The process of the weighted calculation is listed as follows:

Weight = Weights of length * Weights of searching result * Word frequency

A. **Weights of length:** The longer lexical entry has a higher priority according to the lexical entry-building principle. Therefore, the longer the length the larger the weight .
B. **Weight of searching result:** The weight of the searching result changes based on whether this word is an unknown word or not. In principal, the weight of a known word is larger than that of an unknown word. However, according to the principle

Figure 10. The flow chart of the keyword in context comparing system

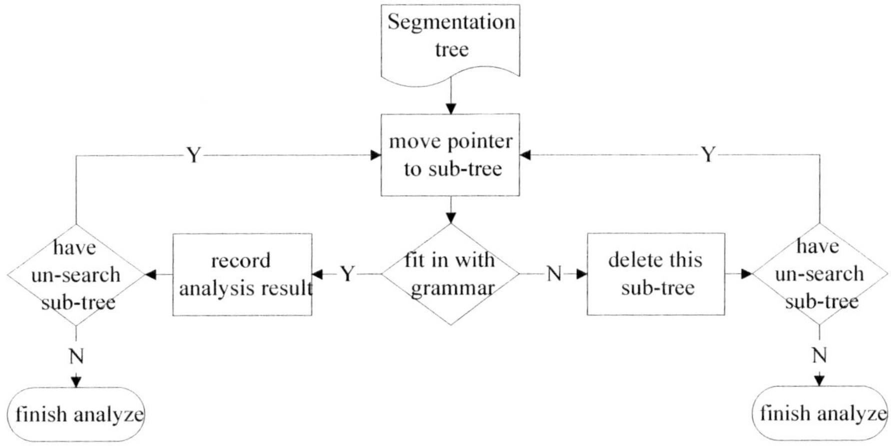

of long lexical entry privacy, the system sets the weight of an unknown word to be the same as N-continuous words. Therefore, the weight of an unknown word is only slightly larger than a one-continuous known word.

C. **Word frequency:** Shows how often the lexical entry appears in the equilibrium corpora. The more often the lexical entry appears, the higher frequency it has.

After calculating the weighted sum of all nodes on every branch the system can find the segmented result that is the most suitable for the lexical entry-building principle.

Syntactic Analysis System

The main function of the syntactic analysis system is to transform the lexical entries of the input sentence into a structure that can represent the relationship of these lexical entries. However, not all the input sentences are legal in syntax, and the system should provide a fault-tolerance mechanism. With a fault-tolerance mechanism, the system can tolerate common mistakes in general oral conversation and thereby increase the level of fluency in the conversation. Figure 11 shows the flowchart of the syntactic analysis system which utilizes the "Word-based Link Grammar" (Sleator & Temperley, 1991) as the parsing method of the syntax.

Word-Based Link Grammar

The method of the Word-based Link Grammar defines the linking rules on each lexical entry for making the link relations. The syntactic analysis system obtains the relations as the syntactic parts of each lexical entry. Table 3 shows the linking rules of each part of speech.

When the syntactic analysis system starts analyzing, it obtains the linking rules of each lexical entry from a dictionary and makes a link according to these linking rules. The parsing algorithm is shown as Algorithm 1.

Fault-Tolerance Mechanism

The sentences that have a syntax error usually appear in oral conversations and those sentences that are difficult to parse. Therefore, it is necessary for the syntactic analysis system to provide a fault-tolerance mechanism. The proposed syntactic analysis system provides the fault-tolerance mechanism by modifying the linking rules of interrelated lexical entries. Figure 12 shows an example of fault-tolerance processing by omitting the preposition "的".

Figure 11. Flowchart of the syntactic analysis system

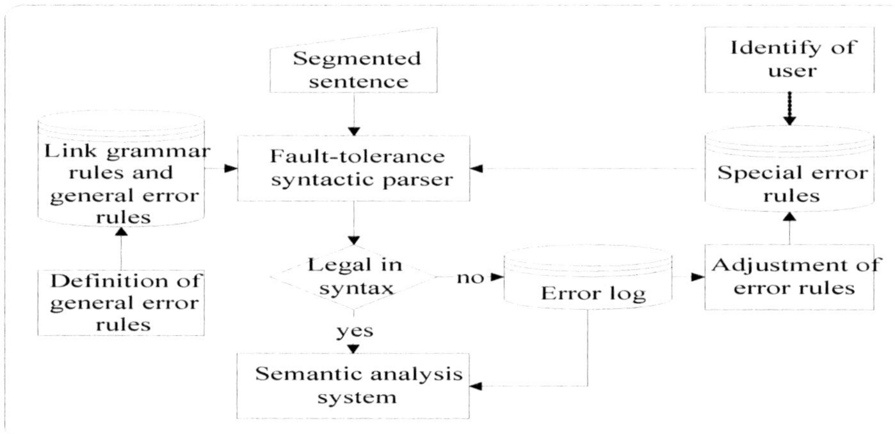

Table 3. The linking rules of each part of speech

part of speech	linking rules
Noun(N)	(S+ or O-)&(Q- or())&(@Adj- or ())&(Do- or ())&(Ds+ or ())&(Cn1+ or ())&(Cn2- or ())
Personal pronoun(Pa)	(S+ or O-)&(@Adj- or ())&(Ds+ or ())&(Cn1+ or ())&(Cn2- or ())
Demonstrative(Pb)	(Bs+ or Pq+)
Doubt pronoun(Pc)	(S+ or O-)
Quantifier (Q)	(num- or Pq- or (Pq- & num-))&(Q+)
Adjective(Adj)	(Adj+ or Bj-)&(Adva- or ())&(Noj- or ())&(Ca1+ or ())&(Ca2- or ())
Adverb-decorate adjective(Adva)	(Adva+)
Adverb-decorate verb(Advb)	(Advb+)
Negation(No)	(Noj+ or Nov+)
Auxiliary verb(Hv)	(Hv+)
Transitive verb(Vt)	(Hv- or ())&(S-)&(O+)&(Advb- or())
Intransitive verb(Vi)	(Hv- or ())&(S-)&(Advb- or())
Preposition(D)	(Ds- & Do+)
Conjunction(C)	(Ca1- & Ca2+)or(Cn1- & Cn2+)
Indicative(Bv)	(Bs- or S-)&(O+ or ())&(Bj+ or ())

In the first block of Figure 12, after the segmentation system process, the correct Chinese sentence “我的朋友” is segmented into “我”, “的”, and “朋友” and their parts of speech are “Pa”, “D”, and “N” respectively. The system obtains the linking rules of each lexical entry from the dictionary and checks if the linkage of each lexical entry is correct. However, in the second block of Figure 12, because of the omis-

Algorithm 1. Syntactic analysis system

```
Comment:
Sentence: sentence inputted by user
Token: segmented lexical entry
First_Token: first lexical entry of sentence
Last_Token: last lexical entry of sentence
Token_Link: flag of whether the lexical entry is linked or not
Link_Grammar: linking rules of lexical entry
Disjuncts: linking rules in disjunctive form
Syntactic_Error: syntactic error flag
Right_Links: right connectors of linking rules
Left_Links: left connectors of linking rules
Syntactic_Part: syntactic part
Syntactic_Error_Procedure: procedure when errors exist on syntax
BEGIN
   get Tokens of Sentence segmented by the segmentation system
END
BEGIN
   FOR(i=First_Token to Last_Token)
   BEGIN
      set Token_Link off
      get Link_Grammar of the ith Token from Dictionary
      make Disjuncts of the ith Token
   END
   set Syntactic_Error off
   FOR(i=First_Token to Last_Token)
   BEGIN
      FOR(j=next Token of the ith Token to the Last_Token and exist Right_Links)
      BEGIN
          IF(one of jth Token's Left_Links matches one of ith Token's Right_Links) THEN
           BEGIN
              1.make a link between the ith and the jth Token and assign Syntactic_Part
              2.set both ith and jth Token's Token_Link on
              3.remove the Disjuncts of the ith Token and the jth Token that are without a link
              4.remove this link from the Disjuncts of the ith Token
           END
      END
      IF(ith Token's Token_Link=off) THEN
      BEGIN
          set Syntactic_Error on
      END
   END
   IF(Syntactic_Error=on) THEN
   BEGIN
      call Syntactic_Error_Procedure()
   END
END
```

sion of preposition "的", the sentence can not make a connection between lexical entry "我" and "朋友" by means of the linking rules. Therefore, in the last block of Figure 12, with the defining of error linking rules "Err_D", the lexical entry "我" and "朋友" can make a connection by linking rules "Err_D" so as to provide the fault-tolerance processing.

Semantic Analysis System

The semantic analysis system, as shown in Figure 13, transforms the structure of the sentence, as constructed by the syntactic analysis system,

Figure 12. Fault-tolerance processing with omitting of the preposition

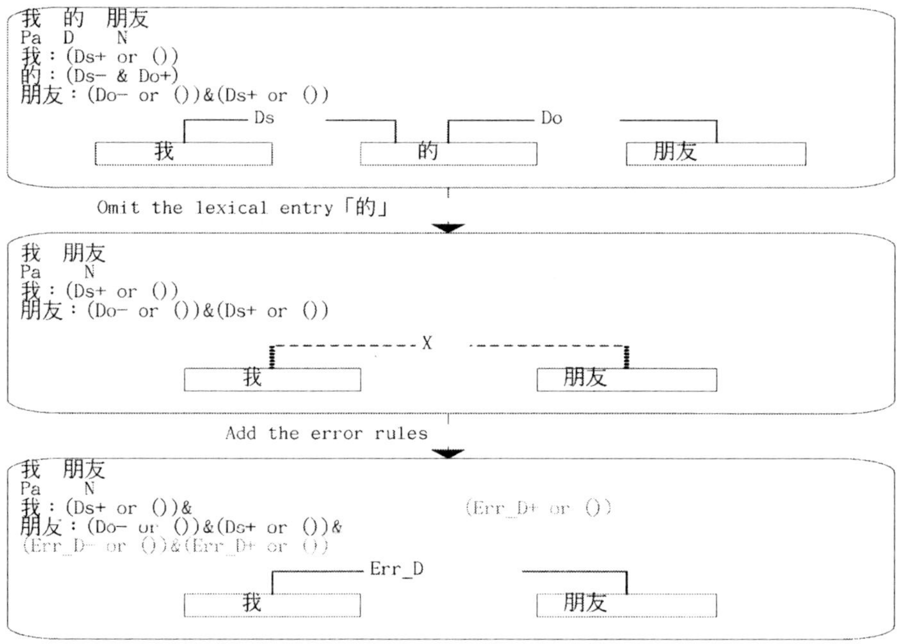

Figure 13. Flowchart of the semantic analysis system

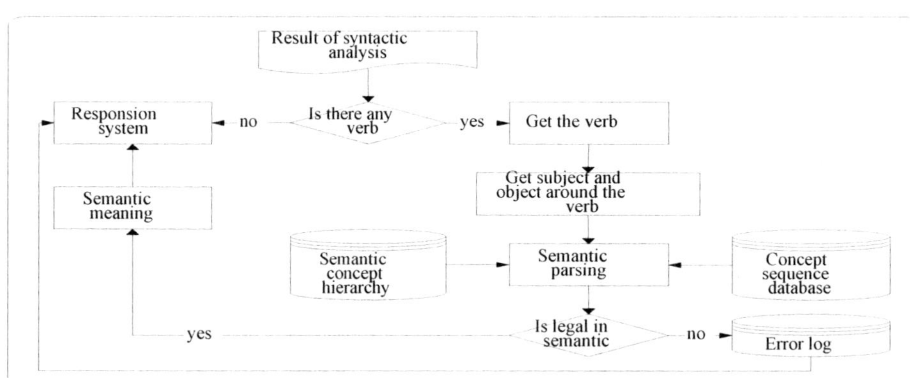

into the semantic meaning. The system judges the correctness of the semantics and provides a semantic learning method based on the user's oral habits.

Because the judgment of semantics only determines the correctness of the subject and the object around the verb, the proposed system searches for the verb of a sentence in advance. If there is no verb in the sentence, the system will continue to the next sub-system after retaining the semantic meaning in the semantic network. The parsing algorithm of semantics is shown as Algorithm 2.

Algorithm 2. Semantic analysis system

```
Comment:
Token: lexical entry
First_Token: first lexical entry of asentence
Last_Token: last lexical entry of a sentence
Syntactic_Part: syntactic part
Verb: the verb of a sentence
Subjective_Token: the lexical entry of a subject
Objective_Token: the lexical entry of a object
Verb_Token: the lexical entry of a verb
Semantic_Error_Procedure: the procedure when an error exist in the semantics
Semantic_Network: semantic network
BEGIN
    FOR(i=First_Token to Last_Token)
    BEGIN
        IF(exist Token which Syntatic_Part is a Verb) THEN
        BEGIN
            search Subjective_Token and Objective_Token that is related to this Verb_Token
            check semantics between Subjective_Token and Verb_Token
            check semantics between Verb_Token and Objective_Token
            IF(semantics is not illegal) THEN
            BEGIN
                call Semantic_Error_Procedure()
                return
            END
            according to Subjective_Token, Verb_Token and Objective_Token create Semantic_Network
        END
    END
    FOR(i=First_Token to Last_Token)
    BEGIN
        IF(Token isn't in Semantic_Network) THEN
        BEGIN
            insert the Token into the Semantic_Network according to the link
        END
    END
END
```

Memory-Based Parsing System

The proposed system utilizes the "Memory-based parsing system" (Chung & Moldovan, 1994b) as the parsing method of the semantics. There are three parts in the memory-based parsing system: the concept sequence layer, the semantic concept hierarchy, and the instance layer.

Concept Sequence Layer

The concept sequence layer keeps both the syntactic and the semantic restrictions of the subject and the object around the verb. As shown in Figure 14, the concept sequence layer takes the verb as the principal element. The verb element links to both the subject and the object elements via the pointers to obtain their restrictions. The detailed contents are explained as follows:

- Structure of the verb:
    - Lexical entry of the verb: Save the context of the verb.
    - S: Link to the restriction of the subject.
    - O: Link to the restriction of the object.
    - Time: Link to the parts of the sentence regarding time.
    - Place: Link to the parts of sentence regarding place.
    - Sentence: Link to the sub-sentence.
- Structure of the subject or the object:

Figure 14. Structure of the concept sequence layer

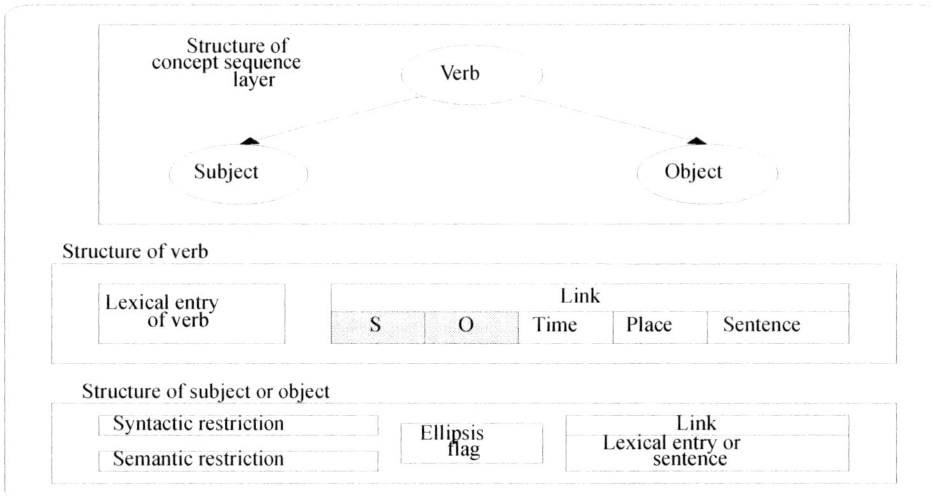

Figure 15. Structure of semantic concept hierarchy

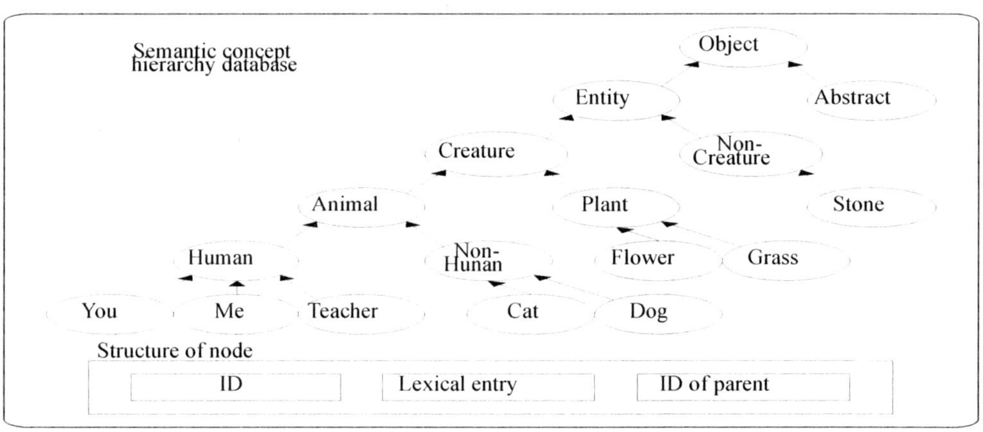

- Syntactic restriction: Record the restriction of the syntax.
- Semantic restriction: Record the restriction of the semantics.
- Ellipsis flag: For judging whether the subject or the object element can be omitted.
- Lexical entry or sentence: Link to the actual lexical entry or sub-sentence of the subject or the object.

Based on the structure of the concept sequence layer, the system provides not only verification of semantic restrictions but also a basis of encoding of the input sentence.

Semantic Concept Hierarchy

The semantic concept hierarchy defines the relation of the nouns according to the meaning of the nouns. The semantic restrictions of subject and object in the concept sequence layer directs them to get their restrictions via the pointers. The structure of the semantic concept hierarchy is shown in Figure 15. The detailed contents are explained as follows:

Figure 16. Example of semantic verification

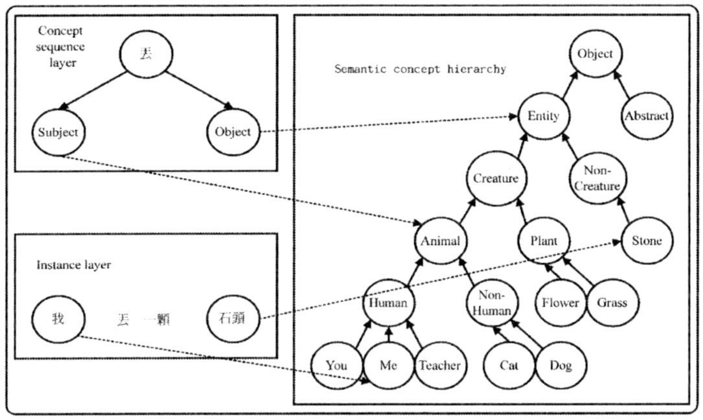

- ID: Store the identity number of the noun.
- Lexical entry: Store the context of the noun.
- ID of parent: Keep up-link of the parent's ID.

Instance Layer

In the instance layer, the proposed system records the lexical entries and obtains the semantic restrictions from the concept sequence layer by comparing the lexical entry of the verb with the verb elements in the concept sequence layer. Figure 16 takes "我丟一顆石頭" as an example for parsing by the above three layers. Because each lexical entry of subject and object could find a path to reach their semantic restrictions, the example sentence is legal. The parsing path of the subject is "「 」➔「 」➔「 」" and the path of the object is "「 」➔「 」➔「 」".

Learning Mechanism of Semantics

In the procedure of semantics processing there could be some inconsistency between the system and the user. Because of this problem, the system should provide a learning mechanism (Kim & Moldovan, 1995) for reducing the differences between the system and the user. The proposed learning mechanism is divided into two parts: generalization and specialization.

Generalization

Generalization of the learning mechanism loosens the semantic restrictions. Figure 17 shows examples of generalization:

There are two conditions of generalization when differences appear between the system and the user:

- The restriction layer of the system is greater and equal to the restriction layer considered by the user, as shown on the left side of Figure 17. Should the user decide that one of the oblique nodes should be corrected, the system would find the lowest common parent node (meshed node) of the oblique node and the restriction node (black node) as the new restriction.
- The restriction layer of the system is less than the restriction layer considered by the user as shown on the right side of Figure 17. If the user decides that the meshed node on top of the restriction node (black node) should be corrected, this meshed node would become the new restriction node.

Figure 17. Generalization

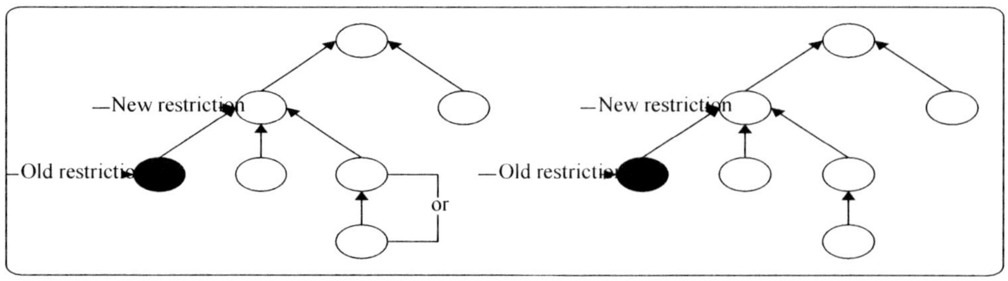

Figure 18. Specialization

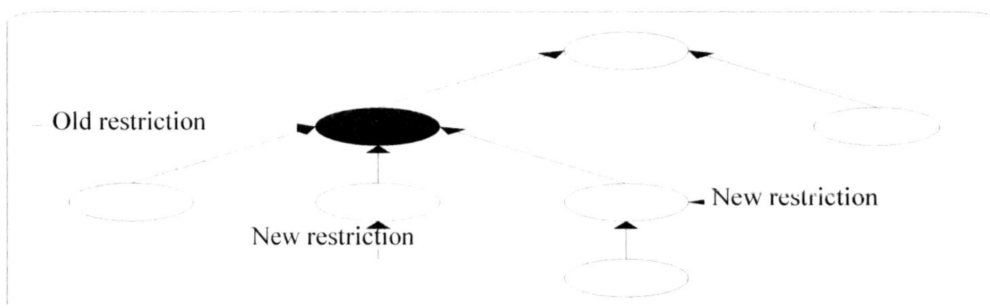

Figure 19. An example of semantic network

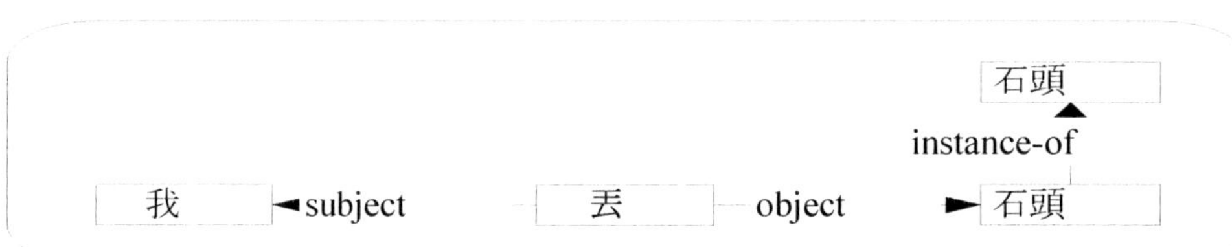

Specialization

Specialization of the learning mechanism shrinks the semantic restrictions. Figure 18 shows an example of specialization.

If a user decides that one of the nodes (oblique node) under the restriction node is illegal in semantics, the system would change the restriction by eliminating all the illegal nodes under the restriction node and the meshed nodes would become the new restriction nodes, as shown in Figure 18. If the illegal node considered by the user is above or the equal to the restriction node, the system would ask the user what the restriction should be.

Semantic Network

The purpose of the semantic network (Quillian, 1968) is to store and represent the meaning of semantics so as to apply it in the inference mechanism. The semantic network describes the relationship between an object and an event. There are three elements in a semantic unit: entity, attribute, and value:

- Entity: The principal part of a semantic unit that represents an object or event.
- Attribute: An arc that describes the attribute of the entity.

- Value: The result of the attribute that describes the entity.

Figure 19 uses the sentence "我丟一顆石頭" as an example. The meshed node is one of the nodes in the concept hierarchy layer, and the actual lexical entry '石頭' in the instance layer uses the arc of the attribute 'instance-of' to form a semantic unit of semantic network with the concept node '石頭'. With the link of the attribute 'instance-of' the actual lexical entry '石頭' inherits the property or the capability from the concept node. The system transforms the linkage (S_我,丟) into the semantic unit subject (丟,我). Consequently, the unit of semantic network is established through linkage by the syntactic parser.

Response System

In the past, learners have had to know exact keywords when using a search engine. However, two identical keywords in different contexts produce different meanings and therefore return different, sometimes undesirable, results. For example, "tell me about the specifications of Bluetooth" and "tell me about the applications of Bluetooth," although having the same keyword, have different meanings. The first sentence concerns hardware specifications of Bluetooth, and the second, software applications of Bluetooth. Learners then would have to filter the data from the results by themselves. The Bayesian Network(BN) and Natural Language Understanding(NLU) (Arai, Wright, Riccardi, & Gorin, 1998; Carpenter & Chu-Carroll, 1998; Kuhn & De Mori, 1995; Miller & Bobrow, 1994; Pieraccini & Levin, 1992) are used to decipher ambiguous sentences and evaluate the searching preferences of different learner.

Before attempting to develop a system, the application domain should be defined as it is very difficult to solve problems of uncertain domain. The application domain of the proposed system is set to the basic computer concept. As shown in Figure 20, understanding natural language queries for a specific application domain involves parsing the input query into a series of domain-specific keywords and searching for the goal of the learner's query. A searching goal assumes that within a restricted application domain, there is a finite set of semantic keywords (M) as well as a finite set of searching goals (N). The searching goals SG_i and keywords K_i are all binary decisions, and the keyword K_i is true if it appears in the speech. In this way, the proposed system can formulate the NLU problem by making M binary decisions with N BNs. The BN for the searching goal SG_i takes the input as a set of keywords K extracted from the learner's query. The BN then gives a posterior probability $P(SG \mid K)$ for the binary decision. The connection of the BN assumes conditional independence among the set of keywords K, meaning that there are direct links between the goal and the concept nodes and no linkages among the concepts nodes. This is equivalent to a naïve Bayes formulation.

When applying the Baysian rule the proposed system assumes that the searching goal SG_i is present if $P(SG \mid K)$ is greater than a threshold θ or absent otherwise. θ may be set to 0.5 for simplicity because $P(SG_i = 1 \mid K) + P(SG_i = 0 \mid K)$ is equal to 1. This formula provides a method to reject out-of-domain queries(OODQ). A query is classified as OODQ when all BNs vote negative for their corresponding goals. Assuming that the searching sentence contains i keywords denoted by KW_i, every keyword affects the searching goal. The searching sentence can be represented as Figure 20 and Formula 1.

According to the Minimum Description Length (MDL) principle, every node in the BN provides the complexity of the network by a magnitude of $L_{network}$. Lower values for the $L_{network}$ reflect lower network complexities. Each node also provides the accuracy in modeling the data by a magnitude of L_{data}. Lower values for L_{data} reflect higher accuracy. In this way, the total description

Figure 20. Belief network of keywords and searching goal

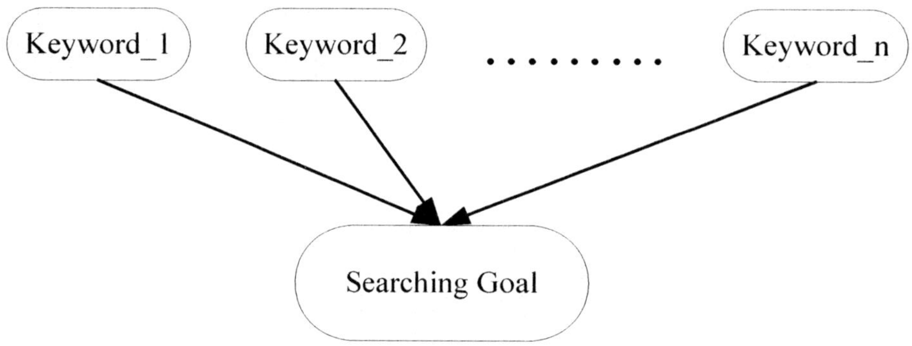

Formula 1.

$$P(SG \mid KW_1, KW_2, ..., KW_n) = \frac{P(KW_1, KW_2, ..., KW_n, SG)}{P(KW_1, KW_2, ..., KW_n)} = \sum P(KW_1, KW_2, ..., KW_i) P(KW_2 \mid KW_1) P(KW_3 \mid KW_2) \cdots P(KW_n \mid KW_{n-1}) \quad (1)$$

KW_1, KW_2, …., KW_n : search keywords
SG : Searching Goal

Figure 21. Trained topology of BN and keyword groups

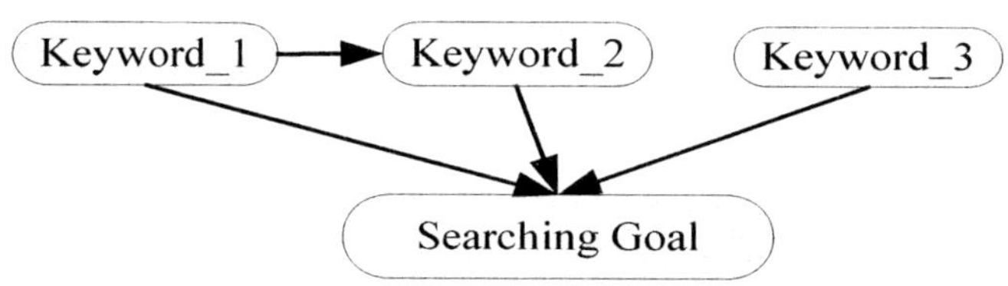

length L_{total} provided by the given node is defined by $L_{total} = L_{network} + L_{data}$. The total description length of a network is the sum of all the concept nodes in the network. The trained BN topologies is shown in Figure 21. There are two keyword groups (maximal sets of nodes that are all pair-wise linked)—(SG, K_1, K_2) and (SG, K_3) which show that the keyword groups can communicate through the separator node SG. Each keyword group K_i relates to a joint probability P(SG, K_i). The keyword group (SG, K_1, K_2) relates to the joint probability P(SG, K_1, K_2), and the keyword group (SG, K_3) relates to the joint probability P(SG, K3). Given a learner's query, the proposed

Formula 2.

$$P^*(SG_i, K) = P(SG_i \mid K)P^*(K) = P(SG_i, K)\frac{P^*(K)}{P(K)} \quad (2)$$

$P^*(K)$: Initialized by the presence or absence of the concepts in the learner's query.
$P(SG_i, K)$: Joint probability obtained from the training set.
$P^*(SG_i, K)$: Updated joint probability.
* : Denotes an updated probability with knowledge about the presence or absence of the various concepts in the learner's query.

Formula 3.

$$P^*(K, SG_i) = P(K \mid SG_i)P^*(SG_i) = P(K, SG_i)\frac{P^*(SG_i)}{P(SG_i)} \quad (3)$$

$P^*(SG_i)$: Updated from instantiating the searching goal node.
$P(K, SG_i)$: Joint probability of the keyword group obtained from the training set.
$P^*(K, SG_i)$: Updated joint probability of the keyword group.

system derives the presence and absence of the various keywords K and updates the joint probability according to Formula 2. The updated joint probability is eventually marginalized to produce a probability for the searching goal $P^*(SG)$.

The BN framework from NLU is extended to mixed-initiative dialog modeling. The idea is to enable BNs to automatically detect missing or spurious keywords according to domain-specific constraints captured by their probabilities. If a missing keyword is detected, the BN prompts the dialog to display the necessary information to the learner. If a spurious keyword is detected, the BN prompts the dialog to notify the learner regarding the unnecessary information. Automatic detection of missing and spurious keywords is achieved by the technique of backward inference which involves probability propagation within the BN. Considering the inferred searching goal SG_i for a given learner's query, the goal node of the corresponding BN is instantiated (to either 1 or 0) to test the network's reliability in each of the input keywords. If the BN topology is assumes conditional independence among the keywords, the updated probability of the concepts would be $P(K_j \mid SG)$. However, in the proposed BN in which the keywords depend on each other, the updated searching goal probability $P^*(K_i)$ would propagate to update the joint probabilities of each keyword group $P^*(K_i, SG_i)$. In this way, each $P^*(K_j)$ can be obtained by marginalization. This procedure is described by Formula 3 and is similar to the procedure described by Formula 2 for updating concept probabilities.

Based on the value of $P^*(K_j)$, the system makes a binary decision (by thresholdθ) regarding whether K_j should be present or absent. This decision is compared with the actual occurrence of K_j in

Figure 22. Bayesian network of knowledge domain

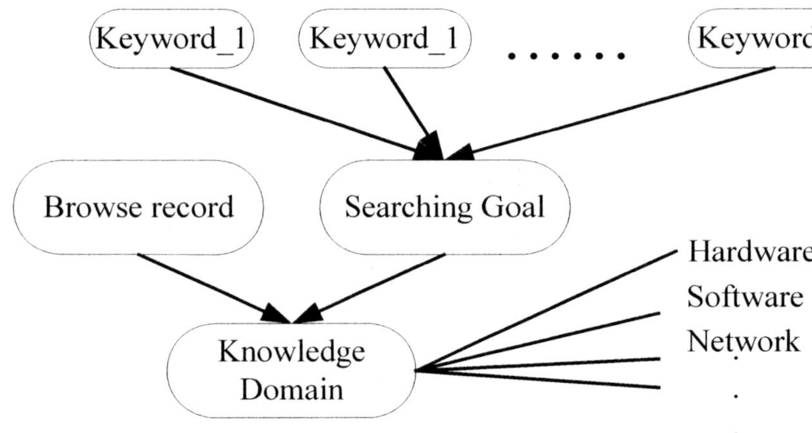

Figure 23. Bayesian network of teaching material difficulty

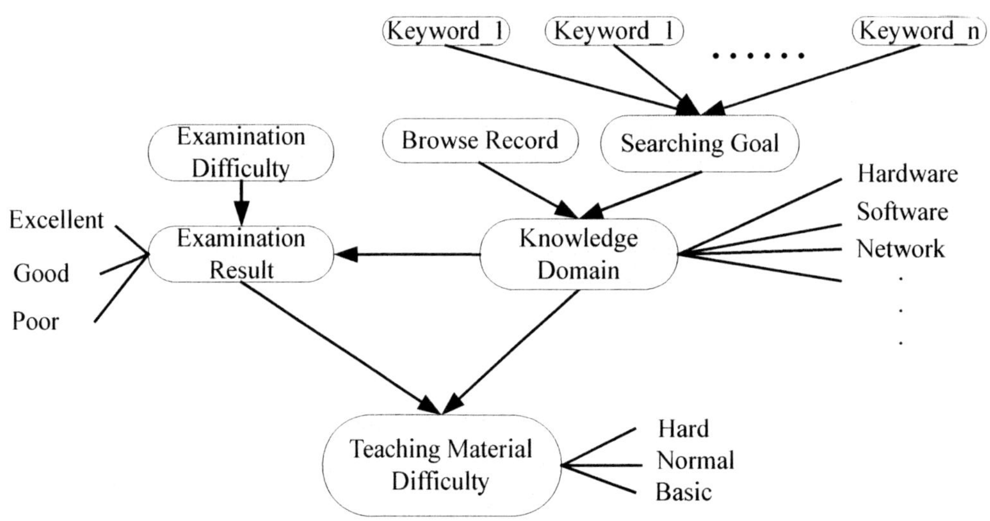

the learner's query. Should the binary decision indicate that K_j is absent and it appears in the input query, the keyword is labeled spurious and the dialog would invoke an explanation. If the binary decision indicates that K_j should be present but it is absent from the query, the keyword is labeled missing and the dialog would invoke the prompting act.

Using keywords and searching goals to categorize knowledge domains is not always desirable as some learners just browse casually in which case a wider variety of search results is preferred. Therefore, the system records browsing habits as another factor that affects the knowledge domain. The corresponding BN is shown as Figure 22 and the probability is described by Formula 4.

The last part is to determine the content and degree of the response to learner. The learning results could be judged by some type of test where a high score indicates a good learning effect and a low score indicates a poor learning effect. The modified BN is shown as Figure 23 and the probability is described by Formula 5 and 6.

Formula 4.

$$P(KW \mid BR, SG) = \frac{P(BR \mid KW, SG) P(KW \mid SG)}{P(BR \mid SG)} \quad (4)$$

P(KD|BR,SG): Probability of knowledge domain
P(BR): Probability of learner's browse record.
P(SG): Probability of searching goal.

Formula 5.

$$P(ER \mid ED, KD) = \frac{P(ED \mid ER, KD) P(ER \mid KD)}{P(ED \mid KD)} \quad (5)$$

P(ER|ED,KD): Probability of examination result.
P(ED): Probability of examination difficulty.
P(KD): Probability of knowledge domain.

Formula 6.

$$P(TMD \mid ER, KD) = \frac{P(ER \mid TMD, KD) P(TMD \mid KD)}{P(ER \mid KD)} \quad (6)$$

P(TMD|ER,KD): Probability of teaching material difficulty.
P(ER): Probability of examination result.
P(KD): Probability of knowledge domain.

EXPERIMENTAL RESULTS

The implementation uses the following example sentence **"這個處理器有許多新的功能"** to describe the process of each step.

Segmentation System

The segmentation system divides the example sentence into lexical entries and gives each lexical entry a suitable part of speech as follows. Figure 24 shows the list branching from the first to the fourth layer. Table 4 shows the segmentation table of sentence in Figure 24

The segmentation system divides the example sentence into lexical entries and gives each lexical entry a suitable part of speech as follows:

這 : Demonstrative pronoun [Pb]
個 : Quantifier [Q]
處理器 : Noun [N]

Figure 24. List of separating from the first layer to the fourth layer

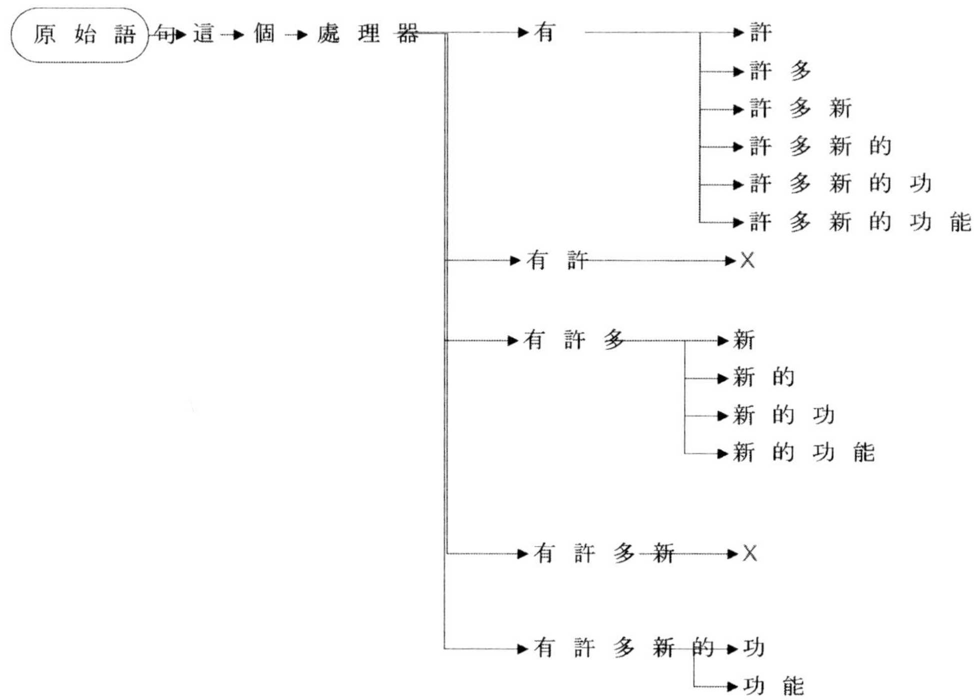

有 : Transitive verb [Vt]
許多 : Adjective [Adj]
新的 : Adjective [Adj]
功能 : Noun [N]

1. 這 : (Bs+ or Pq+)➔
((()(Bs))
個((()(Pq))

2. : (num- or Pq- or (Pq- & num-))&(Q+)➔
((num)(Q))
((Pq)(Q))
((Pq,num)(Q))

3. 處理器: (S+ or O-)&(Q- or())&(@Adj- or ())&(Do- or ())&(Ds+ or ())&(Cn1+ or ())&(Cn2- or ())➔(1)
(({Q},{@Adj},{Do},{Cn2})(S,{Ds},{Cn1}))
((O,{Q},{@Adj},{Do},{Cn2})({Ds},{Cn1}))

4. 有 : (Hv- or ())&(S-)&(O+)&(Advb- or())➔
((S)(O))
((Hv,S)(O))
((S,Advb)(O))
((Hv,S,Advb)(O))

5. 許多 : (Adj+ or Bj-)&(Adva- or ())&(Noj- or ())&(Ca1+ or ())&(Ca2- or ())➔
(({Adva},{Noj},{Ca2})(Adj,{Ca1}))
((Bj,{Adva},{Noj},{Ca2})({Ca1}))

6. 新的 : (Adj+ or Bj-)&(Adva- or ())&(Noj- or ())&(Ca1+ or ())&(Ca2- or ())➔
(({Adva},{Noj},{Ca2})(Adj,{Ca1}))
((Bj,{Adva},{Noj},{Ca2})({Ca1}))

7. 功能 : (S+ or O-)&(Q- or())&(@Adj- or ())&(Do- or ())&(Ds+ or ())&(Cn1+ or ())&(Cn2- or ())➔
(({Q},{@Adj},{Do},{Cn2})(S,{Ds},{Cn1}))
((O,{Q},{@Adj},{Do},{Cn2})({Ds},{Cn1}))

After obtaining the above linking grammars, the system begins to parse the sentence according to the above algorithm. The linking process of the first and second lexical entries are shown in Figure 25.

Because the first lexical entry contains only its relation to the second lexical entry with the

Table 4. The segmentation table of sentence

START	STRING	WORD	RESULT
Start at C(1)			
	C(1)	這	O
	C(1)_ C(2)	這個	X
	C(1)_C(2)_C(3)	這個處	X
	C(1)_C(2)_C(3)_C(4)	這個處理	X
	C(1)_C(2)_C(3)_C(4)_C(5)	這個處理器	X
	C(1)_C(2)_C(3)_C(4)_C(5)_C(6)	這個處理器有	X
Start at C(2)			
	C(2)	個	O
	C(2)_ C(3)	個處	X
	C(2)_C(3)_C(4)	個處理	X
	C(2)_C(3)_C(4)_C(5)	個處理器	X
	C(2)_C(3)_C(4)_C(5)_C(6)	個處理器有	X
	C(2)_C(3)_C(4)_C(5)_C(6)_C(7)	個處理器有許	X
Start at C(3)			
	C(3)	處	X
	C(3)_ C(4)	處理	X
	C(3)_C(4)_C(5)	處理器	O
	C(3)_C(4)_C(5)_C(6)	處理器有	X
	C(3)_C(4)_C(5)_C(6)_C(7)	處理器有許	X
	C(3)_C(4)_C(5)_C(6)_C(7)_C(8)	處理器有許多	X
	⋮ ⋮	⋮ ⋮	

Figure 25. Process of syntactic analysis

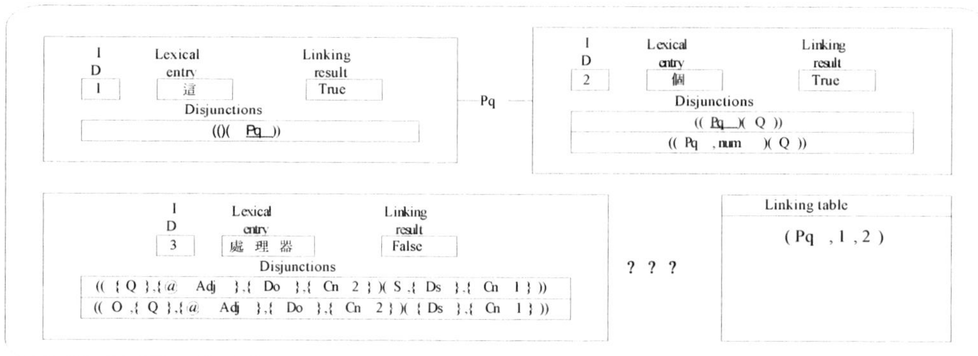

Figure 26. Result of the syntactic analysis

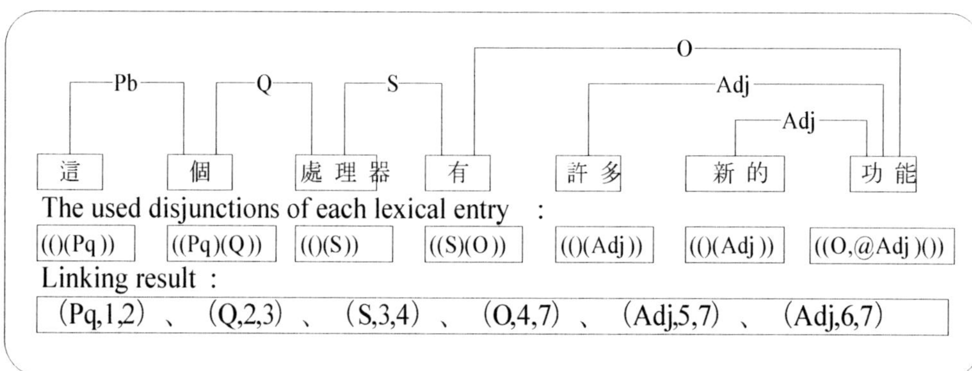

Figure 27. Semantic network of example sentence

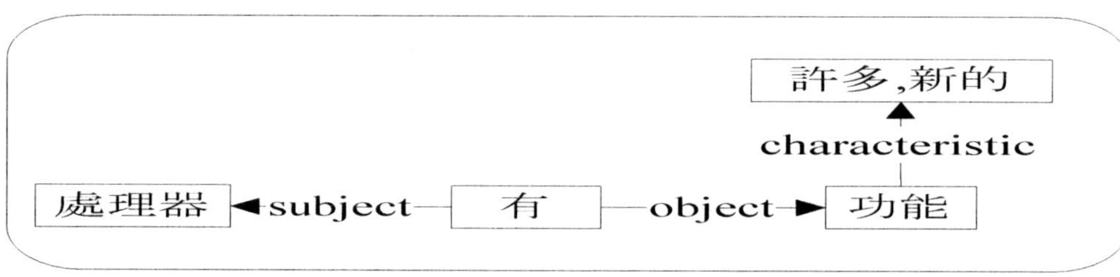

linking requirement 'Pq', the linking results of the first and second lexical entries are set to true and it records the linkage '(Pq,1,2)' in the linking table. The linkage '(Pq,1,2)' denotes that the first lexical entry connects leftward to the second lexical entry via the connector 'Pq'. The linking result of the third lexical entry is still false as a result of having no relationship with the first lexical entry. The final result of the syntactic analysis is shown in Figure 26.

Semantic Analysis System

After the syntactic analysis procedure, the system can determine that the fourth lexical entry is a verb and that the third and seventh lexical entries are the subject and object, respectively, according to linkages (S,3,4) and (O,4,7). The system determines the correctness of the semantics, and the sentence is classified as legal if it conforms to semantic restrictions. Finally, it transforms these linkages into semantic meanings as shown in Figure 27:

- (S,3,4)➔subject (有,功能)
- (O,4,7)➔object (功能,許多)
- (Adj,5,7)➔ characteristic (功能,新的)
- (Adj,6,7)➔ characteristic (有,處理器)

CONCLUSION AND FUTURE WORK

This paper applies the linking of grammar to describe the syntactical construction of sentences and proceeds to verify and record the semantics according to the construction. At the end, the proposed system replies to the user by finding the suitable response derived from the response database. According to the implementation results, the proposed system could correctly describe the relationship between lexicons. Furthermore, with the use of memory-based parsing, the proposed system can check the correctness of the semantics and provide a learning mechanism by changing the semantic restrictions of the concept sequence layer. Finally, by classifying the response databases and using the verb of the sentence as the search key, the response system greatly reduces the amount of response results and increases speed and accuracy. Of the numerous possible applications in the future, one could further develop the interaction between computer and user by utilizing user characteristics and habits, allowing the proposed method to generate a variety of improved responses. With the continual progression of the computing age and the increasing need for improved methods of automated communication, the future of the proposed system remains both worthwhile and practical.

REFERENCES

Arai, J., Wright, G., Riccardi, & Gorin, A. (1998). Grammar fragment acquisition using syntactic and semantic clustering. *The 4th International Conference on Spoken Language Processing.*

Carpenter, B. & Chu-Carroll, J. (1998). Natural language call routing: A robust, self-organizing approach. *The 4th International Conference on Spoken Language Processing.*

Chen, J.-F., Lin, W.-C., Jian, C.-Y. (2003a). Using the keyword in context segmentation method for collaborative design in a Chinese Web site. *The 10th ISPE International Conference on Concurrent Engineering: Research and Applications*, pp. 967–975.

Chen, J.-F., Lin, W.-C., Jian, C.-Y., Ho, T-.Y., & Dai, S.-Y. (2003b). Using the keyword in context segmentation method for a Chinese Web site. *2003 International Conference on Computer-Assisted Instruction*, National Taiwan Normal University, Taipei, Taiwan, pp. 74-80.

Chen, J.-F., Lin, W.-C., Jian, C.-Y., & Hung, C-.C. (2003c). A Chinese automatic interactive feedback system for applying in a Web site. *The Second International Human.Society@Internet Conference*, pp.238-248.

Chen, J.-F., Lin, W.-C., Jian, C.-Y., & Hung, C-.C. (2005). A Chinese interactive feedback system for an e-learning Web site. *Journal of Information Science and Engineering, 21*(5), 929-957.

Chen, K. J., & Liu, S. H. (1992). Word identification for mandarin Chinese sentences. *Proceedings of the Fifteenth International Conference on Computational Linguistics*, Nantes, pp.101-107.

Chung, M. & Moldovan, D. (1993). Parallel memory-based parsing on SNAP. *Parallel Processing Symposium, Proceedings of Seventh International Conference*, pp. 680-684.

Chung, M. & Moldovan, D. (1994a). Applying parallel processing to natural-language processing. *IEEE Expert [see also IEEE Intelligent Systems], 9*(1), 36-44.

Chung, M. & Moldovan, D. (1994b). Memory-based parsing with parallel marker-passing. *Proceedings of the Tenth Conference on Artificial Intelligence for Applications*, pp. 202-207.

Kim, J-.T. & Moldovan, D.I. (1993). Acquisition of semantic patterns for information extraction from corpora. *Proceedings of Ninth Conference on Artificial Intelligence for Applications*, pp.171-176.

Kim, J-.T. & Moldovan, D.I. (1995). Acquisition of linguistic patterns for knowledge-based information extraction. *IEEE Transactions on Knowledge and Data Engineering, 7*(5), 713-724.

Kuhn, R. & De Mori, R. (1995). The application of semantic classification trees for natural language understanding. *IEEE Trans. Pattern Anal. Machine Intell., 17*, 449-460.

Miller, S. & Bobrow, R. (1994). Statistical language processing using hidden understanding models. *The Human Language Technology Workshop*, 278-282.

Pieraccini, R. & Levin, E. (1992). Stochastic representation of semantic structure for speech understanding. *Speech Communication, 11*, 283-288.

Quillian, M.R. (1968). Semantic Memory. In *Semantic information processing*, pp. 216-270. Cambridge, MA: MIT Press.

Sleator, D. & Temperley, D. (1991). *Parsing English with a link grammar.* Carnegie Mellon University Computer Science technical report CMU-CS-91-196.

This work was previously published in International Journal of Distance Education Technologies, Vol. 6, Issue 4, edited by S. Chang; T. Shih, pp. 62-90, copyright 2008 by IGI Publishing (an imprint of IGI Global).

Compilation of References

3GPP TS 23.228 V6.10.0 (2005-06). *IP multimedia subsystem.*

3GPP TS 23.234 V6.5.0 (2005-06). *3GPP system to Wireless Local Area Network (WLAN) interworking.*

3GPP. Third Generation Partnership Project (n.d.). Retrieved from http://www.3gpp.org

6BOOK. (n.d.). Retrieved from http://6book.niu.edu.twf

Adams, D., & Hamm, M. (1990). *Cooperative learning: Critical thinking and collaboration across the curriculum.* Springfield, IL: Charles C. Thomas.

Adams, J., Rogers, B. S., Hayne, S. C., Mark, G., Nash, J., & Leifer, L. J. (2005). The effect of a telepointer on student performance and preference. *Comparative Education, 44*(1), 35–51. doi:10.1016/j.compedu.2003.11.002

Adams, P. C. (1998). Teaching and learning with SimCity 2000. *The Journal of Geography, 97,* 47–55. doi:10.1080/00221349808978827

Adelsberger, H. H., Collis, B., & Pawlowski, J. M. (Eds.) (2002). *Handbook on information technologies for education and training.* Berlin: Springer-Verlag.

Adhvaryu, S., & Balbin, I. (1998). How useful is multimedia on the WWW for enhancing teaching and learning? *Proceedings of International Conference on Multimedia Computing and Systems (ICMCS'98)*, Austin, TX, June 28-July 31.

Advanced Distributed Learning (2006). Retrieved from http://www.adlnet.org/

Ahmadabadi, M., & Asadpour, M. (2002). Expertness-based cooperative Q-learning. *IEEE Transactions on Systems, Man, and Cybernetics-Part B: Cybernetics, 32*(1), 66-76.

Albanese, M. A., & Mitchell, S. (1993). Problem-based learning: A review of literature on its outcomes and implementation issues. *Academic Medicine, 68*(1), 52–81.

Aleven, V., & Koedinger, K. (2002). An Effective Metacognitive Strategy: Learning by doing and explaining with computer-based Cognitive Tutors. *Cognitive Science, 26*(2), 147–179.

Alkit Communications (n.d.). Alkit Confero. Retrieved January 12, 2009, from w2.alkit.se/confero/

Allen, J. (1983). Maintaining knowledge about temporal intervals. *Communications of the ACM, 26*(11), 832-843.

Allen, J. B. (1994). How do humans process and recognize speech? *IEEE Transactions on Speech and Audio Processing, 2*(4), 567–577. doi:10.1109/89.326615

Altmann, E., & Trafton, J. (2002). Memory for goals: An Activation-Based Model. *Cognitive Science, 26,* 39–83.

Alty, J. L. (2002). Dual coding theory and education: Some media experiments to examine the effects of different media on learning. In *Proceedings of EDMEDIA2002: World Conference on Educational Multimedia, Hypermedia & Telecommunications* (pp. 42-47). Denver, Colorado, USA.

American National Corpus. (n.d.). http://americannationalcorpus.org/

Amir, Y. (2002). From total order to database replication. *Proceedings of the 22nd international conference on distributed computing systems (ICDCS'02)* (p. 494).

Anderson, J. R. (1993). *Rules of the mind.* Lawrence Erlbaum.

Anderson, J. R., & Ross, B. H. (1980). Evidence against a semantic-episodic distinction. *Journal of Experimental Psychology. Human Learning and Memory, 6*, 441–466. doi:10.1037/0278-7393.6.5.441

Anderson, J. R., Bothell, D., Byrne, M. D., Douglass, S., Lebiere, C., & Qin, Y. (2004). An integrated theory of the mind. *Psychological Review, 111*(4), 1036–1060. doi:10.1037/0033-295X.111.4.1036

Anderson, J. R., Corbett, A. T., Koedinger, K. R., & Pel letier, R. (1995). Cognitive Tutors: Lessons learned. *Journal of the Learning Sciences, 4*(2), 167–207. doi:10.1207/s15327809jls0402_2

André, E., Finkler, W., Graf, W., Rist, T., Schauder, A., & Wahlster, W. (1993). WIP: The automatic synthesis of multimodal presentations. *Intelligent Multimedia Interfaces,* 75-93, AAAI Press.

André, E., Müller, J., & Rist, T. (1996). The PPP persona: A multipurpose animated presentation agent. *Advanced Visual Interfaces,* 245-247, ACM Press.

Angehrn, A. A., Nabeth, T., & Roda, C. (2001). *Towards Personalized, Socially Aware and Active e-Learning Systems.* CALT White Paper, http://www.calt.insead.edu/Publication/albert.shtm.

Antonacci, D., & Modaress, N. (2008). Envisioning educational possibilities of user-created virtual worlds. *AACE Journal, 16*(2), 115–126.

Apache Tomcat (2007). *The Apache Software Foundation.* Retrieved from http://tomcat.apache.org/

Arai, J., Wright, G., Riccardi, & Gorin, A. (1998). Grammar fragment acquisition using syntactic and semantic clustering. *The 4th International Conference on Spoken Language Processing.*

Arizona Regents University. (n.d.). Retrieved from http://www.azun.net/

Aronson, E. (1978). *The jigsaw classroom.* Beverly Hills, CA: Sage Publication.

Aroyo, L., Dicheva, D., & Cristea, A. (2002, June). *Ontological support for Web courseware authoring.* Paper presented at ITS 2002, the Proceedings of the 6th International Conference on Intelligent Tutoring Systems, San Sebastian, Spain.

Ascione, I. (2006). A Grid computing based virtual laboratory for environmental simulations. *Euro-Par 2006 Parallel Processing* (. *LNCS, 4128*, 1085–1094.

Aylett, R. (2005). And they both lived happily ever after? Digital stories and learning. In G. Dettori, T. Giannetti, A. Paiva, & A. Vaz (Eds.), *Technology-mediated narrative environments for learning.* Amsterdam: Sense Publishers. Retrieved January 15, 2009, from http://www.macs.hw.ac.uk/~ruth/Papers/narrative/Kal-Lisbon.pdf

Aylett, R., Figuieredo, R., Louchart, S., Dias, J., & Paiva, A. (2006). Making it up as you go along - improvising stories for pedagogical purposes. In J. Gratch, M. Young, R. Aylett, D. Ballin, & P. Olivier (Eds.), *Proceedings of the 6th International Conference IVA 2006* (pp. 307-315).

Azevedo, R., & Cromley, J.G. (2004). Does training on self-regulated learning facilitate students' learning with hypermedia? *Journal of Educational Psychology, 96*(3), 523-535.

Baddeley, A. (1990). *Human Memory: theory and practice.* Hove, UK: Lawrence Erlbaum.

Barolli, L., & Koyama, A. (2004). A distance learning system for delivering appropriate studying materials and stimulating learner volition. *Journal of Distance Education Technologies, 2*(1), 1–17.

Barolli, L., & Koyama, K. (2005). A Web-based distance learning system using cooperative. In C. Howard, J. Boettcher, L. Justice & K. Schenk (Eds.), *Encyclopedia of distance learning* (pp. 430-439). Hershey, PA: Information Science Reference.

Barolli, L., Koyama, A., Durresi, A., & De Marco, G. (2006). A Web-based e-learning system for increasing study efficiency by stimulating learner motivation.

Journal of Information Systems Frontiers, *8*(4), 297–306. doi:10.1007/s10796-006-9004-5

Barrows, H. (1985). *How to design a problem-based curriculum for the preclinical years*. New York: Springer.

Barrows, H. (1986). A taxonomy of problem-based learning methods. *Medical Education*, *20*(6), 481-486.

Barrows, H., & Tamblyn, R. (1980). *Problem-based learning*. New York: Springer.

Beacham, N., Elliott, A., Alty, J., & Al-Sharrah, A. (2002). Media combinations and learning styles: A dual coding theory approach. In *Proceedings of EDMEDIA2002: World Conference on Educational Multimedia, Hypermedia & Telecommunications* (pp. 111-116). Denver, Colorado, USA.

Beavers, J., Chou, T., Hinrichs, R., Moffatt, C., Pahud, M., & Eaton, J. V. (2004). *The Learning Experience Project: Enabling Collaborative Learning with ConferenceXP*. MSR-TR-2004-42, Microsoft Research. Retrieved January 12, 2009, from ftp.research.microsoft.com/pub/tr/TR-2004-42.pdf

Beca, L., Cheng, G., Fox, G., Jurga, T., Olszewski, K., Podgorny, M., et al. (1997). Web technologies for collaborative visualization and simulation. *Proceedings of the 8th SIAM Conference on Parallel Processing*. Minneapolis, MN.

Beca, L., Cheng, G., Fox, G., Jurga, T., Olszewski, K., Podgorny, M., et al. (1997b). Java enabling collaborative education healthcare and computing. *Concurrency: Practice and Experience, 9*, 521-534.

Bechhofer, S., van Harmelen, F., Hendler, J., Horrocks, I., McGuinness, D. L., Patel-Schneider, P., et al. (2004 February 10). W3C OWL Web Ontology Language Reference, *W3C Recommendation*..Retrieved from http://www.w3.org/TR/owl-ref/

Beck, J., & Woolf, B. P. (1998). Using a learning agent with a student model, intelligence tutoring system. *Proceedings of 4th International Conference (ITS'98)*, 6-15.

Beck, J., & Woolf, B. P. (2000). High-level student modeling with machine learning. *Proceedings of 5th International Conference Intelligent Tutoring Systems*, 584-593.

Beckett, D. (Ed.) (2004, February 10). RDF W3C, *W3C Recommended.*. Retrieved from http://www.w3.org/TR/2004/REC-rdf-syntax-grammar-20040210/

Bell, P., & Davis, E. A. (1996). Designing an Activity in the Knowledge Integration Environment. In *Proceedings of the Annual Meeting of the American Educational Research Association, New York, NY, USA*.

Benahmed, Y., & Selouani, S.-A. (2006). Robust self-training system for spoken query information retrieval using pitch range variations. *IEEE Canadian Conference on Electrical & Computer Engineering* (pp. 949-952). Ottawa, Canada.

Benlloch Dualde, J. V., et al. (2002). *Osciloscopio Virtual*. Retrieved from http://www.eui.upv.es/ineit mucon/Applets/Scope Osciloscopio.html

Berkson, L. (1993). Problem-based learning: Have the expectations been met? *Academic Medicine*, *68*(1), 79-88.

Berman, F., Fox, G., & Hey, T. (Eds.) (2003). *Grid computing: Making the global infrastructure a reality*. New York: John Wiley and Sons, Inc.

Bernstein, P., & Hadzilacos, V. (1987). *Concurrency control and recovery in database systems*. Reading, MA: Addison-Wesley.

Betz, J. A. (1995). Computer games: Increase learning in an interactive multidisciplinary environment. *Journal of Educational Technology Systems*, *24*(2), 195–205. doi:10.2190/119M-BRMU-J8HC-XM6F

Bielaczyc K, Pirolli P., & Brown A. (1995). Training in self-explanation and self-regulation strategies: investigating the effects of knowledge acquisition activities on problem solving. *Cognition and Instruction*, *13*(2), 221–252.

Birman, K., & Schiper, A. (1991). Lightweight causal and atomic group multicast. *ACM Transactions of Computer Systems, 9*(2), 272-314.

Bisson, C., & Lunckner, J. (1996). Fun in learning: The pedagogical role of fun in adventure education. *Journal of Experimental Education, 9*(2), 109–110.

Blackboard and WebCT. (n.d.). Retrieved from http://www.black board. com/webct

Blanz, V., & Vetter, T. (1999). A morphable model for the synthesis of 3D faces. *Proceedings of The Siggraph 99 conference* (pp. 187-194). New York: ACM Press.

Blanz, V., Basso, C., Poggio, T., & Vetter. T. (2003). Reanimating faces in images and video. *Computer Graphics Forum, 22(3), EUROGRAPHICS 2003* (pp. 641-650). Granada, Spain.

Borkowski, J. G., & Thorpe, P. K. (1994). Self-regulation and motivation: A life-span perspective on underachievement. In D. H. Schunk & B. J. Zimmerman (Eds.), *Self-regulation of learning and performance* (pp. 45-73). Hillsdale, NJ: Lawrence Erlbaum Associates.

Bos, L., & Leroy, S. (2001). Toward an All-IP-Based UMTS System Architecture. *IEEE Network, 15*(1), 36–45. doi:10.1109/65.898820

Bosworth, K. (1994). Developing collaborative skills in college students. *New Directions for Teaching and Learning, 59*, 25–31. doi:10.1002/tl.37219945905

Boud, D. J. (1985). Problem-based learning in perspective. In D. J. Boud, (Ed.), *Problem-based learning in education for the professions* (pp. 13-18). Sydney: Higher Education Research and Development Society of Australasia.

Boud, D., & Feletti, G. (1991). *The challenge of problem based learning*. London: Kogan Page.

Bourlard, H., & Morgan, N. (1994). *Connectionist speech recognition: A hybrid approach*. Kluwer Publisher.

Bowman, R. F. (1982). A Pac-Man theory of motivation. Tactical implications for classroom instruction. *Educational Technology, 22*(9), 14–17.

British National Corpus (n.d.). http://www.natcorp.ox.ac.uk/

Brown, R. (2006). Exploring new speech recognition and synthesis APIs in Windows Vista. *MSDN magazine*. Retrieved January 30, 2009 from http://msdn.microsoft.com/en-us/magazine/cc163663.aspx

Bruer, J. T. (1993). *Schools for thought: A science of learning in the classroom*. Cambridge, MA: MIT Press.

Bruner, J. S. (1960). *The process of education*. Cambridge: Harvard University Press.

Brusilovsky, P., & Nijhawan, H. (2002). A framework for adaptive e-learning based on distributed re-usable learning activities. *Proceedings of the 7th World Conference on E-Learning in Corporate, Government, Healthcare, & Higher Education (E-Learn'02) Canada*, 154-161.

Brusilovsky, P., & Peylo, C. (2003). Adaptive and intelligent Web-based educational systems. *International Journal of AI in Education, 13*(2), 159–172.

Buckingham, D., & Burn, A. (2007). Game literacy in theory and practice. *Journal of Educational Multimedia and Hypermedia, 16*(3), 323–349.

Butz, B. P., Duarte, M., & Miller, S. M. (2006). An intelligent tutoring system for circuit analysis. *IEEE Transactions on Education, 49*(2), 216–223. doi:10.1109/TE.2006.872407

BuyAns (2007). Retrieved from http://www.buyans.com/

CALAT Project. (1998). *Nippon Telegraph and Telephone Corporation*. Retrieved from http://www. calat.com/.

California Virtual University. (n.d.). Retrieved from http://www.california.edu/.

CALsurf. (2000). NTT Software Corporation. Retrieved from http://webbase.ntts.co.jp/

Cameron, B. (2008). Gaming, cognitive style, and feedback in the achievement of learning objectives. In T. T. Kidd, & H. Song (Eds), *Handbook of research on instructional systems and technology* (pp. 416-448). Hershey, PA: Information Science Reference.

Campus, K. V. (n.d.). Retrieved from http://www.kcvu.org/

Canadian Virtual University. (n.d.). Retrieved from http://www.cvu-uvc.ca/.

Candan, K., Prabhakaran, B., & Subrahmanian, V. (1998). Collaborative multimedia documents: Authoring and presentation. *International Journal of Intelligent Systems, 13,* 1059-1111.

Capuano, N., Gaeta, A., Laria, G., Orciuoli, F., & Ritrovato, P. (2003). How to use GRID technology for building the next generation learning environments. In *Proceedings of the 2nd International LeGE-WG Workshop: A Fundamental Challenge for Europe*, France.

Card, O. S. (1995). *What are computers doing at school.* Windows Sources.

Card, S. K., Mackinlay, J., & Shneiderman, B. (1999). *Readings in Information Visualization - Using Vision to Think*. Morgan Kaufmann.

Carol Gaddy, A. (2000). *Training through technology distance learning is more than hardware.* U.S. Army War College, Carlisle Barracks, PA.

Carpenter, B. & Chu-Carroll, J. (1998). Natural language call routing: A robust, self-organizing approach. *The 4th International Conference on Spoken Language Processing.*

Cayzer, S. (2004). Semantic blogging and decentralized knowledge management. Communications of the ACM, 47(12).

CBofN. (2007). *The computational beauty of nature.* Retrieved January 20, 2008, from http://mitpress.mit.edu/books/FLAOH/cbnhtml/

Cellary, W., Walczak, K., Wieczerzycki, W., & Wiza, W. (2001). DIPS - A dynamic system for Web-based business process reengineering. *Proceedings of 7th International Conference on Reengineering Technologies for Information Systems ReTIS, Data and Document Reengineering for the Web* (pp. 33-47). Lyon, France.

Cennamo, K. S., Ross, J. D., & Rogers, C. S. (2002). Evolution of a Web-enhanced course: Incorporating strategies for self-regulation. *Educause Quarterly, 25*(1), 28-33.

Ceri, S. (1985). *Distributed databases principles & systems*. McGraw-Hill.

Chan, T., Sharples, M., Vavoula, G., & Lonsdale, P. (2004). Educational Metadata for Mobile Learning. In *Proc. The 2nd IEEE International Workshop on Wireless and Mobile Technologies in Education 2004* (pp. 197-198).

Chang, G. W. (2005). Teaching photonics laboratory using remote-control web technologies. *IEEE Transactions on Education, 48*(4), 642–651. doi:10.1109/TE.2005.850716

Chang, M. M. (2005). Applying self-regulated learning strategies in a Web-based instruction - An investigation of motivation perception. *Computer Assisted Language Learning, 18*(3), 217-230.

Chang, S.-K. (2002). A growing book for distance learning. *Proceedings of the First International Conference on Advances in Web-Based Learning (ICWL'02)* (pp. 3-18). Hong Kong, China.

Chanlin, L. J., & Chan, K. C. (2004). Assessment of PBL design approach in a dietetic Web-based instruction. *Journal of Educational Computing Research, 31*(4), 437-452.

Chao, H.-C., Wu, T.-Y., & Kao, M. T. C. (2005). Environments for mobile learning. In C. Howard, J. Boettcher, L. Justice, K. Schenk, P. Rogers, & G. Berg (Eds.), Encyclopedia of Distance Learning (pp. 853-856). Hershey, PA: Idea Group Reference.

Charpentier, F. J., & Stella, M. G. (1986). Diphone synthesis using an overlap-add technique for speech waveforms concatenation. In *Proceedings of International Conference on Acoustics, Speech and Signal Processing* (pp. 2015-2018). Tokyo, Japan.

Chase, C. (1978). *Measurement for educational evaluation.* Reading MA: Addison-Wesley.

Chen, J.-F., Lin, W.-C., Jian, C.-Y. (2003a). Using the keyword in context segmentation method for collaborative design in a Chinese Web site. *The 10th ISPE International Conference on Concurrent Engineering: Research and Applications*, pp. 967–975.

Chen, J.-F., Lin, W.-C., Jian, C.-Y., & Hung, C-.C. (2005). A Chinese interactive feedback system for an e-learning

Web site. *Journal of Information Science and Engineering, 21*(5), 929-957.

Chen, J.-F., Lin, W.-C., Jian, C.-Y., Ho, T-.Y., & Dai, S.-Y. (2003b). Using the keyword in context segmentation method for a Chinese Web site. *2003 International Conference on Computer-Assisted Instruction*, National Taiwan Normal University, Taipei, Taiwan, pp. 74-80.

Chen, K. J., & Liu, S. H. (1992). Word identification for mandarin Chinese sentences. *Proceedings of the Fifteenth International Conference on Computational Linguistics*, Nantes, pp.101-107.

Chen, W., Zeng, Q., & Wenyin, L. (2007). A user reputation model for a user-interactive question answering system.

Cheung, K. K. F., Jong, M. S. Y., Lee, F. L., Lee, J. H. M., Luk, E. T. H., Shang, J. J., & Wong, M. K. H. (2008). FARMTASIA: An online game-based learning environment based on the VISOLE pedagogy. *Virtual Reality (Waltham Cross), 12*(1), 17–25. doi:10.1007/s10055-008-0084-z

Chiang, F.-Y., Liang, M.-H., Wu, T.-Y., & Chao, H.-C. (2005). *Pragmatic Lab-Exercises for IPv6 Training.* iCEER-2005, Tainan, Taiwan, March 1-5, 2005.

Childers, L., Disz, T., Olson, R., Papka, M. E., Stevens, R., & Udeshi, T. (2000) Access Grid: Immersive Group-to-Group Collaborative Visualization. *Immersive Projection Technology.* Ames, Iowa.

Chung, M. & Moldovan, D. (1993). Parallel memory-based parsing on SNAP. *Parallel Processing Symposium, Proceedings of Seventh International Conference*, pp. 680-684.

Chung, M. & Moldovan, D. (1994a). Applying parallel processing to natural-language processing. *IEEE Expert [see also IEEE Intelligent Systems], 9*(1), 36-44.

Chung, M. & Moldovan, D. (1994b). Memory-based parsing with parallel marker-passing. *Proceedings of the Tenth Conference on Artificial Intelligence for Applications*, pp. 202-207.

Claroline.net – Open Source E-Learning System (2006). Retrieved from http://www.claroline.net/

CNN. (2004). *http://www.cnn.com/SPECIALS/2004/hurricanes/interactive/hurricane.paths/index.html.*

Cobb, T. (1997). Cognitive efficiency: towards a revised theory of media. *Educational Technology Research and Development, 45*(4), 21–35. doi:10.1007/BF02299681

Cole, M. (1996). *Cultural psychology: A once and future discipline.* Cambridge, MA: The Harvard University Press.

Collins, M., & Loftus, F. (1975). A spreading activation theory of semantic processing. *Psychological Review, 82*, 407–428. doi:10.1037/0033-295X.82.6.407

Colliver J. A. (2000). Effectiveness of problem-based learning curricula: Research and theory. *Academic Medicine, 75*(3), 259-266.

Corbett, A., Mclaughlin, M., & Scarpinatto, K. C. (2000). Modeling Student Knowledge: Cognitive Tutors in High School and College. *Journal of User Modeling and User-Adapted Interaction, 10*, 81–108. doi:10.1023/A:1026505626690

Cordova, D. I., & Lepper, M. R. (1996). Intrinsic motivation and the process of learning: Beneficial effects of contextualization, personalization, and choice. *Journal of Educational Psychology, 88*, 715–730. doi:10.1037/0022-0663.88.4.715

Courtiat, J., Santos, C., Lohr, C., & Outtaj, B. (2000). Experience with RT-LOTOS, a temporal extension of the LOTOS formal description technique. *Computer Communications, 23*(12), 1104-1123.

Csikszentmihalyi, M. (1975). *Beyond boredom and anxiety.* San Francisco: Jossey-Bass.

Csikszentmihalyi, M. (1990). *Flow: The psychology of optimal experience.* New York: Harper & Row.

Dabbagh, N., & Kitsantas, K. (2005). Using Web-based pedagogical tools as scaffolds for self-regulated learning. *Instructional Science, 33*(5–6), 513–540.

Dalgarno, B., Bishop, A. G., & Bedgood, D. R. (2003). The potential of virtual laboratories for distance education science teaching: Reflections from the development and evaluation of a virtual chemistry laboratory. In I. Johnston (Ed.), *Improving Learning Outcomes Through Flexible Science Teaching*. Uniserve Science Conference, Sydney, Australia.

Dasgupta, D., & Michalewicz, Z. (1997), *Evolutionary algorithms in engineering applications*. Springer-Verlag.

Davies, P. (2000). Approaches to evidence-based teaching. *Medical Teacher, 22*(1), 14-21.

Davis, M. H., & Harden, R. M. (1999). Problem-based learning: A practical guide. *AMEE Education Guide*, 15, http://www.amee.org/index.asp?tm=43

de Castro, L. N. (2006). *Fundamentals of natural computing: Basic concepts, algorithms, and applications*. Chapman & Hall/CRC.

de Castro, L. N., & Von Zuben, F. J. (2004). *Recent developments in biologically inspired computing*. Hershey, PA: Idea Group.

de Rosis, F. (2001). Towards adaptation of interaction to affective factors. *Journal of User Modeling and User-Adapted Interaction, 11*(4), 176–199.

DeLisi, R., & Wolford, J. L. (2002). Improving children's mental rotation accuracy with computer game playing. *The Journal of Genetic Psychology, 163*(3), 272–282.

Deliyannis, I. (2002). *Interactive multimedia systems for science and rheology*. Doctoral Thesis, University of Swansea.

Deng, L., & Huang, X. (2004). Challenges in adopting speech recognition. *Communications of the ACM, 47*(1), 69–75. doi:10.1145/962081.962108

Dibiasio, D., & Groccia, J. (1995). Active and cooperative learning in an introductory chemical engineering course. *IEEE Conference on Frontiers in Education*, 3c2.19-3c2.22.

Dietrich, S., & Urban, S. (1998). A cooperative learning approach to database group projects: Integrating theory and practice. *IEEE Transactions on Education, 41*(4), 346.

Dixit, S. S. (2001). Evolving to Seamless All-IP Wireless/Mobile Networks. *IEEE Communications Magazine, 39*(12), 31–32. doi:10.1109/MCOM.2001.968809

Dokeos Open Source E-Learning System (2006). Retrieved from http://www.dokeos.com/

Dolog, P., Henze, N., Nejdl, W., & Sintek, M. (2004). Personalization in distributed e-learning environments. *Proceedings of the 13th International World Wide Web Conference (WWW'04)*, NewYork.

du Boulay, B., Luckin, R., & del Soldato, T. (1999). Human teaching tactics in the hands of a machine. In *Proceedings of the international conference on artificial intelligence in education. Le Mans, France* (pp. 225-232).

Dunlap, J. C. (2005). Changes in students' use of lifelong learning skill during a problem-based learning project. *Performance Improvement Quarterly, 18*(1), 5-33.

Ebel, R., & Frisbie, D. (1991). *Essentials of educational measurement*. Englewood Cliffs, NJ: Prentice-Hall.

Egenfeldt-Nielsen, S. (2007). Third generation educational use of computer games. *Journal of Educational Multimedia and Hypermedia, 16*(3), 263–281.

Ertmer, P. A., Newby, T. J., & MacDougall, M. (1996). Students' approaches to learning from case-based instruction: The role of reflective self-regulation. *American Educational Research Journal, 33*(3), 719-752.

Ertugrul, N. (2000). Towards virtual laboratories: A survey of LabVIEW-based teaching/learning tools and future trends. The Special Issue on Applications of LabVIEW in Engineering Education, *International Journal of Engineering Education, 16*(3), 171–179.

Faculty of Computer Science. (2007). Retrieved from http://www.fiv.upv.es/default_i.htm

Federl, P., & Prusinkiewicz, P. (1999). Virtual laboratory: An interactive software environment for computer graphics. In *Proceedings of Computer Graphics International* (pp. 93–100).

Fordham, J. (2003). Middle earth strikes back. *Cinefex, 92,* 71-142.

Foster, I., & Kesselman, C. (2004). *The grid: Blueprint for a new computing infrastructure*, Amsterdam: Elsevier.

Foster, I., Kesselman, C., & Tuecke, S. (2001). The Anatomy of the grid enabling scalable virtual organizations, *International J. Supercomputer Applications, 15*(3).

Fowler, G. (1996). *Monty Hall (let's make a deal) Problem*. Retrieved January 15, 2009, from http://www.nadn.navy.mil/MathDept/courses/pre97/sm230/MONTYHAL.HTM

Fulk, J., Steinfield, C., Schmitz, J., & Power, J. (1987). A social information processing model of media use in organizations. *Journal of the Communication Research, 14*(5), 529-552.

Gaeta, M., Ritrovato, P., & Salerno, S. (2002). Implementing new advanced learning scenarios through GRID technologies, In *Proceedings of the 1st International LeGE-WG Workshop: Educational Models for GRID Based Services*, Switzerland.

Gagné, R., Briggs, L., & Wager, W. (1992). *Principles of Instructional Design*. (4th ed.). New York: Holt, Rinehart & Winston.

Gao, Y. (2005). Java-Powered Virtual Laboratories for Earthquake Engineering Education. *Computer Applications in Engineering Education, 13*(3), 200–212. doi:10.1002/cae.20050

Garagnani, M., Shastri, L., & Wendelken, C. (2002). A connectionist model of planning as back-chaining search. *The 24th Conference of the Cognitive Science Society. Fairfax, Virginia, USA* (pp 345-350).

Garrison, D. R. (1993). A cognitive constructivist view of distance education: An analysis of teaching-learning assumptions. *Distance Education, 14*(2), 199-211.

Gee, J. P. (2005). *What would be a state of the art instructional video game look like?* Retrieved January 15, 2009, from http://www.innovateonline.info/index.php?view=article&id=80

Gee. J. P. (2003). *What video games have to teach us about learning and literacy*. New York: Palgrave Macmillan.

Ghaith, G. (2002). The relationship between cooperative learning, perception of social support, and academic achievement. *System, 30*(3), 263-273.

Ghaith, G., & Yaghi, H. (1998). Effect of cooperative learning on the acquisition of second language rules and mechanics. *System, 26*(2), 223-234.

Globewide Network Academy. (n.d.). Retrieved from http://www.gnacademy.org/.

Goldberg, M. W. (1996). Student participation and progress tracking for Web-based courses using WebCT. *Proceedings of the Second International N.A. Web conference*, Fredericton, NB, Canada, October 5-8.

Goldberg, M. W., & Salari, S. (1997). An update on WebCT (World-Wide-Web Course Tools) – A tool for the creation of sophisticated Web-Based learning environments. *Proceedings of NAUWeb'97 – Current Practices in Web-Based Course Development*, Flagstaff, AZ, June 12-15.

Goldberg, M. W., Salari, S., & Swoboda, P. (1996). *World Wide Web course tool: An environment for building WWW-based courses.* Computer Networks and ISDN Systems.

Gómez Tejedor, J. A., Barros Vidaurre, C., & Moltó Martínez, G. (2007). Laboratorio virtual. Retrieved from http://personales.upv.es/jogomez/labvir

Gómez Tejedor, J. A., et al. (2002). Laboratorio virtual. In *Proceedings of I Jornadas de Innovación Educativa. Metodologías activas y educación* (pp. 559-564). Institute of Education Sciences and the Vice-rectorate for Academic Organisation and Teaching Staff of the Polytechnic University of Valencia.

Gómez Tejedor, J. A., et al. (2003). *Prácticas de Fundamentos Físicos de la Informática: Facultad de Informática*. Polytechnic University of Valencia.

Gomez, F. J., Cervera, M., & Martinez, J. (2000). A world wide Web based architecture for the implementation of a virtual laboratory. In *Proceedings of The 26th EUROMICRO Conference (EUROMICRO'00)* (Volume 2, pp. 2056).

Gord Mackenzie, G. (2004). *SCORM 2004: Primer*. McGill.

Grau, S., d'Alessandro, C., & Richard, G. (1993). A speech formant synthesizer based on harmonic + random formant-waveforms representation. In [Berlin, Germany.]. *Proceedings of Eurospeech, 93*, 1697–1700.

Gray, J., & Helland, P. (1996). The dangers of replication and a solution. *Proceedings of the 1996 ACM SIGMOD international conference on management of data.*

Grčar, M., Mladenić, D., & Grobelnik, M. (2005). User profiling for interest-focused browsing history. *Workshop on End User Aspects of the Semantic Web (ESWC'05).*

Gredler, M. (2004). Game and simulations and their relationships to learning. In D. Jonassen (Ed.), *Handbook of Research on Educational Communications and Technology* (2nd ed., pp. 571-581). New Jersey: Lawrence Erlbaum Associates.

Greening, T., Kay, J., Kingston, J. H., & Crawford, K. (1996). Results of a PBL trial in first-year computer science. *The 2nd Australasian Conference on Computer Science Education* (pp. 201-206). New York: ACM Press.

Gridsphere (2006). Retrieved from http://www.gridsphere.org/

Guetl C., Dreher, H., & Williams, R. (2005), E-TESTER: A computer-based tool for auto-generated question and answer assessment. *Proceedings of 10th World Conference on E-Learning in Corporate, Government, Healthcare, & Higher Education (E-Learn'05),* Canada.

Gutwin, C., & Penner, R. (2002). Improving interpretation of remote gestures with telepointer traces. In *Proc. of 2002 ACM Conf. on Comp. Supported Cooperative Work* (pp. 49-57).

Habib, S., & Safar, M. (2005). WEBCAP: A capacity planning tool for Web resource management. *Proceedings of the International World Wide Web Conference (WWW2005)* (pp. 918-919). Chiba, Japan.

Habib, S., Ravikumar, C., & Parker, A. (1997). Storage allocation and scheduling problems in Web caching applications. *Proceedings of National Laboratory for Applied Network Research (NLANR) Web Cache Workshop.* Boulder, CO.

Halford, G. S. (1993). *Children's understanding: The development of mental models*. Hillsdale, NJ: Lawrence Erlbaum Associates.

Hall, B. (2006). New Technology Definitions. *Brandon Hall Research*. Retrieved from http://www.brandonhall.com/public/glossary/index.htm

Halverson, R. (2005). What can K-12 school leaders learn from video games and gaming? *Innovate, 1*(6). Retrieved January 15, 2009, from http://www.innovateonline.info/index.php?view=article&id=81

Hammerton, L. S., & Luckin, R. (2001). You be the computer and I'll be the learner: Using the 'Wizard of Oz' technique to involve children in the software design process. In *Artificial Intelligence in Education*. San Antonio, TX, USA.

Hao, T., Hu, D., Wenyin, L., & Zeng, Q. (2007). Semantic patterns for user-interactive question answering. *Journal of Concurrency and Computation: Practice and Experience, 20*(1).

Harasim, L. M., Hiltz, S. R., Teles, L., & Turoff, M. (1995). *Learning networks: A field guide to teaching and learning online*. Cambridge, MA: MIT Press.

Harris, D., Cordero, C., & Hsieh, J. (1996). High-speed network for delivery of education-on-demand. *Proceeding of Multimedia Computing and Networking Conference (MCN'96)*, San Jose, CA, January 29-31.

Hashemi, J., Chandrashekar, N., & Anderson, E. E. (2006). Design and development of an interactive Web-based environment for measurement of hardness in metals: A distance learning tool. *International Journal of Engineering Education, 22*(5), 993–1002.

Heermann, D., & Fuhrmann, T. (2000). Teaching physics in the virtual university: The Mechanics toolkit. *Computer Physics Communications, 12*, 11–15. doi:10.1016/S0010-4655(00)00033-3

Henri, F., & Rigault, C. (1996). Collaborative distance education and computer conferencing. In T. Liao (Ed.), *Advanced educational technology: Research issues and future potential* (pp. 45-76). Berlin: Springer-Verlag.

Henze, N., Dolog, P., & Nejdl, W. (2004). Reasoning and ontologies for personalized e-learning. *Journal of Educational Technology & Society, 7*(4).

Hermann, D., & Harwood, J. (1980). More evidence for the existence of separate semantic and episodic stores in long-term memory. *Journal of Experimental Psychology, 6*(5), 467–478.

Hiltz, S. (1994). *The virtual classroom: Learning without limits via computer networks.* Norwood, NJ: Ablex.

Hmelo-Silver, C. E. (2004). Problem-based learning: What and how do students learn? *Educational Psychology Review, 16*(3), 235-266.

Hoffman, C. M. (1994). Soft lab - a virtual laboratory for computational science. *Mathematics and Computers in Simulation, 36*(4-6), 479–491. doi:10.1016/0378-4754(94)90080-9

Hooper, S. (1992). Cooperative learning and computer-based instruction. *Journal of the Educational Technology Research & Development, 40*(3), 21-38.

Hooper, S. (2003). The effects of persistence and small group interaction during computer-based instruction. *Computers in Human Behavior, 19*(2), 211-220.

Howard, R. (1993). *The virtual community: Homesteading on electronic frontier.* USA: Harper Perennial Paperback.

HTS of Applied Computer Science. (2007). Retrieved from http://www.ei.upv.es/webei/english/in_english/in_english.php

Huang, G. L., & Wenyin L. (2005). Using Web based answer hunting system to promote collaborative learning. *Proceedings of International Conference on Web Learning (ICWL'05),* 387-396.

Huber, G. (2003). Processes of decision making in small learning groups. *Learning and Instruction, 13*(3), 255-269.

Huggins-Daines, D., Kumar, M., Chan, A., Black, A. W., Ravishankar, M., & Rudnicky, A. I. (2006). PocketSphinx: A free, real-time continuous speech recognition system for hand-held devices. In *Proc. of ICASSP, Toulouse, France*.

Humphreys, M. S., Bain, J. D., & Pike, R. (1989). Different ways to cue a coherent memory system: A theory for episodic, semantic and procedural tasks. *Psychological Review, 96*, 208–233. doi:10.1037/0033-295X.96.2.208

Hung Chim, L. (2004). The design and implementation of a Web-based teaching assistant system. *International Journal of Information Technology & Decision Making, 3*(4), 663-672.

Hung Chim, X., & Jie Liu, B (2005). A group decision approach for information assessment. *Proceeding of EUROIMSA* (p. 7-13). Switzerland: IASTED.

Hwang, G. (2003). A concept map model for developing intelligent tutoring systems. *Computers & Education, 40*(3), 217-235.

IBM Developer Works. http://www-106.ibm.com/developerworks/

Ide, N. (2003). The American National Corpus: Everything you always wanted to know...and weren't afraid to ask. Invited keynote, Corpus Linguistics 2003, Lancaster, UK.

Ide, N., Reppen, R., & Suderman, K. The American National Corpus: More than Web can provide proceedings of the third Language Resources and Evaluation Conference (LREC). Las Palmas, Canary Islands, Spain, 839-844.

IETF. The Internet Engineering Task Force (2006). *A Media Resource Control Protocol (MRCP, RFC number 4463.* Jelinek, F. (1997). *Statistical Methods for Speech Recognition.* MIT Press.

ILIAS Open Source E-Learning System (2006). Retrieved from http://www.ilias.de/ios/index-e.html

IMS Global Learning Consortium, Inc. (2002). Draft Standard for Learning Object Metadata, *IEEE Publication P1484.12.1/D6.4.*

IMS Global Learning Consortium, Inc. (2003). *IMS Learning Design Best Practice and Implementation Guide.* Retrieved from http://www.imsproject.org/learningdesign/ldv1p0/imsld_bestv1p0.html

Indiana University. IU Online and Distance Education. (n.d.). Retrieved from http://www.iu.edu /~iuonline/index.html.

Ip, C. W. H., Luk, E. T. H., Cheung, K. K. F., Lee, J. H. M., & Lee, F. L. (2007). A game-based computer supported collaborative learning environment: Learning Villages (LV). In *Proceedings of the 11th Annual Global Chinese Conference on Computers in Education* (pp. 289-292). 26-30 May, Guangzhou, China.

ITU-T(1996) .Recommendation T.120, Data protocols for multimedia conferencing.

ITU-T(2003). Recommendation H.239, Role management and additional media channels for H.300-series terminals.

ITU-T(2007). Recommendation H.323, Packet-based multimedia communications systems, Series H: Audiovisual and multimedia systems, infrastructure of audiovisual services – Systems and terminal equipment for audiovisual services.

Jackson, S. L., Krajcik, J., & Soloway, E. (1996). A learner-centred tool for students building models. *Communications of the ACM, 39*(4), 48–50. doi:10.1145/227210.227224

Jackson, S. L., Krajcik, J., & Soloway, E. (1998). The Design of Guided Learner-Adaptable Scaffolding in Interactive Learning Environments. *CHI 98 Human Factors in Computing Systems* (pp. 187-194).

Jain, A. (1988). *Algorithms for clustering data.* Englewood Cliffs, NJ: Prentice Hall.

Jena – A Semantic Web framework for Java (n.d.). Retrieved from http://jena.sourceforge.net/index.html

Johanson, M. (2001). Stereoscopic video transmission over the Internet. In *Proceedings of the Second IEEE Workshop on Internet Applications* (pp. 12-19).

Johnson, D., & Johnson, R. (1987). *Learning together and alone: Cooperative, competitive, and individualistic learning.* Englewood Cliffs, NJ: Prentice-Hall.

Johnson, D., & Johnson, R. (1990). *Cooperative learning and achievement, cooperative learning: Theory and research.* New York, NY: Praeger.

Johnson, D., & Johnson, R. (1999). Making cooperative learning work. *Theory into Practice, 38*(2), 67-73.

Johnson, D., Roger, T., & Smith, K. (1991). *Active learning: Cooperation in the college classroom.* Edina, MN: Interaction Book Company.

Johnson, S. (2005). *Everything bad is good from you.* New York: Penguin.

Johnson, S., Suriya, C., Yoon, S., Berrett, J., & Fleur, J. (2002). Team development and group processes of virtual learning teams. *Computers & Education, 39*(4), 379-393.

Jonassen, D. H., & Howland, J. (2003). *Learning to solve problems with technology: A constructivist perspective.* Upper Saddle River, N.J.: Merrill Prentice Hall.

Jones, A. Issroff., K., Scanlon, E., Clough, G. & McAndrew, P. (2006). *Using mobile devices for learning in informal settings: Is it motivating?* Paper presented at IADIS International conference Mobile Learning. July 14-16, Dublin.

Jong, M. S. Y., Shang, J. J., Lee, F. L., & Lee, J. H. M. (2006). A new vision for empowering learning and teaching with IT: The VISOLE approach. In *Proceedings of the Hong Kong International IT in Education Conference 2006: Capacity Building for Learning through IT* (pp. 18-25). 6-8 February, HKSAR, China.

Jong, M. S. Y., Shang, J. J., Lee, F. L., & Lee, J. H. M. (2007). *An exploratory study on VISOLE—A new game-*

based constructivist online learning paradigm. Paper presented at American Educational Research Association Annual Convention 2007 (AERA 2007). Chicago, IL.

Jong, M. S. Y., Tse, A. W. C., Zhou, Y. Z., Chen, W. Q., Lee, F. L., & Lee, J. H. M. (2008). Using posting templates for enhancing students' argumentative elaborations in Learning Villages. In *Proceedings of the 2nd IEEE International Conference on Digital Game and Intelligent Toy Enhanced Learning (DIGITEL 2008)* (pp. 180-187). Banff, Canada. Los Alamitos, CA: IEEE Computer Society.

Jou, M., & Zhang, H. W. (2006). Interactive web-based learning system for manufacturing technology education. *Progress on Advanced Manufacture for Micro/Nano Technology 2005, Parts 1 and 2, Materials Science Forum* (pp. 505-507; 1111-1116).

Kagal, L., Paoucci, M., Srinivasan, N., Denker, G., Finin, T., and Sycara, K. (2004, July). Authorization and privacy for semantic Web services. *IEEE Intelligent Systems* (Special Issue on Semantic Web Services).

Kahler, K., Haber, J., Yamauchi, H., & Seidel, H.-P. (2002). Head shop: Generating animated head models with anatomical structure. Proceedings of The ACM SIGGRAPH Symposium on Computer Animation (pp. 55-64).

Kanade, T., Cohn, J., & Tian Y. (2000). Comprehensive database for facial expression analysis. *Proceedings of FG* (pp. 46-53).

Karweit, M. (2000). *Virtual engineering/science laboratory course*. Retrieved May 12, 2007 from http://www.jhu.edu/~virtlab/virtlab.html

Katayama, K., & Kambayashi, Y. (1999). Support of distance lectures using active database. *Trans. of IEICE, D-I, 82*(1), 247–255.

Kauffman, D. F. (2004). Self-regulated learning in Web-based environments: Instructional tools designed to facilitate cognitive strategy use, metacognitive processing, and motivational beliefs. *Journal of Educational Computing Research, 30*(1 & 2), 139-161.

Kelley, T. (1939). The selection of upper and lower groups for the validation of test item. *Journal of the Educational Psychology, 30*(1), 17-24.

Kemme, B. (2000). A new approach to developing and implementing eager database replication protocols. *ACM Transactions on Database Systems, 25*(3), 333-378.

Keyser, M. (2000). Active learning and cooperative learning: Understanding the difference and using both styles effectively. *Research Strategies, 17*(1), 35-44.

Kim, H. R., & Chan, P. K. (2003). Learning implicit user interest hierarchy for context in personalization. *Proceedings of 8th International Conference on Intelligent User Interfaces (IUI'03)*, Miami, FL: 101-108.

Kim, J-.T. & Moldovan, D.I. (1993). Acquisition of semantic patterns for information extraction from corpora. *Proceedings of Ninth Conference on Artificial Intelligence for Applications*, pp.171-176.

Kim, J-.T. & Moldovan, D.I. (1995). Acquisition of linguistic patterns for knowledge-based information extraction. *IEEE Transactions on Knowledge and Data Engineering, 7*(5), 713-724.

Kirriemuir, J., & McFarlane, A. (2004). *Literature review in games and learning* (No. 8). Bristol, UK: Futurelab.

Kirschner, P. (2000). Using integrated electronic environments for collaborative teaching/learning. *Research Dialogue in Learning and Instruction, 2*(1), 1-10.

Klein, J., & Schnackenberg, H. (2000). Effects of informal cooperative learning and the affiliation motive on achievement, attitude, and student interactions. *Contemporary Educational Psychology, 25*(3), 332-341.

Klingner, J., & Vaughn, S. (2000). The helping behaviors of fifth graders while using collaborative strategic reading during ESL content classes. *TESOL Quarterly, 34*(1), 69-98.

Kokinov, B., & Petrov, A. (2000). Dynamic extension of episode representation in analogy-making in AMBR. *The 22nd Conference of the Cognitive Science Society*, NJ. (pp. 274-279).

Koper, R., & Olivier, B. (2004). Representing the learning design of UOLs. *Educational Technology & Society, 7*(3), 97-111.

Kouzes, R. T. J. D., Myers, J. D., & Wulf, W. A. (1996). Collaboratories: Doing science on the Internet. *IEEE Computer, 29*(8), 40–46.

Koyama, A., Barolli, L., Tsuda, A., & Cheng, Z. (2001). An agent-based personalized distance learning system. In *Proceedings of ICOIN-15* (pp. 895-899).

Kruse, K. (2002a). *Using the Web for learning: advantages and disadvantages*. Retrieved May 12, 2007 from http://www.e-learningguru.com/articles/art1_9.htm

Kruse, K. (2002b). *E-learning and the neglect of user interface design*. Retrieved May 12, 2007 from http://www.e-learningguru.com/articles/art4_1.htm, retrieved May 12, 2007. L&H TTS3000. (2006). *Nuance: trademark*. Retrieved February 6, 2007 from http://www.nuance.com

Kuhn, R. & De Mori, R. (1995). The application of semantic classification trees for natural language understanding. *IEEE Trans. Pattern Anal. Machine Intell., 17*, 449-460.

Kuwabara, T., Tamaki, M., Yamada, K., Nakamura, Y., Mistunaga, Y., Konishi, N. & Amano, K. (2000). Support functions for stalled students and their effect in a multi-media assisted education system with individual advance (MESIA). *Transactions of IEICE, J83-D-I, 83*(9) 1013-1024.

Labrou, Y. & Finin, T. (1999). Yahoo! as an ontology—Using Yahoo! categories to describe documents. *Proceedings of the 8th International Conference on Information and Knowledge Management*, Kansas City, MO, November, 180-187.

Lave, J., & Wenger, E. (1991). *Situated learning: Legitimate peripheral participation*. Cambridge, UK: Cambridge University Press.

Lawson, E. A., & Stackpole W. (2006). Does a virtual networking laboratory result in similar student achievement and satisfaction? In *Proceedings of the 7th conference on Information technology education*. 105-114, Minneapolis, Minnesota, USA.

Lawson, E. A., & Stackpole, W. (2006). Does a virtual networking laboratory result in similar student achievement and satisfaction? *Conference On Information Technology Education* (pp. 105-114).

Lawson, E. A., & Stackpole, W. (2006, October 19–21). Does a virtual networking laboratory result in similar student achievement and satisfaction? In *Proceedings of the 7th conference on Information technology education (SIGITE'06)*. Minneapolis, MN.

Lê, T. -.H. & Roy, J. (2005-b). Integrating e-learning and classroom learning. In *Proceedings of CCCT-05, The 3rd International Conference on Computing, Communications and Control Technologies* (Vol. 1, pp. 238-243). Austin, TX, USA.

Lê, T.-H., & Roy, J. (2005-a). LINC: A WEB-based learning tool for mixed-mode learning. *The 7th International Conference on Enterprise Information Systems.* (Vol. 5, pp. 154-160). Miami, Florida, USA.

Lee, J. H. M., Lee, F. L., & Lau, T. S. (2006). Folklore-based learning on the web—pedagogy, case study, and evaluation. *Journal of Educational Computing Research, 34*(1), 1–27. doi:10.2190/3HFM-D9NQ-G7Y7-QC1G

Lee, W., & Magnenat-Thalmann, N. (2000). Fast head modeling for animation. *Journal of Image and Vision Computing, 18*(4), 355-364. Elsevier Science.

Lehman, S., Kauffman, D., White, M., Horn, C., & Bruning, R. (2001). Teacher interaction: Motivating at-risk students in Web-based high school courses. *Journal of Research on Computing in Education, 33*(5), http://www.iste.org/inhouse/publications/jrte/33/5/lehman-s.cfm?Section=JRTE_33_5

Leitner, L. J., & Cane, J. W. (2005, October 20–22). A virtual laboratory environment for online IT education. In *Proceedings of the 6th conference on Information technology education (SIGITE'05)* (pp. 283–289). Newark, NJ.

Li, J., Zhang, L., & Yu, Y. (2001). Learning to generate semantic annotation for domain specific sentences. *In the Workshop on Knowledge Markup and Semantic Annotation at the 1st International Conference on Knowledge Capture (K-CAP 2001)*, October, Victoria, B.C., Canada.

Li, K. C., Wang, H. H., Chen, C. N., Liu, C. C., Chang, C. F., and Hsu, C. W., et al. (2005). *Design issues of a novel toolkit for parallel application performance monitoring and analysis in cluster and grid environments.* Paper presented at I-SPAN 2005, The 8th IEEE International Symposium on Parallel Architectures, Algorithms, and Networks, U.S.

Lindner, R. W., & Harris, B. (1993). Teaching self-regulated learning strategies. In M.R. Simonson & K. Abu-Omar, (Eds.), *Proceedings of selected research and development presentations at the annual conference of the Association for Educational Communications and Technology* (pp. 641–654). Ames, IA: Instructional Resources Center, Iowa State University.

Lindsay, J. (2007, April 2). Shall we call it Collaboration 2.0? *E-Learning Journeys.* Retrieved from http://123elearning.blogspot.com/2007/04/shall-we-call-it-collaboration-20.html

Lintermann, B., & Deussen, O. (1999). Interactive Structural and Geometrical Modeling of Plants. *IEEE Computer Graphics and Applications*, *19*(1), 48–59. doi:10.1109/38.736469

Llinares, J., & Page, A. (1987). *Curso de Física Aplicada. Electromagnetismo y semiconductores.* Polytechnic University of Valencia.

Luckin, R., & du Boulay, B. (1999). Ecolab: the Development and Evaluation of a Vygotskian Design Framework. *International Journal of Artificial Intelligence in Education*, *10*(2), 198–220.

Luckin, R., & Hammerton, L. (2002). Getting to know me: helping learners understand their own learning needs through metacognitive scaffolding. In S. A. Cerri & G. Gouarderes & F. Paranguaca (Eds.), *Intelligent Tutoring Systems* (pp. 759-771). Berlin: Springer-Verlag.

LVCoN. (2007). *Virtual laboratory on natural computing.* Catholic University of Santos (UniSantos). Retrieved January 20, 2008, from http://lsin.unisantos.br/lvcon (Portuguese version), http://lsin.unisantos.br/lvcon_en (English version)

Macdonald, J. (2003). Assessing online collaborative learning: process and product. *Computers & Education, 40*(4), 377-391.

Malassiotis, S., & Strintzis, M. (2005) Robust real-time 3D head pose estimation from range data. *Pattern Recognition, 38*(8), 1153-1165.

Malone, T. W. (1980). *What makes things fun to learn? A study of intrinsically motivating computer games.* Palo Alto: Xerox.

Malone, T. W. (1981). Toward a theory of intrinsically motivating instruction. *Cognitive Science*, *4*, 333–369.

Martens, R. L., Gulikers, J., & Bastiaens, T. (2004). The impact of intrinsic motivation on e-learning in authentic computer tasks. *Journal of Computer Assisted Learning*, *20*, 368–376. doi:10.1111/j.1365-2729.2004.00096.x

Mas, J., et al. (2002). Una experiencia sobre enseñanza distancia de asignaturas básicas de primer curso. In *Proceedings of the I Jornadas de Innovación Educativa en la UPV* (pp. 705-711).

Mason, H., & Moutahir, M. (2006). Multidisciplinary experiential education in Second Life: A global approach. In J. Kemp, & D., Livingstone (Eds.), In *Proceedings of the Second Life Education Workshop at the Second Life Community Convention* (pp. 30-34), San Francisco.

McAndrew, P., Woods, W., Little, A., Weller, M., Koper, R., & Vogten, H. (2004). *Implementing learning design to support Web-based learning.* Paper presented at The Tenth Australian World Wide Web Conference, Gold Coast, Australia.

McDonald, D. (1995). Improving student learning with group assignments. *IEEE Conference on Frontiers in Education,* 2b5.9-2b5.12.

McGuinness, D.L. & Harmelen, F.V. (2004). OWL Web ontology language overview. W3C Recommendation, February 10.

Mcrypt, L. (2006). *A crypotography library as the replacement for the old UNIX crypt under the GPL.* http://sourceforge.net/projects/mcrypt.

Mevarech, Z. (1993). Who benefits from cooperative computer-assisted instruction?. *Journal of the Educational Computing Research, 9*(4), 451-464.

Michigan State University. Virtual University. (n.d.). Retrieved from http://www.vu.msu.edu/site/

Microsoft (n.d.) DirectShow. Retrieved January 12, 2009, from msdn2.microsoft.com/en-us/library/ms783323.aspx

Microsoft Corporation. (2006). *Microsoft English (U.S.) v6.1 Recognizer.* Retrieved June 10, 2006 from http://www.microsoft.com/speech/download/sdk51

Microsoft MSDN online Library. http://msdn.microsoft.com/vstudio/

Microsoft. (2007). *Microsoft learning gateway refresh for SharePoint Server 2007 deployment guide.*

Millard, D., Tao, F., Doody, K., Woukeu, A., & Davis H. (2006). The knowledge life cycle for e-learning. *Journal of Continuing Engineering Education and Lifelong Learning: Special Issue on Application of Semantic Web Technologies in E-learning, 16*(1/2), 110-121.

Miller, S. & Bobrow, R. (1994). Statistical language processing using hidden understanding models. *The Human Language Technology Workshop*, 278-282.

MindEdge. Online Education. (n.d.). Retrieved from http://www.newpromise.com/

Mishra, P., & Foster, A. N. (2007). The claims of games: A comprehensive review and directions for future research. In [San Antonio, Texas.]. *Proceedings of Society for Information Technology and Teacher Education Interactional Conference, 2007*, 2227–2232.

Mitelstedt, P.A. (2001). *Distance learning receives high marks.* U.S. War College, Carlisle Barracks, PA.

Moure, M. J. (2004). Virtual Laboratory as a Tool to Improve the Effectiveness of Actual Laboratories. *International Journal of Engineering Education, 20*(2), 188–192.

Najjar, L. J. (1996). Multimedia information and learning. *Journal of Educational Multimedia and Hypermedia, 5*(1), 129–150.

Najjar, M., & Mayers, A. (2007). AURELLIO – A Cognitive Computational Knowledge Representation Theory. *International Journal of Cognitive Informatics and Natural Intelligence, 1*(3), 17–34.

Najjar, M., Fournier-Viger, P., Lebeau, J. F., & Mayers, A. (2006). Recalling Recollections According to Temporal Contexts – Applying of a Novel Cognitive Knowledge Representation Approach. *The 5th International Conference on Cognitive Informatics.* July 17-19, Beijing, China.

Najjar, M., Mayers, A., Vong, K., & Turcotte, S. (2007). Tailored Solutions to Problems Resolution – An Experimental Validation of a Cognitive Computational Knowledge Representation Model. [iJET]. *The International Journal on Emerging Technologies in Learning, 2*(1), 28–32.

Nakabayashi, K., Koike, Y., Maruyama, M., Touhei, H., Fukuhara, Y., & Nakamura, Y. (1999). CALCAT: An Intelligent CAI System Using WWW. *Trans. of IEICE, D-II, 80*(4), 906–914.

Neely, J. H. (1989). Experimental dissociations and the episodic/semantic memory distinction. *Experimental Psychology: Human Learning and Memory, 6*, 441–466.

Nesbit, J., & Li, J. (2004, July). *Web-based tools for learning object evaluation.* Paper presented at the International Conference on Education and Information Systems: Technologies and Applications, Orlando, FL.

Newman, A. (1996). *Special edition using Java.* Que Cooperation, Indianapolis, IN.

Newman, J. (2004). *Videogames.* London: Routledge.

NMI OGCE Open Grid Computing Environment (2006). Retrieved from http://www.ogce.org/index.php

Norman, G.., & Schmidt, H. (1992). The psychological basis of problem-based learning. *Academic Medicine*, *67*(9), 557-565.

Nota, L., Soresi, S., & Zimmerman, B. J. (2004). Self-regulation and academic achievement and resilience: A longitudinal study. *International Journal of Educational Research*, *41*(3), 198–251.

Noy, N. F., & McGuinness, D. L. (2001). *Ontology Development 101: A Guide to Creating Your First Ontology*. Stanford Knowledge Systems Laboratory Technical Report (KSL-01-05).

O'Shaughnessy, D. (2000). *Speech communication: human and machine*. IEEE Press.

Ohio Learning Network. (n.d.). Retrievcd from http://www. oln.org/

Oregon's One-Stop for Distance Education. (2008). Retrieved from http://oregonone.org/

Osawa, N. (2004). Multipoint remote focus sharing tool: FocusShare. *8th IASTED Int. Conf. on Internet & Multimedia Sys. & Apps. (IMSA 2004)* (pp. 379-384).

Osawa, N., & Asai, K. (2006) Multimedia conference system supporting group awareness and remote management. *12th International Conference on Distributed Multimedia Systems (DMS2006)* (pp. 65-72).

Osawa, N., & Asai, K. (2008). Multipoint Multimedia Conferencing System with Group Awareness Support and Remote Management. *International Journal of Distance Education Technologies*, *6*(3), 23–44.

Osawa, N., Asai, K., Shibuya, T., Noda, K., Tsukagoshi, S., Noma, Y., & Ando, A. (2005). Three-dimensional video distance education system between indoor and outdoor environments. *6th International Conference on Information Technology Based Higher Education and Training (ITHET2005)*, F2C/13-18, CD-ROM.

Osawa, N., Shibuya, T., Yuki, K., Kondo, K., Sastrokusumo, U., Komolmis, T., & Kuroiwa, H. (2005) Multipoint conferencing through a satellite IP network. *8th IASTED Int. Conf. on Comp. and Adv. Tech. in Educ. (CATE 2005)* (pp. 41-46).

Ostermann, J. (1998). Animation of synthetic faces in MPEG-4. *Computer Animation*, 49-51.

Otting, H., & Zwaal, W. (2007). The identification of constructivist pedagogy in different learning environments. In M. K. McCuddy, H. van-den-Bosch, W. B., Martz, A. V. Alexei, & K. O. Morseb (Eds.), *The challenges of educating people to lead in a challenging world* (pp. 171-196). Netherlands: Springer.

Ou, K.-L., Chen, G.-D., Liu, C.-C., &Liu, B.-J. (2000). Instructional instruments for Web group learning systems: The grouping, intervention, and strategy. *Proceedings of the 5th annual SIGCSE/SIGCUE ITiCSE conference on Innovation and technology in computer science education* (pp. 69-72). Helsinki, Finland.

Oz, E. (2002). *Management information systems*, 3rd ed. Boston, MA: Course Technology.

Pacitti, E. (2000). Update propagation strategies to improve freshness in lazy master replicated databases. *VLDB Journal: Very Large Data Bases*, *8*(3), 305-318.

Pankratius, V. & Vossen, G. (2003). Towards e-learning grids: Using grid computing in electronic learning. In *Proceeding of IEEE Workshop on Knowledge Grid and Grid Intelligence*, Canada.

Papert, S. (1993). *The children's machine: Rethinking school in the age of the computers*. New York: Basis Books.

Paquette, G., Marino, O., de la Teja, I., Léonard, J., Lundgren-Cayrol, K., & Contamines, J. (2005). Implementation and deployment of the IMS learning design specification. *Canadian Journal of Learning and Technology*, *31*(2).

Paris, S. G.., & Paris, A. H. (2001). Classroom applications of research in self-regulated learning. *Educational Psychologist*, *36*(2), 89-101.

Parke, F. (1972). Computer-generated animation of faces. *Proceedings of the ACM annual conference*.

Patel, G., & Dennett, S. (2000). The 3GPP and 3GPP2 Movements toward an All-IP Mobile Network. *IEEE Personal Communications*, *7*(4), 62–64. doi:10.1109/98.863998

Paton, R. (1994). *Computing with biological metaphors*. Chapman & Hall.

Paton, R., Bolouri, H., & Holcombe, M. (2003). *Computing in cells and tissues: Perspectives and tools of thought*. Springer-Verlag.

Pazzani, M. J., & Billsus, D. (1997). Learning and revising user profiles: The identification of interesting Web sites. *Journal of Machine Learning, 27*(3), 313-331.

Pennsylvania State University. "World Campus" (2008). Retrieved from http://www.worldcampus. psu.edu/

Perels, F., Gürtler, T., & Schmitz, B. (2005). Training of self-regulatory and problem-solving competence. *Learning and Instruction, 15*(2), 123-139.

Piaget, J. (1964). Development and learning. *Journal of Research in Science Teaching, 2*, 176–186. doi:10.1002/tea.3660020306

Piaget, J. (1970). *Science of education and psychology of the child*. New York: Oxford University Press.

Pieraccini, R. & Levin, E. (1992). Stochastic representation of semantic structure for speech understanding. *Speech Communication, 11*, 283-288.

Pighin, F., Hecker, J., Lischinski, D., Szeliski, R., & Salesin, D. (1998). Synthesizing realistic facial expressions from photographs. *Siggraph proceedings* (pp. 75-84).

Pintrich, P. R., Marx, R. W., & Boyle, R. A. (1993). Beyond cold conceptual change: The role of motivational beliefs and classroom contextual factors in the process of conceptual change. *Review of Educational Research, 63*(2), 167–199.

Podgorny, M., Walczak, K., Warner, D., & Fox, G. (1998). Internet groupware technologies - Past, present, and future. *Proceedings of the International Conference on Business Information Systems*. Poznan, Poland.

Polanco, R., Calderón, P., & Delgado, F. (2004). Effects of a problem-based learning program on engineering students' academic achievements in a Mexican university. *Innovations in Education & Teaching International, 41*(2), 145-155.

Polytechnic University of Valencia. (2007). Retrieved from http://www.upv.es

Poon, W. C., Low, K. L. T., & Yong, D. G. F. (2004). A study of Web-based learning (WBL) environment in Malaysia. *The International Journal of Educational Management, 18*(6), 374–385.

Porto, M. (2001). Cooperative writing response groups and self-evaluation. *ELT Journal, 55*(1), 38-46.

Potter, C. (1996). EVAC: A virtual environment for control of remote imaging instrumentation. *IEEE Computer Graphics and Applications, 16*(4), 62–66. doi:10.1109/38.511856

Preis K. (1997) et al. A virtual electromagnetic laboratory for the classroom and the www. *IEEE Transactions on Magnetics, 33*(2), 1990-1993, Part 2.

Prensky, M. (2001). *Digital game-based learning*. New York: McGraw Hill.

Prensky, M. (2006). *Don't bother me mom – I'm learning*. St. Paul, MN: Paragon House.

Prithvi, R. (2007). IEEE Begins Wireless, Long-Wave Standard for Healthcare, Retail and Livestock Visibility Networks; IEEE P1902.1 Standard to Offer Local Network Protocol for Thousands of Low-Cost Radio Tags Having a Long Battery Life. *2007 North American Supply Chain Visibility Solutions Technology Innovation of the Year Award*. Frost&Sullivan.

Protégé (2008). Retrieved from http://protege.stanford.edu/

Puntambekar, S., & Kolodner, J. L. (2005). Toward implementing distributed scaffolding: Helping students learn science by design. *The International Journal of Research in Science Teaching, 42*(2), 185–217. doi:10.1002/tea.20048

Qin, J., & Hernandez, N. (2004, May). *Ontological representation of learning objects: Building interoperable vocabulary and structures*. Paper presented at the Proceedings of the 13th international World Wide Web conference on Alternate track papers & posters, New York, NY.

Quillian, M.R. (1968). Semantic Memory. In *Semantic information processing*, pp. 216-270. Cambridge, MA: MIT Press.

Rachel, H., & Irit, B. (2002). Writing development of Arab and Jewish students using cooperative learning (CL) and computer-mediated communication (CMC). *Computers & Education, 39*(1), 19-36.

Rachlin, H. (1991) *Introduction to modern behaviorism* (3rd ed.). New York: Freeman.

Ragoonaden, K., & Bordeleau, P. (2000). Collaborative learning via the Internet. *Educational Technology and Society, 3*(3), 1-16.

Ramsay, A., Hanlon, D., & Smith, D. (2000). The association between cognitive style and accounting students' preference for cooperative learning: An empirical investigation. *Journal of Accounting Education, 18*(3), 215-228.

Ravin, Y. (1988). Grammar errors and style weaknesses in a text-critiquing system. *IEEE Transactions on Professional Communication, 31*(3), 1988, 108-115.

Reese, D. D. (2007). First step and beyond: Serious games as preparing for future. *Journal of Educational Multimedia and Hypermedia, 16*(3), 383–300.

Reyero, M., & Tourón, J. (2003). *El desarrollo del talento: La aceleración como estrategia educativa* [*The development of talent: Acceleration as an educational strategy*]. A Coruña: Netbiblo.

Rice, J. W. (2007). New media resistance: Barriers to implementation of computer video games in the classroom. *Journal of Educational Multimedia and Hypermedia, 16*(3), 249–261.

Richards, D. D., & Goldfarb, J. (1986). The episodic memory model of conceptual development: an integrative viewpoint. *Cognitive Development, 1*, 183–219. doi:10.1016/S0885-2014(86)80001-6

Richards, G. (2002). Editorial: The challenges of the learning object paradigm. *Canadian Journal of Learning and Technology, 28*(3).

Risemberg, R., & Zimmerman B. J. (1992). Self-regulated learning in gifted students. *Roeper Review, 15*(2), 98-101.

Roces, C., & González Torres, M. C. (1998). Capacidad de autorregulación del aprendizaje [*Ability to self-regulate learning*]. In J. A. González Pienda & J. C. Núñez (Eds.), *Dificultadesde aprendizaje escolar* (pp. 239-259). Madrid: Pirámide/Psicología.

Rothnie, B. (1980). Introduction to a system for distributed databases (SDD-1). *ACM Transactions on Database Systems, 5*(1), 1-17.

Roweis, S., & Saul. L. (2000). Nonlinear dimensionality reduction by locally linear embedding. *Science, 290*, 2323-2326.

Ryan, B. and & Tschudi-Sutton, M. (2006). *7 development projects for Microsoft Office SharePoint Server 2007 and Windows SharePoint Services Version 3.0.* Washington: Microsoft Press.

Rzepa, H., & Tonge, A. (1998). VChemlab: A virtual chemistry laboratory. *Journal of Chemical Information and Computer Sciences, 38*(6), 1048–1053. doi:10.1021/ci9803280

Safar, M. (2000). *Efficient MBC-based shape retrieval and spatial querying.* Doctoral Dissertation, University of Southern California. Los Angeles, CA.

Safar, M. (2002). Classification of Web caching systems. *Proceedings of IADIS International Conference on WWW/Internet.* Lisbon, Portugal.

Salen, K. (2007). Gaming literacies: A game design study in action. *Journal of Educational Multimedia and Hypermedia, 16*(3), 301–322.

Salton, G. (1968). Computer evaluation of indexing and text processing. *Journal of the ACM, 15*(1), 8-36.

Salton, G. (1971). *The smart retrieval system.* Englewood Cliffs, NJ: Prentice Hall Inc.

Sancho, P. (2006). A blended learning experience for teaching microbiology. *American Journal of Pharmaceutical Education, 70*(5), 120.

Sandras, D. (2001). *Ekiga*. Retrieved January 12, 2009, from ekiga.org/

Sartorius, A. R. S. (2006). Virtual and remote laboratory for robot manipulator control study. *International Journal of Engineering Education*, *22*(4), 702–710.

Scardamalia, M., & Bereiter, C. (2003). Knowledge building. *Encyclopedia of education* (pp. 1370-1373). New York: Macmillan Reference.

Schreiber, A., et al. (2002). Knowledge engineering and management: The CommonKADS methodology. Cambridge, MA: MIT Press.

Segers, M., Dochy, F., & De Corte, E. (1999). Assessment practices and students' knowledge profiles in a problem-based curriculum. *Learning Environments Research*, *2*(2), 191–213.

Shaffer, D. W. (2006). *How computer games help children to learn*. New York: Palgrave Macmillan.

Shaffer, D. W., Squire, K. R., Halverson, R., & Gee, J. P. (2005)... *Phi Delta Kappan*, *87*(2), 104–111.

Shao, J., & Wang, Y. (2003). A New Measure of Software Complexity based on Cognitive Weights. *IEEE Canadian Journal of Electrical and Computer Engineering*, *28*(2), 69–74. doi:10.1109/CJECE.2003.1532511

Shastri, L. (2002). Episodic memory and cortico-hippocampal interactions. *Trends in Cognitive Sciences*, *6*, 162–168. doi:10.1016/S1364-6613(02)01868-5

Sheremetov, L., & Arenas, A. (2002). EVA: An interactive Web-based collaborative learning environment. *Computers & Education, 39*(2), 161-182.

Sifakis, E., Neverov, I., & Fedkiw, R. (2005). Automatic determination of facial muscle activations from sparse motion capture marker data. *SIGGRAPH 2005, ACM TOG 24* (pp. 417-425).

Skinner, B. F. (1938). *The behavior of organisms*. New York: Appleton-Century-Crofts.

Slavin, R. (1989). Research on cooperative learning: Consensus and controversy. *Journal of the Educational Leadership, 47*(4), 52-54.

Sleator, D. & Temperley, D. (1991). *Parsing English with a link grammar.* Carnegie Mellon University Computer Science technical report CMU-CS-91-196.

Sleator, D. K. & Temperley, D. (1991). Parsing English with a link grammar. October, CMU-CS-91-196.

Smith, K. (1996). Cooperative learning: Making groupwork work. *New Directions for Teaching and Learning, 67,* 71-82.

Sonmez, D., & Lee, H. (2003). Problem-based learning in science, http://www.eric.ed.gov/ERICWebPortal/recordDetail?accno=ED482724

Sproat, R. W. (1995). Text-to-speech synthesis. *AT&T Technical Journal*, *74*, 35–44.

Squire, K. R. (2003). Video games in education. *International Journal of Intelligent Games & Simulation, 2*(1). Retrieved January 15, 2009, from www.cyberfest.us/Education/Video_Games_in_Education-MIT_Study.pdf

Squire, K. R. (2005). Changing the game: What happens when video games enter the classroom? *Innovate, 1*(6). Retrieved January 15, 2009, from http://www.innovateonline.info/index.php?view=article&id=82

Stauffer, K. (2005). *XML, IMS LD, and learning object development for Web course delivery.* Unpublished master's thesis, Athabasca University, Athabasca, Alberta, Canada.

Stockinger, H. (2001). Distributed database management systems and the data grid. *18th IEEE Symposium on Mass Storage Systems and 9th NASA Goddard Conference on Mass Storage Systems and Technologies.*

Su, B. (2005). The importance of interaction in Web-based education: A program-level case study of online MBA courses. *Journal of Interactive Online Learning, 4*(1), 1–19.

Sugiyama, K., Hatano, K., & Yoshikawa, M. (2004). Adaptive web search based on user profile construction without any effort from users. *Proceedings of the 13th International Conference on the World Wide Web(WWW'04),* NewYork.

Summers, B. (1998). *Official Microsoft Netmeeting 2.1 Book*. Microsoft Press. Retrieved from http://www.microsoft.com/windows/netmeeting/

Sun Microsystems. (2007). *Java Plugin*. Retrieved from http://java.sun.com/products/plugin/

Sun, C., & Chou, C. (1996). Experiencing CORAL: Design and implementation of distant cooperative learning. *IEEE Transactions on Education, 39*(3), 357-366.

Swain, M. (2001). Integrating language and content teaching through collaborative tasks. *The Canadian Modern Language Review, 58*(1), 44-63.

Sweller, J. (1988). Cognitive load during problem solving. *Cognitive Science, 12*, 257–285.

Tai, C. F., Chen, R. J., & Lai, J. L. (2003). How technological and vocational education can prosper in the 21st century? *IEEE Circuits & Devices Magazine, 19*(2), 15-51.

Tamaki, M., Kuwabara, T., Yamada, K., Nakamura, Y., Mistunaga, Y., Konishi, N., & Amano, K. (2000). Multimedia Assisted Education System with Individual Student Advance. *IPSJ Journal, 41*(8), 2351–2362.

Tattersall, C., Manderveld, J., Hummel, H., Sloep, P., Koper, R., & de Vries, F. (2003). IMS Learning Design Frequently Asked Questions. *Educational Technology Expertise Centre.* Retrieved from http://dspace.learningnetworks.org/retrieve/20

Terzopoulos, D., & Waters, K. (1990). Physically-based facial modelling, analysis, and animation. *Journal of Visualization and Computer Animation, 1*(2), 73-80.

The Globus Alliance (2006). Retrieved from http://www.globus.org

The Open University. (2008). Retrieved from http://www.open.ac.uk/

The University of The Air. (1984). Retrieved from http://www.u-air.ac.jp/

Thiagarajan, S. (1998). The myths and realities of simulations in performance technology. *Educational Technology*, 35–41.

Tinto, V. (1993). *Leaving college: Rethinking the causes and cures of student attrition,* 2nd ed. Chicago, IL: University of Chicago Press.

Tollervey, N. H. (2006). Program# - An AIML Chatterbot in C#. Retrieved January 30, 2009 from http://ntoll.org/article/program-20. Northamptonshire, United Kingdom.

Tsang, H.W., Hung, L.M., & Ng, S.C. (1999). A multimedia distance learning system on the Internet. *Proceedings of IEEE International Conference on Systems, Man, and Cybernetics (SMC), 2*, 243-246.

Tulving, E. (1983). *Elements of Episodic Memory*. Oxford University Press, New York.

University Distance Learning Network. (2005). University digital education development in Taiwan., Retrieved from http://dised.ntu.edu.tw/.

University of Florida Distance Learning. (2008). Retrieved from http://www.distancelearning.ufl.edu/.

University of Illinois Online. (2008). Retrieved from http://www.online.uillinois.edu/.

University of Wisconsin-Platteville Distance Learning Center. (2008). Retrieved from http://www.uwplatt.edu/disted/.

Uskela, S. (2001). All IP Architectures for Cellular Networks. In *Proceedings of Second International Conference on 3G Mobile Communication Technologies* (pp.180-185).

Veenman, S., Benthum, N., Bootsma, D., Dieren, J., & Kemp, N. (2002). Cooperative learning and teacher education. *Teaching and Teacher Education, 18*(1), 87-103.

Vernon, D., & Blake, R. (1993). Does problem-based learning work? A meta-analysis of evaluative research. *Academic Medicine, 68*(7), 550-563.

Viavoice Outloud, I. B. M. (2007). Text-to-speech downloadable for many languages. Retrieved May 12, 2007 from http://www-306.ibm.com/software/voice/viavoice/dev/msagent.html

VLAB. (2007). *Monash University's complexity virtual lab.* Retrieved January 20, 2008, from http://vlab.infotech.monash.edu.au/

VLAI. (2007). *Virtual laboratory of artificial intelligence.* Retrieved January 20, 2008, from http://galaxy.agh.edu.pl/~vlsi/AI/

Vlasic, D., Brand, M., Pfister, H., & Popovic, J. (2005). Face transfer with multi-linear models. *ACM Transactions on Graphics (TOG),* 24(3), 426-433.

Vygotsky, L. (1978). *Mind and society.* Cambridge: MIT Press.

Vygotsky, L. S. (1986). *Thought and Language.* Cambridge, MA: MIT Press.

Walczak, K., Wiza, W., & Podgorny, M. (2001). WebWisdom - Database support for distance learning systems. *Proceedings of 3rd International Conference on Information Integration and Web-based Applications and Services* (pp. 289-299). Linz, Austria.

Walczak, K., Wiza, W., & Podgorny, M. (2002). Managing multimedia educational contents in databases. *Proceedings of the IADIS International Conference on Information Society WWW/Internet* (pp. 152-159). Lisboa, Portugal.

Wald, M. (2005). SpeechText: Enhancing learning and teaching by using automatic speech recognition to create accessible synchronised multimedia. Retrieved June 10, 2006 from http://eprints.ecs.soton.ac.uk/10723/01/mwaldedmediaproceedings.doc

Wallace, R. (2005). Artificial intelligence markup language (AIML) Version 1.0.1. *AI Foundation.* Retrieved January 30, 2009, from http://alicebot.org/TR/2005/WD-aiml

Walton, H., & Matthews, M. (1989). Essentials of problem-based learning. *Medical Education, 23*(6), 542-558.

Wang, C. C., Huang, J. C., Shih, T. K., & Lin, H. W. (2006). A repository-based question answering system for collaborative e-learning. *Journal of Computers: Special issue on E-Learning, 17*(3).

Wang, Y. (2003). Cognitive Informatics: A New Transdisciplinary Research Field. *Transdisciplinary Journal of Neuroscience and Neurophilosophy, 4*(2), 115–127.

Wang, Y. (2005). The Development of the IEEE/ACM Software Engineering Curricula. *IEEE Canadian Review, 51*(2), 16–20.

Wang, Y., & Kinsner, W. (2006). Recent Advances in Cognitive Informatics. *IEEE Transactions on Systems, Man, and Cybernetics, 36*(2), 121–123. doi:10.1109/TSMCC.2006.871120

Wang, Y., & Li, X. (2004). Web-based adaptive collaborative learning environment designing. *Proceedings of ICWL 2004.* Beijing, China.

Wang, Y., & Wang, L. (2006). Cognitive Informatics Models of the Brain. *IEEE Transactions on Systems, Man, and Cybernetics, 36*(2), 203–207. doi:10.1109/TSMCC.2006.871151

Wang, Y., Liu, D., & Wang, Y. (2003). Discovering the Capacity of Human Memory. *Transdisciplinary Journal of Neuroscience and Neurophilosophy, 4*(2), 189–198.

Wang, Y.H. & Lin, C.H. (2004). A multimedia database supports English distance learning. *An International Journal Information Sciences, 158*, 189-208.

Wang, Z., & Crowcroft, J. (1997). Cachemesh: A distributed cache system for the World Wide Web. *Proceedings of the 2nd National Laboratory for Applied Network Research (NLANR) Web Cache Workshop.* Boulder, CO.

Wang,Y.H., Lin, C.H., & Wang, W.N. (2007). Semantic enhanced QA system architecture use link grammar parser for e-learning environment. *Proceeding of Conference Taiwan E-Learning Forum (TWELF) 2007,* May, 18-19.

Wang,Y.H., Wang, W.N., & Lin, C.H. An intelligent semantic agent for e-learning message communication. *Journal of Information Science and Engineering, 21*(5), 1031-1051.

Way, T. P. (2006, March). A virtual laboratory model for encouraging undergraduate research. In *SIGCSE Technical Symposium (SIGCSE 2006).*

Web Services Architecture (2004 February 11). *W3C Working Group Note*, Retrieved from http://www.w3.org/TR/we-arch/

WebCAI Courseware System. (1999). Retrieved from Nihon University, http://iclab.ce.nihon-u.ac.jp/~webcai/.

Weber, G., & Brusilovsky, P. (2001). ELM-ART: An adaptive versatile system for Web-based instruction. *International Journal of AI in Education, 12*(4), 351–384.

Webster, M., & Deliyannis, I. (2002). WWW delivery of graph-based multi-level multimedia systems: Interaction over scientific industrial and educational. *Proceedings of the IADIS International Conference on Information Society WWW/Internet* (pp. 607-612). Lisboa, Portugal.

Weibel, S., Gridby, J., & Miler, E. (1995). *OCLC/NCSA metadata workshop report,* Dublin, EUA. Retrieved from http://www.oclc.org:5046/oclc/research/conferences/metadata/dublin_core_report.html

Weible, D., Kuo, C.-H., Chien, F.-Y., & Taso, N.L. (2001). Automating repeated exposure to target vocabulary for second language learners, Advanced Learning Technologies. *Proceedings, of the IEEE International Conference on,* August 6-8, 127-128.

Weinberger, A., & Fischer, F. (2005). A framework to analyze argumentative knowledge construction in computer-supported collaborative learning . *Computers & Education, 46*, 71–95. doi:10.1016/j.compedu.2005.04.003

Weinstein, C. (1989). Teacher education students' preconceptions of teaching. *Journal of Teacher Education, 40*(2), 53-60.

Wells, L. K., & Travis, J. (1996). *LabVIEW for Everyone: Graphical Programming Made Even Easier.* NJ: Prentice Hall.

Wenger, E. (1998). *Communities of practice: Learning, meaning, and identity.* UK: Cambridge University Press.

Wenyin, L. (2006). BuyAns—An incentive & collaborative platform for knowledge acquisition. *Proceedings of 2nd International Conference on Semantics, Knowledge and Grid (SKG'06),* GuiLin

Wesner, S., & Wulf, K. (2003). How GRID could improve e-learning in the environmental science domain. In *Proceedings of the 2nd International LeGE-WG Workshop: A Fundamental Challenge for Europe*, France.

Wessels, D. (1995). Intelligent caching for World Wide Web objects. *Proceedings of INET-1995 Conference.*

White, T. R., & Gunstone, R. F. (1989). Metalearning and conceptual change. *International Journal of Science Education, 11*, 577–586.

WIDE University, School of Internet. (1997). Retrieved from http://www.sfc.wide.ad.jp/soi/contents.html.

Williams, S. M. (1993). Putting case-based learning into context: Examples from legal, business, and medical education. *Journal of Learning Sciences, 2*(4), 367-427.

Willis, B. (n.d.). Distance education at a glance. Engineering Outreach at the University of Idaho, http://www.uidaho.edu/evo/distglan.html

Winer, D. (2003, July 15). RSS 2.0 Specification. *RSS 2.0 at Harvard Law.* Retrieved from http://blogs.law.harvard.edu/tech/rss

Winnips, K. (2000). *Scaffolding-by-design: A model for WWW-based learner support*, Enschede: University of Twente Press.

Wiza, W., & Walczak, K. (2000). Dynamic Web systems based on XML and database technologies. *Proceedings of 4th Business Information Systems Conference* (pp. 229-241). Poznan, Poland: Springer-Verlag.

Wolfgang, H., & Javier, J. (2000). Data management in international data grid project. *1st IEEE, ACM International Workshop on Grid Computing.*

Wood, H. A., & Wood, D. (1999). Help seeking, learning and contingent tutoring. *Computers and Education.*

Wu, T. Y. (2000). Integrative curriculum planning in technological and vocational education in Taiwan, Republic of China. http://www.eric.ed.gov/ERICWebPortal/recordDetail?accno=ED450230

Wu, T.-Y., & Chao, H.-C. (2008). Mobile e-Learning for Next Generation Communication Environment. *International Journal of Distance Education Technologies, 6*(4), 1–13.

Wu, T.-Y., Wu, J.-C., & Weng, W.-F. (2008, September 10-12). Improvement Security for RuBee Radio-WiMAX Mesh Networks. *The 5th International Conference on Mobile Technology, Application & Systems (Mobility Conference 2008), Ilan, Taiwan.*

Xinyu Zhang, D., & Luo, N. (2004). Web-based collaborative learning focused on the study of interaction and human communication. *Proceedings of ICWL 2004.* Beijing, China.

Xu, J., Lee, W., & Liu, J. (2004). Scheduling Web requests in broadcast environments. *Proceedings of the 13th International World Wide Web Conference* (pp. 280-281).

Yang, O. Y. (2005). ECVlab: A web-based virtual laboratory system for electronic circuit simulation. *Computational Science - ICCS 2005, pt 1* (. *LNCS, 3514*, 1027–1034.

Yang, S. J. H., & Chen, I. Y. L. (2006). Providing Context Aware Learning Services to Learners with Portable Devices. *Advanced Learning Technologies, 2006. Sixth International Conference on 5-7 July 2006* (pp. 840-842).

Yang, Y. (1993). The effects of self-regulatory skills and type of instructional control on learning from computer-based instruction. *International Journal of Instructional Media, 20*(3), 225-241.

Yip, W. (2001). Utilisation of the problem-based learning approach facilitated by information technology to teach information on systems development. http://citeseer.ist.psu.edu/535807.html

Yokomori, T. (2002). Natural computation – new computing paradigm learned from life phenomena. *IPSJ Magazine, 41*, 08–11.

Young, J. D. (1996). The effect of self-regulated learning strategies on performance in learner controlled computer-based instruction. *Educational Technology Research and Development, 44*(2), 17-27.

Zhao, G., & Yang, Z. (2005). Learning Resource Adaptation and Delivery Framework for Mobile Learning. *Frontiers in Education, 2005. FIE '05. Proceedings 35th Annual Conference.*

Zhu, Z., & Ji, Q. (2004). Real-time 3D face pose tracking from an uncalibrated camera. *Conference on Computer Vision and Pattern Recognition Workshop (CVPRW'04), 5,* 73.

Zhuang, Y., & Liu, X. (2002). Multimedia knowledge exploitation for e-Learning: Some enabling techniques. *Proceedings of the First International Conference on Advances in Web-Based Learning (ICWL'02), LNCS 2436* (pp. 411-422). Hong Kong, China.

Zimmerman, B. J. (1998). Developing self-regulation cycles of academic regulation: An analysis of exemplary instructional model. In D. H. Schunk & B. J. Zimmerman (Eds.), *Self-regulated learning: From teaching to self-reflective practice* (pp. 1-19). New York: Guilford.

Zimmerman, B. J., & Martinez-Pons, M. (1986). Development of a structured interview for assessing student use of self-regulated learning strategies. *American Educational Research Journal, 23*(4), 614-628.

Zimmerman, B. J., & Schunk, D. H. (1989). *Self-regulated learning and academic achievement: Theory, research, and practice.* New York: Springer-Veri

Zimmerman, B. J., Bonner, S., & Kovach, R. (1996). *Developing self-regulated learners: Beyond achievement to self-efficacy.* Washington, DC: American Psychological Association.

Zimmermann, H.-J. (1999). *Practical applications of fuzzy technologies.* Kluwer Academic Publishers.

Zwillinger, D. (2003). Standard CRC Mathematical Tables and Formulae (31st ed.). Chapman & Hall/CRC Press LLC.

About the Contributors

Mahbubur Rahman Syed is currently a professor of Information Systems and Technology at Minnesota State University, Mankato (MSU), USA. He has about 25 years of experience in teaching, in industry, in research and in academic leadership in the field of computer science, engineering, information technology and systems. Earlier he worked in the Electrical and Computer Engineering Department at the North Dakota State University in USA, in the School of Computing and Information Technology at Monash University in Australia, in the Department of Computer Science and Engineering at Bangladesh University of Engineering and Technology (BUET) in Bangladesh, and Ganz Electric Works in Hungary. He was a founding member of the Department of Computer Science and Engineering at BUET and served as Head of this Department during 1986-92. He served as the General Secretary of Bangladesh Computer Society and also as the General Secretary of BUET Teacher's Association. He received the UNESCO/ROSTSCA' 85 award for South and Central Asia region in the field of Informatics and Computer Applications in Scientific Research. He won several other awards. He has co-edited several books in the area of e-commerce, software agents, distance education, multimedia systems and networking. He has more than 100 papers published in journals and conference proceedings. He has been serving in different roles such as co-editor-in chief, associate editor, editorial review committee, member of several international journals. Dr. Syed has been involved in international professional activities including organizing conferences and serving as conference and program committee chair.

* * *

Kikuo Asai received the Ph.D. degree in electrical engineering and electronics from Nagoya University, Japan in 1998. He joined the National Institute of Multimedia Education in 1996. He was a visiting scientist at the University of Illinois at Chicago in 2000 and at the University of Alberta in 2002–2003, respectively. He is currently an associate professor at the Open University of Japan. He has been engaged in research and development of human computer interaction, virtual reality, and multimedia systems. He is a member of IEICE, IEEJ, and VRSJ. (as of April 2009)

Leonard Barolli received BE and PhD degrees from Tirana University and Yamagata University in 1989 and 1997, respectively. From April 1997 to March 1999, he was a JSPS Post Doctor Fellow Researcher at Department of Electrical and Information Engineering, Yamagata University. From April 1999 to March 2002, he worked as a Research Associate at the Department of Public Policy and Social Studies, Yamagata University. From April 2002 to March 2003, he was an Assistant Professor at Department of Computer Science, Saitama Institute of Technology (SIT). From April 2003 to March 2005, he was an

Associate Professor and presently is a Full Professor at Department of Information and Communication Engineering, Fukuoka Institute of Technology (FIT). Dr. Barolli has published more than 250 papers in referred Journals and International Conference proceedings. He has served as a Guest Editor for many International Journals. Dr. Barolli has been General Chair, PC Chair and PC Member of many International Conferences. Dr. Barolli is the Steering Committee Chair of CISIS International Conference and is serving as Steering Committee Member in many International Conferences. He is organizers of many International Workshops. His research interests include network traffic control, fuzzy control, genetic algorithms, agent-based systems, ad-hoc networks and sensor networks, Web-based applications, distance learning systems and P2P systems. He is a member of SOFT, IPSJ, and IEEE.

Yacine Benahmed received his B.Sc. degree in computer science in 2005 and M.S. degree in December 2008 in electrical engineering both from the Université de Moncton. He worked as a research assistant at the Human-Machine Interaction Lab. at the Université de Moncton, Campus de Shippagan since 2005. In 2007, the Université de Moncton granted him a performance scholarship for his outstanding results. His main research interests involve distributed interactive systems, dialogue systems on mobile telecommunications, intelligent agents and pervasive technologies.

Arjan Durresi received his BE, MS and PhD at Polytechnic University of Tirana, Albania in 1986, 1990 and 1993, respectively. He holds a Post-Graduate Degree from Italian Telecommunication Institute, La Sapienza University, Italy in 1991. He also got another PhD degree at Tokyo Denki University, Japan in 2006. Presently, he is an Associate Professor of Computer Science at Indiana University Purdue University at Indianapolis, Indiana. In the recent past, he also held roles as Associate Professor at Louisiana State University, Research Scientist of Computer Science and Adjunct Assistant Professor of Electrical and Computer Engineering at The Ohio State University. Dr. Durresi serves as Area Editor of Ad Hoc Networks Journal. He is on Editorial Boards of many International Journals. He has been a Guest Editor for many Special Issues. He was Program Co-Chair of the AINA-2006. He is organizing many International Workshops. He has authored more than 50 papers in Journals and more than 80 in Conference Proceedings. Dr. Durresi's research interest include: network architectures, heterogeneous wireless ad hoc and sensor networks, security, QoS routing protocols, traffic management, grid computing, optical and satellite networks, multimedia networking, and bioinformatics.

José Antonio Gómez-Tejedor received the B.Sc and Ph.D. degrees in Physics from the Universidad de Valencia (UV) in 1991 and 1995. He is professor at the Universidad Politécnica de Valencia (UPV) from 1996. In 1997 he joined the Center of Biomaterials and Tissue Engineering, at UPV. His current interests include tissue engineering for cartilage regeneration and central nervous system regeneration. He is also interested in biomedical applications of spider and silkworm silk. He is also interested in learning and applying innovative active methodologies into classroom and e-learning. Dr. Gómez-Tejedor currently teaches physics to first-year undergraduate students.

Morris S. Y. Jong B.Eng. (HKPolyU), M.Sc. (HKU), Ph.D. (Candidate) (CUHK) Instructor, Centre for the Advancement of Information Technology in Education, The Chinese University of Hong Kong Motivated by his keen interest in education and information technology, Mr. Jong has been teaching teacher education programmes specializing in IT in education, at undergraduate, postgraduate, and master levels, for over 7 years. He became a member of Centre for the Advancement of Information

Technology in Education, The Chinese University of Hong Kong in 2007. Apart from teaching, Mr. Jong has been active in diverse international, global Chinese, and local scholarly activities which promote the integration of IT into teaching and learning. Besides assisting in the organization of these activities, he has published more 30 international and global Chinese journal and conference papers, given presentations in conferences, as well as invited talks in seminars and scholarly visits. Currently, he is pursuing a PhD degree in the area of computer game-based learning at The Chinese University of Hong Kong.

Akio Koyama received his BE and PhD degrees from Yamagata University in 1987 and 1998, respectively. From April 1999 to March 2002, he was an Assistant Professor at the Faculty of Computer Science and Engineering, the University of Aizu. From April 2002 to March 2008, he was an Associate Professor and now is a Full Professor at the Faculty of Engineering, Yamagata University. Dr. Koyama has published about 100 papers in refereed journals and international conference proceedings. Dr. Koyama has been a PC member of many international conferences. His research interests include medical and care communication systems, routing protocols, high-speed network protocols, agent-based systems, distance learning systems and mobile communication systems. He is a member of the IEEE Computer Society, IPSJ and IEICE.

Tang-Ho Lê is currently Full Professor of Université de Moncton, New-Brunswick, Canada. Ph.D. in Computer Science, Université de Montréal (1998). Prof. of Databases, Programming Languages and Software Development courses. Career experiences include: Designer and developer of several software systems: VietVoice (a first Vietnamese Voice Synthesizer - 2004), OCOWS (OnLine Cooperative Working System, a Web-based Learning System - 2007), LINC (Learn IN Context, a Collaborative E-learning system - 2004), DKNS Knowledge Management System (2000), SAFARI Intelligent Tutorial System Planning module (1998), Acupuncture Expert System (1993), Geyser On-Screen Help Book (1990), etc. His areas of interest include Artificial Intelligence, Knowledge Management Systems, E-Learning Systems, and Speech Technology, having more than 30 scientific publications.

Fong-Lok Lee B.Sc., Dip.Ed., M.A.(Ed), Ph.D. (CUHK) Director, Centre for the Advancement of Information Technology in Education, The Chinese University of Hong Kong. Apart from being the Centre Director, Professor Lee is also the Programme Director of the Master of Arts Programme in Information Technology in Education since 2001 and 2003, respectively. He has fifteen years of working experience in his specialist field, twenty-two years of teaching experience in local secondary schools and more than eleven years in conducting teacher training courses for local secondary school teachers. He served as a secondary school teacher, extra-curricular activities master and mathematics panel chairman. Presently he is a member of the executive committee of the Global Chinese Association on Computers in Education, co-chief Editor of Global Chinese Journal of Computers in Education; past-president of Asia-Pacific Society for Computers in Education; Chair of the HK & Macau Chapter, Global Chinese Society on Computers in Education. His research interests include Educational Technology Cognitive Processes, Artificial Intelligence, Mathematics Learning, and Application of Information Technologies in Education.

Jimmy H. M. Lee B.Math., M.Math. (Waterloo), Ph.D. (Victoria) Professor, Department of Computer Science and Engineering, The Chinese University of Hong Kong. Professor Lee read both his BMath (Hons) degree and MMath degree from the University of Waterloo in 1987 and 1988, respectively, and his PhD from the University of Victoria in 1992. Immediately upon graduation, he joined The Chinese University of Hong Kong. His research focuses on the theory and practice of constraint satisfaction and optimization with applications in scheduling, resource allocation, and combinatorial problems. In recent years, Professor Lee has also been conducting research on novel Web-based learning platforms and the accompanying pedagogies, particularly in the development of educational games. He is currently the Associate Director (Research and Development) of the Centre for the Advancement of Information Technology in Education under the Hong Kong Institute of Educational Research, CUHK. Professor Lee has over 100 refereed technical publications in international journals and conferences, and has obtained over $11 million in competitive research funding. He is on the editorial boards of the Journal of Discrete Algorithms, the CONTRAINTS journal, and the Constraint Programming Newsletter. Professor Lee is active in extramural educational activities. He has taught for the Programs for the Gifted and Talented, and was the Chief Examiner of Paper II of the HK A-Level Computer Studies subject from 1995 to 2001. Inspired by his many former good teachers from elementary school to universities, Jimmy's passion for teaching garnered him the Vice-Chancellor's Exemplary Teaching Award in 2005, and the Faculty of Engineering Exemplary Teaching Award in 1999, 2000, 2001, and 2003.

Keita Matsuo received his BE from Fukuoka Institute of Technology (FIT), Japan in 1989. From April 1989 to March 1990, he was an Assistant Teacher at Fukuoka Technical High School. From April 1990 to March 2003, he was a Teacher at Tobata Technical High School. From April 2003 to March 2006, he was a Teachers Consultant at Fukuoka Education Center. From April 2007, he is PhD Student at Graduate School of Engineering, FIT. His research interests include distance learning systems, Web-based education system, P2P systems and Internet Applications.

Germán Moltó received the B.Sc. and Ph.D. degrees in computer science from the Universidad Politécnica de Valencia (UPV) in 2002 and 2007. In 2002 he joined the Grid and High Performance Computing research group, at UPV. Since 2005, he is also an assistant lecturer at the same university. His current interests include Grid Computing, Service-Oriented Architectures, metascheduling and its usage in different scientific fields, such as biomedical applications and protein design. He is also interested in learning and applying innovative active methodologies into classroom. Since July 2008 he holds a title of Specialist in Universitary Pedagogy after having fulfilled a whole-year specialised course for improving the skills of university teachers. Dr. Moltó currently teaches data structures and algorithms to second-year undergraduate students.

Mehdi Najjar is actually a visiting research scientist at the Canadian Space Agency. He received his M. Sc. and his Ph. D. in artificial intelligence from the University of Sherbrooke (Canada). His research interests are related to knowledge representation/engineering and to cognitive/computational modelling within virtual learning environments. He also collaborates with other researchers in the field of human-computer interaction within intelligent systems, during post-doctoral researches at the University of Moncton and the University of Montreal (Canada). Mehdi Najjar is a senior lecturer at the Computer Science Department of the University of Sherbrooke,

Noritaka Osawa received his B.S., M.S. and Ph.D. degrees in information science from the University of Tokyo in 1983, 1985, and 1988 respectively. After working for a software company, the University of Electro-communications, and the National Institute of Multimedia Education, he now works for Chiba

University as a professor. His current research interests include multimedia systems, information visualization, and human-computer interfaces. (as of April 2009)

Douglas O'Shaughnessy has been a professor at INRS-EMT (formerly, INRS-Telecommunications), a constituent of the University of Quebec, in Montreal, Canada, since 1977. He has worked as a in the speech communication field for more than 30 years. His interests and research include automatic speech synthesis, analysis, coding, enhancement, and recognition. He was educated at MIT, and is a Fellow of both the Acoustical Society of America and of the IEEE. He is an Associate Editor for the Journal of the Acoustical Society of America and is a member of the IEEE Technical Committee for Speech Processing, and was the General Chair of the 2004 ICASSP. He is the author of the textbook Speech Communications: Human and Machine (2000, IEEE Press). With Li Deng, he co-authored the book Speech Processing: A Dynamic and Optimization-Oriented Approach (Marcel Dekker Inc.).

Sid-Ahmed Selouani received his B. Eng. degree in 1987 and his M.S. degree in 1991 both in electronic engineering from the Algiers University of Technology (U.S.T.H.B). He joined the Communication Langagière et Interaction Personne-Système (CLIPS) Laboratory of Université Joseph Fourier of Grenoble taking part in the Algerian-French double degree program and then he got a Docteur d'État degree in the field of signal processing and artificial intelligence in 2000. From 2000 to 2002 he held a post-doctoral fellowship in the Multimedia Group at the Institut National de Recherche Scientifique (INRS-Télécommunications) in Montréal. He is currently full professor and responsible of the Human-Machine Interaction Laboratory at the Université de Moncton, Campus de Shippagan. He is also an invited Professor at INRS-Télécommunications. He is a Senior member of IEEE and member of signal processing and computer science societies. His main areas of research include new models in Human-System interaction, E-services, mobile communications, ubiquitous systems and assistive technologies by speech-enabled solutions.

Junjie Shang B.Sc. (Peking U), M.Phil. (Peking U), Ph.D. (CUHK) Associate Professor, Department of Educational Technology, Peking University. Professor Shang read both his BSc Degree and MPhil degree from Peking University in 1996 and 1999, respectively, and his PhD from The Chinese University of Hong Kong in 2007. He is currently an associate professor of the Department of Educational Technology under the Graduate School of Education, Peking University. His research focuses on computer game-based learning and virtual reality in education. Dr. Shang has published more than 35 papers in international and global Chinese journals and conferences.

Tin-Yu Wu is an assistant professor at the Department of Electrical Engineering, Tamkang University, Taipei, R.O.C. He received his PhD degrees in Electrical Engineering from NDHU in 2007. His research interests focus on the next generation Internet protocol, mobile computing and wireless networks.

Fatos Xhafa holds a PhD in Computer Science (1998) from the Department of Languages and Informatics Systems, Polytechnic University of Catalonia, Barcelona, Spain. He was graduated in Mathematics from the Faculty of Natural Sciences (FNS), University of Tirana (UT), Albania, in 1988. During 1989-1993 he was an Assistant Professor at the Department of Applied Mathematics of the FNS, UT (Albania). He joined the Polytechnic University of Catalonia as a Visiting Professor at the Applied Mathematics Department I, and later he entered the Department of Languages and Informatics Systems

(LSI) as a PhD student and in 1996 as an Assistant Professor. Currently, he is an Associate Professor at the Department of Languages and Informatics Systems and member of the ALBCOM Research Group He is also a collaborator of the Open University of Catalonia (Barcelona, Spain). His current research interests include parallel and distributed algorithms, combinatorial optimization and approximation, meta-heuristics for complex problems, distributed programming, Grid and P2P computing. He has published in leading international journals and conferences and has served in the Organizing Committees of many conferences and workshops. He is also member of editorial board of several international journals.

Index

Symbols

A

B

C

D

E

F

G

H

I

J

K

L